THE
CHURCH
VISIBLE

THE CHURCH VISIBLE

THE CEREMONIAL LIFE AND
PROTOCOL OF THE ROMAN CATHOLIC CHURCH

JAMES–CHARLES NOONAN, JR.

THE MOST REVEREND ARCHBISHOP JOHN P. FOLEY, D.D., PH.D.
SPECIAL CONSULTOR

PRODUCED BY AMARANTH

VIKING

✠ The revised Code of Canon Law (1983) reserves the grant of *Imprimatur* and *Nihil Obstat* to studies exclusive to theological, spiritual, and scriptural content. *The Church Visible,* as the reader will find in the study of this text, concerns itself with the external realm of the Church's life: the ceremonial life, protocol, government, and rich history of the Catholic Church.

As a study in the external realm, the revised Code of Canon Law properly precludes the grant of either declaration. In lieu of these grants, however, numerous prelates and officials have come forth to offer statements stressing the importance of this work as the Church moves forward into the Third Millennium. Graciously given, these appear herein in foreword, preface, and commentary form.

VIKING
Published by the Penguin Group
Penguin Books USA Inc., 375 Hudson Street, New York, New York 10014, U.S.A.
Penguin Books Ltd, 27 Wrights Lane, London W8 5TZ, England
Penguin Books Australia Ltd, Ringwood, Victoria, Australia
Penguin Books Canada Ltd, 10 Alcorn Avenue, Toronto, Ontario, Canada M4V 3B2
Penguin Books (N.Z.) Ltd, 182–190 Wairau Road, Auckland 10, New Zealand

Penguin Books Ltd, Registered Offices: Harmondsworth, Middlesex, England

First published in 1996 by Viking Penguin, a division of Penguin Books USA Inc.

10 9 8 7 6 5 4 3 2 1

LIBRARY OF CONGRESS CATALOGING IN PUBLICATION DATA
Noonan, James-Charles.
    The Church visible: the ceremonial life and protocol of the Roman
Catholic Church / James-Charles Noonan, Jr.
        p.   cm.
    Includes bibliographical references and index.
    ISBN 0-670-86745-4
    1. Catholic Church—Customs and practices.   2. Papacy.   3. Church etiquette.   4. Papal decorations
5. Church vestments—Catholic Church.   I. Title.
BX1969.N66   1996
390'.422—dc20   95-49731

This book is printed on acid-free paper. ∞

Printed in the United States of America by Quebecor/Fairfield
Set in Bembo
Produced by AMARANTH, 379 8th Street, Brooklyn, New York 11215
Designed by PublisherStudio, 4 Airline Drive, Albany, New York 12205

Page xvii: photograph of Pope John Paul II courtesy Karsh of Ottawa; coat of arms courtesy Alex Garey. Page xix: photograph of Jacques Cardinal Martin courtesy Arturo Mari; coat of arms courtesy Maria-Helena Bedoya/Maria Mocnik. Page xx: photograph of Bishop van Lierde courtesy Fotografia Felici; coat of arms courtesy Alex Garey.

Contents

One month ago our Holy Father, Pope John Paul II, departed the United States having once again visited our beloved country. During this pastoral visit, which was the latest of his sixty-eight trips outside of Italy, His Holiness once more loudly proclaimed the message of Jesus Christ. As Vicar of Christ, he has visited our country six times. His message gives us strength. His words bring us inspiration. His example teaches us love.

As people witnessed the color and pageantry of his visit, they probably asked many questions concerning various topics. Some may have speculated on life at the Vatican. Others may have wondered about the meaning of terms such as the College of Cardinals, the Roman Curia, the Papal Household, or even the Vesture and Insignia of the Church.

The Church Visible is a masterful effort of research. This text serves as the first post-Second Vatican Council study on the external realm of our Church. It is an authoritative, accurate, and historic presentation of a great wealth of knowledge on Church matters; particularly protocol, vesture, insignia, and historic ceremony.

James-Charles Noonan, Jr., has produced a very interesting book, which as a matter of fact proceeds almost to the point of being fascinating. His text will serve as a reference work on Catholic ceremonial life for years to come. As a teaching tool it will bring our laity, as well as a new generation of religious and clergy, to a better understanding of our history.

John Cardinal Krol

JOHN CARDINAL KROL

November 9, 1995
Dedication of the Lateran Basilica

On retreat in preparation for becoming a bishop, I was deeply lost in the wonder of it all when interrupted by a kindly priest who wanted me to be able to speak intelligently of the new life ahead. He asked me if I knew the origin of the bishop's mitre. I pleaded abject ignorance. He advised me that it would be a question I would be asked more frequently than any other as a bishop, and urged me not to complete my retreat in such ignorance. Unfortunately, he directed me to no source of knowledge, and didn't really seem to know himself.

After frustrating forays to the house library, I gave up. It now seems safe to say that the authoritative answer had not yet been published. Chapter Thirty-six of James-Charles Noonan's fascinating work corrects the deficiency. The same could be said of countless arcane data of ecclesiastical history.

To my knowledge, *The Church Visible* is the first full-fledged post-Vatican II work on "The Ceremonial Life and Protocol of the Catholic Church." I can not imagine the research it had to have required. Students, lay persons, reporters, and editors who write on Church matters will be amazed by the wealth of detail on Church protocol, vesture, ceremonies, and insignia presented from an historical perspective. Undoubtedly, many bishops have forgotten more than I have ever learned about the "tools of the trade;" I suspect that most, if not all, will find this work helpful and fascinating.

Mr. Noonan writes in a sprightly fashion, so that even what could be inestimably tedious often becomes charming. Nor does he ever treat what some might consider hopelessly trivial with less than respect.

The Church Visible does not address even remotely the horrendous moral and social problems of our day or the crucial issues which require the daily energies of the Pope, the Bishops, the Church Universal; nor does it ever purport to do so or apologize for not so doing. It is a work of history, of scholarliness, of meaningful interest to all for whom the Church remains after nearly 2,000 years a wondrous treasure cove. As such, it deserves a warm welcome, indeed.

John Cardinal O'Connor

December 1995

Fascination with the externals of the Catholic Church has often characterized the communications media and even the general public.

The Catholic Church is not only the oldest institution in the world, rich in tradition, but it also reflects in its externals the internal reality of the sacred, the sacramental, the divine. There is an air of mystery, of special significance, of authority about many of the externals of the Catholic Church, reflecting the transcendence and supreme authority of God and at the same time the fact that His Divine Son became man in Jesus Christ. Thus, in external signs we can see reflected the facts of creation, of incarnation and of redemption.

It is most useful to know the origin and the significance of the externals of the Catholic Church; in this way, one can grow in appreciation of sacred history reaching back not only 2,000 years to Christ, but more than 4,000 years to Abraham—and indeed to creation itself—the sacred history of "God with us."

The Church Visible offers not only an introduction but an expanded explanation of the external rites, vestments, and practices of the Catholic Church; it is to be hoped that the reader will be led through these outward signs to the inner reality of God's love for His people throughout history, of redemption in Jesus Christ and of the saving work of the Church founded by Jesus Christ which works in the world, as He worked in the world, through external signs.

ARCHBISHOP JOHN P. FOLEY,
President

N. 5249/95
November 16, 1995

Preface

THE CATHOLIC UNIVERSITY OF AMERICA

James-Charles Noonan has given us the distillate of years of intensive and precise scholarship of the most persevering kind. He has shown that an ardent enthusiasm for the work is fully compatible with painstaking accuracy, bringing both qualities to the task in an abundance unique to himself.

The author's research has taken him to the Vatican Archives, the Archives of the Second Vatican Council, and those of the Secretariat of State. Those of Philadelphia, Baltimore, New York, and Chicago were of value, as were the libraries of The Catholic University of America, the Sorbonne, and the Gregorian in Rome. Both the Knights of Malta and of the Holy Sepulchre of Jerusalem opened their archives to him, and he conducted a total of 367 interviews along the way. It is a tribute to Mr. Noonan's competence that he has fashioned all that data into the volume in hand.

Philosophically, *The Church Visible* attests to a profound Catholic reverence for the physical. Persons are not imprisoned in the wonderfully fashioned material world; rather, we express ourselves in it and through it. The sacraments are prime evidence of this reality, but all the actions, objects, and words in this volume follow right along in their wake. Reverence for the sublime gift of language shines through, along with a deeply human understanding of the role of gestures, and certainly a renewed spirit of awe at the inspired artistry of vessels and vestments from the simplest to the most ornate. That one era or locale may treasure one style or form over another testifies only to the critic's summation of Chaucer: "Here is God's plenty."

At a time when so many cultures veer toward the instant and ephemeral, it is of great worth to be reminded that artistic beauty and reverent precision play a crucial role in the fitting worship of God.

BROTHER PATRICK ELLIS, F.S.C.
President

November 13, 1995
Feast of Saint Frances Xavier Cabrini

Introduction

"The Second Vatican Ecumenical Council was meant as a moment of overall reflection by the Church on herself and on her relationship with the world. The need of an ever greater fidelity to the Lord led her to this reflection. But the impulse was also provided by the great changes of the contemporary world, which, as 'signs of the times,' needed to be interpreted in the light of God's word. Inspired by the Holy Spirit, the Council laid the foundations for a new springtime in the Church. This was not a break with the past but was able to make the most of the Church's entire heritage.

Thirty years later, it is more necessary then ever to return to that moment of grace . . . the question cannot fail to be raised as to how much the Council's message has entered into the Church's life, institutions, and style."*

In nineteen hundred and sixty-two a gentle breeze began to stir in Rome, welcomed by the affable pontiff, John XXIII, who threw open wide the windows and portals of the Church to its soft touch. The breeze quickly grew into a whirlwind as the fathers of the Church gathered with untempered enthusiasm for the opening session of the Second Vatican Council. No one present during the Council's sessions doubted the infusion of the life-breath of the Holy Spirit—not even when that gentle breeze took on the strength of a windstorm which began to change the Church forever.

The history of the Church reveals to us that throughout her life, as each of the many Ecumenical Councils came to a close, some agitation of the faithful resulted. Change of any kind is always unsettling—all the more so when it regards matters of piety and devotion—and the short-term effects of the Second Vatican Council were certainly no different in our own age. Church history also tells us that the period that immediately follows any Ecumenical Council is akin to standing at the foundation of a massive stone wall: standing at its base one sees with clarity only that which is before one's eyes. So it has been in the years immediately following the Second Vatican Council. However, with the passage of time the wall becomes more distant and a wider vista opens to the eye. And as time continues to pass, and we grow further from the immediacy of the Second Vatican Council, we shall come to fully understand the greatness of the fathers' intent, and we shall become more open to the inspiration and work of the Holy Spirit.

The external life of the Church (or the Church Visible) was most clearly effected by the winds of change of the nineteen sixties and seventies. As one studies the Conciliar documents and the various Pauline *motu proprio* of this period, one realizes the thoughtful intent of the Council fathers and Pope Paul VI in discerning and implementing the Spirit's wisdom and guidance in the external life of the Church. Paul VI was keenly aware of widespread disenchantment with the changes he had implemented, and with his own hand he presented his concerns in the remarks of the papal document, *Ut sive sollicite,* issued by the Secretariat of State so as to clear the air and to offer a truly pastoral response to the widespread dissatisfaction existing at that time amongst the clergy and faithful alike.

In this document, the Secretary of State opens with these remarks:

> *In conscientious fulfillment of his obligation over the Universal Church and in his efforts to carry out the directives and teachings of the Vatican Council II, Pope Paul VI has devoted his attention even to the outward symbols of ecclesiastical life. His attention has been to adapt such externals to the altered conditions of the*

---

* Address of His Holiness, Pope John Paul II, Sunday Angelus: 15 October 1995, L'Osservatore Romano, N. 42 (1412).

present time and to relate them more closely to the spiritual values they are meant to signify and enhance.

The late pope's personal remarks follow. He writes:

The issue at hand is disquieting to our contemporaries. It involves harmonizing, without giving in to conflicting extreme demands, propriety and dignity with simplicity, practicality, and the spirit of humility and poverty. These qualities must above all characterize those who, by their admittance to ecclesiastical office, have received a clear duty of service to the people of God.

In retrospect, we now know that much of the disenchantment that had resulted after the Council did not emanate from actions of the Fathers of the Council or the pontiffs of the post-Conciliar era. Rather, these resulted from the actions of the scores of individuals, either well-meaning or self-interested, who took it upon themselves to implement individual or regional preferences in ceremony, protocol, and vesture against the established norm of Rome. So many of the changes that have been received negatively were never the intent of the hierarchy of the Church, and the general acceptance of many unauthorized practices as normative or fundamental Church policy has resulted simply because these practices have not been challenged or publicly questioned in the post-Conciliar era. Appropriately, other important tasks have occupied the Church during this period.

The purpose in undertaking this study, in particular Parts Three and Four—those chapters pertaining to vesture, insignia, ceremony, and protocol—is to clarify in a comprehensive way the direct wishes of the fathers of the Second Vatican Council, the late pontiff, Paul VI, and the present pontiff, John Paul II. It was not the desire to harken back in any way to pre-Vatican II practice. On the contrary, my sole intent is to illustrate in a joyful and definitive academic treatise the present rubrics of Rome, as well as the teaching of our Holy Father on these matters of external life reflective of all the changes made since 1965.

Therefore, in undertaking this study, it has been my intent to present this material solely from a perspective of Church history and protocol. Professional protocolists tend to stress the letter of the law as well as the implications of longstanding custom—a perspective often accused of being formal or rigid. As a professional protocolist, I offer two thoughts in response: the first is my confession of a strong bond of love for Rome, the papacy, and the Church's directives and teaching—all of which remain fresh and alive. The second is my commitment to and love for the law of the Church and a firm interpretation of its codes. As such, this text is not presented as a study in the discipline of liturgy and should not be viewed in that light. Protocol is quite a different animal and my qualifications remain in this latter discipline.

For those who might question any of the positions taken in this academic endeavor, I ask that you review the citations of this text, both in footnote and appendix formats. They are faithful to the teachings of the Council fathers and successive pontiffs. Here, one will find the richness of the present teaching of the Church on matters of vesture, insignia, and non-liturgical ceremony. Nearly all of the citations in this text are citations from post-Conciliar documents (1967-84), and call attention to present practice, although some may be surprised to learn that much of what was believed to be relegated to history is both retained and reinforced. These citations represent the most recent directives from Rome and thus do not reflect local or national interpretations. As this study is meant for a worldwide audience, it must limit itself to the universal directives of Rome and thus cannot explore local practices or adaptations to custom. However, the author holds these locally approved interpretations in the same high esteem that the Church herself holds them.

The presentation of materials in this text concerns itself with topics reflective of the study of Vaticanology and Church history. Once again, it is the intent to present our history, reflective of the Second Vatican Council and all that it offers us, as we move forward into the Third Millennium.

I am happy to offer this treatise at the conclusion of seven years of intense research, study, and interviews throughout the world. In the spirit of the gentle breeze of the great Second Vatican Council, and of the wisdom of the pontificates of Paul VI and John Paul II, I present the current law of the Church with regard to our external life. I bid you many hours of enjoyment and study, and I encourage you to continue to explore the richness of our heritage. In the final analysis, this book serves not only as a celebration of our rich inheritance and history, but also as a celebration of the life of the Church which continues to thrive. After all, we should know ourselves well, yet not harken back— for that which is stagnant shall die.

For a student of Church history, a study of the external life of the Roman Catholic Church approaching the Third Millennium is as exciting as that of the Renaissance period. Albeit different, each reflects the Church of its time and, as intended by Paul VI, the Church Visible must reflect propriety, dignity with simplicity, practicality, and the spirit of humility and poverty.

In faithfulness to the Council's teachings and to the pontifical decrees of Paul VI and John Paul II, *The Church Visible: The Ceremonial Life and Protocol of the Roman Catholic Church* searches the memory of the Church for the origins of what marks us as unique in our external life. It calls the attention of the faithful to the currently mandated practices and ritual prescribed by the Holy See in matters of vesture, insignia, protocol, and ceremony. As John Paul II affirms, that which has been changed has done so not as a break with the past, but as a commitment to our Church's entire heritage.

In closing, I wish to share with you the words of our Holy Father, to whom this work is dedicated as a gift in his golden jubilee year of priesthood, when he spoke of that new springtime, as well as for a call to preserve our heritage: *"May Mary most holy, who was proclaimed 'Mother of the Church' by my predecessor, Paul VI, precisely during the Council, help us on this path. May we feel her presence among us, as did the Apostles on the eve of Pentecost. May she make us docile to God's Spirit, so that the Third Millennium, now at our door, may find believers more steadfast in their fidelity to Christ and fully dedicated to the cause of His Gospel."* *

. . . NOW AND FOREVER

— JAMES-CHARLES NOONAN, JR.

---

* Ibid.

The Church Visible

is dedicated

to Mary,

Mother of the Church,

and to

our Holy Father,

Pope John Paul II,

in joyful celebration

of his golden jubilee

in service to the people of God

Bishop of Rome,

Vicar of Jesus Christ,

Successor of the Prince of the Apostles,

Supreme Pontiff of the Universal Church,

Patriarch of the West,

Primate of Italy,

Archbishop and Metropolitan of the Roman Province,

Sovereign of the Vatican City State,

Servant of the Servants of God

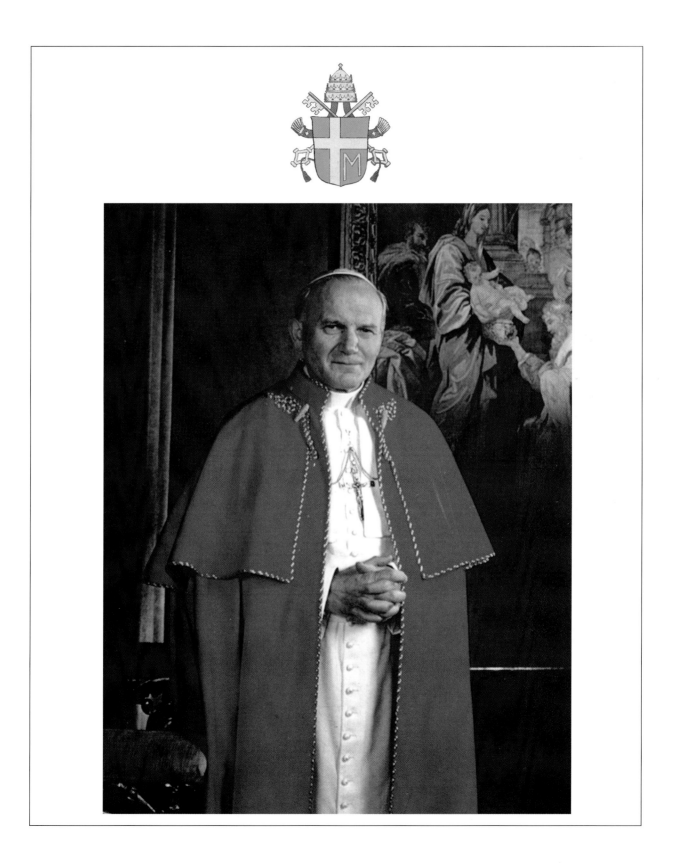

———————————

Jacques Cardinal Martin

Born of this World: 26 August 1908

Elevated to the Sacred College: 28 June 1988

Recalled to God: 28 September 1992

"L'image du Cardinal Martin restera indélébile dans la memoire de ceux qui l'ont connu, comme il demeurera dans les pages de l'histoire de l'Eglise et du Saint-Siege par longue et importante activité qui frit la sienne."

"The image of Cardinal Martin leaves an indelible mark on the memory of those who knew him, for he will remain in the prayer and the history of the Church and of the Holy See because of the long and important work which was his special contribution."

— Pope John Paul II

In gratitude and thanks to my honorary parrain, friend, and inspiration. Go with God and His Angels!

— James-Charles Noonan, Jr.

———————————

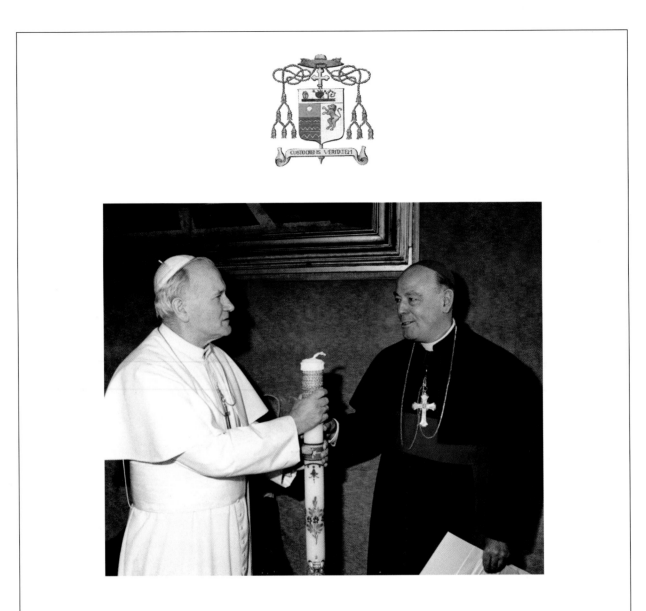

PETRUS CANISIUS JEAN VAN LIERDE
VICAR-GENERAL EMERITUS OF HIS HOLINESS FOR VATICAN CITY
BORN OF THIS WORLD: 22 APRIL 1907
CONSECRATED TITULAR BISHOP OF PORFIREONE: 13 JANUARY 1951
RECALLED TO GOD: 13 MARCH 1995

Bishop van Lierde presents the Paschal candle to Pope John Paul II, Easter, 1988.

Acknowledgments

In undertaking a project of this size and scope, one must repeatedly turn to family, friends, and professionals for the support and assistance required to bring it successfully to fruition. I am truly thankful to so many who offered me an abundance of moral support, active assistance, and technical expertise during the seven years it took to complete *The Church Visible*.

In a firm desire to be certain that I offer public thanks to each and every friend and supporter, I created lists of those involved in this project from its earliest beginnings. I pray that I have not overlooked anyone as I now prepare to offer my public gratitude for their contributions. If an oversight has been made, please know that I am as grateful to you as I am to those I now publicly thank!

To our beloved Holy Father, Pope John Paul II, in the golden jubilee year of his holy priesthood, who has been so kind in his prayerful support of my work, and who received me inside the Apostolic Palace on numerous occasions, I pledge my filial love and continued prayers for the work to which the Holy Spirit has called him as Supreme Pastor of the Universal Church.

From the outset, I was blessed by the support and collaboration of my family. I can never thank them sufficiently for all they have offered me. My single-mindedness must have driven them "around the bend" at times, but each knew how important this work was to me and stood with me as the course of this adventure took many strange turns. I love you all and I owe you much. Especially to my parents, James and Geraldine Noonan, you know how grateful I am for all that you have done for me, and for your unswerving support. I love you! You are the spirit behind me. This work is complete because of your goodness to me, and for instilling in me the real love for God and His Church which we all share. To my sisters and their families, thank you for your help and enthusiastic support throughout my life. To Jerry Porreca, DeChantal Bolger, and Mary Feeney, my three sisters and dear friends, you three girls are the greatest! I love you very much. Thank you for always standing by me and for encouraging me in all that I have done. Thank you all for so much love. Also to Rita and Edward Moore and Mary Walsh who support all my efforts in a special way, and to all members of the Noonan and Gallagher families—too numerous to mention each by name but who remain in my heart, all the same—a profound thanks!

I also must offer public, albeit posthumous, thanks to the two prelates who were the original inspiration for this work, and who facilitated the entrée necessary in Vatican City and around the world at the critical time when I began my research. It was Jacques Cardinal Martin, Prefect-Emeritus of the Papal Household, my *parrain-hon-orifique* and lifelong friend, who wished me to write this work vis-à-vis my professional and academic expertise in Church protocol and diplomacy. He stood by my work until his own death in September of 1993. His assistance with my initial research and his guidance through the myriad of changes of the post–Vatican II era was indispensable. This book was begun because of Cardinal Martin. I owe him all that a godson should and more!

I also have abundant fondness for, and gratitude to, the recently deceased Bishop Peter Canisius Jean van Lierde, O.S.A., Vicar General-Emeritus of His Holiness for Vatican City. The bishop had been a family friend for fifteen years and spent many hours with me inside his apartment at the Vatican assisting in my research and later working to build a proper glossary for a study of this scope. So many of the entries in this glossary were explored through the richness of the immense experience of the late Bishop van Lierde. He, like Cardinal Martin, was the epitome of a gentleman and bishop. I truly miss them both, and I hope that I do each proper justice by the final presentation of the work they were so instrumental in developing. They are with me still.

I must also thank John Cardinal Krol of Philadelphia—one of the greatest American prelates of our age. His early support was instrumental in my completion of *The Church Visible* and his ardent embrace of my finished work, in the beautiful words of the foreword offered by him, was edifying and singular in its support. Thank you Eminence, for always standing by me. For Father Powell, I owe you special thanks for your individual support and friendship.

Archbishop John P. Foley, President of the Pontifical Commission for Social Communications, has served this project as a Special Consultor. When I asked him to take on a task of such magnitude, he did not hesitate to assist me, despite his heavy schedule in Rome. I owe him much and I will always be grateful for his support. He has prayed me through this project. He is one of the finest human beings I have ever known, and a great friend. Thank you, Excellency!

To His Eminence John Cardinal O'Connor, a son of Philadelphia and gift to New York, thank you for the beautiful words of your foreword, and for your continued personal support. You are, indeed, a good friend. I am blessed to know you.

When I began the research stage of this project, I met with then-Archbishop Pio Laghi. He has always been positive and supportive of this project. First in the nunciature in Washington, where we discussed ecclesiastical protocol and diplomatic matters, and, subsequently, in Rome, when I began research on the Sacred College. Now a Cardinal, Pio Laghi always welcomed me with warm cordiality. His Eminence is truly a statesman. Thank you for your continued support and counsel.

In a special way to Cardinals Sodano and Casaroli, who each in his turn deserves a particular note of thanks for securing the appendix documents appearing in this text.

There are many other members of the hierarchy and administration of the Church who helped me with one aspect of this text or another. In simply listing them here, I wish them to know this project would not have come to fruition had they not contributed to it. My gratitude goes to Their Eminences, Cardinals Caprio, Hume, Keeler, Lustiger, Ruini, Bevilacqua, Hickey, Coffy, Arinze, Baum, Cassidy, Daly, Etchegaray, Gantin, Noè, Ratzinger, and Szoka. I owe special thanks to Bishop Dino Monduzzi, who helped me continue on in the research initiated by Cardinal Martin; to Archbishop B.B. Heim for his consistent support of my presentation of ecclesiastical heraldry; to Archbishops Agostino Cacciavillan and Renato Martino; the late Archbishop John F. Whealon of Hartford, who corresponded frequently with me as I began this project, always encouraging in his ideas; to Archbishop Jean-Louis Tauran, Secretary for Relations with the States; Archbishop Lorenzo Antonetti, former nuncio to Paris, now a member of the Roman Curia; and to Bishop James T. McHugh, for whom I studied, and who became involved in *The Church Visible* in the earliest stages—he never wavered in his enthusiastic support of my work. Bishop McHugh has been a tremendous help to me in completing this project and I am blessed to know him. To Bishop Thomas J. Welsh of Allentown; Bishop Edward Egan of Bridgeport; Bishop Thomas V. Daly of Brooklyn; Bishop John Magee, S.P.S., of Cloyne, Ireland; and to Bishops John J. Graham and Louis DeSimone, Auxilliary Bishops of Philadelphia; Bishop James Schad, Auxilliary

Bishop of Camden; and Bishop William E. Lori, Auxilliary Bishop of Washington.

To Reverend Monsignor Piero Marini, Master of Ceremonies of His Holiness, for his permission to translate and reproduce the Burial Rite of Cardinals, and for other valuable research assistance; Reverend Monsignor Stanislaw Dziwisz for his kindness, prayers, and encouragement; Reverend Monsignor Charles Burns of the Vatican Secret Archives for his time, expertise, sense of history, joviality, friendship, and willingness to help in this work; to Reverend Monsignors William Millea and Daniel E. Thomas, and to Rev. Mark Mallak—each of whom applauded my efforts and offered assistance whenever sought; to Rev. Joseph Fox, O.P., and Rev. Leonard Boyle, O.P., and to the latter's superior, Archbishop Luigi Poggi; to Reverend Monsignor Robert Sable; Reverend Monsignor Joseph Kohut; Reverend Monsignor Kevin Whalen; Reverend Carlos Encina-Commentz, F.S.S.P.; to Commander Alois Estermann and Commander Peter Hasler of the Pontifical Swiss Guards. And, finally, to the officials and staffs of the Archives of the Secretariat of State, the Archives of the II Vatican Council, the Archives of the College of Cardinals, Liberia Editrice Vaticana, la Conference des Evêques de France, and the Archives of the National Conference of Catholic Bishops of the United States. You all have been essential to my work. Thank you for your contributions and advice.

I owe personal thanks to Reverend Patrick Brannan, S.J.; Reverend Marcel Chappin, S.J., of the Pontifical Gregorian University; Brother Randall Reide, C.F.X.; Sr. Mary Randal, S.N.D.; Rev. William Ogrodowski; Elena Panti; Carol Salfa; Paul Gamner; John C. Ricardo; Jim Teti; Dan Jones; and Thomas W. Power, Jr., of the Pontifical North American College; to Lory Dominici Mondaini, who deserves a special note of thanks for all her work in this project's completion; Michela Mancini;

and to Meg Ellen Mason—a wonderful, generous American artist living and working in the Eternal City.

At the Grand Magistral Palace on the via Condotti, I wish to express my sincere gratitude to His Most Eminent Highness Fra Andrew Bertie, Grand Master of the Sovereign Order of St. John of Jerusalem, Rhodes, and Malta; and to Fra Hubert Pallavicini, a great gentleman of the old school and a longtime friend who facilitated the history and color for my chapter on the Knights of Malta; I owe immense thanks. With the permission of the Grand Master, the Marquis Pallavicini presented me with the beautiful photographs of the official life of the Sovereign Order seen in these pages. His hospitality and generosity will never be forgotten. Nor will that of Fra Carl Paar, dona Antoinetta Capparella di Boria, Prince Paolo F. Boncompagni Ludovisi, and Fra Gian Luigi Rondi Nasalli.

At the palace of the Equestrian Order of the Holy Sepulchre, in addition to thanks to His Eminence, the Grand Master Giuseppe Cardinal Caprio, who opened wide the doors of his secretariat and archives, and who encouraged my scholarship in such a way as to make my work on the order as authentic and historic as possible, I also wish to specifically thank Prince Lancellotti and Nathalie Donath.

I also owe special thanks to the North American offices of these two orders, whose staffs assisted me early on in obtaining the ceremonials used by these jurisdictions for investing new members in the United States. Both offices are located in New York. Thanks to the late J. Peter Grace, K.M., of the American Association of the Knights of Malta, and to George Doty, G.C.H.S., of the Eastern Lieutenancy of the Equestrian Order of the Holy Sepulchre of Jerusalem, for providing sample invitations and ceremonials included in this work; thanks also to Barbara Brandon.

Special thanks to His Serene Highness, Monsiegneur Rainier III, Sovereign Prince of Monaco; to his son Albert, Prince-Hereditaire of Monaco, whom I am blessed to call a lifelong friend; and to their Ambassadors to the United Nations, M. et Mme. Jacques Boisson, for protocol presentations. Likewise, I also wish to thank His Serene and Her Royal Highness, the Prince and Princess Edouard de Lobkowicz, for photographs, invitations, and other thoughtful assistance.

In the United States, I call my thoughts to all those who supported this project long before it took its final form or title. The list is long, yet each in their own way offered valuable assistance as I continued my work. To the clergy, who have been consistent in their support, especially Rev. William A. Hodge; Reverend Monsignor J. Gerald Gallagher; Rev. Daniel Mackle; Reverend Monsignor Carl Marucci; Reverend Monsignor John Breslin and all the wonderful clergy of St. Christopher parish, Philadelphia; Rev. Vincent Welsh; Rev. Robert Marczewski; the late Rev. Dennis McCann; Rev. Gabriel Rosetti, O.F.M.; also the late Monsignor Louis O'Meara; Rev. Gabriel O'Donnell, O.P.; Rev. Curtis Clark; Reverend Monsignor James Howard; Reverend Monsignor Thomas Hilferty; Reverend Monsignor William Noe Fields; Reverend Monsignor James McGovern; and Deacon John W. Murphy; I extend deep thanks. To Frances Natale, Sister Mary Isabel, R.S.M., and Bernice D'Eramo; to Sister Pauline McShane, S.H.C.J., and to her mother, a gracious hostess and dear lady, Mary (Mrs. John) McShane, and the staff of Kilarney House, County Kerry, Ireland. At the chancery of the archdiocese of New York, a generous thanks to Eileen White, Esq., Susan Fojtik, and Ellen Stafford.

To Brother F. Patrick Ellis, F.S.C., a friend of twenty years, I send a special note of thanks. It was Br. Pat who gave this work a final title, *The Church Visible,* after years of struggle to find one proper for its scope. I owe additional thanks to Br. Pat for also opening every door for me, whenever asked. He remains a big part of this project, as does The Catholic University of America. I extend my thanks to all at CUA who were instrumental in seeing this work to publication—in particular, Vincent P. Walter and Margaret Proctor, the staff of the President's Office, and the Office of Development, for providing sample programs for inclusion in this work; the staff of the CUA Press; Reverend Monsignor Robert Trisco; Rev. Jacques Gris-Gayer; Gloria and Mary Ann of the Department of Church History; Marie of the graduate Religion Department; and, finally, to Dean Raymond Collins.

To my many seminary brothers who have worked diligently to achieve the quality and integrity which I desired for this book, especially Walter Guasp-Santos, Neil Sullivan, Joseph Pettyjohn, Jr., Cecil Spotswood, Scott Buchanan, Peter Idler, Stefan Geisler, and in a very special way to a great friend, Gerald P. Carey, Jr., one of the finest church musicians of our time, who worked with me in designing programs of beautiful music for the samples appearing in the protocol section of this text. These samples are meant to serve only as a starting point for event planners. To Brian L. Quilter, another great friend and brother, who worked tirelessly on archival research, always enthusiastic and encouraging. You have the luck of the Irish and a love for the Church that is genuine in its fidelity. It is a blessing to know you. To each of you, many thanks.

To Jonathan E. Hawley, a special message of thanks for two wonderful years of hilarious humor and dedicated assistance. To Sr. Mary of Victories IHM of the Archives of the Archdiocese of Philadelphia. Also, a special note of thanks to all the parishioners of St. Patrick parish, Woodbury, New Jersey, who befriended a stranger and soon became family. Thank you all for your support and kindness.

To Jack and Vicki Mednikoff, who opened their hearts and doors to this project; to Joan McLaughlin for her magnificent, ever-supportive friendship; to Bob McLaughlin; to Mary Arens of the House of Hansen; to Suzzane Smith; Clint Weiman; Charles Letier; Jennifer Gargiulo; Mike Mintern; Jim Foly; Jim Murray; the Hon. Charles Dougherty; Charles Lewis; Ken McIlvaine; Jeanne McDowell; Lorraine Haggerty; Mary Quilter; and Betty Cardone.

To Lee Ann Chearney of Amaranth; Barbara Grossman, Cathy Hemming, and Dawn Drzal of Viking; and all those involved in the editing, typesetting, and launching of *The Church Visible:* Linda DeMasi and Bruce Sherwin of PublisherStudio, Jim Bristol and Ron Doucette of NK Graphics, Norma Ledbetter, Roni Axelrod, Patti Kelly, Hal Fessenden, David Nelson, Michael Geoghegan, Laurie Rippon, Mary Ellen Curley, Charles Roth, Erin Boyle, Eugene Brissie, Colleen Corrice Clifford, Dave Prout, Cynthia Dunne, James Walsh, Thomas Kwiczola, and William A. Camp.

To Albert W. Tegler, Jr., and to his lovely bride, Janet, and all the Tegler family, who worked tirelessly in achieving publication for this opus. Al, you never forgot how important this project was to me and you never lost confidence in what I hoped to achieve. Your love for the Holy Father and dedication to the papacy is inspiring. Thank you for all you have done to see this dream come true! To Howard S. Browne, James J. Algrant, Brian P. Horan, Esq., and Jacques Ostiguy, Charles L. Williams, and Pierre Merle, Esq., a debt of thanks for years of support and camaraderie. To Rocco and Barbara Martino, thank you for the generous gift of reproductions for the text and for years of friendship.

In a very special way to Clare M. Strenger, who embraced this project in the infant stages, who assisted me when I needed a quiet space to write by offering her home to me as my temporary office, and, most importantly, who facilitated an easy transfer into seminary life by offering storage for my enormous library and personal effects. Clare, I owe you much. Please know how grateful I am to you for all that you have done for me. I lost count of all the generous things you have done. I wish everyone could be blessed by a friend such as you.

There are many professionals and corporations who contributed to my vision of *The Church Visible.* Their individual and corporate generosity has made many of the rich photographs, illustrations, and charts posible for inclusion in this text. I owe special thanks, once again, to Archbishop B. B. Heim, former Nuncio to the United Kingdom and renowned expert on ecclesiastical heraldry, for granting permission necessary to include his artwork in these pages. The Archbishop's newest work, *Or & Argent* (Colin Smythe Ltd.), was most helpful to this study. Likewise, I owe the same indebtedness to Carl-Alexander von Volborth of Belgium, who granted me carte blanche to include his heraldic artwork as illustrations for Chapter 10, Ecclesiastical Heraldry. I wish to credit and thank Mr. von Volborth and his publishers: New Orchard Editions, Villiers House, and its parent company Blandford Press, Ltd., who have been so generous to this project. Mr. von Volborth's work, *Heraldry, Customs, Rules and Styles,* is very impressive.

The staff of L'Osservatore Romano, most especially Dottore Arturo Mari and his senior manager Clara Colelli-Todini, went far beyond the necessary to find the photos that would visually enrich the topics of this study. I spent many hours with Clara and her assistants—each of whom wanted my book to be impressive and rich with detail. My special thanks to them all. The pontifical photographers, Felici, were also most receptive and facilitated the acquisition of the more ancient photos. It was always an adventure visiting them. In conversation, we used a blend of English, Italian, and French to find the photos we needed. Thanks to all at Felici. To the great portrait photographer, Karsh of Ottawa, who offered the dedication portrait of

Pope John Paul II, I am still amazed at your generosity since you do not know me personally. Thank you. To Maria Cusik, Charles Moyer, and Dave Weltz, each of whom offered an education on the procedures of prepublication, it was a wonderful opportunity to learn a new industry. Thank you! To Susan Mozitis, Martine Chauvet, Marie-Renee Martin, Maria Mocnik and Maria-Helena Bedoya, Carol Duplessis, Mr. and Mrs. Alex Garey of Lelli Garey in Rome, Colleen Boyle Sharp, and Robert Halvey. To the Kurt E. Schon gallery of St. Louis Street, New Orleans, and to Rich Moon, for his collaboration in the design of the Holy See organizational chart.

To my legal council, Stradley, Ronan, Stevens and Young of Philadelphia, most especially to my personal attorney and great friend, William R. Sasso, Esq., and to his assistant Jayne Kauffman; to Gillian Facher, Kristine M Jann, Marilyn Boyer, Carolane B. Perreti, Joan V. D'Angelo, Patricia A. Messner, Deborah Rzepela, Cheryl Jackson, and Debra Doxato, who undertook three months of computer scanning so the appendix documents could appear in their original Vatican form.

To my spiritual father and dear friend, Reverend Monsignor Charles B. Mynaugh of the Archdiocese of Philadelphia. You are a wonderful priest and my personal role model. I hope I can achieve your high standards in holy priesthood one day soon. I owe you much. Thank you!

Finally, there are two friends without whose help I would not have been able to complete *The Church Visible*. My brother in Christ, Mario Brunetta, an aspirant for the priesthood in the Order of Preachers of St. Dominic who undertook the first edit of grammar and spelling, completing the task of reviewing seven hundred pages of text in two weeks' time—and who flattered me with a commitment to memory of all things included in those pages. Mario, you are an amazing, genuine scholar! You are also a dedicated friend who will serve God well. Thank you. And now to Amy Joy Mednikoff. There are no words to accurately describe this young lady's dedication to me and to this project. Amy is not a Catholic. In fact, she is not a Christian, and yet she embraced this project one hundred-fold and supported my vision for it from the beginning. If it were not for her generosity of spirit and friendship, *The Church Visible* would not yet be prepared for publication. She is a true friend and professional. Amy also has a deep respect for Pope John Paul II to whom this work is dedicated. For me, this deep respect of a non-Catholic for the head of the Catholic Church is very edifying.

And ultimately to Mary, Mother of God, who has always stood by my side, who never fails to support and love me and to bring me closer to her Son. My filial love and gratitude.

Readers, if you enjoy the materials presented in these pages you, too, share in a debt of gratitude to all those named in these acknowledgments. To each of them, I pledge my prayers of thanks and gratitude.

To you all, *Ad Multo Annos*!

—JAMES-CHARLES NOONAN, JR.

PART ONE

AT THE VATICAN

Sacred College

The Sacred College is not simply a vestige of the Papal Court. In fact, it predates the Papal Court by eleven hundred years or more. In 1587, Pope Sixtus VI, when asked why he limited the number of members of the Sacred College to seventy, declared that long tradition had defined the origins of the cardinalatial office to those seventy elders who were chosen as the special assistants by Moses. It is historically impossible to link these seventy elders of the Old Testament to the cardinals of the Catholic Church, as Sixtus had proposed. Nevertheless, Sixtus went on to specifically define a theological bond that does remain as the original citation for the founding of the Sacred College.

ORIGINS

The original citation is found in Acts 6. The Apostles of Our Lord, from the earliest moments in the life of the infant Church, saw a necessity for assistants who would go among the faithful, relieving the apostles of the mundane tasks thrust upon them so that they might have time for prayer, contemplation, and preaching. The Church looks to these assistants,* if not those others from a more ancient time,

as the original members of the Sacred College.

Some believe the College of Cardinals to be nothing more than an invention of a papacy of the Middle Ages, simply in need of a consultive body in a more turbulent period of the Church's history. Still others believe it to be the embodiment of the self-aggrandizing Papacy of the High Renaissance. Although the theological origins of the cardinalate might be traced loosely to Moses, the historic bonds are surely deeply rooted in the early Christian Church of Jerusalem.

The role of a cardinal, as well as his title, is ancient. For two centuries prior to the Christian era, Roman society had been organized hierarchically, with senators and patriarchs holding the highest office, each having assistants to carry through on their edicts or decrees. These assistants were originally known as *praesides,* then *pro consules,* and simultaneously *prefecti praetoriani.* These important second-level civil authorities were soon considered to be the representatives of the "all highest" rulers of Roman society and took on an importance all of their own.

Simultaneously, the Church continued to flourish, and its structure clearly mimicked that of the

---

* Stephen, Philip, Nicanor, Timon, Nicholas, Parmenas, and Prochorus.

Roman Empire. The original seven assistants chosen by the apostles in Jerusalem passed on, many martyred for their faith. They were replaced, in turn, by others who were consecrated as the need for these special assistants continued to grow alongside the growing infant Church.

By the end of the second century, these select were considered to be an essential part of the Church's hierarchy, yet remained separate from the bishops, priests, and deacons. They remained laymen, continuing the external work of the local Church. As their importance grew, they rapidly took on an importance that necessitated a theological understanding of their expanded role in the Church. *Quator mundi cardines,* a concept meaning the four cardinal, or crucial, points that signify the extremities of the universe and that define the juncture of Heaven to Earth, which is the Church, was applied to the cardinals collectively to theologically define the role of the cardinalatial office. Cardinals were defined, therefore, as the critical supporters of the papacy as early as the mid-third century. By the fourth century, the theology of the cardinalate had taken form, and the title Cardinal was applied to these special consultors to the Bishop of Rome.

The word *cardinal* is derived from two early Latin terms, *cardo* and *cardinis.* For the past three hundred years, the English translation has rendered these two words as "hinge," to signify that important device that serves as a juncture for two opposing forces and that affords harmony as a result. As a hinge permits a door to hang easily upon a framed portal, so too the cardinals, it was believed, facilitated an easy relationship between the theological and governmental roles of the hierarchy of the Church. In actuality, the words *cardo* and *cardinis* take on a more profound theological meaning, which, sadly, has been lost to the English-speaking world for some three hundred years, in no small part due to the

Reformation's attempt to strip any profound theological meaning away from the hierarchy of the Roman Church. *Cardo* and *cardinis* should more accurately be rendered as "pivot" or "tenon," two terms that more accurately depict the role of the cardinalate. Upon this pivot, which is a small nail-like device, symbolically hangs the relationship between Heaven and Earth, between Christ and His Church on Earth. The stem of this pivot is the Sacred College. The pivot's head is the pope, who, together with the College, serve the Church as her guardians on Earth. A hinge is sturdy, whereas a pivot appears fragile. Although fragility is symbolic of our own humanity, the true symbolism is more representative of the College as a body. Although small and appearing fragile, in reality, this pivot's strength is mighty and reaches to Heaven.

At present, that theological symbolism survives. Popes through the ages have viewed the College of Cardinals as the senate of the Church. This is no less the case today. Pope John Paul II depends on the Sacred College for advice in all areas of Church teaching and governance. Its role remains a pivotal one in the Church of the twentieth century.

HISTORIC DEVELOPMENT

By the close of the fifth century, the title Cardinal became synonymous with status and was no longer reserved for the men who served the pope as special assistants. St. Augustine applied the title to those external truths of life, whereas St. Ambrose applied it to the four fundamental Christian virtues. This title was also soon applied to parishes throughout the Church, and by A.D. 845, the Council of Meaux "required Bishops to establish Cardinal 'titles' or parishes in their towns and outlining districts."[1]

In the same year as the Council of Meaux, the Roman popes were calling the cardinal-priests of Rome, that is, all priests directly tied to the papacy serving in the diocese of Rome, to serve as legates and delegates both within Rome at ceremonies, synods, and councils and beyond on diplomatic missions and great councils of the Church. For this latter office, they were granted the titles of Cardinal Legates *(Legatus a latere)* and Special Missions *(Missus Specialis)*.

By the pontificate of Stephen V (A.D. 816–817), the structure of the three classes of the College as we now know them (cardinal-priests, cardinal-bishops, and cardinal-deacons) began to form. Stephen decreed that all cardinal-bishops, the highest of the three classes, were henceforth bound to say Mass on a rotation basis at the high altar in St. Peter's, one cardinal-bishop each Sunday. This decree mentions for the first time the already pre-existing class of cardinal-bishop. Scholars tell us that the final class to form was that of cardinal-bishop. The second to form arose from among the clergy of Rome. The class of cardinal-deacon arose from the original *diaconi* of Rome and was the first to form. Because the last to form was that of cardinal-bishop, we know that the three present classes of the College, therefore, existed as early as A.D. 816. A minor council held at Compiegne (outside Paris) one hundred years prior to Stephen's decree, in a written description of the class of cardinal-bishop, "designated them as Roman Bishops."[2]

As reforms of the clergy became necessary, the successive bishops of Rome turned to their collaborators, the members of the Sacred College. The first of the major reforms occurred during the pontificate of Pope Leo XI (A.D. 1050), who wanted to eliminate "simoniacal clergy from Rome."[3] The cardinals of Rome became more than advisors on local policy; they assumed the roles of both the senate to the popes and guarantors of papal authority as well.

Many papal reformers followed Leo's lead. As early as the pontificate of Stephen III in A.D. 759, a decree of the Third Lateran Council declared that only cardinals could assume the papal throne, a requirement now permitted to lapse. Urban II (A.D. 1130) mandated that all three classes of the cardinalate could take part in papal elections. Until 1130, only cardinal-bishops had the right to vote in conclave.

By the late twelfth century, Popes began nominating cardinals from outside Italy. The period between the twelfth and fifteenth centuries was one of struggle for the College, between various popes and the cardinals of the era. The imposition of papal supremacy over the Church was always the root for the discord between powerful cardinals and the popes, and the most effective means to increase papal power was always to increase the numbers in the College, promoting the supporters of the pope who nominated them. Powerful, political cardinals wanted less papal interference and saw any increase in the numbers of the College as a ploy to dilute their own power and influence, and thus their wealth. The struggle over who had or had not the authority to enlarge the College continued for two hundred years.

In 1517, Leo X created thirty-one new cardinals, which increased the College to sixty-five. His motive was to secure a supportive majority. Paul IV raised that number to seventy and Pius IV to seventy-six. Sixtus V, feeling a need to bring a formality to the College's structure "once and for all," decreed that the number should henceforth not exceed seventy, with fourteen cardinal-deacons, fifty cardinal-priests, and six cardinal-bishops. It was not until the present era that these restrictions were lifted.

TITLE OF EMINENCE

On June 10, 1630, Pope Urban VIII (Maffeo Barberini) decreed that henceforth all members of the Sacred College were to hold and enjoy the title and dignity of "Eminence." All others who applied this title to themselves or who had it accorded them by the states over which they governed were obliged to relinquish the dignity of "Eminence." Most often, this lofty title was exchanged for *"Altezza," "Altesse,"* or *"Highness"* by the secular princes of that era. These qualifications remain the appellations conferred on princes of the blood, whereas that of "Eminence," "Most Eminent Lord," or "Most Eminent Cardinal" are reserved for the clerical princes of the Church.

In fact, the Congress of Vienna and the Congress of Berlin each confirmed that membership in the Sacred College carried with it diplomatic status equal to that of princes of the blood royal and, as such, took official precedence behind emperors, kings, and their immediate heirs, the crown princes. The Versailles Treaty ratified this protocol, as well, in 1918. This precedence remains in effect until this time, and although many present cardinals find the position of clerical prince to be uncomfortable, this nevertheless does not alter their international legal and diplomatic status. They are, indeed, princes of the Church.

As we have seen, the position of cardinal is ancient, with theological roots deep into the Old Testament. By the late Middle Ages, the cardinalatial dignity developed into the powerful office we now know it to be. "In the Middle Ages the loftiness of their position led them to be considered as the successors of the senators of the Roman Empire, with the right to the title of patrician, which gave them the rank below that of kings and above that of the most illustrious princes."[4]

In matters of protocol, cardinals rank just after the crown princes, or heirs apparent, of empires and kingdoms, but before grand dukes and prince sovereigns, except within the actual jurisdiction or territory of these princes. Cardinals likewise rank before all remaining children and all grandchildren of a reigning sovereign. Although legally established in 1812, this special precedence for cardinals existed *de facto* from the decree of Urban VIII (1630); however, strict adherence to the letter of the law is not now observed due to a preponderance of non-monarchial systems of government in the world. Whereas in the past monarchy was the sole form of government, at present presidential and parliamentary systems prevail. Although no formal amendments have ever been made to international conventions, subtle alterations in implementing existing protocol procedures now permit a more equitable manner for proper placement of dignitaries from various forms of government.

By the strict letter of the law, cardinals outrank everyone except emperors, kings, and crown princes, yet modern custom more properly permits heads of state of all types, as well as some other international figures of prominence (such as the head of the United Nations Organization), to enjoy a higher precedence properly due them. With that said, it should be clear to all that cardinals take precedence behind only those royal persons cited above. Heads of state and government, for the duration of their terms of office, and the secretary general of the United Nations, during his or her tenure, are accorded higher precedence today. No other personage, no matter how lofty or self-important, ever outranks a Roman cardinal.*

---

* This may seem trivial or even arcane, but it is an active procedure of protocol remaining in effect today. In 1972, the shah of Iran, during the elaborate celebrations marking the 1,000th anniversary of the Persian nation, invited hundreds of VIPs to Persepolis in the Iranian desert. Royalty and heads of state were housed in tentlike villas in the ancient ruins of the city. All others were housed in nearby hotels. The shah reacted angrily to his chief of protocol, who had incorrectly housed Cardinal de Furstenburg, the pope's representative to the celebrations, at one of the hotels, while a minor royal princess was housed in one of the special tent villas. The princess was moved, and the cardinal, by way of his cardinalatial title and not as the pope's ambassador, was given the villa reserved for senior royalty and heads of state.

The style of "Eminence," with a cardinal's title, may be preceded by the appellation "Most Reverend," or, in Italian, *"Reverendissime."* In Rome, the proper formula is "Most Reverend and Most Eminent, Lord Cardinal." In Italian, this is rendered as *"Reverendissime e Emintissime Cardinale."* The initials *S.R.E.* replace the full appellation on correspondence or social cards. In the United States, Britain, Ireland, and other English-speaking nations, cardinals are most often addressed as "Your Eminence." In Italy, the possessive pronoun is dropped; *"Eminenza"* is used alone. In France, the same holds true; there it is proper to address a cardinal, in conversation, simply as *"Eminence."*

When Urban VIII reserved the style "Eminence" for the cardinalate, he also granted it to the Prince Grand Master of Malta. By so doing, he likewise elevated the Grand Master to the precedence of a cardinal of the Church. To this day, the Grand Master is addressed properly as "Most Eminent Highness" and takes precedence behind the most recently created cardinal-deacon. Until 1630, the Grand Master enjoyed the royal style of "Most Serene Highness" and the lower precedence equal to other princes of the small states of the nonunified Italian peninsula.

From the Urbanian edict of 1630 until the Second Vatican Council, the formula for addressing cardinals was well established by law, decree, and custom. Nevertheless, some confusion has arisen in the era immediately following the close of the Vatican Council regarding the proper placement of the cardinalatial title. It should always be clear that the title Cardinal equates to that of Prince, and yet the office of cardinal is far more significant, as it includes a theological element as well as the social aspect of the office. Cardinals must now always hold the office of bishop, the highest in the Church.

There is only one proper method for applying the cardinalatial title. Using the present archbishop of New York as an example, the proper placement of the cardinalatial title would be this: "His Eminence John Cardinal O'Connor, Archbishop of New York." It is never proper to address the cardinal as "His Eminence, Cardinal John O'Connor." Why? There are two distinct historic reasons for the placement of the cardinalatial title. Each reason for this placement is historic in itself, one simply more ancient than the other.

In the earliest days of the College's development, when these holy men served the bishops of Rome as priests of the original parish churches of Rome and as the pope's special advisors, the use of a surname was not customary because no one actually possessed one. As such, a priest of Rome took the title of his Church to properly distinguish himself from another with the same first name. For instance, he would properly be called "John of St. Clementus" to distinguish himself from "John of Santa Maria." By this time, the cardinal's title also became synonymous with certain parishes of Rome. "Ioannes Cardinale San Clementus" would therefore have been the proper name and title of this early cardinal-priest. This ancient form has remained for eighteen hundred years.

This formula was reinforced in the late Renaissance, when many, if not most, of the Roman cardinals were also of high noble birth. The origins of the princely titles of Europe developed from this same early Roman period when surnames were nonexistent. Titles were derived from the territories over which these noblemen had jurisdiction. As such, the Christian name* was followed by the noble title and then by the territorial jurisdiction. This custom's roots are in the early Roman Empire. The structure of the ancient Latin language would have designated a territory secondary to the title

---

* Possibly followed by a Roman numeral to designate a person of the same name from another in a sequential manner.

itself; therefore, the correct formula for an Italian prince of that time would be Carlo II, Prince of Genoa. Surnames for royal houses are known today, of course, but are never used because of this historic custom. To this day, the ancient Roman formula applies to both cardinals and nobles alike.*

At all times, the proper formula for placement of the cardinalatial title must be the Christian name(s) first, to be followed by the title Cardinal, to be followed by the surname(s). No other formula is correct, and any change would require a papal *motu proprio* to legally effect it. A change of custom alone would not legally suffice in this case.

Cardinals follow the Supreme Pontiff in precedence within the Church. Cardinal-bishops, in order of their creation, precede cardinal-priests. The cardinal-dean always holds the Suburbicarian See of Ostia, as well as his other suburbicarian title, assuming the addition "of Ostia" once he is promoted to the deanship of the College. Cardinal-priests follow cardinal-bishops, with precedence being accorded to cardinals created before others of the same class. Cardinal-deacons follow cardinal-priests. Precedence within each class is set by the date of creation to the College. The Grand Master of Malta follows the last of the cardinal-deacons.[†]

QUALIFICATIONS

Canon law has always set qualifications on those who are eligible for membership in the Sacred College; however, for the most part, the pope "chooses Cardinals how and when he wills."[5] At present, the Code of Canon Law[‡] prescribes the qualifications for membership in the College of Cardinals. Canon 351 § 1 decrees that "those promoted as Cardinals are men freely selected by the Roman Pontiff, who are at least in the order of the presbyterate and are especially outstanding for their doctrine, morals, piety, and precedence in action; those who are not

yet Bishops must receive episcopal consecration."[6] Until Leo XIII's (Gioacchino Pecci) pontificate, simple men were sometimes called to the College of Cardinals, never receiving either ordination to the presbyterate or to the episcopacy. Until that time, the Order of Cardinal-Deacon was open to those outstanding laymen, or more accurately those with minor orders, who were to be raised to the highest ranks of the Church.

During John XXIII's pontificate, it became mandatory for each cardinal to also have episcopal ordination. Although it is still feasible for a single Catholic male with no canonical impediments to be elevated to the pinnacle of the Church, the papacy itself, it is unlikely. If a simple priest were to be elected, before an installation to his new office could take place, he would have to be ordained to the episcopacy, the fullness of the priesthood. Likewise, a Catholic male called to membership in the Sacred College, unless he has been given a special papal indult to the contrary, must receive the episcopal dignity prior to receipt of the red hat in consistory.

The revised Code of Canon Law (1983) supersedes that of 1917, in which an extensive description of the qualifications for the cardinalate had been presented.[§] The 1983 code has incorporated many of the reforms made in the Church, first, by John XXIII and, subsequently, by his immediate successor, Paul VI. These changes have affected the Sacred College directly and, therefore, the Code of

---

* Examples of this practice today would be Rainier III, Sovereign Prince of Monaco, or Charles, Prince of Wales, or Albert, Crown Prince of Monaco—Marquis des Baux.

† See Chapter 12, Ecclesiastical Precedence, and Chapter 13, Ecclesiastical Protocol and Etiquette.

‡ Canons 349–359; Code of 1983.

§ The present revised Code of Canon Law, in reference to the qualifications for the cardinalatial dignity, simplifies the provisions of canons 232 and 233 of the 1917 Code and incorporates the reforms of John XXIII's *motu proprio Cum gravissima*, as well as numerous *motu proprio* of Paul VI.

1983 concerns itself particularly with this aspect. The Code of 1983 does not extensively define the regulations of the College "but leaves the details of the inner operations of the College generally to the College's statutes or particular law,"[7] in other words, to the Pauline *motu proprio,* which directly apply to the reforms of the Sacred College.

Reforms to the College were not unique to Paul VI, as we have already seen. Sixtus V (A.D. 1586) and Innocent XII (A.D. 1692) each implemented reforms that, in particular, attempted to remove nepotism from the College's ranks. Sixtus V was responsible for fixing the number of electors to seventy and began the process of internationalizing the College by opening membership to all Christian nations. "Innocent restricted the pastoral role of Cardinals in their titles in order to open the way for local clergy to provide more effective pastoral care of the people."[8]

PRIVILEGES

The Code of 1983 specifically cites only two unique privileges for cardinals, whereas that of 1917 incorporated centuries of privileges assigned to them. The intent of the present code was not to abolish these many cardinalatial privileges, which of course it did not do; rather it deferred to modern definitions by the papacy of these privileges and responsibilities in statutes specific to the College. The Code of 1983, however, retains two privileges as they effect individual faculties in relation to the local churches. Canon 357 § 2 states: "Cardinals who are staying outside Rome and outside their own diocese are exempt from the power of governance of the Bishop of the diocese in which they are staying in these matters which concern their own person."[9] In searching for the second citation of the cardinalatial privilege of the 1983 code, a student of canon law must go beyond those codes

that concern themselves explicitly to the office of cardinal. In Part IV of the present code, The Office of Sanctifying in the Church, canon 967 § 1 defines this secondary privilege. "Cardinals by law itself possess the faculty to hear confessions of the Christian faithful anywhere in the world."[10] So exist the only two privileges specified in the present code. Decrees of Paul VI throughout his pontificate, however, extensively define the rights and privileges of the cardinals.

In addition to the privileges of protocol and precedence already discussed in this chapter and defined more fully in other sections on protocol and precedence of the Church and the privileges of dress and insignia, cardinals retain certain other unique privileges. Foremost among these privileges are the election of the new pontiff and the trust of the governance of the Church during the *Sede Vacante,* which are discussed in the sections that follow. The Code of 1917 enumerated these privileges because papal directives were not yet in force at that time. These privileges included the universal right to enter a female cloister, the power to choose any priest as a personal confessor, the privilege of administering the Sacrament of Confirmation universally, the privilege of universally conferring minor orders, the unique privilege of saying Mass at sea and using a "portable" altar, the privilege of attending General Councils with the right of decisive vote, the privilege of disposing of their own benefices by last will and testament, and the privilege of being buried within a church. Most of these rights have been either assumed into the general practice of the clergy by papal directive or have become mute as they refer to circumstances in the Church that no longer apply. In either instance, it is clear that cardinals have always held and enjoyed extraordinary privileges as applied by both the law and by custom. Many of these privileges have been retained to the present time.

CLASSES WITHIN THE COLLEGE AND TITULAR TITLES

"The College of Cardinals is divided into three ranks; the episcopal rank which consists of both the Cardinals to whom the Roman Pontiff assigns the title of a suburbicarian church and the oriental patriarchs who have become members of the College of Cardinals, the presbyterial rank, and the diaconal rank."[11]

Until the reforms of the College, which were made early in this century, and later those by John XXIII and his successor, Paul VI, were instituted, these three ranks more or less corresponded to one's office within Holy Orders. For centuries, those with minor orders were assigned diaconal titles and thus became cardinal-deacons upon nomination. Cardinal-priests were from the presbyterial order, although "foreign" residential bishops were also assigned to this class.* The cardinal-bishops were actually once the diocesan ordinaries of those sees surrounding Rome, but this practice was allowed to lapse some centuries ago.

Until the pontificate of John XXIII, the number of cardinals was limited to seventy. With an increase in the numbers in membership, came both a need for new title churches and a stricter adherence in the proper appointment to ranks or classes within the College. In present times, the system of nomination has a simpler structure. Cardinals holding offices within the Vatican or other high offices not linking them to a particular diocese as its ordinary are created cardinal-deacons. Residential bishops who have been raised to the Sacred College are created cardinal-priests. Cardinal-bishops who have been named to one of the six suburbicarian sees[†] surrounding Rome have been nominated specifically by the pope as a sign of additional respect and esteem and, as such, nearly in all cases, they were transferred from one of the other two classes and had been a cardinal for some time prior to nomination to the higher class of cardinal-bishop.

The cardinal-dean of the Sacred College is the cardinal-bishop to whom the Holy Father has given the seventh suburbicarian title Ostia in addition to the suburbicarian title that he already holds.[‡]

On March 10, 1961,[12] John XXIII stripped away the long-standing privilege of cardinals "opting" for a suburbicarian see, that is, to opt for one of the titles of cardinal-bishop. Until that time, the senior-ranking cardinal-priest could apply to the pontiff for a suburbicarian title when the incumbent of that title passed on to eternity. On April 11, 1962, the right to administer one's own suburbicarian see was also removed from the cardinal-bishops who held these titles. Titular (arch)bishops were appointed in their stead to administer these dioceses.

"Cardinals of presbyterial rank, or Cardinal-Priests, are assigned one of the *tituli* in Rome when they are created Cardinals. In Consistory they can later opt to transfer to another vacant title; this requires the approval of the Pope."[13] That transfer would be only from one title to another within the same class. Just as cardinal-bishops have no direct jurisdictional authority over the faithful of the suburbicarian sees to which they have been entrusted, the cardinal-priests have no pastoral authority over the titular churches entrusted to their care.

Cardinal-priests are, however, entrusted with a specific titular church so that they will provide it with symbolic pastoral care as well as necessary financial support. Western European and Northern American cardinals have complained throughout

---

* Cardinal Martel, a Frenchman, was the last cardinal created who had not been ordained to the office of priest. He died in 1899.

† Albano, Ostia, Porto and Santa Rufina, Palestrina, Sabrina and Mentana, Frascati, and Villetri.

‡ The title Ostia is held in addition to one of the other six titles and carries with it the lifetime appointment as dean of the Sacred College.

this century that they were always assigned the more dilapidated of Rome's ancient churches, which is not altogether incorrect. All residential bishops, when nominated to the College of Cardinals, are now seated as titulars of presbyterial churches and take the title Cardinal-Priest.

Just as the six suburbicarian sees are now only titular titles, that is a see to which a cardinal-bishop has been assigned to tie him closely to the Bishop of Rome, the cardinal-priests are assigned a titular title, which has ancient ties to the earliest church at Rome and marks these cardinals in a unique way as members of the clergy of Rome in service to the Bishop of Rome. Today, there are 123 active presbyterial titular churches.

The term *title* does not apply to an individual prelate's personal dignity but to the still common practice of establishing legal title or ownership over a specific property. The original churches of Rome were homes or large villas, which were given by wealthy early Christians to specific clergy to serve as the church of that community. Often these properties were quite extensive. History tells us that the home of Vitas was used for the assembly of bishops at a Council at Rome, in A.D. 341, which decried Arianism. These earliest home-churches were the original parish churches of Rome, and many of the most ancient churches in Rome today were built on the foundations of these homesteads.

The title or legal ownership of these properties was long ago transferred to the Church. The legal term *title* has remained, reminiscent of the origins of these earliest churches. The incorporation of these titular titles* into the Sacred College for the class of cardinal-priest was a natural transition. There existed twenty-five such titles in Rome by A.D. 499, but the number fluctuated to more than thirty between then and 1587, when Sixtus V set the number at fifty. Four of the major basilicas† each had suffragan titular churches assigned to

them; seven cardinal-priests for each basilica. Those cardinals were assigned a rotation to offer masses at those titulars on a daily basis. The fifth, St. John Lateran, the cathedral church of the Bishop of Rome, was reserved for the liturgies of the pope and the six cardinal-bishops.

An increase in the College required an increase in the number of presbyteral, and likewise diaconal, titles. Some of these titles had to be rehabilitated, whereas others had to be created as need arose. In some instances, as circumstances warranted, a cardinal may have received a title from one of the other classes *pro hoc vice tantum,* meaning "for this time only," or for a short time. In the case of John Cardinal Krol, who has the titular title of the Church of Santa Maria della Mercede e S. Adriano a Villa Albani, one of the diaconal titles, but who is himself a member of the class of cardinal-priest, the *bulla* of his nomination to that church reads *Diaconia elevata pro hoc vice a Titolo Presbyteriale* because, at the time of his elevation to the College, all existing presbyteral titles had already been assigned.‡

New Cardinals who are seated as cardinal-deacons are traditionally the heads of the Roman Curia congregations. The titular titles of the cardinal-deacons are the original *diaconia* (way stations) of ancient Rome. These way stations were the original aid stations, or hospices, for the early Christians and remained the place of refuge for persecuted Christians, and later for the poor, well into the Middle Ages.

The original *diaconia,* however, should not be dismissed as simply way stations, for the significance of their role in the Church of Rome through the first millennium was profound. Thousands of the

---

* Titles assigned to one who does not actually govern the place.
† St. Mary Major, St. Peter in the Vatican, St. Paul Outside the Walls, and St. Lawrence.
‡ The diaconal title is transferred and elevated to one of presbyterial degree for the time being (meaning for the lifetime of this incumbent).

hungry were fed at these special posts. Here, also, was provided whatever medical care could be offered at that time to those in need. Scholars agree that the number of these *diaconia* remained at about eighteen. The deacons who headed them were responsible for the distribution of financial support to the poorest in the city and for the administration of the material wealth that the Church had entrusted to them. Rome was not alone in the rise of the *diaconia,* for researchers have found evidence of their existence at the churches of Palestine, Egypt, Constantinople, and Sicily in southern Italy.

"In Rome the staff of a deaconry comprised: the *Pater Deaconiae,* whose duties were similar to those of a Roman *Paterfamilias,* then a *Dispensator* or steward Administrator and servants who were called *Deaconitae.*"[14] This familiar structure later developed naturally into the full status of Roman parishes, and, by the eleventh century, they were headed by archdeacons, just as parishes, or titulars for the presbyteriate, were governed by archpriests. Historians cite many instances where an archdeacon of one of the historic *diaconia* succeeded his bishop as the next Roman Pontiff.

By decree of Paschal II (A.D. 1115), the practice of nominating the archdeacons of these *diaconia* as a cardinal, which had by then become common, became *pro forma.* Henceforth, the cardinal-deacons were required to incorporate their titular titles into their own signatures when serving as protonotaries or witnesses to papal decrees. This was the first time in the Church's history that this age-old custom had become mandatory. "Among the signatories of the more important bullae of Paschal II, we find for instance, Gregory of St. Angeló Cardinal Deacon; Romanus, Cardinal Deacon of St. Mary in Portico; Guy, Cardinal Deacon of SS. Cosmas and Damian etc."[15]

Although there were only eighteen original *diaconia,* as the College grew so did the need for the creation of further titular titles for the diaconate class. Just as one period in the Church's history demanded an increase in the *titulari,* circumstances of history sometimes also resulted in a temporary decrease. Sixtus V limited the number to fourteen, yet Clement VIII, Leo X, and Benedict XII later increased that number. Pius XI, as a result of the Lateran Agreement, suppressed titles effected by that accord and transferred others. John XXIII and his successors have each rehabilitated ancient *diaconia* as the number of new cardinal-deacons increased. At present, there are fifty-two titular sees for the class of cardinal-deacons.

After a tenure of ten years within the class of cardinal-deacon, a cardinal of that class may petition the Holy Father for a promotion to a titular title of cardinal-priest. If granted to him, the precedence of this new cardinal-priest remains as it had been. Although he moves into the higher class of cardinal-priest, his tenure of ten years as a cardinal-deacon is not forfeited. He retains his precedence in the higher class, assuming a precedence inclusive of those ten years, over all other cardinal-priests with less tenure.

Oriental patriarchs who have also been raised to the Sacred College retain their Patriarchal See as their titular title because they alone enjoy a unique bond to the faithful of that rite and should not lose direct contact with them when the additional honor of the cardinalate has been conferred upon them. Oriental patriarchs enjoying the cardinalatial dignity follow the class of cardinal-bishops in the Church's official table of precedence. This has not always been the case, however. At the close of the Second Vatican Council (1965), it was determined that the Oriental patriarchs, by virtue of the unique position they hold over the faithful of their own rite in the Church, should be given official status just behind the cardinal-bishops. This precedence has been assigned specifically for ceremonies at the Vatican.

SECRET NOMINATIONS

The term *in petto* is the Italian translation for the proper Latin *in pectore* (literally "in the breast," but translated to mean "to hold within the heart.") This age-old custom applies to a secret nomination to the Sacred College. Throughout the history of the College, turbulence, war, political strife, and anti-clericalism have required the popes to hold secret the name or names of those who would be in personal danger were it to be known that they had received the highest honor that the Church can bestow. The significance of this protection is evident by the inclusion of an appropriate provision for this practice within the Code of Canon Law.*

The name of a cardinal whose nomination is held *in petto* is not openly declared in the consistory, nor is it known to anyone in the pope's household. The name held *in petto* is placed by the pope in a sealed envelope, where it awaits either the appropriate moment for public announcement or the death of the pontiff who had sealed the nomination. An *in pectore* nomination remains the world's best-kept secret. Because the cardinal-designate is not aware of this honor, he is not bound by the obligations of the cardinalate. Likewise, he may not assume the privileges of his office. Were the nominating pontiff to die before his name was proclaimed publically, this nomination would become void. Once the designate's name has been publically proclaimed, however, no matter how long after the original *biglietto* of nomination had been prepared, he assumes the title and dignity of the office of cardinal in the appropriate class, with all privileges and rights appertaining to it enjoyed.

The precedence of a cardinal named *in petto* is set from the date of his original nomination to the College and not by the date on which he assumes the cardinalatial dignity. As such, within the class or rank of the College to which he now belongs, the cardinal named *in petto* holds that precedence assigned him on the date of his original nomination.

A question that arises from time to time is, May cardinals resign their office? The answer is, of course, yes. Resignation, as defined under the terms of the present code,† is considered only in terms of the curial offices that the cardinals hold and not with the dignity or position of cardinal itself. If a cardinal were to resign his membership in the Sacred College, as some have done, he would return to the dignity he held prior to his rise to the College unless circumstances warranted otherwise, in which case it would become a matter for the pope to determine.‡ As a matter of form, even the customary resignation from curial assignments, which is set by law, requires the concurrence of the pope.

MODERN ROLE

There have been times when the Sacred College served as a means to reward political allies, family, and associates without giving those cardinals any official role in the Church's governance. In its earliest days, the cardinal individually undertook the work of the Church in small parishes or deaconries.

---

* Canon 351 § 3.

† Canon 354.

‡ Although rare, resignations from the Sacred College do occur. These occurrences are not so rare as to be only a part of the distant past. In this century, during the pontificate of Pius XI, French Churchman Louis Cardinal Billot, an active pro-French political figure and professor at the prestigious Roman Pontifical Gregorian University, resigned in anger after the pope publically denounced the doctrines of *l'Action Française,* a movement aggressively supported by the cardinal. Billot returned to the presbyterate as a simple priest and retired to the monastery of Galloro in Italy.

In the modern era, more than in any other, the College serves the papacy as a working advisory body on matters of theology, government, and finance. Never before in history has the College been so international, with members from every continent on Earth included in its ranks, and it has never been more relevant for the work of the Church. Pope John Paul II seeks the advice of the College far more often than did his predecessors. In the past several pontificates, cardinals gathered together only to celebrate the welcome of new members or to mourn the passing of a pope and to elect his successor. John Paul II, remaining faithful to the spirit of the Second Vatican Council, continues to seek out cardinals for their advice and for support of Church policy. No longer are men called to the College for political motives.

During the early summer of 1994 (a month later than anticipated for a convocation of a consistory due to the pope's fall and fracture of his hip), cardinals from the world over gathered in Rome. They came not to welcome newly named members, as had been anticipated in the press, but to discuss the Church's plans for ceremonies marking the two-thousandth anniversary of Christ's birth. "Instead of secret lists of papal candidates or guest lists for receptions, they carried briefing papers on several important Church topics."[16] In the consistory of 1994, Pope John Paul II sought the advice of the cardinals to help him plan for the most significant event of our era, the two-thousandth anniversary of the coming of Christ. "The agenda for the year's brainstorming session was especially rich, with discussions planned on the ecumenical initiatives leading up to the year 2000, a pro-life encyclical and a wider role for retired Bishops."[17]

The work of the consistory of 1994 illustrates the pertinence of the Sacred College in the modern era. Too many critics since Vatican II have decried the Sacred College as anachronistic. In their speech or writing, they pronounce it to be a remnant of the so-called evil Medieval Papacy. In recent press, the College has been described, inaccurately, as noninclusive of all Catholics. Persons who hold these beliefs could not be further from the truth. The Sacred College continues to serve the Church well. It offers her centuries of rich tradition and a contribution that today provides a true international perspective and deep understanding of the needs of the Church, in every area of the world. The Holy Spirit, it is evident, continues to actively participate in the work of the Church through the pope and his senate, the College of Cardinals, in a very profound way. Never before has the College been as important as it now is, and as we prepare to move into the third millennium, the role of the College of Cardinals in the Church is more vital than at any other time in history, including the time of the seventy elders who served Moses and that of the seven disciples in Acts 6. How truly pivotal the College of Cardinals has become.

CREATION OF CARDINALS

Membership in the Sacred College has always carried with it beautiful ceremonies as well as the many responsibilities and privileges attached to the office of the cardinalate. The rituals associated with the bestowal of cardinal's rank are centuries old, little changed, and rich in pomp and pageantry. The post–Vatican II ceremonies mark the unique role of the cardinal, not so much as a prince of the Church—although each still very much is—but as a pastor who serves the Bishop of Rome in a unique apostolic way. We shall see the ceremonial attached to the bestowal of the "red hat" as it has been presented since 1969. We should, however, reach back into the ages for a historic presentation of the pageantry as it once was observed with the bestowal of the red hat.

In the past, once the class of nominees had been prepared by the reigning pope, the official *biglietto,* or list, was announced to the world, very much as it is today. Those persons to be named were always forewarned by prelates who either meant well or who had political motives of their own. The new cardinals resident in Rome seldom were surprised at the publication of the *biglietto.* The ceremonies that followed the announcement differed only upon the place of residence of the new cardinal-designate. Today, a prelate designated a cardinal does not experience the elaborate ceremonial that accompanied his nomination in centuries past. The ceremonies have been simplified substantially, and yet the new cardinals, and those present as witnesses, come away impressed with a feeling of history and pageantry. In all honesty, present-day ceremonies lack some of the beauty of the past; however, as the ceremony of conferral of the red hat, and indeed the title Cardinal, is not a sacramental one, it should reflect the present era, so long as the historic elements linking it to the foundation of the Sacred College remain.

When Paul VI reformed the law to more closely reflect the modern era and to bring the ceremonies of the Church closer to the people, he did not do so maliciously or haphazardly, as many have since claimed. His intent, generally applauded, was to strip only that which no longer had relevance in the world, only that which was not sacred to the Church.*

Public Consistory

As we will see, the ceremony of conferral of the red hat was at one time quite elaborate and beautiful. Although far less so today, it does not lack beauty. Although less elaborate, it does indeed carry with it an aura of dignity. The public consistory, in which the red hat is conferred, follows a private meeting of the entire college, including the newest members, in which the Holy Father officially welcomes each new member. Each cardinal enjoys full membership rights of the College, however, from the moment of the publication of the *biglietto* some weeks before. At the private consistory, the Holy Father introduces each new cardinal to the incumbent cardinals. This concluded, the public consistory commences.†

Because of the large size of the College itself and the numbers of pilgrims that frequently accompany the newest cardinals, the public consistory can no longer be held in the historic Consistorial Hall. In the consistory of 1991, the number of pilgrims was so large that even this hall, which holds 6,500 persons, could not accommodate all who came to witness the ceremony of conferral.‡

In modern times, the public consistory naming new cardinals usually takes place no more than a month before the actual ceremony is to take place in Rome. Although not written in stone, it has been the custom for some time to install the new cardinals on the feast of SS. Peter and Paul on June twenty-nine. The newly named cardinals, however, are quietly informed of their elevation some weeks before public notice is given so that they may make the appropriate arrangements in advance time.

Although the Holy Father receives the new cardinals in secret or semisecret consistory before the public consistory of nomination takes place, these private consistories no longer hold the mystery or ceremonial impact that they formerly held. They are more akin, in present times, to ceremonial "business" meetings than to a gathering of the new princes of the Church of which they were formerly more or less cognizant. This does not infer that the

---

* Since that time, some of the faithful have taken it upon themselves to "adapt" Church practice in ways that do strip away the sacred. This was not Paul's intent, as his many constitutions and *motu proprio* illustrate.
† Not necessarily on the same day.
‡ A large television was set up inside St. Peter's Basilica so that persons not inside the Paul VI Audience Hall could view the ceremony.

celebrations attached to the creation of new cardinals have dwindled down to one simple event. On the contrary, the celebrations marking the elevation of churchmen to the Sacred College still resound with an electric pageantry that lasts a week or longer and for which all in Rome adjust their lives to witness.

Those individuals who have been invited to witness the elevation ceremony firsthand arrive at the Paul VI Audience Hall by ten o'clock on the morning of the appointed day. The Vatican City State is aflutter with excitement. The Swiss Guard are vested in full ceremonial garb and stand their posts around the Vatican State. Inside the Paul VI Hall are seated dignitaries from the world over. Row after row of diplomats and their spouses fill the front of the hall. Each is dressed in uniform, white tie and tails, national costume, or, for the women, long black silk dresses and equally long beautiful black-lace mantillas, many suspended from 6-inch-high ivory combs atop their heads. Behind these sit the dignitaries of dioceses being honored with a new cardinal, as well as the cardinal's family and close friends. In many cases, pilgrims from a diocese accompany their new cardinal to witness his elevation.* It is indeed an honor to witness your (arch)bishop's elevation to the Sacred College.

Row after row of priest, seminarian, and religious fill the hall. In 1991, a solitary figure in white, with blue trim, was seen entering the hall to be a simple witness with all the others, Mother Teresa of Calcutta. Reserved in the front of the hall are seats for the Roman Curia archbishops and bishops, vested in purple choir dress, as well as bishops from throughout the world who have come to be a part of the ceremonies elevating their superior, metropolitan, archbishop, or friend.

Positioned in front of the hall is a row of simple priests, or *monsignori,* the secretaries or attendants of the newly named cardinals. In front of them, a row of beautiful, antique gold and tapestry seventeenth-century French armchairs await the newest members of the Sacred College. Before these thrones are the stairs, ascending to the stage of the hall. At the rear of the stage, along the back wall, is the 1977 sculpture *Risen Christ,* a favorite of Paul VI, designed for him by Pericle Fazzini. In the center of the stage, before the Fazzini sculpture, stands a single throne for the pontiff, positioned on a platform of two beige-carpeted steps. To the right of the pope's throne have gathered the College of Cardinals, those cardinals long ago received into the highest ranks of the Church. To the left of the pope's throne are rows of empty seats, identical both to those used for seated members of the College and to those reserved below the stage where the new member cardinals had begun the day's ceremonies. These empty seats upon the dais await each new cardinal after he exchanges the Kiss of Peace with the entire College.

The last to enter, but one, are the new cardinals. All others have taken their places and await the ceremony's opening hymn. From the salon outside the stage come the new cardinals, officially called "cardinal-designates" until the moment of their installation. Their order of entry into the hall was determined long before this day. In announcing new cardinals, the pope does not list them in alphabetical order but rather in a determinate, specific order that establishes their order of precedence within the Sacred College for the remainder of their lifetimes, unless they are promoted to a higher class within the College itself. So as each one enters the hall, he does so in a way that, once seated, those persons named before their brother cardinals will be received into the College first.

*In 1991, more pilgrims accompanied Anthony Cardinal Bevilacqua of Philadelphia than could be seated in the hall, an unusual sign of the devotion of the people of this see.

A wave of excitement fills the hall as each cardinal appears in the doorway, an excitement that does not subside until long after they all have taken their places. Many of them linger before taking their seats, recognizing this bishop, that cardinal, or this old friend. To add to the electric atmosphere, the Sistine Choir, under the lifetime direction of Monsignor Dominico Bartolucci,* vociferates anthems and hymns at stiletto pace.

Within minutes of the lull and peace that eventually overtakes the hall, the Swiss Guard appear at every entrance, including the stage's grand entrance, and take up their posts on the altar stairs and behind the pontiff's throne, under the *Risen Christ*. Almost immediately, the pope appears, vested in white simar and red silk *mozzetta* and stole, accompanied by Bishop Dino Monduzzi, Prefect of the Papal Household, and Monsignor Piero Marini, Master of Ceremonies of the Supreme Pontiff, along with other Papal Household *officiali*.

The public consistory is held within the structure of the Liturgy of the Word from the Office of the Day. The Sistine Choir provides the music. Before the Liturgy of the Word, the pope presents his *allocutio*, an address on the role of the cardinal and not a spiritual homily. The new cardinals are publicly assigned to their new titular church in Rome at this time, although they had been informed by the Holy See some weeks before the ceremonies of this unique day as to what church they would serve as spiritual protector. This address is also known as the pope's exaltation to the new cardinals; in it, he informs them of their new broadened responsibilities as well as the many challenges that will face them in this extended service to the Church.

At the close of the exaltation, the first in precedence among the cardinals created this day ascends the staircase to a place before a microphone, where he may respond to the Holy Father's address on behalf of all his brother cardinals.† At the close of this address, in which he publicly thanks the pope for this distinction for himself and his brother cardinals, he pledges, on behalf of them all, their unified support and fidelity to the pontiff. At the conclusion of the address, as protocol has dictated for three hundred years, he moves toward the throne and genuflects, setting the tone of the day, one of solemnity and respect for Peter. Rising, he moves to receive the *embracio* (embrace), or Kiss of Peace, from the pope. Once again he genuflects, kisses the pope's ring, and returns to his place alongside the other cardinal-designates soon to be elevated to the Sacred College.

The Epistle follows and then the Gospel, which is chanted by a deacon in either Latin or Greek. The pope, seated at the throne, presents his second address, this time a homily of a spiritual nature reflecting the scripture of the day. His words, by custom, tie the liturgy to the role of the cardinals in a symbolic way. As the homily concludes, the cardinal-designates stand, and, in unison, they approach the bottom step of the stage. Facing the pope, they offer again their Profession of Faith, the Apostle's Creed, in Latin. At its conclusion, the row of scarlet-clad cardinal-designates bow in unison and return to their assigned places.

The moment of installation has arrived. One by one, each of the new cardinals ascends the stairs, often to great cheers and applause from family and friends in the hall. Genuflecting, each then kneels before the pope. Behind the pope are seminarians holding large silver trays, on which are placed the scarlet watered-silk *birette*, atop of which are the scarlet *zucchetti* for each of the cardinals; each bears the cardinal's name inside. (The *birette* and *zucchetti* had been sent over to the Master of Ceremonies

---

* Given the title *Maestro Direttore Perpetuo* by Pius XII.
† In 1991, this was the secretary of state, newly named Angelo Cardinal Sodano.

the day before by each new cardinal in order to ensure the correct size.) The pope immediately places the *zucchetto,* followed by the *biretta,* on the head of the cardinal-designate. As he confers the *biretta* with the following words, the cardinal-designate immediately becomes a full member of the Sacred College:* *In praise of God and in the honor of the Apostolic See, receive the red hat, the sign of the Cardinal's dignity. For you must be ready to conduct yourself with fortitude, even to the shedding of your blood, for the increase of the Christian faith; for the peace and tranquility of the people of God and for the kingdom of Heaven and for the Holy Roman Church.*

Now and forever a cardinal of the Holy Roman Church, the prelate rises, removes the *biretta,* and leans forward to embrace the pope with the Kiss of Peace; he then bows and replaces the *biretta* on his head, proceeds to the members of the College seated on the stage (who have long ago been created cardinals), and, one by one, extends to each the Kiss of Peace. Once completed, he no longer sits on the hall's main floor but remains on the stage, taking his proper place to the left of the pontiff's throne, along with his brothers in the class of cardinals created that day. The ceremony nearing completion, the prayers of the faithful are sung in Latin followed by the papal blessing. At the conclusion, the pope traditionally leaves through the hall's central doors after pausing along the way to greet one group or another.

The cardinals leave through a special door. The newest members of the College are hustled away for comment by a television or news-agency reporter from their home countries or cities. Family and friends surrender this part of the day to the public persona of membership in the Sacred College. Later in the evening, the cardinals receive their families, friends, and pilgrims at a reception within the Apostolic Palace or Vatican gardens—sometimes the magnificent Borgia Apartments, other

times outdoors. This is a festive occasion to publicly greet and thank all those witnessing the unique ceremonies marking admission into the most prestigious body in the world. Private banquets, by invitation only, are held throughout Rome during the next few days, the expense of which falls to the new cardinal himself or to his diocese, if financially possible.

Mass of the Rings

On the actual feast of SS. Peter and Paul, the pope traditionally presents the *pallium* to those metropolitan archbishops who were named to their sees during the previous year. In the years when the College of Cardinals is to receive new members, the pope also presents the cardinalatial ring to its newest members at the Mass of the Pallium.

As the procession of concelebrants—the cardinals and metropolitans—begins to wind its way from the Bronze Door, the other cardinals and curia prelates take their places on the Sacristan, the term used to describe the front steps of the Vatican basilica. To the left, as one faces the basilica, are the cardinals vested in scarlet choir dress. Behind them are seated all others with episcopal dignity, in purple. Farther back in the ranks of prelates are the *monsignori,* priests, and religious. To the right of the Sacristan are seated the diplomatic corps, in full regalia, along with other honored guests from the world over. This is one of the most prestigious events of the year, and all are present to witness it.

For the first time, the newly installed cardinals wear the white damasked mitre and are vested in red silk chasuble (red is the color of martyrs, sym-

---

* Although it must always be remembered that on the day of the publication of the *biglietto* nominating cardinal-designates to the College, they are entitled to vote in the event of the death of the pope even before conferral of the "red hat." The title Eminence is also immediately assumed with the publication of the *biglietto,* although most churchmen are not aware of this privilege.

bolic of Peter and Paul). Preceding them are the metropolitans about to receive the *pallia,* and, closing the *corteo,* is the pope.

The altar has been built under a canopy of wood to protect the pope from the intense Roman summer sun or the wind and rain common in Rome in late summer afternoons. A red-and-gold brocade carpet has been laid across the paving completely covering the 180-by-100 foot expanse of stone. From the rear of the altar, to the portal of St. Peter's itself, is stretched a red carpet runner. Atop the steps is the throne of the pontiff. High above it, suspended from the main balcony 60 feet above, is the papal coat of arms. Vines, flowers, and other decorations abound. Across the top step, wide enough for four rows of chairs, is a single row of antique gold chairs for the new cardinals. Those individuals who are to receive the *pallium* are seated below in two rows facing one another, one to the left in front of the College of Cardinals in choir, and one to the right in front of the diplomatic corps. Only the newest cardinals are placed in proximity to the throne of Peter.

The Mass of the Rings is similar to every other papal Mass to the point of the homily. Just after the Gospel, the pontiff blesses the congregation with the book of the Gospels, which has been presented to him by the Deacon of the Word. He then resumes his throne. The newest cardinals descend the steps, then turn and face the pontiff in unison. As in the public consistory of the day before, one by one they ascend the stairs to receive their ring of office as cardinal.

From their arrival in Rome, to commence celebrations of their rise to cardinalatial dignity, until the morning of the Mass of the Rings, new cardinals use the ordinary ring of the office of bishop. Only on the morning before the Mass of the Rings does someone with episcopal dignity lay aside the ring of office. A new cardinal is not to wear a ring

to the Mass of the Rings, as a new cardinalatial ring will be presented to him by the pope. The new ring symbolizes the fidelity of the new cardinal to Rome. The ring can take any design (see Chapter 32), but the inside always carries an engraving of the reigning pope's coat of arms.

Following the presentation of the rings, the metropolitan archbishops come forward for the *pallium* in the same fashion. The homily follows, and the Mass continues as would any papal Mass, with great pomp and beauty. It is interesting to note that until the cardinal redeems his ring with an honorarium due Rome, he is not entitled to bequeath it or any other personal property to any person or entity other than the Holy See. This rule is an arcane reminder of past difficulties in the history of the College.*

Taking Possession of the Titular Church

The last of the formal ceremonies marking the rise to the College of Cardinals is the taking possession, by the new cardinal, of his new titular church. A titular church is one of the earliest parishes in Rome that has a cardinal as its protector. The origins of the College, as we have seen, were in the Roman clergy. Each cardinal belonged to one specific parish church in Rome. He even took that church's name as part of his own. As the cardinalate expanded, each new cardinal was still given one of the Roman churches so that, in a unique way, he was tied to Rome and could still be considered part of the Roman clergy.

At present, because of the increased numbers of the College, churches other than the earliest

---

* The Mass of the Rings for the Consistory of November 1994 took place inside the Archbasilica of St. Peter in the Vatican. The Holy Father and the new cardinals concelebrated this Mass together on the first Sunday of Advent (November 27). The magnificent purple vestments of the concelebrants provided a colorful contrast to the other cardinals who were seated behind them, vested in scarlet choral (choir) dress.

churches are designated as titular for cardinals. The ceremony of taking possession in modern times differs little from the manner prescribed before Vatican II. The main difference is the change in vesture of the cardinals and the placement of portraits and armorial bearings inside the church. Now no portraits are permitted; arms may be placed outside the edifice, over the portal, or within the vestibule itself. The cardinal now arrives in scarlet choir vesture and then vests in proper sacred vestments to celebrate the Mass. He no longer arrives with the *cappa magna*. The ceremony, although less elaborate, is no less beautiful.

It falls to the cardinal-titular to protect the Church, both spiritually and financially. Claims were made in the not-too-distant past that American and other wealthy western prelates were given the most dilapidated of Rome's churches so that they could be properly restored. (This is still the case somewhat, certainly not out of malice but more out of necessity.) Finally, the week's events wind down with one or more Masses of Thanksgiving in the major basilicas of Rome, along with many formal dinners and receptions. Cardinal Sodano hosted his formal reception outdoors in the Vatican gardens attached to the Belvedere Palace, which provided an alternative method of entertainment very much appreciated by those privileged to attend. It was a very sophisticated event, as one would expect, and was considered very imaginative, by more traditional Roman standards.

FORMER CUSTOM

In past ages, for those designates residing in Rome, the pageantry of the ceremonies began at once. From the moment of the announcement, a room was set aside in their Roman residences, usually a grand palazzo, which was to be sealed. It remained closed until the arrival of the cardinal-secretary of state, who presented the official *biglietto* in person. During the interim between the publication of the names and the official visit of the cardinal–secretary of state, which could be a period of hours or days, the cardinal-designate could receive no other visitors. The level of high esteem of the designate was often gauged by the length of time it took the cardinal-secretary to call upon the designate. The official program of presentation, however, always followed the exact order as prepared by the reigning pope and as listed on the *biglietto*. The twentieth-century practice of alphabetized listing has never applied to the papal *biglietto*.

The cardinal-designate's residence was prepared once the announcement was made public. Care was given not to anticipate the announcement in any way. Proper vesture was commissioned quietly, most often by personal tailors. The recent practice of using independent Roman tailor shops was not always necessary, as many cardinals in former times employed their own personal tailors. (It would be politically incorrect for the vesture to be prepared before the official announcement, no matter how much foreknowledge the designate may have had.)

Within the residence itself, the reception hall was fitted with a throne and *baldachino*. The designate's coat of arms remained covered until the red hat (*galero*) was actually presented to the new cardinal. The reasoning behind this practice was simply one of heraldic protocol. The cardinal-designate was no longer of the rank he had previously held, a rank marked by the proper heraldic hat and tassels, yet he had not yet received the red *galero*, which would now surmount his personal arms as a cardinal. Caught somewhat in the middle, protocol required that the heraldic achievement be entirely covered until the moment that the designate received the red *galero*. A second *baldachino* opposite the first, a requirement for all cardinals of the past, was hung over their throne. It was draped in scarlet velvet or, in summer, scarlet silk. Upon this drape was placed a portrait of the reigning pope. A gilt chair, upholstered in scarlet damask, velvet, or silk, was used as the throne and placed upon a small dais. Until the red hat was presented at the Vatican, this chair was turned to face the wall, illustrating that full privileges to the cardinalate were not assumed until the hat had been bestowed.*

Roman protocol provided for even the most minute details regarding the pageantry associated with the receipt of the red hat. At the door of a new cardinal's throne room, a noble gentleman-in-waiting (not to be confused with a footman or servant) was posted to announce each of the dignitaries calling on the new cardinal to offer congratulations. A second was posted at the entrance of the grand salon adjacent to the throne room and, within the throne room itself, still another who recorded the names, titles, and positions of each of the dignitaries calling that day. Each of these gentlemen were young men of the Roman families known as the Black Nobility (see Glossary). It was a great honor for the Roman nobility to have a son of their house called into service by the princes of the Church.

On the day of the presentation of the *biglietto,* the cardinal-dean was present for the acceptance of congratulations by the diplomatic corps and noble families. The cardinal-dean was vested in simar and *ferraiolo (abito piano).* All present wore their most formal attire: prelates in *abito piano,* nobles of the household in the formal papal costume of their position at the Vatican, and the Roman nobles in formal dress or uniform. The ceremony of presentation was always followed by a formal reception, but, ideally, this was concluded by 1:00 P.M., the time of the Roman siesta. When the reception was over, the throne room was sealed until the red hat[†] was presented at the Vatican.

On the day of the presentation of the *biglietto,* the cardinal-designate was vested in the purple choir cassock with purple sash. The secretary of state entered the throne room, proceeding only to the midpoint of the salon. The parchment was then handed over by the cardinal-secretary to one of the archbishops who accompanied him.[‡] This archbishop then crossed the throne room and presented the *biglietto* to the cardinal-designate. After reading it in silence, the designate handed over the nomination to the one he deemed to be of highest rank in his own entourage, who then read the Latin text aloud. The designate then mounted the stairs of the dais but did not yet sit upon the throne.

Regardless of the number of persons gathered for the ceremony, only ambassadors and ministers to the Papal Court, patriarchs, prelates, and princes were greeted on this first day of ceremonies. Before the reception was over, the Papal Master of Ceremonies came forward to the foot of the stairs for the announcement of the date and hour when the red hat would be conferred at the public consistory.

Because travel was so difficult, even well into our own century, many of those persons named to the Sacred College received word of their nomination by telegram, possibly even by the press, and before that, by courier; consequently, these initial ceremonies, enjoyed by Roman designates, had to be foregone. After the designates and their entourages

---

* This assumption of privileges should not be misunderstood as that of the right to vote in conclave. This right was guaranteed to all designates once the *biglietto* was published, and, were the reigning pontiff to die before the bestowal of the red hat, they could enter conclave as full members of the Sacred College.

† One must remember that the red hat presented today is the *biretta,* whereas that presented prior to 1969 was the red *galero,* or heraldic hat, reserved for cardinals.

‡ Protocol forbade the cardinal-secretary, who outranked all others present, especially the newly nominated cardinals, from proceeding across the room entirely, as this gesture would be an act subservient to the newly named cardinal. As papal decree required the newly named cardinal to receive the *biglietto* on the throne, the diplomatic formula of the attending archbishop had to be devised.

arrived in Rome, the cardinal-designate sent his highest clerical secretary to the office of the Cardinal–Secretary of State to inform the Holy Father of the new cardinal's presence in Rome. Protocol specified the dress of the emissary to be cassock and *ferraiolo* of appropriate rank. The emissary carried a handwritten letter, in Latin text, requesting admittance into audience with the pope. After returning to the temporary residence of the cardinal-designate, word came as to when the Holy Father would formally receive the cardinal-designate, accompanied by his personal staff. Protocol required the designee to be vested not as a cardinal but as a prelate (black simar; red trim; purple sash and *ferraiolo*), and yet concessions to their pending rank were granted. It was customary for the cardinal-designate to don the ordinary black *capella* with the red-and-gold cords and tassels of a cardinal.

The first visit with the pontiff was the most informal of the celebrations during the ceremonies marking the promotion to the Sacred College. This first visit was either a brief courtesy visit or a prolonged business meeting, depending on the cardinal's personal relationship with the Holy Father or the importance of the see over which he had jurisdiction. Following this papal audience, the designate repeated the call on the Secretary of State. The last words of the Secretary of State were ominous. He reminded the new cardinal that custom required that, with this visit concluded, the designee must immediately return to his temporary residence and, once there, was forbidden to leave without the expressed persmission of the pope.

After both Roman and foreign cardinal-designates were properly received, the Vatican published a schedule for official receptions at which Roman society could offer congratulations to the newly named members of the Sacred College. The time for such receptions was limited to between the hours of 10:00 A.M. and 1:00 P.M. Although fewer new members were named at one time than is the case today, it still presented a logistics nightmare for individuals wishing to call on all new cardinals. A mad dash about Rome in antique barouche and landau was often the result.

An emissary of the pontiff arrived at the pre-appointed hour, bearing the scarlet watered-silk *biretta*. This emissary was always a prelate of the Papal Household and was always vested for this occasion in the red velvet, ermine-trimmed cloak known as the *crocia*. He was received in the presence of the assembly, then knelt before the cardinal-designate and presented him with the *biretta,* which he was not entitled to wear until after the reception of the red *galero* in the public consistory.

Although the cardinal-designate was still vested as a prelate of a lesser degree, the red sash with gold tufts and the red *zucchetto* were now also permitted. During the presentation of the *biretta* ceremony, in addition to those dignitaries who had been presented the day before and who had returned for the presentation of the *biretta,* the generals, superiors, and procurators of religious orders; the senior members of the Curia; and abbots resident or visiting Rome were now received. The designate was not permitted to cross the threshold of his throne room although the reception continued in the attached salon. A red gilt chair was prepared for him at a place of honor; however, he was still unable to assume his throne.

First, or "Public," Consistory

On the day of the public consistory, the designate made his way to the Vatican, as protocol demanded, in the purple vesture of a prelate. Inside the Vatican apartments, he donned the vesture of a cardinal: the buckled shoes of red Moroccan leather, the scarlet *zucchetto,* and hat *(cappella)* with gold cords and trimming. The *biretta* previously had been handed over to the Master of Ceremonies for re-presentation at the public consistory. The *mozzetta* was carried over the arm, as the new cardinal would be vested in it during the ceremony.

When properly vested, the new cardinals were led to a formal reception room in the papal apartments. Each new cardinal approached the Holy Father, who was seated on his throne, to receive the *mozzetta* of scarlet watered silk. The red *biretta* was placed upon a head of the designee, who then officially enjoyed all privileges of membership in the Sacred College. The *birretta* was removed by the cardinal as he rose to bow and reverence the ring of the pontiff. As soon as all new cardinals had performed this ritual, the senior within their ranks rose to present an address on all their behalf. A brief private visit followed in the papal apartments, and a formal welcome took place during the subsequent offical call to the office of the Cardinal–Secretary of State.

On the following day, the *galero* (the historical "red hat") was presented in public consistory in the Sistine Chapel. Once inside the Vatican, the new cardinal was vested with the scarlet watered-silk *cappa magna* and was then led into the Sistine Chapel. Upon entering the chapel, he reverenced the altar, followed by a bow to those present on either side. The new cardinal was accompanied by his secretary, who was vested in the purple cassock, sash, and *mantellone*. Traditionally, the secretary was made a papal chamberlain for the occasion if he were not so already; however, the purple vesture was technically one of household or livery and not one of monsignorial rank, a difference that does not exist today.

The *zucchetto* and *biretta* were removed from the head of the cardinal. they were carried by their trainbearers, who all stood along the Gospel side of the Sistine Chapel. After reverencing the Holy Father, who sat upon his throne, the *zucchetto* and *biretta* were returned to the cardinals. "Then the Cardinals-elect, walking between their Cardinal-Deacons as sponsors, came into the presence of the Holy Father surrounded by his court; Cardinal-Priests and Bishops on his right and Cardinal-Deacons on his left. After kissing the Pontiff's hands and cheek and embracing all members of the College of Cardinals in order of their precedence, the Cardinals-elect prostrated themselves on the floor before the altar while the Pope read prayers over them. Then in single file they again kneel before the Pope, the hoods of their Cappa Magna drawn over their heads as the large 'Red Hat' held over each while the Pope recited in Latin: *To the praise of Almighty God and, the honor of His Holy See, receive the red hat, the distinctive sign of the Cardinal's dignity, by which is meant that even unto death and the shedding of blood you will show yourself courageous for the exaltation of our Holy Father, for the peace and outlet of Christian people, and for the augmentation of the Holy Roman Church. In the name of the Father and of the Son and of the Holy Ghost* [Spirit]." [18]

The *galero*—with thirty tassels, fifteen on either side, arranged around its brim—was presented to the new cardinal, never to be worn again. It was stored at the cardinal's residence for the day of his death, when it would be carried before his coffin and then placed at the base of his bier, subsequently to be hung from his church or cathedral ceiling to denote that once a cardinal had jurisdiction there.

Before this ceremony closed, once again the cardinals proceeded into the Sistine Chapel for the singing of the Te Deum. The new cardinals prostrated themselves before the altar and remained there until the final prayers. Rising, they were congratulated by the other cardinals present and again went to the papal apartments to be received by the Holy Father. They remained in *cappa magna* for the duration of this visit, but, as time passed and by the late nineteenth century, permission to vest in *mozzetta* with *mantelletta* was granted. During this ceremony, the household of the new cardinal simultaneously uncovered the coat of arms of the cardinal and placed his throne in the proper jurisdictional position.

Second, or "Secret," Consistory

The secret consistory was the ceremony known as the Opening and Closing of the Mouth. Vested in the *cappa magna,* the cardinals returned to the Vatican Palace. In the Hall of Consistories, they each, in turn, approached the Holy Father. Kneeling before him, the *aperitio oris* (the Opening of the Mouth) took place, in which the pope pronounced, "I open your mouth that in Consistories, Congregations, and in other ecclesiastical functions, you may be heard in the name of the Father, the Son, and the Holy Ghost."[19] After each new cardinal had received *aperitio oris,* and following a hymn, each mounted the steps to the throne a second time for the ceremony of *clausura oris* (the Closing of the Mouth). Whereas the *aperitio oris* symbolized the call for the new cardinal to provide honest, wise counsel, the *clausura oris* symbolized the call for the new cardinals never to divulge the secrets that their office entitles them to learn. In the formula used by the pope for the *clausura oris,* he called them "to keep the secrets of their office and to give wise counsel to the Pope."[20]

At the completion of the *clausura,* each cardinal again approached the pontiff. Kneeling before him, the cardinal was presented with his new ring of office, traditionally a sapphire, which had the name and arms of the reigning pope engraved inside. After receipt of the ring, the cardinal was assigned a church in Rome, over which he served as titular or spiritual head until his death or promotion within the Sacred College.*

Taking Possession of the Titular Church in Past Eras

Before the *biglietto* was announced, the Secretariat of State informed the pope's vicar for Rome which churches would be named the titulars of the new class of the Sacred College. The vicar, in turn, would make the appropriate arrangements for the preparation of these churches for the ceremonies of possession, as they were known.

The church was prepared in festive style. The *cathedra,* if made of marble or wood, was to be covered in red silk. If nonexistent, as was usually the case, as these were simple churches, an ornate gilt chair similar to the one used in the cardinal's residence, covered in red silk, damask, or velvet, was to be placed on a dais with three steps. His arms were hung above the chair but within the drapes of the *baldachino.*

The cardinal traveled from his residence in scarlet choir dress with *mozzetta* and *mantelletta,* then divested himself of these and donned the scarlet *cappa magna* as he arrived at the church. He was accompanied by numerous prelates, including those prelates from his own nation resident or traveling in Rome, members of the Papal Household, and his own retinue—all are vested in choir dress. As the new cardinal arrived at the church, the tower bells, as well as acolytes within the church with bells in hand, rang out in joyful welcome. The organ and choir burst into a hymn of praise to signify the arrival of the new titular head of that church.

At the altar, to the Epistle side, hung a portrait of the new cardinal, almost always on an ornate easel of the Roman baroque style. On the Gospel side hung a portrait of the reigning pope in the same manner. All the clergy already present within the

---

* A promotion within the Sacred College, from rank of deacon to priest or priest to bishop, might entail a change of titular church.

church proceeded from the altar as the hymn began and greeted the new cardinal at the door. All the while, the bells rang and the organ and hymn continued to resound.

After the cardinal had assumed the *cappa magna,* he knelt in silent prayer on a prie-dieu, covered in scarlet silk and emblazoned with his coat of arms, in the vestibule to the church. Before the cardinal rose, his secretary stepped forward to remove the *zucchetto.* The pastor, rector, or superior of the church stepped forward with a crucifix to be reverenced. He then rose. The rector or pastor then stepped forward with the *aspergillium.* The cardinal touched it and blessed himself and then presented it to all prelates present to do likewise. He then sprinkled those directly around him.

The superior or pastor then stepped forward with the thurible for the imposition of incense. The rector or pastor then stepped backward and, using the ancient formula of three double swings of the thurible, he incensed the new titular of the church. The prie-dieu was then removed, and the procession slowly moved down the main aisle of the church as the choir sang "Behold the High Priest" *(Ecce Sacerdos Magnus).* After the cardinal knelt in silent prayer at the Blessed Sacrament altar, the liturgical ceremonies began. The superior or rector sang or chanted the prayers for the solemn reception of prelates. The cardinal rose at its conclusion and took his place on the *cathedra.* A protonotary apostolic de numero stepped forward and read the papal bull conferring the responsibility for that church on the new cardinal, who henceforth would serve as its protector.

The clergy presented then rose to welcome the new cardinal. Archbishops and bishops exchanged the Kiss of Peace. Lesser prelates, priests, and deacons knelt to kiss the ring, a sign of respect and obedience. After remarks from the cardinal, who remained seated on the *cathedra,* a Te Deum was sung. The superior or rector of the church, vested in cope, officiated at the Te Deum. When the Te Deum was completed, the new cardinal rose, with either the *biretta* or the hood of the *cappa magna* on his head, and pronounced his first blessing as cardinal. Once again the bells rang out, and the organ played as the recession wended its way through the church. In the sacristy, after divesting of the *cappa magna* and vesting with the *mozzetta* and *mantelletta,* the cardinal legally took possession of his titular church by signing, in the presence of the protonotary apostolic, the document of possession, which was witnessed by the two most senior members of his retinue, usually vicars general, auxiliary bishops, or the chancellor of his home diocese if that cardinal was a residential archbishop. At the close of the ceremony, prior to the departure of the cardinal, his coat of arms was applied to the portal of the central door of the church to mark it as his own. He was now also financially responsible for this church.

DEATH OF A POPE

The pope is dead. When these urgent words are wired throughout the world, when every news agency worldwide interrupts programming with the announcement of these four words, a sense of wonderment and curiosity about papal Rome takes hold of people everywhere. Our eyes turn to the Vatican for a peek into the ancient ceremonies soon to be relived, the ceremonies surrounding the death and burial of the pope: the calling of the Conclave of Cardinal-Electors* and the installation of the successor to the See of Peter. *Tu es Petres!* From the

---

* *Conclave* comes from Old Latin, *con* or *cum,* meaning "with," and *clavis* meaning "key," which signifies the locked rooms of the enclosure provided for papal elections.

burial to the election, the Church is without Peter. The Holy Spirit guides her, through the Sacred College. It is in these moments, the *Sede Vacante*, that the true significance of the role of the cardinal in the Church is most evident. What may have been viewed as an honorific or gift of gratitude for years of service to the Church is quickly reduced, theologically, to the real foundation of their existence.

The cardinals must open themselves to the grace of the Holy Spirit, as never before in their priestly lives, for it is the Spirit through them, his agents, who elevates to the throne of the Vicar of Christ, the one and only candidate whom Christ wishes to guide His Church on Earth.

The pope is dead. Very little has changed throughout history when these words are spoken. Certainly the modern advancements of each new age contribute their own mystique to the mysteries surrounding the death of a pope. In our own age, modern medicine made it possible to alert the world that the end was near for Paul VI. As the use of medicine became more accurate, the actual certainty of the death of the pope was confirmed. The last hours of recent popes have been made more restful than those of their predecessors because of better medical care. Despite all these modern appointments, death for a pope incorporates a prescribed formula of ceremony that is hundreds of years old and that is not easily laid aside, regardless of advancements of science.

Whereas the lovable John Paul I, Albino Luciano, died so suddenly, which sent the imagination of the world's writers astray, it is best to leave him aside and study his predecessor, Paul VI, still familiar to most of us. Paul died at Castel Gandolfo in the late evening of August 6, 1978. His mentor, Pius XII, likewise died there. Paul's death was not unexpected. The Papal Household had made all the necessary preparations, and the Cardinal–Secretary of State, the Prefect of the Papal Household, and other senior officials of his court were present at his bedside when he entered eternity. The first news of his death came when pilgrims standing vigil outside the papal villa witnessed the age-old custom of closure. The Swiss Guard barred the entrance to the courtyard by hanging a heavy black chain across the doorway. Within minutes, the news was flashed to every news service. Vatican Radio, which broadcasts worldwide, interrupted its normal programming with the tearful announcement of the passing of the pope.

At the Vatican basilica, as the bell of the *Arco delle Campani* tolled the death knell, and as bells all over the city peeled in sorrow at the news of the pope's death, all officials of the Holy See lost their power and position. The Church, for all intents and purpose, came to a grinding halt. The See of Peter was empty. Cardinals had to be notified. Officially, the Camerlengo of the Church—the cardinal who had been nominated by the pope, prior to his death, to serve the Church during the *Sede Vacante,* as administrator rather than as head—assumed his temporary position over the Church.

The Camerlengo under Paul VI, the Frenchman Jean Cardinal Villot, was also the Secretary of State. His immediate tasks were to verify the death of the pope, to announce it to all the cardinals and summon them to Rome for the coming conclave, to notify the diplomatic missions accredited to the Holy See, and to prepare the funeral rites of the deceased pontiff. The funeral of Paul VI was the first of its kind in the history of the Church, as much of the ceremony and pageantry attached to this rite was abolished during his pontificate.[*] Paul was clear in his wishes: He wanted to be buried in simplicity. The Camerlengo's role was to honor those wishes yet to remember that it was the pope, not a simple priest, that he was burying.

---

[*] *On the Vacancy of the Apostolic See,* 1975.

The body was vested in the white simar of the pope, the white alb, cincture, and amice. The modern pectoral cross, which Paul VI favored, was hung over his chest, and a red-and-gold chasuble for burial, which is the sole privilege of the popes, was placed on the body. On his head was placed the golden mitre, again the privilege of the popes.[*] Around his neck was the *pallium,* symbolizing his universal authority. His body was laid in state in the Hall of the Swiss Guard at Castel Gandolfo, where the villagers and pilgrims could come to pay their respects. The body was guarded through the night by the Swiss Guard and by members of the Papal Household who had gathered to pray. Paul's remains were laid in a simple wooden box of a beggar at his own request. In the morning, three Franciscans came to chant the Office of the Dead before the body began the ceremonial transfer to Rome. Nine million people around the world watched the procession as it made its way through the *Castelli* district outside Rome. "Seven motorcycle police led the procession of cars as it filed through the villa's *Gate of the Moor.* About thirty cars bearing those dearest to the Pope followed the hearse as it traveled about twenty-five miles an hour along the Via Appia Nuova."[21] Its first stop was not St. Peter's but St. John Lateran, the basilica of the Bishop of Rome. The cardinal-vicar of Rome, who, along with the members of the Apostolic Penitentiary and the nuncios throughout the world, were the only officials remaining in power during the *Sede Vacante,* as decreed by canon law.

The vicar for Rome prayed the Office of the Dead while the body remained inside the hearse. With the office complete and a final farewell with a blessing of holy water given, the procession continued on to St. Peter's.

As the hearse entered the square, the Swiss Guard and Italian honor guard snapped into a salute. "Forty Cardinals dressed in bright red and carrying lighted candles put the coffin at the steps of the world's largest Church. Accompanied by Cardinals, by lines of white surpliced priests, by black-robed Third Order Franciscan confessors and by his family, Pope Paul's body was carried into St. Peter's."[22]

In the days immediately following the death of Paul VI, many hectic moments caused frustration inside the Vatican. One such event was the fact that no deacon could be found in the city of Rome. The officials of the Prefecture of the Papal Household called the national colleges and seminaries in Rome. It was the height of summer and all those who could get away, had done so. No deacon could be found. Finally, with hands thrown into the air, someone of the prefecture staff asked the Pontifical North American College to appoint one of the newly ordained priests,[†] still present in Rome, to serve as a deacon for the solemn liturgy of the reception of the deceased into the basilica. For this young priest, it was the honor of a lifetime.

The *Novendiales* could thus begin. For nine days, masses were offered in St. Peter's and the basilicas and churches of Rome for the deceased. The body was removed from the simple cypress coffin and once again placed on view at the Confession of St. Peter. Vatican Radio estimated that 10,000 persons an hour passed the bier of the deceased pope to pay their respects.

Whereas twenty-four ten-foot candles surrounded the bier of his predecessors, Paul requested only one Paschal candle. The contrast was notable. Whereas all the funerals of his predecessors had been held inside the basilica for a much smaller number, Paul wished his funeral to be held outdoors so that as many persons who wished to attend, could. The ceremony was carried on live television worldwide to an estimated home audience of sixty million people.

---

[*] All other prelates are to be buried in the white mitre.
[†] Rev. Stephen DiGiovanni of Bridgeport, Conn.

After the solemn obsequies, as prescribed by the rite of burial, had concluded, Paul was laid inside the basilica, alongside his predecessors, in a crypt he had chosen for himself. He wished to be buried in the earth rather than in a sarcophagus. His remains were lowered into a vault below the floor of the crypt. A simple, elegant marble marker designates the place where he now rests.

Paul VI made many changes in the Church, changes that directly affected the faithful and that also affected the governing body of the Church as well as the Sacred College. He did not institute changes that would not affect himself and his successors. Pope John Paul I, whose brief pontificate touched the hearts of all the world, likewise hoped for the simplicity of Paul VI's death and burial. The precedence that was set by these two pontificates is impossible to overlook, yet unlikely to be altered in the near future. This more simplified and dignified burial of the Roman Pontiff has probably taken its place as the proper formula for consigning dead popes to history and their souls to eternity. To offer a historical comparison, until 1978, all pontiffs were subject in death to a series of rituals and ceremonies reminiscent of the early Renaissance, where they had taken root.

The pope is dead. These words reverberated icily throughout the Italian peninsula in past pontificates. The popes were powerful, more for their temporal authority than for their spiritual authority. The court that surrounded them was isolated, and the death of the pope set into motion a court mechanism unrivaled in royal Europe.

Other men die in darkness, in confusion, and amid tears; the Pope, alone in the world, dies in ceremony. Next to the room where he is dying the high dignitaries of the official family form a guard of honor. Around his bed are grouped the resident Cardinals of Rome, standing among them, the Cardinal-Grand Penitentiary, in accordance with his duties, aids the dying Pope.[23]

In past ages, a dying pope was expected to preach his final assessment of his Church and, if strong enough in his last hours to do so, to signify whom he thinks worthy to succeed him on the chair of Peter. This advice, although always sought, was seldom accepted. The entire court of the papacy gathered to watch the pope die. Cardinals quickly made their way from the surrounding cities; others were hastily notified in hopes that they, too, could reach Rome prior to the death of the pope and the formal entrance into conclave.

After the pope drew his last breath, a doctor was called forth to pronounce the death; in some pontificates, no more than a mirror was used to detect breath. To be certain of death, the Church had its own formula: The Cardinal-Camerlengo of the Church would come forward. All others would drop back behind him while he removed from a small red leather bag a small silver mallet engraved with the arms of the deceased. Three times the Camerlengo would gently tap the forehead of the deceased pope as if to say, "Get up!" With each tap, he would call out, in the pope's native tongue, the name given to him at baptism, the name his mother whispered to him as a child. It was thought that no man could remain asleep at the sound of his baptismal or childhood name. Assured of death, the Camerlengo would announce, "The Pope is dead." From that moment, the reverent silence of the Vatican vanished as a flurry of activity began in preparation for the burial and coming conclave.

The body was dressed in state with the red-and-gold chasuble and the fanon of white silk and gold thread. In former times, the body was always carried to the small Chapel of the Blessed Sacrament on the right side of the basilica, midway up the great nave. He was laid in state for two days, for without embalming it was not possible to view the body any longer. At the appointed time, the body was carried in great solemnity to the High Altar for the Mass of the Dead. "Immediately after the general absolution, the body was placed in triple coffins; cypress, lead, and elm, at the side of which stand the chief priest of the Basilica and the Cardinal Camerlengo. Two veils of silk were placed over the face and hands of the pontiff. A great clanking re-echoed from chapel to chapel; it was caused by the taps of the coffin which was being sealed, and crossed with violet ribbons."[24]

Even to this day, three coffins are used. The first, made of cypress, like Paul VI's, is to signify that even the popes are human and are buried like common men. The second, of lead, bears the name of the pontiff, the dates of his pontificate, and copies of the documents of profound importance issued under his seal. The broken seal of office is placed within the lead coffin by the Camerlengo prior to final closure. Finally, the third coffin, made of elm, the most precious of local woods available in Rome, is used to signify the great dignity of the man being laid to his rest. Thanks to this ancient custom, many early documents of the Church have been conserved.

Once the body is sealed within its final coffin, with only the deceased pontiff's family and immediate household present to attend him, he is lowered into the crypt below St. Peter's, through the Confession of St. Peter, where the *sanpietrini* place the heavy cargo on a wagon, to be wheeled to the place the pontiff chose himself for his final resting place. Soon after, a sarcophagus would be fashioned by one of the great artists of the era, marking the grave site for all time.

The pope's vicar for Vatican City, at one time also known as the *papal sacristan,* has the honor of remaining behind all the others to recite the Office of the Dead and to give one last final blessing to the deceased's remains. At that moment, those persons holding titles or honors bestowed for the duration of the pope's lifetime lose them, returning, at least for a time, to their former status, hoping that the successor to the See of Peter will rename them to their posts. Mourning also ended officially, as the Vatican prepared for the *Novendiales* and the coming conclave.

ENTERING THE CONCLAVE

The Camerlengo's job was half complete. In 1978, the conclave opened for the first time under the new regulations as set down by Paul VI in 1975.* One by one, the cardinals arrived in Rome, some in time for the funeral of the dead pope, others missing it but present for discussions leading to conclave.

In modern times, nearly all cardinals are capable of being present for the burial of the pope and are required, if possible, to attend. "After the death of a Pope, the Cardinals must wait fifteen days, and may wait as long as twenty, before entering the Conclave, during which the election takes place."[25] The long-standing custom had been ten days, but as North Americans were named to the College, it became clear that even in the fastest ship of the time, the American and Canadian cardinals could not get to Rome in the brief period allotted them.

The interregnum between the pope's death and burial is known as the *Sede Vacante* (or Vacant See). Vatican postage stamps and official documents bear the *ombrellino* and crossed keys to mark this period as unique. In 1978, two different issues of *Sede Vacante* postage and commemorative coins were

---

* *Romano Pontifici Eligendo.*

issued: one during the period between Paul VI and John Paul I, and the other during the period between John Paul I and his successor, the present pontiff, John Paul II. All insignia of the interregnum bear the name and title of the Camerlengo. Therefore, in 1978, the name *Ioannes Card. Villot, S.R.E. Camerarius,** appeared on all interregnum documents of both periods of the *Sede Vacante.*

With the approaching conclave, the Apostolic Palace is prepared for the important electors soon to occupy the "cells" created especially for them. In 1978, those cells included an iron hospital bed, one chair, a prie-dieu and crucifix, a stand and wash-basin, and a wastebasket. The walls of most cells were made of canvas and were suspended from metal frames because so many of these cells now occupied the magnificent apartments of the Vatican Palace and needed to be freestanding. Most of them had no windows; those that did had been covered over in paint so that no contact with the outside world would be possible.

Election preparations are made also in the Sistine Chapel. The floor is raised by putting a temporary wooden floor over the marble, which is carpeted for warmth as spending long hours on the marble mosaic floor would be difficult for those men, so many advanced in years. Twice each day, morning and evening, the cardinals gather to cast their ballots. Each of these sessions includes two ballots, or a total of four, each day. The late evenings are free for open discussion among the electors. *Pranzo,* the big midday meal, is traditionally followed by the *reposo,* or afternoon nap.

Until 1978, each elector was provided a throne, table, and canopy or *baldachino.* This practice was abolished by Paul VI solely for the consideration of space. When at one time there were eighty electors, now there are upward to 120, a number that requires two rows of desks facing one another rather than the historic row on either side of the chapel.

Because these rows were once placed up against each wall, the canopy could be easily used, but once a front row had to be added on either side of chapel, use of the canopy became an impossibility.

Until the conclave that elected Pius X (1903), the *baldachini* were of varying colors. Seldom more than three were necessary at any one time. Each pontificate was assigned a color of its own so that as the cardinal-electors took their places in the *Sistina,* a glance around the chapel could remind each cardinal in which pontificate his fellow electors had been nominated. Pius X abolished this practice. The *baldachini* were to symbolize like jurisdiction during the *Sede Vacante,* and any segregation according higher precedence due to longevity in the College was undesirable. At the precise moment that the newly elected pontiff spoke the name by which he would be known as pope, each cardinal turned and pulled the cord that collapsed the canopy above them. No longer did they share common jurisdiction, for one of their number had been chosen by the Holy Spirit to lead Christ's Church.

Although governance of the Church falls to the members of the Sacred College collectively, and in particular to the Camerlengo, their competency lies only in matters of ordinary business and issues so critical that they could not be postponed for the new pope to address in ordinary time. In the papal *motu proprio* of Paul VI, *On the Vacancy of the Apostolic See,* these powers are further limited to encompass only matters of Church governance and are not extended to those issues affecting the faithful or the Church's relations with states or governments. "In the same way, while the Apostolic See is vacant, laws issued by the Roman Pontiff can in no way be corrected or modified, nor can anything be added nor a dispensation given from a part of them, espe-

---

* Jean Cardinal Villot, His Most Reverend Eminence, the Camerlengo.

cially with regard to ordering of the election of the Supreme Pontiff."[26]

Soon after the arrival of the "foreign" cardinals in Rome, the General Congregation of the Cardinals is seated, which is to determine who among their number will officiate in the interim, serve as assistants during the conclave, and attend the Camerlengo in the ceremonies attached to the *Novendiales*. Even before the arrival of the non-Roman cardinals, the Particular Congregation had been formed. This body comprises four cardinals: the *Camerlengo* and three assistants chosen from the cardinals present, although the number was restricted by Paul VI to those who had not yet reached their eightieth year. Although the *Camerlengo* will remain at his post until a newly elected pope has been presented to the throngs in St. Peter's Square (even though his power ceased upon election), the three cardinals who serve on the Particular Congregation lose their position after the third day of conclave. Their places are taken by three others who have been chosen by secret ballot and are likewise to serve a term limited to three days.

The issues of lesser import and the more mundane preparatory matters of the funeral and approaching conclave are put to the Particular Congregation. Issues of a higher degree of importance are immediately placed before the General Congregation, which sits before the conclave, inside the Apostolic Palace, and during the sealed conclave, in rooms prepared for that purpose within the Borgia Apartments.

Ironically, the Camerlengo is not automatically the president of the General Congregation. This honor falls to the dean of the College of Cardinals so long as he has not yet reached eighty years, followed by the subdean. If both are beyond the voting age, and therefore barred from entering conclave, then the cardinals themselves elect, by secret ballot, one of their number to serve as president of the General Congregation. It is possible for the Camerlengo to be both Camerlengo and dean. The two posts are not incompatible.

As a prelude to what is yet to come in conclave, the General Congregation votes during the *Sede Vacante* by secret ballot. Only the Particular Congregation, limited as it is to four members, openly discusses each issue among themselves in order to arrive at a consultative decision. Paul VI's two decrees *On the Vacancy of the Apostolic See* and *On Electing the Roman Pontiff* are so expertly designed that conclaves in the future will have little opportunity to experience crippling discord.

During the first full session of the General Congregation, possibly either just before or immediately after entering conclave, these constitutions of Paul VI must be read aloud. Most cardinals have already reviewed them carefully beforehand in their native tongue and thus know of their responsibilities before leaving for Rome. Because modern travel nearly assures that all cardinals eligible to vote will be present in Rome soon after the pope's death, the first full General Congregation will also determine the specifics of the funeral and burial rites of the deceased pope, keeping in mind as they must, the wishes of the deceased. Whenever this opening session is to be held, the first order of business must be the taking of an oath, the first of such oaths to take place in the election process of the new pope. The Pauline *motu proprio* proscribes the exact wording:

> *We, Cardinals of the Holy Roman Church, Bishops, Priests, and Deacons, promise, bind ourselves and swear, as a body and individually, to observe exactly and faithfully all the norms contained in the Apostolic Constitution Romano Pontifici Eligendo of the Supreme Pontiff Paul VI, and scrupulously to observe secrecy concerning everything that shall be dealt with or decided in the Congregations of the Cardinals, both before and during Con-*

clave, and concerning anything that in anyway may pertain to the election of the Roman Pontiff. [This formula continues to include, specifically, each member of the College of Cardinals, present and eligible to vote with the words that follow.] *And I, N. Cardinal N., promise, bind myself and swear* [now placing his hand on the Gospels, each cardinal continues]. *So help me God and these Holy Gospels which I touch with my hand.*[27]

Now the business of the *Sede Vacante* begins. Article 13 of Chapter 2 of the same constitution prescribes in detail how the General Congregation is to fix the date, time, and ceremonial of the funeral of the deceased pope, set the norms for the *Novendiales,* form the commissions for services during conclave, examine budgets, assign conclave "housing," fix the hour of the opening of the conclave, and announce the hour and manner of the destruction of the Fisherman's Ring, the great seal of the office of the papacy. Together, these tasks may seem minor, but individually, because of the historical character of each, they are deliberated upon and carried out with great solemnity and respect.

The late pontiff's secretary is interviewed to determine any further desires of the deceased pontiff in regard to his burial. The Last Testament is opened and quietly reviewed, as this is not only a description of a deceased's desires for the disposition of his belongings, but an open testament to the Church by a pope, including his own personal assessment of his work on earth and his desires for the future of Christ's Church. This testament will be published soon after the new pope's election and installation. For the time being, the cardinals concern themselves with the last wishes of the late pope so that they may attempt to carry through with them as best they can, remembering, as they must, that a Vicar of Christ, not a simple priest, is being consigned to his rest and to history.

The ceremony of the destruction of the Fisherman's Ring is an important one. In this one ceremonial act, the power of the papacy is symbolically extinguished. Until a successor is chosen and a new ring created, the seal of the Vicar on Earth, and thus his power, is nonexistent. The ring, more than any other symbol, therefore represents the successors of Peter.

The General Congregation must determine, under the terms of Paul VI's constitution, if this ceremony will be public, that is, attended by all the College and perhaps covered by television as well, or if they are to be private, reserved for the College itself. Most commonly, this ancient ritual is private, with only a handful of cardinals as well as those senior officials associated with the papacy and the Sacred College present.

The cardinals enter the pope's apartments, each vested in scarlet choir dress. Accompanying them are the Papal Household officials and the commandant of the Swiss Guard as witnesses. The ring is inspected, first by the other cardinals present to verify if it truly is the Fisherman's Ring. This completed, a silver knife is taken in hand by the Camerlengo, who scratches the seal twice, once horizontally and once vertically, in the sign of a cross, although not with theological intent. These scratches, which serve as a simple means of defacing or destroying the symbolic power of the ring, is then inspected by those present. The ring is then placed on a lead block, which stands before the Camerlengo on a marble table. A silver mallet is produced and taken in hand by the Camerlengo, who, swiftly and with as much force as he can muster, administers a blow to the ring. This blow sometimes produces a split, other times a deep crack—either way, the ring is finally destroyed. The Camerlengo must continue to issue blows to the ring if it is not immediately destroyed. All present must visually verify its destruction and affirm this witness to the protonotary present, whose function it is to document these historic moments of the *Sede Vacante.* The ring, along with its broken pieces, is placed in a velvet sack, tied tightly, and carried away by the Camerlengo, who will place it inside the second casket, the lead tomb, along with all the important documents of a papacy now ended.

The papal apartments are now ceremoniously sealed. Each entrance is locked, first from within and then from outside. All telecommunications, telephones, telefax, and telex, have been cut. The curtains have been drawn, and the desk and files locked. No one, including the pope's secretary, who had shared this apartment with his master, may enter it again until its new occupant has been elected.

The Camerlengo, the Particular Congregation of Cardinals, and other *officiali* seal the apartment. The door is locked from outside, and a red silk ribbon is placed across the threshold in two parts, forming an **X**. In the center, at the juncture point, the four-inch-wide seal of the Camerlengo assures enclosure. A Swiss Guardsman remains on duty outside the main doors of the apartment throughout the *Sede Vacante,* linked by telephone to the security station in the event of an attempt to break into the apartments. No one, not even the Camerlengo himself, may enter this sealed apartment for the duration of the Vacant See. After the ceremonies and business of the preconclave and *Novendiales* are over, the General and Particular Congregations of Cardinals prepare for the Mass of the Holy Spirit, which traditionally opens each conclave.

ELECTION

On the morning of the opening of conclave, the cardinals gather at the Apostolic Palace. Until this time, many cardinals have remained in their own Roman apartments, while foreign cardinals have resided in their national colleges and seminaries, with other cardinal friends, or at a Roman hotel or religious house.

This morning is special. A fleet of sleek black cars is sent across Rome to collect the members of the Sacred College from their homes. Some bear the magical SCV license plate,[*] which assures easy passage throughout Rome. Others, because of the sheer number of electors today, arrive in a fleet of leased cars. Altogether, they arrive through the Sant'Anna Gate and proceed through the Belvedere Court, under the arcades of the Belvedere Palace, eventually leading up and into the San Damaso.[†] From here, the cardinals enter the Apostolic Palace, assembling as a body, in the Sala Regia.[‡] Dressed in scarlet choir dress but with the simple rochet, the cardinals proceed two by two into the Pauline Chapel, adorned with Michelangelo's scenes of Peter's crucifixion and Paul's conversion on either wall, for the first Mass of the Holy Spirit, which opens the conclave. The constitution *On Electing the Roman Pontiff* has prescribed an alternative site, the Vatican Basilica of St. Peter's, as suitable for this first Mass of the Holy Spirit. In such a case, a solemn procession must wind its way up into the Sala Regia for the entrance into conclave.

At one time, prior to the reforms of Pope Paul VI, several persons could accompany each cardinal-elector into the conclave. These persons included his personal secretary, a doctor or nurse, chamberlain, and even cooks. Today, every need is provided by the Church itself, including special dieticians, surgeons, nursing care, etc., and no one, not even a clerical secretary, may enter the conclave. All Vatican officials who are present for the opening rituals,

---

[*] *Stato del Città del Vaticano.*
[†] The courtyard of Saint Damasus.
[‡] The "kingly hall" where the Sistine and Pauline Chapels join in the official rooms of the Apostolic Palace.

with few exceptions, must also leave at the appropriate moment. Only those persons with specific needs, such as a lame or infirm cardinal, may be accompanied into the conclave, but even these individuals must first be approved by the Particular Congregation of Cardinals.

On the day before entrance into conclave, each cardinal, and those persons legally permitted entrance, must swear the following oath as prescribed by Paul VI:

> *I, N.N., promise and swear that I will observe inviolable secrecy about each and every matter concerning the election of the new pontiff which has been treated or defined in the Congregations of the Cardinals, and also concerning what takes place in the Conclave or place of election, directly or indirectly concerning every other matter that may in any way come to my knowledge. I will not violate this secret in any way, either directly or indirectly, either by signs, words or writing, or in any other manner. Moreover, I promise and swear not to use in the Conclave, any type of transmitting or receiving instrument, nor to use devices designed in any way for taking pictures: and this under pain of excommunication latae sententiae reserved specialissimo modo to the Apostolic See, should the above norm be violated. I will maintain this secret consciously and scrupulously even after the election of the Roman Pontiff has taken place, unless a special faculty or an explicit authorization be granted to me by the same pontiff. In like manner, I promise and swear that I will never give my help and support to any interference, opposition, or any other form of intervention whereby the civil powers of any order and degree, or any group or individual persons would wish to interfere in the election of the Roman Pontiff. So help me God and these holy Gospels which I touch with my hand.*[28]

The famous words *extra omnes* (all out) are announced loudly by the Prefect of the Papal Household, one of the few noncardinals who play a role in the conclave. All attendants, officials, and observers are ordered out of the Sistine Chapel and, beyond that, out of the sealed rooms that are being used for the conclave. The Prince Assistant to the Papal Throne, one of the Black Nobles of Rome, is granted the permission to seal the external doors from outside while the Prefect of the Papal Household simultaneously seals the doors from inside. To confirm closure, each signals with three taps of a hammer. Except for life-threatening illness, no one may leave the conclave until a new pope has been elected.

The third oath must now be administered by the Camerlengo and taken by each elector. Under Paul VI's constitution, this oath, too, is quite lengthy. It maintains three elements of import: the first, the further pledge of absolute secrecy; the second, the pledge of absolute loyalty to the liberty of the Holy See, both temporal and spiritual; and, finally, the firm pledge that no entity will interfere with the voting judgment of the cardinal-electors, a substantial reference to the privilege of Catholic kings, who could, until World War I, veto a choice of election.

Before election can begin, the entire conclave must be searched for means of a breach of secrecy, be it electronic or by other methods—an unfortunate necessity of modern life. Paul VI provided for this by assigning to the Papal Master of Ceremonies other officials present for the conclave. An architect of the conclave, who knows all the areas of the palace intimately, and two technicians trained in electronic instrumentation are now present throughout conclave. The cardinals retire to their individual cells for the afternoon while this necessary business is being completed. When assured of a thorough search, two documents are drawn: one by the Papal Master of Ceremonies and the other by a delegate of the Camerlengo, each bearing the signatures of the Prefect of the Papal Household, the commandmant of the Swiss Guard, and a delegate of the Pontifical Commission for the Vatican City State.

Officially, the conclave has begun, and no one may enter for any reason. Anyone found inside who does not belong or who has entered surreptitiously "is *ipso facto* to be deprived of every honor, rank, office, and ecclesiastical benefice, or, depending on the condition of the person concerned, subjected to appropriate penalties."[29]

On the morning following the closure ceremonies, a second Mass invoking the Holy Spirit takes place. Because of closure, this Mass is always celebrated inside the Pauline Chapel. No other site within the conclave is large enough to accommodate all the electors, except the Sistine Chapel, but this has been prepared for election and would not offer the proper respect and solemnity for the opening Mass. Immediately following the Mass, the first morning session of election begins. Until a pope is elected, morning and afternoon sessions are scheduled, with two ballots in each session, or four per day.

The cardinals are always vested in scarlet choir dress and the proper rochet. Their *biretta* is worn in procession and placed visibly on their desk as a sign of their cardinalatial dignity and right to vote in conclave. In the evenings, the protocol of the conclave mandates academic dress, that is, the black, red-trimmed simar, sash, and *zucchetto*. The pectoral cross is suspended from a chain for academic dress and the cord for choir dress.*

There are three methods by which a pope may be elected. The first of these is the *acclamation,* or *inspiration*, the least common but most dramatic method. In acclamation, one or more cardinals stand and verbally proclaim one of their brothers to be their choice. When others follow in acclamation, a possible election results. This dramatic means of election would require an outstanding candidate whose qualities and abilities clearly outshine those of all other candidates.

The second method is known in English as the *delegation,* which is a means of breaking a deadlock more than anything else. When the third, and most common, method fails the electors, a delegation may be formed, which entrusts the election of a new pope to a smaller body of electors, who endeavor to arrive at a suitable candidate. Article 64 of the constitution *On Electing a Roman Pontiff* clearly sets forth the boundaries of implementing the delegation method. The entire College must undergo a further pledge that places their right to vote in the hands of this body. It must set the terms, such as the length of competency of this body, and it sets the size of the delegation, which may comprise between nine and fifteen members (the number must always be odd to facilitate the breaking of a tied vote). The delegates vote secretly and apart from the other cardinal-electors in this method. The candidate chosen by delegation must be presented to the entire voting College, who then must promulgate their choice. At this moment, and at the assumption of the new pontifical name, that chosen cardinal becomes pope. In today's sophisticated, less political Church, this method is a rarity; in fact, it may never be seen again, but proper means have been provided by Paul VI to undertake such a method canonically, if needed.

The final means provided for electing a pope, *scrutiny,* is the most common, and most people think it is the only means. The term is derived from the Italian term for "written method." In the English-speaking world, it is known as the *secret ballot* because the chosen's name is secretly written on a card on which is inscribed the words: *Eligio in summum pontificem.*† Until 1975, the formula read *Eligo in summum Pontificeum Reverendissimum dominum meum Cardinalem. . . .* ‡ In this system, each cardinal

---

* *Tenue de Ville* (a black clerical suit) is not acceptable as a part of conclave protocol.

† I elect as Supreme Pontiff.

‡ I choose as Supreme Pontiff the Very Reverend Lord Cardinal. . . .

under the age of eighty who is present in the conclave votes in each ballot for the one he believes to be most capable of leading the Church. Two thirds plus one of the entire body present is required for a canonical election. The conclave structure itself is as it is simply because of the frequency of the use of the scrutiny method. Only two ballots are possible in the morning and two in the afternoon, precisely because of the extent of the preparation necessary for each ballot and the scrutiny of the tallying that follows.

For centuries, the most common method of electing a successor to Peter has been the scrutiny. In affirming the historic significance of this particular method, Paul VI recalled the ancient origins of this mode of papal election and further enforced Pius XII's initiative to add the requirement of two thirds of the electors plus one vote in order for the scrutiny election to be canonically valid.

The constitution *On Electing the Roman Pontiff* defines the scrutiny election as having three phases: the prescrutiny, the scrutiny proper, and the postscrutiny. When and if each is not faithfully carried out as prescribed by this constitution, the election is automatically null and void. At present, this constitution has been translated in all modern languages; the cardinal-electors are now certain of the responsibilities vested with this historic office.

The phase known as the prescrutiny comprises the designing, printing, and preparation of the ballot cards, which historically were folded in quarters to assure total secrecy. Each cardinal-elector is presented four, although the constitution requires only two for each of the ballots. Before the ballots for election of the pope commence, ballots for the cardinal-assistant post must first be cast. The electors choose from among themselves the three who will initially hold the posts of scrutineers, the three who will collect the ballots of the sick or infirm electors, and the three who will be installed as revisors. The most recent, or junior, cardinal-deacon, is entrusted with the task of conducting the election of these posts. The ceremony is simple. On the first batch of ballots provided to the cardinals, each must write his own name. All the ballots are placed in a golden chalice from which is drawn, in succession, nine names, regardless of degree or class within the college.

Now that the *officiali* of the conclave have been chosen, the election begins. The first option for the electors, as we have seen, is the acclamation, or inspiration, method. This method "occurs when the Cardinal-Electors, as it were through the inspiration of the Holy Spirit, freely and spontaneously, unanimously and aloud, proclaim one individual as supreme pontiff."[30] Although the film *Shoes of the Fisherman* depicts this method of election most dramatically, the constitution *On Electing the Roman Pontiff* now requires this more formal formula for the election to be valid. Henceforth, the elector who first steps forth must utilize this formula: *"Most Eminent Fathers, in view of the singular virtue and probity of the Most Reverend N,N, I would judge him worthy to be elected Roman Pontiff and I now choose him as Pope."*[31] Rather than come forth intermittently, the remaining electors must stand and pronounce in a clear voice the word *eligo* (I elect) until the process of unanimous election has been completed. Those sick or infirm electors not present in the *Sistina* must publically verbalize, or when unable so to do, must write the word *eligo* along with the name that has been proclaimed. Acclamation as a method of electing the Roman Pontiff is, paradoxically, both spontaneous and formalized at the same time. Without rigid adherence to the prescribed formula, Paul VI's constitution makes null and void any election by this method.

When election by scrutiny fails and that by acclamation seems unlikely, the same constitution allows for the historic method of election by delegation. A body within a body, the cardinal-electors choose a further select group from among its membership in a desperate attempt to break deadlock in electing the pastor of the world. To move toward delegation, each and every cardinal-elector present in conclave must, without exception, cast a vote for such a canonical procedure. Nothing can be left to chance. For such a ballot, a specific formula is prescribed. Written on each of the ballots to be cast and provided to each elector, who affixes his own signature, the formula is, as follows:

> *In the name of the Lord. Amen. In the year* ____, *on the* ____ *day of the month of* ____, *we the Cardinal-Electors, present in this Conclave,* (signature of each Cardinal), *individually and jointly have decided to carry out the election by delegation, and in agreement, unanimously and without any dissent we elect as our delegates the most eminent fathers* (list of the delegates), *to whom we grant the full faculty and power to provide the Holy Roman Church with its pastor, in this manner, namely* (here the Cardinals list the terms of the delegation), *and we promise to regard as supreme pontiff the person whom the delegates shall have decided to elect according to the aforementioned form.*[32]

How the delegation carries out its entrusted mission depends entirely on the seated College of Cardinal-Electors. Limitations on time, method of balloting, or whether a noncardinal may or may not be elected are all determined when and if the Sacred College must turn to the delegation method for canonical election.

The apostolic constitution *On Electing the Roman Pontiff* prescribes only two dictates. The first requires an uneven number of members in the delegation to assure a tiebreaker (the minimum number possible being nine and the greatest fifteen). The second requires that all electors or conclavists remain locked in conclave. Although the cardinal-electors not chosen for delegation are free for

prayer, discussion, and deliberations, the delegation method is designed to serve as a solution to a prolonged period of deliberation without successful result. Thus, the cardinal-delegates enter delegation confident in their mandate to settle disputes and select the one to be chosen pope. Because surely everything has been a part of papal history when electing the successor to Peter, Paul VI provided the Church with a canonical means to avoid deadlock, as impossible as it seems today.

For the past two hundred years, the cardinal-electors have entered conclave vested in scarlet satin, every inch princes of the Church. Only one in each conclave exits a pope. Each has been chosen by scrutiny, the final and most common of election methods.

Once the voting begins, the apostolic constitution requires that each cardinal be provided with two ballot cards thus imprinted; however, traditionally, four are presented to each cardinal. To be certain that any one cardinal does not mistakenly fold two cards together when casting each ballot, if a *scrutatore* (scrutineer) finds two or more together, and if the name on each is identical, they are counted as only one vote. If each card bears the name of a different candidate, all cards for that cardinal-elector are null and void for this ballot. The election proceeds, nonetheless.

For each balloting session, morning and afternoon, the cardinals process into the Sistine Chapel, two by two. Each is vested in the scarlet choir cassock, *mozzetta,* rochet, and *biretta* of scarlet watered silk.* A desk covered with green felt is provided each cardinal. Upon each has been placed a red Moroccan-leather desk set of blotter, name holder, letter opener, and pens. The tables are small, with barely room enough for the scarlet *biretta* (the out-

---

* See individual chapters on each item of vesture in Part Four of this text.

ward sign of the elector's right to be present in conclave), which protocol dictates be placed on top of the table in full view.

As we have seen, at one time each elector was provided a throne, above which hung a collapsible *baldachino.* Until the 1970s, the College of Cardinals seldom reached the optimum number of eighty members. At present, in spite of the mandatory retirement age—a requirement now barring each cardinal after his eightieth year from participating in the conclave—the numbers of eligible voting cardinals has increased. Paul VI increased the College's membership to one hundred twenty, at the same time limiting electors to those below eighty years. He and his successors have also made a concerted effort to name younger prelates to the College. As a result, there are usually a minimum of one hundred participants in each conclave. Along with the increase in numbers has come an increase in the internationalization of the College. In just two brief pontificates, internationalization has resulted in the election of the first non-Italian pope in eight hundred years.

Today, the *baldachini* are gone. They have been relegated to history because there is simply no longer room for them in the *Sistina* with the increased number of electors. Gone, too, are the thrones; simple leather desk chairs have replaced them. Little else has changed over the years. Just as in conclaves one hundred years ago, today the cardinal-electors follow the same ancient formulae that electors had followed two hundred years prior.

No one may remain inside the Sistine Chapel when the College begins to vote. The chapel doors are closed, effecting a conclave within a conclave. To these few men fall the task of electing Christ's Vicar on Earth, the priest called to serve all God's children as Pastor and Shepherd. It is an awe-inspiring responsibility. After all persons have removed themselves from the chapel, the cardinals

immediately begin the first ballot.* On one of the provided ballot cards, each elector inscribes the name of the one he believes to be the Holy Spirit's choice for pope. "Each Cardinal-Elector, in order of precedence, having written on and folded his card, holds it up so that it can be seen and carries it to the altar at which the scrutineers stand and upon which there is placed a receptacle, covered by a plate, for receiving the cards."[33] For three hundred years, this receptacle has been a 25-inch (63.5 cm)-tall golden, jewel-encrusted chalice, with gold paten.

Upon rising from his knees, the elector places his ballot first upon the paten; then, lifting the paten in full view of all present, he permits his ballot to drop into the chalice. One by one, each elector repeats this ritual. Each one repeats this oath: *I call to witness Christ the Lord who will be my judge, that my vote is given to the one who before God I consider should be elected.*"[34]† He then bows reverently to the crucifix upon the altar and returns to his place.

As for each method of election, three cardinals are chosen as *infirmarii,* who ceremoniously and publicly collect the ballots of those electors too infirm to attend the election in the *Sistina.* After each of the electors has completed his privileged task, the three *scrutatori* (scrutineers) shake the chalice to mingle the ballots. Just after the first *scrutatore* finishes the task of mingling the ballots, the third begins the count. One by one, he retrieves a ballot, opens it, and calls aloud the name inscribed upon it. Each of the two remaining *scrutatori* likewise reads aloud the name. Each of the three make an official note of those chosen, as do many of the cardinal-electors at their places in the *Sistina.* One by one,

---

* Bartolomeo Prignano (1318–89) was the last noncardinal elected pope. He was elected on April 8, 1378, taking the name Urban VI. He was previously archbishop of Bari.

† *Testor Christum Dominum, qui me judicaturus est, me eligere, quem secundum Deum judico eligi debere.*

the ballots are proclaimed and counted. If there is a discrepancy between the numbers present in the conclave and the ballots counted, the balloting session is null and void and a new ballot begins.

If the balloting results in election of the Roman Pontiff, no further balloting is required. Pius XII, however, required a validation of election to provide the College of Cardinals an opportunity to change their minds had they only been wrapped up in the euphoria of quickly electing a popular candidate.

If no election results after the first ballot, a second ballot commences on that first morning. Two ballot sessions will continue in both the mornings and afternoons until a pope is chosen. After seven sessions with no resulting election, a period of prayer is prescribed in the form of a retreat. After each subsequent seven sessions, this retreat is repeated as a means to center this ancient process where it belongs, in prayer. After each session, that is, once in the morning and once in the afternoon, the ballots used in the election, along with any notes or paper scraps, must be burned. This process is best known to the public as it has served as the means of informing Rome, and later the world, that a pope had been elected.

Beyond the sacristy of the *Sistina,* near the Room of Tears, a large metal stove with a 60-foot pipe reaching through the roof of the Sistine Chapel is the historic means of disposing of the ballots of each voting session. Historically, plumes of white smoke have alerted the world that a pope had been chosen. Black smoke means that the process continues. To assure white smoke, wet straw was added when burning the winning election's ballots. Today, a vial of chemicals is added to ensure the famous *bianco,* or white, plumes that announce to the world the beginning of a pontificate.

Before cheers of *"bianco"* can be heard in St. Peter's Square, an election must be canonically carried forth. The apostolic constitution of Paul VI

requires a two-thirds-plus-one majority. The candidate, however, is not yet canonically the successor to Peter with a two-thirds-plus-one vote result. With the election complete, the Camerlengo performs his last official act as Chamberlain of the Church.

Until the pontificate of Paul VI in 1963, the ritual was always the same. His constitution of 1975[*] changed forever the opening moments of every pontificate. Throughout history, the most dramatic moment at the close of each conclave was the act of subservience of the cardinal-electors as the new pope accepted election and announced the name by which history would record his pontificate. It was not until the elected pronounced his new name that the pontificate actually began. (This is so until this day.) At that moment, all cardinals would lose their mutual authority and return to their role as the senate of the Church.

Through 1963, this historic moment was captured in the symbolic act of the collapsing of the *baldachino* of each cardinal-elector. Each elector was seated beneath a *baldachino* of velvet with gold fringe and tassels. Blue was reserved for cardinals created in the previous pontificate, green for that prior, and so forth until cardinals created in each pontificate were provided a *baldachino* identifying their precedence within the College. This practice lapsed early in this century, and blue predominated as the color of protocol for all *baldachini* in conclave. Regardless of color, however, as the final election concluded, the Camerlengo rose from his throne, accompanied by the dean of the College and the senior cardinal-deacon, approached the new pontiff, and, in a formula fixed through the ages, asked the new pope if he accepted election and by what name he chooses to be known.

Paul VI has reaffirmed the canonical language of

---

[*] *On Electing the Roman Pontiff.*

acceptance. *Do you accept your canonical election as Supreme Pontiff?* When the response is a resounding yes, be it in humility or confidence, the chosen cardinal is asked, *By what name do you wish to be called?*[*] At the moment that his breath pronounces his papal name(s), he becomes Peter! Through 1963, and for nearly five hundred years before, the Cardinals then turned to the back of their thrones, pulled the tasseled cord releasing the collapsible panel above them, thus dropping the *baldachini,* simultaneously relinquishing their joint authority over the Church. A pope reigns again. The proper term is *Gloriosamente Regnante* (gloriously reigning), referring to the close of the *Sede Vacante* and a succession to the See of Peter.

From the moment of acceptance and announcement of the pontifical name, the new pope is simultaneously the Bishop of Rome, true Pope, and head of the College of Bishops and *"ipso facto he acquires and can exercise full and absolute jurisdiction over the whole church."*[35] If the pope chosen is not a bishop, the cardinal-dean must now proceed, before the conclave opens, to consecrate him to the episcopal dignity.

Before the world is told that a new pope has been elected, each of the cardinal-electors comes forward to make his own act of fidelity, homage, and obedience. Where the cardinal-assistants and Camerlengo had sat during conclave as *scrutatori,* a throne is now placed, awaiting the new pope who has retired to the Room of Tears behind the Sistine to don the vesture proper to the pope, the white silk simar, white moiré silk fascia without the heraldic device of the new pope, which will not be published in Rome for two to three days to come. He is vested by his valet and the Master of Ceremonies of the Supreme Pontiff, who will assist him throughout those first few days of hectic ceremonial. They assist him in donning a lace or linen rochet and the red *mozzetta,* satin in summer, velvet in winter.

Over the *mozzetta,* he places a richly embroidered stole, after having reverenced it with a kiss, as every priest properly would do when donning his sacred vestments. His black leather loafers and scarlet stockings are replaced by white silk hose and red moroccan-leather loafers. He may also don white velvet slippers embroidered in gold, although the present pontiff prefers the leather loafers.

Once the pontiff has vested, the white *zucchetto* atop his head, he returns to the *Sistina.* One by one, the cardinals approach the new pope. Until 1975, they were required to vest in scarlet choir dress, over which was donned the scarlet watered-silk *cappa magna.* Today, scarlet choir dress throughout the conclave is required.

The first to approach is the cardinal-dean, followed by the Camerlengo, who no longer has the authority of his office, and then the cardinal-bishops; in order of official precedence within each class of the cardinalate, they approach. For some, the pope responds formally, not knowing them intimately. For others, he offers a warm embrace, like that between brothers, and for some others, a hug—a deep embrace of a brother and dear friend of long standing. For centuries, the act of obedience was the genuflection and kiss of the sandal of the pope. Today, protocol demands a genuflection but then provides for an exchange of the *embracio,* or Kiss of Peace, followed by the reverence of the Fisherman's Ring for the first time. In time, the name of the pontiff will be inscribed upon the ring. Already engraved on the inside of this ornate gold ring is the image of Peter casting his net into the sea. It had been prepared by the order of the Camerlengo by the papal jewelers in Rome.

The Master of Ceremonies, Prefect of the Papal Household, and the other *officiali* of the conclave open the doors, thus permitting the hierarchy of

---

[*] *Quomodo vis vocari?*

the Church not permitted inside conclave itself to receive the first papal blessing. It is the first opportunity for the archbishops, bishops, and priests to see for themselves who is the new pontiff. The crowds in St. Peter's Square, and indeed the world, know that Peter's successor has been elected. For two hours they have anticipated the announcement by the senior cardinal-deacon on the central balcony of St. Peter's as to who has been chosen pope. Television and radio crews have all the names and biographies of the *papabile* at hand. The moment the name is announced in Latin from the balcony of St. Peter's, his photograph appears worldwide. It is unlikely today that a total unknown is chosen as pontiff, although John Paul II was a surprise.

The Hall of the Benedictions is a palatial-sized, ornate Renaissance hall crossing the facade of St. Peter's high above the portal and vestibule of the basilica. In this great room, Pope John Paul II prays the rosary each First Friday for the three thousand faithful present in the hall and the world-at-large, which is plugged into the hall through Vatican Radio's worldwide broadcast network. In this hall as well, great ceremonies of state, ceremonies of the College of Cardinals, concerts in past pontificates, and other events are held. The windows of this great hall overlook St. Peter's Square, and from this salon the new pope first appears on the central balcony high atop St. Peter's Basilica. It is this same balcony to which he will come on every important public function of his pontificate, from where he will, as pope, present his address or homily and impart his apostolic benediction *Urbi et Orbi*.

It is to this central balcony that the senior cardinal-deacon comes on the day of election. Within two hours of election, the cardinal-deacon, accompanied by the prefect of the Papal Household and the papal master of ceremonies, enters the central portal of St. Peter's. The curtains draw apart and the doors open wide. Scarlet and violet fill the par-

abolic arch. It is the cardinal-deacon and the *monsignori* of the papal family.

In perfect Latin, in a formula that has not been altered in six hundred years, the cardinal-deacon proclaims: *Annuntio vobis gaudium magnum. Habemus papam . . . Eminentissimum ac Reverendissimum Dominum, Dominum . . . (baptismal name) Sanctae Romanae Ecclesiae Cardinalem (surname) . . . qui sibi nomen imposuit.* *

Having announced the joyful news of the election and who has been selected to occupy the throne of Peter, the crowd erupts in untold, electric joy. The excitement continues for nearly a half hour until the new pope appears before them for the first time.

It seems that Rome ignores the pope during his lifetime. Nevertheless, Romans are present en masse for his burial and rush to St. Peter's Square at the first sign of the *sfumata bianca*.[†] It is amazing how excited they become at the news of election and how possessive they become with "their new pope." Shops close, restaurants pop open wine to celebrate, and everyone who can flocks to the square. In the two hours that it takes to first appear on the central balcony, hundreds of thousands have joined the festivities and anticipation in the piazza below.

One by one the draperies across the facade's windows draw apart. Red blotches are visible at every pane. All cardinals, even those ineligible to enter conclave because of their advanced age, are present in the Hall of the Benedictions awaiting the pope's arrival. The excitement in the piazza below is electric. Biographies of the new pope are already tele-

---

* I announce to you a great joy. We have a Pope! His Most Eminent and Reverend Lord, Lord (baptismal name) . . . Cardinal of the Holy Roman Church (surname), who has chosen for himself the name of (new papal name).
† White smoke!

vised throughout the world. Television crews have scrambled to his home diocese or to his Roman headquarters to obtain that first interview with family, friends, and Church colleagues. Everyone who knows the new pontiff wants to tell the world all that they know from their past acquaintance with him.

Within moments of the cardinals' appearance, the central balcony windows open. The gold patriarchal cross, carried by a violet-robed monsignor of the pope's household, appears. Directly behind him is the new pope, now vested in white simar and red *mozzetta*. The protocol of this first papal appearance has always been the solemn benediction known as the *Urbi et Orbi* blessing. Pope John Paul II broke tradition, in 1978, when he spoke to the crowd below, laughing with them, warming to them and they to him. The first non-Italian pontiff in eight hundred years wanted the faithful of his new diocese, Rome, to feel his love for them from the outset of his pontificate. The Romans, who moments before were dismayed by the election of a non-Italian, embraced this young Italian-speaking son of Poland.

At the outset of his pontificate, the pope can choose to continue the conclave for a time, to be close to those who chose him, to seek council, and to provide direction or he may end the conclave immediately. In the past two pontificates, Pope John Paul I and Pope John Paul II both required the cardinals to return to conclave for one last evening of prayer and reflection. The cardinals and these two popes are said to have relished this last night of togetherness before undertaking the tasks that faced each of them in the coming days.

Traditionally, the new pope will confirm all curialists in their posts. This affirmation is usually short term. In short time, the new pope will make assessments of his own regarding how he wishes to see the Church governed under his leadership. Many will lose their posts—some transferred, others promoted, still others retired to service outside the Vatican. In time, a team will materialize that will serve this new pope best.

INSTALLATION OF A NEW POPE

Romano Pontifici Eligendo,[*] the Pauline constitution of 1975, requires a coronation ceremony for the new pontiff. The coronation symbolizes the religious institution or the sacred rite of ascending the See of Peter. In 1978, John Paul I, feeling the burdens of his office from the moment of election, sought the understanding of the Church in his choice not to be crowned in St. Peter's Square. He opted for a simple installation ceremony. Albeit rich in ceremony, it lacked the pagentry that symbolizes the moment that the one chosen to govern the Church assumes his sacred office. It was a ceremony for the Supreme Pastor. Frankly, the grand ceremonies of coronations past would not suffice today, for so many these ceremonies would be an affront to sensibilities as the spirit of the Second Vatican Council evoked the pastoral role of the papacy rather than its temporal authority.

To those in the Church who would appreciate a return to past ceremonies, an alternative has been put forth as a compromise. The magnificent celebration of the Mass of Installation outside in the piazza for hundreds of thousands to participate in and enjoy should remain. It was, in both instances in 1978, magnificent. To properly return to the ceremonies of our heritage as specifically prescribed by a post–Second Vatican Council Apostolic Constitution (Article 92), protocol suggests a combined ceremony, one as simple and profound as those of

---

[*] *On Electing the Roman Pontiff,* 1975.

1978 and one that also incorporates the thousand-year-old tradition of our Church. This task must fall to the Prefect of the Papal Household, the Papal Master of Ceremonies, the dean of the College of Cardinals, the Camerlengo of the Holy Roman Church, and the Camerlengo of the Sacred College. To these prelates, and to a commission of venerable cardinals, should fall the preparatory work for the next pontificate; that work would be best undertaken during the present pontificate.

The pontifical coronation is prescribed by present Church law, and our heritage provides fine examples from which to choose. To this commission falls the task of combining sacred emblems from our historic past with post–Vatican Council theological doctrine and liturgical practice. In 1978, Pope John Paul II, in his first address presented at his own installation ceremony in St. Peter's Square, called the Church to witness his own installation but reminded her that the law and history of the Church requires a papal coronation, rather than an installation. Although he himself opted for an installation, he did so out of deference to his immediate predecessor, John Paul I, who was burdened by such a grand ceremony and by the papacy itself. John Paul II reminded the world that the ceremony of coronation was not abolished and was expected to return.

With the immediate precedence of two papal installations, it is both unlikely and inappropriate for a total return of the past ceremony of coronation. Once again, to the *officiali* of the Church now falls the task of preparing a proper, theological combined ceremony for institution of a new pontificate. In time, it is possible that such a ceremony will appear.

In the sunshine of St. Peter's Square, future pontificates could open as Paul VI has envisioned. The emphasis should fall to the sacred, the celebration of the Mass central to this liturgy. The act of crowning, symbolic of a pope's authority as Christ's Vicar on Earth and his unique position as head of the Universal Church, incorporated within the Eucharistic celebration, most beautifully combines the sacred and the symbolic as required by the law of the Church.

BURIAL OF CARDINALS

When a cardinal of the Roman Church dies in Rome, often the Holy Father himself arrives at the apartment of the deceased prince of the Church to pray for the repose of his soul. Soon after death, the cardinal is vested in the scarlet choir cassock, the alb, red stockings, and the purple chasuble. Upon his head is placed the *mitra damasco,* in his hands the rosary, on his finger the cardinalatial ring. His body is placed on display, candles placed around it, and a crucifix placed nearby so that his household and family may come to pray together. Most commonly, the first Mass of the Dead is celebrated in the apartment of the deceased.

The body is placed in a casket of oak or mahogany and taken to a site proper for the lying-in-state* so that a wider range of the faithful can gather to pray. Then the lid is closed, all rites of the Church are observed, save for the Mass of Christian Burial, and the body is transferred to the Altar of the Chair in St. Peter's Basilica, where the final Mass is celebrated by the Holy Father himself.

The remains of a Roman cardinal are then transferred to his titular church in Rome, where yet another Mass is celebrated for the faithful of that Church who had looked to the deceased cardinal as

---

* Popes, cardinals, and ordinaries lie "in state." Titular archbishops and bishops lie "in repose," a nicety of protocol that provides for a differential for rank and respect.

a spiritual father and pastor. Soon a proper crypt, emblazoned with the heraldic device of the deceased cardinal, is prepared within his titular church. If the crypt cannot be prepared promptly, then the remains of the deceased cardinal rest in a Roman cemetery, or family vault, until properly prepared. The cardinal's *galero* is still hung high above the crypt, suspended from the ceiling of the church, although the red *galero* itself is not given during the consistory.*

Cardinals who die in their diocese have the privilege of the same special Mass of Christian Burial as is celebrated in Rome. The celebrants, however, would include brother cardinals and the apostolic nuncio of the place. The *pallium* should also be worn by the deceased cardinal in the diocese, though it could not be worn by the deceased in Rome, as only the pope has the privilege to the *pallium* in Rome.

When a cardinal dies in his diocese, possibly at a hospital, his body should be properly prepared (as above) and taken first to his residence or the cathedral rectory or seminary chapel, where his family and household may privately gather in prayer and to celebrate the first Mass for the Dead. The body should then be transferred solemnly to a place suitable for large numbers of the faithful who will gather to pray at the bier. The most suitable of places would be the seminary of his (arch)diocese if in the see (city) and if appropriate in size; if not, a suitable site should be found. The body of the deceased ordinary should lie in state on a bier for at least twenty-four hours to permit all those who wish to gather to pray. An honor guard of papal knights of all orders and ranks present in the (arch)diocese, including the venerable fraternity of the Knights of Columbus, should be posted in uniform or habit. With them, but separated from them, should be posted the seminarians of the (arch)diocese. The body should never be left unat-

tended from the time of transfer until the final commendation. Diocesan priests should be provided a special place to come to pray for their spiritual father.

Religious communities of men, vested in their habits, should also gather there to pray. Religious women should also be encouraged to gather with the faithful. The bier should be surrounded by four large candles. Flowers should be at a minimum for so high a churchman. The *galero,* if available, should be placed on a pillow at the foot of the bier, the tassels gathered around the brim. Any papal honors or decorations could also be properly displayed but should not be more prominent than the *galero,* the symbol of his high rank in the Church. The same holds true for archbishops and bishops.

After a proper period of public viewing and prayer, and, it is hoped, a series of Masses throughout this period celebrated by his successor in the see, if any, or by the auxiliary bishops or the vicars general or visiting prelates, the body is solemnly† transferred to the deceased's cathedral. Whenever possible, the hearse carrying the deceased cardinal should be followed by a foot procession to the cathedral.

The procession to the cathedral should be representative of the archdiocese. Hierarchy, *monsignori,* priests, religious men and women, and the faithful should all be present. The procession should be led by all the seminarians of the place. Preceding the hearse are the crucifer, thurifer, and acolytes with candles. Although outdoors, the transferral of a deceased cardinal to his church is considered a

---

* Today, the red *galero* can be ordered by the titular church or diocesan cathedral from the Roman vesture suppliers. Be certain, however, to order *galero can 30 fiocchi* and not a *cappello romano.*

† The Church specifies that a solemn procession must accompany the cardinal's transfer to his cathedral.

solemn ecclesiastical function. As such, absolute silence is prescribed. Dress for the transferral procession is specified by longstanding protocol: for prelates, choir dress; for the monsignori, choir cassock and surplice; and for priests and seminarians, cassock and surplice, or, if otherwise proper to the place, the alb. Religious vested in habits are followed by the faithful, who should be encouraged to dress respectfully.

At some point in the procession, after a suitable period in the procession itself, the senior presiding prelate* should be driven to the cathedral, where he should vest for the Mass of Christian Burial, according to the Roman burial rite of cardinals, and the reception of the body at the doors of the cathedral. Cardinals are also granted the privilege (not permitted to bishops and archbishops)† of having their red *galero* carried before their caskets in procession. It is never proper to place the mitre on the casket of a dead prelate. The Mass of Christian burial, according to the Vatican's burial rite for cardinals, should always be as solemn a function as possible, both in Rome and in the dioceses.

PROPER DRESS FOR THE CEREMONIES APPERTAINING TO THE BURIAL OF A CARDINAL OF THE HOLY ROMAN CHURCH

The Deceased

THE LYING-IN-STATE

The body of a deceased cardinal can be properly vested in one of two ways for viewing by the faithful:

1. The body can be vested in scarlet choir dress: the cassock, *fascia,* and *mozzetta* of scarlet and the rochet of white lace or linen. The feet should be covered in scarlet stockings and black shoes. On the head of the deceased should be placed the scarlet watered-silk *zucchetto* and *biretta;* in his hands, a rosary; under his head, the *pallium,* if he were entitled to it in life; and on his finger, the cardinalatial ring presented to him in consistory. The precious pectoral cross is suspended from the red-and-gold cord.‡

2. The body is immediately vested in sacred vestments. The choir cassock of scarlet, the watered-silk *fascia* of scarlet, and stockings of the same color and fabric are placed on the deceased. He is then vested in his "best" alb, over which is placed the pectoral cross suspended from the red-and-gold cord. The alb, is girded by a cincture in the proper mode. The amice is worn into the grave by the deceased. Over the alb is properly placed the chasuble. It may be of the liturgical color prescribed by the region: white, violet, or black. (Popes are vested in red and gold.

   Over the chasuble is placed the *pallium,* if the deceased was entitled to it in life. If he were entitled to more than one *pallia* in life, one is worn in the prescribed manner, and all the others are folded and placed beneath his head.

   Upon the head of the deceased is placed the scarlet watered-silk *zucchetto* and the white damasked mitre of the cardinalate. Upon his finger is placed the cardinalatial ring conferred in consistory.§

---

* And other prelates.

† All other prelates are permitted the use of the heraldic *galero* and at the foot of their bier only during the Mass of Christian burial, not during procession. This is an honor reserved for members of the Sacred College.

‡ The crozier is never placed beside the deceased cardinal, as it is an insignia of ongoing jurisdiction that ceases at the death of the cardinal.

§ The precious pectoral cross and ring are removed prior to burial; others of lesser value should be put in their places.

PARTICIPANTS

THE VIEWING

If prelates are attending the public viewing of the deceased two forms are prescribed:

1. If attending for official liturgical events, such as the Office of the Dead, or for a public moment of silent prayer, the prelates should be vested in choir dress.

2. If attending at other moments for private prayer or visitation of remembrance, they should arrive in *abito piano,* that is, black simar with scarlet or red piping, *fascia, zucchetto,* and pectoral cross suspended from the chain, *biretta* in hand (optional).

MASS OF THE DEAD *(also known as the Mass of the High Priest)*

> *Concelebrants:* as prescribed (as usual)
> *In attendance:* choir dress

TRANSFERRAL OF THE DECEASED *(from the place of lying-in-state or repose to the cathedral or church)*

> *In attendance:* Prelates in choir dress; priests and seminarians in either cassock and surplice or alb (stole may be worn by priests only), whichever is appropriate to the place.

MASS OF CHRISTIAN BURIAL AND FINAL COMMENDATION *(according to the burial rite of cardinals)*

> *Concelebrants:* Sacred vestments, simplex mitres, as prescribed, or damasked mitres worn by cardinals.
> *In attendance:* Choir dress with *biretta.*

Monsignori, Priests, Seminarians

At all public functions, other than the various Masses at which the ordained would possibly act as concelebrants, the dress prescribed by Rome is the cassock and surplice. The alb is not acceptable, except for the celebrant and concelebrants of the various Masses or those serving as ministers at the altar. Masters of ceremonies, likewise, are to be vested in cassock and surplice.

Knights and Ladies of the Papal Honors

Knights and Ladies who are present at the various ceremonies of the deceased cardinal's obsequies are present in an official capacity as members of the Papal Family, and, therefore, must not appear dressed as others among the laity. As their presence is official, they are expected to wear the uniform and/or mantle of their respective orders. A proper place in processions and seating should be provided them as their honors are direct from the Holy Father, who considers them part of his household and, therefore, lay officials of the Church.

The Knights of Columbus

The venerable fraternity of the Knights of Columbus should always be invited to participate in the obsequies. Internal protocol provides for the proper dress and insignia for the knights' participation in solemn events. Care should be given to assure an honorable role for the Knights of Columbus at such an important event as the burial of the local cardinal.

IN EXSEQUIIS CARDINALIUM DEFUNCTORUM
THE BURIAL RITE OF CARDINALS OF THE HOLY ROMAN CHURCH:
FUNERAL OBSEQUIES FOR DECEASED CARDINALS[36]

OPENING RITES

While the Holy Father and/or the Concelebrating Cardinals approach the altar, the schola alternating with the entire congregation sings:

ENTRANCE ANTIPHON I

> *Schola:* Give them Lord everlasting rest.
> *All repeat:* Give them. . . .

Psalm 6

> *Schola:* Verses.
> *(after each verse)*
> *All:* Antiphon.

OR

ENTRANCE ANTIPHON II

> *Schola:* Eternal rest grant unto them, O Lord: and let perpetual light shine
> upon them.
> *All repeat:* Eternal rest. . . .

Psalm 64

> *Schola:* Verses.
> *(after each verse)*
> *All:* Antiphon.

ANTIPHONA AD INTROITUM II

PSALM 64

Schola:

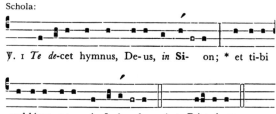

℣. 1 *Te de-*cet hymnus, De-us, *in* Si- on; * et ti-bi

reddétur votum *in Ierú-*sa-lem. Ant. Ré-qui- em.

2. *Qui audis orationem,* * *ad te omnis caro veniet propter iniquitatem.* Ant. Requiem.

3. *Etsi prævaluerunt super nos impietates nostræ.* * *tu propitiaberis eis.* Ant. Requiem.

4. *Beatus quem elegisti et assumpsisti,* * *inhabitabit in atriis tuis.* Ant. Requiem.

5. *Replebimur bonis domus tuæ,* * *sanctitate templi tui.* Ant. Requiem.

Cantu ad introitum absoluto, Summus Pontifex dicit:

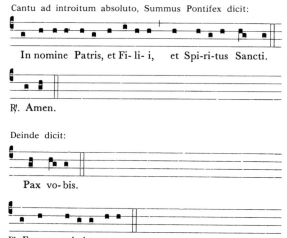

In nomine Patris, et Fi- li- i, et Spi-ri-tus Sancti.

℟. Amen.

Deinde dicit:

Pax vo- bis.

℟. Et cum spi-ri-tu tu-o.

THE PENITENTIAL RITE

A

Ky-ri- e, e-le- ison. *ii.* Christe, e-le- ison. *ii.* Ky-ri- e,

e-le- i-son. Ky-ri- e, * e-le- i-son.

Vel:

B

Ky- ri- e, * e- le- i-son. *bis* Chri-ste, e- le- i-

son. *bis* Ky- ri- e, e- le- i-son. Ky-ri- e,

e- le- i-son.

COLLECT

(Option I[37])

> *Let us pray:* O God, who called Your servant, N., Cardinal-Bishop,* to
> receive the dignity of High Priest and to membership in the Episcopal
> College, grant, we beseech you, that he may be added to their fellow-
> ship forever as well. Through Jesus Christ Your Son, our Lord, Who
> lives and reigns with You in the unity of the Holy Spirit, God, forever
> and ever.
>
> ℟. Amen.

---

* The use in this rite of the term *Cardinal-Bishop* refers to all classes of cardinals, deacons, priests, and bishops. This usage refers to the combined office of bishop with the dignity of cardinal, as required since the
pontificate of John XXIII.

(Option II)

> *Let us pray:* Merciful God, who called Your servant, the Cardinal-Bishop N., to membership in the Episcopal College, grant that he might share in Your Kingdom in the reward promised to the faithful ministers of the Gospel. We ask this through our Lord Jesus Christ, Your Son, who lives and reigns with You in the unity of the Holy Spirit forever and ever.
> ℟. Amen.

OR, AT AN ANNUAL COMMEMORATION OF THE DECEASED CARDINAL:
(Option I)

> *Let us pray:* O God who called Your servants, the Cardinal-Bishops, to receive the dignity of High Priest and to membership in the Episcopal College, grant, we beseech you, that they may be added to their fellowship forever as well. Through Jesus Christ Your Son, our Lord, Who lives and reigns with You and the Holy Spirit, God, forever and ever.

(Option II)

> *Let us pray:* Merciful God, Who called Your servants, the Cardinal-Bishops, to membership in the Episcopal College, grant that they might share in Your Kingdom in the reward promised to the faithful ministers of the Gospel. We ask this through our Lord Jesus Christ, Your Son, who lives and reigns with You in the unity of the Holy Spirit forever and ever.
> ℟. Amen.

THE LITURGY OF THE WORD

The Rite of Burial for Cardinals proposes the following texts for the Liturgy of the Word:

FIRST READING:

Outside the Easter Season:		Easter Season:
1. Job 19:1–23 or to 27a	or	1. Acts 10:34–36, 42–43
2. Wisdom 3:1–9	or	2. Revelation 14:13
3. Wisdom 4:7–15	or	3. Revelation 21:1–7

RESPONSORIAL PSALM

(Option I)

PSALM 41

Psalmista: Ps 41

℣. 1. Quemadmodum desi-de-rat cer- vus * ad fontes

a- qua-rum. ℟. De-si-de-rat a-nima me- a ad te,

De- us.

2. *Sitivit anima mea ad Deum, Deum vivum: **quando veniam et apparebo ante faciem Dei?*
℟. *Desiderat.*

3. *Fuerunt mihi lacrimæ panis die ac nocte, **dum dicitur mihi cotidie: « Ubi est Deus tuus? ».*
℟. *Desiderat.*

4. *Hæc recordatus sum, et effudi in me animam meam; **quoniam transibam in locum tabernaculi admirabilis, usque ad domum Dei.*
℟. *Desiderat.*

5. *In voce exsultationis et confessionis, **multitudinis festa celebrantis.*
℟. *Desiderat.*

℣. As the heart yearns for living fountains.
℟. My soul yearns for You, God.

OR

(Option II)

PSALM 22

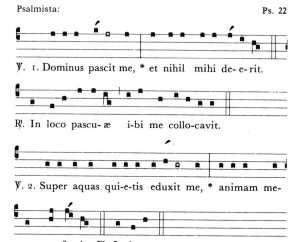

Psalmista: Ps. 22

℣. 1. Dominus pascit me, * et nihil mihi de- e- rit.

℟. In loco pascu- æ   i-bi me collo-cavit.

℣. 2. Super aquas qui-e-tis eduxit me, * animam me-

am re- fe- cit. ℟. In loco.

3. *Deduxit me super semitas iustitiæ * propter nomen suum.*
℟. *In loco.*
4. *Nam et si ambulavero in valle umbræ mortis, non timebo mala, * quoniam tu mecum es.*
℟. *In loco.*
5. *Virga tua et baculus tuus * ipsa me consolata sunt.*
℟. *In loco.*
6. *Parasti in conspectu meo mensam * adversus eos qui tribulant me.*
℟. *In loco.*

Lector: Omnes:

Verbum Domi-ni. ℟. De- o gra-ti- as.

(Option I)

℣. The Lord is my shepherd, I shall not want.
℟. He makes me lie down in green pastures.

THE SECOND READING:

    1. Romans 5:5–11 or

    2. Romans 6:3–4, 8–9

    3. 1 John 3:14–16

The Verse before the Gospel outside the Lenten Season: Alleluia

During Lent in place of Alleluia one sings:

    Schola: Praise to You, Lord Jesus Christ, King of endless glory.

    All repeat: Praise. . . .

THE PRAYER OF THE FAITHFUL

PRESCRIBED PRAYER OF THE FAITHFUL

The Holy Father or Cardinal Presider:

    Let us confidently call upon God our almighty Father

    Who raised Christ His Son from the dead

    for the salvation of all.

The Deacon/Reader:

    That He may receive into the perpetual company of the Saints

    this deceased Cardinal-Bishop, N.,

    who once received the seed of eternal life through Baptism,

    we pray to the Lord.

    That he, who exercised the episcopal office in the Church while on

    earth, may take his place in the Heavenly liturgy,

    we pray to the Lord.

    That He may give to the souls of our brothers, sisters, relatives,

    and benefactors

    the reward of their labor,

    we pray to the Lord.

    That He may welcome into the light of His countenance

    all who sleep in the hope of the resurrection,

    we pray to the Lord.

    That He may assist and graciously console

    our brothers and sisters who are suffering affliction,

    we pray to the Lord.

    That He may one day call into His glorious kingdom,

    all who are assembled here in faith and devotion,

    we pray to the Lord.

The Holy Father or Cardinal Presider:
We ask You, Lord,
that the prayer of Your people may benefit
the souls of Your children
that You may both free them from all sins
and give them a share in Your salvation.

You, who live and reign forever and ever.

℟. Amen.

LITURGY OF THE EUCHARIST

OFFERTORY ANTIPHON

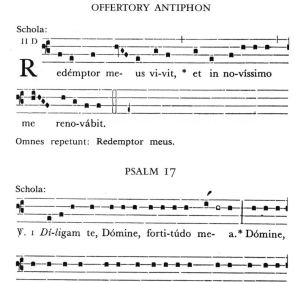

Schola:
II D

R edémptor me- us vi-vit, * et in no-víssimo

me reno-vábit.

Omnes repetunt: **Redemptor meus.**

PSALM 17

Schola:

℣. 1 *Dí-li*gam te, Dómine, forti-túdo me- a.* Dómine,

firmaméntum me-um et refú-gi-um me-um et li-be-

rá-*tor* **me-** us. Ant. Redémptor.

2. *Funes inferni circumdederunt me,* * *præoccupaverunt me laquei mortis.* Ant. *Redemptor.*
3. *In tribulatione mea invocavi Dominum,* * *et ad Deum meum clamavi.* Ant. *Redemptor.*
4. *Exaudivit de templo suo vocem meam,* * *et clamor meus in conspectu eius introivit in aures eius.* Ant. *Redemptor.*

(Option I)

> *Schola:* My Redeemer lives and will renew me on the last day.
> *All repeat:* My Redeemer. . . .
> *Schola:* Psalm 17 *(Schola sings verses; all: Antiphon).*

OR
(Option II)

> *Schola:* I will sing to You, my God, in the presence of the Angels.
> *All repeat:* I will sing. . . .
> *Schola:* Psalm 137 *(Schola sings verses; all: Antiphon).*

PRAYER OVER THE GIFTS

(Option I)

> Receive, Lord, the gifts which we offer You on behalf of Your servant, N.,
> Cardinal-Bishop; You gave the reward of the high priesthood in this
> world; may he be united with the company of Your Saints in the King-
> dom of Heaven. Through Christ our Lord.
> R⃑. Amen.

(Option II)

> Accept, Lord, these gifts which we offer for Your servant, the Cardinal-
> Bishop, N.; You gave him the episcopal charism in the service of Your
> people; receive him into the joyful assembly of Heaven. Through
> Christ our Lord.
> R⃑. Amen.

OR, AT AN ANNUAL COMMEMORATION OF THE DECEASED CARDINAL–BISHOP:

(Option I)

> Receive, Lord, these gifts which we offer You on behalf of Your servants,
> the Cardinal-Bishops; You gave the reward of the high priesthood in
> this world; may they be united with the company of Your Saints in the
> Kingdom of Heaven. Through Christ our Lord.
> R⃑. Amen.

(Option II)

> Accept, Lord, these gifts which we offer for Your servants, the Cardinal-
> Bishops; You gave them the episcopal charism in the service of Your
> people; receive them into the joyful assembly of Heaven. Through
> Christ our Lord.
> R⃑. Amen.

EUCHARISTIC PRAYER

PREFACE OF THE DEAD

On the Hope of Resurrection in Christ

> Father, all-powerful and ever-living God,
> we do well always and everywhere to give You thanks
> through Jesus Christ our Lord.
>
> In Him, Who rose from the dead,
> our hope of resurrection dawned.
> The sadness of death gives way
> to the bright promise of immortality.
>
> Lord, for your faithful people life is changed, not ended.
> When the body of our earthly dwelling lies in death
> we gain an everlasting dwelling place in Heaven.
>
> And so, with all the choirs of angels in Heaven
> we proclaim Your glory
> and join in their unending hymn of praise:

SANCTUS

(Option I)

> Holy, holy, holy Lord, God of power and might,
> Heaven and earth are full of Your glory.
>> Hosanna in the highest.
> Blessed is He who comes in the name of the Lord.
>> Hosanna in the highest.

(Option II)

Sanctus, * Sanctus, Sanctus Dominus De- us Saba- oth.

Pleni sunt cæ-li   et terra glo-ri- a tu- a. Hosanna in

excelsis. Benedictus qui ve-nit in nomine Domini.

Hosanna   in excelsis.

The Rite of Burial for Cardinals recommends the use of Eucharistic Prayer I or III.

AGNUS DEI

(Option I)

> *Cantor:* Lamb of God,
> *All:* Who takes away the sins of the world, have mercy on us.
> *Cantor:* Lamb of God,
> *All:* Who takes away the sins of the world, have mercy on us.
> *Cantor:* Lamb of God,
> *All:* Who takes away the sins of the world, grant us peace.

THE COMMUNION ANTIPHON

(Option I)

> *Schola:* Eternal light shine upon them, Lord, with Your saints forever, because You are holy.
> *All repeat:* Eternal light. . . .

PSALM 129

Schola:

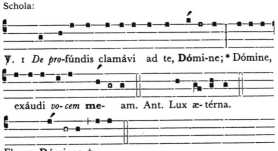

℣. 1 *De pro-*fúndis clamávi ad te, **Dómi-ne;** * Dómine, exáudi *vo-cem* **me**- am. Ant. *Lux æ-*térna.

Flexa: **Dómine;** †

2. *Fiant aures tuæ intendentes* * *in vocem deprecationis meæ.* Ant. *Lux æterna.*

3. *Si iniquitates observaveris, Domine,* * *Domine, quis sustinebit?* Ant. *Lux æterna.*

4. *Quia apud te propitiatio est,* * *et timebimus te.* Ant. *Lux æterna.*

5. *Sustinui te, Domine; sustinuit anima mea in verbo eius,* * *speravit anima mea in Domino.* Ant. *Lux æterna.*

6. *Magis quam custodes auroram,* * *speret Israel in Domino.* Ant. *Lux æterna.*

7. *Quia apud Dominum misericordia,* * *et copiosa apud eum redemptio.* Ant. *Lux æterna.*

8. *Et ipse redimet Israel* * *ex omnibus iniquitatibus eius.* Ant. *Lux æterna.*

Schola:

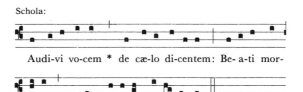

Audi-vi vo-cem * de cæ-lo di-centem: Be- a-ti mor-

tu- i, qui in Domino mo-ri- untur.

Omnes repetunt: **Audivi vocem.**

Schola: Verses.
All: Antiphon.

OR

(Option II)

Schola: I heard a voice from Heaven saying: Blessed are the dead who die in the Lord.
All repeat: I heard a voice. . . .

PSALM 120

Schola:

℣. 1 *Le-vábo* ócu-los me- os in **mon-** tes: * unde vé-ni-

et auxí-li-*um* **mi-** hi? Ant. **Audí-vi vocem.**

Flexa: **custó**dit te, †

2. *Auxilium meum a Domino,* * *qui fecit cælum et terram.* Ant. *Audivi.*

3. *Non dabit in commotionem pedem tuum,* * *neque dormitabit qui custodit te.*

4. *Ecce non dormitabit neque dormiet,* * *qui custodit Israel.* Ant. *Audivi.*

5. *Dominus custodit te, Dominus umbraculum tuum,* * *ad manum desteram tuam.*

6. *Per diem sol non percutiet te,* * *neque luna per noctem.* Ant. *Audivi.*

7. *Dominus custodiet te ab omni malo;* * *custodiet animam tuam Dominus.* Ant. *Audivi.*

8. *Dominus custodiet introitum tuum et exitum tuum,* * *ex hoc nunc et usque in sæculum.* Ant. *Audivi.*

Schola: Verses.
All: Antiphon.

PRAYER AFTER COMMUNION

The Holy Father or the Cardinal Presider says:
(Option I)

> *Let us pray:* We ask, almighty and merciful God, that Your servant, N., Cardinal-Bishop, who on earth fulfilled the office of ambassador for Christ, may be cleansed by this sacrifice and so to take his place with You in the company of Heaven. We ask this through Christ our Lord.
> ℟. Amen.

(Option II)

> *Let us pray:* Almighty and merciful God, we implore You for Your servant, the Cardinal-Bishop N.: You who appointed him as an ambassador for Christ among the people, by this sacrifice of salvation cleanse him of every fault and receive him unto Yourself in glory. We ask this through Christ our Lord.
> ℟. Amen.

OR, AT AN ANNUAL COMMEMORATION OF THE DECEASED CARDINAL-BISHOP:
(Option I)

> *Let us pray:* We ask, almighty and merciful God, that Your servants, the Cardinal-Bishops who on earth fulfilled the office of ambassador for Christ, may be cleansed by this sacrifice and so to take their place with You among the company of Heaven. We ask this through Christ our Lord.
> ℟. Amen.

(Option II)

> *Let us pray:* Almighty and merciful God, we implore You for Your servants, the Cardinal-Bishops: You who appointed them as ambassadors of Christ among the people, by this sacrifice of salvation, cleanse them from every fault, and receive them unto Yourself in glory. We ask this through Christ our Lord.
> ℟. Amen.

THE FINAL COMMENDATION AND FAREWELL

After the prayer after Communion has been said, the Holy Father or Cardinal Presider proceeds to the rite of final commendation and farewell. Standing near the bier, facing the people, he offers the invitation in these words:

(Option I)

> As we complete, according to the custom of the faithful, the services required for the burial of the human body, let us confidently beseech God for whom all things live, that in the power and dignity of the saints He raise up the body of this our brother, N. Cardinal-Bishop, to be buried by us in its weakness and that He bid his soul to be joined with the saints and the faithful.

> May God grant him mercy on the day of judgment, so that, redeemed from death, and freed from debts, reconciled with the Father, and carried on the shoulders of the Good Shepherd he may merit a share of everlasting joy and the company of the saints in the court of the Eternal King.

(Option II)

> Before concluding, in accord with the Christian ritual, the pious duty of burial, let us confidently beg God our Father in Whom and for Whom all things live. We entrust to the earth the mortal body of our brother N., Cardinal-Bishop in the expectation of his resurrection; may the Lord receive his soul into the glorious company of the saints; may He open to him the arms of His mercy, so that this brother of ours, redeemed from death, freed from all fault, reconciled with the Father and carried on the shoulders of the Good Shepherd, may share in eternal glory in the Kingdom of Heaven.

The schola begins the singing:

(Option I)

I believe that my Redeemer lives and on the last days I will rise from the
   earth.
And in my flesh I shall see God my Savior.

   ℣. Whom I myself and no other shall see, and my eyes will behold
      And in my flesh. . . .
   ℣. This hope has been placed in my breast
      And in my flesh. . . .

OR

(Option II)

   Come to his aid, Saints of God, run to him, angels of the Lord:
   Receive his soul and present him to God the Most High.
   May Christ, Who has called you, receive you: and may the angels lead you
      into Abraham's bosom.
   Receive his soul. . . .

(While the singing is going on, the body is sprinkled with holy water and incensed.)
Then the Holy Father or the Cardinal Presider says:

(Option I)

> Into your hands, most merciful Father, we commend the soul of our brother N., Cardinal-Bishop, relying on the sure hope that, just as all who have died in Christ, he will rise again with Christ on the last day. We thank You for all the favors which You bestowed upon Your servant in this mortal life that they might be for us a sign of Your goodness, and of the blessed communion of the saints in Christ. Turn your merciful ears to our prayers, Lord, so that the gates of paradise may be open to Your servant, and that we also, who are left behind, may console one another with words of faith until we all are reunited in Christ, and with You and with our brother forever. We ask this through Christ our Lord.
> ℟. Amen.

(Option II)

> Into Your hands, most merciful Father, we entrust the soul of our brother N., Cardinal-Bishop, with the sure hope that he will rise again on the last day with those who have died in Christ. We thank You, O Lord, for all the favors which you gave him in this life, as a sign of Your goodness and of the communion of saints in Christ. In Your infinite mercy, open the gates of paradise; and grant to us who remain here below Your consolation with the words of faith until the day when, reunited in Christ, we might always live with You in eternal glory. We ask this through Christ our Lord.
> ℟. Amen.

After the prayer has been said, all sing:

(Option I)

> May the angels lead you into paradise; may the martyrs come to welcome you, and may they lead you into the holy city Jerusalem. May the choirs of angels receive you, and with Lazarus, who was once poor, may you have eternal rest.

(Option II)

> I am the resurrection and the life: he who believes in me, even though he die, will live; and everyone who lives and believes in me, will never die.

PSALM 113

Antiphon repeated at the end of Psalm.

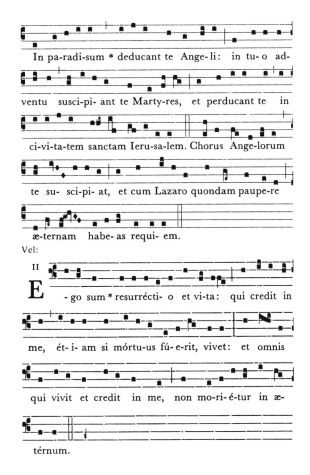

In pa-radi-sum * deducant te Ange-li: in tu- o ad-
ventu susci-pi- ant te Marty-res, et perducant te in
ci-vi-ta-tem sanctam Ieru-sa-lem. Chorus Ange-lorum
te su- sci-pi- at, et cum Lazaro quondam paupe-re
æ-ternam habe- as requi- em.

Vel:

E -go sum * resurrécti- o et vi-ta: qui credit in
me, ét- i- am si mórtu-us fú- e-rit, vivet: et omnis
qui vivit et credit in me, non mo-ri- é-tur in æ-
térnum.

PSALM 113A

℣. 1 *In* éx-i-tu Isra- el de Ægyp- to, * domus Iacob de
pópu-*lo* **bár**baro.

2. *Factus est Iuda sanctuarium eius, * Israel potestas eius.*

3. *Mare vidit et fugut, * Iordanis conversus est retrorsum.*

4. *Montes saltaverunt ut arietes, * et colles sicut agni ovium.*

5. *Quid est tibi, mare, quod fugisti? * et tu, Iordanis, quia conversus es retrorsum?*

6. *Montes, quod saltastis sicut arietes, * et colles, sicut agni ovium?*

7. *A facie Domini, contremisce, terra, * a facie Dei Iacob.*

8. *Qui convertit petram in stagna aquarum, * et silicem in fontes aquarum. Ant. Ego sum.*

SUITABLE FOR THE PROGRAM FOR THE FUNERAL RITE

English:

"May the meek and joyful face of Jesus Christ appear to you to decree that you may be present forever among those who stand before Him." (St. Peter Damian, *Epistola VIII*)

"Jesus Christ is the first born of the dead; to Him be glory and dominion for ever. Amen." (*Apocalypse*, I, 5–6)

"May all of us who have honored the victories of Your resurrection be saved on the final day of resurrection by the accepted sacrifice of this victim." (*Liber Mozaribicus Sacramentorum*, 16)

Original Latin:

"Mitis atque festivus Christi Iesu vobis aspectus appareeat, qui vos inter assistentes sibi iugiter interesse decerneat." (S. Petri Damiani Ep. VIII)

"Iesus Christus est primogenitus mortuorum; ipsi gloria et imperium in saecula saeculorum. Amen." (Apoc. 1: 5-6)

"Omnes qui nunc tuae resurrectionis victorias excoluimus, in resurrectionis novissimo die, huius hostiae litatione, salvemur." (Liber Mozaribicus Sacramentorum, 16)

Roman Curia

The structure of the Church's government is known as the Roman Curia, or in Italian, *la Curia Romana*. It is a formal collection of offices and agencies established for the purpose of the implementation of the work of the Church and of the Holy Father.

The Curia, as most of the ancient governmental structures of the world, evolved from an advisory assembly or council that served the early popes on matters of policy and Church dogma. With time, these various assemblies took on more authority and, as a result, became more formalized. Many of the earliest Curia offices have vanished, their functions and purpose no longer important to the Church or vital to its existence in the modern world. Other offices remain, however, their original purpose having evolved through time into agencies with a much broader scope in the mission of serving the needs of a Church of multitudes of people with twentieth-century spiritual and physical needs. Many traditional offices have been retained, their ancient titles laid aside for more functional modern appellations, whereas others have been newly created to address the specific issues of the modern era.

Most of the present Curia has its roots in the sixteenth century, when the popes formalized the government of the Church. Until 1967, many of the original functions of the various Curia departments remained intact, customarily under the name bestowed upon them by papal bull at the time of their creation three hundred years prior. Pope Paul VI, soon after his election and coronation, began the lengthy process of reorganizing and renaming the Roman Curia.* In 1988, twenty years later, his successor Pope John Paul II promulgated the apostolic constitution *Pastor Bonus,*† which mandated further modifications that resulted in the abolition of arcane titles and that shifted departmental responsibilities in keeping with the demands of the modern world upon the Church.

On December 22, 1988, in his annual Christmas message to the members of the Roman Curia, Pope John Paul II said:

No one is unaware that, more than in any other era, the Church is confronted with tasks which have importance, extent, and multiplicity perhaps never before known. They are challenges which she must meet, and which the

---

* *Regimini Ecclesiae Universae*, March 31, 1968.
† *Pastor Bonus*, June 28, 1988.

Holy See, in particular, feels called upon to respond to by virtue of the Petrine ministry. This has suggested a review of the structure of the Roman Curia in order to improve its functioning in relation to the Church's present demands.[1]

Pope John Paul II went further to declare that the role of the Curia was to bring his brothers in the episcopate closer to the Bishop of Rome. In the years following this message, John Paul II, himself wishing to bring Christ to the people of God, has played a less active role in the life of the Curia than have many of his predecessors, depending heavily upon the capable and talented clergy who serve the Church in the various departments of the Roman Curia.

SECRETARIAT OF STATE

The Secretariat of State is the most senior of the Vatican offices, serving the Holy Father as both his personal office and as an equivalent of a European foreign ministry or the United States Department of State. Historically, the Secretariat was not the most influential department at the Vatican, the position it presently maintains. The Secretariat of State is one of the more recent additions to the governing body of the Church, having been formalized as a consulting body of the Church, by Pope Innocent XII in 1692.

Originally, the Secretariat of State was nothing more than a "kitchen cabinet" of the pontiff and was staffed primarily by his closest relatives. At the head of this council was a member of the Sacred College, who traditionally was also a family member of the reigning pope. As president of this council, he took the title Cardinal-Nepos, a title that derived from the young cardinal's relation as nephew or cousin to the pontiff. Below the president of the council were several secretaries of state, both clergy and lay. By the end of the seventeenth century, the title Cardinal-Nepos was abandoned. It no longer became the practice, within the Papal States, to promote members of the pope's family, a political practice that was the origin of the term *nepotism*. As the Secretary of State, as the president of the council was now formally called, became more influential in the life of the papacy, the practice of nepotism became politically dangerous to maintain. The title Cardinal-Nepos was changed to *Secretaries Papae et Superentendens Status ecclesiastici.*[2]

The post of Secretary of State has thenceforth always been held by a member of the Sacred College; however, many of these cardinals were not members of the clergy. As late as 1800, Ercole Cardinal Consalvi, an Italian minor noble without Holy Orders, held the post of Secretary of State. He was the last lay cardinal to do so. Innocent XII, considered the founder of the Secretariat of State, formalized and restricted the Secretariat of State[3] as the governing body it has become today.

STRUCTURE

Headed by the Cardinal–Secretary of State, who is the closest "official" collaborator with the Holy Father, the Secretariat of State is responsible for the most immediate of the Church's reactions to world events and crises. It is also the department that formalizes the Church's posture on international ecclesiastical policy and shoulders the responsibilities of the daily administration of the Church and the Vatican City State. The appointment to the post of Cardinal-Secretary is most closely watched by the world because this is perhaps the pope's most political appointment and the one that can set the tone of a new pope's pontificate. The Cardinal-Secretary of State, as senior Curia functionary, implements the policies of the reigning pontiff. Today, as a result of canons 401 and 402, the importance of the post of Cardinal–Secretary of State has most often been reflected by the appointment of one of the *sostotore* (substitute)—who has spent years at the side of his predecessor becoming equipped to handle the difficulties of the job—rather than a less-qualified prelate of greater renown, as had historically been the practice.

The Secretariat of State is divided into two sections: the Section for General Affairs, which has responsibility over the daily life of the Curia, governing appointments, and coordinating intercurial meetings; and the Section for Relations with States, which has responsibility for the relations with civil governments and political authorities.

Each of these two departments is headed by a *sostituto,* or "substitute," who manages the affairs of his own department on a daily basis. He reports to the Cardinal–Secretary of State and to the pope directly on those matters of great import. The *sostituto's* job is to be certain that all information vital to the pope's decision-making process be presented first to the Cardinal-Secretary and, if need be, to the Holy Father. There is no codification in the law that stipulates the extent of the responsibilities of the *sostituto.* As the *sostituti* are the two chief aids to the Cardinal-Secretary, it is up to him to determine the extent of the authority each *sostituto* will have over his section within the Secretariat. It is therefore solely a preference for a particular managerial style, and nothing more, that governs how the two sections will conduct business. Regardless of style, the role of the two substitutes in the work of Secretariat is vital.

Section for General Affairs

The Section for General Affairs is the administrative arm of the Secretariat; from it flows the daily administration of the Church, the Holy See, and the Vatican. The department is responsible for the preparation of papal decrees and documents and for the coordination of the work of the *Acta Apostolicae Sedis (AAS),* the Vatican Press Office, and the Secretariat's own archives, which are maintained separate and apart from the Secret Vatican Archives. It is to the Section for General Affairs that falls the responsibility for the rapport of the Secretariat with all other Curia ministries, formerly known as dicasteries, and today known independently as congregations, councils, and offices.

This section of the Secretariat is also responsible for the issuing of lay awards, honors (see Chapter Six), and testimonials in the name of the Holy Father, as well as for the overseeing of the governance of the Vatican City State through a Commission of Cardinals established for that purpose.

Section for the Relations with States

Under the watch of the Sostituto, the Section for the Relations with States concerns itself with the Church's relations with foreign governments, princes, (and all other heads of state), and matters of international diplomacy.

The Vatican possesses one of the world's most efficient and highly trained foreign service corps (see Chapter Four, Papal Diplomacy). The Section for Relations with States is responsible for the care of the Church's interests worldwide. Through use of formal diplomacy, the Holy See maintains relations with states and international organizations. This section of the Secretariat of State coordinates the diplomatic efforts of the Holy See and keeps the Holy Father fully abreast of world events as they unfold. The pope's personal secretaries are officially posted to the Secretariat of State for this purpose. International news and diplomatic briefs are prepared by this section of the Secretariat each day so that the Holy Father is fully cognizant of changing international events. The Section for Relations with States most resembles other nations' foreign offices or the U.S. Department of State. This section, like its counterparts worldwide, maintains the staff and apparatus necessary to remain as informed and prepared to respond to world events as it must always be in order to effect sound policies of the Holy See.

All concordats or treaties with foreign states are written by this section of the Secretariat. In former times, beautifully arcane titles applied to the work of this office, as well as to the work of other areas within the Secretariat. The *Secretaria Brevium* was the historic title applied to the work of preparing papal briefs. This department was founded by Innocent XI in 1678.[4] The *Secretaria Brevium Ad Principes* had been responsible for the formal letters, briefs, and addresses to princes. Today this work continues, but the scope includes all foreign heads of state and government. This department has always been staffed by experts of the most formalized Latin, in both composition and style, who are commonly known as Vatican Latinists.

Under the care of the Secretariat of State, and under the patronage of the Cardinal-Secretary, who serves as its chancellor, is the Pontifical Ecclesiastical Academy, which serves the Church as the training ground for future papal diplomates (see Chapter Four). The Secretariat of State is the most flexible of the Vatican departments because its character and operational style change during each pontificate, reflecting the reigning pontiff. As this department is the closest to the pontiff, it follows that this body most reflects his personal-management style.

CONGREGATIONS

Doctrine of the Faith

At present, senior among the papal congregations is the Congregation for the Doctrine of the Faith *(Congregatio pro Doctrina Fidei),* formerly known as the Congregation of the Holy Office and, more historically by its founding title, the Holy Office of the Inquisition. Although the latter title resounds negatively in the minds of the faithful and in the minds of the world at large, today, the Congregation for the Doctrine of the Faith is positive in nature, design, and character. Its chief role is to protect and encourage the faith, not to condemn randomly or arbitrarily, as some historians distort.

The Congregation for the Doctrine of the Faith was founded by Pope Innocent III in the thirteenth century as a safeguard against the heretical movements common to that era. Two hundred years later, in 1542, Paul III restructured the office, placing it under the guardianship of a body of first three and then five cardinals whose responsibility it was to root out and eradicate heresy. Abuses continued, as they had throughout the previous two hundred years; however, subsequent pontificates eventually restricted the activities of the congregation in order to safeguard against these abuses.

To mark the change in mission, Pope St. Pius X renamed the congregation the Holy Office. Paul VI, in his reorganization of the Roman Curia,[5] restricted the work of the congregation to reflect his desire to promote the teaching of the Church with a positive and loving, yet firm, hand. This document followed his earlier *motu proprio,*[6] in which he renamed the Congregation of the Holy Office the Congregation for the Doctrine of the Faith.

Presently, it is the congregation's responsibility to maintain the accuracy and truthfulness of the teachings of our faith. It examines, therefore, questions relating to doctrine. It evaluates the theological writing and teachings of churchmen of the day and has the power to reprove them if they are found to be opposed to the fundamental teachings of our faith. In all matters concerning the faith, the congregation is consulted when a doctrinal issue becomes a matter for discussion by the Holy See and the Church Universal.

Oriental Churches

Known also by its official Latin title, *Congregatio pro Ecclesiis Orientalibus,* this congregation is responsible for the faithful who live in predominantly Eastern rite localities or who are themselves members of one of the Eastern rites of the Catholic Church wherever they may reside.

The congregation has its roots in two former departments of the Curia, the *Propaganda Fide* and the Oriental Church Congregation. United, and subsequently expanded, the competency of this congregation includes the proposing of new Eastern Rite bishops, the interaction between the Holy See and the Eastern rite hierarchy, the protection of the liturgy of the Eastern rites, and the codification of the law as it pertains to the Eastern Church.

The Congregation was founded by Pope Pius IX in 1862[7] and later restructured by Benedict XV. When Benedict granted autonomy to the congregation in 1917[8] by removing the Christians of the Orient from under the Curia governance of the Congregation for the Propagation of the Faith, he affirmed the universality of this saying: "It (the Church) is neither Latin, nor Greek, nor Slav, but Catholic. We repeat beloved St. Paul when We affirm; 'Herein there is not gentile and Jew, circumcision and uncircumcision, barbarian and Scythian, slave, freeman, but Christ is all and in all.'"[9]

For centuries, Christians living in a predominantly Muslim world have clung to Rome for spiritual guidance, as have minority rites within orthodoxy. These Christians pledge loyalty and fidelity to Rome and to Peter's successor, and proper care and protection must be provided them by the Holy See.

In modern times, the Congregation for the Oriental Church is most active and concerned with matters protecting the liturgy and law of the individual rites of the "Orient." The Church has always been careful to preserve the individual traditions and practices of these Christians, all the while preserving the catholicity of the Church.

Divine Worship and the Discipline of the Sacraments

Two separate Curia departments, the Congregation for Divine Worship and the Discipline of the Sacraments, were united into one senior congregation by Pope John Paul II in 1988, after years of merging together and then again splitting apart.[10] The original Congregation for Divine Worship is a recent Pauline creation (1969), whereas the Congregation for the Discipline of the Sacraments was created by *motu proprio* of Pope St. Pius X as a replacement for the former Congregation of the Rites.

It falls to the Congregation for Divine Worship and the Discipline of the Sacraments to maintain the liturgical life of the Church and foster its growth, and to assure orthodoxy with Rome. It is also the task of the *Congregatio de Cultu Divino et Disciplina Sacramentorum,* its formal Latin title, to rectify abuses to the sacred liturgy and the sacraments. The congregation's primary concern, therefore, is with the sacraments and the sacramental life of the Church. This department works closely with the Congregation for the Doctrine of the Faith when questions of abuse arise within the Church.

Under the scope of this congregation also falls the work of the special commissions on "treating cases of nullity of sacred ordinations and dispensations from obligations of sacred ordination of deacons and priests."[11]

Causes of Saints

The most mysterious of the offices of the Roman Curia, the Congregation for the Causes of Saints *(Congregatio de Causis Sanctorum),* deals in miracles. Much has been written about this office and its work. Entire volumes have been dedicated to the history and study of what transpires behind the walls of its offices on the Piazza Pius XII.

First and foremost, this office deals with faith—faith in God and His Church, which leaves room open for embracing the idea that miracles, the touching of humankind by the Finger of God, can still happen in the world, even a world that is fast approaching the twenty-first century. During this congregation's entire existence, its purpose was to foster the naming of men and women, known by their sanctity, to be saints. The congregation bore two names since its inception more than four hundred years ago. Created by Pope Sixtus V (Felice Peretti) in 1588 as the Congregation of Rites, it held this name until the apostolic constitution of Paul VI in 1969.* Thereafter, it took its present title, the Congregation for the Causes of Saints.

For nearly four hundred years, the process remained the same. The *minutanti* (the ecclesiastical employees of the lower ranks of the congregation) in 1925 followed the identical formula utilized by their predecessors in 1625. In 1930, the process was modernized, making room for improved techniques in both medieval research and historical study. Finally, in 1983, Pope John Paul II, by apostolic constitution,† reformed the process for declaring saints of the Church.

"The investigation and gathering of proofs are now under the authority of the local Bishop. Before initiating a cause, however, he must consult with other Bishops of the region about the value of seeking canonization for the candidate."[12] Once the local ordinary begins the public process, the cause of the individual begins to gather some notoriety, most notably within the ecclesiastical community of that province. An electricity begins to build when a candidate has possibility and other bishops readily support the cause.

"The Bishop then appoints the officials necessary to investigate the life, virtues, and/or martyrdom of the candidate."[13] In the late twentieth century, this process is exact and often rapid. In nearly every case today, the need for eyewitnesses to the life, work, and chastity of the candidate is essential. Every aspect of the life of the potential *beata* is researched; only then does the local bishop submit his findings to Rome. If Rome concurs that there is evidence sufficient to proceed, the candidate is given the title Servant of God. The cause is then assigned two *officiali,* the realtor and the postulator, the former being the more vital of the two. It falls to the realtor to search through the history of not only the individual but also the histories of the place and the events and circumstances of that era, to properly create a bibliographical study on this "servant" for further study at the congregation.

After the work is completed, a series of reviews begins at the congregation. The first of these reviews, which sometimes takes months to complete, is that made by the historical experts. These consultors study the dossier closely to judge if what has been found is both historically accurate and verifiable, as it concerns the actual participation of the Servant of God.

When the reviews are completed, the congregation's panel of six to ten of some of the best theologians of the Curia, under the direction of the *Promotore Generale della Fide* (prelate theologian), study the cause in light of the candidate's orthodoxy in word, action, writings, and life example to the teaching of the Church. Once assured of this adherence, the *Promotore Generale* submits the cause to the thirty cardinals, archbishops, and bishops who have been personally appointed to serve in this capacity by the pope.

This commission now authenticates the miracles attributed to the cause. One miracle for the first

---

* *Regimini Ecclesiae Universae.*
† *Divinus Prefectionis Magistro.*

step to *Venerable,* and one subsequent miracle for each of the two remaining stages, if the cause progresses that far. No miracle, under the terms set for by Pope John Paul II, is required of a martyr. A just investigation on the martyr's sanctity and circumstance is sufficient, if so decided by the pope, to declare a martyr both Blessed and a Saint.

Bishops

Officially known as the *Congregazione per i vescovi,* (Congregation for Bishops), this office of the Curia has the heavy responsibility of naming the world's bishops, the future leaders of the Church. Each year, hundreds of vacancies are effected by death, retirement, illness, or expansion of a diocese, as in the case of a need for auxiliary bishops. The Congregation for Bishops, in conjunction with the papal representative of a country or region, makes inquiry into the suitability of one priest or another and submits to the Holy Father nominees for each post to be filled.

It is not as simple a process as it seems. First of all, the congregation must gather information on the exact needs of the local churches so that any eminent appointment would meet the need of the local church. To do so, the congregation employs priests and religious men and women who gather information from local ordinaries, bishop's conferences, presbyterates, and laity so that, when a vacancy arises, the congregation will be prepared for an appointment based upon the needs of the church in that locality.

The nominating process has been perfected over the centuries since the congregation was created in 1588 by Pope Sixtus V under the title of the Consistorial Congregation, the name held by that office until the congregation was reformed by Paul VI on August 15, 1967. Prior to these reforms, this congregation was concerned with not only the causes for bishops but also matters concerning the Sacred Liturgy and the works of the liturgical books. With the expansion of the Pauline Curia came numerous new departments, each concerned with a singular area of the Universal Church. The Consistorial Congregation was divided, and the Congregation for Bishops was created in an attempt to meet the needs of the expanded episcopacy.

In seeking potential new bishops, ordinaries within each diocese canvass the priests of their diocese to see if they believe one among them to be worthy of the office of bishop. In addition, from time to time, lay persons active in the Church are often consulted as well.

As soon as it becomes apparent that one or two persons within a jurisdiction are considered by his peers and by the laity to be worthy of consideration, the ordinary consults with the metropolitan of the province, as well as with his brother bishops of the province, to ascertain their opinions on this or that candidate. Beyond this consultation, the name is submitted to the Nuncio of the place, who has also made separate inquiries on various candidates. From these consultations, the nuncio begins to compile a list of suitable candidates.

Three names are eventually submitted to the Congregation for Bishops. This list is called a *terna,* Latin for "three." The *terna* is ranked by preference of the nuncio from most likely to least likely for any given appointment. Once the *terna* has been submitted to Rome, the congregation is free to nominate any one of the three. For that matter, the congregation may nominate one whose name does not appear on the *terna* yet who is known to them to be the most qualified for that vacancy, given the needs and circumstances of the local church.

After consultation and investigation within the congregation, the cardinal-prefect, during his weekly meeting with the Holy Father, submits the name deemed to be most suitable. Of course, the Holy

Father can choose any priest* to fill the vacancy; he need not choose from the *terna* at all.

After the Holy Father has made his decision, the candidate is notified. He is bound by secrecy until the announcement is made at noon on the following Thursday. Once the hour of noon passes in Rome, he is free to break the news to family, friends, and the faithful of the local church.

It is important to note that the Holy Father ordains new Bishops in Rome only once each year, on the feast of the Epiphany. Any bishop nominated at other times throughout the year is traditionally ordained to the episcopacy at the cathedral of his home diocese or the new diocese he is to govern.

Evangelization of Peoples

The Congregation for the Evangelization of Peoples, or *il Congregatio per L'Evangelizzazione dei Popoli* as it is known in Italian, is one of the more important of the Curia offices and one of its most historic. For centuries, it was known worldwide as *di Propaganda Fide.* The cardinal-prefect of the *Propaganda Fide* was known as the "Red Pope" because of the blood that was shed by the missionaries under his jurisdiction. The congregation was also one of the wealthier of the Curia offices, being endowed by Catholics worldwide; its finances were independent of the Holy See's budget.

The *Propaganda Fide* was created by Pope Gregory XIII in 1580 as a commission of cardinals who looked after the Church's activities in the foreign missions. As the mission work of the Church mushroomed, the commission expanded into a full Curia dicastery. On July 22, 1622, Pope Gregory XV erected the Congregation for the Propagation of the Faith.

In present times, the congregation bears the more pastoral name Evangelization of Peoples, which is a concern dear to Pope John Paul II. Its responsibilities include the coordination of mis-

sionary efforts worldwide. "Accordingly, it has competence over those matters which concern all the missions established for the spread of Christ's kingdom without prejudice to the competence of the Congregations."[14] In other words, whenever possible, its activities for the spread of the Gospel are encouraged and promoted.

The direct activities of this congregation's competence include the establishment of societies and organizations bringing aid and missionary work to the people, the promotion and encouragement of mission vocations to the priesthood and religious life, the erection of episcopal jurisdictions and ordinary authority, the nomination of mission territory bishops, the assignment of missionaries in their work, and the finance of mission works. The Congregation for the Evangelization of Peoples has jurisdiction on every continent including North America. The diocese of Fairbanks, Alaska, one of the largest ecclesiastical territories, is still designated a mission diocese and therefore falls under the jurisdiction of the cardinal-prefect of this congregation.

Clergy

Until 1967, the Congregation for the Clergy was known as the Congregation for the Council. It held that name for 350 years. Prior to this, it was called the Council of Cardinal Interpreters of the Council of Trent. It was founded for the purpose of interpreting the text of the Council of Trent (1545–63) and to bring into practice its teaching. As such, it grew rapidly, taking on many of the heated issues of that era. By the beginning of the eighteenth century, the Congregation for the Council concerned itself chiefly with the finances of the diocesan clergy worldwide and the supervision of diocesan clergy outside Rome.

---

* The pope is not bound by the nomination list of the congregation yet almost always trusts their competency in these matters.

It was not until Paul VI began the reform of the congregation in 1967, renaming it the *Congregazione per il clero,* as it is known in Italian, that its responsibilities came into the modern era. Pope John Paul II further widened the scope of this office. As a result, it now has three sections, with competencies over "the life, discipline, rights, and duties of the clergy; the preaching of the Word, catechetics, norms for religious education of children and adults; preservation and administration of the temporal goods of the Church."[15]

In present times, when even the clergy are forcibly entangled in world events, it falls to this congregation to exercise the Church's wisdom and guidance in sensitive matters between governments and the local clergy.

Institutes of Consecrated Life and Societies of Apostolic Life

Predating both the Congregation for Bishops and the Congregation for the Causes of Saints by two years each, the *Congregazione per gli Istituti di vita Consacrata e Le Societá di vita Apostolica* was founded in 1586 by Sixtus V, with competence over the growing number of religious institutes and societies. Almost immediately thereafter, it was merged with another congregation, Consultation with Bishops, where it remained until Pius X reestablished its full competency in 1908 under the name Congregation for Religious. In 1988, Pope John Paul II reformed the Curia once more in an attempt to bring it further into the twentieth century. Many of the Curia offices had a name change, including the Congregation for Religious. At the present time, it holds the title Congregation for the Institutes of Consecrated Life and Societies of Apostolic Life so as to more accurately identify the competency of this commission.

In addition to having authority over institutes of religious and societies of consecrated life,* this con-

gregation also has authority over secular or third orders, the establishment of councils or other consultative bodies whereby the superiors of all bodies may consult with one another, the suppression of defunct institutes or societies, and the erection or expansion of others.

Catholic Education

The newest of the major offices of the Roman Curia, *the Congregazione per L'Educazione Cattolica,* was not created until November 4, 1915, by Pope Benedict XV. Prior to that time, its important work concerning education in general and, more specifically, Catholic education in seminaries and universities, came under the competency of various offices in the Curia and, from time to time, special commissions of cardinals as well. Its work has always been vital to the Church; however, the growth in the number of universities and seminaries late in the last century and early in this century demanded that an office be established specifically for the care and oversight of Catholic education.

This office was founded under the title of the Congregation of Seminaries and Universities, a title it held for fifty-two years until Paul VI changed it to the Congregation for Catholic Education. This is the title by which it is most commonly known; however, Pope John Paul II qualified it in 1988 when he added, in parentheses, "for Seminaries and Institutes of Study." Very few persons, however, take notice of this change, insisting on referring to it as "Catholic Education."

The importance of the work of this Curia office is evident in its structure. The congregation is divided into three separate sections, each concerned with a specific relevancy of the faith with regard to education. The first of these sections concerns itself with seminaries in that it "handles matters con-

---

* Canons 573–746.

nected with the direction, discipline, and temporal administration"[16] of seminaries worldwide. This section also concerns itself with the ongoing education of diocesan and religious clergy, of religious, and of the secular institute membership. This office has the responsibility of assuring that the seminaries of the world are closely adhering to the priestly formation formulae as set forth by Rome. The second section has competency over matters concerning Catholic universities and colleges inasmuch as these institutions work within the structure of the Church. The third section concerns itself with preuniversity preparation and formation. By concentrating its efforts in this area, this congregation can strive to foster a formidable Catholic foundation in school systems throughout the world.

The cardinal-prefect and his staff work closely with local bishops' conferences, as well as with the Congregation for the Evangelization of Peoples, which has authority over seminaries in the remaining mission territories. The congregation often comes under extreme criticism. Its critics claim it has no right to "interfere" in their work or administration, despite their claim to be "Catholic" in foundation. Recently, some seminaries have even let it be known that they would prefer less direction from Rome. For critics of the work this congregation performs in the name of the Holy Father, a quote of Pius XII summarizes the role of the cardinal-prefect and the staff of his congregation: "When the Holy See seeks to inform itself on the teaching practiced in some seminaries, colleges, athenaeums, and universities concerning the subject matter which is subject to its authority, it is only fulfilling the mandate that it has from Christ and the duty which it has before God to defend and preserve, pure and intact, true doctrine. This vigilance, furthermore, also tends to defend and emphasize your right and duty to feed the flocks entrusted to you with the truth of the authentic words of Christ."[17]

The Congregation for Catholic Education, as with all the offices of the Curia, has a serious mandate from the Holy Father, one that requires a great deal of work and diligence. At its head, as in the case of all congregations, is a cardinal-prefect who is assisted by a secretary, who is always a titular archbishop. Together with their staff, they concern themselves with every aspect of Catholic education worldwide. The growth of new parochial systems, universities, and seminaries, as well as the guidance and care required by existing seminaries and Catholic universities, is a formidable task in the modern area.

TRIBUNALS

"Christ is teacher, legislator, and judge; the Pope, His Vicar, must also be teacher, legislator, and judge."[18] And through the tribunals of the Roman Curia, the Holy Father exercises his rights and responsibilities as the successor of Peter.

Throughout the five centuries of the modern Curia's existence, the successive popes have modernized and streamlined the functions of the numerous departments that compose the present Curia. Because of the unique functions that each of the tribunals of the Holy See performs, these bodies alone have survived the vicissitudes of time, remaining firmly resolved in their mission of serving the pontiff in his threefold role as teacher, legislator, and judge.

Apostolic Penitentiary
The senior of the tribunals, the Apostolic Penitentiary, or to give it its proper Italian title *Penitenzieria Apostolica,* was created in the twelfth century by Pope Honorus III. From the early Middle Ages, the Church was concerned with the need for the pope's legate to provide absolution in the name of the pontiff on grave matters presented at court for the pope's opinions. Quickly, these matters moved into

1.

2.

3.

4.

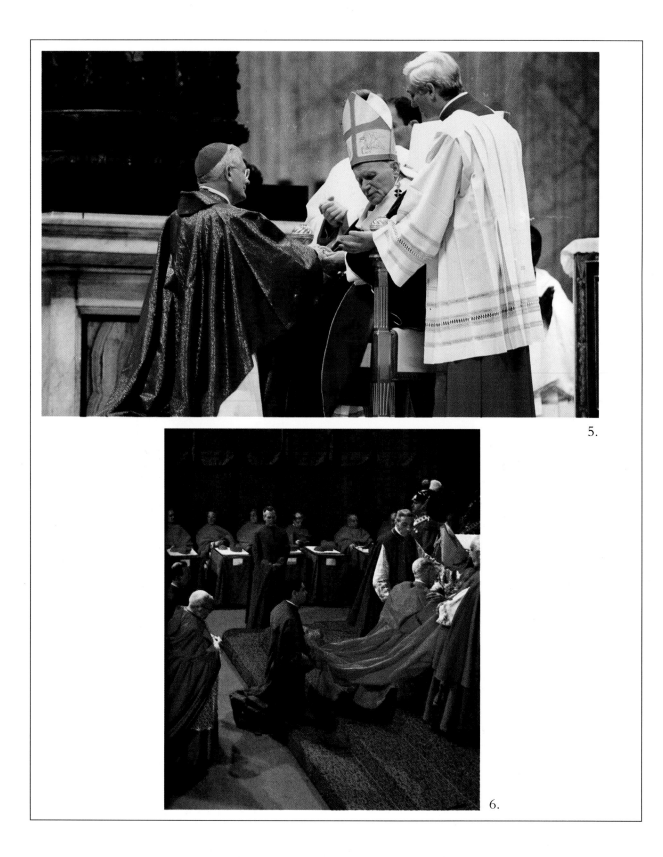

5.

6.

7.

8.

9.

10.

11.

12.

13.

14.

15.

17.

16.

18.

19.

20.

21.

22.

23.

24.

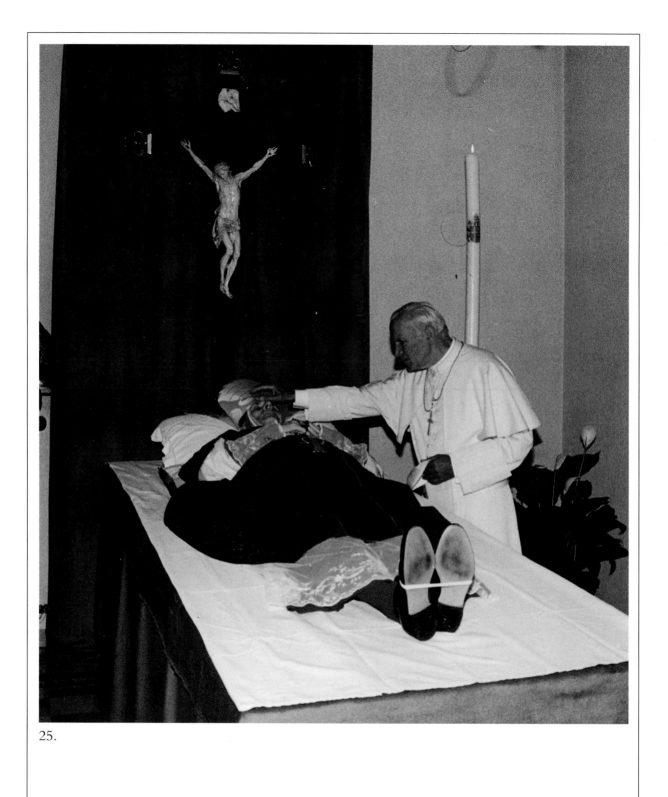

25.

26.

27.

28.

29.

30.

31.

32.

33.

34.

35.

36.

37.

38.

39.

the realm of internal forum, and matters under the penitentiary's jurisdiction fell into areas of absolution from grave sin, sins reserved to the Holy Father, dispensations, commutations, and so forth.

The Apostolic Penitentiary developed naturally, with very little need for radical reform or outside interference. Over time, however, the pontiffs did bring into modern practice procedures that governed the tribunal's work. In addition to matters of internal forum, with which the penitentiary is primarily concerned, the tribunal also has under its competence the maintenance of the Raccalta of Indulgences. Until 1917, all matters of indulgences were under the protection of a Curia office concerned with nothing else, and the penitentiary remained strictly in the realm of internal forum, as it had for the previous seven hundred years; however, Benedict XV, in his Curia reforms, merged the competency of these two offices.

The cardinal-prefect of this tribunal is known as the Major Penitentiary of the Holy Roman Church. He maintains offices in the Palace of the Chancelleria off the Corso Vittorio Emmanuel. The major penitentiary, at one time known as the Grand Penitentiary of the Holy Church, is the only Curia official who remains in power, with the full authority of his office, during the *Sede Vacante*. This is so that he may continue to confer necessary pardon and dispensations during the duration of the vacancy of the See of Peter. The major penitentiary is also the only cardinal who may maintain a steady stream of outside contact during the sealed conclave as the nature of his office requires his continued attention in severe matters of internal forum. "In the event that he dies during Conclave, the conclavists must immediately elect a successor for the duration of the Conclave. The mystery of the mercy of God, which is exercised through the Penitentiary, thus does not suffer interruption."[19]

The major penitentiary, also known as the cardi-nal-prefect, is assisted in his work by a regent, rather than the traditional secretary, as in the congregations. He is always a titular archbishop. In addition to the regent, the penitentiary has assigned to it a designated theologian who, following a four-hundred-year-old tradition, is always a Jesuit. This is one of the privileges assigned to religious orders and congregations in the Curia organization. Numerous *officiali* assist in the work of this tribunal as well. It is important to note that every petition to the penitentiary is given a confidential response within five days of petition.

Apostolic Signatura

The Supreme Tribunal of the Apostolic Signatura, to give it its formal title, is the supreme court of the Catholic Church. Whereas the Apostolic Penitentiary concerns itself with matters of the internal forum, only this tribunal has competency over all matters of the Church in the external forum. This tribunal bears the name "Signatura" because it was the first authoritative body of the Church to be granted the privilege of assigning the pope's proper name and title to documents in his absence. By affixing the pope's signature, the signators, or signers, acquired the name of the court to which they belonged.

The Apostolic Signatura is a special court presided over by a council of judges, who are cardinals appointed by the pontiff for five-year terms. At present, there are eight cardinal-judges. This court is of mid-fifteenth century creation, having been established by Eugene IV and redefined in the next pontificate of Nicholas II in 1449. For three hundred years, it served as one of the courts of the Church, as well as of the sovereign Papal States, two separate legal entities. It was designated as the supreme court of the Catholic Church by papal decree of Pius X in 1908.

After Nicholas V confirmed the rights and privileges of the *Signaturi* and the body now known as the Signatura, subsequent pontificates hastened its growth and development. Alexander VI further defined the competency of members of the Signatura. As a result, specific functions within the tribunal began to develop. Julius II ordered the tribunal subdivided into the Signatura for Promoting Justice and the Signatura for Grace, which later was assumed by the datary, the office that concerned itself with papal functions and documents.

This early split in responsibilities within the Signatura is significant in that it set a tribunal precedent for having two distinct functions within the Signatura body, a distinction remaining to this day, albeit functionally different in nature. Today the Signatura is divided into the first and second sections. Their competency was defined by Paul VI when he ordered first major reorganization of the Curia of the modern era.[*]

In the apostolic constitution concerning the Roman Curia, Paul VI wrote concerning the specific competency of this section of the Signatura when he said, "It extends to the competence of tribunals, even those established for matrimonial cases; until other provisions are made, it extends the forum of strangers [*pellegrini*] in the city of Rome to process dealing with nullity of marriage but only in extraordinary circumstances and for the most serious reason."[20] Paul VI further expanded the jurisdiction of the first section of the Signatura by placing in its competence "those rights which are assigned to it in concordats between the Holy See and the various nations,"[21] a protection that enables the Holy See to involve itself in jurisdictional matters in the international arena.

The first section of the Signatura derives its responsibilities from the earliest Curia offices. In 1245, at the close of the Council of Lyon, the staff of the Chancelleria (as it was known as a governing body of the Church) were officially recognized as advisors to the Pope. The first title to be granted to the staff of this office, most commonly laymen in the earliest era, was *Breviatores.* In 1467, these *breviatores* were divided by command of Calistus III into three classes: *abbreviators, primae visionis,* and *de parco minori.* This body of *breviatores* took the formal name of *Collegii abbreviatores* in 1463 by decree of Pius II.

By 1558, the divisions were further clarified when Paul IV ordered the separation of responsibilities of clerics and laity. The lay positions took the name *Substituti Minutantes,* the first time that the title *Minutantes* appeared in Curia usage. This title remains in use to this day as a designation for mid-level clerics, particularly in service at the Secretariat of State.

The second section of the Signatura is the more modern of the two judicial bodies within the Signatura. It resolves "contentions which have arisen from the exercise of an art of administrative ecclesiastical power which are referred to it because of an interposed appeal or recourse against a decision of a competent department."[22] In other words, this body serves as a court of appeals and cassation within the Curia.

It must be remembered that the Apostolic Signatura serves the Curia and the Holy See alike as supreme court, and, as such, it has jurisdiction over all matters referred to it, matters involving a judicial nature of the Holy See in the international arena and matters referred from the Rota, which serves the Church as the Court of Ordinary Appeal.

Tribunal of the Roman Rota

Known in the Latin as *Tribunal Rotae Romanae,* the title of this court of appeals is derived from the 1331 decree of John XXII, which referred to the court as a wheel-like assembly, because jurists sat at a large round table during the exercise of their authority. This was drastically different from the

---

[*] *Regimini Ecclesiae Universae,* August 15, 1967.

practice, then common throughout the Italian peninsula, in which jurists and all those with jurisdictional authority, temporal as well as spiritual, were seated at the most prominent position in the hall, elevated over all present.

John XXII set the oath to be administered to all Rota jurists, composing it himself. He further required that the oath be administered by himself and his successors, a practice that waned by the fifteenth century. In the earliest days of the court, the Rota comprised fifty jurists; in less than a century, that number had fallen to twelve. Today, the number of jurists is closer to twenty, with an additional staff of senior clergy, in varying classes, for a total of approximately thirty.

The competency of this court is defined in *Regimini Ecclesiae Universae*. Any request for "nullity of matrimony duly referred to the Holy See is extended to cases involving a Catholic and a non-Catholic party, or to two non-Catholic parties, whether one or both of the baptized parties belongs to the Latin Rite or to Oriental rites."[23]

Very few cases come to the Rota directly; nearly all are referred to the court under the terms of the internal regulations and norms governing the Rota itself. Eventually, many famous cases do reach the Rota, and this is often seen as an act of favoritism for the parties involved—which is not the case. Whereas the large majority of cases involving the nullity of matrimony are heard on the diocesan level, as is proper under the law of the Church, the law requires certain cases to be automatically transferred to Rome for hearing and deliberation. Specific instances of such cases would include the request for the nullity of a marriage of a head of state, his or her children, grandchildren, brothers, sisters, and other prominent personages. The reason for such laws is not favoritism. On the contrary, the law has been formulated to avoid just that, sometimes to the detriment of the petitioners who may

have to wait far longer for a verdict than common laypersons.

There are strong historic reasons for the existence of such a law, which is universally praised for its soundness and political thoughtfulness. In order to avoid all political pressure, involvement, or coercion upon the Holy See, the decision for these few, albeit famous, personages, must be made in Rome, far away from political and diplomatic pressures in the petitioner's homeland.

One of the more famous cases involved Henry VIII of England. As everyone knows, Henry wanted to divorce his wife, Catherine of Aragon, because she could not bear him an heir. This case is very complicated and forms a study of its own, as already undertaken by numerous historians; nevertheless, it is important to stress the implications of this case in the present law regarding heads of state. Henry's pressure upon the bishops of England to force an annulment ruling in Rome was tremendous.[*] When Rome refused, Henry forced the bishops to annul locally his marriage—which some agreed to do in violation of Rome's edict. This political pressure and other major events connected to it led, of course, to Henry VIII's split from Rome and eventually to the establishment of the Church of England. To avoid such unlawful and dishonest pressure, often life-threatening in nature on the local bishops, the Holy See long ago imposed the stipulation that removes the local ordinary from the petition process and thus from local political influence.

Of course, these and other famous cases get much press attention, which is usually unkind to the Church and which illustrates the ignorance of the press to many respects of standard, long-

---

[*] Any visitor can see this when visiting the Secret Vatican Archives, where bishop after bishop signed and sealed his approval to Henry's request. Almost all historians assert that this approval was given under life-threatening pressures from the king.

standing Church practice. What is often branded as favoritism in the press is nothing more than faithful adherence to Church law and practical concern for the Catholic petitioner, all too often caught in the vortex of the subsequent press storm.

PONTIFICAL COUNCILS

In studying the reorganization of the Curia in the modern era, two documents must be carefully examined in order to come to a full understanding of what Pope Paul VI and Pope John Paul II desired in promulgating the extensive changes to the governing body of the Church. The foremost intent has been the effort to adjust the Church's government to more faithfully and accurately address the needs of the faithful and to further the message of the Church throughout the world. To accomplish this, both popes have seen the need for a more modern, efficient, and international Curia. In implementing these much needed changes, historic roles, titles, and responsibilities needed to be altered, redefined, or, in some instances, abolished.

Although the congregations and the tribunals were affected by the many changes that followed *Regimini Ecclesiae Universae* and *Pastor Bonus,* the pontifical councils and papal offices were most directly affected. Most of these came into existence as a result of one of these decrees. *Pastor Bonus* clearly furthered the work of *Regimini Ecclesiae Universae.* Today's Curia is efficient, modern, and intentionally international, much more reflective of the Church Universal than in past pontificates. It is also a body that continues to evolve and modernize from within, often without papal initiative. As such, changes will continue to arise, most probably more so before the close of this millennium than in the past three hundred years combined. The competency of these bodies, therefore, continues to evolve, and it is the intent, within the following pages, to present an overview of the work of the Holy See in the remaining departments of the Curia.

The Pontifical Council for the Laity, known in Italian as *Pontificio Consiglio per i Laici,* is headed by a cardinal-prefect. All councils, in contrast to the congregations, are not headed by a cardinal-prefect by right. This is one of the newest of the Curia departments, having been established on December 10, 1976, by the papal *Motu Proprio Apostolotus Perogendi* of Paul VI in the last years of his pontificate. He established it for work on the apostolate of the laity as they are involved in the life and activity of the Church worldwide.

The Pontifical Council for Promoting Christian Unity, known in Italian as *Pontificio Consiglio per la Promozione Dell'Unita Dei Cristiani,* is likewise a new commission. It predates both reorganizational decrees, owing its foundation to John XXIII, before the Second Vatican Council. In fact, he established this body as a precouncil research and advisory commission. Having performed this work to the highest standards possible, it was retained by Paul VI after the council, having by then been raised to the level of Secretariat, a title later abolished by *Pastor Bonus* for all Curia bodies except the Secretariat of State. In 1988, it took its present title.

The main thrust of the work of this council is in the discipline of ecumenism. It "undertakes dialogue regarding ecumenical questions and activities with Churches and ecclesial communities separated from the Holy See."[24] The work of this office is extremely important as volatile issues continue to face the Church in relation to other churches and ecclesial communities. Issues such as female ordination, in relation to the posture of the Church of England and its ongoing dialogue, are concerns of this office. Attached to this commission as well is the Commission for Religious Relations with Jews, and, although primarily the work of the Secretariat of State, the recent diplomatic recognition of Israel, as well as Israel's concurrent recognition of the Holy See, was a matter of immediate concern for this commission.

The Pontifical Council for the Family is the next organization encountered within the Curia were one to follow along the official organizational chart of the Holy See. Like so many other councils, this office was established in recent times. Erected by Paul VI on January 11, 1973, and given its present name by Pope John Paul II in 1981, the Council for the Family, or as it is known in Italian *Pontificio Consiglio per la Famiglia,* is concerned primarily with providing pastoral care, education, and the spreading of the Gospel to the family worldwide. It is always headed by a cardinal-prefect.

The Pontifical Council for Justice and Peace was erected by Paul VI in 1976 after nine years of existence on a semipermanent basis as an advisory commission. It was raised to the status of pontifical council in 1988 by John Paul II and is headed by a cardinal-prefect. Based solely in the Gospel teaching, the council's work is to promote justice and lasting peace throughout the world by means of the extension of the message of Christ's Church.

The Pontifical Council "Cor Unum" was erected for the purpose of fully integrating the Church's participation in the assistance of aid and succor in coordination with other world organizations likewise involved. It was created in 1971 by Pope Paul VI and is intimately linked to the work of Justice and Peace.

The Pontifical Council for Providing Pastoral Care to Migrants and Travelers was erected as a subcommittee of the Council of Bishops in 1970 and later raised to a fully constituted council by Pope John Paul II in 1988. Its work is diversified because of the problems facing migrants and travelers worldwide. As a recent council, and one involved in an area not fully understood by most governments of the world, this council is most certainly going to see change to its mission and structure in the near future as problems with displaced peoples continue to intensify.

The Pontifical Council for the Apostolate of Health Care Workers is probably the least known and least understood of the Curia departments. Erected as a commission in 1985 and later changed to a council in 1988, its function is to promote the education, vocation, and interests of the various degrees of international health care providers in Catholic organizations. Because many of these providers fall under the competency of other Curia departments, such as the Congregation for Religious or Consecrated Life, whose members are engaged in health care activity, these departments continue to maintain a close rapport with one another.

The main responsibility of the Pontifical Council for the Interpretation of Legislation Texts is to provide the Church Universal with an accurate interpretation of Church laws and promulgations. It is headed by a cardinal-prefect and was erected by Pope John Paul II on January 2, 1984. It assumed the title Pontifical Council in 1988.

The Pontifical Council for Interreligious Dialogue was known by its original title, the Secretariat for Non-Christians, until it took its present title in 1988. It was the creation of Paul VI (1965) in response to the Second Vatican Council's wish to further more sincere dialogue between Christians and non-Christians. Attached to the council is the Special Commission for Religious Relations with Muslims, whose competence is to foster open dialogue and understanding with the peoples of Islam.

Of the remaining councils, the first, the Pontifical Council for Dialogue with Non-Believers, concerns itself with the ongoing discourse about the prominent issues of the day, as they affect Christian belief, with the sector of nonbelievers such as atheists and godless philosophies. It was erected in 1965, as a post–Vatican II commitment to furthering dialogue with nonbelievers, and was later raised to its present status and title by Pope John Paul II in 1988.

The Pontifical Council for Culture's role in the Curia is to continue the mission of the Church and the Gospels, into the plurality[25] of the world's cultures. One of the later Curia bodies, it was founded by Pope John Paul II in 1982. It is headed by a cardinal-prefect.

The final Council, the Pontifical Council for Social Communications, was founded by Pope Pius XII in 1945 as a direct result of the needs that faced the Church as the Second World War closed and as the technological age opened. John XXIII erected it as a permanent commission with initial competence over the spreading of the message of the social communications of the forthcoming Second Vatican Council. Its competency was expanded through the 1960s and 1970s as the age of technology and international public relations became more sophisticated. At present, the Council for Social Communications is responsible for the fostering of the Church's mission through the extensive use of the most sophisticated tools presently available to the world in technology and media science. It is one of the Curia councils that continually experiences growth as the tools for its work continue to develop on a daily basis. Pope John Paul II relies heavily on this council as he continues to increase his worldwide evangelization efforts. Like all of the papal commissions, the constitution *Pastor Bonus* altered the title of this pontifical council in 1988.

OFFICES AND AGENCIES

As we continue along the organizational chart of the Holy See, we find the numerous offices and agencies necessary for the extensive work of the Church through the legal entity of the Holy See or for the proper governance of the Vatican City State. In similar fashion to the previously discussed Curia

departments, these offices and agencies are a mix of the ancient and the modern; those attached to the papacy tend to be more historic in character, whereas those attached to the Vatican City State tend to be modern governmental agencies necessary for the smooth operation of the work of the Church in Rome.

The Apostolic Camera is of ancient origin. It developed in the beginning of the eleventh century and has been a continual entity of the Church, unbroken through time, since its appearance on the scene of the medieval papacy. The title of this office is derived from that of the individual who served the popes of the eleventh century, beginning with Nicholas II, as director of finance. The title conferred on the first "finance minister" was *Camerarius domini papae,* who held, along with that office, a position of authority over several staff clerics in service to the pope. In 1150, the position of *camerarius* also carried with it the dignity of "cardinal" under the pontificate of Blessed Pope Eugene III.

Because of the connection to finance, the title *Chamberlain of the Apostolic Camera* (a late Renaissance development) was said to derive from the archdeacons of the seven regional deaconries of Rome who were responsible for the giving of succor or aid to the poor (thus the financial connection), but the ancient link between the two cannot be verified and may be nothing more than Renaissance lore.

The Camera, headed by the Camerlengo of the Holy Church, soon became the most powerful post after the pope himself because, by the twelfth century, the responsibility for governing the Church during the *Sede Vacante* fell to him. In medieval times, the vacancy of the papacy was often a lengthy period, and the safeguards against personal gain, which are time honored, were not in place during this era. The Camerlengo, if not spiritually grounded, could prove to be a major political power with whom to reckon.

The Camera, as we know it, began to develop in the late fifteenth century, yet the fundamental responsibilities existing today in this office were present as early as the twelfth century. It is to the Camerlengo that falls the responsibility of verifying the death of the pope; summoning his successor's electors, the College of Cardinals; burying the deceased pope; and presiding at the conclave (see Chapter One, Sacred College).

In present times, the Camerlengo is always a Rome-based cardinal of the highest esteem. Traditionally, he has served the Church, in particular the Curia, for many long, devoted years and is well versed in the financial protocol and precedence that this position demands.

In contrast, the next Curia department to be discussed, as one moves along the Holy See's organizational chart, is a very modern necessity, being founded as late as 1967—the Prefecture of Economic Affairs of the Holy See. Responsibility for the internal fiscal affairs of the Holy See—budgets, salaries, pensions, and stipends—are all in the domain of this office. The modern Church faces an annual shortfall on the balance sheet and counts on the generosity of the faithful worldwide through the annual Peter's Pence Collection. The proceeds of this twelfth-century English invention are applied to the work of the Prefecture of Economic Affairs. This office is headed by a cardinal-prefect.

Whereas the Prefecture of Economic Affairs concerns itself with the balance of the annual operational budget of the Holy See, the Administration of the Patrimony of the Holy See is concerned solely with the largesse of the Church accumulated over time, much of it the result of the payment made to the Vatican at the Lateran Treaty of 1929 in reparation for the lands taken by the Italian state in the previous century. This largesse is known as the Patrimony or Estate of the Church. The funds generated as annual dividends form the major source of revenue for the Church's work each year, as well as the annual operating budget of the Vatican. The principal is seldom touched, and correctly so, for to do so could spell the end of the wonderful charitable works of the Church as we know them. Once gone, the funds will never be retrieved. In the hands of cardinal-commissioners, the Administration of the Patrimony of the Holy See has an important function, a function supported by experts in the financial field. The administration dates to the pontificate of Leo XIII; it was reorganized by Paul VI and later by the present pontiff, John Paul II.

The Prefecture of the Papal Household is a body that is responsible for organizing the pope's daily life. Because of its involvement with the Supreme Pontiff on a daily basis, it is discussed more fully in Chapter Three, The Papal Household and the Papal Family.

The Office of Liturgical Celebrations of the Supreme Pontiff is the department of the Curia that organizes the liturgical life surrounding the papacy. The Papal Master of Ceremonies heads an office of sixteen or more clerics and religious. It is the responsibility of this office to make proper arrangements for all liturgical functions bearing the designation "papal." These include the burial of members of the Sacred College, as well as normal celebrations throughout the liturgical year. This office does not concern itself with the arrangements surrounding other aspects of the pope's official life, however, as these responsibilities fall under the aegis of the Prefecture of the Papal Household.

There are at least fifteen agencies that complete the study of the present *Curia Romana*. Nearly all function under a competency redefined in 1988 in *Pastor Bonus*. Some of these reach deep into Church history while others are recent creations, yet each serves the pope and the Church well by fulfilling a present need of the faithful; a need addressed by the competency of each of these offices. Below, we will look at just a few of these remaining offices; those that are most recognizable to Catholics the world over.

The Pontifical Biblical Commission was instituted by Leo XIII on October 30, 1902, and has been restructured twice since its erection. It is attached permanently to the Congregation for the Doctrine of the Faith and is therefore headed by its cardinal-prefect, who additionally holds the secondary title President of the Pontifical Biblical Commission. The Disciplinary Commission of the Roman Curia handles matters arising from a breach of confidentiality in Curia affairs. The "Fabric of St. Peter's" is a misnomer in English, as the Italian name, *Fabrica di San Pietro,* refers to the physical makeup of the basilica, what we would call in English "the physical plant." Under the care of the Cardinal-Archpriest of the Patriarchal Basilica of St. Peter in the Vatican, the everyday maintenance, as well as the extraordinary decoration and preparation for papal events, is under the domain of this office. It is a massive task to keep a plant this size in proper order, considering that 100,000 persons per day go through its doors in the height of the travel season. The men who clean, repair, and set up for papal Masses are known as *sanpietrini,* literally, "the little ones of St. Peter's."

The Secret Vatican Archives and the *Biblioteca Apostolica Vaticana* (the Vatican Library) are two world-renowned agencies. Anyone visiting the Eternal City for a prolonged period would be wise to seek the permission of each of these bodies for a tour and further study. Each is headed by a cardinal; the Vatican Library by a cardinal-protector and the Secret Vatican Archives by a cardinal referred to as the "Most Eminent and Most Reverend Archivist." The two departments have been responsible, through the centuries, for the guardianship of much of the greatest treasures of the modern era. Original manuscripts from our greatest authors and documents and historic memorabilia from the most important events in the history of mankind are housed within the walls of the Vatican and are carefully protected for future generations to study.

The Office of Papal Charities, the *Elemosineria Apostolica,* is the agency that distributes funds to persons in need in and around Rome and throughout the world. Pleas for assistance arrive in every mail delivery at the Vatican. Through this office, the Holy Father is able to disburse funds directly to people in need. In 1993, the office made gifts to the needy in the amount of $1.3 million. Each year, thousands of requests for papal blessings arrive at this office. Just inside the Sant'Anna gate on the via del Pellegrino, the office of the papal *Elemosineria* handles all requests for assistance and the bestowal of formal papal blessings.

Of the remaining offices of the Curia many are certainly worthy of special note. These include the Press Office of the Holy See, the Office of Statistics, the Commission on Sacred Archaeology, and the Theological Commission. The continuing list is quite extensive and worthy of further study.

Each congregation, tribunal, council, office, and agency that makes up a part of what the world calls the Roman Curia fulfills a highly specialized, necessary function in the life of the Church as she prepares for the third millennium. Both Pope Paul VI and Pope John Paul II have established a government for the Church that is self-adjusting, even capable of growth and adaptation to change as the world changes. The Curia is certainly the oldest governing body of the world. It remains probably the most perfected as well, despite its arcane titles and odd-sounding functionaries. It is a governmental body envied for its efficiency and expertise. Despite its critics from outside and from within the Church itself, all who fully understand the extensive work of this body, collectively and individually, admire its success in service to the Church.

THE ORGANIZATION OF THE HOLY SEE

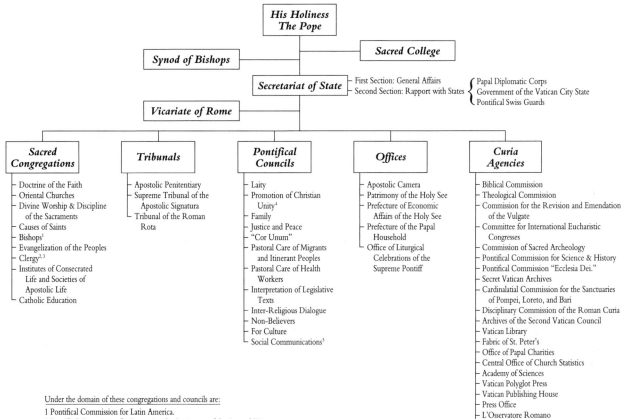

His Holiness The Pope

Synod of Bishops

Sacred College

Secretariat of State — First Section: General Affairs
— Second Section: Rapport with States
{ Papal Diplomatic Corps
Government of the Vatican City State
Pontifical Swiss Guards

Vicariate of Rome

Sacred Congregations
- Doctrine of the Faith
- Oriental Churches
- Divine Worship & Discipline of the Sacraments
- Causes of Saints
- Bishops[1]
- Evangelization of the Peoples
- Clergy[2,3]
- Institutes of Consecrated Life and Societies of Apostolic Life
- Catholic Education

Tribunals
- Apostolic Penitentiary
- Supreme Tribunal of the Apostolic Signatura
- Tribunal of the Roman Rota

Pontifical Councils
- Laity
- Promotion of Christian Unity[4]
- Family
- Justice and Peace
- "Cor Unum"
- Pastoral Care of Migrants and Itinerant Peoples
- Pastoral Care of Health Workers
- Interpretation of Legislative Texts
- Inter-Religious Dialogue
- Non-Believers
- For Culture
- Social Communications[5]

Offices
- Apostolic Camera
- Patrimony of the Holy See
- Prefecture of Economic Affairs of the Holy See
- Prefecture of the Papal Household
- Office of Liturgical Celebrations of the Supreme Pontiff

Curia Agencies
- Biblical Commission
- Theological Commission
- Commission for the Revision and Emendation of the Vulgate
- Committee for International Eucharistic Congresses
- Commission of Sacred Archeology
- Pontifical Commission for Science & History
- Pontifical Commission "Ecclesia Dei."
- Secret Vatican Archives
- Cardinalatial Commission for the Sanctuaries of Pompei, Loreto, and Bari
- Disciplinary Commission of the Roman Curia
- Archives of the Second Vatican Council
- Vatican Library
- Fabric of St. Peter's
- Office of Papal Charities
- Central Office of Church Statistics
- Academy of Sciences
- Vatican Polyglot Press
- Vatican Publishing House
- Press Office
- L'Osservatore Romano
- Institute of Religious Works

Under the domain of these congregations and councils are:

1 Pontifical Commission for Latin America.
2 Pontifical Commission for Preserving the Patrimony of the Art and History.
3 Standing Interdiscasterial Commission for Clergy Distribution.
4 Commission for Religious Relations with the Jewish People.
5 Vatican Film Archives.

PRESENT INCUMBENTS OF THE ROMAN CURIA

SECRETARIAT OF STATE

Cardinal–Secretary of State: Angelo Cardinal Sodano
Sostituto: Archbishop Giovanni Battista Re
Secretary: Archbishop Jean-Louis Tauran
Assessor: Mons. Leonardo Sandri

THE SACRED CONGREGATIONS*

The Congregation for the Doctrine of the Faith
Prefect: Joseph Cardinal Ratzinger
Secretary: Archbishop Alberto Bovone

The Congregation for the Oriental Churches
Prefect: Achille Cardinal Silvestrini
Secretary: Archbishop Miroslav S. Marusyn

- Special Commission for the Liturgy
- Pontifical Mission for Palestine
- Catholic Near East Welfare Association

The Congregation for Divine Worship and Discipline of the Sacraments
Prefect: Antonio Cardinal Javierre Ortas
Secretary: Archbishop Geraldo Majella

The Congregation for the Causes of Saints
Prefect: Angelo Cardinal Felici
Secretary: Archbishop Edward Nowak

The Congregation for the Bishops
Prefect: Bernardin Cardinal Gantin
Secretary: Archbishop Jorge María Mejía

- The Central Office for the Coordination of the Military Ordinates
- The Pontifical Commission for Latin America

The Congregation for the Evangelization of Peoples
Prefect: Josef Cardinal Tomko
Secretary: Archbishop Giuseppe Uhač

- Theological Commission
- Catechism Commission
- Review Commission
- Pastoral Care of Workers
- Other related commissions

The Congregation for the Clergy
Prefect: José Cardinal Sánchez
Secretary: Archbishop Crescenzio Sepe

- International Council for Catechists
- The Pontifical Commission for the Preservation of Artistic and Historic Patrimony of the Church

The Congregation for Institutes of Consecrated Life and Societies of Apostolic Life
Prefect: Eduardo Cardinal Martínez-Somalo
Secretary: Archbishop Francisco J. Errázuriz Ossa

- Council for the Rapport with the Congregations and International Unions of Superiors and Superiors General

The Congregation for Catholic Education
Prefect: Pio Cardinal Laghi
Secretary: Archbishop José Saraiva Martins

THE TRIBUNALS

Apostolic Penitentiary
Cardinal Penitentiary: William Wakefield Cardinal Baum
Regent: His Excellency, Mons. Luigi De Magistris

* No longer referred to as "Sacred."

Supreme Tribunal of the Apostolic Signatura
Prefect: Gilberto Cardinal Agustoni
Secretary: Archbishop Zenon Grocholewski

The Tribunal of the Roman Rota
Dean: His Excellency, Mons.
Mario Francesco Pompedda

THE PONTIFICAL COUNCILS

The Pontifical Council for the Laity
President: Eduardo Cardinal Pironio
Vice President: Bishop Paul J. Cordes

The Pontifical Council for Promoting Christian Unity
President: Edward Cardinal Cassidy
Secretary: Bishop Pierre Duprey

The Pontifical Council for the Family
President: Alfonso Cardinal López Trujillo
Secretary: Bishop Elio Sgreccia

The Pontifical Council for Justice and Peace
President: Roger Cardinal Etchegaray
Vice President: Archbishop F.X. Nguyên Van Thuân
Secretary: Mons. Diarmuid Martin

The Pontifical Council "Cor Unum"
President: Roger Cardinal Etchegaray
Secretary: Mons. Iván Marín-López
Sustituto: Mons. Karel Kasteel

The Pontifical Council for the Pastoral Care of Migrants and Travelers
President: Archbishop Giovanni Cheli
Special Delegate: Archbishop Emmanuel Milingo
Secretary: Rev. Silvano Tomasi

The Pontifical Council for the Pastoral Care of Health Workers
President: Fiorenzo Cardinal Angelini
Secretary: Rev. José Luis Redrado Marchite

The Pontifical Council for the Interpretation of Legislative Texts
President: Archbishop Julian Herranz
Secretary: Bishop Bruno Bertagna

The Pontifical Council for Interreligious Dialogue
President: Francis Cardinal Arinze
Secretary: Bishop Michael Louis Fitzgerald

The Pontifical Council for Culture
President: Paul Cardinal Poupard
Secretary: Mons. Franc Rodé

The Pontifical Council for Social Communications
President: Archbishop John P. Foley
Secretary: Bishop Pierfranco Pastore

• Vatican Film Office

THE OFFICES

The Apostolic Camera
Camerlengo of the Holy Roman Church:
Eduardo Cardinal Martínez-Somalo
Vice Camerlengo: Archbishop Ettore Cunial

The Administration of the Patrimony of the Apostolic See
President: José Cardinal Castillo Lara
Secretary: Archbishop Giovanni Lajolo

The Prefecture of the Economic Affairs of the Holy See
President: Edmund Cardinal Szoka
Secretary: Bishop Luigi Sposito

CURIA AGENCIES

The Prefecture of the Papal Household
Prefect: Bishop Dino Monduzzi
Regent: Mons. Paolo Nicolò

The Office of the Liturgical Celebrations of the Supreme Pontiff
Papal Master of Ceremonies: Mons. Piero Marini

The Pontifical Biblical Commission

The International Theological Commission

The Pontifical Commission for the Revision and Emendation of the Vulgate

The Pontifical Committee for International Eucharistic Congresses

The Pontifical Commission of Sacred Archaeology

The Pontifical Committee for Science and History

The Pontifical Commission "Ecclesia Dei"

The Archives of the Second Vatican Council

The Cardinalatial Commission for the Sanctuaries of Pompei, Loreto, and Bari

The Disciplinary Commission of the Roman Curia

The Secret Vatican Archives

The Vatican Library

The Fabric of St. Peter's

The Office of Papal Charities

The Vatican Press Office

VICARIATES AND GOVERNMENT

The Vicariate for Vatican City
Vicar General: Virgilio Cardinal Noè

The Vicariate for Rome
Vicar General: Camillo Cardinal Ruini
Vicegerent: Archbishop Remigio Ragonesi
Prelate Secretary: Mons. Luigi Moretti

THE PONTIFICAL COMMISSION FOR THE VATICAN CITY STATE (*GOVERNATORATO*)

President: Rosalio José Cardinal Castillo Lara
Secretary: Mons. Gianni Danzi
Special Delegate: Marquis Don Giulio Sacchetti, G.C.H.S.

CHAPTER THREE

The Papal Household and the Papal Family

The Papal Chapel and the Papal Household are separate entities supporting the modern papacy, and each is of decidedly ancient origins. "The origin of the papal court dates back at least as far as the Carolingian Era, but as an institution, the court developed most during the period of the Avignon papacy (1306–74) and by the time of Urban VIII it had reached much the same form as it perseveres today."[1]

Both the Papal Household, which today forms part of the Roman Curia and is therefore a legal entity within the governing structure of the Holy See, and the Papal Chapel, which formalizes the participation of various officials at papal events, serve the Holy Father in his external, ceremonial life, which, in the final analysis, furthers his mission for the Church. Together they form what was once called the Papal Court. From the fourteenth century until Vatican Council II, the Papal Court did not differ much from other royal courts of Europe. Its ceremonies, although religious in nature, more closely resembled the pomp and pageantry of other royal events. A British diplomat who was posted to Rome as one of the members of the official delegation to Pope Pius XI's jubilee celebration described in his diary the extent of that pageantry:

The great procession is now marshalled and ready for its slow march up the center of the Church to the High Altar. First comes the Papal Master of Ceremonies, accompanied by the procurators of the ecclesiastical colleges and two Swiss Guards. Then comes the Capuchin Preacher to the Holy See, in his brown habit, the Father-Confessor, by tradition a member of the Servite Order, in black, then representatives of all the chief religious orders whose habits, plain black and brown and white, contrast with the Monsignorial purple of those who follow, the chaplain bearing the Papal mitre, the judges of the Rota and Vatican legal officials carrying the candles; then two of the deacons, one Latin, one Greek, who are to assist in the Mass to follow, and so on to higher and higher ranks of clergy. The Abbots, Bishops, and Archbishops of the Latin rite are preceded by two clergy carrying staves decked with flowers; then come the Bishops, Archbishops, and Patriarchs of the various Eastern Churches in communion with Rome, all in their traditional vestments. The procession begins to glow with more and more color as the Cardinals come in their crimson robes, followed by a single figure, in black with silk hose and a white lace fichu, * the Prince Assistant at the Pontifical Throne, always either Prince Colonna or Prince Orsini, the two great historic families, mortal enemies in the Middle Ages, but long reconciled and united in this traditional personal service to the Pope.*

Then come the Papal Chamberlains, in their gala court uniforms, surrounding the Pope aloft on his throne, over him a canopy held high by eight Monsignori. *The Pope is dressed in a robe of white silk, with a short cape of red velvet; his tiara seems heavy to bear for such a long time as the procession takes to reach its end. Accompanying the Pope, who gives his blessing to the kneeling crowds as he passes, are the Swiss Guards, some carrying staves representing the Swiss cantons; officers of the Noble and Palatine Guards; Knights of the Order of Malta in black with a white Maltese Cross; Knights of the Holy Sepulchre, in white with red crosses; two Privy Chamberlains carrying the* flabelli; *and the Dean of the Rota, who has the duty of holding the tiara when at length the Pontiff can take it off. Bringing up the end come the Papal Major Domo, various other Papal officials, and the Generals of all the religious orders.*[2]

Today, most of that pageantry has been relegated to history by Pope Paul VI in his *motu proprio* document, *Pontificalis Domus,* reorganizing the Roman Curia. The primary functions of both the Papal Household and the Papal Chapel are to bring the papacy closer to the faithful.

The Papal Chapel has been streamlined, abolishing many of the colorful titles and posts of the ancient court. Today's papal ceremonies, although certainly less colorful than those in centuries past, are more concerned with the liturgical life of the Church than they are with pageantry itself. The Papal Household forms part of the Curia, officially known as the Prefecture of the Papal Household *(Prefettura della Casa Pontificia).* "The Prefecture of the Pontifical Household oversees the Papal Chapel, which is at the service of the Pope in his capacity as spiritual head of the Church, and the Pontifical Family, which is at the service of the Pope as a sovereign."[3]

It falls to the Prefect of the Papal Household to arrange the official life of the Holy Father. It is he who arranges the daily official schedule of the pope, and it is he who arranges the official visits of foreign dignitaries with the Holy Father. The Prefecture is also responsible for the arrangement of the foreign travels of the pontiff in association with the Secretariat of State and the bishops' conferences of the host nation.

The prefect of the Papal Household at one time held the venerable titles *Maestro di Casa,* Chamberlain of His Holiness, and Majordomo of the Sacred Palace. "He was always endowed with extraordinary and unique privileges. For example, he is the only prelate of the Roman Curia who may enter the Pope's library unannounced at any time: he is at the Pope's side at audiences that are not strictly private and he accompanies the Holy Father on all his travels in and outside Rome."[4] He is also the first Vatican official to see the pope each day.

Jacques Cardinal Martin, a renowned author and devoted servant of God and His Church, held the post of Prefect of the Papal Household longer than did all his predecessors, serving under the pontificates of Popes Paul VI, John Paul I, and John Paul II. The privilege of combining (marshaling) his own coat of arms[†] with all three of the reigning popes whom he had served as prefect was a privilege none of his predecessors could claim. Jacques Martin received the "red hat" from Pope John Paul II upon his retirement from the Prefecture. He has been succeeded by the former Regent of the Prefecture Bishop Dino Monduzzi.

The residence and offices of the Prefecture are within the Vatican territory. The Apostolic Palace,

---

* A name once used to refer to *rochet* or *rochetta.*

† See Chapter 10, Ecclesiastical Heraldry.

adjacent to the Bernini colonnade, houses the offices of the Papal Household. The palace was constructed in 1553 by Pope Julius III.

The following table sets forth the official rank and precedence of both the Papal Chapel and the Papal Household as they are presently organized.

ORGANIZATION OF THE PAPAL CHAPEL AND THE PAPAL HOUSEHOLD

THE PAPAL CHAPEL

College of Cardinals

College of Patriarchs
   (All patriarchs are named automatically to the Papal Chapel, but those who rise to the Sacred College take the higher precedence in that College.)

Assistants to the Papal Throne
   (Assistants include those archbishops, bishops, and eparchs of the Oriental rite who have been given this honor by the Supreme Pontiff.)

Vice Camerlengo of the Holy Roman Church

Presidents of the Pontifical Councils

Secretaries of the Roman Congregations

Secretary of the Synod of Bishops

Regent of the Apostolic Penitentiary

Secretary of the Supreme Tribunal of the Apostolic Signatura

Dean of the Tribunal of the Sacred Rota

Prelates Superior of the Pontifical Councils and the Pontifical Commissions

Abbot of the Abbey of Monte Cassino

Abbot General of the Canons Regular

Abbots General of the Monastic Orders

Superiors General and Procurators General of the Mendicant Orders

Auditors of the Sacred Rota

Votanti of the Supreme Tribunal of the Apostolic Signatura

Canons of the Patriarchal Basilicas

Consistoral Advocates *(laymen)*

Parish Priests of the Diocese of Rome

Chaplains of the Papal Household
   (These chaplains are not to be confused with the Chaplains of His Holiness who hold the title Monsignor.)

Closest Working Associates of the Holy Father

THE PAPAL FAMILY

Clergy

Substitute Secretary of State for General Affairs

Substitute Secretary of State for the Rapport with the States

Almoner of His Holiness

President of the Pontifical Ecclesiastical Academy

Theologian of the Papal Household

College of Protonotaries Apostolic
- de Numero
- Supranumerary

Papal Master of Ceremonies

Prelates of Honor of His Holiness

Chaplains of His Holiness

"Predicatore" of the Papal Household

Laity

Lay Assistants to the Throne

Lay Delegates to the Pontifical Commission for Vatican City State

General Council for the Vatican City State

Commandant of the Swiss Guards

Consultors of the Vatican City State

President of the Pontifical Academy of Sciences

Gentlemen of His Holiness

Procurators of the Apostolic Palace

Attachés of the Anticamera

Lay Familiars of the Holy Father
- Valets
- Assistants

Papal Diplomacy

Other than its legal status as the diocese of Rome, the Holy See has no international legal status of its own. It is through the Vatican City State's unique independent sovereignty that the Holy See exercises its worldwide mission. Pope John Paul II summarized the position of the Holy See during his first United Nations address on October 2, 1979:

The territorial extent of that sovereignty is limited to the small state of Vatican City, but the sovereignty itself is warranted by the need of the Papacy to exercise its mission in full freedom, and to be able to deal with any interlocutor, whether a government or an international organization, without dependence on other sovereignties.[1]

The Vatican's sovereignty is but a conduit for the extensive works of the Holy See. Part of that work is to extend the Church's message and to respond to the needs of the Catholic faithful wherever and whenever necessary. For that purpose, the Holy See, not the Vatican City State, maintains both a passive and an active diplomatic service.

The Holy See's diplomatic service has existed for centuries and is, in fact, one of the oldest continuous services in the world. Medieval popes sent delegates to represent them in both the Church and political affairs of Rome. Later they sent representatives, known as *legates,* a position existing throughout the history of the Church. "These Legations assumed even more importance when, especially after the eleventh century, they were entrusted to Cardinals whom we called *de Latere.*"[2] Legations headed by illustrious Archbishops, under the direct authority of the pope, were called *Legati nati.*

The title Nuncio was originally granted to bishops who were appointed a specific task or "to whom the management of business of a specific nature or of minor importance"[3] was entrusted. This rank officially developed during the fourteenth and fifteenth centuries. As Europe entered its Renaissance, the Church's influence and power grew. The popes established permanent missions, called *nunciatures,* at the royal courts of Europe. The nunciatures were headed by permanent nuncios "who were given duties similar to those *Legates a Latere,* who were then no longer sent except in very special cases."[4] The nuncios were responsible for political issues of the day, as well as matters directly concerning the local churches. The dual nature of the nuncios' responsibilities set them apart from other diplomatic emissaries of their day and, likewise, marks the modern nuncio.

At present, the nuncio and his staff serve as both the ambassador of the Holy See in the host nation and as the representative of the pope to his Church in that nation. A nuncio must therefore concern himself with the critical issues facing the Church in that locality as well as the most complex political issues facing the government to which he is accredited and the relationship between that state and the Church.

There are two distinct forms of papal representation, the nunciature and the apostolic delegation. Until 1993, the nunciature was headed by either a nuncio or a pro-nuncio. This level of representation was the most formal relationship possible between the Holy See and a nation-state. Until this time, when the Church's representative was accorded precedence over all other diplomats in the host nation regardless of rank, he was called the Dean of the Diplomatic Corps and was granted the senior title Apostolic Nuncio.

As of 1994, however, all representatives of the Holy Father in the higher degree of nunciature bear the title Nuncio, regardless of the religion or relationship of the host state. Pro-nuncio, as a diplomatic ranking, has been placed in abeyance, although for the present this change affects only new appointments. The apostolic nuncio was always given precedence over every foreign representative, regardless of rank. Until 1993, in nations where a nunciature-level relationship existed but where the Holy See's representative was not accorded the status of doyen, or dean, the title of Pro-nuncio was granted. Though the responsibilities of nuncio and pro-nuncio were identical, in the intricacies of diplomatic protocol the pro-nuncio was always viewed as a step below the nuncio. The title Nuncio was usually found in the traditionally Roman Catholic states, whereas the title Pro-nuncio was found in the major states that were not considered Catholic by majority.

Whereas the nuncio took immediate and permanent precedence within his host nation, the pronuncio's precedence was set by the date on which he presented his credentials to the host country's head of state in like manner to all other ambassadors accredited within that host nation. A pronuncio was equal to his fellow ambassadors, whereas the nuncio was first among equals. The title Inter-nuncio had once been used to describe the present position of pro-nuncio; however, these terms were updated in the last twenty years, and the term *Inter-nuncio* now applies to the prelate who temporarily fills the vacant post of the nuncio (or, until 1993, that of the pro-nuncio) and no longer refers to one with a permanent appointment.* Once the Holy Father appoints a new head of mission, the position of inter-nuncio is dissolved and that prelate returns to former duties or takes on a new assignment elsewhere.

The second form of papal representation is the apostolic delegation.† "Apostolic Delegates are nondiplomatic representatives of the Supreme Pontiff who, within the territory entrusted to them which generally includes several dioceses or vicarages and apostolic prefectures, oversee conditions in the Church and report to the Supreme Pontiff."[5] It is also possible for an apostolic nuncio of one state to serve another state as an apostolic delegate. This is most common in regions where several small states exist in proximity and where the nunciature staff would not be overtaxed by the additional responsibilities of the apostolic delegation, or

---

* The first nation where the title Pro-nuncio was employed for the senior diplomatic post equal to Minister Plenipotentiary was Kenya in Africa. Inter-nuncio was at that time a title of lesser degree and that of Nuncio was not granted by the Holy See, to Kenya, because that government would not accord the Church's representative the status of dean in Nairobi.
† The Secretariat of State assigned this title to all nondiplomatic, permanent observerships or missions in 1916.

when the faithful of both jurisdictions would not be negatively affected by joint responsibilities of the papal legate.

The apostolic delegate's responsibilities are no less important than those of the apostolic nuncio in the eyes of the Church. The apostolic delegate represents the Holy Father in the matters of the Church within the host nation. His role is to study possible changes in the episcopate (promotion, transfers, and nominations to the *terna* for new bishops), as well as changes in the canonical structure of the local churches (elections of new dioceses and new archdioceses and the creation of new apostolic prefectures and vicariates). It is his role, as well, to monitor and react to changes within the local church. These responsibilities are also inherent in the posts of nuncio and the now abeyant pro-nuncio.

Prior to 1994, when the post of pro-nuncio was filled by a prelate with the personal title Nuncio, he was referred to as the "pro-nuncio nuncio." In such cases, he would not be the dean of the diplomatic corps. As it had been up until 1993, the relationship between the Holy See and the host nation determined the privilege of deanship and not the personal, additional title Head of the Diplomatic Mission from the Holy See. A pro-nuncio nuncio, although holding the personal dignity of "nuncio," if posted to a pronunciature, could not enjoy the status of dean.

The Code of Canon Law (§362–367) stresses the importance of the work of the Holy Father's legates. The role of the emissaries of the Holy See, in papal diplomatic service, is to strengthen and enhance the bonds that exist between the local church and the Holy See and, as a result, to encourage the mission of the Church whenever possible through discourse with the states.

The Church, that is, the Holy See, exercises both passive and active diplomacy: passive being the reception of delegations at the Vatican; and active, as we have seen, through the missions of the Holy See at work in the world's capitals.

Diplomats, either on personal or permanent missions, have been accredited to the Holy See for centuries. In the fifteenth century, the royal courts of Europe began to recognize both the spiritual and temporal powers of the Supreme Pontiff and sent to Rome high-ranking diplomatic missions to represent their interests and to hopefully gain influence.*

Pope Paul VI, in 1969, set forth his interpretation of the diplomatic role at the Vatican, saying:

> The primary and specific purpose of the mission of a papal representative is to render ever closer and more operative the ties that bind the Apostolic See and the local Churches. The ordinary function of a pontifical representative is to keep the Holy See regularly and objectively informed about the conditions of the ecclesiastical community to which he has been sent, and about what may affect the life of the Church and the good of souls. On the other hand, he makes known to the religious and faithful of the territory where he carries out his mandate, and forwards to Rome their proposals and their requests; on the other hand, he makes himself the interpreter, with those concerned, of the acts, documents, information, and instructions emanating from the Holy See.[6]

From the perspective of the modern powers, the Holy See serves as the greatest listening post in the world, offering accurate insight and a healthy detached opinion on every possible modern issue. The Church is represented in formal fashion through its diplomatic missions and informally through the eyes and ears of the thousands of the

---

* Even prior to that time, the great Mongol king, Kublai Khan, sent a diplomatic mission to Pope Innocent IV in A.D. 1250 demanding that the pope and other "potentates" come to him at once to pay him homage as the "greatest king on earth."

world's bishops, who provide the Church with valuable local insight, which is necessary to formulate Church policy. Foreign representatives at the Vatican strive to tap into this unequaled, efficient network of information.

The Holy See places certain constraints upon new ambassadors when their countries seek diplomatic approval or acceptance. The Church will not accept an individual *(persona non grata)* who publicly opposes Church teaching on such issues as divorce, abortion, and anti-Catholicism, nor will it accept shared status, that is, the sharing of one ambassador from a foreign country with both the Holy See and Italy. This posture dates to the reunification of the Italian peninsula and the forfeiture of the Papal States. In opposition to the royal House of Savoy, which governed unified Italy, the popes went into self-imposed Vatican exile, where they remained until the Lateran Treaty of 1929. The popes would not accept an ambassador who was also accredited to the Italian royal court; they viewed the royal family and court as usurpers. Even today, despite the cost of maintaining two embassies in Rome, the Vatican's independent-sovereignty status requires exactly that.

Depending on the rank and precedence accorded to papal diplomats abroad, the Holy See establishes relationships that govern the title and rank for ambassadors accredited to the Holy See. There are two ambassadorial ranks, or degrees of emissaries, accredited to the Church, special and plenipotentiary ambassadors and envoys or plenipotentiary ministers. These ranks directly correspond to those of apostolic nuncio and apostolic pro-nuncio.

The diplomatic service of the Holy See is under the governance of the Cardinal–Secretary of State. The Secretariat of State, similar to other nation's foreign offices, oversees and directs the works of the Church through diplomatic missions abroad. The Cardinal–Secretary of State also "invites"

priests to join the papal diplomatic corps. In ancient times, distinguished laymen served the Church as diplomats and even as cardinals. In modern times, however, laymen are excluded from both posts. A papal diplomat begins his career as a priest earning a doctorate in sacred science and possibly a second in canon law.

If a priest is "invited" to join the papal diplomatic service, he is first posted to a two-year course of intense studies at the Pontifical Ecclesiastical Academy, which is housed in a grand burnt sienna palazzo on the Piazza Minerva in Rome, just above the famous Gammarelli clerical house. The academy was founded by Pope Clement XI in the early 1800s, when diplomacy was at its apex. At one time, it was called the Academy for Noble Ecclesiastics, and, as the name suggests, it was reserved for the sons of Europe's noble families. It was rumored that "sixteen quarterings" were required for admittance into the academy, which meant that all sixteen great-grandparents had to have been of noble birth. At present, it is opened to the most promising and scholarly priests who are chosen to serve the Church, away from their home dioceses and families, for the majority of their careers. A thorough working knowledge of Italian is required, as is an understanding of upward to five other languages, including Latin.

With the internationalization of the Curia, and likewise the diplomatic service, non-Italians have joined the ranks of papal diplomats. The Holy See usually makes it known to a residential archbishop or bishop that an opening exists and that a candidate would be welcome from their diocese. The ordinary then proposes a priest who has "an international scope," as well as being one who is up to the rigors of the Pontifical Ecclesiastic Academy's two-year course of studies. Often, if a local bishop believes that he has such a priest in his diocese, he makes known this man's potential as a possible candidate for the diplomatic service by informing the nuncio, pro-nuncio, or apostolic delegate who, in turn, informs the Secretariat of State. When an opening occurs, this candidate is likely to be invited to study at the academy. It is also common practice for the president of the academy to canvass the rectors of the national colleges and seminaries in Rome for potential candidates.

Priests who graduate from the Pontifical Ecclesiastical Academy are well versed in Latin, modern languages, international law, and politics, as well as Church history. Priests begin their careers in papal diplomacy in either a post at the Secretariat of State or at one of the nunciatures or delegations throughout the world. Usually they begin as attachés, or *addetti di nunziatura;* moving up the chain of command, the priest would then be appointed secretary, or *segretario di nunziatura.* There are two grades, second and first class. The next gradation is that of auditor of the nunciature, *uditore di nunziatura,* second and first class. The most senior post below that of the head of the mission, nuncio (formerly pro-nuncio) or apostolic delegate, is the counselor, or *consigliere di nunziatura.*

The title Chaplain of His Holiness is customarily bestowed upon the lower ranks of the nunciature staff, that is, secretary, auditor, and, in some instances, attaché. The title Prelate of Honor is granted to the counselors, although exceptions to these rules are possible and, indeed, frequent. Of course, the heads of missions are always created titular archbishops.

In addition to formal relations with states, the Holy See additionally establishes permanent missions to certain international organizations, as well as temporary missions to international gatherings and convocations. These missions are most commonly called observerships.

The Church's diplomatic role is often subtle and not often visible; however, at times it is thrust into the thick of international affairs.* As one of the world's longest-standing diplomatic services, the papal corps continues to serve as a superior model of efficiency, which other nation's diplomatic missions continue to emulate.

---

* For example, in the case of General Noriega of Panama, when the general sought refuge at the nunciature in Panama City, the nuncio had to seek a diplomatic solution in full view of the world while under intense pressure from the U.S. government and military establishment.

CHAPTER FIVE

Swiss Guard:
Defensores Ecclesiae Libertatis

Although most of the credit for the creation of the papal regiment of the Swiss Guard is given to Pope Julius II (1503–1513), the practice of hiring Swiss nationals as paid mercenaries predates Julius by two hundred years. For centuries, the Swiss have been known for the ferocity of their fighting men. In fact, the Swiss were the predecessors of modern guerilla warriors.

Prior to 1471, the Holy See made use of the talents of the Swiss by placing Catholic nationals from Switzerland in the papal service. Pope Sixtus IV formalized an agreement to recruit Swiss fighting forces and included into the papal regiment a company of Swiss national militiamen. The first formal agreement between the then Papal States and the Federal States was signed on January 21, 1480. "But the idea of creating a stable disciplined corps, composed entirely of Swiss, goes back to Julius II in whose reign two hundred Swiss were enlisted under the command of Peter von Hortenstein. Only one hundred and fifty reached Rome in their triumphal entry into the city from the Piazza del Popolo and were afterward blessed in St. Peter's Square by the Pope, who appeared on the loggia of Paul II."[1] Today, the *Cohors Helvetica* (Corps of Swiss Guards)

is the sole remnant of the ancient Pontifical Guard. The practice of hiring Swiss militiamen was not unique to the Papal States. In fact, most of the royal houses of old Europe maintained a regiment of these fierce warriors. Austrian Iberia, Lorraine, Tuscany, France, Piemonte, Savoy, and even Prussia made use of the Swiss Guard, who were known for their loyalty as well as for their military strength. Often Europe's crowned heads, in more turbulent times, could not trust their own countrymen for protection and turned to the foreign Swiss as lifeguards.

Until 1471, a varying number of Swiss fighting men were employed not only to guard the popes but also to enter battle for the defense of the Papal States, oftentimes finding themselves fighting against their own countrymen who were hired out by the opponents. Try as they did, the governors of the Swiss cantons could not put a halt to mercenary soldiering. It was the livelihood of these mountain folk, in particular, and was also viewed as a means to support the Church.

Some of the most honored names in the guard's history were men of this period who headed the corps in their service to the Church: Von Hortenstein, Schiner (who went on to become a cardinal), and Roist are but a few of the renowned. These men served with the Swiss regiments serving in the Papal

States. "On July 5th, 1512, with the bull *Etsi Romani Pontifices,* Pope Julius decreed, as a special mark of gratitude to the Swiss, the title of *Defensores Ecclesiae Libertatis* (Defenders of the Freedom of the Church), a title still carried proudly by the Papal Swiss Guard."[2]

It was not until the defense of the Vatican Palace and Pope Clement VII, during the sack of Rome in 1527—in which 147 of the Swiss Guard lost their lives in a gallant fight with the invading German and Spanish armies of Charles V—that the concept of a permanent Swiss Guard became a reality. The surviving forty-two soldiers saw the pontiff to the safety of Castel Sant'Angelo on the Tiber by scurrying along the *passetto,* or crenelated wall, along what is now the Burgo Sant'Angelo. Most of the men were butchered on the steps of St. Peter's, whereas others were slaughtered on the steps of the high altar inside the basilica. The remaining troops guarding Clement VII that May day fled at the sight of the size of Charles V's approaching armies. Only the Swiss stood to fight. Clement VII, his court, and the remaining Swiss Guards held up inside Castel Sant'Angelo until the siege was ended. For several days, the invaders raped, pillaged, and destroyed everything in their sight, including an extensive violation of the known tombs of the dead popes, looking for booty to take home with them as a souvenir of the siege. A later description of that week is attributed to the canons of St. Augustine, who said, "The Germans were bad, the Italians were worse, the Spanish were the worst."[3]

In remembrance of that violent week, the anniversary of the battle has become the most important date on the calendar of the corps. Each May 6, the reigning pope celebrates a Pontifical Mass in St. Peter's Basilica. What follows is one of the most colorful ceremonies of past eras, still played out in the modern world.

A senior Curia cardinal represents the Holy Father at the oath-taking ceremony in the San Damaso courtyard of the Apostolic Palace. Also present is the ambassador from the Swiss Federal States to the Holy See, the military attaché from the Swiss embassy, numerous bishops and priests, as well as honored guests from the recruits' homeland and from Rome. The ceremony opens with the "Pontifical March" (the papal anthem) and the "Hymne Nationale Suisse," and the unfurling of the papal flag and Swiss Guard banner. The banner, which is made of silk, incorporates the arms of the founding pope, Julius II, the arms of the reigning pope, the colors of the corps, and the arms of the present commandant. "When his name is called, each new Guard, in full armor and sixteenth century pageantry, marches up to the Swiss Guard's flag, which is rolled up and held parallel to the ground. The flag itself bears the coat of arms of the founder of the Swiss Guards, Pope Julius II; the coat of arms of the reigning Pope; and the coat of arms of the present colonel of the Swiss Guards."[4]

Nearly every tourist who has come to Rome has seen a photograph of the oath-taking ceremony, either on postcards or souvenir collectibles. The new recruit grasps the unfurled banner in his left hand. In full armor and plumed helmet, he raises his right gloved hand with only the thumb, index, and middle fingers extended. This gesture is symbolic of the Holy Trinity: Father, Son, and Holy Spirit. The chaplain of the guard reads aloud the oath of fidelity and allegiance in German, the official language of the guard. The words have not been altered for four hundred years:

I swear to serve faithfully, loyally, and honorably the person of the Sovereign Pontiff, His Holiness Pope John Paul II, and his legitimate successors canonically elected, as well as, to dedicate myself to them with all my strength by sacrificing, should it become necessary, even my own life in their defense. I likewise assume this promise toward the members of the Sacred College during the period of the

Sede Vacante. Furthermore, I pledge to the Commandant and to my superiors, respect, obedience, and fidelity. By this I swear. May the Almighty and His Saints protect me.[5]

After the chaplain has finished the oath of allegiance, each new recruit, in his own turn, proclaims to swear to loyally and faithfully uphold the oath and likewise seeks the protection of the Almighty. He has the privilege to respond in his own native tongue—German, French, Italian, or Romansch.

Recruitment for the Swiss Guards used to be restricted to the Swiss-German cantons in Switzerland. In 1505, the Swiss, always adept in international diplomacy, convinced Julius II to enter into an official agreement regarding the recruitment of the guard as a means of placing a wedge between themselves and France, who would not attack the Federal States if they were closely aligned to the papacy. Originally, the traditionally Catholic cantons (Swiss German) were the only regions permitted to send citizens to the guard.

Since 1803, citizens from all parts of Switzerland may enter the guard; however, certain requirements must be met. First and foremost, the honor of protecting the life of the pope falls only to Catholic men who are between the ages of nineteen and thirty years, although that limitation was at one time twenty-five, and who must be bachelors at the time of their recruitment into service. Applicants must also be at least 5 feet 9 inches in height, and along with their application must come letters of recommendation from past members of the guard, now returned to Switzerland—priests, local police and government officials, and employers.* As in all European nations, military service in Switzerland is compulsory, but Switzerland will release a young man from his service at home if he is accepted by the Holy See for service in the guard. The Federal States have abolished all other external service for

its citizens. What was formerly both a tradition and a source of financial support is forbidden today. Only those Swiss seeking service in Rome are permitted the privilege of serving a foreign power.

The main purpose for the guard remains the protection of the pope. The exercise of that duty has changed drastically in the past thirty years, and, since the assassination attempt on Pope John Paul II in St. Peter's Square, the focal point of the Swiss Guards' training has shifted to include all aspects of modern security and protection. Although one would not know it from looking at a guardsman in his colorful uniform, each of the one hundred guardsmen has completed rugged training in karate, self-defense, judo, and the use of firearms and heavy assault weaponry. Guardsmen must also be able to utilize their ceremonial halberds (axelike spears) and lances in defense of the pope. The state of the world today requires the Guard to be fully versed in the most modern techniques of security and protection.

Despite the primary purpose of the Swiss Guard in protecting the life of the pope, the world has also come to view this crack regiment as a ceremonial remnant of past glories. In part, the reason for this is their celebrated uniform. "On great ceremonial occasions the guards wear the medieval cuirass (armor) over their red, yellow, orange, and dark-blue striped uniform."[6]

The uniform is in the colors of the Medici family—red, blue, yellow—which gave the Church many popes during the Renaissance. Red was

---

* Recruitment, by agreement with the modern Swiss state, must be undertaken informally and without fanfare. As a result, it is often the younger family members of past guardsmen or neighbors who are recruited into service. It is not unheard of to see brothers serving simultaneously or successively. It is also common in the history of the corps to have a family history of service in the guards. Papal service is worn as a badge of family honor.

added to the original blue and yellow by Pope Leo X, who was of the Medici family. Red, blue, and yellow were the Medici livery colors, whereas blue and yellow, of the previous uniform, were the livery colors of the Delle Rovere family. For centuries, it was claimed that Michelangelo designed the uniform. This tale is told time and again in Rome for the tourist trade. Others have claimed, with less success, that Raphael was the designer. Neither story is exactly true. Michelangelo played no role at all, as history illustrates, whereas Raphael had more of an indirect influence through his colorful paintings of the period, which illustrated the guardsmen. All indications were that the Swiss arrived with a style of uniform very similar to that which we still see today, and, during one of the Delle Rovere pontificates, their house or family colors took the place of the drab browns and reds of the traditional Swiss country soldier.

The uniform saw many changes through time until Pope Pius X returned it to its ancient design. It was at this time that the tale of Michelangelo's designing the uniform took preeminence. Each of the uniforms is made by hand in the barracks of the guard off the Sant'Anna Gate in Vatican City. They may be kept, upon retirement, by those guardsmen (halberdiers) and officers who have served more than two terms (five years). "There are 119 separate pieces to a Swiss Guard's uniform and each one is made by hand in the Guard's own tailor shop. A separate, less elaborate uniform is utilized for routine assignment and, given Rome's seasonal temperature fluctuations, uniforms are made with both summer and winter materials."[7] The less ceremonial of the uniforms, used at business posts within the Vatican and at Castel Gandolfo, are blue and take on a Napoleonic appearance although they have developed from uniforms of the sixteenth century. These blue uniforms, often seen with matching capes with large black tassels in cool or inclement weather, are most often seen at the Sant'Anna Gate by tourists visiting Rome.

In 1910, Jules Respond, from French-speaking Fribourg, was appointed by Pius X to serve as commandant. It is thanks, in large part, to his superb historical research that the Swiss Guard uniforms were reformed. He based his final designs on the depictions of Raphael; thus it is said that Raphael was the uniform's designer. In reality, Respond used Raphael as a resource rather than a "designer." Respond abolished all the headgear that was adopted after the French Revolution and adopted the simple beret, which has on it an emblem marking the rank of the guardsmen. "Furthermore, he replaced the pleated gorget or throat piece with a plain white collar. Nowadays only the full dress uniform is worn with a special gorget, white gloves, and pale gray metal morion."[8] The gray morion is referred to within the corps as white and is reserved for the most solemn occasions of state or corps life.

Ostrich plumes are always worn on the gray morion, "white for the Commandant and Sergeant Major, purple for Lieutenants, red for Halberdiers, and yellow/black on a black morion for the drummers."[9]

Although Pope Leo X, a Medici, substituted the colors of his noble house for the simple yellow and blue of the house of Della Rovere, he and subsequent popes did nothing to alter the insignia of the Della Rovere on the morion itself (oak leaves) or the standard of the corps, which depicts the coat of arms of the founding pope, Julius II, a Della Rovere, on the lower exterior quarter of the banner.

The structure of the corps has been modified throughout its history. At present, there are seven ranks within the guard. The senior officer holds the rank of colonel. Guardsmen of the lowest ranks are called halberdiers and are not permitted to marry until reaching the rank of corporal, usually during their second tour of duty. The Cardinal–Secretary of State's permission is necessary prior to a young officer's marriage. Once permission has been granted for a guardsman to marry, the marriage date cannot be set until an apartment within the barracks of the corps becomes available. The corps is divided into three equal squads, each protecting the pope at either the Vatican or Castel Gandolfo or during his many overseas trips.* During the Pope's more public events, all three squads are posted to service. Nowadays, the pay schedule of the guard is not the bone of contention it formerly was. In the 1930s, recruitment became extremely difficult because of the poor pay schedule offered to the guard by the Vatican, which had not upgraded its pay scale for forty years.

The *Cohors Helvetica* is the most colorful military unit in the modern world. It is also one of the most finely trained. To assist the guard in its work of protecting the pope and to address all the additional security demands required at so public a sight as the Vatican, Pope Paul VI created the *Vigilanza,* which replaced the former Papal Gendarmerie. The *Vigilanza,* whose members are Italian nationals, is the closest thing the Vatican has to a police force. It is as modern as any force in the world and quite capable of serving the general police and tourist control needs of the Vatican City State. In addition to the Papal Gendarmerie, Paul VI abolished the Noble Guard. The Noble Guard, as one would assume from the corps' title, was chosen from the Italian aristocracy. To be posted to the Noble Guard, a candidate had to "possess a gallant nobility of at least a century and an income sufficient to live decently in Rome."[10]

Before the Lateran Treaty of 1929, only those candidates from the territories of the former Papal States† were admitted. After 1929, every Italian noble house was permitted application for admission. In 1930, King Alfonso XIII of Spain wrote to the pope, petitioning him to permit all Catholic nobles the right to join the Noble Guard. In his petition, the king urged the pope to open the most prestigious regiment in the world to all Catholic noblemen. His request was denied, and the Noble Guard remained Italian until its demise in 1969.‡

What made the Noble Guard unique was its lack of foot soldiers. Every member of the guard became an officer upon acceptance. The Noble Guard had its origins in the two horse regiments, the *Guardia dei Cavalleggeri* (the Light Horse Guard) and *Guardia delle Lance Spezzate* (the Broken Lance Guard), that had protected the papacy during the Napoleonic invasions.

Also abolished by Pauline *motu proprio* was the Palatine Guard. As its name indicates, the guard served as the palace guard at the Vatican and Lateran palaces. It must be remembered that the main purpose of the Swiss Guard was to protect the pope's life, and, as such, most of their responsibilities kept them in proximity to the pope. It was not until after the abolition of the Noble Guard (used primarily on ceremonial occasions) and the Palatine Guard that the Swiss Guard became the primary and most visible of the Papal forces. Whereas the Swiss Guard required Swiss nationality§ and the Noble Guard required one hundred years of noble ancestry, the Palatine Guard had among its ranks men from every

---

* When the Swiss Guard accompanies the Holy Father during all of his overseas travels, they dress in civil attire, resembling that of the U.S. Secret Service.

† Rome, Latium, Umbria, The Marche, and Romagna.

‡ *Pontificalis Domus.*

§ Even sons of a Swiss Guard with an Italian wife are banned from following in their father's footsteps, as these children, under Swiss law, are not considered Swiss nationals.

walk of life. Requirements were limited only to age, height, the Catholic faith, and a character beyond reproach.

The Noble Guard and the Palatine Guard, by virtue of their impressive uniforms, most resembled the soldiers of the royal courts of Europe. Their steel helmets, with long, dyed horse-tail plumage and armored plates, and their high fur caps and leather boots were viewed, along with their regiments, as arcane vestiges of royal, nonpapal tri-umphalism and were abrogated to history by Pauline *motu proprio.*

At the present time, one can visit the Papal Court exhibit within the Lateran Palace to view the uniforms and insignia of these regiments on the first Sunday of each month, or one can study these historic regiments in the books listed in the bibliography section of this text as well as in time-honored films such as *The Shoes of the Fisherman* or *The Scarlet and the Black.*

PART TWO

PAPAL HONORS

Papal Honors: Laity

GENTLEMEN OF HIS HOLINESS

The highest honor bestowed on a layman in the Church is not one of the pontifical orders or one of the Vatican decorations; it is the post of Chamberlain to His Holiness, which is formally known by its Italian title, *Gentiluomo di Sua Santitá* (Gentleman of His Holiness). The bestowal of this title carries with it the high honor of membership in the Holy Father's official household, the privilege of serving the Holy Father as a gentleman of honor during a period of one week each year. During the honoree's term of service at the Vatican, he is posted close to the Pope and is often seen during official ceremonies at St. Peter's Basilica. Always dressed in formal attire (*tenue pontificale,* or white tie and tails), he wears the gold *Chi Rho* lapel pin, the more common symbol of his high office. The Prefect of the Papal Household is always nearby to direct the participation of the faithful in papal ceremonies. The Gentlemen of His Holiness are also presented with the impressive collar of office; usually worn at only the most solemn of papal events, it is recognized the world over for both its beauty and the respect that it implies.

When the Papal Court was reorganized in 1969, the post of Gentleman of His Holiness was created to mark those among the laity who earned the special recognition of the papacy. Today, the ordinary of a diocese petitions the Holy See for the nomination of one of the faithful of his diocese. Sadly, in the United States, ordinaries seldom make use of this request; however, in Europe and elsewhere, the honor is vested generation upon generation within the same family to those who work generously for the Church.

The predecessor of the title Gentleman of His Holiness was the title Chamberlain of the Cape and Sword, or, as these chamberlains were officially known, *Camerieri Segreti di Spada e Cappa*. The service of the Papal Court has always required the aid of laymen, and the Chamberlains of the Cape and the Sword performed this function. The Chamberlains of the Cape and Sword were divided into four classes: participating and the honorary *(Partecipanti e d'Onore),* and de Numero and Supranumerary.

These lay officials, like their successors the Gentlemen of His Holiness, were always visible at papal events in the presence of the Holy Father and were always on hand to welcome official visitors at the Apostolic Palace. The world knew them by their uniform of velours, with knee breeches, flat cap, a little brocade cloak, and the ruff, all in satin or black velvet, except for the white starched, ruffled collar "which resembles an aureole with its white plaits."[1] Their Palatine name, *Camieri di Capa e Spada,* derives from their costumes—*cubicularii intimi ab ense et lacerna.* The Chamberlains of the Cape and Sword also wore the badge of their office, a spectacular gold chain, which was retained for use by the Gentlemen of His Holiness.

Today, the Renaissance costume and fanciful title are gone, vestiges of papal history. The only remnant of their existence is the chain of office, worn with pride by newly appointed Gentlemen of His Holiness. The insignia of office is made of two gold chains, interlocked at intervals of three inches by golden medallions bearing the monogram of the pontiff. At the base, as the chains and medallions fall upon the chest of the wearer, is suspended the gold triple tiara of the papacy and the two crossed keys, each nearly 3 inches in length.

Although the Gentlemen of His Holiness wear less elaborate costumes and have responsibilities more ceremonial in nature than their predecessors had, the title Gentleman of His Holiness is the highest dignity the Holy Father can presently bestow upon Catholic laymen and is one of the most coveted awards of the papacy.

GOLDEN ROSE

The most exclusive award worldwide reserved for women is in the gift of the Roman Pontiff—The Golden Rose. It is bestowed upon Roman Catholic female sovereigns who, by their living examples, have illustrated the highest ideals of Catholic womanhood. By its own regulations, the Golden Rose is rarely bestowed. There are no living recipients of this decoration. The late Grand Duchess Charlotte of Luxembourg was awarded the "Rose" on July 8, 1956. The ceremonies marking the honor's conferral on the Grand Duchess lasted for three days in Luxembourg and the Golden Rose itself was placed on display as thousands passed through the basilica to view it. Although Charlotte of Luxembourg was the last recipient of the Rose, it surely will be awarded in the future. In addition to being presented to royal Catholic sovereigns,* the Golden Rose may be bestowed upon sacred shrines under the patronage of Our Blessed Lady. The Golden Rose has been presented to more of these shrines than it has to royal women.

Until two hundred years ago, the Golden Rose was also presented to male sovereigns. This practice was abolished when the Supreme Order of Christ was reserved for them. The Rose has romantic origins. A society of religious sisters in Tulle, Alsace, was granted independence from the local bishop by Pope Leo IX in 1049. In gratitude for this mark of papal respect and in natural gratitude for independence from local authority, the community sent a delegation to Rome each year to present the pope with a "golden rose."

"The first historical instance of the conferring of the Golden Rose by the Pope is in 1096, when Urban II (1088–1099), passing through Angers during the preaching of the First Crusade, bestowed this distinction on the Count Fulco d' Angio [Falk d'Angers]."[2] Pope Clement VIII was the last pontiff to bestow the Golden Rose on a male. He did so in 1759, in the first year of his pontificate, when

---

* Evita Peron attempted to bully Pius XII into awarding her the Golden Rose and the papal title Marquise (Marchioness), but the Pope would have none of it.

he presented it to Francesco Lardani, Doge of Venice.

The Golden Rose can be presented to individuals only once in their lifetimes, but may be presented by successive pontificates to Marian shrines whenever a reigning pope wishes to bring singular honor to that shrine. Award of the Rose, however, may be granted to a shrine only once in each pontificate.

This decoration has always been held in the highest esteem. The Papal Family included the post of Bearer of the Golden Rose as late as 1969.* "The presentation of the Golden Rose is performed with great pomp and ceremony. If the recipient is in Rome, it is customary for the Sovereign Pontiff himself to confer it in the Sistine Chapel. Otherwise a Special Mission is entrusted with the presentation of the Rose and the accompanying Apostolic Brief announcing the bestowal and giving the reason for sending it, and recounting the merits and virtues of the recipient."[3]

Although receipt of the Rose has become one of the world's highest honors, it has often been a source of great jealousy and envy. Its award in past centuries was filled with intrigue and malice, but modern popes have been careful to award it on merit alone, leaving all politics aside. Despite past political intrigue, the Golden Rose is viewed as a special honor and a unique mark of favor from the papacy.

When the Grand Duchess Charlotte of Luxembourg died in 1985, the Golden Rose that had been presented to her in 1956, by Pius XII was carried by an officer of the Luxembourg forces at the position of honor at the head of the funeral procession. The Rose stood in its simple velvet-lined case, doors thrown open. It was followed by the late grand duchess's other orders, including those of Luxembourg itself, preceding her coffin, the royal mourners, and the government of Luxembourg. During her lifetime, when formal occasions required her to wear her orders and decorations, the grand duchess could always be seen wearing a gold-and-diamond rosebud brooch, symbolizing her award of the Golden Rose.

Although the Rose itself has taken many forms of design through the ages, it is always made of solid gold. The original design was quite simple, but later, with the influence of the baroque period, it became quite ornate. During the modern pontificates of Paul VI and his successors, it has once again taken a more simplified design.

In the past, the Golden Rose was encrusted with sapphires, gems usually reserved for members of the Sacred College. Sapphires were chosen as a symbolic reference to the high esteem of the Golden Rose and its recipients. The base of the Rose, regardless of its design, has always had a hidden basin as a repository for balsam and musk. The Rose is bestowed on those recipients who, through the virtue of their lives, exude the fragrance of all virtues,[†] thus the incorporation of symbolic fragrances. The basin also incorporated a reliquary for a relic of the True Cross.

When the decoration is to be presented, it is first blessed by the Sovereign Pontiff with great pomp during a Pontifical Mass in the Basilica of Santa Croce in Gerusalemme, on the square in Rome bearing that same name, on Laetare Sunday,[‡] also known as Rose Sunday, or in Latin, *dies dominica in Rose.* The Rose is placed on the high altar throughout the Mass, which precedes the presentation ceremony or the sending forth of the official delegation from Rome. The present pontiff, Pope John Paul II, has made no award of the Rose to a Catholic sovereign, but he has presented the Rose to a Marian shrine, most recently the Shrine of Our Lady of Czestochowa in Poland.

---

* *Pontificalis Domus.*
† Pope Innocent III defined it as an "odor of sanctity."
‡ The fourth Sunday of Lent.

SUPREME ORDER OF CHRIST

The Supreme Order of Christ, also known as the Militia of Our Lord Jesus Christ, is the highest order of knighthood that the Vatican bestows. Unlike the title Gentlemen of His Holiness, which is an honorary chamberlaincy in the Pontifical Household, or the Golden Rose, which is a special class decoration, the Supreme Order of Christ is an order of knighthood in the gift of the Supreme Pontiff. In present times, it is reserved for Catholic male heads of state and sovereigns.

The Order of Christ was founded on August 14, 1318, by the king and queen of Portugal, who responded to both the invasion of Iberia by the Moors and to Pope Clement V's abolition of their former defenders, the Knights Templar, in 1312. Clement's successor, John XXII, officially recognized the order as a religious body in 1319 and once again in 1321. The order spread throughout Catholic Europe under the protection of John XXII, who later gave the governorship of the order, in Portugal, to King Denis I. For two hundred years, the order was governed as a religious community under monastic rule. In 1507, Pope Julius II released the community from their vows of poverty, chastity, and obedience.

With the lack of religious character, the governors of the order in Portugal assumed grand mastership of the Portuguese branch. In short form, as sovereigns of Portugal, the Order of Christ became an independent royal decoration under the House of Bragança. It remained so actively until the fall of the monarchy in Portugal in 1911. The Portuguese state, both socialist and democratic, claimed governorship over the order, maintaining that it had always been an official state order rather than a royal-house order in Portugal and, thus, placed it in the gift of the Portuguese head of state. At present,

as the highest state decoration in Portugal, it is awarded to foreign dignitaries and prominent statesmen. The order in Portugal, long separate from the church's order by the same name, has no religious character.

The order's life outside Portugal diminished with the demise of its religious character in 1507. It became one of the orders in the gift of the pope within the Papal States. Between the *Risorgimento* of Italy (1878) and the pontificate of Pope St. Pius X, the order was reorganized. Its new statutes were granted by Pope Pius X in 1905. It was, thereafter, considered the highest order in the pope's gift and has had some of this century's outstanding luminaries as members.

The Militia of Christ officially became the Supreme Order of Christ by papal bull in 1905.* Unlike other papal distinctions, the Supreme Order of Christ must be bestowed either by a cardinal-delegate in the presence of the Supreme Pontiff or by his own hand in the Apostolic Palace. It is not a decoration that may be sent to the recipient by delegation.

Only Roman Catholic heads of state and sovereigns may receive the Supreme Order of Christ. It is not, however, automatic to them. The head of state of Spain, King Juan Carlos I, was given the Grand Collar of the Pian Order rather than the Order of Christ, and yet he met all three requirements for receipt of the Order of Christ: He was a Catholic, a head of state, and a sovereign. In fact, the kings of Spain maintained the style "Most Catholic Majesty" for centuries, relinquishing it only as late as the 1980s.

The order comes in one class only, that of Grand Collar. It consists of two gold filigree chains joined together by alternating filigree knots and white

---

* *Multum Ad Excitandos.*

enamel medallions, upon which are emblazoned the papal tiara and crossed keys. At the bottom of the chain, where it is properly joined together, hangs a solid-gold military trophy consisting of the helmet, armor, flags, and axes placed above two golden cannons, on which is displayed the badge of the order. Suspended from the trophy is an Italianate royal crown, below which hangs the cross of the order in white on red enamel, trimmed in gold.

The star *(placca)* of the order, worn on the left breast, consists of the badge (cross) of the order, in miniature, surmounted on a silver eight-rayed star. The cross is completely surrounded by a gold wreath. The cross has eight gold rays. This decoration is granted by the *motu proprio* of the reigning pontiff and, like the Golden Rose, is presented with Old World ceremony and pomp.

Knights of the Order have their own uniform, to be worn only at state ceremonies. Since the reforms of 1905, however, only male foreign Catholic heads of state may receive this award. As such, they would not make use of this uniform because, as sovereigns, they would wear the order on their own national military uniforms. The order's uniform is a vestige of the past, to be sure, but it is still considered appropriate for wear on state occasions under Vatican protocol. "It is bright scarlet fabric with facings of white cloth and rich gold embroidery on the collar, breast, and cuffs. Knee breeches of white smooth silk with gold side stripes, shoes of white silk with gold buckles, hat with plumes and ornamented with a knot of twisted gold cord terminating in tassels of gold. A sword with a gold and mother of pearl hilt and pendant tassels or twisted gold cord complete the costume."[4] One would venture to guess that this costume has not been seen at papal functions in two generations, yet it is still available through the Roman ateliers for those recipients who choose to purchase it.

ORDER OF THE GOLDEN SPUR

The Order of the Golden Spur, also known as the *Militia Aurata* or the Golden Militia, is the second-highest honor of the Holy See. It is entirely in the gift of the Roman Pontiff, who awards it by *motu proprio,* on Catholic and non-Catholic heads of state. It is the only Vatican honor dedicated to and placed under the patronage of Our Lady. On the fiftieth jubilee of the promulgation of the dogma of the Immaculate Conception, Pope Pius X presented the Order of the Golden Spur to the spiritual care of the Mother of the Redeemer. "Most historians agree that this ancient Order was founded by Pope Saint Sylvester in 332. It remained inactive for many centuries, but in 1539 Pope Paul III permitted high dignitaries of the Papal Court and Roman royal families the privilege of conferring the Golden Spur."[5]

These leading families of the Papal States were so abusive of the pope's trust that the award of the Golden Spur became meaningless. With the conferral of the order came the hereditary title Palatine Count and Count of the Lateran Palace *(Palatini et Aulae Nostra Lateranensis Comes*[6]) for the laity, and the title Protonotary Apostolic for clerics. In 1841, Pope Gregory XVI abolished the privilege of protonotary apostolic for clerics and two months later decreed that thenceforth the order would be in the gift of the Supreme Pontiff; it was to be called the Order of the Golden Militia and St. Sylvester. This decision was the cause of great discontent among the Roman clergy and the Roman, or Black, nobility, which viewed the privileges attached to the order as a means of personal recognition and honor. The hereditary title Palatine Count was also abolished. The 1841 reorganization also stipulated that the order could be bestowed upon non-Catholics as well. The Golden Spur, likewise the Order of Christ, became an award in one class only—the Grand Collar.

The order consists of a Grand Collar of two gold-filigree chains interlocking in an ornate pattern. Suspended from the chain is the insignia of the order, a gold and yellow eight-pointed enameled cross. The center medallion is white and depicts the gold crowned monogram of the Mother of God. Between the two points of the bottom arm of the insignia is suspended a golden spur. Between the chain and the insignia is a gold military trophy rather than the royal crown or pontifical tiara. In 1929, at the final session of the signing of the Lateran Treaty, Pope Pius XI bestowed upon the Italian king and crown prince the Order of Christ, whereas the actual leader of the Italian state, Benito Mussolini, was given the less exalted Golden Spur. Il Duce absolutely refused to accept the papal decoration, and his refusal resulted in a near break in the treaty discussions. Cardinal Pacelli, later Pius XII, who was then secretary of state, ordered the *Maestro di Casa* of the Holy Father to substitute the silver-edged red moiré neck ribbon of the order with the chain of the formerly combined Order of the Golden Militia and St. Sylvester. Mussolini accepted this face-saving tactic, and the order was henceforth awarded as a Grand Collar instead of on the ribbon of a simple knight commander.

In modern times, the Golden Spur is awarded to Catholic princes and non-Christian heads of state, including non-Catholic kings and presidents. The order also is awarded with the *placca* (star), which is worn on the left breast. The yellow and gold eight-pointed cross, with suspended spur, is mounted on an eight-rayed silver star.

The uniform of the Order of the Golden Spur is less ornate than that of the Supreme Order of Christ but more so than the other papal orders. It has not changed for two hundred years. Like the recipients of the Supreme Order of Christ, the Knights of the Golden Spur are most commonly foreign heads of state and, therefore, make little use of this colorful ceremonial garment. The tunic of the uniform is deep red, with two rows of gold buttons; on each is emblazoned the cross of the order. The collar and cuffs are of black velvet and are embroidered with gold threads. The trousers are of black cloth, with a gold-thread military stripe. Napoleonic epaulets, emblazoned with the insignia of the Golden Spur, complete the tunic. A knight also is granted actual golden spurs in the award of the order. A gold-thread belt binding the waist, a sword, and a bicorn black hat, with insignia and gold tufts, are worn as well.

ORDER OF POPE PIUS IX

Also known as the Pian Order, the Order of Pius IX, or the *Ordo Pianus,* is the third of the Vatican orders but the highest to have more than one class or rank. The class of Grand Collar is bestowed by the *motu proprio* of the reigning pontiff. The lower classes of the order can be bestowed upon the specific recommendation of either the Secretariat of State or the local bishop.

The order was founded by Pope Pius IX in 1847 in honor of his predecessor Pope Pius IV (1559–1565). During the pontificate of the fourth Pius, a group of loyal knights served as the Pope's elite guard. They took the name of Pian Knights, but they did not survive the reign of Pius IV, whose favorites they were. Three hundred years hence, Pope Pius IX honored his predecessor and these brave knights by founding the new Pian Order. It soon became known, however, as the Order of Pius IX rather than, as was intended, in recognition of the fourth Pius. It remains, today, officially the Order of Pius IX.

The Pian Order has four classes, all of which are now open to women. In addition to the Grand

Collar, also known as Knights of the Golden Collar, the order is bestowed in the ranks of Knight, Knight Commander, and Knight Grand Cross. The insignia of the three lowest grades is suspended from a dark blue moiré ribbon, with two red stripes on each edge. For the grade of Knight, the insignia is suspended from a breast ribbon. For the class of Knight Commander, the insignia is suspended from a neck ribbon, and for that of Grand Cross, the insignia is suspended from a sash worn over the right shoulder, across the breast and resting on the left hip.

Pope Pius XII instituted the grade of Grand Collar, reserving it for heads of state and heads of government, as a special mark of distinction for those who are not eligible for the award of the two highest Vatican honors. The collar consists of two gold chains interlocked by medallions and knots. The knots are of gold filigree. Of the twelve medallions, one type is a representation of the coat of arms of the Collar's founder, Pope Pius XII, and is worked in enamel; the second is a representation of the papal emblem (the tiara and crossed keys) worked in gold. At the base of the chain is the papal tiara, or *triregno,* in gold. On either side, each facing the tiara, is a golden dove, the heraldic emblem of Pius XII. The insignia of the order is suspended below the tiara. It consists of an eight-rayed blue enamel star. Between each ray is a golden flame. The center medallion is white enamel and has on it the name of its founder, Pius IX, in Latin, as well as the order's motto, *Virtuti et Merito.* The award of the Collar also includes the *placca* (star), which is similar to the insignia, except for size, and with flames of silver rather than gold. The *placca* is also awarded with the class of Grand Cross.

The Pian Order was never designed as a religious order. It was created as an Order of merit for the Papal States, similar to the awards bestowed by foreign states and royalty. The ancient Pian Knights were awarded the hereditary title Count Palatine, a common practice of the Renaissance pontificates. In 1847, the newly instituted order conferred the same privilege on only the highest class, the Grand Cross. On November 11, 1939, in the Papal constitution *Litteris Suis,*[7] Pope Pius XII abolished all such privileges. It was then that he also instituted the new class of Grand Collar, which had further reforms in 1957.

Although the Pian Order continues to be awarded to Catholic laymen at the request of the local ordinaries, the order is more commonly known as the award bestowed upon the diplomats accredited to the Holy See from foreign states. The Grand Cross is usually presented to foreign ambassadors to the Holy See shortly before they prepare to retire from service at the Holy See or, if their accreditation extends for a prolonged period, after a suitable period of service has elapsed. The lesser classes of the order are presented to members of the diplomatic missions and other official visitors to the Holy See.

ORDER OF ST. GREGORY THE GREAT

The Order of St. Gregory the Great, also known by its Latin name, *Ordo Gregorianus,* and affectionately by the anglicized familiar term *the Greg,*[*] is the most recognizable of the papal awards and the most frequently awarded. It is the award of choice of the Secretariat of State in honoring the request of the local bishops who wish to bestow papal favor on one of the faithful of their dioceses.

Artistically, the Order of St. Gregory is also one of the more handsome of all decorations, both papal and otherwise. The St. Gregory does not share the ancient origins of higher papal awards such as the Golden Spur and the Supreme Order of Christ, having been instituted on September 1,

---

* Not to be confused with the same familiar name for the Pontifical Gregorian University, Rome.

1831. It was founded by Pope Gregory XVI, who named it after his holy predecessor Pope St. Gregory the Great, whom the pontiff intended to honor. In naming it after him, Gregory XVI placed the new order under his spiritual patronage.

Established during a period of great turbulence for the temporal realm of the Church over the Papal States, the Order of St. Gregory the Great was founded in two divisions, military and civil, as a reward for those outstanding citizens of the Papal States and for persons who defended the temporal territory of the Church. It originally came in four classes in each of the two divisions. At present, there are three classes within each division, although the class of Knight Commander is divided into individuals who are also awarded the *placca* (star) and those who are not, which often allows for some confusion over the number of classes.

The Order of St. Gregory does not include the award of the rank of Collar or Chain. The highest class is that of Grand Cross, a much-sought-after award by laymen in the service of the Church. The class of Grand Cross is awarded by both papal *motu proprio* and by nomination of the Secretary of State. It is reserved for statesmen, senior politicians, and any outstanding laity of the Church. The class of Grand Cross is always awarded with the star.

The class of Knight Commander is subdivided by the award with the star, which is the higher of the two awards, or the award without the star. Customarily, one is awarded the lesser class initially; the award of the star is subsequently awarded for continued service to the papacy. On the diocesan level, the rank of Commander is usually reserved for promotion or further award.

The class of Knight is the lowest grade within the Order of St. Gregory and the most frequently bestowed on the diocesan level as a special mark of favor of the Holy See for persons who diligently serve the Church on the local level.

The Order of St. Gregory the Great can now be bestowed upon any individuals who serve the Catholic Church or who have distinguished themselves by their accomplishments benefiting society, regardless of their religion or gender. Until 1991, the order was reserved for men only; then, for the first time in papal history, Pope John Paul II conferred a papal award, one that was created specifically as an award for males, on a group of Swedish Catholic women.

The insignia of the Order of St. Gregory the Great is recognizable by its brilliant color. It consists of an eight-pointed, gold-rimmed red enamel cross with a gold ball on each of the tips of the eight points. The center medallion is blue enamel and portrays the image of Saint Gregory the Great, Doctor and Pontiff. The blue center medallion is surrounded by a gold circle, on which are inscribed the words *Sanctus Gregorius Magnus;* on the reverse of this medallion are the words *Pro Deo et Principe,* the order's motto. The insignia is suspended from a green and gold laurel wreath in enamel for the civil division, and from a golden military trophy of armor, flags, and swords for the military division. The ribbon of the order is red moiré silk, edged in yellow. For the rank of Knight, the ribbon is usually presented in the triangular military form of old Italy rather than the presently accepted rectangular form, and it is worn on the left breast.

For the two grades of Commander, the insignia is worn at the neck. For the higher class, Grand Cross, the order is suspended from a sash of the order's colors worn over the right shoulder, across the breast, and resting on the left hip. The insignia is suspended from a stylized bow. The star *(placca)* is worn on the left breast. The star includes a representation of the order's insignia mounted on an eight-pointed silver star.

The order has its own uniform. Unlike the uniforms of the higher papal awards, which are not frequently seen at papal or diocesan ceremonies, the uniform of the Order of St. Gregory the Great is a fixture both in Rome and in the local church. Whereas the uniforms of the Orders of Christ and of the Golden Spur are somewhat fanciful and obsolete, the uniform of the Order of St. Gregory is based on the diplomatic costume of the early part of the twentieth century. The degree of its embroidery depends on the class of the order bestowed. "It is a dark green tail-coat closed at the front with a row of silver buttons embossed with the emblem of the Order, and silver braiding."[8] The cuffs, pockets, rear waist and collar of the tunic are embroidered with silver oak leaves. For the higher classes, especially that of Grand Cross, the oak-leaf motif is quite lavish. The trousers are also of green cloth and have silver brocade military stripes on the outside of each leg. A plumed silk hat, sword, and military gloves complete the uniform.

On the diocesan level, knights should wear their uniforms and insignia at the most solemn liturgical ceremonies. They should also wear them when serving the ordinary or the apostolic pronuncio or nuncio as honor guard. Knights, in uniform and insignia, are always a common sight at papal ceremonies in Rome.

EQUESTRIAN ORDER OF POPE ST. SYLVESTER

Known also as the *Ordine di San Sylvestro Papa,* the Order of Pope St. Sylvester was established by Pope Gregory XVI on October 31, 1841, ten years after he founded the Order of St. Gregory the Great. In its founding, Gregory XVI intended the order to replace the Order of the Golden Spur, which by that time had fallen into disrepute. Rather than replace the Golden Spur, the St. Sylvester remained joined to it under the name the Order of the Golden Militia and St. Sylvester. In combining the two, the pontiff was able to regain authority over the Golden Spur, which had been lost to the Black Nobility of Rome, who were traditionally permitted to award the order and the privileges that it carried. The order remained joined to the Golden Spur for sixty-four years until, under the pontificate of Pope St. Pius X, the two were permanently separated. The Golden Spur had been sufficiently rehabilitated in the eyes of the popes. The new Order of Pope St. Sylvester took its place as the fifth of the pontifical awards, bestowed as an award for Catholic laymen who by their examples in business, the professions, the military, and society have lived exemplary lives. At present, it is also bestowed on non-Catholics.

The Order of Pope St. Sylvester is awarded in three classes. As is the case of the Order of St. Gregory, the Order of St. Sylvester is divided into the ranks of Grand Cross, Commander, with star and without, and Knight. The Order of St. Sylvester is the least known of the papal orders. Its unique ribbon, however, immediately identifies it as one of papal awards. The ribbon of the order is of black moiré silk. In the center of the ribbon and on the edges are red moiré stripes, a total of three, appearing as alternating equal stripes of red, black, red, black, and red.

The insignia of the Order of St. Sylvester is composed of a gold-rimmed, eight-pointed white enamel cross. Gold rays generate from the center medallion between each of the four arms of the cross. The center medallion is worked in midnight blue enamel and portrays the golden effigy of Saint Sylvester, who reigned as pope from A.D. 314 to 335 and for whom Pope Gregory XVI named the order. Surrounding the central medallion is a gold band inscribed with the name of the order. On the medallion's reverse is the founding date (1844) and the reorganization date (1905) of the order. The *placca* (star) of the order has the insignia of the order mounted onto an eight-pointed silver star. The star is always worn on the left breast.

The rank of Grand Cross is worn over the right shoulder on a sash in the order's colors. The insignia rests at the left hip, where it is suspended from a stylized bow. The rank of Commander, both with *placca* and without, is worn suspended from a neck ribbon in the order's colors. The class of Knight is suspended from a ribbon and is worn on the left breast. The ribbon can be either triangular or rectangular. The shape depends where and when the insignia was obtained.

As is the case with all pontifical orders, the Order of St. Sylvester has its own uniform, which should be worn at all papal ceremonies in Rome and at all solemn diocesan ceremonies of the local church. Like the uniform of the Order of St. Gregory, the uniform of the St. Sylvester claims its origin in the diplomatic costume of the early twentieth century. Likewise, the degree of embroidery on the uniform itself depends on the class within the order of the recipient.

The color of the cloth used for the Order of St. Sylvester is known as Sylvester black or jet black. Like the tunic of the St. Gregory, the Sylvester tunic is a tailcoat with a high-fronted waist. The tunic is fastened by a single center row of gilt buttons, upon which is emblazoned the insignia of the order. The cuffs and collars of the uniform are made of black velvet. The oak-leaf motif of the embroidery is worked in gold thread. The trousers are also of Sylvester black cloth. On the outside of each leg is a gold military stripe. The plumed hat is made of silk cloth. On the right side of the hat is a yellow and white cockade, that is, a silk circlet in the papal colors. Gloves and a sword complete the uniform.

CROSS PRO-ECCLESIA ET PONTIFICE

The Cross for the Church and Pontiff, or *Cross Pro-Ecclesia et Pontifice,* is not a pontifical order; it is characterized as a papal award. Founded by Pope Leo XIII on July 17, 1888, it was intended as an award to mark his fiftieth priestly jubilee, not as a long-standing award. The Cross Pro-Ecclesia et Pontifice was intended as Leo XIII's specific mark of honor, but it continues to outlive the founder. In present times, the award is bestowed on persons, both laypersons and clergy, who have given service to the Church. It is also the papal award that had been traditionally bestowed upon women throughout this century, but, as we have seen, this has changed with the award of the Order of St. Gregory to women.

The original award consisted of the effigy of the reigning pontiff on a round medallion in either gold or silver. The ribbon was of red and white stripes, with a thin yellow stripe imposed upon the white stripe. From the time of Leo XIII until late into the pontificate of Paul VI, the award remained true to this design with the exception of the ribbon, which was altered to half yellow and half white, the heraldic colors of the Holy See. Pope Paul especially loved modern art and altered the insignia of the Cross Pro-Ecclesia et Pontifice when he replaced the papal effigy and medallion with a gold Greek cross. In the center of the squarelike cross are the images of the apostles Peter and Paul. On the cross bar of the Greek cross is the name of the award perpendicular to each of the apostles' effigies. At the base of the Cross is the name of the reigning pope in Latin, above the papal arms, in modern stylized fashion. At present, the Cross is awarded in gold or gilt only.

It is important to note that the reigning pope is not bound by the *motu proprio* of his predecessors, although seldom are these reversed in the pontificates that immediately follow. The creation of new awards or the suppression of existing orders, however, is within the jurisdiction of the reigning pope. As such, a return to the traditional form of the

Cross Pro-Ecclesia et Pontifice or a substitution of yet another design is, of course, possible in future pontificates.

BENEMERENTI MEDAL

The term *benemerenti* literally translates to "good merit." "Several medals ('To a well-deserving person') have been conferred by popes for exceptional accomplishment and service."[9] The Benemerenti Medal is awarded to individuals of both genders who have merited special recognition by the Holy See. The award seldom comes more than once during a pontificate; however, the Benemerenti of successive popes can be bestowed on the same individual.

The first papal Benemerenti Medal was bestowed by Pope Pius VI (1791) as an award for military courage in the defense of the temporal Papal States. The award was not created as a perpetual decoration in the gift of the Holy Father. Later, Pope Gregory XVI, the same pontiff who had instituted both the Order of St. Gregory and the Order of St. Sylvester, officially founded the Benemerenti, specifically and exclusively as a military reward. It could not be awarded to civilians or to the clergy.

In 1925, the concept of awarding the Benemerenti as a mark of recognition to persons in service to the Church, both civil and military, lay and clergy alike, became acceptable. The medal has since been bestowed during Holy Years and during special jubilees in the life of the Church and of the reigning pope.

Pope Paul VI redesigned the traditional decoration at the same time that he redesigned the Cross Pro-Ecclesia. Similar in design, the Benemerenti depicts the image of Christ on a gold Greek cross. The Savior, depicted in radiant splendor, has His hand raised in blessing. On the left of the transverse arm of the cross is a modern depiction of the tiara and crossed keys; to the right, the shield of John Paul II and his motto. On the reverse, the word *Benemerenti*. The insignia is suspended from a ribbon of the papal colors, yellow and white.

OTHER LAY AWARDS

The Holy See additionally recognizes the talents and contributions of laymen by bestowing upon them titles that tie them to the person of the pope and to the Holy See. These honorifics can be bestowed upon laymen of all faiths.

In the past, the Holy Father bestowed noble titles on the faithful as his highest mark of esteem. These titles derived from the powers of the pontiffs as sovereigns of the temporal Papal States, and later from their dual legal role as sovereign of the Vatican City State and Supreme Pontiff of the Universal Church. Pope John XXIII was the last pope to ennoble a layman. His predecessor, Pius XII, continued the practice of his predecessors by creating new titles of nobility for prominent laymen. The titles Prince, Marquis, and Count were the titles most frequently bestowed by the Roman pontiffs. The bestowal of these titles was not relinquished by one pope, as they are theirs by right of their position; however, the exercise of this privilege more accurately can be said to have lapsed into disuse.

Although Pope Paul VI did not further the creation of new members of the papal nobility, it was not until the *Motu Proprio Pontificalis Domus* that it became clear that their role at the Papal Court had been extinguished. *"Jean XXIII a refusé d'anoblier sa famille comme cela s'était toujours fait. Depuis Paul VI le pape n'a procédé a aucun anoblissement."* (John XXIII refused to enoble his family as it was the usual custom. Since Paul VI there has been no further enoblements by a pope.)[10] The pope and his successors have the legal right to reestablish the honors system if they were to decree it in keeping with the times.

A few of the papal honors have been retained while yet another has been recently instituted. The new papal honorific, Stewards of St. Peter, was created by the present pontiff at the behest of John Cardinal Krol, Archbishop-Emeritus of Philadelphia and President of the Papal Foundation, whose aim it is to establish a financial foundation capable of generating income to aid the Holy See in the offset of its annual deficit, a task well on its way to success. Laymen who, through their largesse and generosity, have benefited the work of the Papal Foundation have been formally vested by the Church with the new title Stewards of St. Peter. This honorific, however, has no legal standing in the same sense that honorees of papal decorations have by virtue of their creation by formal decree of the Secretary of State. Although this is a new title or honorific, a similar award was granted during the pontificate of Leo XIII. The award was in the form of a white enamel and gold cross with a medallion of cobalt blue encircling a golden effigy of St. Peter enscribed with the name of the award, the Advocates of St. Peter. The cross was suspended from the cross keys and tiara on a lavender, gold-edged moiré ribbon.

The title Pontifical Academician continues to be awarded to the most distinguished scientists worldwide. This title is granted for the lifetime of the recipient and carries with it the style of "Excellency." There are presently seventy-five active members, along with numerous honorary members. The headquarters of the Pontifical Academy is within the territory of the Vatican City State and is housed in the beautiful Casino Pio IV in the Vatican gardens. The title Pontifical Academician is as time honored as the award of the Nobel Prize. It is open to scientists in all disciplines and to men and women of all faiths. It is in the personal gift of the Supreme Pontiff.

The last of the ancient titles retained by the modern papacy, and in the gift of the Holy Father for the honor of laymen, is the title *Lay Assistant to the Throne*. This title is reserved for members of great Italian noble families whose members have served the papacy for generations and who most frequently continue to serve in the actual administration of the Church. The number of honorees is extremely restricted and is, in fact, the remnant of the many privileges once enjoyed by the Black Nobility at the papal court.

INVESTITURE CEREMONIES

There are three basic types of ceremonies for investiture of papal awards. The simplest of these is known as the private presentation ceremony. This method is usually reserved for non-Catholics who are being honored by the Holy See. The presentation usually takes place in the bishop's residence or at the diocesan chancellery office. In addition to the staff of the bishop, the honoree's family and a few invited guests are welcome to witness the presentation ceremony. The diocesan photographer should be present to mark the occasion. In the event that the honoree is a local dignitary, the press office of the diocese should also alert the local press corps.

After a few opening remarks by the bishop, a history of the order or of the award being bestowed should be read by either the bishop or by a diocesan official. The letter of nomination to the award should be read aloud so that it is clear why the honoree has been singled out by the Church. The bishop then confers the award on the recipient. He may either present it in its case or by pinning or draping the insignia on the recipient. A few moments should be set aside for remarks from the honoree when planning the ceremony. A photography session should follow the close of the ceremony. The bishop should always be vested in *abito piano*.

The second form of investiture is the official presentation ceremony. The official presentation is an extension of the private method in that it takes place at a site other than a church, either at the diocesan chancellery office or at a public forum, such as a banquet. As in the private presentation, the award is most frequently bestowed with little fanfare. Usually, at the official presentation ceremony, several awards would be presented. Traditionally, a reception follows this presentation ceremony.

Finally, the most common form of representation is that of the public presentation. It is also the most solemn form of celebration. The public presentation investiture always takes place in a church, and most commonly in a cathedral. The ceremony of investiture may be designed to include the full pomp of Church ceremony or to reflect humble simplicity.

It would be appropriate either to include the investiture in a Pontifical Mass or as part of the Liturgy of the Hours, preferably Evening Prayer. The timing, schedule, and personal style of the ordinary determines the presentation form. In cases where many awards are to be presented, care should be given to exact precedence and to protocol. In contrast to ceremonies of other nations' awards, wherein the highest honors to be bestowed are presented last, the honors system of the Holy See traditionally calls for the investiture of its highest honors first.

As such, the award of the highest Vatican honors are presented first, followed by each of the lower orders, with the highest class of each award being presented prior to the lower classes of the same order. In other words, the award of the Pian Order precedes that of the St. Gregory, whereas the rank of Knight Commander of St. Gregory precedes that of the rank of Knight of that same order.

In dioceses that are capable and willing to include all the pomp of the Church in the presentation of lay papal awards, the following guidelines, based on long-standing formal protocol practices, are put forth to serve as an example:

- All guests should be in place by the appointed hour. Care should be given in the planning of the investiture to provide seating to all invited and anticipated guests. It is best to preassign seating whenever possible. Precedence in seating should be accorded to honored guests. The director of the diocesan choir or the director of the Office of Music should prepare a musical program befitting the solemnity of the event. All the ecclesiastical officials of the diocese should be encouraged to attend and should be provided a fitting role to play. If the event is to include the celebration of the Mass, the celebrants and concelebrants should be vested in gold and white. All concelebrants should be vested in chasuble, not simply the stole, as this is a very formal occasion. If the auxiliary bishops are to be present but are not concelebrating, they should be vested in choir dress. The ordinary in this case would be vested in chasuble and precious mitre. If the investiture does not include the Celebration of the Mass, the ordinary should be vested in cope and precious mitre.

- A procession should include all the dignitaries of the diocese. It may also include a contingent of Papal Knights, Knights of Malta, and Knights of the Holy Sepulchre serving as the bishop's honor guard. The awards may be carried in procession. This option, when included in the ceremony of investiture, adds color and pomp to the occasion. In this case, however, just one insignia or one insignia of each class or order to be awarded should be carried in procession. All the insignia should be blessed as part of the ceremony.

- The actual presentation of papal honors should be made at the *cathedra*. Each recipient should be called forward by one of the masters of ceremonies, or diocesan official, who recounts the outstanding merits of the recipient, as well as clearly announces the title and class of the award being conferred.

- The bishop should be seated with mitre. As each recipient approaches the *cathedra,* a second master of ceremonies leads the recipient forward. The honoree kneels before the bishop, who either pins or drapes the papal award on the recipient, or who presents the award in its decorative case, whichever is most in keeping with the local custom. After each presentation, the bishop then either offers the kiss of peace or a congratulatory greeting to the recipient, who then rises and returns to his or her place in the sanctuary.

- Diocesan officials should be aware of a secret known for years in the diplomatic and military communities. When an award needs to be publically presented by pinning it on the recipient's breast, especially in the case of a female recipient, a large safety pin should be attached by the honoree, prior to the ceremony, inside the dress or jacket so that the bar of the pin is on the exterior of the garment, with just enough slack between the pin and the garment. (Be sure to have just enough slack because the weight of the insignia may otherwise pull down the material.) The insignia, and, additionally, the star when also awarded, can be placed without any difficulty and without a lack of decorum by hooking it onto the pin rather than the garment.

- A program should be prepared by the diocese so that the press and those present in the church or cathedral are kept informed as to the movement of the ceremony and to the history of the award being presented. A brief biography of the honorees, as well as the reasons for the conferral of the papal award, should also be included. As this event is a joyous celebration in the life of the local church, the Catholic press of the locality should provide appropriate coverage of the events and the backgrounds on each of the awards and recipients.

- Finally, bishops should be aware that even when one of their faithful has a papal order, or multiple papal decorations, that person may still be honored for further supportive activity for the (arch)diocese, or can be honored as a continued enticement for dedicated service, by the award of a promotion to a higher class or grade in one or more of their orders.

PRECEDENCE OF PAPAL AWARDS

Supreme Order of Christ
Order of the Golden Spur
Order of Pope Pius IX *(Grand Collar, Knight and Dame Grand Cross, Knight and Dame Commander, Knight and Dame)*
Order of St. Gregory the Great *(Grand Cross, Knight and Dame Commander, Knight and Dame)*
Order of St. Sylvester *(Grand Cross, Knight and Dame Commander, Knight and Dame)*
Cross Pro-Ecclesia et Pontifice
Benemerenti Medal

HONOR GUARD

In dioceses where Papal Knights have been appointed or where there is a strong tradition of the Order of Malta and the Order of the Holy Sepulchre, the ordinary has the right to make use of these gentlemen at solemn liturgical functions.

The following guide provides the ranking of these orders, which determines the proper placement of these knights in processions. Members of the highest ranked orders are placed at the rear of this contingent and nearest to the celebrant or the highest ranking Church official. Within each order, if there are more than one knight of each papal order present, the lower ranking class of that order precedes the higher class of the same order.

Papal Knights are knights who have received one of the five papal orders of knighthood. They take precedence over the ecclesiastic orders of Malta and of the Holy Sepulchre. As such, the Knights of Malta and the Knights of the Holy Sepulchre precede the Papal Knights in procession. Proper ranking among the two orders has always been a thorny problem, with each historically claiming precedence over the other. To avoid such problems, it would be wise to place one knight of each order side by side with the other order. The accompanying chart illustrates an ecclesiastical procession including an honor guard of papal knights, the Order of Malta, and the Order of the Holy Sepulchre.

Traditionally, only the orders of St. Gregory, Malta, and the Holy Sepulchre are found at the diocesan level. In the event that Gentlemen of His Holiness are present in the diocese, these honorees should directly precede the ordinary, walk alongside him, or follow him in procession.

The use of Papal Knights and members of ecclesiastical chivalric orders as an honor guard should always require the mantle or habit for the Malta Knights, the mantle for the Holy Sepulchre Knights, and the uniform for Papal Knights. Insignia should never be worn on business attire when serving as a guard of honor. When Gentlemen of His Holiness are serving as guards of honor, they, too, should be

ECCLESIASTICAL PROCESSION

(Honor Guard)

THE KNIGHTS OF COLUMBUS

THURIFER

CRUCIFER

SEMINARIANS

DIOCESAN PRIESTS

MONSIGNORI

CONCELEBRANTS

VISITING PRELATES

AUXILIARY BISHOPS

HOLY SEPULCHRE	MALTA
MALTA	HOLY SEPULCHRE
KNIGHT OF ST. SYLVESTER	KNIGHT OF ST. GREGORY
COMMANDER OF ST. GREGORY	COMMANDER OF ST. SYLVESTER
KNIGHT OF THE PIAN ORDER	COMMANDER OF THE PIAN ORDER

PRELATES IN CHOIR

ORDINARY

ORDINARY'S ATTENDANTS*

* Either Gentlemen of His Holiness, with chain of office and wearing white tie and tails (*tenue pontificale*), or the two most senior honorees of the highest order present.

119

in ceremonial attire. Often, they will have the uniform of one of the papal orders that they have also been awarded. The chain of their office as Gentlemen of His Holiness should be worn to signify their position in the Papal Household. If they are not otherwise entitled to a uniform of a Papal Knight, their costume would correctly be white tie and tails *(tenue de soirée),* which might be considered somewhat out of place, but correct dress all the same; therefore, a dark business suit would be unacceptable.

BURIAL OF A PAPAL KNIGHT

There are no Vatican prescriptions for the burial ceremonies of a knight; however, certain assumptions can be made based upon ancient traditions and present protocol directives regarding the placement of honors and insignia at a funeral of the recipient. Also, military protocol, which serves as the common heritage of the ceremonial life of all orders of knighthood, also sets forth certain guidelines.

The Order of Malta and the Equestrian Order of the Holy Sepulchre each maintain a ceremonial that describes the official procedures for a knight or lady member's burial ceremony. As for Papal Knights, the common practice in most nations is to prominently display the honoree's awards at the burial ceremony. For Catholics, this would include the Mass of Christian Burial or the Mass of the Resurrection, as well as during the procession to the funeral in instances of state or official funerals.

All the recipient's honors, both civil and religious, should be properly displayed if the family makes the choice to display the deceased's Church awards, unless the deceased honoree had specifically decided to the contrary. As a general rule, display of Church honors also would require similar respect for the civil awards that the recipient received in his or her lifetime.

On the occasion of a funeral for a deceased Catholic statesman or politician, the master of ceremonies for the local church and the official protocol liaison should carefully plan the proper display and procession of orders and awards. On all other occasions, the time-honored custom of placing the decorations on velvet cushions at the foot of the bier (Style I) or surrounding it, if the deceased had been awarded numerous decorations during his or her lifetime, is the most dignified method of displaying the decorations. The family's representative, possibly the funeral home official, and/or the master of ceremonies, should work closely together in the planning of the presentation. Usually, other surviving Papal or Ecclesiastical knights can be called upon for assistance in this regard.

If the deceased is either a Gentlemen of His Holiness, a recipient of the Golden Rose, or of one of the pontifical orders in the highest classes (i.e., Grand Collar or Grand Cross), custom requires that these awards be as prominently displayed in death as they were in life because of the direct, personal involvement of a pope in their original presentation. As such, the Golden Rose should be placed nearby on a pediment or on a credence table, whereas each of the highest classes of the pontifical orders and the chain of office for the title Gentlemen of His Holiness should each be presented on a cushion of its own. Protocol accords the place of honor of the highest award of the deceased at the foot of his or her bier. When the bier is placed in a vertical position in the center aisle (Style I), the place of honor is the center position. When the coffin is placed horizontally during the viewing as one approaches it (Style II), the place of honor would be the central cushion. The next senior honor is placed to the right (as viewed from the front), the next highest to the left, and so on, alternating across the front of the coffin.

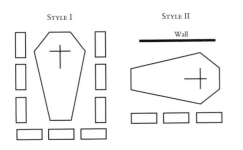

STYLE I   STYLE II

Wall

Likewise, the classes of Grand Collar and Grand Cross of other civil or national orders should be each provided a cushion. Lesser classes could be placed together in groups of two (for ranks of Commanders with star), three or four (for ranks of Commanders without star), and five or six (for the simple insignia of Officer and Knight).

Often one is asked about the inclusion of the chapeau and sword at the funeral for a Papal or Ecclesiastical Knight. For those who would prefer the formality and solemnity that the inclusion of this regalia would provide, the proper placement of these items would be on the closed lid of the deceased's coffin. They would be placed there after the coffin had been closed for the last time. During the viewing of the deceased's remains, this regalia would not be displayed but would, however, remain on the coffin throughout the funeral ceremony and during the final procession to the graveside. The regalia should be removed prior to burial. If these items are to be displayed, the white gloves of a gentleman Knight should also accompany the chapeau.

The insignia of the papal and ecclesiastical orders should never be worn by the deceased to the grave. If the family insists on dressing the knight or dame of the ecclesiastical or papal order with the insignia in death, these should be removed before burial. As such, it should be remembered that the proper display of one's membership in any order is as described above. The Church recalls that one enters

life without pageantry and we are recalled to God just as simply. Protocol also recognizes this view by placing the awards near to, but not on, the faithfully departed. All things can be overdone, so simplicity is the best path in these matters.

Other than as a guard of honor or as honorary pallbearers, Papal and Ecclesiastical Knights in attendance at the funeral play no prescribed role. It must be remembered that the funeral is a celebration of one's life and rebirth in Christ, and therefore temporal ceremonies take a secondary role. If the deceased were, in life, a member of several papal or ecclesiastical orders, a guard of honor composed of members of each of these orders would be appropriate.

These knights should always appear in the dress of their own orders. Papal Knights would wear their ceremonial uniforms, each wearing the uniform of the order to which they belong, and the Knights of the Holy Sepulchre and of Malta would wear either their mantles or uniforms. The Knights of Malta could also appropriately wear the habit of their order known as the *cuculla*.

The diocesan protocol official or the master of ceremonies should be informed of the intention of the deceased's family to include the papal honors in the funeral rites. Simultaneously, these officials should be prepared to orchestrate a papal honoree's funeral in accordance with the various order's customs and by the precepts of ancient tradition.

In the event that the deceased's civil honors are to be displayed as well, the following official list will serve as a guide in the event that the chore of placement of these awards for display, or at minimal a listing of the appropriate civil awards, would fall to a diocesan official. As far as the Church is concerned, the dignified display of its own honors is preeminent. The following is presented as a reference guide in the event the need arises for its use:

PROPER ORDER FOR CIVIL AWARDS

The Congressional Medal of Honor
  (Army or Air Force)
The Congressional Medal of Honor (Navy)
The Distinguished Service Cross
The Navy Cross
Air Force Cross
Distinguished Service Medal
  (Army or Air Force)
Distinguished Service Medal (Navy)
Silver Star
Legion of Merit
Distinguished Flying Cross

Soldiers Medal
Navy and Marine Corps Medal
Airman's Medal
Bronze Star Medal
Purple Heart
Air Medal
Joint Service Commendation Medal
Army Commendation Medal
Navy Commendation Medal
Air Force Commendation Medal
Presidential Medal of Freedom
Campaign Medals (by date of authorization)

KNIGHTS OF COLUMBUS

The history of this noble organization is rich and long. Whenever and wherever the Church has called the Knights of Columbus to support her work both on the universal and the local levels, they have readily answered the call of the Church.

An honor guard comprising members of the local organization of the knights should always be included in Church ceremonies. Their contribution adds to the beauty and pageantry of our liturgies.

It is the custom in the United States, even when papal honorees are present, to have the knights constitute the opening honor guard in ecclesiastical processions. The master of ceremonies should coordinate the placement of the Knights of Columbus and the Papal Knights in processions. It must be remembered that papal honorees have been given a place of honor because of their status in the Papal Family and as such, when Papal Knights are used as the senior honor guard, the Knights of Columbus should not be incorporated with them but rather utilized in some other prominent manner.

CHAPTER SEVEN

Papal Honors: Clergy

The gift of papal honors is not exclusively reserved for the laity. Like the honors conferred by the reigning pontiff upon the laity, honors bestowed upon the clergy are derived from the days of the temporal powers of the Holy See in the former Papal States. In ancient times, the clerics honored by the papacy were officials of the Palatine Court and held colorful and arcane titles associated with their positions at the Papal Court.

In 1969, Pope Paul VI dismantled the centuries-old Papal Court, along with its honors system, and replaced it with a simplified structure of honors for clergy and the laity that reflected his personal discomfort with pageantry and his desire to reshape the entire Church in a more pastoral mode. This *motu proprio* document took on the first two words of the decree that reflected the name of his household, *Pontificalis Domus* (1969).

Prior to *Pontificalis Domus,* there were numerous ranks or degrees of honors that conferred the style of "Monseigneur" (or "Monsignor") and that carried with it membership in the honorary prelature, the lower-ranking, nonepiscopal prelature. By 1900, there were sixteen various degrees of the

Monsignori. The majority of these titles derived from a personal or domestic service to the reigning pope, and the majority of recipients were also clerics residing in the Roman province.

Despite the age-old custom of conferring the title Monsignor upon members of the Roman clergy serving in the Papal Court, membership in the *prelaturae gratiae* was not granted to the non-Roman clergy until Pope Pius VI conferred it to non-Italian priests residing in Rome. These priests were the first supranumerary, or honorary members, of the Papal Court. In subsequent pontificates, the practice of honoring "foreigners" was once again restricted. Even within the Italian peninsula, suspicion of non-Romans ran so high that it was not uncommon for the Roman clergy to distrust other Italians, let alone other Europeans.

During the pontificate of Pope Pius IX, the honors system, for both the laity and the clergy, flourished. Pius IX systematized papal titles and honors, awarding each for a specific service to, or responsibility in, the Church. For the clergy, the papal honors system included sixteen various lesser or inferior prelature classes, both actual and honorary. Each carried with it specific pontifical privileges. Following the decree of *Pontificalis Domus* in 1969, nearly all these richly arcane titles and positions were relegated to history. In their place, four honors were reserved for the clergy.

Prior to *Pontificalis Domus,* the monsignorial ranks included the title Domestic Prelate, which carried with it the official style of "Right Reverend Monsignor" and rights to purple vesture. It was the most frequently bestowed papal clerical honor. This title was granted to the recipient for life without requirement of any specific responsibility in Rome or within the diocese.

Continuing in descending order of precedence, the Private Chamberlain Supranumerary was granted to non-Roman clergy for the duration of the pontificate of the pope who had bestowed that honor. Shortly following that pope's death, at the time of his burial (more accurately, as the *Bussolanti* laid him in his crypt below the High Altar of St. Peter), their title and position was lost. The succeeding pope, however, usually confirmed the honor upon a petition from the recipient, but once again, it would be lost at that pontiff's burial if he, too, predeceased the recipient. The private chamberlains supranumerary were accorded the style of "Very Reverend Monsignor," and they were entitled to purple vesture.

Following these prelates were the Chamberlains of Honor in *abito paonazzo,* who were identical to the private chamberlains supranumerary but who were, as time progressed, only differentiated for purposes of precedence. Similar to the lay award of a papal knighthood of a lower class, the chamberlains of honor in *abito paonazzo* were considered worthy of a high papal honor, and yet the papacy reserved the higher degree or rank from within the honorary prelature for an anticipated further award at a later time. The Chamberlains of Honor *extra Urbem* were, like the chamberlains in *abito paonazzo,* a lesser degree of the title Private Chamberlain Supranumerary. These honorary prelates held their positions and privileges outside Rome. In reality their honors, although bestowed by Rome, were limited to use within the recipient's own diocese. Among the sixteen monsignorial positions were also the titles Private Chaplain of Honor and Private Chaplain of Honor *extra urbem,* each of which bestowed the rank of honorary prelate upon the recipient and which permitted the use of purple vesture. The qualification of *extra urbem* was granted for use only within the recipient's diocese. These and the other categories of the Roman prelates were officially and collectively known as *Romanae Curiae Antistites.* Prelates who lost their titles upon the pope's death held these honors because of their positions or offices within the Papal Court. They wore a distinct costume known as the *mantellone,* and they were collectively referred to as the *prelates di mantellone.*

In addition to clerics who were entitled Domestic Prelate and who held honorary positions at the former Papal Court or within the modern Papal Household, were those greater prelates within the Roman Curia and Papal Court who were also collectively known as domestic prelates. These two distinctions should never be confused as the same. The greater prelates who were collectively known as the domestic prelates, because of their placement in the Papal Chapel, were the non-Oriental patriarchs, the archbishops and bishops who had been appointed as assistants to the papal throne, and the protonotaries apostolic, as well as other dignitaries of the Curia and Household, most notably the dean of the Rota and the auditors and the votanti of the Signatura. Grouped together, these senior Roman prelates were collectively referred to as domestic prelates, meaning prelates of senior position in the Papal Chapel.

Of the sixteen clerical papal honors existing prior to 1969, two have not as yet been presented for study in this text: the Assistants to the Papal Throne and the College of Protonotaries Apostolic. These two ancient titles are the only vestiges of the Papal Court that have been retained by the modern papacy.

ASSISTANTS TO THE PAPAL THRONE

Other than membership in the Sacred College, the highest honor in the gift of the Roman Pontiff exclusively for the clergy is the title and rank *Assistant to the Papal Throne*. This post is a vestige of the Renaissance court of the papacy; however, as it has been adapted throughout the years, it serves as a means to bestow honor on the highest levels of the clergy of the Church.

All patriarchs are automatically nominated assistants to the throne, both of the Latin rite, if they are not already members of the Sacred College, and of the Oriental rites. In addition to these automatic nominations, which have their roots in the Renaissance Church when political strife required a firm bond between Rome and the far-off patriarchates, the special privileges attached to the title Assistant to the Papal Throne have been conferred upon prominent churchmen of other ranks as well. Archbishops and bishops of the Latin rites and eparchs of the Oriental rites may have this dignity attached to them by special favor of the Roman Pontiff. The title is solely in the gift of the pope. Many archbishop secretaries to Roman congregations and a few diocesan archbishops are given this honor during each pontificate.

In addition to the honorary title, the post carries with it a place of honor in the Papal Chapel, as well as a higher precedence than their ecclesiastical rank would normally permit. In the past, these prelates were permitted the exclusive use of silk in their everyday vesture as a mark of their unique proximity to, and favor by, the Roman Pontiff; however, the title Assistant to the Papal Throne is a ceremo-

nial one and does not carry with it a special post within the Papal Household or Curia.

PROTONOTARIES APOSTOLIC

The monsignorial titles of protonotaries apostolic were retained by the papacy of Pope Paul VI after the issuance of the *Motu Proprio Pontificalis Domus;* however, only two of the original four classifications were retained. Until 1968, the College of Protonotaries Apostolic was divided into four classes, the first being that of protonotaries apostolic participating, whose responsibilities were to serve as the notaries at the Vatican. Today these officials number seven prelates and take the name "protonotaries apostolic de numero."

Prior to 1968, the second class in this prelatial college was the protonotaries apostolic supranumerary. These prelates were the canons serving in the three great Roman patriarchal basilicas: St. Peter's in the Vatican, St. Mary Major, and St. John Lateran. The third class within this college was the protonotaries *ad instar participantium,* which was purely an honorific from the Holy See. Finally, the college also included the title Titular Protonotary Apostolic, which was purely a diocesan honor reserved to the highest classes of the local *monsignori.* The nonepiscopal vicars general of the dioceses held this title *ipso uire.* All the last three classes of the former College of Protonotaries Apostolic have been combined and today take the title *Apostolic Protonotary Supranumerary.*

All the former privileges of the College of Protonotaries have been abolished. Individuals who were granted the privileges of use of pontificals prior to the *Motu Proprio Reform of the Use of Pontifical Insignia,* in 1968, were permitted to retain the privileges that were granted to them by apostolic letter until the time of their death; "however they may give up these privileges spontaneously in accord with the law"[1]—a clear hint that Rome preferred they do so after 1968.

Persons holding the title Protonotary Apostolic Supranumerary are the highest-ranking nonepiscopal prelates at the diocesan level. They are styled "Reverend Monsignor," whereas the protonotaries apostolic de numero still have retained the style "Right Reverend Monsignor." The de numero protonotaries are responsible for countersigning all Vatican official documents, including papal bulls and the *rogito,* which consigns a deceased pontiff to history.

The protonotaries apostolic, as a college, date from the first century, when Pope Clement I nominated certain men (both laymen and clerics) as notaries for the city of Rome, where they served as the city's archivists and diarists. The ancient city of Rome was divided into seven districts or communes. "At the head of each district a notary was appointed, and because of his dignity as well as to distinguish him from other notaries, he was called *proto* or first notary."[2] As diarists for the city, each chronicled the life of the early Church in Rome. Momentous events were recorded for posterity because of the diligence of these notaries. Many of the histories of our most glorious saints and martyrs have been documented by their hands. Pope Julius I was the first pontiff to grant these working notaries special privileges. "Pope Sixtus V (1585-1590) increased the number of protonotaries to twelve and granted them further privileges."[3] In 1838, Pope Gregory XVI reorganized the Roman government with a resulting decrease in the number to seven, although for a time the total number dropped to six. This number was once again increased to the present total of seven by Pope John XXIII.

All seven protonotaries apostolic de numero serve well the Church of God and must reside in Rome.

As recently as the 1800s, prominent Italian noble laymen were named as protonotaries apostolic de numero. One fine example was Cardinal Consalvi, who remained a layman for most of his long service to the Church. He rose to the College of Cardinals and to the post of cardinal–secretary of state while still a layman. He was later created a deacon but served as a protonotary while also a layman.

The position of protonotaries apostolic supranumerary, prelates of this class who reside outside Rome, can be traced back to the sixteenth century. As we have seen, several classes of the Supranumerary title were merged into one title, presently granted to the highest ranks of the honorary prelature at the diocesan level.

Protonotaries apostolic are entitled to purple vesture. The seven de numero prelates are additionally permitted to wear the purple *mantelletta* and the rochet, a privilege formerly granted to most of the *monsignori.* They are also permitted to wear the black *biretta* with red tuft, a privilege no longer granted to other honorary prelates. Both the de numero and the supranumerary protonotaries are permitted the purple *ferraiolo.*

PRELATES OF HONOR

The former title Domestic Prelate, the most frequently bestowed of the monsignorial or honorary prelatures, was renamed Prelate of Honor, or as it is known in Italian, *Prelato d'Onore di Sua Santita,* in 1968. It is the most frequently bestowed of the papal honors at the diocesan level.

The title Prelate of Honor is conferred on the recipient for his lifetime. It entitles the recipient to the style of "Reverend Monsignor," although in the past the recipient of the equivalent title bore the style of "Right Reverend Monsignor." Persons who have been named to the honorary or inferior prelature receive the letter of their nomination from the Vatican Secretariat of State, and their title does not officially become valid until the date is applied to the sealed *bulla* in Rome. The title Prelate of Honor is usually conferred on outstanding members of the local clergy, and the nomination of the honoree is traditionally announced simultaneously with the group of other papal honors being conferred at that time within a diocese.

CHAPLAINS OF HIS HOLINESS

In 1968, the title of Chaplain of His Holiness was created to replace a collection of lesser monsignorial appointments from within the reorganized Papal Household. At present, the title is granted, by the pope, to a member of the diocesan clergy upon the request of the ordinary, and more frequently upon clerics in service in the Curia or in the papal diplomatic service.

Chaplains of His Holiness are now styled "Reverend Monsignor." The predecessors of this title held the style of "Very Reverend Monsignor," but this style is no longer accorded to the honorary prelature. The title Chaplain of His Holiness is now granted for the lifetime of the recipient, but prior to 1969, those monsignorial titles equivalent to the present title Chaplain of His Holiness, known in Italian as *Cappellano di Sua Santita,* surrendered their honors and title at the burial of the Pope who had conferred it. The title Chaplain of His Holiness is the lowest grade or class of papal honors for the clergy.

CEREMONIES OF INSTALLATION FOR CLERICAL HONOREES

As in the case of the award of papal honors to the laity, the conferral of prelatial status upon a member of the clergy is a time for rejoicing and celebration on the diocesan level, although when awarded to a Rome-based cleric no ceremony accompanies the appointment. A formal presentation of the papal honor would be appropriate in the cathedral of the diocese. It would be appropriate to combine the ceremonies of installation or investiture with that for the laity, if lay papal honors are simultaneously to be conferred. Prominence, not priority, however, must be accorded in the presentation of the papal honors upon the clergy.

As described previously in the investiture section for lay papal honors, the ceremony of installation for "monsignorial honors" should be conducted with all the solemnity available in the diocese of the honoree. The honorees, both lay and ecclesiastic, can either be previously seated in the sanctuary or be included in the procession into the cathedral or church. If several classes of clerical papal honors are to be bestowed, the procession of these honorees would be as follows: chaplains of His Holiness (by order of their names' appearance in the letter of notification to the ordinary or, if unavailable, by individual ranking within the diocese), the prelates of honor (again by order of their individual names' appearance on the rescript or, if unavailable, by individual ranking within that diocese), and finally the class of protonotaries apostolic (supranumerary). Seating in the sanctuary should be similarly organized, allowing for the higher classes to present themselves to the ordinary first.

As the presentation begins, the bishop should be seated on the *cathedra* and should be vested in either chasuble or cope, depending on the chosen liturgy, as well as the precious mitre. A dignitary of each of the classes to be honored should be seated nearby so that each one can easily come forth to read the official letter of nomination for his class.

If for some unforeseen reason a protonotary apostolic de numero is to receive his appointment at the diocesan level (perhaps while home from his assignment in Rome or perhaps prior to assuming his new posting in Rome), a special formula should be designed to signal out this high honor. While the ordinary is seated on the *cathedra,* a protonotary apostolic de numero, or if there is none present in the diocese, a vicar general of the diocese should come forward to read aloud the letter of nomination of the new prelate, as well as the reasons for its conferral.

The protonotary apostolic de numero is entitled to both the rochet and the *mantelletta,* each a garment of jurisdiction and authority. One of the assigned masters of ceremonies should present each of these garments to the ordinary at the *cathedra,* where he pronounces the appropriate blessing.* The honoree, in choir cassock and *fascia,* is escorted to the *cathedra,* where the bishop vests him, first in the rochet and subsequently with the *mantelletta.* The brief of appointment is then presented to him, and the honoree and the ordinary exchange the sign of peace prior to the recipient's return to his assigned seat within the sanctuary.

The next to be honored are the protonotaries supranumerary and then the prelates of honor. A prelate of these classes should come forth to read the letter(s) of appointment for each of the honorees. One by one, these recipients should come forward to have the brief of appointment presented to him, the higher class before the lesser. The bishop remains seated on the *cathedra.* Only one honoree should be brought forward at a time. All the other recipients should remain seated. To guarantee a smooth flow to the ceremony, two or three masters of ceremonies should be called into service. Rehearsal is always a requirement. One by one, the honorees are presented to the ordinary at the *cathedra.* Their accomplishments, the reason for their receipt of this honor, and the class and title of the honor to be presented should be read as the honoree comes forth.

Finally, the chaplains of His Holiness are presented one by one in the same fashion. If the ordinary wishes his remarks to each honoree to be heard by those gathered in the cathedral (such as a greeting, a blessing, or words of congratulations), the appropriate technology should be prearranged. If this is not desired, light liturgical background music should be played while the ceremony proceeds.

All the new lesser prelates—that is, the *monsignori*—should be vested in the appropriate vesture of their rank. Because the de numero protonotaries are to be vested at the *cathedra,* they process in purple choir cassock and sash only. Prelates of honor wear the purple cassock and sash and a surplice, whereas chaplains of His Holiness wear the black, red-trimmed cassock and a purple sash. "It has been an almost inviable practice that no appointments to honorary papal titles are conferred without the recommendation or at least the endorsement, of the recipient's Ordinary and/or the Ordinary of the place."[4] This has been the case for nearly a century; nevertheless, individuals who are in service in the Curia or in the papal diplomatic service receive this honor, traditionally, at the direct behest of the department or mission chief. Of course, the cleric's ordinary is always consulted in these matters. The various degrees of the honorary prelature should never be sought out by any cleric. On the other hand, persons to whom this honor has been conferred should never refuse it. "Normally, appointment to prelatial rank is made by a rescript from the Vatican Secretariat of State, the validity of which does not depend on the designee's willingness to accept. In view of current canonical legislation, it would seem that the appointment cannot be renounced since it is purely a personal favor."[5]

The prelatial title is not only a personal honor conferred upon the recipient, but it is also an honorary position within the Papal Household, bonding the recipient to the pope himself, who alone is

---

* Refer to *Benedictio Sacerdotalium Indultorum* for the traditional formula, if desired.

the font of honor of the Church. Therefore, individuals who have been singled out for this distinction, either because of their individual service to the Church or because of the esteem of the local ordinary for their worthiness to receive it, have no rights to decline the honor. Likewise, a recipient of a papal award has no right to flaunt the privileges associated with that honor or neglect them in any fashion.

Simultaneously, a person to whom one of these titles has been conferred must always carry this honor with the dignity and decorum associated with it, as it is not only a gift of great personal esteem from the Holy Father, but also an honor that brings recognition to the Church and faithful of the recipient's diocese and parish. Any papal award, but most significantly one of the clerical awards, is part of a centuries-old tradition within the Church to which relatively few have ever been singled out. Proper care to live accordingly, as is also the mandate for a lay honoree, requires an understanding of the history and traditions of the prelatial title, as well as of the privileges and responsibilities that the award carries. It must always be remembered by papal honorees, both lay and ecclesiastical, that, for whatever reason the award may have been conferred, the recipient has been singled out by Rome as an exemplary example of his vocation of life within the Church, and that individual must always live up to the Church's trust in him.

NONPAPAL AWARDS: AN OFFICIAL GUIDE FOR WEARING OTHER DECORATIONS

Oftentimes, priests are the recipients of honors, awards, and decorations of nations or chivalric orders as a reward for their service to the Church Universal. As such, they may accept these non-Vatican honors under the terms and conditions discussed below. Each diocesan bishop, however, has

certain prerogatives that could negate general custom and practice.

- The clergy are entitled to both accept and to wear decorations and orders of knighthood that are legally offered to them. It is customary for them to seek the permission of either their ordinary, superior, or Curia superior prior to any acceptance of a non-Vatican honor.

- Members of the papal diplomatic corps, as well as Curia appointees, are most likely to be given nonreligious foreign orders. These orders should be accepted in accordance with the policies of the Secretariat of State and of the civil government of the honoree, as some governments do not permit their citizens to accept foreign decorations without formal governmental permission.

- Religious decorations, other than those bestowed directly by the Holy See, are frequently granted to the clergy. These are most prominently the Order of Malta and the Order of the Holy Sepulchre. Guidelines for acceptance of these orders are outlined in the application process for each order.

- Care should be given to follow the customs and traditions of the order involved. Proper care should also be given to the proper placement of the order's insignia on the vesture of priests and prelates.

The following guidelines are provided for persons who are permitted to wear on their vesture an award or decoration that has been legally granted them.

Abito Piano
(The Simar and Ferraiolo)
- The miniature decoration should be arranged on a decoration bar, along with all other awards,

which should be worn on the left side of the chest or on the left cape of the simar.

- The star, or *placca,* if awarded as part of the decoration, should be placed on the proper side (traditionally the left side of the chest) and above the *fascia,* or sash. Usually the clergy wear only one order's star at a time, although laymen may wear three at once.

- If the class of Grand Cross, which requires a sash to be worn over the chest, has been awarded, the prelate should forgo the sash and wear the star only, although the miniature of that order would also be worn on the decoration bar.

- The neck ribbon of a bailiff of the Order of Malta may be worn over the simar and below the collar of the *ferraiolo,* but it must never take the place of the pectoral cross. It may also be worn over the scarlet choir cassock and *mozzetta* (purple for bishops) when attending functions at the order's headquarters.

Cappa Magna

- The star, or *placca,* may be worn on the *cappa magna* on the upper-left breast. Miniatures are never worn on the *cappa magna.*

- The neck ribbon of the Order of Malta and the collar of the Holy Sepulchre may be worn over the *cappa magna* at the neck for persons awarded these honors.

Crocia

- In present times, only the prelates of the Rota make use of the *crocia;* however, they may wear their awards at functions that require "decorations" and that would, at the same time, require use of the *crocia.*

- The star of any order may be worn on the upper chest. Papal awards such as the Pro-Ecclesia et Pontifice and the Benemerenti should be worn full size. Although miniatures of these awards have recently been seen for the first time, these are not orders, but decorations, and as such should be worn in the style in which they were awarded (full size).

Choir Dress

- No orders should be worn with the choir dress of prelates; however, the collar of a bailiff of the Order of Malta as well as its star *(placca)* may be worn at the order's functions, as may the insignia of the Order of the Holy Sepulchre.

As papal honors for the laity reach throughout the world and extend to every diocese, post-nominal initials (the legal abbreviation for each class of papal decoration) need some clarification so that an understanding of these abbreviations is uniform. In the accompanying chart, the reader will find the presently accepted post-nominal initials for Church honors for the laity.

AN OFFICIAL GUIDE TO POST-NOMINAL INITIALS

Papal Honors: Laity

The Supreme Order of Christ (Grand Collar)	G.C.O.C
The Order of the Golden Spur (Grand Collar)	G.C.G.S.
The Order of Pope Pius IX	
• Golden Collar	G.C.P.
• Knight Grand Cross	K.G.C.P.
• Knight Commander	K.C.P.
• Knight	K.P.
The Order of St. Gregory the Great	
• Grand Cross	G.C.St.G.G.
• Knight Commander with Star	K.C.St.G.G.
• Knight Commander without Star	K.C.St.G.G.
• Knight	K.St.G.G.
The Order of Pope St. Sylvester	
• Grand Cross	G.C.S.S.
• Knight Commander with Star	K.C.S.S.
• Knight Commander without Star	K.C.S.S.
• Knight	K.S.S.
Cross Pro-Ecclesia et Pontifice	P.E.P.
Benemerenti Medal	B.M.
Lateran Cross	none
The Golden Rose	none
Gentlemen of His Holiness	Gent di S.S.
Pontifical Academician	P. Acad.
Stewards of St. Peter	none

Papal Honors: Clergy

Protonotary Apostolic	
• de Numero	P.A.
• Supranumerary	P.A. Supra.
Prelates of Honor	none
Chaplains of His Holiness	none

Ecclesiastical Orders

The Equestrian Order of the Holy Sepulchre of Jerusalem	
• Knights of the Grand Collar	G.C.H.S.
• Knights Grand Cross	K.G.C.H.S.
• Knight Commanders with Star	K.C.*H.S.
• Knight Commander without Star	K.C.H.S.
• Knight	K.H.S.
The Sovereign Military Order of Malta	
• Grand Cross	G.C.M.
• Knight Commander	K.C.M.
• Knight	K.M.
The Order of Merit of Malta	
• Grand Collar of Merit	G.C.M.M.
• Grand Cross	K.G.C.M.M.
• Knight Commander	K.C.M.M.
• Knight	K.M.M.

Sovereign Military Hospitaller Order of St. John of Jerusalem, of Rhodes, and of Malta

There are few organizations in the world with as long a history rich in custom and tradition as the Sovereign Military Hospitaller Order of St. John of Jerusalem, of Rhodes, and of Malta. It is the oldest order of chivalry and predates the Crusades as a religious hospitaller fraternity.

HISTORY

The historians of the Order of Malta place its founding in A.D. 1070 at the time of the relief of the Holy City by the Christians. Its founder, Blessed Gerard, built a hospice for the Christian pilgrims in Jerusalem, naming it in honor of St. John the Baptist. A chapel was soon erected, and the community of religious men grew in support of the hospital complex.

On February 15, 1113, Pope Paschal II approved the legal status of the hospital, by papal bull, thus placing it under his personal care and protection. This papal bull established the independence of the order by granting to the confraternity's members the right to elect the successor to Blessed Gerard. It further guaranteed that the hospital would remain independent of all ecclesiastical authority other than the pope. Paschal's immediate successor, but one, confirmed these privileges, as did successive pontificates.

Blessed Gerard was the first of the Grand Masters of Malta but was called simply "Rector" of the religious house and hospital that he had founded. The title Master of the Order of St. John of Jerusalem, as the order was then known, was used by Blessed Gerard's successor, Blessed Raymond du Puy, who later also assumed the title Grand Master.

In A.D. 1126, the order underwent its first major transformation. The religious brotherhood, in a call to its own defense, welcomed members who were not professed to religious life. The Muslims had renewed their attacks on the sites of Christian presence in the Holy Land, and pilgrims and religious communities suffered under Muslim cruelties. In response to this siege, the Order of St. John of Jerusalem transformed itself into both a "religious" and a "militarist" brotherhood. This act enhanced its prestige at the Western courts, which had been horrified by the brutality of the Muslim attacks and which responded by waging the first of the great holy wars, the Crusades.

Kings and princes of Europe showered funds and large tracts of land on the order. The number of recruits to the order's call was so great that the newly proclaimed "Grand Master" could not assimilate them into the community. The Order of St. John grew both in numbers and in territory to house them. Its presence was felt throughout the Holy Land. Great fortresses began to appear in defense of the order and Christianity. The number of "Knights of St. John" became so great that they became the first modern standing army in the West. The order maintained its own calvary, composed of local Christians, who took the name *turcopoles.* Together with the founding religious brothers, these fighting knights became the first order of chivalry with the mandate of defense of the Faith and service to the poor. Within twenty years of its founding, the hospital of the order in Jerusalem was caring for more than fifteen hundred pilgrims, soldiers, and sick religious.

Despite the efforts of the Crusaders, the Holy Land fell to the Muslims in A.D. 1187. The armies of Saladin killed 8th Grand Master Fra Roger des Moulins, and Jerusalem became an Islamic fiefdom. The once mighty Latin Kingdom of Jerusalem was reduced to the acreage surrounding the city of St. John d'Acre. By A.D. 1291, the Christian presence throughout the Holy Land was extinguished.

The Order of St. John reestablished itself on Cyprus, at Limesol, and entered into its second transformation. It became a great naval power. Out of necessity, the order continued the fight against the Muslims, but the conflict shifted to the Mediterranean off the coasts of Lebanon and northern Palestine. The order utilized the treasures it had been given earlier to create a mighty naval power. The Greek island of Rodhos (Rhodes), until now the possession of the Islamic Turks, was seized, and in A.D. 1310 became the home of the Order of St. John of Jerusalem and Rhodes under the grand mastership of Fra Fulk de Villaret. The order now had substantial territory of its own. It constructed a beautiful villa complex to serve as its headquarters and as a hospital. It covered almost a single acre and was the first new hospital of the modern age.

The order became sovereign of Rhodes and its predominately Greek populace. It also became a wealthy entity in its own right, as it was located in a strategic position on the eastern Mediterranean trading routes. It minted its own silver coins and opened diplomatic missions at the courts of Europe. The red banner with white Maltese cross became a sovereign flag, no longer the simple banner of an order of chivalry. The Knights of St. John were now more commonly called "of Rhodes."

The order did not forget its mission in defense of the Faith and service to the poor and continued to fight the Islamic raiders throughout the eastern Mediterranean. It also continued to maintain its strong ties to the Church of Rome. With the development of nations in Europe came nationalistic pride. At the same time, the order's growth necessitated a reorganization from within, with leadership at the national or regional level. The order recognized national jurisdictions known as "Langues" or "Tongues." These Langues were first created in A.D. 1302 and continue today as Priories, Grand Priories, and National Associations.

It was also during this period that the "auberge" developed. The concept of living in community was not new, but it became more of a necessity for the knights on Rhodes. A grouping of several auberges in a geographic area became known as a "convent," or a religious community, which is the predecessor of the "convent" of the Grand Magistral Palace.

With the Crusades behind them and a sense of balance and calm pervading through the order, a formula for admittance into the order began to develop. The leading families of Europe began to send their sons to the prestigious Order of St. John at Rhodes to be educated and to come into manhood within the order. A candidate for knighthood entered the order as a youth, serving as a page to one of its officials. Several years within the convent followed, where the art of war was mastered; however, the religious life of the young postulants was never overlooked. Each convent had a spiritual director who strenuously protected the young men's spirituality. Medical training was also provided to assure that the knights could not only defend, but provide succor as well.

The relative tranquility of the order's life came to an end in A.D. 1522, when Suleiman the Magnificent laid siege to Rhodes. The order was outnumbered thirty-three to one, but withstood the siege for six months. When all hope of victory waned, 44th Grand Master Fra Philippe de Villers surrendered Rhodes to the invading forces. In recognition of the great position the order held, the Grand Master was permitted to enter exile with the wealth and archives of the order in tact. The Grand Master applied the name "Convent of the Fleet" to the order when in exile. This title recalls the duality of the order, both military and religious; in reality the order became a stateless state.

After eight years at sea, the Habsburg emperor Charles V ceded the Maltese islands to the order in full sovereignty. They had belonged to the southern Italian state of Sicily, which made up part of the emperor's Spanish domains. Three months following this grant, a former knight, Pope Clement VII, officially recognized the order's sovereignty over Malta and referred to them for the first time as the "Knights of Malta."

For four months in 1565, the order faced the great siege of Malta, in which the Turkish empire attacked with a force of fifty thousand soldiers and slaves. Unlike the siege of Rhodes forty years before, the Knights of Malta were properly prepared to defend their fortifications on the harbor. An estimated thirty-six thousand Turks were killed, and much of their fleet sank off the coast of what was to become Malta's capital, Valetta, named for the defending Grand Master Jean de la Valette-Parisot (1494–1568).

The order continued to grow and to build, and the beautiful hospital of Rhodes was overshadowed by a great modern complex constructed at Malta. According to the official history of the Order of Malta, the sick knights were henceforth served on silver salvers befitting their position as "our lords the sick" and as victorious soldiers for the Faith. The Order of Malta moved into the modern world.

The Grand Master held the position of an international figure of great import, and honors were showered upon him. In A.D. 1620 the Holy Roman Emperor, the leading figure of his day, granted the 55th Grand Master the title Prince of the Empire with the qualification of "Serene Highness." The Holy See, in recognition of five hundred years of service to the Faith, accorded the Grand Master the precedence of a cardinal of the Church with the qualification of "Most Eminent Highness." This precedence and appellation is still reserved for the Grand Master of Malta.

In the ensuing centuries, the power of the order declined as, initially, Protestantism, and, later, revolution, flourished. The order lost influence in some states altogether. On his way to Egypt in 1798, Napoleon I attacked the islands of Malta. The order was devastated, and the Grand Master fled with only the relic of the right hand of St. John the Baptist. The order was once again stateless. Of all the possible defenders of the order's rights, the oddest of these was the orthodox Russian tsar, Paul I, who not only claimed protectorship of the order but sovereignty of the islands, which would provide the Russian empire with a Mediterranean port for its growing fleet.

The tsar deposed the authentic Grand Master (Ferdinand von Hompeasch) and declared himself the new Grand Master. The Holy See refused to recognize the tsar's illegitimate act. The legacy of the Order's sojourn in orthodox Russia is the flourishing of orthodox orders of St. John, which sprang from this odd twist in the order's history and are active today. Numerous Protestant groups under the name of Hospitallers of St. John arose in defiance of the tsar's actions, more out of political motives than chivalric or charitable ones; many of these groups exist today. The Order of Malta does not recognize most of these groups and views many as spurious.

Finally resettling in Italy, first in Ferrara and later in Rome, where a wealthy professed knight bequeathed his palace to the order, the Knights of Malta found their final home. Strong in faith and conviction, it remains both the smallest state in Europe and a symbol of Christian charity and chivalry.

GOVERNMENT

The Order of Malta is a sovereign power and is recognized as an independent nation-state by many nations in the world community. As such, despite its territorial limitations, the Sovereign Military Order of Malta (S.M.O.M.) is governed by a traditional European constitution based on the Napoleonic Code. Within the Order, the constitution is referred to as "the code," which stipulates the activities of the order in relation to the Church and to foreign governments and which aids in the formulation of internal policy, reflecting the traditions of its nine-hundred-year history. Although comprehensive, the code is surprisingly brief, consisting of twenty-two general articles. It is through edicts of the Grand Master and the Supreme Council that interpretation of this code brings the order into modern life.

The government of the S.M.O.M. is headed by the elected Prince Grand Master, who bears the style "Most Eminent Highness" and the precedence of a cardinal of the Church in regard to rank and protocol. His official title in Latin is *Dei gratia Sacrae Domus Hospitalis Sancti Johannis Hierosolymitani et Militaris Ordinis Sancti Sepulchre Dominici Magister humilis pauperumque Jesu Christi Custos.* He is elected in conclave by members of the Council Complete of State. As in all governments, the Grand Master is assisted by officials of the order who have been granted a portfolio, or official position, within the government of the order. These officials, along with the Grand Master, form the Sovereign Council of the Order of Malta. The highest of these officials are the grand commander, the grand chancellor, the hospitaller, and the receiver of the common treasure. Assisting the Grand Master on general affairs are those officials named as "councilors." Always professed knights, these councilors are always resident in Rome and play a formidable role in the daily affairs of the order worldwide.

To accomplish its programs abroad, as well as to maintain its sovereign status, the Order of Malta maintains both an active and a passive diplomatic apparatus. Prominent nation-states have posted senior diplomats to the order's headquarters in Rome and receive, in return, fully accredited ambassadors of the Prince Grand Master. The order issues its own passports, which are most commonly issued for specific diplomatic missions of the order's officials rather than ordinary use.

VESTURE

The habit of the Order of Malta is of ancient origin, dating from A.D. 1125, when it was ordained as the official garb of the brother-knights by Blessed Raymond de Podio (a Frenchman of the House of du Puy) who served as "master" and "rector" (later as first Grand Master) of the order from A.D. 1125 to 1158. It was of black wool and had the eight-pointed white cross on the left breast which symbolized the eight Beatitudes, which were to become the constitution of chivalric life. It later became known as the Maltese cross in honor of the order that first adopted it.

The habit has seen only a few changes through the centuries. In modern times, it is known as the *cuculla,* and it remains as it first appeared in A.D. 1125, except for the addition of white silk cuffs and a cowl, which originally served as a hood to bar the elements in bad weather. The *cuculla* is worn loose and full and does not make use of a cincture to bind it.

The *cuculla* is also referred to in Italian as the *abito da chiesa,* which can be loosely translated as "church, or choir, habit." It is worn by the knights when they are participating in the religious life of the order. Although the *cuculla* remains basically a religious habit, due to the duality of the nature of the order, religious and chivalric, modern knights are permitted to ornament their habits with the collar of their individual ranks in the order. The insignia of the cross is to be worn suspended by the embroidered cloth collar and is worn outside and below the cowl.

The national Langues, or subdivisions, are permitted to emblazon their habits with the Maltese cross that is most representative of their regional associations. For this reason, at international gatherings of the order, one sees the cross with the fleur-de-lis of France between each arm of the cross or the double-headed eagle of the Austrian association. Although these adaptations are permitted throughout the insignia of the order and take their legitimacy from the ancient principles of heraldry, they are regulated by the Grand Magistry to assure legitimacy.

In A.D. 1248, the reigning pontiff, Innocent IV, authorized the fighting knights to lay aside the religious habit and vest in a military tunic. The tunic has seen many adaptations through history, always mirroring the military garb of the times. The Malta tunic originated in the mantle, or cape, which is still in use today. As the need for armor disappeared, the tunic developed into a more customized uniform. The mantle was retained, but the black tunic became a symbol of a member's fidelity to the order and to the defense of Christianity. On its breast was emblazoned the white Maltese cross. In A.D. 1259 Pope Alexander IV ordered the tunic's color to be changed to scarlet, which was to reflect (in the same way as the scarlet worn by the College of Cardinals) that the order's members would be called to shed their blood in the defense of the Faith. It remains red to this day. The present tunic is a modernization of the Napoleonic period's uniform.

The Malta tunic varies in degree from simplicity to quite ornate, depending on the rank of the individual and the category of his membership within the order. It is, however, only in adornment that the uniform differs. From the simple Knight to the Grand Master, the uniform is the same. The Malta uniform consists of a tunic of red or scarlet merlino (wool) and dark blue trousers. For the category of Magistral Grace, the cuffs and facings (lapels), along with the collar, are of black velvet, and the tunic is closed by twelve gold buttons emblazoned with the Maltese cross. The trousers are ornamented with a gold-braid stripe, bordered on each side by a red stripe. The belt is embroidered with lace spun of pure gold threads in the motif of the Crown of

Thorns or of filigree. Epaulets of gold, a cocked hat, and an enameled, engraved sword complete the uniform. Within each category of the order's membership, as one progresses in grade, the uniform receives further ornamentation. The exact specifications are set forth by the master of ceremonies for the Grand Magistry and are well known to the tailors throughout Rome.*

The more senior categories of membership (of Justice and of Obedience) forgo the facings in black velvet and adapt either white silk or elaborate gold braiding, depending on their individual class and rank. The tunic of the Prince Grand Master is entirely of scarlet wool and gold embroidery in the motif of the Crown of Thorns and the insignia of the order.

The mantle of the Order of Malta, mandated by Pope Innocent II in A.D. 1130, remains nearly as it did nine hundred years ago. With its large white cross on the left breast, it has become the most recognizable symbol of the Order of Malta. It calls to mind the commitment of the order to Christian charity and chivalry. It is made of black wool and may have a black velvet collar. Its facings (opened lapels) and its lining are of black silk, and it is fastened by a gold chain and two buttons emblazoned with the Maltese cross.

There are presently three classes of the Order of Malta. The Knights of Justice must make monastic vows of poverty, chastity, and obedience and pledge to live a life of service, whereas the Knights and Dames of Honor and Devotion must provide, as must Knights of Justice, a proof of nobility and, additionally, pledge to adhere to the monastic vows as they can best be applied to their individual secular lives. Finally, the class of Knights and Dames of Magistral Grace makes up the majority of the order's members worldwide and does not demand the commitment of vows upon its members.

INSIGNIA

The Collar of the Grand Master is a chain of gold with nine red medallions, on each a red shield with the white eight-pointed cross of the order, symbolizing the eight Beatitudes. Suspended from the chain is the white Maltese cross.

The insignia of a professed bailiff consists of a black ribbon of simple cloth, known as a *gorgerin,* with a white Maltese cross suspended from it. The sash is worn from the right shoulder and rests on the left hip, where a Maltese cross is suspended from a stylized bow. The Grand Cross of a professed bailiff is a neck ribbon embroidered with a motif of the Crown of Thorns in gold (the motif of the Crown of Thorns is reserved for the division of Justice). Suspended from it is a full military trophy with the shield of the order emblazoned on it. Suspended from this is the white Maltese cross below a gold Grand Magistral crown.

The insignia of a Knight Grand Cross of Obedience is of black cloth from which is suspended a gold filigree crown, below which hangs the white Maltese cross. The Knight of Obedience wears his insignia suspended from a neck ribbon of black silk, with the insignia suspended from a full military trophy.

The Knights of Honor and Devotion wear their insignia suspended from a black watered-silk ribbon. Below a half trophy with a shield, helmet, and crossed swords are suspended the filigree crown and the cross of the order. The Knight Grand Cross of Grace and Devotion has a ribbon of black watered silk with a central white watered-silk stripe. It is worn from the right shoulder to the left hip and has suspended from it a Grand Magistral crown and the

---

* Barbiconi, the Roman clerical-attire house, is at present perhaps the most adept in manufacturing these historic uniforms.

order's cross. The Grand Cross of a Knight of Grace and Devotion is similar to that of the Grand Cross of Justice in that it is suspended from an embroidered ribbon worn at the neck. The embroidery is of gold but less ornamental than the motif of the Crown of Thorns, reserved for the category of Justice. The insignia is suspended from a half trophy and the filigree crown.

The insignia of the Knight Grand Cross of Magistral Grace is suspended from a black watered-silk sash, with a central red watered-silk stripe worn from the right shoulder to the left hip. Suspended from it are a shield and Grand Magistral crown above the Maltese cross. The Grand Cross of Magistral Grace is identical to the Grand Cross of a Knight of Grace and Devotion except that the insignia is suspended from a shield rather than the half trophy.

ORDER OF MERIT OF MALTA

The Order of Merit of the Order of Malta was established by Prince Grand Master Galleazzo von Thun und Hohenstein in 1916. It may be awarded to members and nonmembers alike and may also be bestowed upon non-Catholics.

The Collar, or Chain, of Heads of State is bestowed personally by the Prince Grand Master to special sovereigns and heads of state whom the order wishes to honor. It comprises a gold interlocking chain with three alternating motifs. Two of the three motifs are filigree in design; the third is the Meritorious cross in miniature. The chain's two segments join in the center at a shield of the order in red and white enamel. Suspended from the shield is a gold Grand Magistral crown, below which hangs the white gold-trimmed meritorious cross (similar in design to the Cross Moline). The Chain or Collar of the Heads of State is also awarded with the star *(placca),* which has eight rays. The top ray of the star is surmounted by a gold Grand Magistral

crown. The center of the star is worked in white enamel with the motto MIL. ORD. EQUITUM MELIT BENE MERITI (well meriting the Military Order of the Knights of Malta), in gold, surrounding the inner circle of red enamel, on which is mounted the white Meritorious cross.

There are five classes of the Order of Merit. The special Civil Class for Gentlemen is suspended from a white watered-silk ribbon with red and white edges. The Military Class of Merit is of red watered silk with white and red edges; two crossed swords are mounted behind the insignia to mark it as a military distinction. The Class of Merit for Ladies is identical to that of the civil award for gentlemen but is in the appropriate scale for ladies. In this class, the junior grades are suspended from a bow, as is the traditional custom for female honorees.

DEATH AND BURIAL OF THE GRAND MASTER

Like the simplest of men, the Prince Grand Master of Malta makes his journey from life to death alone, having been given the comfort of the sacraments and the benediction of the Holy Roman Church. The rites that follow reflect the glories of his former position, and the simplicity of death is forgotten in the pomp of the burial of a prince.

The official life of the order comes to a halt, but, just as life across the Tiber within the Vatican walls appears serene after the death of a pope, it is only an impression of serenity. Just as life within the Church becomes frantic at the moment of the death of a pontiff, so too it does when his servant, the Prince Grand Master of Malta, passes from this life. For a brief while following the death of the Grand Master, the Grand Magistral Palace becomes the focus of the world's gaze.

The responsibility of announcing the death of the Grand Master falls to the lieutenant of the Grand Master (a post held by a professed knight of

62.

63.

PAX IN VIRTUTE

MAGNUS MAGISTER
ORDINIS EQUESTRIS S.SEPULCRI HIEROSOLYMITANI

64.

65.

Pax Per Obedientiam

66.

67A.

68A.

67B.

68B.

69A.

70A.

69B.

70B.

71A.

72.

71B.

73.

74.

75.

76.

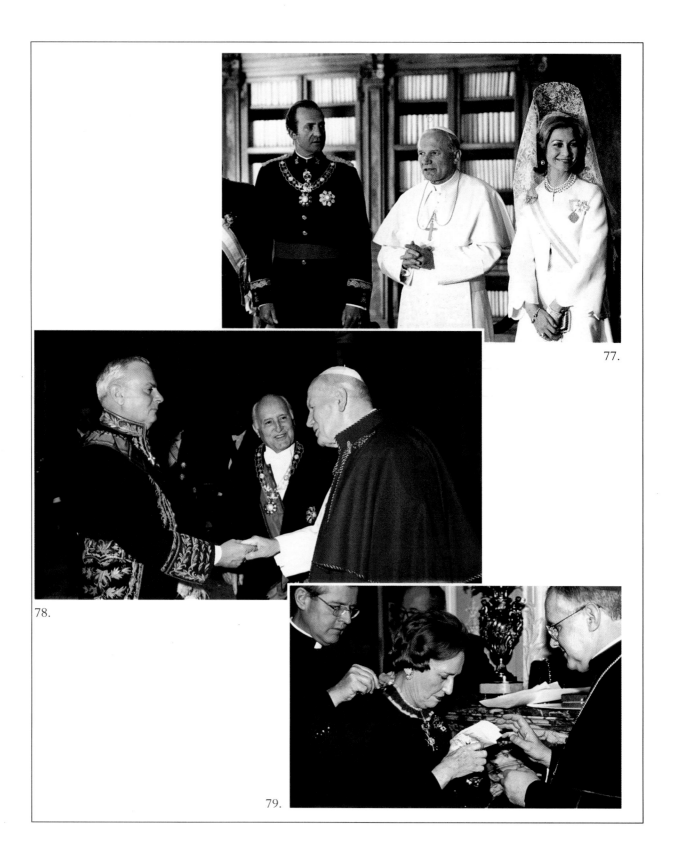

77.

78.

79.

80.

81.

82.

83.

84.

85.

86.

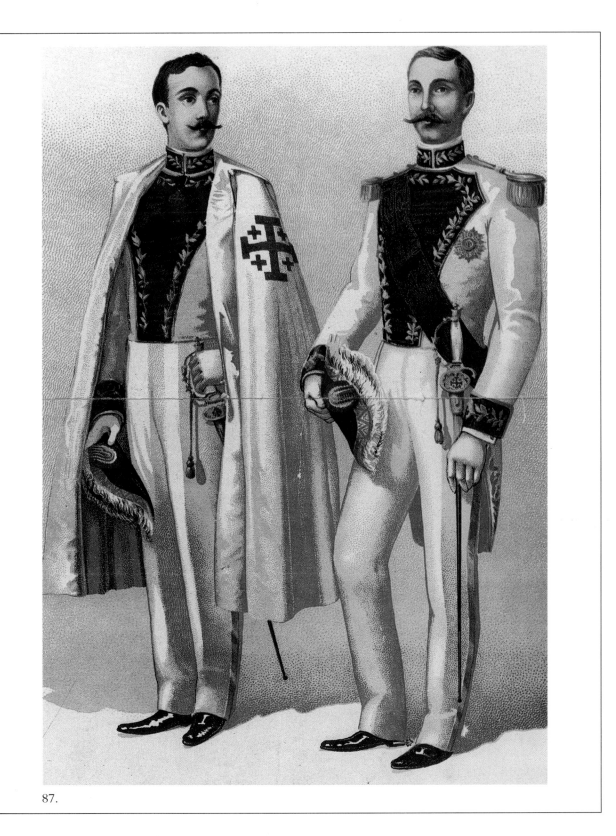

87.

88a.

88b.

89.

the highest repute), the master of ceremonies of the Grand Magistry, and the Sovereign Council of Professed Knights, who are responsible for the governing of the order during the interregnum.

The first to be informed of the death is the cardinal-patronus, who, in turn, informs the Holy Father and the Cardinal–Secretary of State. The news is announced to the jurisdictions of the order, to the diplomatic corps accredited to the Grand Magistral Palace, and to the world. The interregnum begins, and the ancient formula of preparing for the Grand Master's burial overtakes the Aventine and the via Condotti. All senior officials of the order are summoned to Rome. The lieutenant assumes temporal authority of the order in the name of the Council Complete of State.

In the sanctuary of the Chapel of Santa Maria del Prioria, the body is laid in a wooden coffin lined with scarlet and white satin, the colors of the Order of Malta. It is dressed, not as a prince with the splendor of the red tunic and a display of the pontifical, royal, or civil decorations awarded in life, but as a simple professed brother in the black woolen habit of the order. In his hands is placed a simple wooden rosary.

The open coffin is placed before the altar on a black carpet, upon which is embroidered a skull and crossbones at each corner. A Paschal candle is positioned at the head of the coffin. The throne of the Grand Master, given a place of honor under a crimson satin *baldachino* emblazoned with the arms of the dead Grand Master, is turned to face the wall, symbolizing the vacancy of the grand mastership.

Those knights assembled in Rome gather at the Chapel of Santa Maria del Prioria on the Aventine for the first of the rites of burial. The cardinal-patronus (who, at the time of the death of 77th Grand Master Fra Angelo de Mojana was Sebastian Cardinal Baggio),* and as the Camerlengo of the Holy Church, vested in the white satin pontifical

mitre (mitre damasco) and the black cope embroidered with symbols of the order, intones the prayers for the repose of the soul of the dead prince. All knights present are in the black habit of the order, with no outward sign of dignity or wealth. Suspended from their backs and permitted to drape around the hips and over the left forearm is the great stole of the Order of Malta, resembling both the maniple of ancient vestments and a large monastic rosary, symbolizing the Passion of Christ. It is worn to recall the need to give atonement for our earthly failings. Known officially in Italian as the *manipule,* it bears symbolic reference and reminder to the betrayal, passion, and death of Our Lord. Emblazoned on embroidered panels throughout the 1.6 meter long stole appear, respectively, a cloth bag of silver coins received as the price Judas extracted for Christ; a *coq,* or rooster, representing the three-times denial by Peter; three dice representing the casting of lots for Our Lord's robe; and a column representing the scourging at the pillar. These representations remind the professed bailiff and knight of the deep suffering and humiliation of the Savior. The knights now enter the chapel in silence.

At the same time, via Condotti is flooded with acknowledgments of bereavement from heads of state and chiefs of government. Chiefs of diplomatic missions, resident in Rome, come to sign the book of condolences on behalf of their governments. Telegrams from cardinals and archbishops and from the order's jurisdictions arrive within hours of the Prince's passing.

The first message to arrive is the chirograph of the pope, followed by telegrams from the Cardinal-Secretary of State and from the cardinal-grand master of the Equestrian Order of the Holy Sepulchre of Jerusalem. In 1988, at the death of the 77th

---

* Cardinal Baggio died in April 1993, and was replaced by Pio Cardinal Laghi as patronus.

Grand Master, telegrams arrived the first day from the kings of Belgium and Spain, the presidents of Italy, France, Ireland, Austria, and Brazil; the sovereign prince of Monaco; and from the royal families of the Two Sicilies, Savoy, Habsburg, and Bragança. In all, nearly one hundred nations offered condolences to the lieutenant of the Grand Master, the Sovereign Council, and the order at large, illustrating its esteem and importance in the modern world.

After the semiformal farewell on the Aventine, the coffin is sealed. Six candles, joined together in two sets of three and bound by black cords, are placed beside it to symbolize the lighting of the way ahead. The lieutenant welcomes those present and receives the first of the personal condolences. The body is solemnly transferred to one of the great Roman churches. In 1988, the funeral rites were celebrated at the Church of the Twelve Apostles in the piazza of the same name.

In contrast to the monastic silence on the Aventine, the body processes in dignity and pomp surrounded by the professed knights of the order. In the choir of the sanctuary are seated all the cardinals of the Church residing in Rome. They wear the scarlet vesture, the *mozzetta,* cassock, and *biretta,* for they, more than others, have been called to shed their blood for the Faith. In life, the Grand Master ranks just after the cardinal-deacons of the Church in precedence.

Joining the cardinal-patronus is the Cardinal-Secretary of State; together they celebrate the Mass of Resurrection. Each of the papal orders, as well as the other great Catholic orders, are represented, each bearing the magnificent colors on their uniforms and mantles. Most of the Catholic royal families send representatives; many are members of the Order of Malta. In deep contrast to the solemnity of the previous rites, the knights are permitted their scarlet tunics and badges of rank. The brilliance of color in the red and gold vestments of the celebrants and the scarlet of the Sacred College is enhanced by the spectrum of colors that fills the magnificent basilica.

From the medieval city of Sienna, halberdiers, wearing the medieval costume of multicolored velvet and satin with plumed caps and pantaloons, are posted as an honor guard throughout the church, each carrying a banner of the order. The Mass is solemn and dignified, befitting the state burial of a prince.

After the Mass, but before the private burial, the Cardinal-Secretary greets the family of the deceased Grand Master, as well as the senior dignitaries present in the church. For a period of thirty days following the burial, Gregorian Masses are offered for the soul of the dead Prince. Once the funeral rites are finally concluded, the order prepares for the election of its new Grand Master.

CONCLAVE AND ELECTION

The electors are called to the Aventine for the election of the new Prince Grand Master of Malta at a time agreed upon, previously, by the Holy See. Gathered in the chapel owned by the Grand Magistral Palace are the professed knight-electors. Their number is restricted to the lieutenant of the Grand Master (or, if he is deceased or incapacitated, by the lieutenant "ad interim"), the professed knights of the Sovereign Council, the prelate of the order, the professed priors and grand priors, the professed bailiffs, two professed representatives of each priory and grand priory, the regents of the subpriories, the representatives of the national associations according to the constitution of the order, and other dignitaries permitted by the Holy See in accord with the General Chapter of the Order.

All knights are vested in the simple black *cuculla* as required by the directives of the program—forwarded on to each by the master of ceremonies—

which stipulates *abito da chiesa*. The Aventine conclave, as in the conclave called to elect a pope, begins with a Mass of the Holy Spirit, invoking the Third Person of God to guide them in a just and honorable election. The prelate of the order, traditionally an archbishop, is chief celebrant of the Mass. The cardinal-patronus is present in choir (hearing Mass in the sanctuary on a throne and priedieu). The procession begins with the *Veni Creator* as the knights take their place in the Chapel of Santa Maria del Prioria. At its conclusion, the professed brother-knights process, two by two, out into the square of the chapel, preceded by a knight carrying the banner of the sovereign order.

The procession continues into the Hall of Deliberations within the Aventine Palace. As in the Vatican during conclave, the chamber is sealed to the outside world; only the knight-electors and the two prelates are permitted inside. Each participant must take the oath of secrecy, and, under the terms of articles 198 and 208 of the Code, the mandate of election is then verified.

On each side of the great hall, floor-to-ceiling windows overlook the palace gardens. In the center of this ornate room is a large table capable of seating all the electors. At the 1988 election, thirty-four electors were present. The table is covered in red cloth, on which a large white Maltese cross is embroidered every several meters. At the far end of the table stands a wooden crucifix, reminding the knights of their oath and their allegiance to the Church of Christ. At the opposite end of the table, a smaller table is placed under a crimson *baldachino,* at which preside the cardinal-patronus and the lieutenant of the Grand Master. It is covered in red watered silk, the material reserved for cardinals. To the left of this table is placed an easel, upon which hangs the portrait of the deceased Grand Master draped in red velvet. Behind it is the banner of the order, which had been carried in procession from the Chapel of Santa Maria. To the right is a smaller table, at which sit the grand chancellor of the order and his assistant. They serve as the *scrutatori* of the election.

At each place there is a red Moroccan-leather ink blotter and a matching nameplate. After everyone has taken his place, the lieutenant rises to read the instructions of the Sovereign Pontiff and of the Secretary of State. Procedures for the coming election are set forth, and the lieutenant presents his opening remarks in Italian. Article 209 of the Code requires each knight-elector to make a Profession of Faith and to vote by individual conscience and in total secrecy. Ballots are distributed to each of the electors. Voting is by secret ballot, as in the papal election. Each knight rises, in turn, and having inscribed the name of the knight whom he believes to be the most worthy of election, places his folded ballot in a chalice set upon a credence table at the end of the Hall of Deliberations.*

If the election is successful on the first ballot, the morning's events could be completed in fewer than six hours. The *scrutatori* verify the tally and announce either election or default. Once a new Grand Master has been elected, the lieutenant of the Grand Master rises. Approaching his newly elected Prince, the lieutenant asks, in Italian: *Accetto l'elezione a Principe e Gran Maestro del Sovrano Militare Ordine Gerosolemitano di Malta?†* If accepted, the lieutenant and the grand chancellor lead the new Grand Master to the table under the *baldachino.* When the applause has subsided, the cardinal-patronus issues the oath to the new Grand Master of Malta. Placing his hand on the open Bible, with his back to the knight-electors but facing the cardinal-patronus who represents the person of the Holy

---

* Election requires a majority of two thirds plus one.
† Translation: Do you accept election as Prince Grand Master of the Soverign Military Order of St. John of Jerusalem, Rhodes, and Malta?

Father, the Grand Master pronounces the oath of office. His signature is applied to the document of election, and he assumes the place next to the cardinal under the *baldachino.*

A small leather case is brought forward. In it is the Collar of the Grand Master, designed and manufactured in Vienna at the beginning of this century, for Galleazzo von Thun und Hohenstein, 75th Grand Master. It consists of a long gold chain with nine red enamel medallions. Upon each is the white eight-pointed Maltese cross, symbolizing the eight Beatitudes. Suspended from the chain is the simple white Maltese cross.

After the new Grand Master is invested with the Grand Magistral collar, the symbol of his authority over the order, the knights come forward, each in turn, to offer their congratulations and to swear their fidelity. The election does not become official, however, until it has been ratified by the Sovereign Pontiff. The results of the election are carried to him personally by the cardinal-patronus. The election of 1988 was rapidly approved by Pope John Paul II.

The election completed, the Grand Master, his council, and household call on the Holy Father at the Vatican. Following this audience, the new Grand Master receives the diplomatic corps and the dignitaries who call at the Aventine in full uniform with decorations or in their national costumes. A Mass of Thanksgiving is sung at the chapel in the Villa Malta. The throne, which was reversed at the time of death of his predecessor, is now placed in the position of honor for the new Grand Master.

His arms replace his predecessor's and now hang below a crown and mantle under the crimson *baldachino.* The first official reception of the reign of the new Prince Grand Master of Malta follows. Once again life returns to normal, and the Sovereign Order of St. John of Jerusalem, of Rhodes, and of Malta returns to its works of charity throughout the world.

INVESTITURE CEREMONIES

The ceremonies of the investiture of Knights and Ladies of the Sovereign Order vary from one national association to another, each incorporating the liturgical tradition of the local church, while maintaining the thousand-year history of the ceremonies of the sovereign order. The investiture ceremonies at the Grand Magistral Palace are, of course, the most elaborate, as they are orchestrated in the beautiful surroundings of the order's headquarters, with the Prince Grand Master performing the ancient rituals of installation. In the United States, as in other national associations, the ceremonies reflect the personality of the people of that region. As such, the American associations each reflect a more democratic style of ceremonial. Presented below is a sample program as it was used by the National Association in 1984.[*]

---

[*] A ceremony of investiture, as prescribed for modern ceremonies by the Grand Magistral Palace, follows that of the customary American Investiture Ceremony, provided herewith.

CEREMONIAL OF THE SOLEMN INVESTITURE
VOTIVE MASS OF ST. JOHN THE BAPTIST

(UNITED STATES CUSTOM)

This Mass commemorates the church and hospice in Jerusalem that were home to the knights before and during the crusades. Both church and hospice were dedicated to St. John the Baptist.

ENTRANCE HYMN

> O God, our help in ages past,
>   Our hope for years to come,
> Our shelter from the stormy blast
>   And our eternal home.
>
> Under the shadow of Thy throne
>   Thy saints have dwelt secure
> Sufficient is Thine arm alone
>   And our defense is sure.
>
> Before the hills in order stood,
>   Or earth received her frame,
> From everlasting Thou art God,
>   To endless years the same.
>
> A thousand ages in Thy sight
>   Are like an evening gone;
> Short as the watch that ends the night
>   Before the rising sun.
>
> Time, like an ever-rolling stream,
>   Bears all its sons away;
> They fly, forgotten, as a dream
>   Dies at the op'ning day.
>
> O God, our help in ages past,
>   Our hope for years to come,
> Be Thou our guide while life shall last,
>   And our eternal home.

PENITENTIAL RITE

GLORIA

OPENING PRAYER

God our Father, You raised up John the Baptist to prepare a perfect people for Christ the Lord. Give Your Church joy in spirit and guide those who believe in You into the way of salvation and peace. We ask this through our Lord Jesus Christ, Your Son, who lives and reigns with You and the Holy Spirit, one God, for ever and ever.

All: Amen.

LITURGY OF THE WORD

FIRST READING (1:4–10)

A reading from the book of the prophet Jeremiah

The word of the Lord came to me thus:
"Before I formed you in the womb I knew you,
    before you were born I dedicated you,
    a prophet to the nations I appointed you,"
"Ah, Lord God!" I said,
    "I know not how to speak; I am too young."

But the Lord answered me, "Say not, 'I am too young.'
    To whomever I send you, you shall go;
    whatever I command you, you shall speak
    Have no fear before them, because I am
    with you to deliver you," says the Lord.

Then the Lord extended his hand and touched my mouth,
    saying, "See, I place my words in your mouth!
    This day I set you over nations and over kingdoms,
    To root up and to tear down, to destroy
    and to demolish, to build and to plant."

The Word of the Lord.

RESPONSORIAL PSALM (71:1–2, 3–4, 5–6, 15, 17)

℟. Since my mother's womb, You have been my strength.
    In You, O Lord, I take refuge;
        let me never be put to shame.

In Your justice rescue me, and deliver me;
incline Your ear to me, and save me.

SECOND READING (1:8-12)

A reading from the first letter of Peter

It is true you have never seen Jesus Christ, but in the present age you believe in Him without seeing Him, and rejoice with inexpressible joy touched with glory because you are achieving faith's goal, your salvation. This is the salvation which the prophets carefully searched out and examined. They prophesied a divine favor that was destined to be yours. They investigated the times and the circumstances which the Spirit of Christ within them was pointing to, for He predicted the sufferings destined for Christ and the glories that would follow. They knew by revelation that they were providing, not for themselves but for you, what has now been proclaimed to you by those who preach the gospel to you in the power of the Holy Spirit sent from Heaven. Into these matters angels long to search.

The Word of the Lord.

GOSPEL (1:5–17)

ALLELUIA

A reading from the Holy Gospel according to Luke

In the days of Herod, king of Judea, there was a priest named Zechariah of the priestly class of Abijah; his wife was a descendant of Aaron named Elizabeth. Both were just in the eyes of God, blamelessly following all the commandments and ordinances of the Lord. They were childless, for Elizabeth was sterile; moreover, both were advanced in years.

Once, when it was the turn of Zechariah's class and he was fulfilling his functions as a priest before God, it fell to him by lot according to priestly usage to enter the sanctuary of the Lord and offer incense. While the full assembly of people was praying outside at the incense hour, an angel of the Lord appeared to him, standing at the right of the altar of incense. Zechariah was deeply disturbed upon seeing him, and overcome with fear.

The angel said to him: "Do not be frightened, Zechariah; your prayer has been heard. Your wife Elizabeth shall bear a son whom you shall name John. Joy and gladness will be yours, and many will rejoice at his birth; for he will be great in the eyes of the Lord. He will never drink wine or strong drink, and he will be filled with the Holy Spirit from his mother's womb. Many of the sons of Israel will he bring back to the Lord their God. God himself will go before him, in the spirit and power of Elijah, to turn the hearts of fathers to their children and the rebellious to the wisdom of the just, and to prepare for the Lord a people well-disposed."

The Gospel of the Lord.

Ceremonial for the Investiture of Knights in the Sovereign Military Order of Malta

After the Gospel, all remain standing for the singing of the hymn:

COME, HOLY GHOST

Come Holy Ghost, Creator blest
    And in our hearts take up Thy rest;
    Come with Thy grace and heavenly aid
    To fill the hearts which Thou hast made,
    To fill the hearts which Thou hast made.

O Comforter, to Thee we cry,
    Heavenly gift of God most high;
    Thou font of life and fire of love
    And sweet anointing from above,
    And sweet anointing from above.

Celebrant: Send forth Your Spirit and they shall be created.

All: And You shall renew the face of the earth.

Celebrant: Lord, hear my prayer.

All: And let my cry come to You.

Celebrant: The Lord be with you.

All: And also with you.

Celebrant: Let us pray.

O God, You have instructed the hearts of the faithful by the light of the Holy Spirit. Grant that through the same Holy Spirit we may always be truly wise and rejoice in His consolation. Through Christ our Lord.

All: Amen.

The Celebrant blesses the insignia of the Order.

Celebrant: Our help is the name of the Lord.

All: Who made Heaven and earth.

Celebrant: The Lord be with you.

All: And also with you.

Celebrant: Let us pray.

Almighty God and Father of us all, bless these Crosses of Malta that they may contribute to the sanctification of those whom they are to be given. May they be a reminder of faith, an inspiration to good works, and an aid in their salvation. May they be a comfort and a protection against all that is evil. Through Christ our Lord.

All: Amen.

The Celebrant sprinkles the emblems with holy water.

After the Oration, all are seated. The Master of Ceremonies reads the decree of the newly appointed Knights. Each Knight stands as his name is mentioned and remains standing.

At the conclusion of the reading, the Knight(s) kneel.

The Celebrant asks the Knight(s):
Do you accept this grant of Knighthood in the Order of Malta?

The Knight(s) answer:
(I) We do accept it.

The Celebrant:
Do you promise to be faithful to the noble purposes of the Order, to participate in its services, to have a special care for the poor, the needy and the sick, and to live as exemplary Catholics and true Knights of Malta?

The Knight(s) answer:
(I) We do so promise.

The Celebrant:
In virtue of the decree received and by the authority invested in me, I confer upon you the honor of Knighthood in the Order of Malta.

The Knight(s) enter the sanctuary. Each kneels while the Celebrant confers the Cross, the emblem of the Order.

The Celebrant:
> Accept this Cross and the call to apostolic service which it signifies, in the name of the Father, and of the Son, and of the Holy Spirit.

After receiving the Cross, each Knight responds:
> Amen.

LITURGY OF THE EUCHARIST

All remain seated and are led by the choir in singing:

> Faith of our fathers! living still
> In spite of dungeon, fire, and sword;
> Oh how our hearts beat high with joy
> When e'er we hear that glorious word:
>
> Faith of our fathers, holy faith
> We will be true to Thee till death.
>
> Faith of our fathers! Mary's prayers
> Shall win our country unto Thee;
> And through the truth that comes unto Thee;
> Our people shall be truly free;
>
> Faith of our fathers, holy faith
> We will be true to Thee till death.
>
> Faith of our fathers! We will love
> Both friend and foe in all our strife;
> And preach Thee, too, as love knows how,
> By kindly deeds and virtuous life:
>
> Faith of our fathers, holy faith
> We will be true to Thee till death.

THE EUCHARISTIC PRAYER

> *Celebrant:* Let us proclaim the mystery of faith.

> *All:* Lord, by Your cross and resurrection
> You have set us free.
> You are the Savior of the world.

During the distribution of Holy Communion, the choir sings hymns and motets. Toward the close of the distribution, all are led by the choir in singing:

O God of loveliness,
   O Lord of Heaven above,
How worthy to possess
   My heart's devoted love.
So sweet Your countenance,
   So gracious to behold,
That only glance were bliss untold.

You are blest Three in One,
   Yet undivided still;
You are the one alone
   Whose love my heart can fill.
The Heavens and earth below,
   Were fashioned by Your word;
How great You are, O holy Lord!

O Loveliness supreme,
   And beauty infinite!
O overflowing stream
   And ocean of delight!
O life by which I live,
   My truest life above,
I give You undivided love.

RECESSIONAL HYMN

Now thank we all our God,
   With heart, and hands, and voices,
Who wondrous things hath done,
   In whom His world rejoices;
Who from our mother's arms
   Hath blessed us on our way
With countless gifts of love,
   And still is ours today.

O may this bounteous God,
   Through all our life be near us!
With ever joyful hearts
   And blessed peace to cheer us;
And keep us in His grace,
   And guide us when perplexed

And free us from all ills
  In this world and the next.

All praise and thanks to God
  The Father now be given,
The Son and Him who reigns
  With them in highest Heaven,
Eternal, Triune God,
  Whom earth and Heaven adore;
For thus it was, is now,
  And shall be, evermore.

CEREMONIAL OF THE SOLEMN INVESTITURE

(ROMAN CUSTOM)

As Prescribed for Professed Knights by the Grand Magistral Palace, 1994.

THE BLESSING OF THE SWORD

The blessing of the sword by the priest is customarily carried out in community before Mass.

℣. Our help is in the name of the Lord.

℞. Who made Heaven and earth.

℣. Blessed be the name of the Lord.

℞. Now and for ever.

℣. O Lord, hear my prayer.

℞. And let my cry come unto Thee.

℣. The Lord be with you.

℞. And with your spirit.

Let us pray: O Lord, we beseech Thee, be pleased to bless this sword and this, Thy servant, N., who by Thy guidance wishes to take it up. Defend him with Thy righteousness, guard him with Thy power and keep him free from harm. Through Christ our Lord.

℞. Amen.

Then the sword is sprinkled with Holy Water and the Grand Master or his representative (M) says the following words to the Postulant (P), who kneels:

M.: Receive this sword in the name of the Father and of the Son and of the Holy Spirit. Use it to guard your own person, to defend the Church and to confound the enemies of the Cross of Christ and the Christian Faith. As far as human frailty allows, wound no man unjustly with it. For your sake may Christ Himself grant you this prayer; who lives and reigns with the Father and the Holy Spirit, one God, for ever and ever.

P.: Amen.

THE GIVING OF THE SWORD

The Postulant, wearing the Surcoat and having previously gone to Confession and (if he is unwilling to do so at Mass) Holy Communion, appears before the Grand Master or his representative, kneeling before the altar at which Mass will be said and holding a lighted candle symbolizing that Charity which every true Knight must always show. After the reading of the Epistle, the Postulant presents himself, without the candle, and kneels before the Grand Master or his representative.

M.: Noble sir, what do you ask?

P.: I ask, my Lord, to be counted and enrolled in the Order and company of the Knights of the Religion of St. John of Jerusalem.

M.: What you ask is of great import. It is by custom granted only to those who because of their ancient lineage and personal virtue are counted worthy to be enrolled in this way. This presents no obstacle, for we have received certain information as to your nobility, your virtues, and the honorable condition of your person. Accordingly, what you ask will be granted if you promise to keep those precepts which you will hear from us and chiefly if in your soul you are willing to be a defender of our Holy Church and of the Catholic Faith in all circumstances, even if danger to your own life is required of you in her service.

P.: I promise that with all my strength and at all times I shall apply myself to it.

M.: In the same way you shall strive never to desert the colors under which you will stand: for if you were to desert them, you would be expelled from this honorable Order in the greatest disgrace and infamy.

P.: I will strive to stand fast with all my strength.

M.: You must promise to have particular care and concern for those who are poor, dispossessed, orphaned, sick and suffering.

P.: I promise to do so, with the help of Almighty God.

The Grand Master or his representative gives the unsheathed sword to the Postulant.

M.: Since you have shown a ready will in all these matters which we have put to you, take this sword in your hand as the means to carry out the promises you have made, in the name of the Father and of the Son and of the Holy Spirit. With the help of God, you will be inflamed with hope, justice, and charity and you will bravely offer your spirit to God and your body to the dangers and toils of this world. In this way you will be able to defend the Poor and the Sick, and fight against all the enemies of the Catholic Faith. If, then, this is your intention, put your sword into its scabbard and take care that you do no harm to any innocent person.

The Grand Master or his representative gives the scabbard to the Postulant, who sheathes the sword and hands it back, receiving in return the belt, with which he girds himself.

M.: Chief among the virtues of a Knight of God is Chastity. This belt is to gird you from the outset and to put out the fire of the passions in you. May God give you the grace to remain in chastity throughout your life.

The Grand Master or his representative gives the sheathed sword to the Postulant, who fastens it onto his belt.

M.: It is not considered honorable among worthy Knights that they should always carry their sword in their hand. Hang your sword, then at your left side, so that with your right hand you may serve the Lord your God, His Immaculate Mother and St. John the Baptist, into whose Order you ask to be admitted.

The Postulant rises and gives the unsheathed sword to the Grand Master or his representative, who then strikes his left shoulder three times with the flat of the sword.

M.: Although this deed is one of great disgrace for noble men, it will recall to your mind that you have received these blows as your last humiliation.

The Grand Master or his representative gives the unsheathed sword to the Postulant, who brandishes it three times in the air as a symbolic threat to the enemies of the Faith.

M.: You must know that this your gesture of brandishing your sword three times indicates that in the name of the Most Holy Trinity you will challenge all enemies of the Catholic Faith in the hope of victory. May the Lord God always grant you the victory. Put the sword in its scabbard now, and keep it always pure and clean.

The Postulant wipes the sword against his left arm and sheathes it.

M.: The purity and spotlessness of the sword signify that it is the duty of a Knight to be pure and free from every vice and a lover of all the virtues, especially that of honor, which is ever in the company of the four Cardinal Virtues. With the help of Prudence, the first of the Cardinal Virtues, you shall bear in mind the past and the present and take thought for the future. With the help of the second, which is Justice, you shall dispose your public duties and your private interests, holding them in balance. With the help of the third, which is Fortitude, you shall show magnanimity on occasions worthy of a true and religious Knight. With the help of Temperance, the fourth, you shall so govern your senses and feelings as to become a very perfect, gentle Knight. With these four Virtues you shall ever seek honor.

The Grand Master or his representative shakes the shoulder of the Postulant and says:

M.: Never hesitate so to value and magnify these virtues, if you will, that they may earn you honor and recognition from other men. Arise now above your sloth and vices and be vigilant in the virtues of which we have spoken, and particularly in the Faith of Christ, for Whose sake you shall do all in your power to oppose any man who wishes in any way to assail the Faith or offend against it.

The Grand Master or his representative gives the spurs to the Postulant and two Knights fasten them to his feet.

M.: Much might be said of the significance of these golden spurs. But now we shall say only this to you: just as instruments such as these are used to quicken horses to vigor and swiftness, so you too must keep a spur in your heart to urge you toward the virtues and the service of God in all your enterprises and endeavors, to show the world that in your deeds you are a stranger to greed and that you place but little value upon gold—as witness the humble place where you wear it. These spurs, in accordance with their true purpose, are worn on the lowest part of the body, that is the feet, as a reminder that you should hold gold always in contempt and never allow any greed or avarice to corrupt you throughout your life.

The Postulant takes the lighted candle and goes to the altar.

M.: Receive this candle and go with the grace of the Holy Spirit to hear the Word of God.

THE CEREMONY OF CLOTHING

The ceremony of clothing takes place after Mass.

M.: What do you ask?

P.: I ask, my Lord, that I may be counted worthy to enter the Order of Brothers of the Holy Religion named after the Hospital of St. John of Jerusalem.

M.: We reply to you that what you ask is indeed of great moment and high importance. This favor is by custom granted only to men of many virtues, as you have recently heard. This is no obstacle to you; for we know that in love you are willing to perform works of mercy and that in charity you are willing to serve this Holy Religion of St. John of Jerusalem, which has been honored and rewarded by many Supreme Pontiffs and Catholic Princes with countless favors and privileges, enabling us by our own labors to work for the defense of the Holy Catholic Faith against the Infidel and against the enemies of the Christian Religion; to do our duty in the service of the Sick, the Poor, the Afflicted, the Dispossessed, and the Orphaned; and finally, by living in accordance with this rule of life, to earn the reward of life everlasting, which will most certainly be granted to you if you keep the precepts of the Lord your God, of your Holy Mother the Church of Rome and of our Religion, in which, as time passes, you will find easier the practice of self-denial and mortification of the flesh. If you bear in mind that you have chosen chastity for service of Religion, it will never be difficult or painful for you to resist any temptation. Tell me, then, in particular, whether you are ready to obey any Superior who may in future be appointed over you by the Grand Master and by this Holy Religion, having no regard for personal status, even if he be your inferior in his state of life; and tell me whether you are willing thus to give up your liberty.

P.: I am willing to give up liberty in this sense.

M.: You shall now inform us whether in the past you have thus given up liberty because you have been bound by vow to any other Religion or in any other way. You shall answer me sincerely and truthfully: are you a professed member of any other Religion?

P.: No, my Lord.

M.: Have you now any matrimonial obligations?

P.: No, my Lord.

M.: Have you any obligations to other men, either of personal security or of significant debt?

P.: No, my Lord.

M.: Take heed, sir Knight: if anything of what you have denied in our presence is later proved to the contrary, then with great shame your Habit will be stripped from you and you will be expelled from our Order in disgrace. However, assuming the truth of your declarations, in accordance with the form of our Constitutions we accept you as a member of our Order.

An acolyte presents a Missal to the Grand Master or his representative, opened at the beginning of the Canon. The Postulant, placing both hands on the Crucifix, makes his Profession:

P.: I, N., VOW AND PROMISE TO GOD ALMIGHTY, TO THE BLESSED MARY, THE EVER-VIRGIN MOTHER OF GOD, AND TO ST. JOHN THE BAPTIST THAT WITH THE PERPETUAL HELP OF GOD I WILL OBSERVE TRUE OBEDIENCE TO ANY SUPERIOR WHO WILL BE APPOINTED OVER ME BY OUR SACRED RELIGION AND BY OUR MOST EMINENT GRAND MASTER. I ALSO VOW AND PROMISE THAT I WILL LIVE HENCEFORTH IN POVERTY AND CHASTITY.

The Grand Master or his representative gives the Accolade to the Postulant.

M.: I NOW ACKNOWLEDGE YOU AND TRULY COUNT YOU AS ONE OF OUR BROTHERS.

P.: I, too, so consider myself, by the grace of the Lord our God and the favor of our Most Eminent Prince and Grand Master.

M.: From this day forth, with all your relatives, you will have a share in every Indulgence and Grace which has in the past been granted to this Holy Religion by the Holy Apostolic See.

An Acolyte presents the Missal to the Grand Master or his representative.

M.: As your first act of obedience, will you take this Missal to the Altar and then bring it back to me here?

The Postulant rises and, as an act of obedience, takes the Missal to the altar and then brings it back to the Grand Master or his representative, who gives it to the Acolyte. The Postulant then kneels.

> M.: As your second act of obedience and as your chief obligation, by virtue of your devotion, you shall recite daily the Office of the Blessed Virgin Mary, or the Office of the Dead, or five Decades of the Holy Rosary.

The Grand Master or his representative shows the Habit to the Postulant.

> M.: This is our Habit, in the form of the garment of camel-hair which our Patron, St. John the Baptist, wore in the desert for his severe penance. Therefore you shall strive to wear it as a penance for your sins, bearing in mind that from this time until the end of your life you must follow the virtues.

The Master of Ceremonies presents the Habit to the Grand Master or his representative.

> M.: The sleeves of this Habit are not only to bind your arms but to remind you of your true obedience to our Holy Religion and to urge you to the defense of the Poor and the Sick. Remember this often!

The Grand Master or his representative shows the Postulant the Cross displayed on the Habit.

> M.: This is the sign of the True Cross. We commend it to you. Wear it always on your left side, over your heart, so that you may defend it with your right hand, keeping ever in your heart its shape of eight points, which stand for the Beatitudes, which we seek to deserve through our own endeavors and the grace of God.

The Master of Ceremonies places the Habit on the Postulant and presents the Stole to the Grand Master or his representative, who returns it to him. He then places into the hands of the Grand Master or his representative, one by one, the mysteries of the Passion depicted on the Stole.

> M.: We show you this Stole to remind you of the bitter Passion of our Lord Jesus Christ, who suffered on the Cross for us. Remember often the Cords with which our Lord was bound; these were the Whips with which He was bound and fiercely scourged; these were the Dice; this was the Sponge; and finally, this was the Cross on which our Lord Jesus Christ suffered for our sins. Let these be your traveler's guide and standard in all your endeavors throughout your life.

The Grand Master or his representative places the Stole on the neck of the Postulant and the Master of Ceremonies adjusts it.

M.: This is your yoke, which, in the words of our Redeemer, is sweet and light. May it lead you to eternal life, if you bear it with the patience and charity which are expected of you as a true Brother of Religion and an honored Knight. May our Lord grant you this grace in this world and give you the reward of eternal glory in the next.

ORATIO EQUITUM
(PRAYER OF THE ORDER)

Domine Jesu, qui me Militiae Equitum Sancti Ioannis Hierosolymitani participem fieri dignatus es, Te humiliter deprecor ut Beata Maria Virgine a Filermo, Sancto Ioanne Baptista cunctisque Sanctis intercedentibus, ad sacra Ordinis nostri instituta servanda benigne me adiuves.

Religionem Catholicam, Apostolicam, Romanam firmiter colam ac adversus impietatem strenue defendam.

Caritatem erga proximum, praesertim erga pauperes atque infirmos, diligenter exerceam.

Concede mihi virtutes, quibus indigeo, ut ad Evangelii normam haec pia vota ad maiorem Dei gloriam, totius mundi pacem nostrique Ordinis profectum, mei immemor animoque penitus Christiano, valeam implere.

ENGLISH TRANSLATION

Lord Jesus, Thou hast seen fit to enlist me for Thy service among the Knights of St. John of Jerusalem. I humbly entreat Thee, through the intercession of the Most Holy Virgin of Philermo, of St. John the Baptist and all the Saints, to keep me faithful to the traditions of our Order.

Be it mine to practice and defend the Catholic, the Apostolic, the Roman Faith against the enemies of religion.

Be it mine to practice charity toward my neighbors, especially the poor and sick.

Give me the strength I need to carry out this my resolve, learning ever from Thy holy Gospel a spirit of deep and generous Christian devotion, striving ever to promote God's glory the world's peace and all that may benefit the Order of St. John of Jerusalem.

THE RITE OF OBEDIENCE
IN THE SOVEREIGN MILITARY ORDER OF MALTA

Before the Promise of Obedience is made, the Candidate shall receive the Sacrament of Penance. Before the beginning of Mass, the Candidate (in Church Dress without scapular) shall enter the Church carrying a lighted candle in the left hand. On arrival, he sits in front of the Grand Master before whom one of the attendants shall carry the Book of Ceremonial. When the sign is given, the Candidate (C) kneels and replies to the questions of the Grand Master (GM). The English translation follows the Latin text.

G.M.: *Quid petis?*
(What do you seek?)

C.: *Misericordiam Dei et habitum fratrum militum oboedientiae Sacrae Domus Hospitalis Sancti Ioannis in Ierusalem.*
(The mercy of God and the habit of a Knight of Obedience of the Order of St. John of Jerusalem, of Rhodes, and of Malta.)

G.M.: *Desiderium tuum grave est et magni momenti. Perfectionem christianam consequi vis et oboedientiam praestare legitimis tuis superioribus, sicut regula militum oboedientiae praescribit. Ideo rogo te: legisti regulam quam suscepturus es?*
(Your desire is a serious one and of great import. You seek to emulate Christian perfection and to promise obedience to your legitimate superiors as the Rule for Knights of Obedience prescribes. Therefore I ask you, have you read the Rule by which you now seek to live?)

C.: *Legi.*
(I have read it.)

G.M.: *Es igitur paratus in nomine Domini, ad promissionem?*
(Are you ready, therefore, in the name if God to make the Promise?)

C.: *In nomine Domini, ego, NN., paratus sum.*
(In the name of God, I, NN., am ready.)

G.M.: *Ad emittendam promissionem accede.*
(Therefore, you may make the Promise.)

C.: *Ego, NN., nomen Dei invocans promitto: observantiam, in fidelitate christiana quae militem decet, legum Supremi Militaris Ordinis Hospitalis*

Sancti Joannis in Ierusalem, Rhodiensis vel Melitensis nuncupati; institutionem vitae meae secundum regulam, praesertim adimplendo obligationes militis oboedientiae, ut sic christianam perfectionem consequar; oboedienriam debitam Sanctae Matri Ecclesiae, Eminentissimo Principi et Magno Magistro, et eius legitimis successoribus, fideliter et diligenter adimplendo superiorum mandata. Sic me Deus adiuvet, et Sanctissima Virgo de Philermo, et Sanctus Joannes Baptista, patronus noster, et omnes Sancti Ordinis nostri. Ego, NN., haec omnia promitto.

(I, NN., invoking the name of God promise: to observe in the Christian faith of a true Knight the Laws of the Sovereign Military Order of St. John of Jerusalem, of Rhodes, and of Malta; to regulate my life according to the Rules laid down, fulfilling in particular the obligations of a Knight of Obedience, thus striving after Christian perfection; to fulfil the obligations which l owe to the Church, to His Most Eminent Highness the Prince and Grand Master, and to all his legitimate Successors, and faithfully and diligently to carry out the orders which have been given to me by my superiors. To this end, my God be my help and the Most Holy Virgin of Philermo, St. John the Baptist, our glorious Patron, and all the Saints of the Order, I, NN., promise all this.)

There follows now the signature of the documents on a table placed on the right of the Grand Master's throne. Two witnesses stand to the right and left of this table. The Candidate carries the candle to his own place where the candle is put in a candlestick. Next, he proceeds to the above-mentioned table and signs the document, as do the witnesses. He then kneels before the G.M. and brings him the document. When this has been done, he stands again before the G.M., who says:

G.M.: *Quid ultra quaeris?*
    (What else do you seek?)

C.: *Quaero togam scapularem.*
    (I seek the scapular.)

With the help of an attendant, the Grand Master imposes the scapular and says:

G.M.: *In nomine Sanctae et Individuae Trinitatis, in nomine Beatissimae Mariae Virginis, in nomine Sancti Joannis Baptistae, accipe hoc signum in defensionem nominis Christi, in propagationem fidei; in servitium pauperum. Ad hunc finem damus tibi, Frater, hanc Crucem ut eam diligas ac defendas. Si contingat, ut in certamine pro Christo et Ecclesia eam deseras, Sacrum Signum a te auferetur et tu ipse tamquam indignus ex Ordine nostro dimitteris.*

(In the name of the Holy Trinity, in the name of the Blessed Virgin Mary, in the name of St. John the Baptist, receive this sign in defense of the name of Christ, in the propagation of the Faith, in the service of the poor. To this end, we give you, Brother, this Cross that defending it you may love it. If it should happen that in battle for Christ and His Church you abandon or lay down your arms, then according to the custom of the Order, the Holy Sign shall be taken from you and you yourself shall be dismissed from our Order as unworthy as the law demands.)

After the new Knight of Obedience has received the scapular, the Grand Master hands a Cross to him saying:

GM: *In nomine Sanctae et Individuae Trinitatis, iubeo te hanc crucem ostendere testibus promissionis tuae. Ita hoc signum tibi est gestandum "ut virtutes adnunties eius qui de tenebris te vocavit in admirabile lumen suum."* (1 Peter 2:9).

(In the name of the Most Holy Trinity, I order you to show the Cross to those who, by its manifestation, are made the witnesses of your promise. "Thus you should carry this sign in the world to proclaim the Glory of Him who has called you out of darkness into his marvelous light.") (1 Peter 2:9).

The new Knight of Obedience receives the Cross from the hands of the Grand Master and, holding the Cross with two hands in front of him, walks down the aisle. Returning to his place, he hands the Cross back to the Grand Master. The signed documents are placed on the Altar, where they remain until the end of the Mass.

All the national associations and tongues of the order have committed to the solemnity of the investiture ceremony. For this reason, the investiture is traditionally held at a cathedral in the presence of many of the hierarchy of the Church. Beautiful music and long processions mark the event. To be called to knighthood in a modern world is no easy task. It often means the symbolic shedding of blood because of the often abusive and violent attacks on the supportive posture of the order for the Church and its dogma by its members, and yet it is a great honor to the knight himself, his family, and to the local Church. He or she is accepting membership in an organization that has stood by the Church for more than one thousand years and that continues to stand by her side today.

Equestrian Order of the Holy Sepulchre of Jerusalem

"In the year 1070 Jerusalem was conquered by the Seljuk Turks who immediately suppressed Christianity and frequently captured, murdered, or sold into slavery Christian pilgrims on their journey to the Holy Sepulchre. Pope Urban II answered by preaching the first Crusade. Its success, in part, resulted from the great battle cry first uttered by him at Clermont in A.D. 1095— DEUS LO VULT, 'God wills it.' Though of ancient origin, the motto is ever alive and vibrant, for it inspires the Knights and Ladies of the Holy Sepulchre to crusade for equality of men, justice for all, and peace in the Holy Land so that Christian, Jew, and Muslim may live side by side in love of God and each other—'God wills it.' "[1]

HISTORY

The Equestrian Order of the Holy Sepulchre of Jerusalem can trace its origins to Godfrey de Bouillon of the first Crusade, who gathered around him a group of knights who were entrusted with the protection of the religious Chapter of Canons who were present at the Holy Sepulchre of Christ. For twenty years, these knights, and those who came to join their number, protected the Christian presence at the Holy Sepulchre, taking as their banner the red Jerusalem cross popularized by the crusading knights. By 1113, Pope Paschal II officially recognized their existence and purpose. It was not until 1122 that Pope Callistus II issued a *bulla* establishing them as a lay religious community with specific responsibilities of guarding the Basilica of the Holy Sepulchre and the city of Jerusalem in defense of Christianity against Muslim attack.

The Latin Kingdom of Jerusalem was established, and the knights of the Holy Sepulchre played an integral role in advancing peace in the territory. The Muslim attacks, however, did not cease, and defense of the Basilica of the Holy Sepulchre— which was built by the earliest knights of the order and still stands today, covering both the site of the crucifixion of Christ and His burial place—became impossible.

The earliest band of knights fled to the city of Acre, to the fortress of St. John, where they were received by other groups of besieged crusaders. They remained there from 1245 until the great fortress fell to the Muslims in 1291, ending the Latin Kingdom of Jerusalem. A diaspora then took place among the Christians in Palestine. Many of the knights of the Holy Sepulchre remained in the Mediterranean basin; others fled as far as France and

Spain. The works of the order continued as far away as Poland, where knights had settled and later their descendants continued in the spirit of the defense of Christianity.

The activity of the order, indeed its identity, in Palestine shifted from the knights, who returned to their own countries, to the religious Order of St. Francis, which had custody of the monastery of Mt. Zion. This group of Franciscans preserved the mission of the crusading knights of the Holy Sepulchre for centuries, mindful of the original *bulla* of appointment that entrusted the basilica, as well as the faithful, to the order's protection.

In 1330, Pope John XXII named the prior of the Franciscan house Custodian of the Order of the Holy Sepulchre. The custodian served as deputy to the pontiff, who reserved unto himself the governing authority of the order, and yet, the custodians, in all effect, were responsible for all aspects of the order's growth and governance, including the calling of new knights.

In 1489, Pope Innocent VIII desired to suppress the order and decreed that it was to be merged with the order of St. John (Malta). For seven years, the two lived an uneasy, yet peaceful, union. In 1496, Innocent's successor, Pope Alexander VI, recognized the folly of this uneasy merger and restored the Holy Sepulchre to independent status. Alexander VI decreed that the Order of the Holy Sepulchre would no longer be governed by the office of custodian and further decreed that the senior post of the order would henceforth be raised to the rank of Grand Master, reserving this title for himself and his successors of the See of Peter.

The darkest period of the order's history began shortly after the pontificate of Alexander VI, when little is recorded of its work or activity. Throughout this prolonged era, with the blessing of the Holy See, the Franciscans of the Holy Land continued to welcome into the order, under the emblem of the red Jerusalem cross, men of great faith and strength of character always willing to defend the faith, even to the shedding of their blood, and to death when necessary.

It was not until 1847, after four hundred years of vacancy, that the Latin Patriarchate of Jerusalem was restored and, with it, the order of the Holy Sepulchre rose from its dormancy, from a period of occasional growth to its revitalization under the pontificate of Pope Pius IX. The ecclesiastical superior of the order was then vested in the Latin Patriarch of Jerusalem, who eventually assumed the title Grand Prior. The office of Grand Master still remained vested in the papacy.

In keeping with the customs of the royal houses of Europe prevalent at that time, Pius IX undertook a restructuring of all papal honors, which included the restructuring of the order of the Holy Sepulchre so that it was more closely linked to the papacy and more formalized and uniform in structure. For twenty years, form 1847 to 1867, Pius IX fostered the growth of the order throughout Europe. He removed the requirement that a knight be invested in Jerusalem. He also encouraged a structure to form, with both an ecclesiastical and jurisdictional hierarchy, so that investiture and other works of the order could take place throughout the world.

Continuing to care for the rebirth of the order, Pius IX, in 1868, redefined the new classes or ranks of membership in the order, that of Grand Cross, Commander, and Knight. In 1888, Leo XIII permitted the Holy Sepulchre to confer membership upon ladies of "society and noble birth," the first international order so to do. Ladies were welcome in each of the classes of membership without prejudice. Actually, the first female member was the Contessa Maria Francesca di Tomas, who received the rank of Grand Cross in 1871, predating the "official" welcome of female members by seventeen years.

In an attempt to assert its own unique identity in the world, the membership of the Order of the Holy Sepulchre petitioned the Holy Father (Pius XI) to nullify the terms identifying the order as military and sacred, seeking a conferred sovereign status. The Holy See was neither prepared nor capable of doing so, as the order did not enjoy diplomatic sovereign status. Agreeing that the appellation "sacred and military" was commonly used by chivalric societies not closely linked to the Holy See, Pius XI conferred in their place the appellation "equestrian." At present, the full title of the order remains The Equestrian Order of the Holy Sepulchre of Jerusalem.

In the first few decades of the twentieth century, the senior leadership position of the order was held by the reigning pontiff. The offices of Grand Master, Protector, and Custodian were used interchangeably, albeit incorrectly, by historians and members alike, when referring to the Latin Patriarch's role in the governance of the order. During this period of time, Pius IX intended the title Grand Master to be reserved for the papacy, a political move that linked the order personally to the pope without the order becoming assimilated into the Holy See's own honors system. The role of Grand Prior, which had supplanted that of Custodian, was vested in the person of the restored Latin Patriarch of Jerusalem. Pope Pius X, in a post-*risorgimento* posture, inserted an additional level of administration into the order's structure as he was now in a self-imposed Vatican exile. The office of Cardinal-Protector was established to facilitate the order's work in and around Rome in lieu of the pontiff, who remained behind the Vatican walls.

In 1949, Eugene Pacelli, Pope Pius XII, restructured the order once again and relinquished for himself and his successors the title and post of Grand Master, vesting it in the person of a cardinal of the Church who assumed the title. The post of Cardinal-Protector, no longer necessary in a post–Lateran Concordat world, was placed in abeyance.

Pius XII additionally bestowed the ancient fifteenth-century palace of Giuliano Cardinal della Rovere, later Pope Julius II, as headquarters of the Equestrian order. Officially known as the *Palazzo dei Penitenzieri,* it was built by Julius's ancestor Domenico Cardinal Della Rovere between 1480 and 1490. It was built to resemble the much-admired Palazzo Venezia. It took its name from the Jesuits, who, after Julius's pontificate, occupied it as their Roman headquarters. As they were the penitentiaries (or confessors) at St. Peter's, the palazzo took that name. After the Lateran pacts were sealed, Mussolini attempted many gestures to warm relations with the new Vatican City State. One such gesture was the demolition of a width of 150 yards of the city of Rome, between the Square of St. Peter's and the Tiber River, known as the Borghi, in order to cut a broad boulevard, *à la Parisienne,* as a ceremonial entrance into the Vatican. Named via della Conciliazione* this new broad boulevard was created by demolishing hundreds of ancient buildings and palaces. After its completion, the new facade on either side of the new boulevard revealed that which was formerly well hidden: the palaces and shops of Renaissance Rome. One such "hidden" palace was that of Julius II, the Palazzo dei Penitenzieri. Today, it is best known as the Hotel Columbus, fronting the via della Conciliazone on the left as one prepares to enter St. Peter's Square. The headquarters of the order are housed in this palace, a part of which was set aside as a hotel to earn income for the order and to house pilgrim knights. The offices, chancellery, and residence of the Grand Master are housed here. The church of the order is the very small, ancient Chapel of St.

---

* Translation: Avenue of the Reconciliation (referring to the Lateran pacts).

Humphrey (S. Onofrio), under the care of the Franciscans of Mt. Zion, adjacent to the Bambino Gesù Hospital and the Pontifical North American College on the Janiculum Hill above the Vatican.

The new constitution of the order was promulgated by Pope Paul VI in 1977, and the order now enjoys protection under canon law. This constitution clearly sets forth the reasons for its continued existence:

> *The Order relives in a modern manner the spirit and ideal of the Crusades, with the arms of faith, of the apostolate, and of Christian charity. To this end the Order (a) fosters in its members the practice of the Christian life; (b) is zealous for the preservation and spread of the faith in Palestine; (c) champions the defense of the rights of the Catholic Church in the Holy Land, the cradle of the order.*[2]

The Equestrian Order has grown tremendously in defense of the Faith during the twentieth century. With a strong allegiance to the papacy, serving it as soldiers of Christ, the members of the order are linked to the Church in a unique way, carrying with membership in the order a responsibility of faithful witness, as well as the dignity of being in the service of the papacy.

"The Order now comprises five classes: Knights of the Collar, a rank established by Pius XII in 1949. There are twelve in number; Knights Grand Cross; Commanders with Star, who are also called Grand Officers, an honor given for special merit; Commanders; simply Knights."[3] Female honorees hold the same ranks or classes but are known as Dame or Lady of (rank), depending on the local custom. It is more correct, from a protocol posture, to refer to female members as Dames of (rank); however, local practices have established the customs for each jurisdiction.

Finally, unlike some chivalric orders whose membership is open to non-Catholics and even the papal orders of knighthood that admit non-Catholics and, in some cases, non-Christians alike, the Equestrian Order of the Holy Sepulchre is reserved solely for practicing Roman Catholics. It is precisely that faith that bonds them so closely to the Sovereign Pontiff. The investiture ceremony itself requires the pledge of defense of the Faith with a Profession of Faith, which, of course, only the Catholic faithful could undertake.

GRAND MASTER

At the present time, the order is governed by the much-loved Giuseppe Cardinal Caprio. His Eminence was appointed by Pope John Paul II as Grand Master in 1988. He has served the Church well through fifty years of service in the priesthood, including many years abroad in the papal diplomatic service, including nearly ten years in China. His Eminence held posts in the Secretariat of State under Popes Paul VI, John Paul I, and John Paul II and subsequently served as president of the Prefecture of Economic Affairs of the Holy See before retiring, at seventy-five, from active Curia service under the terms of canon 401.1. He was appointed to succeed Maximilian Cardinal de Furstenburg (1973–1988), who was also a prince of the German noble house that bears his name.

There have been two other cardinals who served as Grand Master of the Equestrian Order since the post was canonically established by Pope Pius XII. The first was Nicholas Cardinal Canali, who was succeeded by the famous Frenchman and Dean of the Sacred College Eugene Cardinal Tisserant. Cardinal Tisserant was legendary in the Vatican from the 1940s–1970s, when he held great power. He was a former WWI French paratrooper and was also the arch-nemesis of Mother Pascalina (*La popesa*) and of Vatican II. The cardinal was a force to be reckoned with and a famous figure in the twentieth-century Church.

GOVERNMENT

The Equestrian Order is governed, as are all parts of the Church, by a formalized, hierarchal structure. At its head is the Sovereign Pontiff, represented by the cardinal, who serves unto death from the date of his appointment as Grand Master.

The Grand Master is followed in rank by the Grand Prior, who is now always the Latin Patriarch of Jerusalem, and by the Assessor of the Order, who holds the title of archbishop and who traditionally serves in another Curia post within the Vatican. The most senior layman of the order holds the title Lieutenant General. The post is presently held by Prince Massimo-Lancellotti, who holds the rank Knight of the Collar. He is followed by the Governor General of the order, who is presently Count Carducci. Three vice governor generals follow in descending order, then the Chancellor, the Master of Ceremonies, and numerous members of the Grand Magistery, who tend to be appointed from large national jurisdictions from around the world.

Each nation has its own national jurisdiction, which is usually subdivided into smaller jurisdictions known as "Lieutenancies." Each Lieutenancy has a lieutenant who is elected or appointed by a senior Churchman of the area, usually one or more of the cardinals in the locality. The term is fixed. He is assisted by a governing council similar in structure to that of the Grand Magistery in Rome, allowing for local practice and custom to some extent. Investitures are held locally, although Grand Magistral investitures do take place annually as well.

INSIGNIA AND VESTURE

The insignia of the Equestrian Order is easily recognizable the world over. The use by the order of the blood-red Jerusalem cross of the early Crusaders has been continual since its adoption by Godfrey de Bouillon in A.D. 1071. It is the visible insignia of the order, marking it in a special, historic way. The mantle of the order, revived by Pius X, is the oldest link to the Crusaders, who originally adopted a creamy white woolen cape marked by a large red Jerusalem cross on the left breast. In 1888, a black silken mantle, with the red Jerusalem cross emblazoned in the same fashion, was adopted for the newly accepted women with the title Lady. The collar is of black velvet, and a mantilla of fine, long black lace in the Vatican and Spanish mode completes the official garb for the Ladies of the order. The Jerusalem cross predates Godfrey's adoption of it; in fact, it can be traced to Charlemagne in the year 800.[4] "It consists of five red and gold trimmed crosses, with a gallow cross in the center, inset at the intersections with four small Greek crosses, representing the five wounds of Christ."[5]

The mantle of knights in modern times varies from jurisdiction to jurisdiction; some are shorter than others, and some are bound differently than others, yet in style they are fundamentally the same: white for purity of intent in serving the Church; and the Jerusalem cross, red for the blood shed in former times by knights of the order in defense of the Faith and for a reminder that we are all called to the shedding of our blood for the defense of that Faith.

The knights make use of a chapeau as well. In all of Europe, except Spain, the chapeau is an extended military-style beret—black velvet and marked by the Jerusalem cross on the brow. In Spain, an ancient black *biretta* with white ostrich plumes is still in use. In the United States, some Lieutenancies make use of the black beret, whereas others do not, but protocol requires it to complete the official regalia of the order.

The vesture of the order also includes a uniform that is not seen much today but that still makes up a part of the order's official vesture. It is no longer obligatory but is nevertheless utilized by many jurisdictions of the order worldwide. The uniform is of white broadcloth, cut in the Napoleonic style of the nineteenth-century diplomatic habit, similar to those of the orders of the Holy See. The collars, cuffs, and facings are in rich black velvet, with embroideries and epaulets in thinly woven gold thread. The epaulets have the Jerusalem cross insignia worked into them, as do the buttons. The black velvet facings, or breast front, are embroidered more richly for the higher degree or rank of the members. The motif is of gold intertwined palm leaves, reminiscent of the palm used at Palm Sunday and Christ's triumphal entry into Jerusalem. That same motif is worked onto the white broadcloth on the borders of the tailcoat, on the lower-back region, and on the black-velvet cuff. The trousers are white, with gold military stripes on the outside. The uniform is completed by a sword, engraved with the Jerusalem cross in red enamel and gold, and the chapeau. The chapeau used with the uniform is the same as that of the papal orders in design; a black-velvet eighteenth-century naval ceremonial hat with white plumes and the red Jerusalem cross. The soft beret is worn only with mantle when vested in civilian or formal attire but never with the uniform.

The insignia of the order of the Holy Sepulchre has always remained simple, yet consistent, after 1847, with the other orders of the Holy See. The Jerusalem cross is the main theme, always worked in red enamel and trimmed with real gold. For gentlemen, the cross is suspended from a gold military trophy comprising an armor breastplate including a smaller red Jerusalem cross, helmet, plumes, and four unfurled banners on each side—all worked in gold. From the top of the helmet's plumes is a ring, on which the insignia is suspended from a black watered-silk ribbon. For Ladies, the cross suspends from a bow worked in red enamel, on which the insignia is suspended from a black watered-silk ribbon.

KNIGHTS OF THE COLLAR

The highest rank of the order is Knight of the Collar. There may be only eleven knights and the Grand Master at any one time. It is an honor held for life and is reserved for those of the highest esteem from within the order and from the world at large. The most recent vacancy, for example, occurred at the death of Baudouin of Belgium, who, although a member of the order, would be more commonly viewed as from "the world at large" because of his sovereign, royal status.

The insignia of this rank is the chain, or collar. Pius XII founded this new class of highest precedence in the order that took the name "collar." It can best be described as a red enamel Jerusalem cross suspended from a silver military trophy. On the cross itself is a golden medal with the image of Godfrey de Bouillon. Surrounding the cross, in a manner that encircles it entirely, are golden palm leaves, symbolic of the Palm of Jerusalem used to welcome Christ. The chain comprises six medallions of gold, on which are worked in red the Jerusalem cross. Between each medallion are two interlocking rectangular plaques: On the first is the word DEUS; on the second, the words LO VULT, the motto of the Equestrian Order.

A star (*placca*) accompanies this award. It is an eight-rayed star, often set in diamonds, otherwise worked in silver. A medallion of gold and enamel in the center reproduces the insignia with green palm leaves surrounding a red Jerusalem cross and the likeness of Godfrey de Bouillon in gold above it.

The insignia of Knights and Dames of the Grand Cross is identical to that of all the classes, as described above. The sole difference is the size of the insignia, which is two times the size of that of the other ranks. It is also suspended from the *cordon,* or black watered-silk ribbon, worn over the left shoulder, resting on the right hip. The star of the order is identical to that presented to members of the class of Knight of the Collar. Knight Commanders and Dame Commanders with star suspend their insignia from the black ribbon. For gentlemen as described above, the insignia is surmounted by a military trophy and is worn at the neck. For ladies, it is surmounted by a red enamel bow and is suspended from a larger bow of black watered silk and worn high on the left breast. The star for both is worn on the left side below the breast. Knight Commanders and Dame Commanders wear the same insignia as the Knight Commanders and Dame Commanders with star, but they are not entitled to the star, as this is a special award and class in itself.

Finally, the rank of Knight and Dame: The insignia of this class is worn on the left breast, gentlemen in military fashion and ladies with a much smaller black bow of watered silk to differentiate them from the higher class of award and membership.

ORDER OF MERIT

The Order of Merit class was established in 1949 by Cardinal Canali, the Grand Master, under the guidance of Pope Pius XII, to honor non-Catholics who would otherwise be excluded from the Equestrian Order. Originally of five classes, mirroring the structure of the order itself, the constitution of 1977 limited the award to three classes: the Cross of Merit, with the rank of Knight (Dame) Commander; the cross of Merit, with the rank of Silver Star or Grand Officer; and the Cross of Merit, with Gold Star or Knight (Dame) Grand Cross.

The insignia of this special award comprises a ribbon of equal stripes, four white and three red. The insignia itself is a red cross (gallow cross), similar in style to the Jerusalem cross without the four Greek crosses. Surmounted from the top by a golden Crown of Thorns, the insignia is suspended from the ribbon by a simple golden clasp.

The rank of Grand Cross and Knight (Dame) Commander are awarded with a star. For the rank of Grand Cross, the eight-rayed silver star is surmounted by the insignia in full size. For the rank of Knight (Dame) Commander, the insignia surmounted on the star is a smaller, more traditional size.

OTHER AWARDS

The Pilgrim's Shell (*Conchiglia del Pellegrino*) is recognized worldwide as the insignia of an individual who has made his or her way to Jerusalem to pray at the site of Christ's birth, crucifixion, death, burial, and resurrection. The shell is awarded by the Grand Prior, the Latin Patriarch of Jerusalem, who verifies to the headquarters in Rome that a knight or lady of the order has made the pilgrimage. The insignia is the traditional golden pilgrim's shell surmounted by a red enameled Jerusalem cross. The insignia has come to be commonly worn on the mantle at the center of the cross, although originally it was worn below the star on the lower breast, which is still proper.

The Jerusalem Palm (*Palma di Gerusalemme*) is the award of special service of the order. It comes in one class and is awarded to males and females alike who render a special act or service to the work of the order. It is suspended from a black watered-silk ribbon and is worn on the left breast.

The award of merit, the Holy Land Pilgrim's Cross, has been abolished under the Constitution of 1977; however, anyone who was awarded this honor prior to 1977 may continue to wear it at all functions of the Equestrian Order.

INVESTITURE CEREMONIES

The ceremonies of investiture of the order may take place in Rome or in the localities of the local jurisdictions so long as they are held with the appropriate respect for the tradition of the order and solemnity of the ceremony of investiture. The Grand Magistery is careful to permit local custom; however, there remains a set formula for investiture that is in keeping with both history and practices set in the Constitution of 1977. When the investiture is held in the local church, the see's cathedral should always be used.

When, on occasion, the Grand Master is presiding, the local clerical officials should either join him in concelebration or attend vested in choir. If the Grand Master is present, the honor falls to him, by right of his appointment by the pontiff as Grand Master of the order, to preside at the investiture ceremony and to personally invest each new knight and dame.

The following two programs are presented as fine examples of local investiture ceremony.*

---

* The United States custom has been provided by the gracious permission of the Eastern Lieutenancy of the United States. The Roman custom has been provided by gracious permission of the Office of the Grand Master and was formulated by a decree of the Sacred Congregation of Rites, which approved the norms of the Ceremonial of the Knights and the Ladies of the Holy Sepulchre of Jerusalem.

CEREMONIAL OF THE SOLEMN INVESTITURE

Minor changes have been made in an effort to bring the ceremonies into closer conformity with approved liturgical guidelines. Ceremonies of the Order vary in minor degree from nation to nation. At present, many investitures are conducted within the structure of the Holy Mass. When the investiture is to be conducted within the Mass, the following ceremonial should be closely followed.

VOTIVE MASS OF THE TRIUMPH OF THE CROSS
INVESTITURE WITHIN THE MASS

(UNITED STATES CUSTOM)

PRELUDE

Praeludium, Fugue, and Chaconne in C Major   D. Buxtehude

PROCESSIONAL HYMN: LIFT HIGH THE CROSS

Refrain:
Lift high the cross, the love of Christ proclaim
Till all the world adore His sacred name.

Come, Christians, follow where the Master trod,
Our King victorious, Christ, the Son of God. *(refrain)*

Led on their way by this triumphant sign,
The hosts of God in conquering combine. *(refrain)*

Each newborn follower of the Crucified
Bears on the brow the seal of Him who died. *(refrain)*

O Lord, once lifted on the glorious tree,
Your death has bought us life eternally. *(refrain)*

So shall our song of triumph ever be:
Praise to the Crucified for victory! *(refrain)*

PENITENTIAL RITE

GLORIA

Glory to God in the highest,
and peace to His people on earth.

Lord God, Heavenly King,
almighty God and Father,
    we worship You, we give You thanks
    we praise You for Your glory.

Lord Jesus Christ, only Son of the Father,
Lord God, Lamb of God,
You take away the sin of the world:
    have mercy on us:
You are seated at the right hand of the Father:
    receive our prayer.

For You alone are the Holy One,
You alone are the Lord,
You alone are the Most High,

    Jesus Christ,
    with the Holy Spirit,
    in the glory of God the Father, Amen.

OPENING PRAYER

Let us pray: God our Father, in obedience to You, Your only Son accepted
death on the cross for the salvation of mankind. We acknowledge the
mystery of the cross on earth. May we receive the gift of redemption
in Heaven. We ask this through our Lord Jesus Christ, Your Son, who
lives and reigns with You and the Holy Spirit, one God, forever and
ever.

All: Amen.

LITURGY OF THE WORD

FIRST READING (Num. 21:4–9)

A reading from the book of Numbers

> With their patience worn out by the journey, the people complained against God and Moses. "Why have you brought us up from Egypt to die in this desert, where there is no food or water? We are disgusted with this wretched food. In punishment the Lord sent among the people saraph serpents, which bit the people so that many of them died. Then the people came to Moses and said, "We have sinned in complaining against the Lord and you. Pray the Lord to take the serpents from us." So Moses prayed for the people, and the Lord said to Moses, "Make a saraph and mount it on a pole, and if anyone who has been bitten looks at it, he will recover." Moses accordingly made a bronze serpent and mounted it on a pole, and whenever anyone who had been bitten by a serpent looked at the bronze serpent, he recovered.

The Word of the Lord.

All: Thanks be to God.

RESPONSORIAL PSALM *(sung)*   Haig Mardirosian

Antiphon (Unison): Do not forget the works of the Lord.

Hearken, My people, to My teaching:
  incline your ears to the words of My mouth.
I will open My mouth in a parable,
  I will utter mysteries from of old.

Antiphon

While he slew them they sought him
  and inquired after God again.
Remembering that God was their rock
  and the Most High God, their Redeemer.

Antiphon

But they flattered him with their mouths
  and lied to him with their tongues,
Through their hearts were not steadfast toward Him,
nor were they faithful to His covenant.

Antiphon

Yet He, being merciful, forgave their sin
  and destroyed them not;
Often He turned back His anger
and let none of His wrath be roused.

Antiphon

SECOND READING (Phil. 2: 6–11)

A reading from the letter of Paul to the Philippians

Christ Jesus, though He was in the form of God,
    did not deem equality with God
    something to be grasped at.

Rather, He emptied Himself
    and took the form of a slave,
    being born in the likeness of men.

He was known to be of human estate
    and it was thus that He humbled himself,
    obediently accepting even death,
    death on a cross!

Because of this,
    God highly exalted Him
    and bestowed on Him the name
    above every other name,

So that at Jesus' name
    every knee must bend
    in the Heavens, on the earth,
    and under the earth,
    and every tongue proclaim
    to the glory of God the Father:
    JESUS CHRIST IS LORD!

The Word of the Lord.

All: Thanks be to God.

GOSPEL (John 3:13–17)

A reading from the Holy Gospel according to John

Jesus said to Nicodemus:

> "No one has gone up to Heaven
> except the One who came down from there—
> the Son of Man [Who is Heaven].
> Just as Moses lifted up the serpent in the desert,
> so must the Son of Man be lifted up,
> that all who believe
> may have eternal life in Him.
> Yes, God so loved the world
> that He gave His only Son,
> that whoever believes in Him may not die
> but may have eternal life.
> God did not send the Son into the world
> to condemn the world,
> but that the world might be saved through
> Him."

The Gospel of the Lord.

All: Praise to You, Lord Jesus Christ.

HOMILY *(All are seated.)*

After the Homily, all remain seated and are led by the choir in singing:

COME, HOLY GHOST

> Come Holy Ghost, Creator blest.
> And in our hearts take up Thy rest;
> Come with Thy grace and heav'nly aid.
> To fill the hearts which Thou hast made.
> To fill the hearts which Thou hast made.
>
> O Comforter, to Thee we cry.
> Thou heav'nly gift of God most high;
> Thou fount of life, and fire of love.
> And sweet anointing from above.
> And sweet anointing from above.
>
> O Holy Ghost, through Thee alone
> Know we the Father and the Son;
> Be this our firm unchanging creed.
> That Thou dost from them both proceed.
> That Thou dost from them both proceed.

Praise be the Lord, Father and Son.
And Holy Spirit with them one;
And may the Son on us bestow.
All gifts that from the Spirit flow.
All gifts that from the Spirit flow.

CEREMONIAL FOR THE INVESTITURE OF KNIGHTS AND LADIES IN THE EQUESTRIAN ORDER OF THE HOLY SEPULCHRE OF JERUSALEM

Celebrant: Send forth Thy Spirit and they shall be created:

All: And Thou shalt renew the face of the earth.

Celebrant: Let us pray.

O God, You have instructed the hearts of the faithful by
the light of the Holy Spirit. Grant that through the same
Holy Spirit we may always be truly wise and rejoice in
His consolation. Through Christ our Lord.

All: Amen.

The celebrant blesses the insignia of the Order.

Celebrant: Our help is in the name of the Lord.

All: Who made Heaven and earth.

Celebrant: The Lord be with you.

All: And also with you.

Celebrant: Let us pray.

Hear, we pray You, O Lord, our prayers and deign through the power
of Your majesty to bless these insignia of office. Protect Your
servants who desire to wear them, so that they may be strong to
guard the rights of the Church, and quick to defend and spread
the Christian faith. Through Christ our Lord.

All: Amen.

The celebrant sprinkles the emblems with holy water.

The Master of Ceremonies reads the decree of the newly appointed Knights and Ladies and of those promoted in rank. Each member stands as his or her name is mentioned and remains standing.

It is proper in preparing the program of ceremonies to list all honorees here by rank, lowest to highest. List Knights, followed by Ladies, followed by Priest Knights.

At the conclusion of the reading, The Knight(s) to be invested kneel(s). All others are seated.

> *Celebrant asks the Knight(s):*
> What do you ask?

> *The Knight(s) answer:*
> I ask to be invested as a Knight of the Holy Sepulchre.

> *Celebrant:*
> Today, being a Knight of the Holy Sepulchre means engaging in the battle for the Kingdom of Christ and for the extension of the Church; and undertaking works of charity with the same deep spirit of faith and love. Are you ready to follow this ideal throughout your life?

> *The Knight(s) answer:*
> I am.

> *Celebrant:*
> I remind you that if all men should consider themselves honored to practice virtue, so much the more should a soldier of Christ glory in being a Knight of Jesus Christ and use every means to show by his actions and virtues that he is deserving of the honor which is being conferred upon him and of the dignity with which he is invested. Are you prepared to promise to observe the Constitutions of this holy Order?

> *The Knight(s) answer:*
> With the grace of God I promise to observe, as a true soldier of Christ, the Commandments of God, the precepts of the Church, and the Constitutions of this holy Order.

> *Celebrant:*
> In virtue of the decree received, I appoint and declare you Soldiers and Knights of the Holy Sepulchre of Our Lord Jesus Christ. In the name of the Father, and of the Son, and of the Holy Spirit.

The Knight(s) enter the Sanctuary kneeling while the Celebrant confers the Jerusalem Cross, the emblem of the Order.

Celebrant:

Receive the Cross of Our Lord Jesus Christ for your protection and salvation, in the name of the Father, and of the Son, and of the Holy Spirit.

After receiving the Jerusalem Cross, each Knight responds:

Amen.

When all the Knights have returned to their seats, the Ladies to be invested kneel.

Celebrant asks the Ladies:

What do you ask?

The Ladies answer:

I ask to be invested as a Lady of the Holy Sepulchre.

Celebrant:

I remind you that if all women ought to consider themselves honored to practice Christian virtue, so much the more should a Lady of the Holy Sepulchre use every means to obtain Christian perfection and, by her actions and virtues, show herself worthy of the honor that she receives and the dignity with which she is invested.

The Ladies answer:

With the help of God, I promise to be faithful to the honor and responsibility of a Lady of the Holy Sepulchre.

Celebrant:

As Ladies of the Holy Sepulchre, try to imitate those holy women who followed our Lord; ministering to his daily needs, and then, with living faith and tears, kept vigil at His Holy Sepulchre. May your thoughts and deeds always be directed toward the Land of the Redeemer. Always aim to make His holy Name known and loved everywhere, so that you will merit the reward of the Risen Lord.

The Ladies:

This is my desire. May our Divine Savior, through the prayers of Our Blessed Lady, grant us the grace that we need.

Celebrant:

In virtue of the decree received, I pronounce and declare you Ladies of the Holy Sepulchre and commit to your care the Cross, which is the emblem of the protection of the Lord in this life and the pledge of future glory in eternity.

The Ladies enter the Sanctuary kneeling while the Celebrant confers the Jerusalem Cross, the emblem of the order.

Celebrant:

Receive the Cross of Our Lord, Jesus Christ for your protection and salvation in the name of the Father, and of the Son, and of the Holy Spirit.

After receiving the Jerusalem cross, each Lady responds:
Amen.

LITURGY OF THE EUCHARIST

OFFERTORY MOTET

Exultante Justi   L. Viadana

HOLY HOLY

Holy, holy, holy Lord. God of power and might, Heaven and earth are full of Your glory. Hosanna in the highest, Blest is He who comes in the name of the Lord. Hosanna in the highest.

MEMORIAL ACCLAMATION   R. Proulx

Christ has died. Christ is risen, Christ will come again.

GREAT AMEN   R. Proulx

LAMB OF GOD   R. Proulx

Lamb of God, You take away the sins of the world: have mercy on us. Lamb of God, You take away the sins of the world: have mercy on us. Lamb of God, You take away the sins of the world: grant us peace.

COMMUNION MOTET

Ego Sum Panis   J. Esquivel

COMMUNION HYMN: SHEPHERD OF SOULS

Shepherd of souls, refresh and bless
Your chosen pilgrim flock.
With manna in the wilderness,
With water from the rock.

We would not live by bread alone,
But by Your word of grace.
In strength of which we travel on.
To our abiding place.

Be known to us in breaking bread.
But do not then depart;
Savior, abide with us, and spread
Your table in our heart.

Lord, sup with us in love divine;
Your Body and Your Blood.
That living bread, that Heavenly wine
Be our immortal food.

CLOSING HYMN: NOW THANK WE ALL OUR GOD

Now thank we all our God
With hearts and hands and voices.
Who wondrous things has done,
In whom His world rejoices;
Who from our mothers' arms
Hath blessed us on our way
With countless gifts of love,
And still is ours today.

O may this gracious God
Through all our life be near us,
With ever joyful hearts
And blessed peace to cheer us;
Preserve us in His grace,
And guide us in distress,
And free us from all sin
Till Heaven we possess.

All praise and thanks to God
The Father now be given.
The Son, and Spirit blest,
Who reigns in highest Heaven,
Eternal, Triune God,
Whom earth and Heaven adore:
For this it was is now,
And shall be ever more.

CEREMONIAL OF INVESTITURE FOR THE EQUESTRIAN ORDER OF THE HOLY SEPULCHRE OF JERUSALEM

(ROMAN CUSTOM: HISTORIC)

The present Ceremonial, since it evidently in no way contradicts the decree of the Sacred Congregation of Rites, may properly be followed by the Equestrian Order of the Holy Sepulchre of Jerusalem in its own proper ritual, anything whatever to the contrary notwithstanding.

✠ Enrico Dante
Secretary of the Sacred Congregation of Rites
July 25, 1962

The Celebrant, assisted by the Ecclesiastical Master of Ceremonies, enters the Sanctuary and kneels for a moment of silent prayer. All present likewise kneel.

The Celebrant then begins the following hymn, which is continued by all present:

VENI CREATOR

Come, Holy Spirit, Creator blest,
And in our souls take up Your rest;
Come with Your grace and heavenly aid,
To fill the hearts which You have made.

O Comforter, to You we cry,
You, heavenly gift of God Most High,
You, fount of life and fire of love,
And sweet anointing from above.

You, in your sevenfold gifts are unknown;
You, finger of God's hand we own;
You, promise of the Father, You
Who do the tongue with power imbue.

Kindle our senses from above.
And make our hearts o'erflow with love;
With patience firm and virtue high
The weakness of our flesh supply.

Far from us drive the foe we dread,
And grant to us Your peace instead;
So shall we not, with You for guide,
Turn from the path of life aside.

Oh, may your grace on us bestow
The Father and the Son to know;
And You, through endless times confessed.
Of both the eternal Spirit blest.

Now to the Father and the Son,
Who rose from death, be glory given,
With You, O Holy Comforter,
Henceforth by all in earth and Heaven.
Amen.

℣. Send forth Your Spirit and they shall be created:

℟. And You shall renew the face of the earth.

℣. Lord, hear our prayers:

℟. And let our cry come unto You.

℣. The Lord be with you.

℟. And also with you.

Let us pray: God, who instructed the hearts of the faithful by the light of the Holy Spirit, guide us by Your Spirit to desire only what is good and so always to find joy in His comfort. This we ask through Christ Our Lord.

℟. Amen.

BLESSING OF DECORATIONS

℣. Our Help is the name of the Lord.

℟. Who made Heaven and earth.

℣. The Lord be with you.

℟. And also with you.

Let us pray: Hear, we pray, O Lord, our prayers and deign through the power of Your Majesty, to bless this insignia of the office, and protect these Your servants who desire to wear it, so that they may be strong to guard the rights of the Church and quick to defend and spread the Christian faith. This we ask through Christ Our Lord.

℞. Amen.

The celebrant sprinkles the emblems with holy water.

After the Oration, the M.C.s return to their places and the Celebrant occupies the chair placed on the altar platform. When the Celebrant gives the signal, the Knight Master of Ceremonies reads the decree of the newly appointed Knight. Toward the end of the reading, the newly appointed Knight* kneels on the lowest step of the altar, before the Celebrant, who asks him:

Celebrant:

What do you request?

Knight:

I desire to be invested a Knight of the Holy Sepulchre.

Celebrant:

I remind you, that if all men should consider themselves honored to practice virtue, so much the more must a soldier of Christ, who should glory in being a Knight of Jesus Christ, use every means never to sully his good name. Finally, he ought to show by his actions and virtues that he is deserving of the honor which is being conferred upon him and of the dignity with which he is invested. Are you prepared to promise by word and in truth to observe the constitutions of this holy military Order?

The Knight puts his folded hands into the hands of the Celebrant.

Knight:

I declare and promise by word and in truth to God Almighty, to Jesus Christ, His Son, to the Blessed Virgin Mary, to observe, as a true soldier of Christ, all that I have been charged to do.

The Celebrant then places his right hand on the head of the Knight.

Celebrant:

Be a faithful and brave soldier of Our Lord Jesus Christ, a Knight of His

---

*When there are to be invested more than one Knight, all are seated in the Church proper and kneel in unison for the Interrogation.

Holy Sepulchre, strong and courageous, so that one day you may be admitted to His heavenly court.

The Celebrant hands the golden spurs to the Knight saying (when used by a jurisdiction):

Celebrant:
Receive these spurs that are a symbol of your Order for the honor and defense of the Holy Sepulchre.

The Knight Master of Ceremonies hands the unsheathed sword to the Celebrant who, in turn, hands it to the newly appointed Knight.

M.C.:
Receive this sword that symbolizes the defense of the Holy Church of God and the overthrow of the enemies of the Cross of Christ. Be on guard never to use it to strike anyone unjustly.

After the Knight Master of Ceremonies has returned it into the scabbard, the Celebrant hands the sword to the newly appointed Knight.

Celebrant:
Bear well in mind that the Saints have conquered kingdoms not by the sword, but by faith.

The following two parts of this ceremony must be repeated for each candidate. The Celebrant is given the unsheathed sword and touches the Knight's right shoulder three times with the sword, saying:

Celebrant:
I appoint and declare you a Soldier and Knight of the Holy Sepulchre of Our Lord Jesus Christ. In the name of the Father, and of the Son, and of the Holy Spirit.

After returning the sword to the Knight Master of Ceremonies, the Celebrant places around the neck (according to his degree) the Cross, the emblem of the Order, saying:

Celebrant:
Receive the Cross of Our Lord Jesus Christ for your protection, and for that purpose repeat unceasingly: "By the sign of the Cross, deliver us, O Lord, from our enemies."

The Knight arises, bows to the Celebrant, and goes to the dignitary highest in rank to receive the cape from him. He then receives from the Knight assistant, the beret, which he puts on immediately. He then goes to his place in the pews.

The ceremony is repeated for the other candidates who might be present.

CEREMONY OF THE INVESTITURE
AND CONSIGNMENT OF THE CROSS
TO THE LADIES OF THE HOLY SEPULCHRE

When the investiture of the Ladies immediately follows that of the Knights, before the Te Deum, at the signal of the Knight Master of Ceremonies, the newly appointed Lady leaves the place that was assigned to her and comes to the Sanctuary, accompanied by two Ladies. Here she remains standing; the Celebrant, assisted by the ecclesiastical Master of Ceremonies, is seated in a chair at the altar rail at the bottom step of the altar, and at the signal of the ecclesiastical Master of Ceremonies, the Knight Master of Ceremonies reads the decree of appointment.

When the reading is completed, the Lady* kneels before the Celebrant, while the two assisting Ladies remain standing.

Celebrant:

What do you request?

Lady:

I desire to be invested a Lady of the Holy Sepulchre.

Celebrant:

I remind you that if all men ought to consider themselves honored to practice Christian virtue, so much the more should a Lady of the Holy Sepulchre use every means to obtain Christian perfection, and, by her actions and virtues, show herself worthy of the honor that she received and the dignity with which she is invested. Do you promise, therefore, in all your actions and virtues, to show yourself worthy of the honor that you are to receive and of the dignity with which you are to be invested?

Lady:

With the help of God, I promise never to fail in the honor and dignity of a Lady of the Holy Sepulchre.

Each candidate in turn approaches the Celebrant and kneels before him. To each he says:

Celebrant:

I pronounce and declare you a Lady of the Holy Sepulchre and commit to your care this Cross, which is the emblem of the protection of the Lord in life and the pledge of future glory in eternity.

---

* When more than one is to be invested this oath is presented in unison by the Knights and Ladies while standing.

The Celebrant hands the cross, the emblem of the Order, to one of the Lady assistants, who places it around the neck of the newly appointed Lady. She arises and remains standing in the sanctuary, if space permits, until all Lady candidates have been invested.

Celebrant:

Now that you are a Lady of the Holy Sepulchre, strive to imitate those pious women who followed the Savior providing Him with the necessities of life, and with lively faith and tears of compassion watched at His Holy Sepulchre. Therefore, let your actions and your mind be turned to the Land of the Redeemer, and take care that His Holy Name be spread and loved everywhere, so that you may merit for yourself the praise of the Risen Lord.

Lady or Ladies in unison:

Thus do I hope to act, and may the Divine Redeemer and the Virgin Mary grant the necessary help.

The newly appointed Ladies bow to the Celebrant and return to their pews.

CEREMONY FOR THE INVESTITURE OF A PRIEST

The Celebrant is seated for the reading of the decree. The priest-candidates come before the Celebrant, each holding the mozzetta in his hands. The Celebrant stands for the following blessing.

℣. Our help is in the name of the Lord.

℟. Who made Heaven and earth.

℣. The Lord be with you.

℟. And also with you.

Let us pray: Almighty and eternal God, You consecrated the sign of the Cross with the blood of Your Son; and You willed to redeem the world by this same Cross of Our Lord Jesus Christ. Through the power of this same Cross You freed mankind from the dominion of our ancient enemy. We humbly beseech You to bless this garment ornamented with the cross. May he who wears it keep in his mind and in his heart the holy places where Your Beloved Son, our Redeemer, spent his mortal life; and may he receive the fullness of Your heavenly graces together with the protection of Your blessing. This we ask through Christ Our Lord.

℟. Amen.

The Celebrant then blesses the mozzetta with holy water. Then he sits and takes from the hands of the candidate the mozzetta, which he then places on the candidate's shoulders, saying:

Celebrant:

I clothe You with this garment adorned with the saving Cross of our Lord Jesus Christ. May it bring you firmness in faith, progress in good works, and assistance for spreading the kingdom of Christ.

The Celebrant then takes the Cross of the Order and places it around the neck of the new priest knight. The priest knight arises, bows to the Celebrant, and returns to his assigned place.*

The Celebrant then rises and says:

Let us pray: Lord Jesus Christ, You are truly almighty God, the perfect image of the Father, eternal life. You told us whoever wishes to be Your disciple must deny himself, take up his Cross, and follow You. This servant of Yours now wishes to live in accord with Your words: to deny himself, to take up his Cross and follow You, and to fight against our enemies to further the salvation of Your people. Lead them safely through all dangers and let their desires be fulfilled, so that they might rejoice with You in Your death and resurrection for all eternity. This we ask through You who live and reign forever and ever.

℟. Amen.

TE DEUM

We praise You, O God: we acknowledge You to be the Lord.
All the earth worships You, the Father everlasting.
To You all the angels cry aloud, the Heavens and all the Powers therein.
To You the Cherubim and Seraphim continually do cry:
Holy, Holy, Holy, Lord God of Hosts.
Heaven and earth are full of the majesty of Your glory.
The glorious choir of the Apostles praise You.
The admirable company of the Prophets praise You.
The white-robed army of Martyrs praise You.
The holy Church throughout the world acknowledges You,
The Father of infinite majesty,

---

* When only one priest is to be invested, or but a few, the celebrant might also offer the *embracio* (Kiss of Peace) at this time.

Your adorable, true, and only Son.

And the Holy Spirit the Comforter,

You are the King of Glory, O Christ.

You are the everlasting Son of the Father.

When You would take human nature to deliver man,

To not disdain the Virgin's womb.

When You had overcome the sting of death,

You did open to believers the kingdom of Heaven.

You are seated at the right hand of God, in the glory of the Father.

We believe that You shall come to be our Judge.

We beseech You, therefore, help Your servants,

Whom You have redeemed by Your precious Blood.

Make them to be numbered with Your Saints in glory everlasting.

O Lord save Your people, and bless Your inheritance.

Govern them, and exalt them forever. Day by day we bless You:

And we praise Your name forever, and ever.

Vouchsafe, O Lord, this day to keep us without sin.

Have mercy upon us, O Lord, have mercy upon us.

Let Your mercy be upon us, O Lord, as we have hoped in You.

O Lord, in You have I hoped, let me not be confounded forever.

The Celebrant recites the Antiphon:

℣. Strengthen, O God, what You have wrought in us.

℟. From Your holy temple, which is in Jerusalem.

℣. O Lord, hear my prayer.

℟. And let my cry come unto You.

℣. The Lord be with you.

℟. And also with you.

Let us pray: O Lord God of Hosts, Who this day has deigned through our hands to receive these faithful servants among the number of those who are dedicated to the defense of the most holy Sepulchre, grant, we beseech You, that through the ministry of the Angels, they may one day merit to be among the triumphant Hosts of Heaven. This we ask through Christ Our Lord.

℟. Amen.

℣. The Lord be with you:

℟. And also with you.

℣. Our help is in the name of the Lord.

℟. Who created Heaven and earth.

The Celebrant gives the final blessing:

Celebrant:

> May the Almighty God bless You.
> Father, Son, and Holy Spirit.

CONFERRING OF PROMOTIONS

If promotions are to be conferred, the Celebrant is seated while the decree is read. Individuals to be promoted then approach the Celebrant, coming forward in the proper order of rank, beginning with the lower rank. Each in turn kneels before the Celebrant, receives the insignia, rises, bows to the Celebrant, and returns to his place.

If promotions are to be conferred on Knights, Ladies, and Priest Knights, it would seem preferable to follow the same procedure used in the Ceremony of Investiture: the reading of the decree and bestowal of insignia for Knight promotees; the reading of the decree and bestowal of insignias for the Lady promotees; and finally the reading of the decree and bestowal of insignia for the Priest Knight promotees.

When all have returned to their places, the Celebrant rises and begins the Te Deum, which is continued by all present.

Ecclesiastical Heraldry

Heraldry is both art and science. It is a phenomenon very much a part of the legal and social structures of practically every continent on earth. It originated nearly a thousand years ago in Europe and has been carried throughout the world by both the migrating peoples of continental Europe and by the Church, which is represented in every corner of the globe.

PRIVILEGES AND RESPONSIBILITIES OF ECCLESIASTICAL HERALDRY

Heraldry originated in the warrior classes as a means of differentiating combatants on the field of battle. As Europe developed and the feudal warrior class disappeared, the practice of identifying one's possessions, lands, and holdings with personal emblems flourished. Every noble family could easily be identified by the arms that it displayed, as could all the newly developing municipalities, communities, and nations. The Church also incorporated the practice of adopting heraldic achievements in order to differentiate between the various degrees of the clerical estate.

As a science, heraldry requires adherence to specific regulations governing the design, implementation, and display of armorial bearings. Everyone is entitled to design and bear symbols reflecting his or her individuality; however, no one has the right to simply assume a new heraldic achievement without first giving proper care to one's own national conventions. "The rights of others should be respected, and since a coat-of-arms is the property of its bearer, to adopt the armorial bearing of another family that happens to have the same or similar name, is misleading and could be considered theft."[1]

Heraldry is not independent of the law and is, in fact, strictly governed by international custom and individual state law. In many nations, it is an offense to bear and display arms not previously granted by a recognized heraldic authority of that state or another. "Yet it is the birthright of any human being to bear names and signs which distinguish him from another person. This right is limited by the corresponding rights of the others, and it is clearly inadmissible for someone to appropriate the emblems of rank, office or dignity to which he is not entitled."[2] Therefore, "there is an important point which must be made: The right to arms is not the privilege of any particular group of society and anyone may assume new arms for himself or for his family, unless it is not considered legal or customary in his own country."[3]

It has become the accepted practice of newly created prelates of the Catholic Church to assume an individual heraldic achievement. Prior to 1960, the process of designing and displaying prelatial coats of arms was in the strict domain of the Heraldry Commission of the Roman Curia. When this office was abolished by Pope John XXIII, prelates began to assume their armorial bearings without the official mandate or advice of the Church. Many abuses resulted, due both to an ignorance of the strict requirements of the heraldic science and to the historic precedence of the Church in this regard.

It is impossible to offer a complete study of this discipline in the relatively few pages set aside for this chapter. For those whose interest is piqued by this topic, I suggest further study of the volumes appearing in the bibliography section of this text. For newly named prelates and for clerics with interest in ecclesiastical heraldry, I lay down the following points by which one may properly design and implement armorial bearings for oneself and for religious institutes. This chapter will likewise serve as a starting point for those among the laity who would wish to assume individual arms.

The most significant advice that any heraldist can provide is that all ecclesiastical heraldry should be designed with great care in order to assure overall dignity. It should additionally be clear that the Holy See has set forth very specific regulations as to what symbols are permitted the clergy and, likewise, which symbols are to be reserved for the various degrees within the hierarchy.

It is perfectly acceptable for a priest or prelate to use his own family arms as his own, if these armorial bearings were used by him prior to ordination or episcopal nomination and if these arms are not offensive to the religious state. One of the more common errors found in ecclesiastical heraldry after the demise of the Heraldry Commission at the Vatican, which served as a safeguard against abuses, has been the inclusion of warlike symbolism (swords, crossbows, maces, bows, arrows, and spears) into religious heraldry. This is strictly forbidden in newly created arms, and yet it is seen time and time again. What is appropriate and often beautiful in the individual or family arms of the laity may not be appropriate for the son of a family who enters into religious life.

"The right to bear arms, *la capacité héraldique,* is a general right, not a privilege, and belongs to any man excepting one from whom the right may have been withdrawn by public authority as a result of certain crimes."[4] In the Church, the right to bear arms or to have that right abrogated is determined by both Church law and by the individual initiative of the Roman Pontiff.

HERALDRY AND CHURCH LAW

"Ecclesiastical heraldry is not determined by heraldic considerations alone but also by doctrinal, liturgical, and canonical factors. It not only produces arms denoting members of the ecclesiastical state but also shows the rank of the bearer."[5] The role of Church law is to protect the dignity of the hierarchy and the priesthood in regard to heraldry. The Church concerns herself with those insignia permitted the clergy and the prelature by virtue of their individual ecclesiastical estate and safeguards against illicit adoption of arms by individuals seeking self-aggrandizement at the expense of the Church.

In his text *Heraldry in the Catholic Church,* Archbishop B. B. Heim argues for the proper creation and registration of new episcopal arms. He writes that "the choice of prelatial arms is often a disastrous defiance of the rules of heraldry, if only as a breach of good taste."[6]

Taking this argument to its logical extension, it may be suggested that the task of properly designing and registering episcopal arms and the armorial bearings of newly created dioceses or religious institutes, in order to ensure their conformity with the norms of heraldic law and with the Church's law,* should return to an authority under the direction of the Roman Curia, which could properly advise, without abrogating or limiting the free choice of prelates in assuming new arms. This would ensure ecclesiastical dignity and would avoid breaches of good taste resulting from ignorance. It is important to remind the reader that religious heraldry should, above all else, be dignified. Simplicity in design and proper attention to Church directives will ensure a beautiful artistic achievement.

Everyone within the Church has the right to armorial bearings; however, the Church places limitations on the assumption of arms by the clergy according to their rank. It precludes the use of warlike or inappropriate symbolism but otherwise concerns herself only with the appropriate display of insignia of rank.

Unlike the symbols in civil heraldry (crowns, coronets, helmets, crests, etc.), ecclesiastical heraldry makes use of actual insignia utilized by the prelature in the exercise of this ordinary jurisdiction and authority. These insignia are emblems of their individual rank within the hierarchy (the mitre, crozier, *pallium*, archiepiscopal cross, etc.). Additionally, religious heraldry makes use of the historic vesture of the clergy by ensigning each coat of arms beneath the *galero*.

ECCLESIASTICAL SYMBOLS

Papal Tiara

The most respected of the ecclesiastical symbols, the tiara, or *triregno*, is also the symbol of the pope's authority over the Church. No one knows for certain when the tiara originated, and it has undergone many changes since it first appeared at the Papal Court. The tiara comprises three separate crowns, or diadems. The bottom crown appeared in the ninth century as ornamentation at the base of the mitre.

When the pontiffs assumed the temporal role of sovereign princes, they further adorned the base decorations with the jeweled crown of the princes of the time. The second crown was added by Pope Boniface VIII in A.D. 1298 to represent his spiritual dominion. By A.D. 1315, the *triregno* appears in the documentation of the Papal Treasury. "Since the thirteenth century it has had two ribbons, which were originally black, hanging from the back, like a mitre."[7]

The triple tiara represents first, the Vicar of Christ's universal episcopate; second, his jurisdictional supremacy; and third, his temporal power. The tiara has also been described as representing the pope's power—militant, penitent, and triumphant—and his role as priest, pastor, and teacher.

In heraldry, the *triregno* is always depicted as having a white "beehive" form, with three gold and jeweled diadems. The tiara is surmounted by an orb and a cross. The infulae are depicted as red lined, gold fringed, and gold backed. (See Plates 40 through 45.[†])

Crossed Keys

Known as the "keys of the Kingdom" and the "keys of Peter," the crossed keys first made their appearance on papal arms in the thirteenth century. They are borne during the lifetime of a reigning pope but pass at his death to the Cardinal-Camerlengo. The

---

* Governing canons §381, 382, 450, 470, 545, 1205, 1283, 1287, 1450, 1455, 1643, 1715, 2041, 2055, 2056, 2063, 2073, 2360, 2362, 2406.
† Color plates illustrating the heraldic designs discussed in this chapter can be seen by turning to the second full color insert section of *The Church Visible*.

keys, along with the *ombrellino* and the Camerlengo's personal arms, form the heraldic achievement of the *Sede Vacante.*

"The symbolism of the keys is brought out in an ingenious and interpretive fashion by heraldic art."[8] The keys are placed below the tiara and behind the papal shield, in saltire. The greater of the keys is gold (or); the lesser is silver (argent). The golden key is placed in dexter (from the viewer's perspective: the left) and extends to Heaven. The silver key is placed in sinister (to the right as one looks upon the achievement) and is symbolic of the power of the keys and their keeper over the earth. The two are joined by a red (gules) cord with tassels. The key's handles, or wards, are always pointed downward as they should be within easy grasp for the pope, who has the power over them. It is this power that Christ entrusted to Peter and to his successors and that is represented in the depiction of the crossed keys.

The emblem of the crossed keys, ensigned with the *triregno,* has also been granted to the departments of the Roman Curia as a symbol of their special bond with Peter's successor.

Ombrellino

The *ombrellino* is also known as the basilica pavilion. It is one of the most ancient symbols in Church heraldry. The *ombrellino* was actually used as a canopy in processions not only by the hierarchy but also by the nobility. It was used to protect officials from the hot Mediterranean summer sun during long journeys. It came to be identified with the papacy as early as the eleventh century and thereafter was reserved for the arms of the popes and their households.

The privilege of adorning the arms of the great Roman basilicas with the *ombrellino* was later granted. As part of the papal establishment, the granting of this privilege was not unusual. Later, the privilege was extended to minor basilicas and to some insti-

tutes and seminaries. At present, the *ombrellino* is the symbol for all basilicas, linking them to the pope in an unique way. It may be displayed on all heraldic achievements of the individual basilicas and is incorporated into sculpture and bas-relief throughout the world. The major basilicas were permitted the additional distinction of richly ornamenting the *ombrellino,* whereas the minor basilicas, as well as all other institutes or individuals[*] granted the privilege of the *ombrellino,* may not ornament it in any way.

The *ombrellino* is most familiar during the *Sede Vacante,* when the arms of the Cardinal-Camerlengo, placed in saltire beneath the crossed keys and beneath the pavilion, can be seen on Vatican postage and coins and on interregnum documents. (See Plate 46.)

The *ombrellino* is heraldically represented as a half-umbrella, or parasol. It is composed of alternating vertical stripes of gold (or) and red (gules) while the flaps of each stripe take the alternating color. It can be artistically represented as having either seven, nine, or eleven stripes. The staff of the *ombrellino* is always illustrated as gold (or) and should be depicted as sturdy, recalling its original purpose as a canopy used in processions.

Mitre

Despite the liturgical significance and import of the mitre as an emblem of episcopal rank, it is no longer used in the individual arms of prelates within the Church. What was formerly common practice has been abolished by Pope Paul VI. At present, only the arms of a diocese, an archdiocese, an abbey, or a prelature nullius are permitted the heraldic use of the mitre.

When depicting a mitre, the color should always

---

[*] Families who have provided the Church with a pope have the privilege of depicting the *ombrellino* within their shields. It should not appear outside the shield but should be given prominence within the shield proper.

be white (technically argent), although rich adornment is permitted. The infulae, if depicted, should always be illustrated with a red (gules) lining.

Crozier

The crozier, like the *pallium*, recalls the most ancient traditions of the prelature and yet, ironically, modern ecclesiastical heraldry forbids the use of the crozier in the armorial bearings of cardinals, archbishops, and bishops with whom it is most closely identified. As a symbol of jurisdiction and authority, the crozier is permitted in the arms of abbeys, abbots, provosts, abbots nullius, and prelates nullius, and, in certain cases, by abbesses.* The crozier for these prelates and certain abbesses is always depicted as veiled. (See Plates 53 and 54.)

Galero

The pontifical or Roman hat is officially called the *galero*. It is also known in English as the "pilgrim's hat." The *galero* has been in use for more than a thousand years and was first bestowed to a cardinal, in the color red, by Pope Innocent IV at the First Council of Lyons (A.D. 1245). As the processions at the council were quite lengthy, Innocent wanted his favorites to be recognizable and distinct; consequently, the precedent was established, and all future cardinals received "the red hat" at the hands of the pope at the consistory accepting them into the Sacred College. The presentation of the red *biretta* is a new phenomenon. Although a prelate may still obtain a *galero* in the clerical ateliers of Rome, it is no longer presented to him by the pope at the time of his elevation to the Sacred College.

When the *galero* became widely accepted as the *de rigueur* headgear for the prelature, the Church adopted it into official ecclesiastical heraldry. Initially, often both the *galero* and the mitre were depicted in the same achievement, but this practice has been abolished. Both Pope Saint Pius X and

Pope Paul VI, through individual initiative, set the rules that presently govern the arms of the clergy.

It is important to note that priests, as well as prelates, are entitled to the *galero*.† The simple black *galero*, with one tassel on either side, heraldically denotes one's ordination to the priesthood. By *motu proprio*, Pius X regulated the use of the *galero* among the clergy and all grades of the hierarchy. The arms of all priests and newly named prelates should adhere to these directives.

Heraldic Emblems of Rank

Cardinals

The heraldic achievement of a cardinal of the Catholic Church comprises his personal shield, above which is placed (ensigned) the red cardinalatial *galero*. Suspended from the *galero* on red cords are fifteen red *fiocchi* (tassels) on either side. They are suspended in rows of one, two, three, four, and five. Behind a cardinal's shield is placed the symbol of his episcopal rank. If he is an archbishop at the time of his elevation to the Sacred College, the archiepiscopal, or double-barred, cross is placed behind the shield. The entire cross should be visible above the shield. Only the base of its staff should be visible below the base of the shield.

---

* Abbesses no longer have the jurisdictional right to the crozier; however, use of it within their abbeys and in their personal arms is considered no more than maternal affection for the abbey and, although rarely seen today, it is tolerated in newly created armorial devices.

† There are many different artistic representations of the *galero*. One should not permit a heraldic artist to ensign one's individual achievements with a style that one does not personally prefer. Plate 48 illustrates the form most preferred by North American heraldic artists. The arms of Cardinal Martin (see dedication page) and Cardinals Laghi and Caprio (see Plates 47 and 64) represent the two Roman artistic styles currently in vogue. Plates 49–61 illustrate a second preference, which is found in Europe and which is historically realistic as well as practical. These latter examples of size and shape offer a better overall appearance to the achievement; however, it remains purely a matter of individual preference.

If he is a bishop or a simple priest at the time of his elevation to the Sacred College, the jeweled episcopal, or processional, cross is used. All cardinals, unless they have been granted a special dispensation from the Holy Father at the time of their elevation, must now be consecrated bishops if they were not so previously. In the 1991 Consistory naming new cardinals, Pope John Paul II named the bishop of Berlin, Cardinal Sterzinsky, to the Sacred College. As a bishop, his arms would make use of the jeweled processional cross behind the shield. He would not be entitled to an archiepiscopal cross unless the See of Berlin was raised to an archdiocese or if the dignity of "archbishop" was accorded to him personally.*

The mitre, crozier, *pallium*, or other similar ancient symbols are no longer permitted in the heraldic achievements of cardinals. The motto of a cardinal is to be placed at the base of the achievement in an appropriately dignified artistic manner. (See Plates 47, 48, 64, and that of Cardinal Martin in the sub-dedication.)

Patriarchs

Patriarchs who are not also members of the College of Cardinals have heraldic achievements identical to those of members of the Sacred College except that the *galero*, cords, and *fiocchi* (tassels) are green rather than red. Since the mid-eighteen hundreds, it has become the accepted practice to differentiate between the green used for patriarchs and that used by archbishops, bishops, and abbots by illustrating the cords and *fiocchi* as green with gold threads intertwined. There is no foundation in papal documentation for this practice, nor is there any historic precedence for such ornamentation; however, this practice in itself is harmless and has become somewhat time-honored. It is the option of the prelate and his heraldic artist. (See Plate 49.)†

Archbishops

The heraldic achievements of archbishops consist of their personal shields, behind which is placed the archiepiscopal cross. Above the shield is placed a green *galero*, with ten green *fiocchi* on either side. The *fiocchi* are placed in rows of one, two, three, and four. The motto is placed below the shield. No other adornment is permitted. (See Plate 50.) It is also proper, but not common, to see prelatial arms depicted without the *galero*. (See Plate 51.)

Bishops

Bishops also make use of a green *galero*, cords, and *fiocchi*, but the number of *fiocchi* on either side of the shield is six, consisting of rows of one, two, and three. Behind the shield is placed the jeweled processional cross. Below is placed the motto. No other adornment is permitted. (See Plate 52 and the armorial achievement of Bishop van Lierde in the subdedication.)

Abbots and Provosts

The arms for an abbot and provost are similar to that of a bishop; however, the veiled crozier is placed behind the shield rather than the processional cross. The *galero*, cords, and six *fiocchi* are black. (See Plate 53.)

Abbots Nullius and Prelates Nullius

The arms of an abbot nullius and prelate nullius are identical in presentation to that of a bishop with the

---

exception of the placement of a veiled crozier behind the shield in place of the jeweled processional cross. The *galero*, cords, and six *fiocchi* are green. (See Plate 54.)

Prelates di Fiocchetto (Defunct)

This rank of prelates, now abolished, enjoyed enormous privileges. Prelates *di fiocchetto* held the highest posts in the Papal Court. They took the name *di fiocchetto* from the tassels and plumage that adorned their horses and carriages, not from the additional *fiocchi* permitted them on their *galero*.

As a point of historic interest, the arms of a prelate *di fiocchetto* consisted of their personal or family arms, above which hung a violet *galero*. Although the *galero* granted to these prelates was violet, the two tassels at the brim, the cording emanating from inside the crown of the hat and the ten *fiocchi* suspended on either side of the shield were all scarlet, which symbolically linked these few privileged prelates to the highest levels of authority in the Vatican. (See Plate 55.)

Protonotaries Apostolic de Numero and Supranumerary

These prelates are the highest grades of the *monsignori* in the post–Vatican II Church. The personal or family arms of these prelates are ensigned with a violet *galero*. The cording and *fiocchi* are of scarlet. On either side of the shield are arranged six red *fiocchi* in rows of one, two, and three. The motto is permitted, but as for all priests and prelates, it should never be a family motto if that motto is warlike (such as a Celtic *cris de guerre*) or otherwise inappropriate for a priest in any manner. (See Plate 56.)

Prelates of Honor

Honorary Prelates of His Holiness are permitted to ensign their arms with the violet *galero*. Suspended on either side of these prelates' shields are six violet *fiocchi* in rows of one, two, and three. They are permitted a motto, but it must be one appropriate for a priest as described above. (See Plate 57.)

Chaplains of His Holiness

The armorial achievement of the Chaplains of His Holiness are identical to the honorary prelates with the sole exception of the color of the *galero*, which is black. The *fiocchi* and cords are violet. (See Plate 58.)

Canons

Canons are priests with special responsibilities and privileges. This special standing is also reflected in heraldry. The achievements of canons are ensigned by a black *galero* with three black *fiocchi* and black cords on either side of the shield in rows of one and two. The *fiocchi* can be traditional in design or somewhat more artistic as illustrated in Plate 59. If the canon has the higher monsignorial dignity, as has traditionally been the case with European canons, his arms are ensigned by the *galero* appropriate to his higher rank.

Deans, Vicars Forane, and Minor Superiors

Deans, vicars forane, vicars episcopal, and minor superiors have been granted a black *galero,* black cords, and two black *fiocchi* on either side, which may be displayed one below the other or side by side, whichever better suits the total artistic achievement. The appropriate motto is permitted and appears below the shield. (See Plate 60.)

Priests

Once a gentleman has been ordained, he lays aside the heraldic achievements of his secular life. Although his family or personal arms remain, the shield is now ensigned with a simple black *galero* with one black *fiocchi* on either side (see Plate 61). The motto is permitted but is not obligatory. It may not be worldly or warlike and must be in keeping with the religious character of a priest. If a priest or prelate of any rank is a member of the Sovereign Order of Malta and/or of the Equestrian Order of the Holy Sepulchre of Jerusalem, the insignia of those orders may be displayed in a prominent manner.

Examples of the proper and accepted means for displaying these orders in ecclesiastic heraldry are as follows: When the priest or prelate is a knight of only the Equestrian Order of the Holy Sepulchre, his shield may be placed on the Jerusalem cross, or on the Maltese cross for an individual who is only a Knight of the Order of Malta. In cases where these ecclesiastical orders are represented, the *galero* and *fiocchi* should frame the entire achievement in a manner that brings symmetry to the presentation.

In instances where membership in both these orders is to be depicted, it is not permissible to include in the heraldic achievement the ecclesiastical orders' crosses in a position behind the shield (pale-wise). In order to illustrate one's membership in both orders, it is proper to depict the insignia of each order with their black ribbons as either below the shield and emanating from behind it or encircling the shield entirely, depending on the cleric's rank in that order. For clerics, care must always be given to assure dignity and simplicity in the presentation of heraldic achievements. No other adornment is permitted priests and minor prelates; likewise, no other orders may be depicted in a cleric's achievement.

ARCHIEPISCOPAL AND PROCESSIONAL CROSS

As seen, cardinals and patriarchs who are archbishops, both titular and residential, at the time of their elevation to the Sacred College make use of the archiepiscopal cross. Heraldically, this cross is depicted as a double-barred cross (see Plates 47, 48, 49, 50, and 51) and is often illustrated as jewel encrusted. It is the heraldic representation of the actual cross carried before archbishops in procession.

If the cardinal was a bishop or a simple priest* at the time of his nomination to the Sacred College, the cross to be depicted in his arms would then be the processional cross, which may or may not be depicted as jewel encrusted.

Archbishops, as we have seen, and patriarchs make use of the archiepiscopal cross, whereas bishops use the simple processional cross (see van Lierde subdedication and Plate 52). The entire cross should be visible above the shield, whereas just the base of its staff should be visible below the shield.

PALLIUM

The *pallium* is a sacred liturgical garment that represents jurisdictional authority; as such, it should be given proper treatment if it is to be included in a prelate's arms. It should never be displayed by persons not entitled to its use. Such an abuse would be an affront to both heraldic and canon law. The *pallium* should not be depicted in an inappropriate manner by those entitled to bear it. Of all the symbols of rank permitted the prelature, in heraldry, the *pallium* is the most difficult to depict with reverence. It should not surround the entire achievement, as a knight would do with an order's ribbon, although it may be displayed at the base of the shield. It should never appear above the shield or in place of the motto ribbon. In Anglican heraldry, it is most commonly placed within the shield itself, which is not permissible in the Roman Catholic Church. It is best to depict it at the base of the cross's staff in a stylized fashion. Individuals granted the *pallium* need not include it in their arms. It is a privilege to which they are entitled but which is not required in heraldry.

---

* All newly named cardinals must have episcopal ordination. If they are not bishops when raised to the Sacred College, they must receive episcopal ordination within forty-eight hours.

MOTTO

One of the abuses that developed after the demise of the Heraldry Commission of the Holy See was the adoption of a family motto by priests and prelates. Although these mottos served as a link to one's own family, they were often inappropriate. Many ancient family mottos developed as *cris de guerre* and were not in keeping with the clerical state.

An ecclesiastical motto need not be in Latin; it is perfectly acceptable for it to be in the vernacular. With the introduction of the vernacular into the Church, we now see mottos in English, German, Lithuanian, Japanese, Swahili, Spanish, Portuguese, Greek, and, of course, Latin. The motto should be reflective of one's own philosophy of life, and for Churchmen it should also be appropriate to their clerical state. Above all else, a motto should be a personal statement that reflects the identity of the bearer. The artistic representation of a motto can vary from quite simple, without the motto ribbon, to very ornate, depending on both the abilities of the heraldic artist and the personal taste of the individual bearer.

HERALDRY FOR PAPAL AND ECCLESIASTICAL KNIGHTS

The Order of Malta and the Order of the Holy Sepulchre are the only orders whose insignia are permitted, in heraldry, to members of the clergy. Priests and prelates who have been granted papal, dynastic, royal, or national decorations may not depict them in their armorial bearings. These restrictions, however, do not apply to Catholic lay persons. A Catholic who has been awarded one or more of the papal honors should carefully include them in the presentation of his or her armorial achievement.

Order of Malta

The Grand Master of the Order of Malta quarters his personal, or family, arms with the simple arms of the order. The badge of the order, the large white Maltese cross, is placed behind the shield. A silver rosary surrounds the achievement and is depicted as intertwining through the arms of the Maltese cross. Each of the five decades of the rosary is marked by a larger silver ball, and, in place of the crucifix, a white Maltese cross is suspended below. The entire achievement is placed below the Grand Magistral crown and a black, ermine-lined mantle, corded and fringed. (See Plate 62.) The arms of the Sovereign Order, the official emblem of the Knights of Malta, is presented in the same fashion as those of the Grand Master, with the exception of the shield which is entirely represented with the white cross on a red background. (See Plate 63.)

Professed Bailiffs of the Order of Malta place their shield on the badge of the order. The simple arms of the order are placed "in chief." The entire achievement is surrounded by the silver rosary of a professed Knight.

The pattern of arms for a Bailiff of Honor and Devotion places the simple arms of the order, in chief, and mounts the shield on the badge of the order. The ribbon of his individual rank surrounds the total achievement. Members of all other divisions of the order simply surround their shield with the ribbon and insignia of their rank within the order.* They may also place the white Maltese cross near their arms to denote their membership in the

---

* Members of the Order of Malta who are also members of other orders of knighthood may depict their membership by placing the ribbons and insignia of these orders at the base of the shield. Care should be given to proper placement and precedence. In such cases, the actual insignia with ribbons and insignia would be depicted rather than one order's cross being placed behind the shield while another order's insignia would be displayed below.

Order of Malta but would not do so if they also depict the ribbon and insignia of the order.

Order of the Holy Sepulchre

Knights of the Holy Sepulchre of Jerusalem can place their arms on the badge of the order, the red Jerusalem cross. Knights Grand Cross may also choose to place the order's insignia on the black ribbon surrounding the shield. Other ranks in the order may place the ribbon and insignia of the order at the base of the shield. (See Plate 66.) If they choose to display several orders to which they may belong, the ribbons should be displayed at the shield's base in proper precedence.

Ladies of the order of the Holy Sepulchre also have the privilege of depicting their arms on the badge of the order, or for those with the rank of Grand Cross, by surrounding the shield with the ribbon and insignia of the order. Ladies awarded lesser ranks in the order may depict their memberships by placing the black ribbon and insignia at the base of their shield. Both ladies and gentlemen of the Order of the Holy Sepulchre of Jerusalem may depict their membership by placing a red Jerusalem cross in proximity to their shields; however, they would not depict their membership in the equestrian order by both the ribbon and insignia and the red Jerusalem cross in proximity.

Papal Orders

Persons who have been honored with a papal order of knighthood have the privilege of depicting this honor in their individual armorial bearings. Only the insignia of their actual rank within one of these orders may be depicted. For instance, individuals who have been given the rank of Grand Cross of the Pontifical Order of St. Gregory the Great have the privilege of surrounding their shield with the red and gold ribbon and the insignia of the Order of St. Gregory the Great. Persons who have been

granted this order in the rank of Knight Commander would depict their rank by placing the order on its ribbon at the base of the shield in a manner simulating the style of wearing the insignia around the neck. Likewise, persons given the rank of Knight would depict this award at the base of the shield, either alone or with other orders, and would artistically represent the actual ribbon of the rank of the honoree, just as it appears in actuality.

The Order of Christ and the Order of the Golden Spur are awarded in one class only, the Collar. The Order of Pius IX's most senior grade is also the Collar. Individuals who have been awarded the grade of Chain, or Collar, of a pontifical order have the right to depict this award by artistically depicting the Collar completely surrounding the shield.

Gentlemen of His Holiness

Laymen who have been awarded the special title Gentleman of His Holiness and who, as a result, offer personal service to the Holy Father and the papacy, are granted a beautiful, stylized gold chain with medallions depicting the papal seal as an insignia of their position in the Papal Family. Suspended from this chain is the papal tiara and crossed keys. "There is no prohibition or prescription for use of the chain in heraldry."[9] Heraldically, the award of this title and its insignia may be depicted by persons so honored by completely surrounding the recipient's shield with this beautiful stylized chain, as, since the Pauline changes of 1968–69, this office carries with it a dignity akin to a papal decoration that may be depicted heraldically.

HERALDIC TERMINOLOGY AND NORMS

This study has, until this point, concerned itself with the regulations governing the insignia that accompany the arms of prelates and priests and papal honorees. For readers who wish to use this study as a reference point for designing new ecclesiastical and personal arms, we must give proper attention to the basic principles of the heraldic science. Understanding the following terminology, rules, and regulations will assure a faithful adherence to the ancient principles that govern heraldry when creating and implementing new arms.

Heraldic emblems need not be symbolic and, indeed, in ancient times were seldom displayed for symbolic reasons. If the bearer so chooses, however, he may depict his arms in a symbolic way, as armorial bearings are, after all, an expression of one's own individuality. Although symbolism is not required, a strict adherence to the laws, regulations, and principles of heraldry remains a requirement.

The vocabulary or terminology of heraldry comes to us from Old English, by way of French. William the Conqueror brought with him to England the continental practice of bearing arms. The base for the coat of arms is the shield. This derived from the actual practice of painting the warrior's shield with his individual emblems, which enabled friend and enemy alike to identify each participant in battle and in tournament. Later, these emblems were depicted on banners, and eventually they appeared on the cloaks, or coats, of these warriors. The term *coat of arms* dates from this period.

The shield is also known as the escutcheon,* from French, and the *scutum*, or *stemma*, from Latin. It can take many shapes and forms.† There are only a few colors, termed *tinctures*, which are permitted in heraldry. Use of other hues is strictly forbidden and would identify the bearer as one not conversant with heraldic law and practice. Two of the tinctures are termed *metals*: These are *or* (gold) and *argent* (silver). Gold is represented artistically as yellow and silver as white. It was a long-held belief for metal upon metal to be impermissible. In other words, silver objects on a gold field would not be permitted, with the further logic, however, that a blue object

on a gold field would be acceptable. Archbishop Heim recently has debunked this misconception in an excellent treatise entitled *Or & Argent,* which is widely acclaimed for its historic research on the topic.

There are five colors in common heraldic practice, although old English heraldry permits two additional colors. The base colors are *azure* (blue), *gules* (red), *vert* (green), *sable* (black), and *purpure* (purple). These five colors are the only ones permitted in heraldry.‡

When an artist is depicting arms without employing actual color and when also depicting arms incorporating the metals in the same fashion, there is a universally prescribed manner for depicting each of the acceptable colors. In representing gold, a plain shield with dots throughout is used. When depicting silver, a plain white field is used, whereas blue is depicted with horizontal lines. Red is depicted with vertical lines, and green makes use of a diagonal line, right to left. Purple also uses the diagonal line, but the pattern is represented left to right. Black does not use the logical representation but rather combines the patterns for red and blue by depicting the color as horizontal and perpendicular lines crossing through each other, creating a grid pattern.

---

* The proposed new money for European unification is the "écu," which is derived from the word *escutcheon*. The money of old France had the seal, or shield, of emblems on it, taking the same name. The écu was proposed to recall the historic European traditions.

† Persons who are adopting new ecclesiastical arms should refer to the sources listed in this text's bibliography on heraldry. Many fine examples are illustrated and offer the individual a wide range of historic shapes from which to choose.

‡ *Tenny* (orange) and *sanguine* (blood red), which traditionally appear in the arms of individuals with ancient Anglo-Saxon roots, and even then only rarely, are two others. These two old English colors are depicted as follows: for tenny, diagonal lines, left to right, crossed by horizontal; and for sanguine, diagonal lines from each direction crossing through each other at the center.

In addition to the metals and the colors, certain furs are utilized as well. The two most common of these are ermine and vair. The first of these, ermine, is the most popular and is represented as black spots of a tail-like design on a white background. It very much resembles the black tails on royal robes and on robes of state. The second of these is vair, more commonly known as miniver, and it is represented in a fashion opposite to that of ermine, that is, as a white pattern on a black field.* Furs may be used in lieu of other emblems if desired.

The term applied to emblems that actually appear on the shield is *charges*. The charges do not have to be symbolic in any way; however, it is perfectly acceptable to choose charges that are symbolic to one's own individuality, providing they are in keeping with the norms of heraldry. Charges should never be detailed to the degree where they depict the exact physical characteristics of the emblem in question.† It is desirable to depict the concept and to maintain beauty and simplicity rather than authentically depicting an object.

In ecclesiastical heraldry, one often finds that the bearer wishes to incorporate his filial devotion to Our Lady or to a particular saint. This is both natural and acceptable; however, the means to depict Our Lady or patron saints without depicting the physical image of them were long ago determined by heraldic custom. Each of the saints, as well as our Blessed Lord and His Mother, have symbols associated with them that could more easily be incorporated into a bearer's arms. For example, the inverted cross is the symbol of St. Peter, as are the keys; the organ is the symbol for St. Cecilia, whereas the broken wheel is the symbol for St. Catherine of Alexandria. Many symbols exist for Our Blessed Lord and Our Lady. Caution should be given to incorporating symbols of Our Lord, in particular, as these may be more appropriate for the Church Universal than for individual bearers.

Finally, some direction should be provided as to the proper means of subdividing a shield. There are numerous patterns from which to choose. For ecclesiastics, however, only a few are generally used. The process of subdivision is known as "partitioning the fields." In ecclesiastical heraldry, the more complicated patterns are found only among the European clergy who have retained ancient family arms. Most commonly, Church heraldry depicts a single shield, or arms divided quarterly—that is, four equal sections with two of the quarters depicting the same charges, whereas the remaining two sections depict charges similar to each other but different from the other two quarters. An example of this would be the placement of an archbishop's personal arms in two quarters and the diocese's arms in the remaining two.

Another common method of partition of the field is "per pale." A shield divided per pale is equally split down the center—vertically. It is this style of parted shield that we see most often in North America. Although it is not required to do so, bishops and archbishops in the United States have often marshaled, or united, their arms with those of their new diocese by placing their own arms "in dexter" (left, as one views the shield) and the arms of the diocese "in sinister" (right, as one views the shield). (See Plate 48.) This practice has arisen only since the late eighteen hundreds and is most common in North America. It is a concept foreign to most other regions and to most non-American prelates. It is, of course, the prerogative of the ordinary, and, unless the diocesan statutes

---

* There are other representations of fur in heraldry, and patterns for these are depicted in the studies of heraldry listed in the bibliography. Additionally, heraldic artists may provide the bearer with numerous options from which to choose.
† For example, it is perfectly acceptable to represent a sailing yacht as an ancient wooden sailing vessel, but it would be inappropriate to depict it as a streamlined, modern, polyurethane racing yacht.

require it, the new bishop has the right not to do so. If this practice is adopted, however, the place of honor (dexter) is given to the ordinary for his personal arms, whereas the sinister is reserved for the diocesan arms. This practice is also known as "impaling of arms."

CONCLUSION

"Heraldry is a celebration, based on ancient symbols, of the sense people have of themselves, personally and in groups. The tradition of using distinguishing marks goes back more than eight centuries."[10] In the Church, this practice is just as time-honored as it is in nobiliary and civil heraldry. Adherence to the few principles and regulations put forth in this chapter will afford all ranks of the clergy who either wish to become armigerous or,

by virtue of their promotion to the prelature, are subsequently required to assume armorial bearings, the tools necessary to design and display proper and beautiful ecclesiastical coats of arms.

Under the pontificates of St. Pius X and Paul VI, the use of heraldic emblems for the ecclesiastical state was regulated and codified. It is unlikely that there will be further changes for generations, with the possible exception of the office of Permanent Deacon, which has flourished in the post–Vatican II era and which was not addressed in the modernization of heraldry in the Church by Paul VI. As described in detail in the text of this chapter, certain emblems or symbols have been restricted to particular ranks of the Church. Likewise, colors have also been codified. The accompanying reference chart illustrates the present rules and regulations regarding attributes of ecclesiastical heraldry.

HERALDIC REFERENCE CHART
THE HIERARCHY OF THE CATHOLIC CHURCH

OFFICE	COLOR OF ECCLESIASTICAL HAT	NUMBER AND COLOR OF *FIOCCHI* ON EACH SIDE	INSIGNIA ACCOMPANYING THE SHIELD; REGULATED BY LAW
POPE	*triregno**		crossed keys; one silver, one gold
CARDINAL	scarlet	15 scarlet	archiepiscopal or episcopal cross, according to office
PATRIARCH	green	15 green, interlaced with gold	archiepiscopal cross, palewise
ARCHBISHOP	green	10 green	archiepiscopal cross, palewise
BISHOP	green	6 green	Latin processional cross, palewise
ABBOT AND PRELATE NULLIUS	green	6 green	vellum or veiled crozier, palewise
ABBOT AND PROVOST	black	6 black	vellum or veiled crozier, palewise
PRELATE DI FIOCCHETTO	violet	10 scarlet	(title now abolished)
APOSTOLIC PROTONOTARY	violet	6 scarlet	
PRELATES OF HONOR OF HIS HOLINESS	violet	6 violet	
CHAPLAINS OF HIS HOLINESS	black	6 violet	
CANONS ORDINARY	black	3 black†	
DEAN AND MINOR SUPERIOR, VICARS FORANE AND EPISCOPAL, VICARS GENERAL	black	2 black	
PRIEST	black	1 black	
ABBESS	none	none	veiled crozier with rosary encircling the shield

* The *triregno,* or the triple tiara, is heraldically represented in silver (white) and gold (yellow), with gemstones in natural colors.
† Some canons have extraordinary privileges including, heraldically, that which enabled them to make use of various prelatial colors and increased numbers of *fiocchi.*

PART THREE

CHURCH PROTOCOL

CHAPTER ELEVEN

Forms of Address

E ducated and courteous people, both within the Church and external to it, are careful to address one another correctly and appropriately. This is simply a case of good manners and common sense, even in a modern world all too often unconcerned with formalities. In commerce and diplomacy, this is vital to the success of one's activities. It should be no less so in the Church, where prelates, priests, and all others engaging in the activity of the Church are customarily viewed by the world at large as highly educated and well versed in correct form.

ECCLESIASTICAL FORMS OF ADDRESS

The Holy See, through custom and long-standing tradition, has set forth a proper form for the hierarchy of the Church. These ancient, time-honored, and historic titles and styles should be held in respect not only by the faithful but also by those persons honored to have received them. Unfortunately, the affording of such respect is not always the case.

In the following pages, charts are presented that not only address the proper titles and styles for the hierarchy and dignitaries of the Church but also provide the clergy and faithful with the correct and official English-language forms of address for the hierarchy of the Roman Catholic Church.

THE POPE

ENVELOPE	His Holiness Pope John Paul II The Apostolic Palace 00120 Vatican City Europe
SALUTATION	Your Holiness *or* Most Holy Father
COMPLIMENTARY CLOSE	Respectfully yours, *(laity, clerics)* *or* Devotedly yours in Christ, *(Brother Bishops)*
INVITATION *(inside envelope)*	All invitations *(requests)* should be forwarded through the appropriate channels *(Nuncio, Pronuncio, Delegate, appropriate Curia Office, or through the secretary of the Holy Father)*.
PLACE CARD	His Holiness Pope John Paul II *(outside Vatican City)*
INTRODUCTIONS/PRESENTATIONS	His Holiness*
IN CONVERSATION	Your Holiness *or* Holy Father

* Everyone, regardless of rank or title, is presented *to* the pope.

CARDINAL

ENVELOPE	His Eminence John Cardinal Doe, D.D., J.C.D. Archbishop of *(place)* (Residence: *for personal correspondence*) (Chancery: *for official correspondence*)
SALUTATION	Your Eminence *(normal)* *or* Most Eminent Cardinal *(formal)* *or* My Lord Cardinal *(very formal)*
COMPLIMENTARY CLOSE	Respectfully yours, *or* Sincerely yours in Christ, *(when relationship makes it appropriate)*
INVITATION *(inside envelope)*	His Eminence, John Cardinal Doe
PLACE CARD	His Eminence, John Cardinal Doe
INTRODUCTIONS/PRESENTATIONS	His Eminence, John Cardinal Doe Archbishop of *(place)*
IN CONVERSATION	Your Eminence

Note: It is improper to refer to a cardinal in any form other than John Cardinal Doe. The recent practice of Cardinal John Doe is improper and has no foundation in the law. The exact Latin formula would be, using John Cardinal Krol, Archbishop-Emeritus of Philadelphia as an example, Johannes S.R.E. Cardinalis Krol.

PATRIARCH

ENVELOPE	His Beatitude* John Doe, D.D. The Patriarch of the East Indies *(local address)*
SALUTATION	Your Beatitude
COMPLIMENTARY CLOSE	Respectfully yours, *or* Sincerely yours in Christ, *(when appropriate)*
INVITATION *(inside envelope)*	His Beatitude The Patriarch of the East Indies
PLACE CARD	His Beatitude Archbishop Doe†
INTRODUCTIONS/PRESENTATIONS	His Beatitude Archbishop Doe *or* His Beatitude The Patriarch of the East Indies, The Archbishop of Goa and Damao
IN CONVERSATION	Your Beatitude

* Patriarchs who are also cardinals, traditionally Lisbon and Venice, take the higher title, precedence, and rank of the cardinalate. Therefore, these patriarchs are styled as "Eminence," and all else remains consistent with the cardinalate; however, the title Patriarch and the Patriarchal See take the place of the title Archbishop of (place).

† Patriarchs who hold the rank and title between Cardinal and Archbishop or who are titular patriarchs with the jurisdiction of a patriarch should be referred to by use of this title (to be followed by the patriarchal designation when appropriate) but are styled as "Beatitude" rather than "Excellency."

THE APOSTOLIC NUNCIO OR PRO-NUNCIO

ENVELOPE	The Most Reverend Valerio Agostino Doe, D.D. Titular Archbishop of *(place)* The Apostolic Pro-Nuncio to the United States The Apostolic Pro-Nunciature 3339 Massachusetts Avenue NW Washington, DC 20008
SALUTATION	Your Excellency *or* Most Reverend Sir *or* Dear Archbishop *(when relationship is appropriate)*
COMPLIMENTARY CLOSE	Respectfully yours, *or* Sincerely yours in Christ, *(when appropriate)*
INVITATION *(inside envelope)*	His Excellency, The Apostolic Pro-Nuncio
PLACE CARD	His Excellency, The Apostolic Pro-Nuncio
INTRODUCTIONS/PRESENTATIONS	As the Pro-Nuncio represents the Holy Father in the United States, everyone is presented *to* him.
IN CONVERSATION	Your Excellency

Notes: A nuncio is accredited to nations who accord the Holy See's emissary the deanship of that nation's diplomatic corps (see Chapter 4, Papal Diplomacy, for recent changes to these titles).

A pro-nuncio is an emissary equivalent to an ambassador extraordinary and plenipotentiary but is not automatically recognized as the dean of the diplomatic corps (as in the United States); yet henceforth the title Nuncio will be accorded to all senior postings.

The Pro-Nuncio to the United States is additionally accredited as Nuncio Apostolic "Ad Personam" as the Permanent Observer to the Organization of American States.

ARCHBISHOP (RESIDENTIAL)

ENVELOPE	The Most Reverend John Joseph Doe, D.D., J.C.D. Archbishop of *(place)* (Residence: *for personal correspondence*) (Chancery: *for official correspondence*)
SALUTATION	Your Excellency *(normal)* *or* Most Reverend Sir *(formal)** *or* Dear Archbishop *(when appropriate)*
COMPLIMENTARY CLOSE	Respectfully yours, *or* Sincerely yours in Christ, *(when appropriate)*
INVITATION *(inside envelope)*	His Excellency, Archbishop Doe, D.D., J.C.D. *or* His Excellency The Archbishop of *(place)*
PLACE CARD	His Excellency, Archbishop Doe
INTRODUCTIONS/PRESENTATIONS	His Excellency Archbishop Doe *or* The Most Reverend John J. Doe, Archbishop of *(place)*
IN CONVERSATION	Your Excellency

* Rarely used today.

Note: Retired archbishops (with jurisdiction) assume the title Archbishop-Emeritus upon retirement. All else remains consistent.

BISHOP (RESIDENTIAL)

ENVELOPE	The Most Reverend Carlos Garcia Mestre, D.D., S.T.D., J.C.D. Bishop of *(place)* (Residence: *for personal correspondence*) (Chancery: *for official correspondence*)
SALUTATION	Your Excellency *(normal)* *or* Most Reverend Sir *(formal)** *or* Dear Bishop *(when appropriate)*
COMPLIMENTARY CLOSE	Respectfully yours, *or* Sincerely yours in Christ, *(when appropriate)*
INVITATION *(inside envelope)*	His Excellency, Bishop Garcia Mestre, D.D., S.T.D., J.C.D. *or* His Excellency The Bishop of *(place)*
PLACE CARD	His Excellency, Bishop Garcia Mestre
INTRODUCTIONS/PRESENTATIONS	His Excellency Bishop Garcia Mestre *or* The Most Reverend Carlos Garcia Mestre Bishop of *(place)*
IN CONVERSATION	Your Excellency

Note: Retired bishops (with jurisdiction) assume the title Bishop-Emeritus upon retirement. All else remains consistent.

* The recent practice of referring to the ordinary in conversation as "Bishop" rather than "the Bishop" is both incorrect form and improper interpretation of Roman practice. The most common argument for referring to the ordinary as "Bishop," without the definite article, is that "this usage incorporates the fullness of his authority." As a bishop's authority derives from apostolic succession in the fullness of Holy Orders, it would be erroneous to look to linguistics to somehow further stress that authority. One would never refer to the pope without the definite article as "Pope." It would be correct to refer to him only as "the Pope" or "Pope John Paul." Roman etiquette specifies the use of the article *the* when referring to a prelate, as does standard English when referring to proper titles (e.g., the president, the prime minister). Standard English drops the definite article only when also naming the titled person (e.g., President Bill Clinton, Prime Minister John Major), as is the case in the Roman etiquette (e.g., Bishop Doe, not the Bishop Doe).

TITULAR ARCHBISHOPS AND BISHOPS

ENVELOPE	The Most Reverend James Francis Doe, D.D. Titular Archbishop (Bishop) of *(place)* Secretary, The Congregation for Bishops 00120 Vatican City, Europe *or* Auxiliary Bishop of *(place)* *(local address)*
SALUTATION	Your Excellency *(normal)* *or* Most Reverend Sir *(formal)* *or* Dear Archbishop (Bishop) *(when appropriate*)*
COMPLIMENTARY CLOSE	Respectfully yours, *or* Sincerely yours in Christ, *(when appropriate)*
INVITATION *(inside envelope)*	His Excellency, Archbishop (or Bishop) Doe
PLACE CARD	His Excellency, Archbishop (or Bishop) Doe
INTRODUCTIONS/PRESENTATIONS	His Excellency Archbishop (Bishop) Doe *or* The Most Reverend James Francis Doe Secretary, Congregation for Bishops *or* Auxiliary Bishop of *(place)*
IN CONVERSATION	Your Excellency

*In all these examples, the relationship is appropriate when it is either personal or equal in status.

ABBOT

ENVELOPE	The Right Reverend James Francis Doe Abbot of *(place)* Abbey of *(name)* *(local address)*
SALUTATION	Your Excellency *(normal)* *or* Most Reverend Sir *(formal)* *or* Father Abbot *(fraternal)*
COMPLIMENTARY CLOSE	Respectfully yours, *or* Sincerely yours in Christ, *(when appropriate)*
INVITATION *(inside envelope)*	His Excellency, The Abbot of *(place)*
PLACE CARD	His Excellency, Abbot Doe
INTRODUCTIONS/PRESENTATIONS	His Excellency The Abbot of *(place)* *or* The Right Reverend James Francis Doe Abbot of *(place)*
IN CONVERSATION	Your Excellency

Note: Archabbots, abbots general, titular abbots, and abbots emeritus follow the same protocol.

MONSIGNOR

ENVELOPE	Reverend Monsignor Joseph Paul Doe, S.T.L. *(local address)*
SALUTATION	Dear Monsignor Doe *or* Reverend Sir
COMPLIMENTARY CLOSE	Respectfully yours, *(laity)* *or* Sincerely yours, *(clergy)*
INVITATION *(inside envelope)*	Monsignor Joseph Paul Doe
PLACE CARD	Monsignor Joseph Paul Doe
INTRODUCTIONS/PRESENTATIONS	Monsignor Doe
IN CONVERSATION	Monsignor Doe *or* Monsignor

Notes: The usage of the style "Very Reverend Monsignor" and the higher style of "Right Reverend Monsignor" are no longer granted to Honorary Prelates and Chaplains of His Holiness, except for certain positions within the Papal Household. The style of "Very Reverend," however, is still granted to monsignors who are Auditors of the Sacred Rota, Promoters of Justice and the Defenders of the Bond of the Signatura, Apostolic Protonotaries de Numero, and the clerics of the Apostolic Chamber.

The style of "Excellency" is accorded to the Dean of the Sacred Rota, the Secretary of the Apostolic Signatura, and the Vice Camerlengo of the Holy Church (if they had not previously been raised to the Episcopate).

In the U.S.A., the accepted abbreviation for *Monsignor* is *Msgr.* Nearly everywhere else, the accepted abbreviation is *Mons.*

Canons, although sometimes of monsignorial rank, are a class of their own within the hierarchy of the Church. The correct form of address for canons in English is "John Canon Doe." The title is placed between the Christian and surname as in the case of the cardinalate. In the Italian language, this is not so. This is not so much a concern of protocol as it is a matter of linguistics.

PRIEST, DIOCESAN

ENVELOPE	The Reverend John T. Daniel *(local address)*
SALUTATION	Reverend Sir *or* Dear Father Daniel
COMPLIMENTARY CLOSE	Respectfully yours, *(laity)* Sincerely yours, *(clergy)*
INVITATION *(inside envelope)*	Reverend John T. Daniel
PLACE CARD	Reverend John T. Daniel
INTRODUCTIONS/PRESENTATIONS	Father Daniel
IN CONVERSATION	Father Daniel *or* Father

Note: The style "Very Reverend" should be used, appropriately, when a priest holds this privilege (dean, minor superior, etc.).

PRIEST, RELIGIOUS

ENVELOPE	The Reverend Terrence Doe, O.P. *or* The Reverend Terrence Doe, Order of Preachers
SALUTATION	Reverend Sir *or* Dear Father Doe
COMPLIMENTARY CLOSE	Respectfully yours, *(laity)* Sincerely yours, *(clergy)*
INVITATION *(inside envelope)*	Reverend Terrence Doe, O.P.
PLACE CARD	Reverend Terrence Doe, O.P.
INTRODUCTIONS/PRESENTATIONS	Father Doe of the Order of Preachers *or* Dominican Father, Terrence Doe
IN CONVERSATION	Father Doe *or* Father

Note: The style of "Very Reverend" is reserved, in religious life, to the prior or superior of a province or jurisdiction.

DEACON, PERMANENT

ENVELOPE	Deacon Thomas Murphy *(local address)*
SALUTATION	Dear Deacon *or* Dear Deacon Murphy*
COMPLIMENTARY CLOSE	Respectfully yours, *(laity)* Sincerely yours, *(clergy)*
INVITATION *(inside envelope)*	The Deacon Thomas Murphy
PLACE CARD	Deacon Thomas Murphy
INTRODUCTIONS/PRESENTATIONS	Deacon Murphy
IN CONVERSATION	Deacon

* Transitional deacons (those in preparation for priesthood) are properly referred to as "Reverend Mr.," using the surname above; it would be appropriate to say Reverend Mr. Murphy rather than Deacon Murphy.

BROTHER, RELIGIOUS

ENVELOPE	Brother Patrick Ellis, F.S.C., Ph.D. President, The Catholic University of America Washington, DC 20064
SALUTATION	Reverend Brother* *or* Dear Brother
COMPLIMENTARY CLOSE	Respectfully yours, *or* Sincerely yours,
INVITATION *(inside envelope)*	Brother Patrick Ellis, F.S.C., Ph.D.
PLACE CARD	Brother Patrick Ellis
INTRODUCTIONS/PRESENTATIONS	Brother Patrick *or* Brother-President†
IN CONVERSATION	Brother, Brother Patrick *or* Brother-President

* The use of this title has not been abolished yet has fallen into disuse. It is not indicative of Holy Orders and, as such, is seldom seen today.
† Brother-President should be reserved for the academic setting, in particular, at the institution itself.

SISTER, RELIGIOUS

ENVELOPE	Sister Marie-Claire Duchêne, D.C. President, The Daughters of Charity *(local address)*
SALUTATION	Dear Sister *or* Dear Sister Marie-Claire
COMPLIMENTARY CLOSE	Respectfully yours, *or* Sincerely yours,
INVITATION *(inside envelope)*	Sister Marie-Claire Duchêne, D.C.
PLACE CARD	Sister Marie-Claire
INTRODUCTIONS/PRESENTATIONS	Sister Marie-Claire *or* Sister-President* *or* President Duchêne
IN CONVERSATION	Sister *or* Sister Marie-Claire

* The title Sister-President is not commonly used. The titles Reverend Mother, Mother Superior, or Mother, although not abolished had fallen into general disuse, but are now, once again, on the revival. They are still used in religious orders of ancient origins and by those new institutes structured upon more ancient rules. Where not used, in their place one finds more common use of Sister, Sister-President, or President when referring to heads of communities of sisters or congregations. Each order or community determines the norm, it appears.

SEMINARIAN/THEOLOGIAN

ENVELOPE	Mr. John Doe Seminarian for the Archdiocese of Washington House of Formation The Catholic University of America Washington, DC 20064
SALUTATION	Dear Mr. Doe *or* Dear John
COMPLIMENTARY CLOSE	Sincerely yours,
INVITATION *(inside envelope)*	Mr. John Doe
PLACE CARD	John Doe, Seminarian for the Archdiocese of Washington
INTRODUCTIONS/PRESENTATIONS	Mr. John Doe, Seminarian for the Archdiocese of Washington
IN CONVERSATION	Mr. Doe *or* John

Notes: It is improper to refer to a seminarian in speech or written form as Seminarian John Doe. Until Holy Orders, a seminarian properly retains the appellation "Mister," which is commonly abbreviated as *Mr.*

If a seminarian is entitled to the use of postnominal initials to denote a degree or some rank, it would be appropriate to continue their use during seminary formation when appropriate; for example, John Doe, J.D., Ph.D., K.M. One also occasionally finds Europeans and some Asians who entered formation from a noble family. On formal documents, their formal titles would still be used until the call to the transitional deaconate. Permanent deacons would likewise relinquish the use of any family titles at ordination.

PRINCE GRAND MASTER OF MALTA

ENVELOPE	His Most Eminent Highness, Fra Andrew W.N. Bertie Prince Grand Master of Malta* The Grand Magistral Palace 68 via Condotti Rome, Italy
SALUTATION	Your Highness *or* Monseigneur *or* Sir
COMPLIMENTARY CLOSE	Respectfully yours, *or* Confraternally yours, *(from members of the order)*
INVITATION *(inside envelope)*	His Most Eminent Highness, The Prince Grand Master of Malta
PLACE CARD	His Highness The Prince Grand Master of Malta
INTRODUCTIONS/PRESENTATIONS	As a head of state, everyone is presented to the Prince Grand Master.
IN CONVERSATION	Your Highness *or* Monseigneur *or* Sir

* Italian translation: S.A. Em.ma il Principe e Gran Maestro, Di Ordine Sovrano Militare Di San Giovanni, Di Gerusalemme Di Rodi e Di Malta.

Note: The Prince Grand Master of Malta holds the rank and precedence of a cardinal in the Church, having the qualification of "Eminent" Highness. In international law, the Prince Grand Master holds the position of sovereign head of state.

THE GRAND MASTER, THE EQUESTRIAN ORDER OF THE HOLY SEPULCHRE OF JERUSALEM

ENVELOPE	His Eminence, Giuseppe Cardinal Caprio Grand Master The Equestrian Order of the Holy Sepulchre of Jerusalem 00120 Vatican City
SALUTATION	Your Eminence, *or* Most Reverend Sir, *or* My Lord Cardinal,
COMPLIMENTARY CLOSE	Respectfully yours, *or* Confraternally yours, *(from members of the Order)*
INVITATION *(inside envelope)*	His Eminence, Giuseppe Cardinal Caprio
PLACE CARD	His Eminence, Giuseppe Cardinal Caprio, Grand Master
INTRODUCTIONS/PRESENTATIONS	His Eminence, Giuseppe Cardinal Caprio, Grand Master of the Equestrian Order of the Holy Sepulchre*
IN CONVERSATION	Your Eminence

* The use of the order's full title would be proper for events outside the order itself.

QUICK REFERENCE TABLE

ECCLESIASTICAL TITLE	FORMAL STYLE
The Pope	His Holiness; Your Holiness; Most Holy Father
Cardinals	His Eminence; Your Eminence
Patriarchs	His Beatitude; Your Beatitude
Archbishops	His Excellency; Your Excellency
Bishops	His Excellency; Your Excellency*
Eparchs (Oriental rites)	His Excellency; Your Excellency
Exarchs (Oriental rites)	Father†
Monsignors (all ranks)	Monsignor
Abbots	Father Abbot
Priests	Father
Superiors	Father *(unless they hold a higher personal title that confers a higher style)*
Vicars General/Forane	Father *(unless they hold a higher personal title that confers a higher style)*

* The British and the Canadians sometimes adhere to the practice of calling archbishops and bishops "Your Grace," but this practice is no longer authorized and should be abandoned.

† Unless he also holds a higher personal rank or is a legate of a patriarch, then use "Excellency."

Notes: The use of the title Doctor (Dr.) is permissible, but it should be restricted to academic settings and never used if a higher ecclesiastical title is held, which takes precedence. Clerics holding doctorates should present these credentials by postnominal initials (Ph.D., D.D., J.C.D., S.T.D., J.U.D., J.D., etc.). It would be proper, however, to refer to one holding a doctorate as "Reverend Doctor." One occasion for such usage would be during an introduction of a speaker who holds a doctoral degree.

The Oriental rites have additional titles beyond those most commonly found in the Latin rite. An example of one such title is Archimandrite, which has its origins in the monastic traditions of the East but now is conferred, like the title Monsignor, on deserving Eastern rite priests.

ACADEMIC TITLES

A.B. and B.A., Bachelor of Arts
B. Arch., Bachelor of Architecture
B.B.A., Bachelor of Business Administration
B.Ch., Bachelor of Surgery
B.D., Bachelor of Divinity
B.E., Bachelor of Engineering
B.E. Chem., Bachelor of Engineering in Chemistry
B.Ed., Bachelor of Science in Education
B.F.A., Bachelor of Fine Arts
B.S., Bachelor of Science
B.S.E.E., Bachelor of Science in Electrical Engineering
B.S.M.E., Bachelor of Science in Mechanical Engineering
D.A., Doctor of Arts
D.D., Doctor of Divinity*
D.D.S., Doctor of Dental Surgery
D.Ed. and Ed.D., Doctor of Education
D.Eng., Doctor of Engineering
D.Th., Doctor of Theology
His. Ecc. D., Historiac Eccesiaticae Doctoris (Doctor of Church History)
J.C.D., Doctor of Canon Law
J.C.L., Licentiate in Canon Law

J.D., Doctor of Law
J.U.D., Juris Utriusque Doctor (Doctor of both laws)
Litt.D., Doctor of Literature
L.L.B., Bachelor of Laws
L.L.D., Doctor of Laws
L.L.M., Master of Laws
L.Th., Licentiate in Theology
M.A., Master of Arts
M.B., Bachelor of Medicine
M.B.A., Master in Business Administration
M.D., Doctor of Medicine
M.Div., Master of Divinity
M.Ed., Master of Education
M.F.A., Master of Fine Arts
M.Th., Master of Theology
Mus.D., Doctor of Music
Ph.D., Doctor of Philosophy
Sc.D., Doctor of Science
S.Mus.D., Doctor of Sacred Music
S.S.D., Doctor of Sacred Scripture
S.S.M., Master in Sacred Sciences
S.T.D., Doctor of Sacred Theology
S.Th.B. and S.T.B., Bachelor of Sacred Theology
S.T.L., Licentiate in Sacred Theology
S.T.M., Master in Sacred Theology

* The doctor of divinity degree, required for all newly named bishops, was once bestowed upon the new prelate by decree of one of the pontifical universities and, in more ancient times, by one of the Curia congregations or the pope. Today, however, it is a title, style, and degree automatically assumed by a newly named bishop, both residential and titular.

Note: Honoris Causa (honorary doctorate) degrees, when conferred, carry with them all the privileges entitled to the honoree of an academically earned degree. Therefore, the honoree is entitled to both the title Doctor and the appropriate postnominal initials as well as the proper vesture and insignia of that title.

CHAPTER TWELVE

Ecclesiastical Precedence

I n the beginning of the nineteenth century, the western world was in turmoil
following the fall of Napoleon I. All sense
of the order that previously had ruled
now disappeared. The Congress of
Vienna in 1815 was called not only to
divide the spoils but to stabilize the West, politically and socially, and to lay down regulations
governing international relations based upon a
foundation of Christian principles and values. At
this congress, diplomatic and parliamentary protocol and precedence were determined once and for
all. The Church adopted the Congress of Vienna's
terms in regard to precedence and to the external
life of the Church and adjusted its own external life
to reflect the uniform regulations adopted in
Vienna.

ORDER OF PRECEDENCE

Ecclesiastical protocol must deal not only with
external issues—the Church's relations with the
States—but also with internal issues—the integrate
orders of precedence within the Church as well
as the relationship to the ceremonial life of the
Church.

Within the structure of the Church, regulations
governing precedence are clearly and historically
defined. The Roman Pontiff holds the unique position of both Head of the Church Universal and
Sovereign of the Vatican City State. In the international diplomatic community, he is accorded
precedence before all other heads of state because of
the dual character of his position. This duality views
him not only as spiritual leader to the world's eight
hundred million Catholics and the premier spiritual
leader of the world, but also as sovereign of an independent state, much like a benevolent monarchy in
terms of governmental structure. As such, the pope
holds a unique international position of head of
state of the smallest nation on earth, yet leader of
more people than all but the largest of nations.
Emperor, kings, princes, and presidents all defer
their precedence to the pope when in his presence
due to this singular duality of character.

All clerics and laymen of the Church hierarchy
strictly follow the tables of precedence set forth at
the Congress of Vienna in 1815.

College of Cardinals

Precedence of the Sacred College is governed by the Secretariat of State and by the personal initiative *(motu proprio)* of the reigning pope. During the 1815 Congress of Vienna, the long-standing practice of referring to cardinals as "Princes of the Church" was formally recognized by according all newly elevated cardinals the rank and privileges equal to princes of royal birth.*

The senior members of the College of Cardinals are the six cardinals who hold the seven suburbicarian sees. The cardinal-dean holds the See of Ostia as well as one of the other six sees held by the Order of Cardinal-Bishop. These are Ostia, Albano, Frascati, Palestrina, Porto-Santa Rufina, Sabina-Poggio Mirtelo, and Velletri-Segni. The order of Cardinal-Bishops additionally includes cardinal-patriarchs of the Eastern rite of the Church. They take precedence equal to, but immediately following, the six suburbicarian sees.

The dean of the Sacred College is considered *primas inter aequales* within the College. His see is always that of Ostia in addition to the see held at the time of his election, by his fellow cardinal-bishops, to the post of dean. Although elected by the cardinal-bishops, both the dean and the subdean must have their election confirmed by the reigning pope. Precedence within the Order of Cardinal-Bishops is accorded by the date that the cardinals were promoted to a suburbicarian see.

The order of Cardinal-Priests follows in precedence. Within the Sacred College, cardinals take their precedence primarily by date of appointment and secondarily by order of nomination on the *biglietto* appointing them. Therefore, the longest-standing members of the College take precedence within their order over newly named cardinals. Because the papal document naming new cardinals is not alphabetized, precedence among those named on the same day is accorded by strict order of their appearance on the *biglietto*.

Cardinal-deacons form the third order in the Sacred College and take their precedence in the same manner as do the cardinal-priests. It is important to remember that although segregated into different divisions, each member of the Sacred College is equal to all others.

It should be noted that cardinals named *in petto,* that is, silently for reasons deemed necessary by the reigning pope, take their precedence from the date of their nomination once they have been publically proclaimed cardinal and, therefore, have precedence over those who have been named subsequently.

Patriarchs

Following the College of Cardinals, the patriarchs take precedence over all other prelates of the Church and form a college of their own. Additionally, they are granted the title Assistants to the Papal Throne, a post that holds high honors and that automatically accords them a special position in the Papal Chapel. If a patriarch has been named a cardinal, his precedence, rank, and privileges become those of a member of the College of Cardinals.

Archbishops

There are several degrees of archbishop. For matters of protocol and precedence the highest of these is *Major Archbishop.* Major archbishops have jurisdiction over large territories or specific groups of the faithful. At present, there are two such titles only, Lviv of the Ukraine and Ernakulam-

---

* Even today, in the colorful language of diplomacy, kings refer to cardinals, in correspondence, as "dear cousin," and the Sovereign Order of Malta immediately confers upon newly named cardinals the rank of Bailiff of Justice in the order, which is strictly reserved for the nobility.

Angamaly of the Sino-Malabaresi rite. If one of the major archbishops were to be promoted to the Sacred College, then this prelate would assume the precedence of cardinal in the class of his appointment.

The archbishops follow the patriarchs in descending order of precedence. Among their number there are archbishops with jurisdiction (with a residential archdiocese to govern), titular archbishops, and archbishops *ad personam*. As a group, archbishops come before all other prelates and officials of the Church. The personal honor of naming an archbishop "Assistant to the Papal Throne" brings with it additional precedence and honors, but this is not accorded to every archbishop. Prelates who have been so named have the right to a place of honor before all other archbishops at the Papal Chapel.

Bishops, Abbots, and Minor Prelates

After the archbishops, precedence is accorded to all bishops and abbots (although certain abbots have a higher precedence gained through history and still retained). The titular bishops assigned to Rome may have a higher precedence if the post they hold carries with it further honors. In this case, however, the higher precedence is accorded to the post a prelate holds and not to the prelate personally.

The College of Protonotaries Apostolic de Numero (of which there are presently seven) follow in the order of precedence. These prelates have unique responsibilities in service to the Holy Father and are accorded special honors and precedence in the Papal Chapel. The protonotaries apostolic supranumerary are honorary and diocesan in character and, along with the prelates of honor and the chaplains of His Holiness, precede (in descending order) priests and deacons. When present, the religious superiors; canons; vicars apostolic, forane, and episcopal; and the prefects apostolic precede priests and deacons.

The importance of the order of ecclesiastical precedence is felt both in Rome and on the diocesan level. It determines the proper placement of prelates in processions and in their seating and placement at religious functions. It also determines the role they are to play at liturgical functions, as well as their placement at nonliturgical social functions, all of which guarantees the proper dignity and respect owed to members of the Episcopate. Protocol and precedence serve as a tool to arrive smoothly at the desired effect and to maintain order and decorum at all times. When properly mastered, the implementation of protocol and the proper adherence to precedence will provide the appearance that a logistically awkward occasion has been effortlessly presented. Protocol additionally removes the possibility of thorny problems or personal preferences from defacing the sacredness of religious occasions.

THE TABLES OF PRECEDENCE WITHIN THE CHURCH

International tables of precedence were set forth in 1815 at the Congress of Vienna. These tables remain in force today, with few changes, governing all diplomatic protocol as well as professional and social interaction. Church precedence, however, preceded the formulation of official protocol at the Vienna Congress, yet the Church incorporated the diplomatic formulae of the day into its own usage in order to actively participate in the world and its accepted mode of social behavior. These modifications, in a way, were a modernization of the Roman High Renaissance formula in force until 1815.

PRECEDENCE WITHIN THE CHURCH

The Supreme Pontiff
Cardinal-Dean
Cardinal-Vice Dean
Cardinal–Secretary of State
(*de facto* by responsibility)
Cardinal-Bishops
(by date of their appointment to the subur-
  bicarian see)
Oriental Patriarchs
Cardinal-Priests
(by date of creation)
Cardinal-Deacons
(by date of creation)
Patriarchs
Primates
Major Archbishops
Archbishops
• Residential
• Titular
Bishops
• Residential
• Titular

Prelates Nullius
Abbots Nullius
Abbots
Exarchs Apostolic (of the Oriental rites)
Vicars Apostolic
Prefects Apostolic
Apostolic Administrations
Prelates of Personal Prelatures
Protonotaries Apostolic
• De Numero
• Supranumerary
Superiors/Provosts
Canons
Prelates of Honor of His Holiness
Chaplains of His Holiness
Vicars General
Vicars Forane and Episcopal; Deans
Diocesan Notaries
Archpriests
Priests
Deacons, Permanent and Transitional
Religious Brothers and Sisters

Within each category or rank, precedence is derived from the date of ordination, promotion, or nomination into that specific category. For example, a prelate of honor who holds this title longer than all others in his diocese is the highest ranking of this class in the hierarchy in that specific jurisdiction; however, if he were to be nominated as a protonotary apostolic supranumerary, by Rome, he would then become the lowest ranking prelate of this higher class within his own jurisdiction. The same rule applies to each class within the hierarchy.

A special note must be made of the pope's delegate within each nation. Nuncio, Pro-Nuncio, and Apostolic Delegate are titles of a diplomatic nature and not of prelatial nature. These prelates usually hold the title *Titular Archbishop*. The titles *Nuncio, Pro-Nuncio,* and *Apostolic Delegate* are accorded precedence by diplomatic convention, that is, by international common law and treaty. In Catholic countries, the nuncio is head of that nation's diplomatic corps, whereas a pro-nuncio takes his precedence within a nation's capital by his date of appointment to that post. The Holy See, however, has redefined the usage of the title Pro-Nuncio (these changes are explored further in Chapter 4, "Papal Diplomacy"). Apostolic delegates, on the other hand, have no official diplomatic standing in a nation's capital because their responsibility is to represent the pope to his Church in that country and not to represent the Holy See to the government of the country. With that said, however, the issue of precedence for these officials must be discussed because the ranking Vatican official in each nation will maintain a presence at the diocesan level from time to time.

When an apostolic nuncio or pro-nuncio is present in a diocese on official business, he is representing the person of the pope and therefore should be accorded the highest precedence. Examples of occasions requiring the nuncio's official presence would be during a priestly jubilee of the ordinary, the installation of a new ordinary, the raising of a new diocese, a local bishop's conference, etc. During these events, despite the fact that cardinals would be present who would normally always outrank an archbishop, it must be remembered that the pope's representative takes the pontiff's place at these events; therefore, official precedence should be accorded to him. Outside his jurisdiction, however, the papal representative is accorded the precedence required only for his personal title. As most senior papal diplomats are titular archbishops, the papal representative would then be placed among those of this rank in matters of precedence.

Precedence at Major Ecclesiastical Processions

When a large procession is to be formed prior to a special diocesan Mass, the planners and masters of ceremonies of the forthcoming event should always be sure to plan well ahead so that care is given to the rank and position of those Church dignitaries who plan to participate.

A large chart should be prepared so that as replies return to the Chancery, the planning committee can meet to assign seating, procession order, and roles for the liturgy itself. On this chart, care should be given to assign the proper order to the clergy. Seminarians, if present, should follow the crucifer, but only when vested in cassock and surplice. Never is the alb or civil dress acceptable, by long-standing Church custom, for seminarians in procession. Following the seminarians would be nonconcelebrating priests in alb, stole, and, optimally, matching chasuble. The *monsignori* of the diocese and visiting monsignors who are also concelebrating follow. If a monsignor is not concelebrating, he precedes the clergy, vested in choir cassock and surplice. The vicars general and forane follow. All bishops and archbishops vested in choir follow next. Beyond them are the concelebrating bishops, followed by the archbishops.

The following processional charts are derived by protocol. They illustrate the proper structure of the ecclesiastical procession and the proper positioning of participants in the procession as well as present special variables for unique cases.

I. Processional Order When Apostolic Nuncio or Delegate Is Present as a Major, Vested Concelebrant

ALTAR

	Aisle	
	•	Master of Ceremonies
	•	Thurifer
	†	Crucifer
	• •	Acolytes
	• •	
	• •	
	• •	Seminarians
	• •	
	• •	
(carrying the Gospels)	•	Deacon of the Word
	• •	
	• •	Clergy
	• •	
	• •	
	• •	
	• •	
	• •	
	• •	Monsignori
	• •	
	• •	Vicars Forane
	• •	
	• •	Vicars General
	• •	(Arch)bishops
	• •	in choir
When vested as concelebrants, the simplex mitre is worn.	• •	(Arch)bishops vested as Concelebrants
	•	M.C.
1–6: two chaplains each	• 1 •	Main Celebrant
	• 2 •	Apostolic Nuncio
	• 3 •	*Cardinals vested in*
	• 4 •	*scarlet choir dress;*
	• 5 •	*first to process is the*
	• 6 •	*most recently named.*
	•	M.C.
	• • •	Vimps/Acolytes

Note: Main celebrant wears precious mitre; apostolic nuncio wears simplex.

II. Processional Order When the Metropolitan Presides at a Suffragan Diocesan Event and When the Apostolic Nuncio/Delegate Is Present in Choir

ALTAR

	Aisle	
	•	Master of Ceremonies
	•	Thurifer
	†	Crucifer
	• •	Acolytes
	• •	
	• •	
	• •	Seminarians
(carrying the Gospels)	•	Deacon of the Word
	• •	
	• •	Clergy
	• •	
	• •	
	• •	
	• •	Monsignori
	• •	
	• •	Vicars Forane
	• •	
	• •	Vicars General
	• •	(Arch)bishops
	• •	in choir
	• •	
	• •	Bishops (Auxiliary)
Concelebrants all wear the simplex mitre.	• •	Bishops (Residential)
	• •	
	• •	
	•	M.C.
Simplex mitre, without crozier	• 1 •	Bishop of the place
Precious mitre, and pallium	• 2 •	The Metropolitan
Vested in choir; two chaplains each	• 3 •	The Apostolic Nuncio
	• • •	Vimps/Acolytes

Note: The Metropolitan alone carries the crozier. The deacons for the main celebrant may be vested in dalmatic.

III. PROCESSIONAL ORDER WHEN THE MAIN CELEBRANT IS A CARDINAL ARCHBISHOP; THE CONCELEBRANTS ARE OTHER CARDINALS, ARCHBISHOPS, BISHOPS, AND THE APOSTOLIC NUNCIO; AND WHEN OTHER CARDINALS ARE PRESENT IN CHOIR

ALTAR
Aisle

(Procession begins as illustrated in I and II.)

	• •	Vicars Forane
	• •	
	• •	Vicars General
	• •	
	• •	(Arch)bishops
	• •	*in choir*
When vested as	• •	(Arch)bishops
concelebrants,	• •	vested as
simplex mitre is worn.	• •	concelebrants
Simplex mitre	1	Vested Nuncio
The most recent is	•	Cardinals; vested as
the first in procession.	•	concelebrants with
	•	*damasked mitre*
	•	M.C.
Precious mitre/pallium/	2	Vested Cardinal-
crozier		Archbishops
	• • •	Vimps/Acolytes
Two chaplains escort each	• • •	cardinals vested in
cardinal (either monsignori	• • •	scarlet *choir;* the
or knights).	• • •	first to process is the
	• • •	most recently created.
	•	Seminarian/Acolytes
	• • •	Papal Knights

Note: Use of the papal knights, as prescribed by Rome, requires a place of honor for them in the procession as they are members of the Papal Family. Knights of Columbus, an esteemed and valuable fraternity, does not hold and enjoy this same privilege; however, their contribution and role is always welcome as a guard of honor. The Church in the United States has always placed the Knights of Columbus in the opening of the procession as a way of marking their special contribution to Church ceremonies.

IV. PROCESSIONAL ORDER FOR THE MASS OF TRANSFER OF ORDINARY AUTHORITY OF AN (ARCH)BISHOP TO HIS SUCCESSOR, WITH THE APOSTOLIC NUNCIO/DELEGATE AS CONCELEBRANT

ALTAR
Aisle

	•	Master of Ceremonies
	•	Thurifer
	†	Crucifer
	• •	Acolytes
	• •	
	• •	
	• •	Seminarians
	• •	
(carrying the Gospels)	•	Deacon of the Word
	• •	
The clergy of the place is	• •	Concelebrating
seated prior to procession.	• •	Bishops in *simplex*
	• •	*mitre and chasuble*
	• •	
	• •	
	• •	
	• •	Concelebrating
	• •	Archbishops in
	• •	*simplex mitre*
	• •	
	• •	
	• •	
	•	M.C.
Precious mitre and chasuble	• 1 •	Newly named
		(Arch)bishop
Simplex mitre and chasuble	• 2 •	Apostolic Nuncio
	•	M.C.
Precious mitre/cope/crozier	• 3 •	Retiring Ordinary
	• • •	Vimps/Acolytes
	• 4 •	
	• 5 •	Cardinals *in choir*
	• 6 •	Most recent first in
	• 7 •	order of procession
	• 8 •	
Acolytes/Seminarians or	• •	Papal Knights

Note: Chaplains may accompany each of the main concelebrants, typically the chancellor, vice chancellor, or rector of the cathedral.

Planning Processional Order

When planning processional order, it is important to keep these points in mind:

1. When a patriarch without cardinalatial dignity is present, he is placed in choir or, if vested as a concelebrant, in a position of honor in the procession to follow the archbishops.

2. If primates are present, within their primatial jurisdiction, they too would be given preeminence, similar in degree to a metropolitan archbishop when present in his own jurisdiction.

3. If a primatial see has lapsed, as in the case of the United States, that same historical see can be accorded a place of honor nonetheless by placing the incumbent ordinary of the place in a senior position among those whose rank he shares—in other words, with his brother archbishops.

4. Papal honorees, both lay and cleric, by long-standing papal custom, are to be given a place of honor in the processional order. For this reason, the *monsignori* follow the clergy of the place as concelebrants or in choir. Placement should follow this order: Chaplains of His Holiness, Prelates of Honor, Apostolic Protonotaries. (Lay papal awards are just as significant and most definitely have a role to play in diocesan functions. Please refer to the chapter on these awards and become familiar with those faithful who have been so honored by the pope, as these papal awards hold great dignity internationally. They are not the same as fraternal associations that carry the title Knight or Lady; therefore, precedence should be given to them, whereas lesser roles should, by protocol, be assigned to these loyal fraternal organizations.)

5. At very large diocesan events, such as the installation or funeral of an archbishop or a bishop, the processions tend to be very long because of the large number of participating hierarchy. Therefore, with the exception of cardinals, patriarchs, or the nuncio, all those vested in choir should not process; they should be seated in the sanctuary just prior to the beginning of the procession. The same is true for the seminarians, other than those designated as the "ceremonies crew," and all clergy, including the *monsignori*, unless otherwise few in number.

6. The senior master of ceremonies (M.C.) is placed closest to the presider, whereas others are placed throughout to ease the flow of traffic and to direct the hierarchy and ceremonies crew as need be.

7. Only the main celebrant makes use of a precious mitre; all others must make use of the simplex mitre. The practice of matching mitre and chasuble is discussed in the chapter on mitres (see Chapter 36).

Large processions should be formed one-half hour before the procession is to begin. This is often difficult, of course, because of late arrivals and last-minute changes. Planning for large liturgical ceremonies should always be done well in advance, especially for the processional order. If done correctly, the event itself will run far more smoothly.

Notes should be written or telephone calls made to all the senior clergy—visiting bishops, archbishops, and cardinals—so as to inform them of the exact place and time they are expected. A reminder of what vestments or vesture is expected of them should be clarified at this time as well.

Once gathered, the senior master of ceremonies and some assistants should arrange into groups the various ranks of the clergy. If the staging facilities permit, it is best to separate the ranks to better organize the order of procession. For instance, the ceremonies crew and seminarians gather at one site, while the priests, *monsignori,* and vicars gather at another. As these two groups are led into place and the procession takes its proper form, the hierarchy, placed in proper processional order at the cathedral sacristy, rectory, or other suitable site, joins them to complete the order of procession and begin the ceremonies.

The organization described above works best! It, however, requires an excellent master of ceremonies and ceremonies crew, who are well rehearsed and well versed in the setup of the processional units, as well as the time and proper place each unit is to join the full procession as it begins to enter the cathedral.

The recessional, with occasionally few exceptions, takes the same order for exiting the cathedral but relies on the memory of the participants more than on the direction of the master of ceremonies.

A special note should be made concerning an old custom still honored in many (arch)dioceses by the hierarchy as they enter and exit the cathedral. Whenever the Blessed Sacrament is reserved somewhere other than the main sanctuary, if the procession passes by the tabernacle, the ordinary may pause in silent prayer for a few moments. In some places, where size permits, senior concelebrants join the Ordinary in prayer at a prie-dieu prepared for them. The assembly should also kneel quietly for a few moments, rising when the hierarchy does. The entrance hymn continues as usual during this prayerful pause. This same act of reverence may occur as the ordinary exits the cathedral. When this act of reverence occurs, the master of ceremonies should be nearby to remove the mitre of the ordinary so as to be handed off to a ready vimp (mitre bearer). The other bishops remove and replace their own mitres. The *zucchetto* is not removed unless the Blessed Sacrament is exposed for some reason.

State Ceremonial Precedence

From time to time, the Church becomes the center for state ceremonies. Weddings and funerals of prominent Catholic government dignitaries are events wherein Church and state protocol must

ORDER OF PRECEDENCE AT STATE CEREMONIES

President of the United States (spouse)

Foreign Heads of State present, with precedence given to royalty in proper rank

Vice President of the United States (spouse)

Secretary-General of the United Nations

Governor of the State (spouse)

Past Presidents of the United States (spouses)

Chief Justice of the Supreme Court

Secretary of State (spouse)

Ambassadors of Foreign States *(ranked by the date of presentation of their credentials)*

Justices of the Supreme Court

Cabinet of the President *(by formal precedence)*

President Pro Tempore of the Senate

Senators *(according to length of service)*

Governors *(from other states; ranked by the date of each state's entry into the Union)*

Members of the House of Representatives *(according to length of service)*

Mayor of the Place (spouse)

State Officials *(as set by local custom)*

Local Officials *(as set by local custom)*

merge. At such events, Church protocol must always take the forefront. As a general rule, civil or state protocol should be employed for seating and processions only. The diocese should always appoint a clerical official from within its Chancery to oversee the program of events that take place on Church property. He should also serve as liaison with the appropriate government counterpart if one has been assigned. As a general rule, the accompanying list provides the order of precedence of state officials of the United States. In nations where royalty still reign or where they may be in attendance, special care should be provided to give them the precedence that is always their due because of their special rank. The order of precedence of the United States is set by the Office of Protocol of the U.S. Department of State. Periodically, the official tables of precedence are adjusted to take into account changes within society.

At the local level, precedence begins with the highest civil official present and descends through the ranks of those remaining dignitaries present. When time allows for the proper scheduling of these events, the diocesan official in charge of protocol should preassign the appropriate place in processions, as well as seating, for persons invited or expected to attend. In so doing, problems that could otherwise arise are avoided. Although some mention has been made of royal guests, this might seem to be a foreign concept in some dioceses. There are occasions when the local church is faced with the participation of foreign titled dignitaries at its Church functions. On such occasions, it should be remembered that royal protocol is the most prescriptive. By tradition, Roman Catholic royalty are accorded the privilege of separate seating within the sanctuary of the church or cathedral. At state occasions, such as the funeral of a president or of a statesperson, this privilege need not be accorded. It would be appropriate at special Church events, however, such as Eucharistic Congresses or state weddings. Non-Catholic royalty are not accorded this same privilege; neither are civil authorities of any rank.

Special Notes

1. The Cardinal-Secretary is given *de facto* precedence by virtue of his office within the Curia as he is the closest collaborator with the Holy Father. Senior precedence within the College, however, must always go to the dean of the College, always a suburbicarian cardinal-bishop, the vice-dean, and then the Camerlengo, if this position has been separated from that of dean, vice-dean, or even Cardinal–Secretary of State.

2. Paul VI raised the Oriental patriarchs who were not also members of the Sacred College to a precedence below that of cardinal-bishops but above that of cardinal-priests and deacons as a sign of the Church's acknowledgement of their esteem and importance. They are not members of the Sacred College unless otherwise nominated and, therefore, enjoy no other privileges of the College of Cardinals.

3. For cardinals within each category who were created on the same day, higher precedence is accorded to each in the exact order in which their name appeared on the *biglietto* that named them to the Sacred College.

4. When vicars, prefects, and administrators apostolic, as well as personal prelates, hold the higher dignity of "Bishop," "Archbishop," or even "Cardinal," they naturally assume the correct precedence of their positions in these offices.

5. When vicars general, forane, and episcopal, as well as deans, hold a higher dignity of "Bishop" or one of the monsignorial classes, they naturally enjoy all the privileges and precedence of that rank.

6. The lay honorees of the papacy also enjoy a strict precedence, which is more fully discussed in Chapter 6. Special details are provided for the ranking of the honors themselves, as well as the classes within each order.

Ecclesiastical Protocol and Etiquette

"The term 'protocol' is derived from the Greek word *protokollen; protos* means the first and *kolla* means 'glue.' This refers to a sheet of paper glued to the front of a notarial document giving it authenticity."[1] This narrow meaning of the term *protocol* is still used today in referring to official Church, governmental, and diplomatic documents.

"Not everyone realizes that protocol has been a part of life for thousands of years. Scenes painted in Egyptian tombs and writings of early times tell of the strict rules that applied to various phases of life and death. The sculptural reliefs on the ruined walls of Persepolis show the order of procession imposed upon the tribute bearers at the court of Cyrus the Great 2,500 years ago."[2]

Throughout the Middle Ages and into the Renaissance, protocol developed to meet the changing needs of society. As life became more complex, protocol filled the need to bring control and a sense of calm to governments and society. In the High Renaissance, the Church began to implement a code of behavior for all aspects of life, both ceremonial and mundane. Protocol took two forms: that governing the ceremonial life of the Church and the liturgy, and that governing the Church's relations to states, known as the external life of the Church.

At the time of the founding of the United States, protocol was viewed by the founding fathers as a good thing. Both Thomas Jefferson and Benjamin Franklin spoke of it "as a means to achieve a desired effect in the governing of peoples." Despite the general principles of protocol then existing, often serious rifts between states arose due to a lack of understanding or mistrust of one another's customs and traditions. The Church was not immune to these problems, as it was part of the existing international fabric.

As we have seen, the Congress of Vienna in 1815 bought formulae into practice that have lasted to the present. These formulae govern the relationship of one state to another, the reaching of accord between feuding states, the diplomatic discourse throughout the world, and the relationships that the Church maintains throughout the world.

The protocol established in Vienna was also social in nature. Royalty, the nobility, and the bourgeoisie alike adopted social customs and practices that were defined as universal at Vienna. These same customs survive today in the world of formal entertaining.

Entertainment in the Church is a necessity. The pope receives visitors of all ranks and positions in a fashion to be described as entertainment. It is not so in any modern sense but is very much so in the diplomatic sense. The Cardinal–Secretary of State, in his official capacity as head of government of the Vatican City State, likewise offers official entertainment. This "entertainment" is usually in the form of receptions, which are official in nature and not generally conceived to be entertainments in any modern sense or understanding of the term. Likewise, at the local level, all sorts of official entertainments are expected and required of the local ordinary and his officials in order to accomplish the work of the Church in any given area.

Just as any diplomatic or social host would be expected to follow long-standing formulae in precedence and protocol in regard to entertaining, a local cardinal, archbishop, or bishop is obliged to do so as well. The success of the event, after the success of the endeavor itself, therefore, often depends on the perceived success of the social event attached to it, or the style of the prelate(s) presiding as host(s). This is very much the case when dealing with sophisticated, erudite laity who attend many of these events and who are being pulled in several directions for financial contributions as well as for contributions of time and talent.

The intent of this chapter is to educate and enlighten all persons who host, plan, or participate in any way in official entertainments for the benefit of Church causes. The proceedings set forth were, indeed, formulated in Vienna long ago. Like all things in society, however, they have been brought up to date and are, therefore, the most modern of accepted practices in social, diplomatic and, most important, Church protocol with regard to official entertaining.

VATICAN PROTOCOL

In the diplomatic environment, the term for the most formal criteria for dress and deportment is commonly referred to as *Vatican protocol*. Strictly speaking, Vatican protocol would apply only to those regulations set in place within the Vatican—governing official and private visits there as well as the social customs set forth for the employees of the Holy See in their daily routine. The term *Vatican protocol* is applied commonly, although not exclusively, to the Holy See because in the years since these procedures were first employed, the Church has always maintained the highest standards of formal style of dress and deportment.

Technically, present Vatican protocol comprises only those regulations presently in place at the Vatican, which never have been meant to be static. Nonetheless, whenever the most formal protocol is employed somewhere in the world today, it is commonly referred to as Vatican protocol.

Papal Audiences

Style and deportment at the Vatican, especially in association with a visit to the pontiff, has always been highly formal. Regulations for clerics are defined throughout this study and need only a brief mention in this section. Present regulations governing visits between the pope and members of the hierarchy make use of the *ferraiolo* optional. The *ferraiolo* is still seen from time to time, contrary to what one would expect. (It seems that when something becomes optional today, it tends to fall into disuse; this is not the case with the *ferraiolo*, yet, it is not worn all that frequently.) All clerics and seminarians are still expected to appear in the presence of the pope in cassock or the simar for the hierarchy. The black clerical suit, or vesture other than the religious habit, are contrary to Vatican protocol.

For the laity, the most formal protocol of dress is known as *tenue pontificale,* comprising a black tailcoat, black waistcoat, white bow tie, and one's decorations or orders. This most formal dress is now reserved for persons on formal or official visits to the pontiff and for functionaries at papal ceremonies and within the Papal Household. Ladies during these same occasions are required to make use of a long sleeved, full-length black dress with a long black mantilla. Ladies from European nations and from the Hispanic culture often make use of the high ivory hair comb, over which is placed the mantilla. This is the correct Vatican protocol for females on very formal occasions. Ladies may likewise wear any decorations or orders conferred upon them. Jewelry should always be discreet and tasteful. Royal and noble ladies are presented the option of wearing a tiara or diadem rather than the Spanish comb. Catholic queens and the Grand Duchess of Luxembourg are entitled to the diplomatic privilege known as the *privilège du blanc.*

"Formal dress," somewhat less formal than "official dress" or *tenue pontificale,* for gentlemen is always the black business suit and black four-in-hand necktie. For ladies, this protocol would include the black calf- or knee-length dress with long sleeves or a black shawl that covers the arms and a black mantilla without the comb. "Less formal dress" for gentlemen, which was unacceptable in the pope's presence until the 1970s, is a dark business suit and conservative necktie. For ladies, this dress would include a conservative calf- or knee-length dress with long sleeves. Head coverings for ladies at Papal Masses are still correct under present Vatican protocol.

Roman Visits

The Church's protocol extends beyond papal visits. In fact, the "less formal dress" described above is still expected for men and women when visiting the Roman basilicas, churches in Rome, public rooms within the Vatican Palace, and the Vatican gardens. The tremendous number of visiting tourists to the Vatican museums makes it impossible to enforce this dress code in the museums even though, technically, these sites are also included in this protocol directive.

Although one might get away with wearing informal "tourist" dress in the museums, one should not attempt to enter St. Peter's in casual clothing, such as shorts, and for women, even a sleeveless dress. The *sanpietrini* will bar your entrance.*

Finally, a protocol exists, as well, for those who need to conduct business within the confines of the Vatican City State. Anyone attempting to pass by the Swiss Guards who are posted on duty at the Sant'Anna or Holy Office gates and who are improperly attired will be turned back no matter who they may be.

When paying a visit to an official of the Roman Curia, whether he be a prelate, priest, or layman, one should always dress in the most conservative manner. Although less observed today, this protocol extends to the use of the black business suit or black conservative dress for those calling on a cardinal at all times.

ETIQUETTE FOR OFFICIAL CHURCH ENTERTAINING

There are many reasons why the ordinary should host official entertainments. Fund-raising is, of course, a necessity, and entertaining potential donors or organizers of a fiscal campaign is an excellent motivation. Entertaining also provides the ordinary the opportunity to greet both donors and dedicated workers in a more intimate social environment. There is an old business adage, and I can attest to it myself, that "more business is done over lunch, dinner, and on the golf course than in the office." This benefit should not escape the Church.

---

* The author has seen a young American couple visiting St. Peter's who, with only one pair of long slacks between them, publically stripped to their underclothes so that they might each take a turn wearing the pants in order to visit the basilica in a more respectful attire. It meant nothing at all to passersby as they viewed the couple changing clothing in the open air of St. Peter's Square.

Because official entertainments are a necessary part of the ordinary's role as corporate head of the diocese, the ordinary should take full advantage of techniques that have been successfully utilized by the worldwide diplomatic service and official governments for years.

Some attention should be devoted to the proper procedures for official entertainment within the Church. The local ordinary is often called upon to host official functions that require proper attention to protocol. Often questions arise as to the proper seating of distinguished guests according to their rank and precedence, and, by tradition and custom, for both Church officials and laity. The following diagrams and seating plans have been designed to serve as a guide for the staff of the host to an official evening of entertainment where members of the hierarchy are to be present. (See pages 255–60.)

Protocol calls for an alternating seating arrangement between ladies and gentlemen at mixed dinners or luncheons. Often in the Church, however, the protocol for all-male affairs is more appropriate, as women might not be present. A few basic principles should be understood before planning an official event.

The first of these rules is that the host, who in the case of Church protocol is usually either the ordinary of the diocese, the metropolitan in his province, or the nuncio within his jurisdiction, is always placed at the center of the head table or dais. If a podium is placed at the center of the table, the host should be placed at right center (as viewed from the front). In the place of honor, which is always to the immediate right of the host, would be placed the guest of honor, or if there is none, either the cohost or the master of ceremonies.

When the dais or head table is reserved for prelates of the Church, the seating of these prelates would follow the same pattern as described above for both the host and guest of honor, whereas all other prelates would be seated in an alternating pattern to the right of the guest of honor and to the left of the host. In a descending fashion, the most senior prelates would be placed close to the center at either side, whereas the lesser ranking prelates would be placed to the outside.

The second rule to follow is that of precedence. The highest ranking prelate present should be accorded the place of honor. If a priest or lesser prelate is designated to be the guest of honor, it is customary for the higher dignitary to forgo the honors of precedence in order for the guest of honor of a lesser rank to be seated appropriately. In cases such as these, several solutions can be found in order to honor the ranking dignitary and to properly place the official guest of honor. One solution would be to invoke the principle of "courtesy to a stranger." This diplomatic device works well when a lower ranking foreign dignitary is to be honored. Regardless of his rank in the Church, he is accorded a one-time precedence under the principle of courtesy to a stranger.

A second possible solution would be the use of round tables or, more correctly, two equal tables. The first would be headed by the host. To his immediate right would be placed the guest of honor. Heading the second table would be the other, more senior-ranking prelate. This arrangement works well when the other ranking prelate present is a member of the Sacred College and when the guest of honor is a lesser ranking prelate, priest, or layman. Because protocol requires that a cardinal always be accorded the higher precedence, the round table seating plan accomplishes this requirement by making the cardinal the *de facto* cohost. Two tables are also employed when there are a number of governmental officials and a like number of ecclesiastical dignitaries. The senior-ranking dignitary from each respective group would host one of these two tables.

When the affair is to be mixed, that is, when both sexes are to be present, the rules of protocol and etiquette are clear and should always be followed. More accurately, they are to be mingled with Church etiquette as described above. The host of the event will most likely be the bishop of the place. The guest of honor could be either a Churchman or a member of the laity. When female guests are present at the head table, they should be seated in alternating places whenever possible.

When an important civil dignitary such as a president or vice president or governor is to be entertained, most commonly at luncheons, the basic mixed seating plan should be used. The honored guest, however, would sit opposite the host, whereas the guest's spouse would sit next to the host. The same is true for visiting royalty, who may be entertained most commonly at a luncheon.

Planning Procedures for Official Diocesan Entertaining

It usually falls to an ad hoc committee to plan entertainments associated with special events that occur within a diocese. Such events include the welcoming of a new ordinary, the return of a new cardinal to his diocese, and the jubilee of an ordinary or auxiliary. The secretary to the ordinary should always be included on this ad hoc committee. The secretary, better than all others, knows the likes and dislikes of his superior, the bishop. He also has firsthand knowledge as to who should or should not be included on a guest list for the event at hand. The following is a list of all the topics that an ad hoc committee should be prepared to present:

- Guest list: size and makeup
- Invitation: style, components, wording, and choice of engraver
- Site for function
- Decorations: flowers, banners, lanterns, etc.
- Menus: choice of caterer and choice of menu, keeping in mind dietary restrictions and the likes and dislikes of the host and the many guests of honor, as well as the capabilities of the kitchen staff of the site
- Receiving line: procedures to be set when all the assembly will be received, as well as the makeup of the receiving line (who stands where)

TOASTS

Toasts should fall on the shoulders of the bishop's secretary to compose or to assign to appropriate guests. Guests who are to offer a toast should be informed that they have been asked to present a toast and that an appropriate "outline" for it will be provided them by the secretary of the bishop. This assignment should always be undertaken diplomatically so as not to offend a high-ranking clergyman and to appear to assume that he has already undertaken the desired theme for the toast on his own; the secretary's job is to assure that he has.

PRESS OR PUBLIC RELATIONS

A full description of the event should be prepared in press-packet format by the ad hoc committee. The packet should include histories of the guest(s) of honor as well as a history of the event. A staff member of the diocese should be designated to be on hand to facilitate smooth relations with any press who are present at the event.

SECURITY

In present times, it is a necessity to make the appropriate security arrangements at the site of the event, as well as with the local police and diocesan security, if senior Churchmen or other dignitaries are to be present.

PROTOCOL

The diocesan protocolist should be assigned to the ad hoc committee and make appropriate arrangements for the necessary protocol of the event(s).

CHECKLIST FOR OFFICIAL ENTERTAINING

Choice of Date
Choice of Luncheon, Dinner, or Banquet
Nomination of Planning Panel
Nomination of Master of Ceremonies
Choice of Site
Guest List
Invitations
Menu, Caterer, Table Shape, Seating
 Arrangements
Music, Entertainment, Audiovisual
Photographer
Printed Programs
Public Address System
Public Relations/Press Release

RECEIVING LINE

The following placement (in reverse order) is the correct formula for an ecclesiastical receiving line:

• Host (usually the ordinary of the place)

• Guest of honor

• Official assigned for protocol (possibly the secretary to the ordinary or the master of ceremonies)

OR

• Host

• Guest of honor

• Senior prelate also present (cohost)

• Official assigned for protocol

If the entertainment follows a liturgical ceremony at which the host either presided, celebrated, or concelebrated and where he greeted the faithful at the liturgy's end, no receiving line would be required at the entertainment. A simple procession to the head table at the opening of the evening would be appropriate.

INVITATIONS

It may appear frivolous in the modern world to remain faithful to age-old customs and traditions regarding the issuance and acceptance of invitations, whether they be social or liturgical, and yet the fact that these customs have existed for as long as they have is evidence that they play a unique role in the life of society and within the Church.

The rules that apply to society, and by this I include the "official" world such as the diplomatic corps, the state or the official governmental world, as well as the social world of charitable events and fund-raisers, are also relevant to the Church in the external arena, that is, in the nonliturgical role that the Church plays in society. Many of the rules that govern social intercourse today were refined at the courts of Europe, including the Papal Court, and as we have seen, the present system of protocol by which all social intercourse is derived was formalized at the Congress of Vienna in 1815, at which the Church played a significant role.

Any diocesan or Church official who wishes to participate in the social or external work of the Church for the benefit of the local Church or the Church Universal must be well versed in the niceties of the modern social world, and he must be able to utilize these abilities to the benefit of the Church.

Dos and Don'ts

A good starting point is the issuance and proper acceptance of social invitations. In no other area of social discourse are the clergy found to be so lacking as they are in this area. First and foremost, when one has received a social invitation, one should realize that he or she is considered "honored company" by the host and hostess issuing it. Such an honor demands a prompt reply. Many members of the clergy ignore invitations issued to them. Some individuals even attend the event without having responded in the affirmative (definitely inappropriate). They do not realize that the host and hostess must have an accurate head count in order to prepare the many aspects for entertaining that evening. Some persons take the attitude that "one person won't make that much of a difference," but social gatherings are made up of many "one persons." Always, always respond by the requested date! Remember, large social events of all kinds take a great deal of preparation and often generate confusion all around. Do not rely on the memory of the host or hostess to recall a passing comment that you will or will not attend that event. Always reply by note or response card so that your answer may be recorded properly.

Next, always pay careful attention to the dress requirements on formal invitations. Many clergymen are invited during the course of their lifetimes to very formal events where a vest or tab shirt would not be appropriate. To arrive improperly dressed is very similar to a priest's complaint that the faithful arrive in shorts, T-shirts, and sandals for Sunday Mass. One should always show respect for the host or hostess of an event by dressing appropriately.

In the ecclesiastical world, one must never refuse an invitation from an ordinary. It is just plain rude to do so. Although some bishops may issue late invitations when it would be impossible to find a replacement for your responsibilities, invitations that are issued in proper time should always be accepted. This is both a long-standing Church tradition and a sign of good manners. It should go without saying, nevertheless, that all invitations from an ordinary should be responded to promptly and in writing to either the bishop personally or through his priest secretary.

The dos and don'ts of good manners also require that all persons invited to an event arrive at the appointed time. This would rule out the half-hour-late arrival because of a late wedding rehearsal at the parish. Once one has accepted a formal invitation, it is one's responsibility to make the necessary arrangements to be present at the requested time!

Guest Lists

A special note to the secretary, to the bishop, or to the host of the event must be made. A list of appropriate individuals within the diocese or jurisdiction should be compiled in order to form a base for creating guest lists for a given function. This list should be substantial, and input from the deans or vicar forane is always appropriate. Individuals who support the Church at the local level are not always known to the bishop and yet are deserving of reward. An invitation to join the bishop and the diocesan officials at a specific function is often ample reward. This database should never make up more than 70 percent of the guest list. Variety makes for a successful function. At least 30 percent of the guests should come from other areas, certainly not all Catholic.

For instance, when the function is to be a party for a visiting prelate from a foreign country, it would be wise to include some distinguished person of that country who resides in the host nation. The local embassy's social secretary will be able to supply you with a list of such persons, but you must always cross-reference this list with the visiting prelate's secretary (via fax, preferably). In the case of a foreign prelate's visit, perhaps industrialists and distinguished bankers would be an excellent addition to the diocesan database of invitees (70 percent) so that these persons can offer to the visitor advice or counsel, which he might carry home with him.

Guest lists should always be prepared with proper care well in advance. Any additions or uncertainties should be reviewed with both the bishop's (host) and the guest of honor's secretary. If the guest of honor is also to be the houseguest of the ordinary or host, a listing of all the guests attending each of the events should be prepared and placed in his accommodations for his familiarization.

Also be careful to be aware of language difficulties. If the guest of honor is a foreigner with little working knowledge of English, be certain to obtain some idea of the languages that the guest does speak; and it is hoped that one of those languages is understood by a priest or staff member of the diocese.

Style and Form for Invitations

In society, there are many styles and types of invitations; some are considered correct by long-standing norms and traditions, and others are more inventive or reflective of the times. Both types have become socially correct for the social world. Within the Church, however, one must be always careful to avoid the trendy. The best forms for invitations, therefore, are the traditional styles, and yet even this category affords a great variety from which to choose. This rule should apply not only to members of the clergy but also to organizations within the Church or associated with it that are formal and/or that benefit the Church's work.

The following are the traditional components of an invitation:

THE BODY

The body is what we have come to call the "invitation." This includes all the particulars of the event in question such as who is the host or hostess, which organization is involved (if any), date, time, address, and dress required. The body could be on single-card stock (vellum) or bifolded stock. White or off-white with black ink are traditional. For the most formal events, it would be appropriate to emboss the prelates' coat of arms or to engrave it in color at the top of the stock.

THE R.S.V.P.

The response card comes in many forms, occasionally requesting a letter or call to the appropriate person by a requested date or by a *pro forma* card to be returned. Whichever type is used, the invitees should always refer to this card as soon as they have reviewed the body of the invitation and, after checking their schedules, should immediately respond in the affirmative or negative. It would be appropriate to add a handwritten personal note at the bottom, whatever the response may be.

R.S.V.P. is the standard abbreviation for *Répondez s'il vous plaît* ("please respond"). It takes its name from French, which is the language of international diplomacy.* You will see this abbreviation associated with all sorts of formal entertainments.

For prelates and priests in chancery service or the diplomatic corps, the most formal invitations will often come via telegram, such as for a reception for a posthaste foreign visit. Always respond within the hour to such invitations—preferably by phone, if not by telegram or telefax.

If an event is on a large scale and the reception that follows is more along the line of light refreshments, such as cookies and punch, as well as an opportunity to mingle with other guests, an R.S.V.P. is not necessary unless some idea of a head count is required for catering. If an event follows in a church hall or social center and the seating capacity of the Church is known, then no R.S.V.P. card would be required.

---

* Just as English is the international business language and, of course, Latin remains the language of the Universal Church.

RECEPTION CARDS

It is customary to invite many persons to a specific event—such as an ordination, a celebration of a First Mass, or a jubilee—and not invite all who came to witness the event to the reception that would follow at a suitable time. When this is the case, it is proper to issue the body of the invitation without any mention whatsoever of a reception. Enclosed within the packet to persons who are to be invited to a reception would be a separate reception card with the appropriate information, such as the site, the time, and the hours, if limited. Under no circumstances should one combine the information onto one card in order to save money. In the long run, it will cause more headaches and cost more money if persons who misread the combined card arrive for the reception. This situation is not only an affront to individuals not included in the invitation to the reception, but it is simply bad manners to let one officially know of a party to which one is not invited. Never combine the two.

As a rule, never combine two events on one invitational body. For instance, it has become "acceptable" practice to combine both an ordination invitation or announcement with a First Mass invitation. As most cathedrals could not hold the number of persons wishing to attend ordinations, the local Church limits the number of invited guest per *ordinandi*. The remainder attend the First Mass the following day or later that evening. By combining these events, the invitees are totally confused, and some are rightly offended. The proper form in such a case would be to announce the "semi-private ordination" ceremony (Ordinations are always diocesan events even when most of the faithful would not normally attend) and to invite, on a separate card, persons desired for the First Mass. The announcement of an anticipated ordination could be issued separately or could be printed separately but included in the packet sent. At all costs, be careful to avoid assuming that people understand modern styles of invitation. They generally do not, and the *ordinandi* often have angry family and friends turned away from a cathedral because "they were not invited." Always be clear as to what events your invitees are to be included. Separate cards for each event are always required.

PROTOCOL CARD

Protocol cards are utilized for formal entertaining during the installation ceremonies of a new bishop, ceremonies marking the return of a newly named cardinal, jubilees of the ordinary, funerals of the ordinary, etc. These cards take the same shape and style as do the reception cards. Sometimes the event requires the cards to be the size of the actual invitation. Whichever demands the occasion places on the organizer of that event warrants the size and context of this card.

A protocol card should always have the heading "Protocol" in bold, centered at top. Below it, the text should be of the same print type used on all other printing for the occasion. These cards are meant as informational so that important information can be relayed to the invitees prior to the event. Information about the style of the event or the procedures to be followed during the event would be items included on the protocol card. Titles of individuals present might also be listed so that the invitees will know the proper forms of address to use. Perhaps, for important occasions, security, protocol, etiquette, or even parking information should be included. (See Fig. 13-13 on page 275.)

The most formal invitations, both within the Church and external to it in the social world, require the proper formula of introduction. In the Church, the invitation should begin with words "In the presence of His Eminence, Michael Cardinal Doe," and continue with "His Excellency, James Francis Smith, Bishop of Portland, requests the honor of your presence, etc."

Engraved Invitations

The completely engraved invitation is the most familiar kind. All the pertinent information is included in an engraved fashion. The most formal invitation always includes the wording "requests the pleasure of the company of," and a space is provided for that person's name to be inscribed in calligraphy. This is not only the most formal manner, as it clearly states who is to be invited (which also eliminates the often delicate situation of a guest's response that he or she plans to bring along someone who was not invited), but it also is the most personal, as it illustrates the care provided in inscribing the guest's name. Other acceptable means are "requests the honor of your presence" or "requests the pleasure of your company."

Semiengraved Invitations

If an ordinary wishes to maintain some degree of formality in all of his entertaining and yet avoid the costs of continual engraving and/or printing, the long-standing tradition of the semiengraved invitation would serve him well (see Fig. 13-2 on page 262). In the semiengraved style, the arms of the bishop and his name, as well as the basic wording of all invitations, are printed in bulk. The remainder of the information, such as the date, the occasion, and the time, are hand lettered or written in calligraphy. The bulk printing provides both less expensive printing costs and on-hand availability of invitations that permit a sense of the desired formality.

It should be noted that persons in public life, especially those in the Church, often forget what an honor it is for the public to be invited by a high-placed official. It is all the more the case when one of the faithful of the diocese or a local business leader is being invited by a bishop. A little effort toward formality goes a long way in public relations and is almost always welcomed and appreciated by persons who are invited.

Printing and Engraving

Some mention needs to be made of the terminology used by printers and engravers when accepting commissions for invitation printing. There are different types of engraved invitations, and an individual who is responsible for commissioning a job on his bishop's behalf should be prepared to discuss the matter in appropriate terminology.

The most formal of invitations is, of course, the engraved invitation. Nearly everyone in the western world has seen an engraved invitation—most commonly, a wedding invitation. The most formal invitations are written in the third person (individual's name, then he/she/they). The heading of a formal invitation should be placed below the body of the invitation. The proper order of information, that is, the date on the first line, with the address or the site of the event appearing on the second line, is the reverse of that for standard invitations. The date is always spelled out.

Informal invitations are always written in the second person (you). All paragraphs, the date, complimentary close, and signature should always be indented as would a formal letter. The R.S.V.P. notation should appear in the lower-left corner of the invitation. Any response note, whether it be an acceptance or a regret, should follow the same format as the invitation, repeating the pertinent facts from the body of the invitation.

Formal and informal invitations may be handwritten or engraved but may not ever be typed or computer generated.

If envelopes are to be lined with tissue paper, as is the custom in Europe, it should be noted that white, off-white, or cream is the most formal. Also, red for cardinals; green for patriarchs, archbishops, and bishops; and violet for monsignorial classes, is proper if the intended mailing is issued in the name of that prelate himself.

CALLING CARDS AND SOCIAL CARDS

Most clerics in present times would think it unnecessary to have either calling or social cards; they would consider them obsolete. For a relatively inexpensive investment, however, clerics can be prepared for any sort of encounter, be it in liturgical circles or the social world.

Calling cards and social cards are not the same; each has its own function.

Calling Cards

The calling card is older than the social card and is of diplomatic convention. It is, therefore, the least popular in the modern world. In more gentle eras, one sent a calling card ahead, prior to one's intended visit. This card had one's name engraved upon it, and if the card was acceptable to the intended host, a visit would follow. Sometime following the presentation of a calling card, a return visit would follow. In this way, a diplomat or an official dignitary did not have to risk having the door slammed in his face, which, in former times, could lead to war. As time developed, this custom became refined, and the calling card, in general society, also took on the purpose of sending brief personal notes.

Although calling cards are still in use in diplomatic circles and in the highest levels of the Roman Curia, they are not seen often by the general populace or the diocesan clergy. For the purpose of proper definition, however, the following is the accepted form for these cards: The stock, or heavy paper, used should always be white or off-white, and the lettering should always be in black ink regardless of one's rank. Although the dimensions for these cards traditionally vary according to the rank of the bearer, the standard dimensions are 3½ by 2 inches.

Social Cards

The social card developed as the "child" of the diplomatic calling card and, as such, permitted more informality. These cards may be of smaller dimension, although the 3½- by 2-inch size works well. Envelopes should be purchased to match the size of the card. A reputable printer will be able to provide appropriate samples. Whereas the calling card required the formality of just the individual's name, the social card might also include one's home or chancery address. The social card would also be appropriate for papal honorees and should include their postnominal initials denoting membership in the Orders of the Holy See. This information would also permit the use of the heraldic colors on white or off-white stock—for example, red for cardinals; green for patriarchs, archbishops, and bishops; and violet for the ranks of monsignor.

The social card is used for correspondence and, in particular, brief notes. It is permissible to use a folding note card for a social card; in this case, however, the inside must be entirely blank. The outside flap could have either the priest's or prelate's coat of arms (the same for a papal gentleman) or the name and rank of the individual. The folding card may not, however, have an address or any other markings on the outside flap, nor can both the name and the arms appear simultaneously, as this would be redundant (see Chapter 10, Ecclesiastical Heraldry).

Proper Uses for Calling and Social Cards

Calling and social cards may serve a variety of purposes other than the traditional official use of calling cards or the effectiveness of social cards as personal notes. They may be sent with flowers, in place of an impersonal card supplied by a florist, as well as with gifts of all types. They can be used as a means of issuing a very informal invitation to one's home. Prelates and chancery officials might make use of them as a personal means of congratulating a staff member or one of the faithful. Such messages should always be handwritten by the sender rather than typed. In using calling and social cards in this manner, a sense of the personal and informal is the desired effect.

A member of the hierarchy, especially one in frequent contact with Rome, persons exposed to "official" society, as well as knights and ladies of the papal and sovereign orders, will often see a series of initials penned onto the calling or social cards that they may receive. Those abbreviations, like R.S.V.P., signify, in French, a specific meaning as defined by the Congress of Vienna. The most common abbreviations and the most likely to be seen by prelates, diocesan officials, and papal honorees are these:

- *p.f. (pour féliciter),* used on a card sent to offer congratulations to someone on special occasions

- *p.r. (pour remercier),* used to offer thanks for a kindness extended or for a gift

- *p.p. (pour présenter),* used to introduce another person. This abbreviation would be used most frequently by a bishop wishing to introduce one of his staff or a diocesan faithful to a member of the Roman Curia.

   N.B. (Nota Bene), used to signal out a specific point to be noted. Many Americans most commonly tend to use this in sentence format by starting the sentence with "Please note" or "Please note well." The proper format, however, is to end with a specific *Nota Bene.*

- *p.c. (pour condoléances),* used to extend one's condolences at the time of a death of a loved one. For Church use, a further social note commending the deceased unto God's mercy and a pledge of prayers for the deceased's soul and for the surviving family is more appropriate.

TABLE ETIQUETTE

At large functions, a brief reception usually precedes a dinner or banquet. Smoking is permitted although not encouraged. At all major events, smoking is to be expected; however, once the call to come to dinner has been given, all smoking must cease. Smoking at table is never permitted and is always considered the height of rudeness. Even Europeans, who enjoy smoking as a collective group more so than many other groups, never bring cigarettes or cigars to the table. At all-male events, a very common occurrence in the Church, cigars often follow dinner but even these are better still left behind until after the adjournment to another room unless a meeting is scheduled to follow at table.

One of the hardest tasks for hosting a party or banquet is to keep conversation going. Part of the success of this falls to the shoulders of the host or his secretary (as in the case of the ordinary), who should place persons of varied backgrounds together to incite interest and smooth conversation. Sadly, modern society has not produced the best of listeners. One tends to talk more than listen. To be a successful partner at table requires the ability not only to listen (and I do not mean sitting quietly for the opportunity to jump into the conversation to recount one's own stories or adventures), but rather to truly listen to what has been said by your partners and, in so doing, attempt to judge the things that he or she spoke of with a bit more enthusiasm or interest. These items of specific interest to your dinner companion are matters to explore with them more fully, as they are obviously important to him or her. Ask further questions about the points your dinner partner discusses, and the conversation will begin to roll. Everyone loves to speak about themselves, to relate their own life stories and adventures. The key to successful table conversation is to listen well and to ask about that which seems most important to your partner. Remember, however, that you will be seated next to a second person as well as across from yet another. Just repeat the same process with them, tying together the three or four persons around you, and you will be surprised how much you can learn in one evening and how enjoyable the evening is.

Here are a few steps that take away that feeling of nervousness when arriving at a big event. They work well in the social and business world and have been used to train diplomats and high-ranking employees of some of the world's largest companies.

When you arrive at the reception for a large social gathering, you will most likely be greeted by either the hostess or a receptionist who will show you to a table or desk where the seating assignments are posted or displayed. As soon as you have ascertained your assignment, excuse yourself quietly. If you arrive in a group, from the main reception area quietly review the names for persons also listed at your table. Seating lists at large events are usually designed by alphabetical order or by table numbers. If the list is designed by alphabetical order, you have a bit of research to do; otherwise a quick glance will let you know who will be seated with you. At large social functions, spouses are often seated at different tables. This is more common in Europe than America, yet it is possible that you will eventually come across this practice. If this is the case, you will have double the amount of last names to remember. Banquet tables seat anywhere from six to ten persons.

When you have obtained the names of those persons to be seated with you, you should do your best to commit these names to memory. If you have a knack for this, you will see how handy it comes when you have met one of the parties and they then, in turn, begin to introduce their spouses to you. Before they can complete the introduction, you will be able to say something along these lines, "Oh yes, Bill, it is a pleasure to meet you" or "Oh yes, you must be Sue; I am happy to meet you." This informal approach should only be undertaken, however, with Americans, who appreciate this type

of informality. Europeans, even those resident in the United States for a prolonged period, never come to appreciate this type of informality at social functions.

When making introductions at the table, always repeat that person's name as you shake his or her hand or nod. Do your best to commit that name to memory. It is not always easy but you should make the effort. Later on, you may be called upon to introduce that same person to someone else, and it would be very embarrassing to be unable to recall the name after having conversed with that person for the past hour. Do not be afraid to ask someone to repeat the name a few moments after your meeting. It is always wise to do so with those seated around you and can be accomplished delicately by saying, "The noise was so loud I could not quite make out your name." They will always be happy to repeat it, but be certain to commit it to memory from here on. The table listing comes in handy. Keep it open on your lap and glance at it occasionally. In reviewing the names of the persons around you, you should be able to connect the proper face with the proper name.

When an individual "re-introduces" himself or herself to you, and you do not have a indication who they are, it is best not to blatantly say so, as this might lead to dejection or hurt feelings. It is better to welcome such a person with a warm handshake, a smile, and words such as "Refresh my poor memory, won't you, it's been so long" or "You know, last time I didn't get your card, may I have one now?" If all else fails, and you have not given yourself totally away, it always works well to open the guest list and ask where they are seated and let them point to themselves on the list. Get the name quickly! Remember, you will need to remember these names as you may be called upon to introduce them to someone else, which is an important point. If someone comes up to you at the table, when all your tablemates are lost in deep conversation, you should always introduce that person to them.

All members of the clergy should remember that they stand out in the laity's mind. With this honor comes the responsibility to diplomatically recall as many "strangers" as possible, a responsibility that is always put to task at banquets and dinners.

Remember that you should spend equal time in conversation with everyone around you, not just with the partner who piques your interest the most. Leaving others out of the conversation is both rude and disappointing to them. Remember, the clergy are always looked up to, and ignoring others at the table is a personal affront. Please be mindful that you should speak to all present, especially to persons nearby.

Seating Charts

At formal functions where a bishop is host and when other members of the hierarchy are to be present alongside lay dignitaries, proper care should be provided to satisfy the demands of official protocol, which prescribes the approximate seating arrangement for the dais. Care should also be provided for the remaining guests so that both a variety and a balance promote conversation. As a result of such attention, a successful dinner or banquet will be accomplished. As described previously, planning the seating charts for a diocesan event falls to the ad hoc committee formed for the event and to the ordinary's secretary, who brings the bishop's desires and wishes to the floor. As already discussed, a proper mix of the diocesan community and additional invitees from the guest of honor's country, field of interest, or particular group would be appropriate.

The dais should always be reserved for the highest-ranking dignitaries present. The charts at the end of this chapter display sample arrangements that depict a variety of scenarios for official diocesan or more universal Church events. These designs have been the acceptable format for nearly a century and work very well in achieving the desired attention to proper precedence as well as flow of conversation.

PRINTED PROGRAMS

Finally, the last component of an official diocesan Church function is the printed program. This is an information card printed or engraved in a style similar to that of the event's invitation. Modern computer software packages have made desktop publishing quite simple. Ideally, at the most formal diocesan events, such as episcopal ordinations or the welcoming ceremonies of a new ordinary, the cards should be engraved or printed; otherwise, a desktop publisher can provide a suitable high-quality program. If the program is to be engraved, the engraving should be done on heavy stock in white or off-white with black ink. In the case of a dinner that is to follow a liturgy, the program would then be placed at each table setting, awaiting the guest's arrival.

When programs are required for liturgical events, the two options above remain viable; however, the heavy printed program would take the place of the protocol card, mentioned previously, and would accompany the mailing. If the desktop-publishing method is chosen, the protocol card remains, if necessary, and the program is handed out at the doors of the cathedral, church, or other site.

The key to issuing a proper program is to choose a design that is simple yet dignified and that matches the design of the invitations. The program should be written in a succinct, clear format so as to relay the desired information as efficiently as possible.

There are as many different types of programs as there are different events. In the Church, these types can be narrowed down to two divisions: the liturgical and the social. Both the liturgical and the social programs, regardless of the number required for distribution, should be photocopied and enclosed with appropriate notations for a prepared press release. In so doing, this will minimize improper press reporting due to a lack of accurate information. Copies of all official programs should always be prepared for the diocesan archives.

Liturgical Programs

Liturgical programs have a long-standing history of their own. All liturgical programs should include the following information:

- the names of the chief celebrant and all concelebrants
- the names of the presiding prelates (listed in proper descending order, from the highest to the lowest)
- the names of deacons and other ministers, including the readers and cantors
- the list of officials or officers for the organization, as in the case of an investiture of papal honorees
- the order of the Mass, including music
- perhaps a note of thanks to the choirmaster, the choir, and, of course, the pastor of the church, if he is not either the celebrant or concelebrant

A special note should be given about the program of music for the Mass at important liturgical events. Often proper care is not given to the choice of music at the local-church level. Music has always played a vital role in the liturgical life of the Church. For many centuries, the Church has always promoted high standards in liturgical worship. The great treasury of Gregorian chant, polyphonic music, and the use of the pipe organ as the primary liturgical instrument have always been upheld.

With the advent of the Second Vatican Council, the Catholic Church made many rapid developments in the area of sacred music. Clearly, the most radical change that occurred at this time was the use of the vernacular in the liturgy to facilitate "full and conscious participation" among the faithful. Thus, the Church generously opened its doors to publishers and composers to draw upon the rich treasuries of mainstream hymnody among Christian Churches and to compose new hymnody and Mass settings for the new liturgical rite.

In the years immediately following the Second Vatican Council, and even in present times, growth within the Church in the area of sacred music has become extremely diverse. Perhaps this is because the Church has never been given a standard hymnal of repertoire to serve as a core foundation of worship. On the other hand, because of this embracing of mainstream Christian hymnody and Mass settings, Catholics have had at their disposal some of the best music written in past times and contemporarily as well. As we move beyond the first quarter century of the Second Vatican Council, we can see that the Church has had its share of both good and bad quality music.

The editors of the *Worship Hymnal* series have been at the forefront in providing some of the best quality music as a core foundation for Catholic Americans. This hymnal, since the early 1970s, has done a fine job in moving Catholics to a better mainstream of hymnody and service music. The selections listed in the programs that follow are primarily taken from this hymnal, which has done so much to improve the quality of worship among Catholics. These liturgical selections have been suggested in light of the tremendous work the Gregorian Institute of America (GIA) has done in promoting high standards in Church music, and, of course, Church musicians. It draws upon the rich heritage that Catholics already share. The following musical programs have been designed as samples for specific Church events, such as ordinations, a First

Mass, episcopal ordination, and a funeral of dignitaries of the Church. These samples are meant to be guides upon which the local churches may make additions of their own by way of local custom.

In designing these sample programs, experts in Church music were consulted in order to present samples that properly reflect present liturgical guidelines as well as those that would truly inspire all persons present in a manner befitting the Church of God.

Liturgical programs are best put to use at special events in the life of the Church, such as at a funeral of a member of the hierarchy. They serve the prelates who are present as well as the "invited" mourners.

A description of the burial rite, the order of procession into and out of the Church, and the staging areas for visiting dignitaries are all items that could be included on a funeral program. Of course, burial

or reception information would also be most appropriate. In some dioceses, both local custom and the cathedral's facilities permit a burial in a crypt beneath the church. In other dioceses, where facilities do not exist or have been exhausted with time, alternative burial procedures are required. In both instances, a program that describes the exact procedure for burial (time, place, who is to participate, and who is to witness the internment) would be most helpful. Examples: "The late Archbishop will be interred in the Cathedral Crypt in a private ceremony of interment presided over by the Apostolic Nuncio," or "The late Archbishop's body will be carried from the Cathedral after the final commendations and will be transferred to St. Patrick's Cemetery, where burial will take place. All present in the Cathedral are invited to follow in procession; the Apostolic Nuncio will preside."

ORDINATION OF A PRIEST

Prelude:	Prélude, Adagio et Choral varié sur le thème du "Veni Creator" Op. 4	M. Durufle
Entrance Hymn:	To Jesus Christ, Our Sovereign King	Ich Glaub an Gott
Kyrie:	Mass of Jubilee	R. LeBlanc

Liturgy of the Word

First Reading Responsorial Psalm:	Forever I Will Sing the Goodness of the Lord (Worship III)	A. della Picca
Second Reading		
Gospel Acclamation: Gospel	Alleluia (Worship III, #286)	M. Vulpius

ORDINATION RITE

Calling of the Candidates
Presentation of the Candidates
Election by the Bishop and Consent of the People

Homily
Examination of the Candidate
Promise of Obedience

Invitation to Prayer
Litany of the Saints
Laying on of Hands

Prayer of Consecration
Investiture with Stole and Chasuble

Anointing of the Hands:	Veni Creator Spiritus	G. Romanum

LITURGY OF THE EUCHARIST

Presentation of the Gifts:	Air (from Suite in D)	J. S. Bach
Kiss of Peace:	This Is My Commandment (Worship III)	Routley
Holy, Holy, Holy:	New Plainsong Mass	D. Hurd
Memorial Acclamation:	New Plainsong Mass	D. Hurd
Great Amen:	Mass of Jubilee	R. LeBanc
Lamb of God:	Mass of Jubilee	R. LeBlanc
Communion Procession:	We Shall Go Up with Joy To the House of Our God (Worship III)	A. Gregory Murray
Song of Praise (Choir):	Ubi Caritas et amor (from Quatre Motets Op. 10)	M. Durufle
Recessional Hymn:	Christ Is Made the Sure Foundation	Westminster Abbey
Postlude:	Carillon-Sortie	H. Mulet

PRIEST'S FIRST MASS

Prelude:	Festival Piece (Ut Queant Laxis)	Gerard Farrell, OSB
Entrance Hymn:	I Bind Unto Myself Today (Worship II)	St. Patrick's Breastplate
Rite of Sprinkling:	Vidi Aquam	G. Romanum
Gloria:	A Community Mass	R. Proulx

LITURGY OF THE WORD

First Reading		
Responsorial Psalm:	This Is the Day the Lord Has Made, Let Us Rejoice and Be Glad (Worship III, #836)	R. Proulx
Second Reading		
Gospel Acclamation:	Alleluia (Worship III, #281)	R. Proulx
Gospel		
Homily		
Intercessions		

LITURGY OF THE EUCHARIST

Presentation of the Gifts:	Prière a Notre-Dame (from Suite Gothique Ap. 25)	L. Boellmann
Holy, Holy, Holy:	A Community Mass	R. Proulx
Memorial Acclamation:	A Community Mass	R. Proulx
Great Amen:	A Community Mass	R. Proulx
Lamb of God:	A Community Mass	R. Proulx
Communion Procession:	Arise, Come To Your God, Sing Him Your Songs of Rejoicing (Worship III, #53)	J. Gelineau
Song of Praise (Choir):	Draw Us in the Spirit's Tether	H. Friedell
Postlude:	Nun Danket Alle Gott	S. Karg-Elert

ORDINATION OF A BISHOP

Prelude:	Grand Chorus Dialogue	E. Giogout
Entrance Procession:	Entrada Festiva Op. 93	F. Peeters
Kyrie:	Cum Jubilo	G. Romanum
Gloria:	A Festival Eucharist	R. Proulx

LITURGY OF THE WORD

First Reading		
Responsorial Psalm:	Forever I Will Sing the Goodness of the Lord (Worship III)	J. R. Carroll
Second Reading		
Gospel Acclamation:	Alleluia (Worship III, #281)	R. Proulx
Gospel		

ORDINATION RITE

Hymn:	Veni Creator Spiritus	G. Romanum

Presentation of the Bishop Elect
Apostolic Letter
Consent of the People

Homily
Examination of the Candidate
Invitation to Prayer

Litany of the Saints   G. Romanum

Laying on of Hands
Book of the Gospels
Prayer of Consecration

Anointing of the Bishop's Head
Presentation of the Book of the Gospels
Investiture with Ring, Mitre, and Pastoral Staff

Sung Antiphon:	Go Out to All the World and Tell the Good News (Worship III)	A. Peloquin
Kiss of Peace		

LITURGY OF THE EUCHARIST

Presentation of the Gifts:	Andante Sostenuto (from Symphonie Gothique)	C. M. Widor
Holy, Holy, Holy:	A Festival Eucharist	R. Proulx
Memorial Acclamation:	A Festival Eucharist	R. Proulx
Great Amen:	A Festival Eucharist	R. Proulx
Lamb of God:	A Festival Eucharist	R. Proulx
Communion Procession:	The Lord Is My Shepherd There Is Nothing I Shall Want (Worship III)	R. Proulx
Song of Praise (Choir):	Ecce Sacerdos Magnus	E. Elgar
Hymn of Thanksgiving and Blessing:	Te Deum (Solemn Tone)	G. Romanum
Solemn Blessing		
Recessional:	Finale (Symphony No. 1, Op. 14)	L. Vierne

FUNERAL OF A BISHOP

Prelude:	In Paradisum	Daniel-Lesur
Introit:	Requiem Aeternam (Mass for the Dead)	G. Romanum

LITURGY OF THE WORD

First Reading Responsorial Psalm:	My Shepherd Is the Lord	J. Gelineau
Second Reading		
Gospel Acclamation: Gospel	Easter Alleluia	Chant-Mode II
Homily		

LITURGY OF THE EUCHARIST

Presentation of the Gifts:	Arioso (Cantata No. 156)	J. S. Bach
Sanctus:	Mass of the Dead	G. Romanum
Memorial Acclamation:	Plainchant	Sacramentary
Great Amen:	Plainchant	Sacramentary
Agnus Dei:	Mass of the Dead	G. Romanum
Communion Procession:	Precious in the Eyes of of the Lord Is the Death of His Friends (Worship III)	A. G. Murray, OSB
	He Is Risen, Alleluia!	E. Engieri

FINAL COMMENDATION AND FAREWELL

Responsory:	I Know That My Redeemer Lives	H. Hughes, SM
Closing Prayer		
Recessional:	In Paradisum (Mass for the Dead)	G. Romanum

The Social Program

A social program should be used at all large social functions and formal events. As it ties together the entire event, it brings a sense of totality or completion to the evening while, at the same time, informing the guests of the program of events for the evening.

There are many items that could be included on the program for the social segment of an event. One such item is the menu card, which should always be provided at formal luncheons and dinners (see samples provided). This is also a nice added touch for smaller, less formal dinners at a bishop's home or diocesan center. In this case, the staff of the bishop's office should obtain plain white or off-white stock cards from a local printer. The bishop's staff may then inscribe each by hand, in calligraphy, or, if the diocesan-office printer is equipped to receive card stock, they may have them printed in an appropriate font by the computer. Little effort is involved, and the menu card makes a wonderful impression when the occasion calls for just that.

The social program should also provide an order of events, such as the rotation of speakers, the calling for toasts, the playing of the national anthem, and the conferral of awards or citations. Finally, this program is often best suited to provide informational tidbits about the evening, the organization, or the purpose for the gathering, such as the mission statement or some brief biographical information on the guest of honor.

The social program is meant to bring elegance to any entertainment segment of an evening or afternoon function. It also affords the host a secondary opportunity to educate the guests about a given project, the purpose for the gathering, the intent of the appeal, and the plans for the funds pledged. Beyond that, when fund-raising is not the goal, the program offers a wonderful opportunity to inform the guests about the guest of honor or, as in the case of papal honorees, the history of the award and the reason for its bestowal.

Social programs are used in the diplomatic and formal social world all the time because they are successful tools for not only "getting the message across," but, more important, for "covering all the bases" so that each guest has an understanding of what is to transpire and what food and beverages are to be served.

Social program cards, if done well, are usually the one item the laity remove from the event as a souvenir, a sure sign that the event was a success!

Conclusion

Official entertainment is both necessary and expected at the diocesan level. There are some events in the life of the Church that simply demand a full-fledged entertainment. The laity often finds it confusing when a major campaign of some sort has been announced with great fanfare, and then the accompanying "drive" dinner falls flat. The same is so when a VIP is hosted by the local Church hierarchy. Often the visit holds the interest of that locality for days, sometimes weeks as in the case of the pontiff or visiting royalty, yet formal precedence that adheres, primarily, to protocol and, secondarily, to good common sense is most often not followed.

The intent of this chapter has been to aid the host and planners of such events. It is hoped that these basic, universally accepted formal proceedings will serve well the local Church as need arises.

SEATING CHART DIAGRAMS

DESIGN FOR BANQUET WITH DAIS
(all clergy)

(10)	(8)	(6)	(4)	(2)	(P) (1)	(3)	(5)	(7)	(9)

STYLE I

(P) Podium
(1) Host (Ordinary)
(2) Cohost or Guest of Honor
(3) Ranking Prelate
(4) 2nd-ranking Prelate
(5) 3rd-ranking Prelate
(6) 4th-ranking Prelate
(7) 5th-ranking Prelate
(8) 6th-ranking Prelate
(9) 7th-ranking Prelate
(10) 8th-ranking Prelate

STYLE II

(P) Podium
(1) Host
(2) Guest of Honor
(3) Master of Ceremonies (layman or clergy)
(4) Ranking Prelate
(5) 2nd-ranking Prelate
(6) 3rd-ranking Prelate
(7) 4th-ranking Prelate
(8) 5th-ranking Prelate
(9) 6th-ranking Prelate
(10) 7th-ranking Prelate

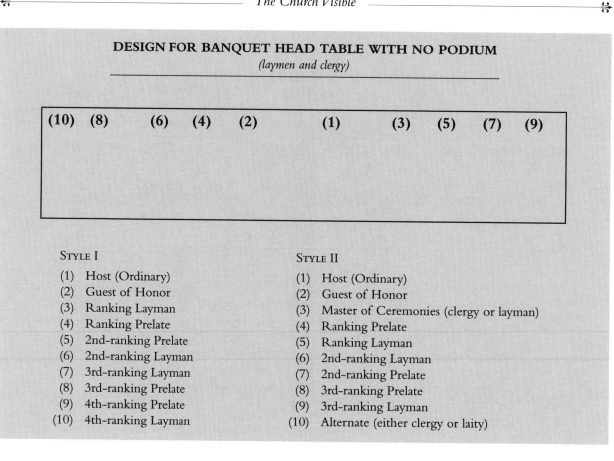

DESIGN FOR BANQUET HEAD TABLE WITH NO PODIUM
(laymen and clergy)

| (10) | (8) | (6) | (4) | (2) | (1) | (3) | (5) | (7) | (9) |

Style I

(1) Host (Ordinary)
(2) Guest of Honor
(3) Ranking Layman
(4) Ranking Prelate
(5) 2nd-ranking Prelate
(6) 2nd-ranking Layman
(7) 3rd-ranking Layman
(8) 3rd-ranking Prelate
(9) 4th-ranking Prelate
(10) 4th-ranking Layman

Style II

(1) Host (Ordinary)
(2) Guest of Honor
(3) Master of Ceremonies (clergy or layman)
(4) Ranking Prelate
(5) Ranking Layman
(6) 2nd-ranking Layman
(7) 2nd-ranking Prelate
(8) 3rd-ranking Prelate
(9) 3rd-ranking Layman
(10) Alternate (either clergy or laity)

DESIGN FOR SEATING RANKING CHURCHMAN AS HOST
(VIP layman as guest)

```
20        19
16        15
12        11
 8         7
 4         3
 2         1
 6         5
10         9
14        13
18        17
```

(1) Host (Cardinal/Nuncio/Archbishop/Bishop)
(2) VIP Guest (U.S. President/Vice President/Governor)
(3) Spouse of Guest of Honor
(4) Auxiliary Bishop/Vicar General
(5) Senior male member of guest's entourage
(6) Vicar General/Vatican Mission Councilor
(7) Senior Prelate
(8) Spouse of entourage
(9) Honored Clergy
(10) Spouse of entourage
(11) Spouse of entourage
(12) Honored Clergy
(13) Spouse of entourage
(14) Honored Clergy
(15) Male member of guest's entourage
(16) Male member of guest's entourage
(17) Male member of guest's entourage
(18) Priest/Secretary of the host
(19) Honored Clergy
(20) Male member of guest's entourage

DESIGN FOR ROUND TABLE ARRANGEMENT
(mixed clergy and laity)

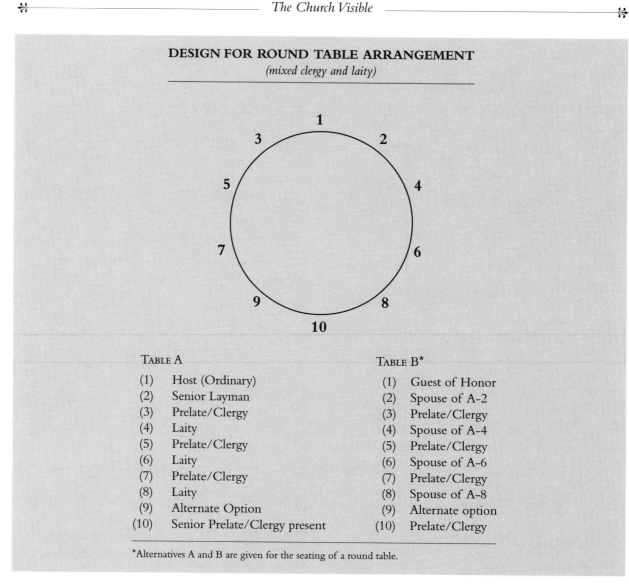

TABLE A

(1)   Host (Ordinary)
(2)   Senior Layman
(3)   Prelate/Clergy
(4)   Laity
(5)   Prelate/Clergy
(6)   Laity
(7)   Prelate/Clergy
(8)   Laity
(9)   Alternate Option
(10) Senior Prelate/Clergy present

TABLE B*

(1)   Guest of Honor
(2)   Spouse of A-2
(3)   Prelate/Clergy
(4)   Spouse of A-4
(5)   Prelate/Clergy
(6)   Spouse of A-6
(7)   Prelate/Clergy
(8)   Spouse of A-8
(9)   Alternate option
(10) Prelate/Clergy

*Alternatives A and B are given for the seating of a round table.

DESIGN FOR SEATING RANKING CHURCHMAN AND
ROYAL GUESTS

20	19
16	15
12	11
8	7
4	3
2	1
6	5
10	9
14	13
18	17

(1)   Host (Cardinal/Nuncio/Archbishop/Bishop)
(2)   Ranking male royal
(3)   Ranking female royal
(4)   Auxiliary Bishop/Vicar General/or Chancellor
(5)   Female of royal entourage
(6)   Senior spouse of local official (governor's or mayor's wife)
(7)   Auxiliary Bishop/Honored Clergy
(8)   Female of royal entourage
(9)   Senior male official of locality
(10) Honored Clergy

(11) Female of royal entourage
(12) Honored Clergy
(13) Female guest
(14) Local dignitary (male)
(15) Male of royal entourage
(16) Female guest
(17) Honored Clergy
(18) Priest/Secretary of the host
(19) Honored Clergy
(20) Male dignitary

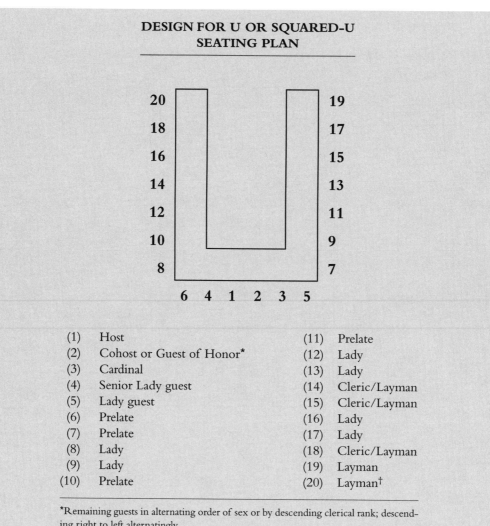

DESIGN FOR U OR SQUARED-U
SEATING PLAN

(1) Host	(11) Prelate
(2) Cohost or Guest of Honor*	(12) Lady
(3) Cardinal	(13) Lady
(4) Senior Lady guest	(14) Cleric/Layman
(5) Lady guest	(15) Cleric/Layman
(6) Prelate	(16) Lady
(7) Prelate	(17) Lady
(8) Lady	(18) Cleric/Layman
(9) Lady	(19) Layman
(10) Prelate	(20) Layman†

*Remaining guests in alternating order of sex or by descending clerical rank; descending right to left alternatingly.

†A Lady should not be placed at the end of a table following this design.

INVITATIONS

A l'occasion de l'anniversaire de
S. A. S. le Prince Souverain de Monaco
le Représentant Permanent de la Principauté de Monaco
auprès des Nations Unies et
Madame Jacques Boisson
ont l'honneur d'inviter

Mr. James Charles Noonan

à la réception qu'ils offrent le 31 mai à partir de 18 heures.

111 U. N. Plaza, Apt. 36 A/B
327 East 48th Street
New York, 10017

Regrets seulement
(212) 832.1721

13-1.

Le Nonce Apostolique

prie ..... S.A.S.

..... La Princesse Marie-Gabrielle de Lobkowicz .....

de lui faire l'honneur de venir à une réception

chez lui le Mardi 21 Mars

à 18:30 heures précises

R.S.V.P
47.23.58.34

10, Avenue du Président Wilson
Paris XVI.

13-2.

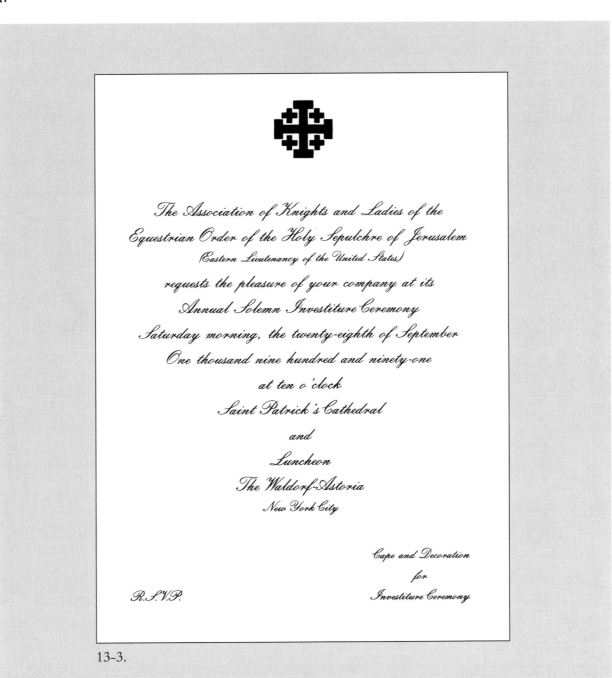

The Association of Knights and Ladies of the
Equestrian Order of the Holy Sepulchre of Jerusalem
(Eastern Lieutenancy of the United States)
requests the pleasure of your company at its
Annual Solemn Investiture Ceremony
Saturday morning, the twenty-eighth of September
One thousand nine hundred and ninety-one
at ten o'clock
Saint Patrick's Cathedral
and
Luncheon
The Waldorf-Astoria
New York City

Cape and Decoration
for
Investiture Ceremony

R.S.V.P.

13-3.

PREFETTURA DELLA CASA PONTIFICIA

Giovedì 7 aprile 1994

alle ore 18 nell'Aula Paolo VI

alla presenza di Sua Santità

Giovanni Paolo II

avrà luogo un concerto

per commemorare la « Shoah »,

l'Olocausto degli Ebrei

Vaticano, 1° aprile 1994

Programma

MAX BRUCH	« Kol Nidrei » per violoncello e orchestra Opera 47 (1881) *Violoncellista*: Lynn Harrell
LUDWIG VAN BEETHOVEN	Sinfonia n. 9 in Do minore opera 125 Terzo movimento: adagio molto e cantabile
FRANZ SCHUBERT	Salmo 92 per solo coro *Cantore*: baritono Howard Nevison
LEONARD BERNSTEIN	Sinfonia n. 3 « Kaddish » (1961-1963) brano *Narratore*: Richard Dreyfuss
LEONARD BERNSTEIN	Chichester Psalms (1965) Secondo movimento: Salmo 23 (tutto) Salmo 2 (versetti 1-4) Andante con moto, ma tranquillo *Solista*: Gregory Daniel Rodriguez Terzo movimento: Salmo 131 (tutto) Salmo 133 (versetto 1) Sostenuto molto, lento possibile

ROYAL PHILHARMONIC ORCHESTRA

DIRETTORE
GILBERT LEVINE

CORO « CAPPELLA GIULIA »
DELLA BASILICA DI SAN PIETRO IN VATICANO
•
CORO DELL'ACCADEMIA FILARMONICA ROMANA

MAESTRO DEI CORI
PABLO COLINO

INGRESSO ALL'AULA PAOLO VI
DA PIAZZA SAN PIETRO
COLONNATO DI SINISTRA
CANCELLO SANT'UFFIZIO

L'INGRESSO SARÀ DATO
DALLE ORE 16 ALLE ORE 17.30

ABITO SCURO
(ECCLESIASTICI: ABITO PIANO)

Reparto A/S   № 473

13-4.

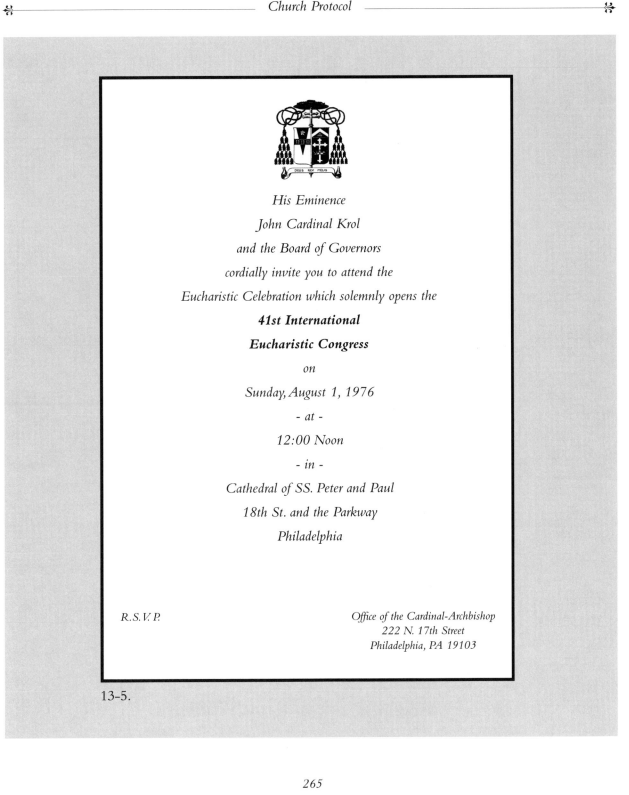

His Eminence

John Cardinal Krol

and the Board of Governors

cordially invite you to attend the

Eucharistic Celebration which solemnly opens the

41st International

Eucharistic Congress

on

Sunday, August 1, 1976

- at -

12:00 Noon

- in -

Cathedral of SS. Peter and Paul

18th St. and the Parkway

Philadelphia

R.S.V.P.

Office of the Cardinal-Archbishop
222 N. 17th Street
Philadelphia, PA 19103

13-5.

With great joy

The Pontifical
North American College

announces
the Ordination of those called by the Church
to the

ORDER OF DEACONS

through the imposition of hands
and the invocation of the Holy Spirit

by His Eminence

WILLIAM CARDINAL BAUM

Major Penitentiary of the Apostolic Penitentiary

Saturday, the eighteenth of December
nineteen hundred and ninety three
ten o'clock in the morning
Basilica of Saint Peter
Vatican City

Luncheon reception to follow
Pontifical North American College
Via del Gianicolo 14

13-6.

YOU ARE RESPECTFULLY INVITED TO

THE FUNERAL OF

HIS EMINENCE

D. CARDINAL DOUGHERTY

LATE ARCHBISHOP OF PHILADELPHIA

IN THE CATHEDRAL OF PHILADELPHIA

ON THURSDAY MORNING, JUNE THE SEVENTH

NINETEEN HUNDRED FIFTY-ONE

AT TEN-THIRTY O'CLOCK

DAYLIGHT SAVING TIME

FAITHFULLY YOURS IN CHRIST,

✠ **HUGH L. LAMB**
ADMINISTRATOR

DIVINE OFFICE
TUESDAY, 4:00 P.M.

13-7.

Dress for Ecclesiastics: Sacred vestments for concelebrants, simplex mitre (bishops); choir dress for prelates in attendance

Dress for Papal Honorees: Uniforms, habits, mantels, and insignia

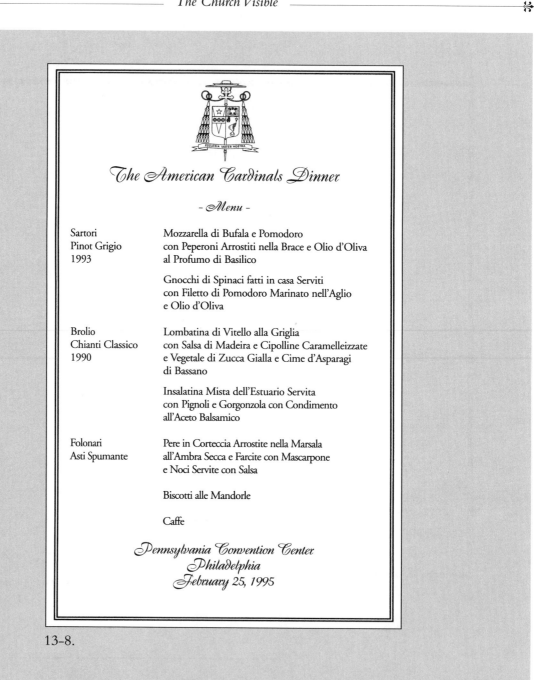

The American Cardinals Dinner

- Menu -

Sartori Pinot Grigio 1993	Mozzarella di Bufala e Pomodoro con Peperoni Arrostiti nella Brace e Olio d'Oliva al Profumo di Basilico
	Gnocchi di Spinaci fatti in casa Serviti con Filetto di Pomodoro Marinato nell'Aglio e Olio d'Oliva
Brolio Chianti Classico 1990	Lombatina di Vitello alla Griglia con Salsa di Madeira e Cipolline Caramelleizzate e Vegetale di Zucca Gialla e Cime d'Asparagi di Bassano
	Insalatina Mista dell'Estuario Servita con Pignoli e Gorgonzola con Condimento all'Aceto Balsamico
Folonari Asti Spumante	Pere in Corteccia Arrostite nella Marsala all'Ambra Secca e Farcite con Mascarpone e Noci Servite con Salsa
	Biscotti alle Mandorle
	Caffe

Pennsylvania Convention Center
Philadelphia
February 25, 1995

13–8.

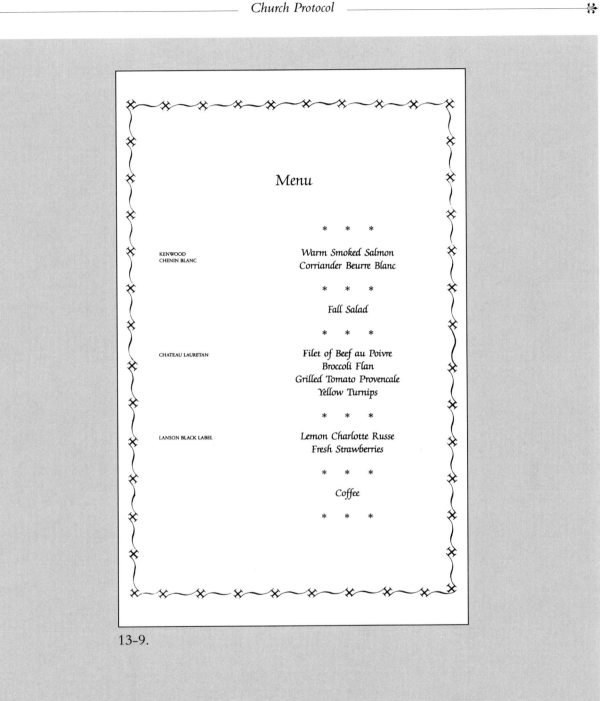

Menu

*   *   *

KENWOOD
CHENIN BLANC

Warm Smoked Salmon
Corriander Beurre Blanc

*   *   *

Fall Salad

*   *   *

CHATEAU LAURETAN

Filet of Beef au Poivre
Broccoli Flan
Grilled Tomato Provencale
Yellow Turnips

*   *   *

LANSON BLACK LABEL

Lemon Charlotte Russe
Fresh Strawberries

*   *   *

Coffee

*   *   *

13-9.

13-10.

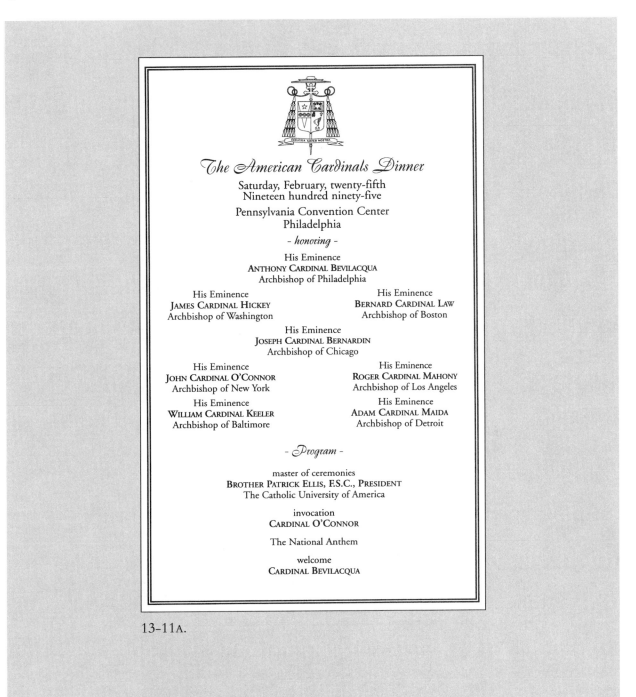

The American Cardinals Dinner

Saturday, February, twenty-fifth
Nineteen hundred ninety-five

Pennsylvania Convention Center
Philadelphia

- *honoring* -

His Eminence
ANTHONY CARDINAL BEVILACQUA
Archbishop of Philadelphia

His Eminence
JAMES CARDINAL HICKEY
Archbishop of Washington

His Eminence
BERNARD CARDINAL LAW
Archbishop of Boston

His Eminence
JOSEPH CARDINAL BERNARDIN
Archbishop of Chicago

His Eminence
JOHN CARDINAL O'CONNOR
Archbishop of New York

His Eminence
ROGER CARDINAL MAHONY
Archbishop of Los Angeles

His Eminence
WILLIAM CARDINAL KEELER
Archbishop of Baltimore

His Eminence
ADAM CARDINAL MAIDA
Archbishop of Detroit

- *Program* -

master of ceremonies
BROTHER PATRICK ELLIS, F.S.C., PRESIDENT
The Catholic University of America

invocation
CARDINAL O'CONNOR

The National Anthem

welcome
CARDINAL BEVILACQUA

13-11A.

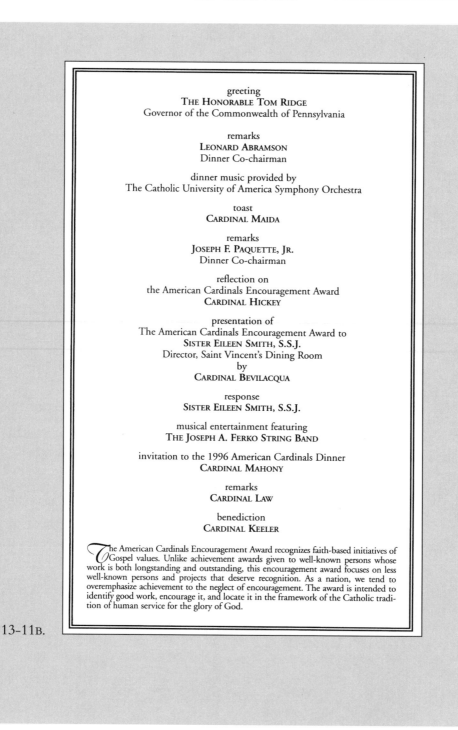

greeting
THE HONORABLE TOM RIDGE
Governor of the Commonwealth of Pennsylvania

remarks
LEONARD ABRAMSON
Dinner Co-chairman

dinner music provided by
The Catholic University of America Symphony Orchestra

toast
CARDINAL MAIDA

remarks
JOSEPH F. PAQUETTE, JR.
Dinner Co-chairman

reflection on
the American Cardinals Encouragement Award
CARDINAL HICKEY

presentation of
The American Cardinals Encouragement Award to
SISTER EILEEN SMITH, S.S.J.
Director, Saint Vincent's Dining Room
by
CARDINAL BEVILACQUA

response
SISTER EILEEN SMITH, S.S.J.

musical entertainment featuring
THE JOSEPH A. FERKO STRING BAND

invitation to the 1996 American Cardinals Dinner
CARDINAL MAHONY

remarks
CARDINAL LAW

benediction
CARDINAL KEELER

The American Cardinals Encouragement Award recognizes faith-based initiatives of Gospel values. Unlike achievement awards given to well-known persons whose work is both longstanding and outstanding, this encouragement award focuses on less well-known persons and projects that deserve recognition. As a nation, we tend to overemphasize achievement to the neglect of encouragement. The award is intended to identify good work, encourage it, and locate it in the framework of the Catholic tradition of human service for the glory of God.

13–11B.

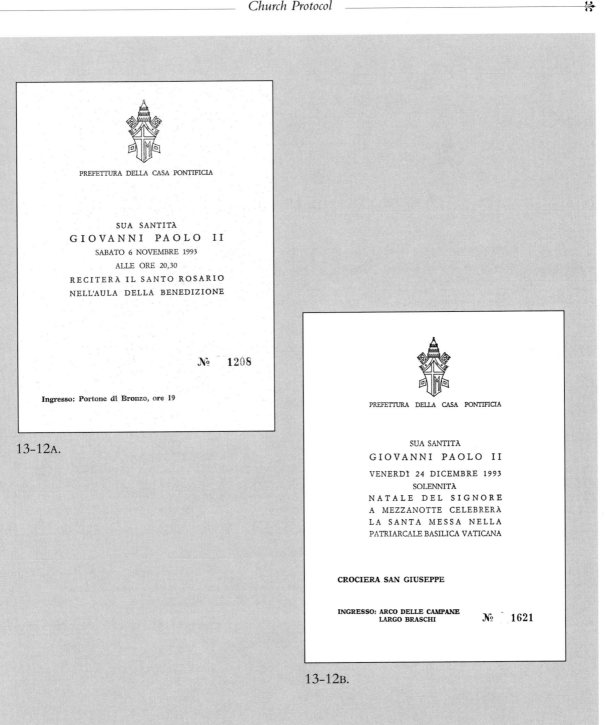

PREFETTURA DELLA CASA PONTIFICIA

SUA SANTITÀ
GIOVANNI PAOLO II
SABATO 6 NOVEMBRE 1993
ALLE ORE 20,30
RECITERÀ IL SANTO ROSARIO
NELL'AULA DELLA BENEDIZIONE

№ 1208

Ingresso: Portone di Bronzo, ore 19

13-12A.

PREFETTURA DELLA CASA PONTIFICIA

SUA SANTITÀ
GIOVANNI PAOLO II
VENERDÌ 24 DICEMBRE 1993
SOLENNITÀ
NATALE DEL SIGNORE
A MEZZANOTTE CELEBRERÀ
LA SANTA MESSA NELLA
PATRIARCALE BASILICA VATICANA

CROCIERA SAN GIUSEPPE

INGRESSO: ARCO DELLE CAMPANE
LARGO BRASCHI   № 1621

13-12B.

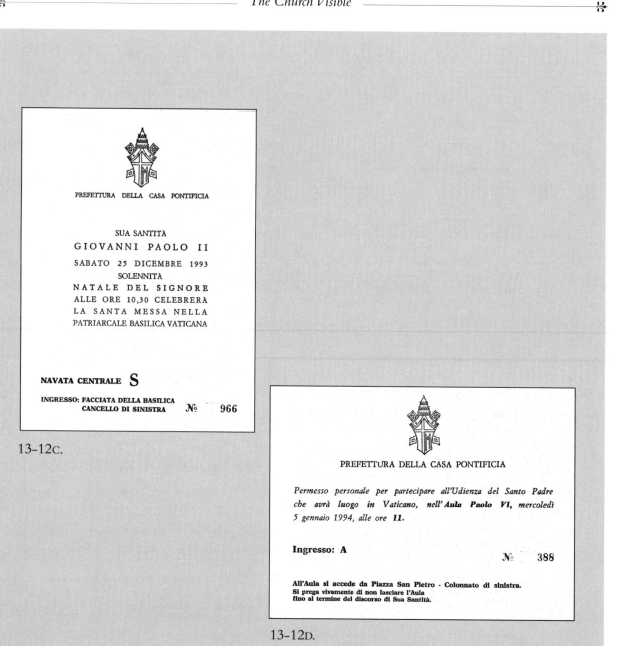

PREFETTURA DELLA CASA PONTIFICIA

SUA SANTITÀ

GIOVANNI PAOLO II

SABATO 25 DICEMBRE 1993
SOLENNITÀ
NATALE DEL SIGNORE
ALLE ORE 10,30 CELEBRERÀ
LA SANTA MESSA NELLA
PATRIARCALE BASILICA VATICANA

NAVATA CENTRALE   S

**INGRESSO: FACCIATA DELLA BASILICA
CANCELLO DI SINISTRA**   № 966

13-12C.

PREFETTURA DELLA CASA PONTIFICIA

*Permesso personale per partecipare all'Udienza del Santo Padre
che avrà luogo in Vaticano, nell'**Aula Paolo VI,** mercoledì
5 gennaio 1994, alle ore **11.***

Ingresso: A   № 388

**All'Aula si accede da Piazza San Pietro - Colonnato di sinistra.
Si prega vivamente di non lasciare l'Aula
fino al termine del discorso di Sua Santità.**

13-12D.

PROTOCOL

Official Visit of His Holiness
Pope John Paul II
The Cathedral of Mary Our Queen

ADMITTANCE

All guests holding valid seating assignments are to present themselves at the west entrance of the cathedral by four o'clock P.M., October 8, 1995. Presentation of a photo-identification card and a valid ticket will be required for admittance.

SECURITY

Both the Swiss Guard security forces accompanying His Holiness and the Secret Service of the United States require individual security examination upon arrival. Umbrellas will not be permitted inside the cathedral.

PRESS INFORMATION

The press will be represented by pool coverage. No other press will be admitted to the cathedral.

WELCOME CEREMONIES

The Holy Father will arrive with His Eminence Cardinal Keeler and the familiars of the Papal Household. His Eminence, Angelo Cardinal Sodano, Cardinal-Secretary of State, will be present in the cathedral, as will American members of the Sacred College, the Archbishop-Emeritus of Baltimore, William Borders, auxiliary bishops of Baltimore, and the bishops of the Baltimore province. Cardinal Keeler will offer official words of welcome and greeting upon arrival.

PRESENTATIONS

Only those seated in the sanctuary will be formally presented to His Holiness, although, as is his custom, it is expected that the Holy Father will greet as many persons present as possible.

CLOSE OF EVENTS

At the close of the prayer service, the Holy Father will depart the cathedral for the remainder of his schedule in Baltimore. There will be no formal reception line and no one will be permitted to leave their seats until the Holy Father and the papal entourage have left the cathedral. Please remain seated until an announcement has been made by the Secret Service.

LITURGICAL NOTE

The Holy Father will pause in silent prayer, as is the custom of the Church, at the Blessed Sacrament Chapel. While the Holy Father kneels in prayer, those seated in the cathedral are asked to kneel as well, to join our Holy Father in silent prayer.

PHOTOGRAPHY

Cameras and hand-held video recorders are permitted, but professional equipment and tripods are prohibited due to space limitations. Please note that all equipment must pass through an electronic security check. Additional lighting will not be permitted.

PARKING

Parking is not permitted on the cathedral grounds or by security directive in the immediate vicinity of the Cathedral of Mary Our Queen.

13-13.

CORRESPONDENCE CARDS AND NOTES

Dimensions: 3½ by 2 inches (white vellum stock with ink color appropriate to rank)

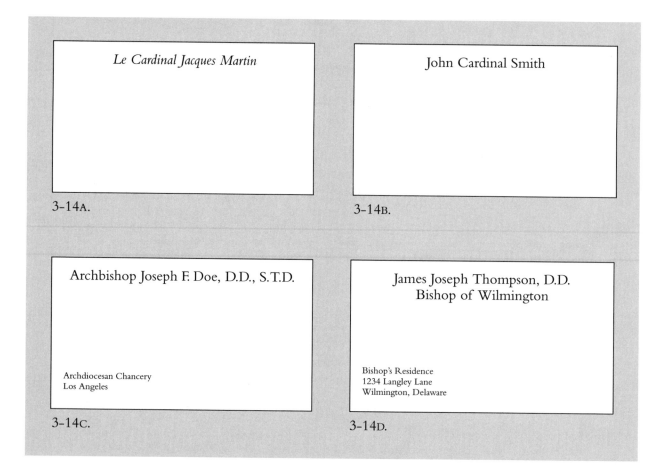

Le Cardinal Jacques Martin

3-14A.

John Cardinal Smith

3-14B.

Archbishop Joseph F. Doe, D.D., S.T.D.

Archdiocesan Chancery
Los Angeles

3-14C.

James Joseph Thompson, D.D.
Bishop of Wilmington

Bishop's Residence
1234 Langley Lane
Wilmington, Delaware

3-14D.

Reverend Monsigner
Louis A. Jones

St. Mary Magdalene
1234 Carlisle Drive   TEL. 210/451/1234
Woodston, ME 60419   FAX. 210/451/1235

3-14E.

Reverend Gerald J. Mahoney
St. Patrick Parish
64 Copper Street
Monroeville, TN 41067

3-14F.

Albert L. Martin, K.ST.G.G., K.M., K.C.✱H.S.

3-14G.

Reverend Monsignor Thomas M. Kwiczola,
K.M., K.H.S., K.C.N.

3-14H.

James-Charles Noonan, Jr.

3-14I.

BRIAN LEONARD SMITH

3-14J.

FIGURE CAPTIONS

FIGURE 13-1. The most formal method of invitation provides a space for the name(s) of those invited to be personalized in calligraphy or print. Blind embossing of one's insignia (here that of H.S.H. Prince Rainier III of Monaco) is considered in the diplomatic world to be the most formal and elegant presentation.

FIGURE 13-2. A formal, semi-engraved invitation for diplomatic functions (but which works well in all aspects of formal entertainment). Employed by the Apostolic Nunciature in Paris, this invitation was issued to the daughter of Her Royal Highness Princess Edouard de Lobkowicz on the occasion of the princess's installation as dame commander of the Equestrian Order of St. Gregory the Great at the hands of Papal Undersecretary of State, Archbishop Jean-Louis Tauran. A request for a reply by telephone is made at the lower left corner; the address for the reception appears in the opposite lower right.

FIGURE 13-3. A formal engraved invitation should always include all pertinent information including date, place, and time, as well as proper dress requirements. Oftentimes, Church-related events include reception information within the body copy. This sample illustrates a required response and dress information. The insignia of the organization (or individual) traditionally appears above the body of the invitation.

FIGURE 13-4. The combination of invitation, program, and ticket information into one beautiful presentation is favored in Europe. This sample is a Papal Household invitation to the concert commemorating the fiftieth anniversary of the Holocaust, in the presence of the Holy Father. The presentation is made on a double-sided, three-fold velum card. On page one appears the papal arms and the body of the invitation. Page two consists of the concert program. Page three gives the artistic credits of those performing. The reverse consists of entrance, seating, and dress instructions. When folded closed, the frontispiece appears most elegantly with the insignia of the host, in this case, the papal coat of arms.

FIGURE 13-5. A formal invitation with an ordinary as host. A request for a reply is made through the traditional abbreviation, R.S.V.P., and an address is provided opposite, rather than including an inserted reply card. In cases where a reply is requested and no card provided, the response should be carefully scripted to mimic the body of the text of the invitation itself. Another method for the form of reply is by telephone. In such cases, a dedicated telephone number to facilitate incoming responses is required. This number is included on the invitation.

FIGURE 13-6. A formal invitation scripted to open as an announcement of the occasion. The font chosen is simple and the text includes reception information. No direct response is required with this method.

FIGURE 13-7. This archival reproduction is a fine example of an invitation to a funeral of a deceased ordinary, which actually serves as an admission ticket and program of information. Although from a bygone era, this information remains the proper form for the occasion. No insignia should appear above the text, as the administrator does not carry the same heraldic privileges as does the Camerlengo of the Holy See during the *Sede Vacante*. The text should include the opening, the date, place, and time, as well as any other pertinent information. Here, one sees a reference to the Divine Office (now referred to more commonly as Evening Prayer). It is also proper to include information concerning the dress of clerics and papal honorees.

FIGURE **13-8.** A wonderful example of a banquet menu card following the diplomatic formula, which should either be placed at each table setting or included in the program to be presented upon arrival. Menu cards are wonderful for opening table conversation—everyone wants to review the offered menu. These cards also add a rich appearance to the table when they are placed at each setting. Colored ink on white or cream velum stock works best. This sample employed scarlet on cream. Menu cards always include a full list of each course's offering; wine is also listed by course. It is proper to include the insignia of the host, organization, or other decorative insignia.

FIGURE **13-9.** A luncheon menu card does not present the delicacies to the same extent as would a banquet card. It should be less ornate, but should include all pertinent information.

FIGURE **13-10.** A formal, decorative card used for smaller dinners (ideally at the ordinary's home, a rectory, or private home), upon which is etched in calligraphy the evening's menu.

FIGURES **13-11 A AND B.** Program cards should always be prepared and included in the information kit presented to each guest upon arrival or placed at each table setting. They should follow the style of the menu card and other event printing. Program cards should include as many facts about the event as possible, including a mission statement or special program (not illustrated).

When a program card is used to detail parking or dress information, it should *always* be mailed well in advance to the guest. In such cases, a second program card, specific to the events to unfold, should be prepared as well.

FIGURES **13-12 A THROUGH D.** Often tickets need to be prepared quickly for a special event in the life of the Church. Simple differences of color offer the simplest means to differentiate between placement and seating. These examples are from different Vatican events. Each includes the papal arms, the event's name, date, and site, as well as the gate or door to enter, a ticket number, and other pertinent information.

FIGURE **13-13.** This sample of a formal protocol card is of the design to be mailed or distributed before the date of the event. Another type of design would be that which awaits guests' arrival, but this type should never include protocol information too late to be useful to the guests. Logos and artwork complete a protocol card when appropriate.

FIGURE **13-14A.** Cardinal's correspondence card of the European style (red ink).

FIGURE **13-14B.** Cardinal's correspondence card of the Anglo/American style (red ink).

FIGURE **13-14C.** Correspondence card with business address included (green ink).

FIGURE **13-14D.** Correspondence card with the bishop's residence address (green ink).

FIGURE **13-14E.** Correspondence card with parish name/address/telephone/fax (violet ink).

FIGURE **13-14F.** Correspondence card with parish address (black ink).

FIGURE **13-14G.** Correspondence card for a papal knight (black ink).

FIGURE **13-14H.** Correspondence card for a chaplain of the equestrian orders (violet ink).

FIGURE **13-14I.** Correspondence or presentation card for a layman, of the European style (black ink).

FIGURE **13-14J.** Correspondence card for a layman following the death of a close family member.

PART FOUR

VESTURE AND INSIGNIA

Regulations Governing Color and Material

COLORS

The Church began to regulate colors for the hierarchy and the clergy as early as the 1200s; these colors were formalized because of heraldry rather than as a result of directives concerning the livery of the Papal Household and its functions. For example, the color for bishops and archbishops was green for most of the long history of the Church. Even today, the color green is used as the heraldic color for these prelates as seen in their *galero* and *fiocchi* (see Chapter 10, Ecclesiastical Heraldry).

By A.D. 1059, the color green became customary for prelates but it was not until the fourth Lateran Council (1215) that it was required for patriarchs, archbishops, and bishops, whereas red became the color for cardinals at the Second Council of Lyon; Pope Gregory X, in 1274, granted his favorites the red *galero* in order for them to be more prominent in the council's processions. Since the 1700s, however, the Holy See has mandated the colors appropriate to prelates and priests alike. The present vesture colors are white, scarlet, amaranth red, purple, violet, black, and green. In the past, the colors rose (saffron) and gray were additionally used, but these were abolished in 1969 by *motu proprio* of Paul VI, who minimized the vesture in the Church, as well as the ritual of the liturgy and in Vatican ceremonies.

Prior to the decree *Pontificalis Domus,* during mourning periods and penitential seasons, the vesture of all prelates, other than for the Holy Father himself, changed. Rose (saffron) vesture replaced the scarlet vesture for the cardinals, but the piping and trims remained scarlet. The archbishops and bishops took on black vesture, but the piping and trim remained amaranth red, as did the *zucchetto* and sash.

For the lower ranks of the *monsignori,* black vesture with piping and trim, in purple, replaced the choir habit. For these prelates, however, the *zucchetto* and sash were in the traditional purple.

The color gray, or ash, was also a color for vesture, but it no longer is used by prelates. All the religious orders who provided the Church with prelates each had its own color of habit adapted to prelatial vesture. Whereas a Franciscan bishop in the past would wear a gray cassock and *mozzetta* with amaranth-red piping, he would never appear in the full purple of secular bishops. In present times, however, a Franciscan bishop wears purple choir vesture very much like that of any other bishop.

White is reserved for the Holy Father. A custom dating from the pontificate of Pope Saint Pius V who reigned as pontiff from A.D. 1566 to 1572. As a Dominican priest, Antonio Ghislieri wore only the white of his order's habit. So saintly was Pius V that all his successors adopted from his Dominican attire the pure color white for their papal garb. Although several orders use white in their habits, these habits are not prelatial vesture. The cassock of the Holy Father is of either white silk or light wool merlino although he traditionally makes use of the white silk simar most of the year. The *zucchetto* is of white moiré silk, as in his *fascia,* or sash, and the fringe is of narrow gold threads. Embroidered on the sash is the pope's personal coat of arms, traditionally surrounded by an oak or laurel wreath and topped by the crossed keys and the papal tiara, the emblems of his office. The stockings are also white, traditionally cotton, whereas the shoes are red moroccan leather. It has only been since the pontificate of John XXIII that the shoes were exclusively red. For centuries, the popes also made use of richly embroidered velvet slippers, often sewed with gems, which matched the colors of the liturgical vestments. At present, the pope uses only the red moroccan-leather loafers. The pope also makes use of the *cappa* (cape) of red wool (not be confused with the *cappa magna*). It is best described as a "traveler's cape," piped with gold chords and bound by frogs of the same cloth. The traveler's hat of the pope used for everyday wear is the *cappella*, not the *galero*. It is known in English as the "Roman hat" and takes the shape of a saucer. It is red and has gold cords at the brim.

Scarlet

Technically, it is not proper to refer to cardinals as wearing "red." In actuality, the color scarlet, which is a distinct form of orange-red, is reserved for members of the Sacred College. The *biretta, mozzetta,* choir cassock, *ferraiola, zucchetto*, and sash are all scarlet for cardinals.

Amaranth Red

Although the name seems foreign, we all are very familiar with the color of amaranth red, which is a mixture of reddish-purple hues and scarlet. We see this red used in the piping for the cassocks of bishops, archbishops, and minor prelates. Amaranth is known to most of us as the name for the annual flower, love-lies-bleeding. It is also a grain. The word is sometimes used to denote an imaginary flower that never fades or dies; it has been employed by the Church for four centuries.

Purple and Violet

The term *being raised to the purple,* which comes from the Roman empire's practice of vesting new dignitaries with a purple toga (or the present Roman usage of *violetta*), is used to describe choir or choral dress proper to prelates of the Church. Neither purple nor violet, truly speaking, is used in the Roman Catholic Church.

Roman purple is a bit more reddish than true purple. The violet described in Roman vesture corresponds more to amaranth red. In actuality, the prelates of the Roman Church are vested in a purple hue more accurately described as fuchsia or magenta. The terms for these colors derive from heraldic terminology of the Middle Ages and not from modern terminology assigned to describe various hues in the spectrum of colors as we know them today. Throughout this text, references will be made to red and purple. In reality, the colors referred to are properly, unless otherwise specified, amaranth red and fuchsia.

Green

Prior to the sixteenth century, green was not only the heraldic color of bishops, archbishops, and patriarchs, it was also their vesture color. As such, the choir dress of these prelates before the end of the sixteenth century was made of a cloth akin to the present color of forest green. Historical paintings provide us with fine examples of this early choir dress although several green hues are depicted incorrectly; perhaps they suffer from age and have faded. Cloth of darkest green would have been used most commonly although a certain hue was never prescribed. The actual shift to fuchsia or purple for these prelates began as early as the pontificate of Gregory XIII (1578); by that of Urban VIII (1590), the change was complete in Rome.

Except for the heraldic usage of green for major or greater prelates, the only vestige of green associated with them today is found on the cushions of their *cathedra*, the velvet cover of their prie-dieu, and any drapery remaining around the *cathedra*. In recent times, due to changes proscribed by Paul VI throughout his pontificate, the cloth-covered prie-dieu, drapery, and other embellishments are not seen frequently except for historic reasons.

MATERIALS

The materials of the Church for vesture are velvet, watered silk, satin, damask, wool cloth known as both merlino or broadcloth, linen, and lace of various degrees or types. The vestment chapter of this text will expand upon the types of cloth permitted for sacred vestments.

Only the Sovereign Pontiff may make use of velvet in his ecclesiastical vesture. Cardinals make use of watered silk as prescribed, a mixture of silk and merlino, which is a light wool blend similar to the material used in cassock making. At present, the seasons are the only factors that determine a change of material, whereas in the past the liturgical calendar and time of mourning were factors as well. Patriarchs, by virtue of their automatic appointment as Assistants to the Papal Throne, as well as archbishops who are singularly appointed to that title, may make use of silk for their vesture. They may also make use of the material reserved for all other archbishops and bishops—light wool or merlino in the appropriate color. The silklike fabric known as faille, used in the production of the *fascia* and the *ferraiolo*, is permitted to all ranks of the clergy in the appropriate color of rank because it is not silk *per se*. The pontiff and cardinals make use of a specially processed silk, known as moiré, for their *fascia*, white and scarlet respectively.

All lining, trim, facings, buttons, and accessories, such as the *zucchetto*, are traditionally worked in silk unless otherwise prescribed. This holds true for the *monsignori* as well. Priests and seminarians make use of light wool (merlino) for the cassock, whereas faille is permitted them for the *fascia* (optional) and the *ferraiolo* (optional).

CHAPTER FIFTEEN

Cassock

The Roman cassock as we have come to know it today is of early fifth-century French origins, but it was known by its Latin name *pellicia* and the early French *pelisse*, which meant "skin" or "hide" (taken from the Latin *pellis*). Prior to the twelfth century, the majority of the populace, including the laity, made use of a heavy, long cloak lined with animal skin or fur for warmth. By the end of the twelfth century, the laity assumed other forms of clothing and sources for warmth, and the *pellicia* was laid aside by all but the clergy. This predecessor of the cassock was retained by the clergy because churches were unheated year-round. During the twelfth and thirteenth centuries, the cassock became identified exclusively with the Church, and as the Renaissance approached, the cassock took on the general form that it has today.

The cassock, as it is known in English, is more commonly known worldwide by its formal French name, *soutane*, which ironically is derived from the Medieval Latin/Early Italian *sottana*, which means "beneath," a reference not to the cassock's use under the alb but to the linings of skin and fur that once formed part of the *pelisse*. The cassock is also seen spelled as casaque (which provides us with a familiar alternative English pronunciation), but for the past fifty or so years this previously common alternative spelling was only found in France and the Basque region of northern Spain. The official Latin term for the modern cassock is *vestis talaris,* which connotes the style of the garment—covering the body from head to toe.

During the cassock's early development, prelates lined their cassock with ermine, the richest of furs. This fur could be seen at the hem, cuffs, and collar. The higher the prelate was, the more precious was the fur. Simple priests made use of muskrat, beaver, or lamb's wool. The Roman collar did not form part of the cassock until many centuries later.

The *pellicia* existed all through the Dark Ages and can be traced to Roman documents as far back as the beginning of the fifth century. It is one of the most ancient items of vesture of the Church and one with the richest of histories. The cassock has seen many adaptations and alterations. As the Renaissance approached, the roughness of the garment was laid aside, and the brilliance of that age was incorporated into this garment in a manner reflected in no other item of vesture in the Church. Color and rich materials were applied to it. The simple cloak, closed by a sash, became "roman-ized." Buttons were added—silk for the prelature and broadcloth for simple clergy. The scarlet of cardinals was granted for their use on the cassock. In some regions of Europe, the heraldic color of bishops, green, was applied for their use; however, this practice later lapsed and the "household color" of purple* was assumed. The councils of Nicaea II, Vienne, and Constance regulated the use of clerical attire, most commonly the cassock, for all members of the clergy. Strong penalties were prescribed for those who abrogated this obligation.

From the eighth to the late thirteenth centuries, the practice of adapting the religious habit to prelatial vesture flourished. Although a prelate raised from the various orders and communities vested as a prelate rather than as a religious, he would have retained the color of his religious order's habit to denote membership in that order despite his personal rise to the prelature. For instance, the cassock of the prelates of the "Calmadolise, Cistercians, Carthusians, Dominicans was always white; of Sylvestrians, dark blue; of Jeromites, gray; of Minor Conventionals and Minor Observants, ash colored; of Franciscans, brown."[1] This practice was retained until March 1969 when papal *motu proprio* required all those from religious orders and communities to lay aside the habit of their order and its color and assume the prescribed prelatial vesture when that prelate was nominated to the prelature.

DESIGN

There have always been two different types of cassock for the prelature: the choir cassock and the ordinary cassock. Until the Pauline modifications of 1969, the two were very different, indeed. The choir cassock was not only distinct in its color, scarlet for cardinals and purple for other prelates, but it was unique in its design.

Choir Cassock

"The choir cassock is so-called because it is worn by Prelates *in choir* at the public ceremonies of the Church."[2] The choir cassock was also required for all public events on church grounds. Perhaps the most obvious difference between the choir cassock of former times and that of today is its train, which, when unraveled, would trail the prelate for 26 inches. The "opening of the train" was permitted only when prescribed by the *Ceremoniale*; under normal circumstances, the train† was fastened to a button at the rear of the waist. It always remained fastened when the wearer was outside his jurisdiction or in the presence of the metropolitan of the province unless express permission by the resident ordinary or Metropolitan had been granted whereby the train was permitted to be opened. This was a rare privilege!

"The train of the choir cassock, according to Roman Etiquette, was [sic] not a piece added to the bottom of the cassock but was [sic] the normal extension of the lower part of it."[3] The train was made of the same color and material as the choir cassock and was lined with a 2-inch-wide scarlet (for cardinals) or amaranth red (for all other prelates) silk strip, which, when carried in procession and viewed by onlookers, appeared to be a special border rather than part of the lining of the garment.

The choir cassock for cardinals was made entirely of scarlet watered silk,‡ whereas that of other prelates was made of purple silk, with amaranth-red

---

* Archbishops in Rome were usually appointed Assistants to the Papal Throne or members of the Papal Household, where purple was used as the livery color.

† The train is abolished for all ranks of the clergy.

‡ For persons wishing to view a fine example of the former style choir cassock, it is recommended that they view the film *The Cardinal*. Both the opening and closing scenes of this film depict the former choir cassock on the main character, an archbishop, as he receives the *biglietto* of nomination to the Sacred College.

silk piping and buttons. In what was termed "penitential" times (i.e., during Lent or for a prelate's funeral or at the death of the pontiff), a second choir cassock was donned by all prelates. For cardinals, this vesture was purple but was designed in exactly the same manner as the primary choir cassock. For prelates, the secondary choir cassock was black with purple trim and, like that of cardinals, was worn during the penitential seasons. Cardinals donned yet a third choir cassock, made entirely of rose-colored watered silk on two Sundays of the liturgical calendar: *Gaudete* (the third Sunday of Advent) and *Laetare* (the fourth Sunday of Lent). All trimmings were in scarlet.

In addition to the choir cassocks, cardinals also made use of nonwatered-silk vesture during the winter season, when vesture was of light wool trimmed in silk. The purple silk for prelates, likewise, was laid aside in winter, replaced by merlino or wool. Only prelates appointed as assistants to the papal throne and inferior prelates serving as household livery at the Lateran and Apostolic Palaces retained the use of silk the year round. This privilege, however, was associated with their positions in the Papal Household and not reflective of Church vesture. The only time the prelates of the Papal Household donned a choir cassock of black wool was during the vacancy of the papacy. As these prelates were members of the Papal Household, at the vacancy they served no one and therefore lost their privileges and titles. These privileges were traditionally restored, however, by the succeeding pope.

Certain inferior or lesser prelates, known collectively as the *Monsignori*, had privileges to the former style of choir cassock. The senior classifications of the *monsignori* were called prelates *di mantelletta* because their rank entitled them to the use of the *mantelletta*. These prelates only vested in black vesture donned by bishops in penitential times at the time of the death of the pontiff. During the

vacancy of the papacy and until a successor was installed, these prelates laid aside all purple vesture.

The prelates *di mantellone,* inferior prelates of the Papal Household, never technically went into mourning as they lost their title, rank, and privileges at the death of the pontiff who had created them. Their privileges were traditionally restored by his successor; however, during the vacancy of the papacy, they vested as simple priests. The *di mantellone* were never permitted a train, whereas the *di mantelletta* were, yet this train was seldom permitted to be opened.

In present times, the choir cassock is retained for use at the most solemn liturgical occasions where prelates are called to vest in choir. It should be understood that the term *in choir* additionally requires the use of the *mozzetta* and rochet. Prior to the Pauline modifications of 1969, the *mantelletta* was also part of choir vesture. The most significant changes in the choir cassock after 1969 were the abolishment of the train on all choir cassocks for all the ranks of the prelature and the placing in abeyance* of the watered-silk material for the cassock and *mozzetta* of cardinals.† All else remains the same.

The Roman protocol requires that the choir cassock be worn under the alb when celebrating the liturgy even when the alb chosen is one that has no lace or when the cassock cannot be seen at all. The standard black cassock with either scarlet or amaranth-red trim is not properly to be worn under the alb as a substitution for the proper choir cassock.

Ordinary Cassock

The ordinary cassock is very simple in design although there are several varieties to this garment.

---

* Described by the Holy See as the laying aside, at this time in history, of something not in keeping with present practice yet not an outright abolishment by the competent authority of the Church.
† Although watered silk has been retained for *fascia, zucchetto,* and *ferraiolo.*

The first point to be discussed is the difference between the Roman cassock and the French cassock. Some historians define the two as what we now would call the Roman and the Jesuit cassocks, but this is incorrect. The most common cassock is the Roman, a one-piece bell-shaped garb fronted by buttons from the Roman collar to the toes. It is a full-cut, loose-fitting garment, with no trim for simple priests and seminarians, and with purple, amaranth-red, or scarlet buttons, piping, and trim for the various ranks of the prelature.

The second style of familiar cassock has become known as the French cassock, but this is a misnomer. The proper terminology is the "french-cut Roman cassock," as both types of cassock are Roman cassocks. The french-cut cassock is so named because it was popularized by the French clergy, especially the hierarchy, after 1800. Both the ordinary Roman and the french-cut Roman cassock are acceptable for the clergy of the Catholic Church.

The french-cut Roman cassock is the more formal of the two types and most resembles the design of the choir cassock. In fact, since the Pauline modifications of 1969, the present choir cassock for prelates is always made in the french-cut design, which is more fitted and makes use of three inverted pleats, one at the center rear and one each on the hips. At the top of each pleat is an embroidered inverted triangle known as the "dart" because it resembles an arrowhead or dart. At present, some manufacturers apply leather darts rather than the hand-stitched version. These darts, along with buttons and trim, are always to be in the appropriate color of rank.

The torso segment of the french-cut cassock is more tapered and its bottom is less bell-shaped and more tubular than the standard Roman cassock. Both styles, the french-cut and the simple Roman, are quite acceptable. The latter is more formal; the former is somewhat more informal or relaxed. Both are quite comfortable to wear.

It has been the tradition in the Church to close the Roman cassock with a series of buttons.* Since the Renaissance, thirty-three buttons were employed, regardless of the height of the individual, in remembrance of the number of earthly years of Christ. The french-cut Roman cassock additionally places five buttons on each sleeve cuff, symbolizing the five wounds of Christ. The cuffs of the french-cut Roman are approximately 6 inches in length, with space between the cuff and the sleeve, to place items such as programs or notes. "The collar of this cassock is of standing model, cut square with an opening extending from a half to three quarters of an inch so that the Roman collar may show."[4] For this reason, the french-cut Roman cassock is used most often by masters of ceremonies. The french-cut Roman additionally makes use of the cords that are destined to support the *fascia*, or sash. These cords are attached at the seams of the underside of the arm and should drop to the top of the hip, allowing for both the sash and a certain fullness to the cords, which makes for a better appearance.

Other Styles of Ordinary Cassock

There are other examples of the cassock. These, however, are not given the name "Roman" because they were not in vogue by the general clergy of the Roman Church for any prolonged period. The most well-known of these types are the Jesuit cassock, worn by a community that never took on a habit *per se;* the semi-Jesuit cassock; the Anglican cassock, in vogue by some of the Roman clergy but not part of the Roman tradition at any time; and the Byzantine cassock, a part of the tradition of the

---

* So decreed by the fourth Lateran Council (A.D. 1215).

clergy of the Oriental rites of the Catholic Church.

The Jesuit and semi-Jesuit are free-flowing cassocks that close at the neck by a hook-and-eye device and that do not permit the Roman collar to be fully seen. A sash of light cloth with small fringe is used as a belt to bind it closed at the waist. The Jesuit and semi-Jesuit are always entirely black; no trim or color may be added. As in the case of all religious when raised to the prelature, even Jesuits must lay aside their habits or previous vesture and assume the prescribed vesture for prelates.

Of the remaining historical styles of cassock, all are similar in origin and design. Whereas the Roman cassock closes in the front by a row of buttons and the Jesuit and semi-Jesuit by a hook-and-eye device and sash, the remaining cassock styles, namely the Anglican, the Byzantine, and the Russian, all fasten by a series of buttons on the chest.

The Anglican cassock buttons on the chest close to the neck. The garment is wrapped around one's front, resulting in closure at the right side; there are snaps underneath to assure the proper closure. It is traditionally bound by a sash of the same cloth and color. Small fringe on either end of the sash is permitted. There is no choir cassock in the Anglican tradition although the "choir colors" of red and purple are worn by Anglican prelates on the ordinary Anglican cassock; the cloth is traditionally woolen, never silk. The purple used by Anglicans is traditionally more bluish in hue than that referred to as purple in the Roman Catholic Church, which is more reddish in hue, yet both are seen. The bluish hue is not a part of the Roman tradition and is, therefore, never permitted to the Roman prelature.

Although the Anglican cassock has never been a part of the Roman tradition, from time to time one sees a Roman cleric making use of it. This most frequently occurs in nations where there is a strong Anglican influence. In this event, however, all Roman norms regulating the color, trim, and material of the garment must be respected. One is strongly recommended to make use of the Roman or french-cut Roman at all times, as these garments are within the universal tradition of the Roman Church and supersede any ethnic or national preference in clerical dress.

The Byzantine cassock is not synonymous with the Greek Orthodox cassock. It is most common in the Russian Orthodox Church but is somewhat familiar to the Roman Church, as it is often worn by the clergy of the Oriental rites of the Church. The fullest of all the styles of cassock, it, too, is a wraparound-style cassock, closing at the neck and fastening at both the neck and hip by a set of snaps and buttons. This cassock does not allow for a collar, Roman or otherwise. Whereas the Anglican cassock closes to the right, the Byzantine cassock closes across the left side of the chest. The sleeves are cut full, and the folds of the cassock fall in a fashion similar to pleats, although that is not the intended effect. Often this full cassock can be removed to reveal another tighter-fitting cassock below, known as the Greek cassock. This principal cassock is traditionally of prelatial hue although the Byzantine is traditionally black without trim. The Byzantine is always made of light wool.

Outside the Oriental rites of the Church, most especially within the Russian Orthodox Church, the Byzantine cassock can be found in many color varieties that range from blue-gray to white. Depending on which branch of the Orthodox communion one might belong as a member of the clergy, the rank of the cleric within that Church makes the determination of the color of the cassock.

The Greek cassock closes at the neck and waist, as does the Byzantine, but it is more form fitting—somewhat in the style of the Anglican cassock. Often, a pocket is evident on the outside right chest. The waist is girded by a silk or woolen cord, rather than by a sash, which is not part of the heritage of this style of garment. The cassock closes in the front in the wraparound style, being buttoned on the left side of the chest.

The Anglican, Byzantine, and Greek styles are, strictly speaking, cassocks; however, their traditions are not of the Roman Church and should not be adopted for wear by the Roman clergy with the exception of the Oriental rites.* Even Anglican clergymen who have been received into the Holy Roman Church should lay aside the Anglican style and don the Roman or french-cut Roman cassock.

COLOR

The color of the ordinary Roman cassock is black in all cases.† For cardinals, the buttons, trim, and inside hem are scarlet silk. For patriarchs, archbishops, bishops, protonotaries apostolic, and prelates of honor, the buttons, trim, and inside hem are amaranth red, and for chaplains of His Holiness, purple.

LENGTH

The cassock should always be worn at ankle length, never longer and never shorter. The practice of wearing the cassock 8 to 10 inches above the instep developed in the academic world, where the individual could avoid having to gather the cassock in order to frequently climb stairs. The cassock has always been worn at ankle length. When purchasing a new cassock, if the individual intends to make use of the *fascia*, he should inform the manufacturer so that the length will be made slightly longer. The sash always pulls the hem of the cassock upward by approximately 2 inches.

Note: It is important to note that the Holy Father does not make use of the cassock. By tradition, he dons only the white simar on all occasions.

---

* Although the double-breasted cassock was commonly in use in Roman seminaries to mark each in a unique way. The North American College's cassock was black, piped and buttoned in sky blue, whereas the Urbanianum made use of black with red trim and buttons.
† For all priests and prelates residing in or traveling to tropical climates, a papal indult is provided to don a cassock made of fine, lightweight white cloth. Trim should always be in the appropriate prelatial color for the hierarchy. Customs vary for simple priests with either all white cloth (absolutely no silk) or white cloth with black trim.

CHAPTER SIXTEEN

Simar

The most familiar ecclesiastical dress of the Catholic hierarchy is the simar (or *zimarra*), and yet this garment was not officially recognized as part of episcopal or clerical vesture until 1872, when it was granted status at the Papal Court as acceptable garb for papal audiences. Until the pontificate of Pope Pius IX, the simar was an optional garment available to all the clergy, but reserved for use at home—thus the modern name "house cassock." The simar has origins earlier than the late nineteenth century. Mention of it is made in apostolic briefs as early as 1760, but it did not become official vesture until 1872.

The simar is often described as a cassock with shoulder cape, but it is not, strictly speaking, a cassock at all.* The hierarchy came to make use of the simar, which later came to replace the cassock for those elevated to the prelature, for wear outside the liturgical life of the Church. The shape of the simar is very similar to that of the cassock, but the simar has an elbow-length shoulder cape, which does not meet in the front, thus exposing the buttons from the collar to the toe. The simar traditionally included oversleeves of matching black wool, trimmed in the appropriate color of rank. These sleeves extended from the shoulder to the elbow and were opened in front and were closed by a row of five buttons, symbolizing the five wounds of Christ. The oversleeves were abolished by Pope Paul VI in 1969. This garment, together with the cape and oversleeves, was known in the seventeenth and eighteenth centuries as the "pelerine." Later the name *zimarra*, or simar, became more prominent.

The simar and the ordinary cassock were never interchangeable; they were distinct garments with unique origins. Since the Pauline modifications of 1969, which abolished the unique feature of the oversleeves, some prelates have economized by having a small shoulder cape made to attach to their ordinary cassock with the aid of a hook-and-eye device. Some have gone so far as to use a device known as a "frog," a sort of cloth figure-eight with two buttons, which fasten this cape at the neck. Neither practice has been condoned by the Holy See, and these devices are therefore not officially part of Roman vesture. Despite the added cost of purchasing both the ordinary cassock and the simar, protocol requires the purchase of both distinct items of vesture, as they are not interchangeable.

---

* Secretariat of State Directive No. 135705.

The simar is always made of black wool, which is lined, piped, and trimmed in the color of the rank of the prelate: scarlet for cardinals and amaranth red for patriarchs, archbishops, and bishops. As with the cassock, each cuff of the simar sleeve has five buttons, representing the five wounds of Christ. The simar also traditionally made use of a frontal of thirty-three buttons, which represented the number of earthly years of Christ's life. In present times, many manufacturers, including the Roman ateliers, have fallen away from the custom of symbolic representation. The appropriate scarlet or amaranth-red sash, with matching silk fringe, is always worn with the simar, as is the *zucchetto*.

The winter simar of the pontiff is made of light white wool, which gives it the appearance of ecru or light beige against the pure white silk sash. In summer, the pontiff makes use of a simar made entirely of silk. The oversleeves were not abolished for the Roman Pontiff, and therefore it is still possible to see them in use. In both seasons, all trim, buttons, and piping are of raw watered silk (moiré) as are the cuffs on the sleeves. The *fascia* of the pontiff is of white moiré silk and always includes the papal coat of arms represented on the lower section of both flaps of the sash.

The only variation seen in the modern simar is the style of edging on the shoulder cape. Modern styling allows for a preponderance of a squared edge at the base of each frontal piece of the shoulder cape. Pope John Paul II has rejuvenated the style of earlier pontificates, with a preference for a rounded edge of each frontal piece. Either style is acceptable, neither preferable, and most manufacturers of liturgical vesture should be able to provide a client with either style.

The simar is a garment of jurisdiction and not of the clerical state. Its use is now restricted to members of the prelature who possess episcopal dignity; therefore, it may not be worn by seminarians, priests, or monsignors of any grades at any time. Although it was once permitted to irremovable pastors and professors of Sacred Science, the use of the simar has been clarified by papal decree,* and, at present, it is formally restricted to reflect its true jurisdictional significance.

It should be remembered that prelates who have been elevated to episcopal dignity from religious life are to properly lay aside their habit and don the simar—the vesture proper to prelates today. The habit may be retained in the privacy of the prelate's home or among his brethren in a closed environment; however, all religious bishops are required to forgo the habit of their order at all other times and vest as all other bishops do.

---

* It is important to note that even Vatican documents of the Pauline pontificate referred to the simar simply as a cassock for prelates "with cape," which it is not. This misunderstanding results in an incorrect translation from the original Italian. The simar, or house cassock, is a jurisdictional garment reserved for the prelature with episcopal dignity and is never to be considered simply the cassock "with cape."

Fascia

The *fascia,* also most commonly known as the "sash" or "cincture," and in previous centuries as the "zingulum," became mandatory for wear with the cossack in 1624 by papal *motu proprio* of Urban VIII.* This papal decree has never been abrogated. The use of the *fascia,* however, has become somewhat misunderstood, being mainly associated with the hierarchy; in fact, Urban VII's decree specifies its use by all in formation, as well as by priests and the prelature. At present, the *fascia,* as it is properly called, is incorrectly considered optional for all but the hierarchy. It remains, nonetheless, officially *de rigueur* for all when wearing the Roman cassock.† The sashes required by some religious orders, such as the Jesuits, are so in adherence to the papal mandate of 1624.

Originally, the *fascia* became commonplace because of the looser-fitting nature of the cassock style of the day; however, Urban VIII mandated its use as a symbol of one's commitment to a life devoted to Christ. For the same reason, the *fascia* was forbidden to altar servers and to all other persons who adopted the cassock for specific liturgical functions unless they were either seminarians or individuals ordained to the priesthood. Urban VIII

further clarified the use of the *fascia,* and two centuries later it was made significant as an additional symbol of jurisdiction and dignity for the prelature. From this clarification developed the codification of colors of the sash as well as the actual width of the sash according to ranks within orders and the hierarchy.

Paul VI, in his *motu proprio* of March 1969, restricted the *fascia* in no way—neither in its entitlement to seminarians and priests nor in color and width. Until 1969, there were two types of *fascia* for each rank within the hierarchy, including that of the Sovereign Pontiff: the normal *fascia* and the formal *fascia,* introduced in the sixteenth century. This formal *fascia,* which employed tufts rather than fringe, was a late Renaissance adornment that was used only on solemn occasions, notably with choir dress, and was abolished by Pauline *motu proprio.*

The formal cincture, or *fascia,* was 1 inch wider than the ordinary sash. Worn in the same manner as the modern *fascia,* the formal sash terminated in either tassels or large tufts, one suspended from each

---

* Priests in mission countries seldom followed this edict because of economic necessity. The United States, a mission territory long into its civil history, shared in this experience, which is why so many persons incorrectly believe that the *fascia* is not mandatory.
† Although few seminarians make use of it at this time.

flap of the sash. Each tuft or tassel was made of silk and matched the color of the *fascia,* except in the case of the reigning pontiff and cardinals, who wore tufts made entirely of gold threads. Gold-threaded tufts soon became a mark of ecclesiastical dignity. The pontiff later accorded the honor of gold tufts to nuncios and other legates of His Holiness; however, they were restricted the use of this honor within the jurisdiction assigned to them as nuncios or during the special mission for which they were accredited. Patriarchs and primates had no special privileges regarding the *fascia.*

In abolishing the formal *fascia,* Paul VI neither intended to minimize its significance in the vesture of the Roman Church nor did he wish to abrogate the rulings of his predecessor Urban VIII.* Nevertheless, abuses in the use of the formal *fascia* required some reform. As such, the standardization of the *fascia* with the knotted silk fringe returned the sash to the style originally desired by Urban VIII when he mandated its use in 1624. Sadly, by abolishing the formal *fascia,* which had existed for nearly three hundred years, the clergy wrongly assumed that the *fascia* itself was abolished for all but the prelature.

At present, there are five colors for the *fascia:* white (watered silk for the pontiff, cloth for religious habits), scarlet (watered silk for cardinals), violet (silk for patriarchs, primates, archbishops, bishops, apostolic protonotaries, and prelates of honor), purple (wool cloth or faille for chaplains of His Holiness), and black (wool cloth or faille for priests and seminarians).

The pontiff and cardinals make use of a wider sash than all other prelates and priests. It is acceptable for their sash to be as wide as 10 inches, but the 8-inch sash is most common. All others wear a 5- or 6-inch-wide *fascia* in the appropriate color of their individual rank.

Prior to 1969, the penitential color for cardinals was rose or saffron—with the exception of trim, buttons, and, of course, the scarlet *fascia*—and would be worn on penitential days and during the vacancy of the papacy. All other ranks of the hierarchy "went into mourning," as well. Amaranth-red trim was replaced by purple, and purple by black. Likewise, the *fascia* color also changed at the appropriate season and period of mourning. The use of penitential colors was abolished by Pauline *motu proprio* in March 1969.

Only the reigning pontiff and members of the Sacred College are permitted watered silk by right of their position; nevertheless, the watered-silk *fascia* may be worn, in the appropriate color, by members of the Papal Household and persons formerly described as in "cardinalatial livery," that is, members of the household of a cardinal. These *fascia,* however, should be worn within that jurisdiction and not universally. This privilege, although not abolished, has all but disappeared through disuse.

Silk may be used by all patriarchs, primates, archbishops, and bishops. Wool cloth or faille of the appropriate color should be worn by all other persons. The fringe is to be made of silk and should be hand-knotted according to the present motif.

The *fascia* should be approximately 5 to 6 inches in width and should be made so that no seams are shown on either side; the stitching should not be obvious. The sash should be stiffened by appropriate heavy broadcloth or buckram so that the section of the cincture that encircles the waist will be firm.

The section of the sash that is designed to fall in two folds or flaps should not be stiffened. It should be mentioned that long-standing tradition requires that the ends of each sash be worn so as to overlap. In this way, the lower part of the sash's entire fringe will be exposed. The upper part of the sash should

---

* Secretariat of State Directive No. 135705; and *On the Reform of Choral Dress,* Sacred Congregation for Clergy (SRC), October 30, 1970.

drop directly on top of the under part, but, when properly worn, the fringe of the upper part will fall above the lower part, thus exposing the fringe of both sections of the *fascia*. The cincture has been worn thus for three hundred years. The practice, since 1960, of draping the *fascia* bands one directly on top of the other, without the under section being entirely exposed, is contrary to historical practice.

The *fascia* is always draped down the left side, slightly forward, yet not entirely beyond the left hip. It is important to note that the sash is not meant to be worn as a belt; the proper placement of the circular segment of the *fascia* is above the belt line and just below the breastbone. The closure of the *fascia* may be fastened by either snaps or Velcro; either method is acceptable today.

CHAPTER EIGHTEEN

Roman Collar and Rabat

The Roman collar, as we know it today, did not take its present form until the middle of the last century. The clerical collar originated in the fifteenth century, when the clergy adapted the secular practice of turning the linen collar up and over their outer garment. Well into the seventeenth century, the "collar" became universally accepted and began to resemble a primitive version of what we see in use today.

Paintings of the fifteenth to seventeenth centuries show many versions of the clerical collar. National differences are exhibited in the portraits of the prelates of the day: The French preferred to adapt the linen and lace collar of the noble class, which extended to the shoulder with lace trim, whereas the English preferred a collar that took a primitive appearance of the present ascot tie. These various exaggerations became so frivolous that Rome eventually forbade worldly decorations on the clerical collar. Early on, a linen band was placed over the collar at the neck in order to protect it from being soiled, as is often the practice with the stole. With the abolition of the more frivolous lace collars, known in the Italian as *collarino,* all that remained was the linen band, which had originally served as a protective overlay piece. It was later stiffened, resulting in a form of choker. By the late eighteenth century, the linen "choker" was worn by the hierarchy, whereas diocesan priests wore a more simple white cloth or scarf out of financial necessity. In the late nineteenth century, especially among North American priests, the clergy made use of an adaptation of this choker, which was nearly 4 inches high. It was made of starched linen and was fastened to the shirt and vest.

The collar took its final form in Rome in the nineteenth century, when it became customary to place a 3-inch-wide starched linen *collaro* onto the rabat, also known as the "rabbi," for use under the cassock and simar. The linen collar, which was held in place by posts, had a soft leather band inserted into it in order to keep its desired form. This *collaro* became so popular that it rapidly became the accepted form of clerical collar. The insertion of this linen collar into the black cloth collar of the rabbi, rabbi vest, or working shirt replaced the smaller choker form popularly preferred well into the early decades of the twentieth century. At present, the collar is usually made of white plastic,*

---

* *Plastic* is a term applied to the present manufacture of the collar in acetate.

which allows for easier cleaning and durability. Until the 1960s, starched linen was used, and this material is still available for persons who prefer it to plastic. Roman vesture suppliers are now offering the permanently starched linen collars at a very reasonable rate. These collars are the most comfortable available today, and they provide modern easy care in contrast to the laborious methods of maintaining the linen collars of former times.

Rabbi is a familiar or slang derivative of the formal French word *rabat*. In the archives of the Church, the Latin form, *rabattu,* is also seen; however, *rabat* as a term employed by the Church is derived from seventeenth-century French usage. Although similar in spelling to the Jewish word for teacher, it is correctly pronounced *rab́-bee.* The rabat, or rabbi, is actually the section of cloth that stiffens at the top and that is molded to rest fit around the neck. The top of the rabbi fits snugly into a linen or plastic collar, and, together, they form the neckwear for use under the cassock and simar.

For priests, the rabbi is always black and is made of the same material as the cassock, either summer or winter wool. For chaplains of His Holiness, the rabbi is purple cloth. For prelates of honor and the apostolic protonotaries, the rabbi is amaranth red and is made of cloth. For bishops, archbishops, and patriarchs the rabbi is always made of silk and is amaranth red. Cardinals make use of scarlet red moiré (watered silk) rabbi. The Holy Father uses white, and, depending on the season, it may either be silk or light wool broadcloth.

90.

91.

92.

93.

94.

95.

96.

97.

98.

99.

100.

101.

102.

103.

104.

105.

106.

107.

108.

109.   110.

111.

112.

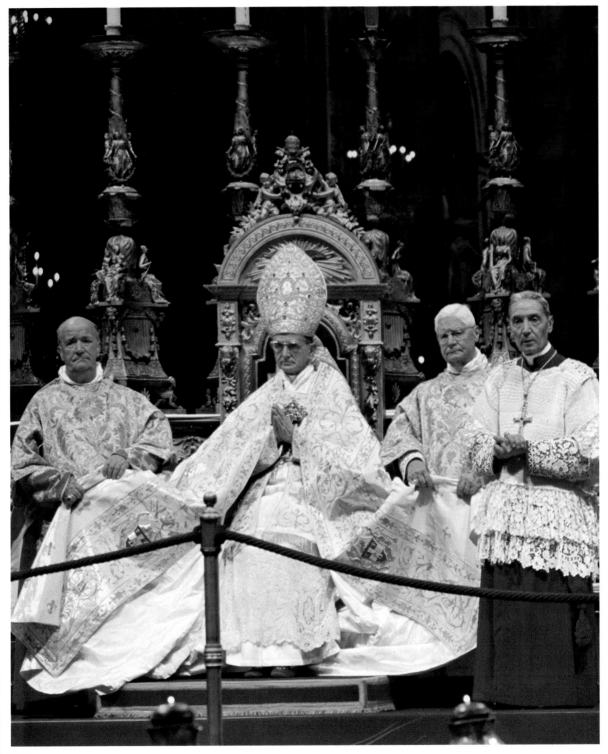

113.

114.

115.

116.

117.

118.

119.

120.

121.

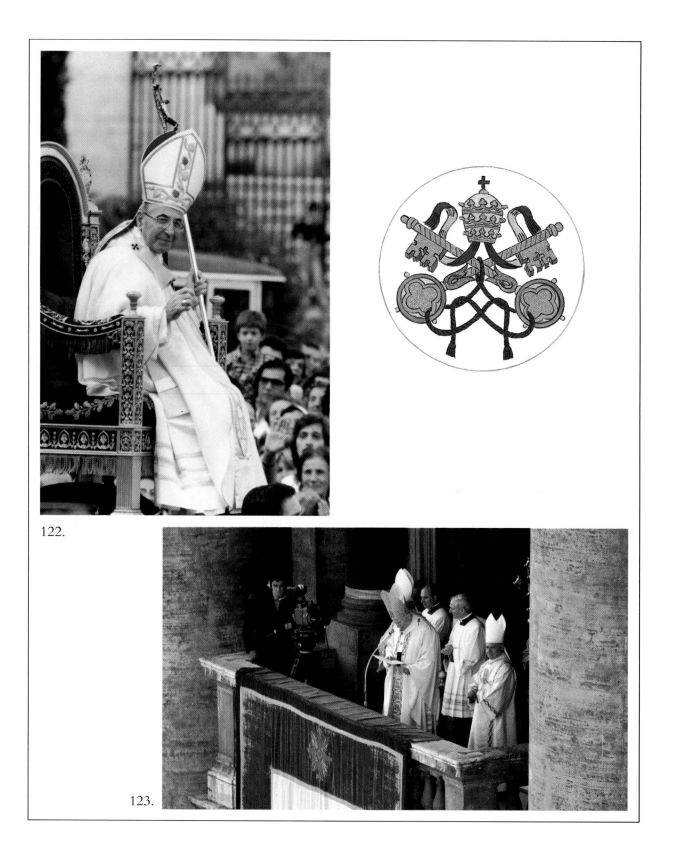

122.

123.

Biretta

The *biretta* is, in present times, most often seen on clerics with episcopal rank. The *biretta* has never been abolished although many clerics have the mistaken opinion that the *biretta* for priests was abolished by Pauline *motu proprio*. The *biretta* has fallen into disuse, due only to changing times.* Since the 1960s in the United States, the use of headgear for men has fallen out of fashion. The general demise of the *biretta* is a result of this shift in society's general outlook to more formal attire. The *biretta* has never been listed among the liturgical or sacred vestments, with the exception of the scarlet moiré *biretta* of a cardinal. A cardinal is restricted, by papal decree, to make use of this *biretta* only with choir dress.

The *biretta* (known also in Italian as *beretta,* in Old Latin as *birettume,* and Latin as *biretum*) is a square ecclesiastical cap that is worn over the *zucchetto*. From the top of the cap rise either three or four "horns." The Roman *biretta* is reserved for the Roman Catholic clergy and has three horns. Until the mid–nineteenth century, it was common to see the four-horned *biretta* in use among the clergy. Even today, some Spanish, French, and Portuguese clerics maintain the four-horned *biretta* for ecclesiastical use, and this usage is not incorrect, as time-honored tradition and custom warrant continuation of this practice. Nevertheless, the four-horned *biretta* should technically be reserved for use by clerics who hold doctoral degrees in the Sacred Sciences and Canon Law.

The doctoral *biretta* is identical to the Roman *biretta* with the exception of the fourth "horn." The tuft and trim may also represent the color associated with the individual's academic discipline. The doctoral *biretta* may be worn only in an academic setting; therefore, its use is permitted only at convocations, commencements, while teaching, or while presenting addresses. This *biretta* may never take the place of the episcopal *biretta*. The episcopal purple or red *biretta* ranks higher than the doctoral cap at all times, and once a priest has been raised to episcopal rank, he no longer makes use of a doctoral *biretta*.

---

* It once was directly proscribed by the *Ritus Servandus* but is not now proscribed by the *General Instruction of the Roman Missal*. Papal documents in the post–Vatican II era continue to make mention of its use as well as pronouncements on the limitations to color for the hierarchy; therefore, its use continues even though rarely seen.

In addition to the three horns, the *biretta* has a tuft of silk at the conjunction of the horns. This tuft, or pompon, is not a tassel and should never appear as one. It should always be given full shape, almost ball-like. A thread fastened to the inside of the cap allows for the tuft to be made firm by a quick tug from inside. At present, manufacturers offer two types of tufts for the *biretta*. The Roman ateliers tend to prefer much fuller, larger tufts, whereas domestic manufacturers prefer the smaller pompon style. Both are correct. It is simply a matter of the taste of the priest or prelate.

HISTORY

Although there are many reputed origins of the *biretta*, there is no single definitive documentation of its creation. The most probable origin of the ecclesiastical cap is the academic hat of the high Middle Ages. This soft, square cap, familiar in paintings from the period, included cords and tassels. In France and Spain, velvet or silk cording surrounded the brim, which included knots and tassels at the top. This cap is the ancestor of both the academic mortarboard and the soft doctoral cap in secular universities.

With the approach of the Renaissance in Italy, this cap took on a more fanciful appearance. During the Renaissance, the "horns" appeared, the cording and tassels disappeared, and the silk tuft became prominent. The *biretta* evolved to a form we recognize today over a period of one hundred years. By 1527, the *biretta*, appearing as we now recognize it, was referred to as "of long-standing tradition." Archival documents of the period refer to the *biretta* as the "scholastic cap," thus alluding to its early origins. Regulations permitting its use by priests and the hierarchy did not come into effect for another one hundred years.

DESIGN

The Roman *biretta* is square-shaped although at first glance it appears to be quadrangular. It has three "horns," or peaks, and a tuft of silk threads. The hat, or cap, is made of stiffened cardboard and covered with material proper to the rank of the cleric. *Birettas* are permitted to seminarians (without tuft), but, as in the case of most modern priests, use of the *biretta* is seldom seen during seminary formation. The *biretta* may be collapsible (folding) or stationary. Clerics who make use of a *biretta* should consider the collapsible type for ease of packing and modern travel.

The *biretta* for priests is always made of black merlino (light wool); it should never be made of silk. In the past, members of a cardinal's household were entitled to the black silk *biretta*, but this privilege has lapsed with time. Velvet or other cloth should never be used.

Although cardinals have long made use of a scarlet silk *biretta*, all other members of the hierarchy and clergy were permitted only the black *biretta* until the pontificate of Pope Leo XIII in 1888. Leo XIII permitted the purple *biretta* for patriarchs, archbishops, and bishops, and the black *biretta*, with either red or purple tuft and trim, for the various ranks of the *monsignori*.

In 1969, Pope Paul VI reorganized the structure of the Papal Household as well as the rules for vesture and insignia of the clergy. Prior to this ruling, monsignors known as prelates *di mantelletta* and *di mantellone* were entitled to a black silk *biretta* with either red or purple trim. The cap of the prelates *di mantellone* was lined in purple, whereas that of the *di mantelletta* was lined in crimson or amaranth red. The tuft of the *biretta* of domestic prelates and all other prelates *di mantelletta* was crimson red, with red cording as trim; that of prelates *di mantellone* was purple, with purple trim.

At present, the regulations of the Secretariat of State* define the proper use of the *biretta* for the episcopacy and the lesser prelates. Further regulations, set forth by Pope Paul VI, for the *biretta*'s design are to be strictly adhered to, as follows.

For Cardinals

The scarlet watered-silk *biretta* is to be reserved for choir dress only. It is not to be worn as a headdress for everyday use. The cardinal's *biretta* has three peaks, but it never has the tuft, or pompon. When Pope Paul II (1468) granted the *biretta* to the members of the Sacred College, he specifically denied them the tuft. The popes have never made use of the *biretta*; rather, they make use of the *camauro,* which shares the same early origins as the *biretta,* but, for some unknown reason—perhaps the whim of a pope of that time—it never took on the stiffened shape of the later Renaissance cap. When Paul II, Pietro Barbo, finally granted the *biretta* to cardinals for everyday wear, he reminded them of the lack of a tuft on the pontiff's *camauro.* As they were closest to him as the senate of the Church, he affirmed that he withheld the tuft to mark the College members as special and uniquely bound to the papacy. In place of the common tuft, a loop of scarlet silk was granted to remind the cardinals of their simpler clerical origins and subjugation to the pontiffs of the Renaissance era. Although it may appear that the absence of a tuft for cardinals was a slight, the removal of the tuft on the cardinal's *biretta* was a cogitative act to distinguish them from other prelates.

The *galero* and the *cappello Romano* were more prominent than the *biretta* until toward the end of the pontificate of Pope Paul VI. Prior to that time, the red *galero* was *the* red hat that had, for centuries, been presented to new cardinals in the consistory of elevation. The *biretta* was always sent prior to the consistory, carried by a pontifical emissary who announced the conferral of membership in the Sacred College. This special *biretta* was never worn by a new cardinal. It was immediately placed on display in his salon or reception room, usually on a credence table between two candles.

In present times, the red silk-moiré *biretta* is the red hat presented by the pope at the consistory that confers membership in the College of Cardinals. Cardinals make use of two types of *biretta*s. The watered-silk (moiré) and the scarlet merlino, or light scarlet wool. The watered-silk cap, as stated above, may never be worn as everyday wear. It is reserved only for use with choir dress and with the *cappa magna.* The scarlet wool *biretta* may be worn with the simar and ferraiolo.

For Archbishops and Bishops

Patriarchs of the Latin rite, primates, archbishops, and bishops each make use of the purple *biretta* with purple tuft. It is always to be worn over the *zucchetto.* The purple episcopal *biretta* may be worn with both choir dress and academic dress; in fact, it should be considered obligatory for both. Prelates of episcopal dignity may make use of either a silk (not moiré) *biretta* in summer or a purple merlino, or light wool, *biretta* in winter. The tuft on each is of purple silk. The proper lining for a *biretta* of a prelate of episcopal dignity is green. The size of the tuft depends entirely on the manufacturer; the Roman ateliers prefer to offer the larger pompon style.

For Apostolic Protonotaries

Apostolic Protonotaries de Numero are entitled to a black *biretta,* silk if given by a special indult of the pontiff. The tuft, trim, and lining are crimson red. Apostolic Protonotaries Supranumerary may make use of the black *biretta* and black silk tuft only. For this class, the purple tuft has been abolished.

---

* Secretariat of State Directive No. 135705.

For Prelates of Honor and Chaplains of His Holiness

As in the case of priests and seminarians, lesser prelates are permitted only the black *biretta* and black silk tuft (priests only). An exception is made for priests and lesser prelates who hold a doctoral degree. They are permitted the appropriate doctoral *biretta*, with the corresponding color for the tuft and trim associated with the academic discipline of the cleric, but only for use in an academic setting. For clerics with episcopal dignity, the doctoral *biretta* may neither replace the liturgical or vestural *biretta* nor be used at any time outside the academic environment.

PROTOCOL

As we have seen, the *biretta* is required for all prelates of episcopal dignity for both choir and academic dress. Misinterpretation of the rubrics, Pauline *motu proprio,* and directives of national bishop's conferences have led many persons among the clergy to view the *biretta*, for all but the hierarchy, as abolished. This is not the case, nor has it ever been. Those individuals who make use of the *biretta* or who wish to see it revived for themselves or others should be aware of the protocol required at sacred ceremonies today.

The cap should never be worn loosely on the crown of the head; it should fit firmly at the brow. The "hornless" peak should always be to the left. The *biretta* can be worn outdoors, like any other hat, but never without cassock or vestments (as at the exit of church). Inside a church, during sacred ceremonies, the following guidelines should be followed:

- The cap should be worn only when walking in procession, although it would also be appropriate to carry it during processions and when seated. It should not be worn when the bearer is standing or kneeling when present or attending "in choir."

- When removing or replacing the *biretta* during liturgical functions, the center or frontal horn should be grasped between the index and middle fingers.

- During solemn processions, tradition requires that all but cardinals remove the *biretta*. The cap should therefore be carried, using both hands, at breast level. This would also be the proper pose for formal photography when incorporating the *biretta*.

Although it is very rare in present times to see celebrants of nonepiscopal rank making use of the *biretta* during the liturgy, those who still make use of it must do so according to present custom and protocol. All former practices have been abrogated.

MODERN RUBRICS FOR OPTIONAL LITURGICAL USE OF THE BIRETTA

Although current circumstances identify primary use of the *biretta* with the hierarchy, the following rubrics detail proper form for clergy were they to make use of the *biretta* during the liturgy. These procedures for use of the *biretta* during the sacred liturgy are currently in practice in Rome and are subject to change at a future time.

Procession

- Celebrants wear the *biretta* in procession rather than carry it when they opt to make use of it unless, of course, they enjoy episcopal dignity, in which case they would properly use the mitre. Concelebrants have the option to either wear it or to carry it at the breast while processing. Canons and all those vested "in choir" likewise have the option to wear or to carry the *biretta* in procession.

- All persons who wear the *biretta* in procession must remove it at the foot of the stairs to the sanctuary. The correct form would be for all to remove the *biretta* in unison, that is, all together; however, if the numbers in procession are large, it would be best for each group of two or four to remove their *birette* as they approach the bottom step.

Liturgy

- After the altar has been reverenced, the *biretta* is returned to the head, as the celebrant, concelebrants, and prelates and priests vested "in choir" assume their positions within the sanctuary.

- The *biretta* is always removed for the incensation of the altar and/or for the opening prayer. At times, it is proper not to return the *biretta* to one's head after reverencing the altar. Such a case would occur when there is not a choral group present and the invitation to prayer begins immediately.

- The *biretta* is always returned to the head as the prelates and priests take their seats for the first reading. It remains on the head until the Alleluia before the Gospel.

- During the reading of the Gospel, the *biretta* is properly placed on the seat or on the prie-dieu, or it is held at the breast. The *zucchetto*, for prelates, properly remains on the head, despite some recent occurrences to the contrary.

- The *biretta* is returned to the head during the homily, but not by the prelate or priest who is presenting the homily. At present, only bishops may preach with any symbol or insignia of office; for them, it must be the mitre. Even bishops remove the *biretta*, keeping on the *zucchetto*, when preaching a homily on occasions outside the Mass where use of the mitre would not be appropriate.

- The *biretta* is once again removed after the preparation of the gifts, just after the lavabo. Of course, the celebrants and concelebrants remove the *biretta* before approaching the altar after the homily, whereas the homilist would already be without his *biretta*.

- During the incensation, after the gifts, altar, and crucifix have been incensed, those persons attending are incensed as well. At this point in the liturgy, the *biretta* is properly removed. The *biretta* should be held at the breast, not laid down, until after the incensation is complete.

- The *biretta* remains off until after the Blessed Sacrament has been returned to the Blessed Sacrament chapel or tabernacle, at the same moment that the presiding bishop returns the *zucchetto* to his own head. The *biretta* remains on the head throughout the conclusion of the Communion rite.

- At the oration before the final benediction, the *biretta* is again removed from the head and held at the breast for the conclusion of the Mass.

Recessional

- After the benediction, the celebrant and the concelebrants are invited to reverence the altar in unison. If this act takes place in the sanctuary, those "in choir" may also join in the proper reverence. The *biretta*, however, should not be returned to the head until after the procession turns to leave down the nave aisle. If the reverence takes place when the procession is gathered at the front of the steps to the sanctuary, then the *biretta* is returned to the head at this time.

- It is common for all but the concelebrants to carry the *biretta* in procession, at the breast; however, it would also be proper to wear the *biretta* during the procession. In such cases, it should be removed if the procession passes the

Blessed Sacrament chapel or a place where the Blessed Sacrament is exposed, returning it to the head as the procession continues on to the sacristy. The *biretta*, properly, should remain on the head until entrance into the sacristy.

N.B.: In present times, use of the *biretta* is optional for inferior or lesser prelates and priests attending in choir, but it is never optional for bishops vested in choir, as many persons seem to believe. Bishops vested in choir must make use of the *biretta*. In addition, practices governing the use of the *biretta* have been changed, as described above, and careful attention should be given to the present customs. Former practices and protocol for the *biretta* are now null and void, and present customs are subject to change over time.

CHAPTER TWENTY

Zucchetto

The *zucchetto,* or *calotte,* as it was formerly more commonly called, is also known as the skullcap. It is also known in the Old Latin as *pilleolus.* From time to time when searching through old documents, one will also see the term *solideo* in Italian. Because most of the Holy See's documents in this century refer to the skullcap as the *zucchetto,* I, too, will exclusively make use of this term. "It is derived from the Italian *zuccha* (a gourd) and is a closely fitting skullcap, saucer shaped, in color white, red, violet, or black, suitable to the rank of the wearer. Originally introduced to protect the crown of the head bared by the tonsure, it is now worn oblivious to that need. It is called also *calotte* (shell), *pilleolus* (small cap), *biretina (biretta)* and *sub-mitrale,* because it is worn under the Bishop's mitre."[1]

The use of the *zucchetto,* despite popular misconceptions of the past thirty years, is not restricted to the hierarchy. In fact, it is the option for all clerics. It is not permitted seminarians, altar servers, or choir members, although abuses by the latter two are sometimes seen. These abuses are for theatrical effect and in no way suggest an understanding of the rubrics concerning vesture of the Church.

The *zucchetto* was developed for the utilitarian purpose of covering the tonsure of the cleric, protecting him from the elements. It was initially of rough wool, with a circumference three times the present shape, which it had adopted nearly two hundred years ago. During the Renaissance, and subsequent to it, the application of color and material became prevalent. In 1464, Pope Pius II granted cardinals the red *zucchetto.* This primitive version of the present scarlet silk *zucchetto* was deep, blood red and made of wool; it also covered most of the crown of the head.

Once cardinals were permitted a *zucchetto* of rank, it was only a matter of time for other members of the hierarchy to obtain license to adopt the appropriate color of their own rank within the hierarchy. Green was incorrectly applied to bishops for a short period of time.* Early on, the pontiff made use of the *camauro,* so it was not until the fifteen hundreds that the popes also adopted the *zucchetto.* Once adopted, however, the color white was always reserved for pontiffs.†

---

* Green remains the heraldic color of the Episcopacy. Officially, the *zucchetto* of all ranks other than that of cardinal remained black until the papal brief of Pius IX on June 17, 1867, which granted the amaranth-red skullcap to patriarchs, archbishops, and bishops alike.

† With the exception of religious orders whose habits are also white, made of wool or cloth, such as the Norbetines.

Members of the inferior prelature eventually assumed, and were later confirmed, the privilege of a colored or ornamented *zucchetto*, whereas the simple black cloth *zucchetto* is the privilege of all clerics. The Papal *Motu Proprio* of 1968* did not abolish use of the *zucchetto* for clerics not of episcopal dignity. This practice of making use of a *zucchetto* has simply fallen into disuse. This same document, however, reinforces the use of the *zucchetto* for the hierarchy. The pontiff makes use of a white silk (summer) or merlino (winter) *zucchetto*.

Cardinals make use of only one type of *zucchetto*, red silk. It is the preference and privilege of members of the Sacred College to make use of scarlet watered silk (moiré), and nearly all members do assume this singular mark of distinction.

Patriarchs, archbishops, and bishops all make use of a silk amaranth-red *zucchetto*.

Each *zucchetto* is made from age-old patterns in Rome. Very few, if any, non-Roman clothing suppliers know the secret for making this uniquely shaped headgear. Often suppliers that have attempted to make them on their own have found that the closest that they have come to the proper design is a version of the Jewish yarmulke, which, of course, it is not, nor has it developed from it, as is often suggested.

Nearly all non-Roman suppliers have purchased their stock in Rome. The *zucchetto* should always be lined with white chamois, a soft suedelike cloth, which helps it keep its shape. At present, the chamois is usually white, whereas formerly the color of the chamois varied by the rank or preference of the wearer. All *zucchetti* today, however, are not made with chamois. Two reasons for this have been put forth: One reason is that prelates often complained that the use of chamois helped along the natural tonsure process, which, most likely, it did not; the other reason put forth is that forgoing the chamois lining helps keep the cost of the *zucchetto* down. In effect, chamois offers more of a support to the *zucchetto* than it does an increased cost. All *zucchetti* hold their shape best if they have a chamois lining. The use of chamois, however, remains a matter of personal preference.

The *zucchetto* is made of silk in eight equal triangular parts and is lined in chamois of one piece. Usually, *zucchetti* are offered in only three sizes: small, medium, and large. At the top junction of the triangular points is a silken loop of matching color. This is not only in place to facilitate an ease of taking off and putting on the *zucchetto*, but it actually is the historic remnant of the tuft from the *biretta,* for these two share common origins; in fact, ancient documents refer to them both as *biretum.*†

The *zucchetto* has become identified solely with the hierarchy in the past thirty years because, as we have seen, members of the hierarchy make use of it by law. In fact, the *zucchetto* is required of them at all times. The *zucchetto* must always be worn under the mitre. Celebrants and concelebrants at the liturgy of the Mass must remove their *zucchetto* from the time of the Sanctus to just after communion. The main celebrant is to have his *zucchetto* removed from him by the master of ceremonies,‡ whereas concelebrants remove their own, discreetly placing them in sleeve, cuff, or pocket.

Prelates attending the liturgy in choir, that is not vested in chasuble and mitre, must remove their own *zucchetto* when they approach the altar for reverencing prior to taking their assigned place in the

---

* Secretariat of State Directive No. 135705.
† Refer to Chapter 19, Biretta.
‡ It is proper for the master of ceremonies to fold the *zucchetto* and place it in his sleeve or cuff until he can quietly place it upon the seat of the presiding prelate, who will place it upon his own head prior to taking his seat after Communion. At no time is it proper to place, drop, or lay aside a *zucchetto* on the altar. Concelebrants would place their *zucchetti* in their own sleeves or pockets at the Sanctus. It must be noted that masters of ceremonies and choir directors and the like should never make use of a *zucchetto* while functioning in those posts.

sanctuary. For them also, the *zucchetto* must be removed at the Sanctus. Each ought to remove his own and best place it on the arm rest of the priedieu or upon his own seat.

The *zucchetto* is always removed in the presence of the Blessed Sacrament when exposed, in processions of the Blessed Sacrament, and during the veneration of, or blessing with, a relic of the true cross.

The *zucchetto* is never removed at the recitation of the Lord's Prayer as has become the practice of many senior prelates of late, or at the Gospel. Although removal of the *zucchetto* is certainly a sign of deep respect for Our Lord's own words in prayer to the Father and to the Gospels, the *zucchetto*, in more than six hundred years of use has not, until the present era, been removed at these times. Any prelate choosing to do so does so solely as a personal gesture and not according to any rubric, law, or long-standing practice.

A cleric of nonepiscopal dignity (not including abbots) may not celebrate, concelebrant, or attend the Mass "in choir" with the *zucchetto* on the head. Clerics who do not have episcopal dignity yet still make use of the *zucchetto*, are to leave it in the sacristy. In the case of the celebrant of the liturgy who insists on the use of the *zucchetto*, it is to be removed prior to entering the sanctuary and not returned to the head until leaving the sanctuary again afterward. At one time, the general clergy who made use of the *zucchetto* were permitted to do so during the Mass if they were attending. In those instances, it had to be removed for the reverencing of the altar, when they were incensed, when reciting the *Confiteor* (now properly known as the Penitential Rite prayer), and at the Penitential Rite within the Liturgy of the Hours (commonly known as the Divine Office). Today, this practice has been modified so that all clerics without episcopal dignity should remove the *zucchetto* in the sacristy.

Absolutely everyone must remove the *zucchetto* in

the presence of the Holy Father. At one time, cardinals had the singular privilege of wearing the *zucchetto* in the pope's presence, but time has elapsed since that privilege was widely assumed. At present, everyone removes their *zucchetto* when the Holy Father enters a room, and should not replace it on the head until all formal greetings and salutations have taken place. There are persons who argue that it should not be returned to the head of the prelate until the Holy Father exits; however, Pope John Paul II prefers to participate in lengthy meetings, and, in these instances, it would be acceptable to replace the *zucchetto* once greetings and salutations have been made. The senior prelate present should be aware of this, and all others, simply out of good manners, should take their cue from him, especially if he is a cardinal, who is due deference and respect.

During papal Masses or other liturgical celebrations in the presence of the Holy Father, as well as during all other public ceremonies in the presence of the pontiff, as a cardinal or other prelate reads aloud an address or presents a homily or other discourse, he is to first lift the *zucchetto* from his head, turning to the pontiff as he does so, in a sign of filial deference to the Holy Father. He should, by age-old custom, repeat this act each time he refers to the pontiff by name or title within that discourse. This is not an ancient practice lost to the ages. It is still observed in Rome and is still expected, as a sign of respect and good manners, in all other parts of the world when one is in the presence of the pope. If the pope is not present, regardless of the number of times to which he is referred in a discourse, a reverence in this manner is not observed. Lesser prelates, priests, and laymen, under the same conditions, would always observe this custom by a slight inclination of the head, turning to face the pontiff from time to time as circumstances warrant.

Finally, it has been the time-honored custom for four hundred years or more that anyone who is to be presented to the pope in private may choose to make a presentation of a white silk *zucchetto* to the Holy Father. Custom requires that the Holy Father, in turn, replace it for his own, giving his to the guest as a token of his appreciation.* In keeping with longstanding Church custom, this is a practice that is also observed in some countries for local prelates. The present pontiff, Pope John Paul II, does not encourage this practice; nevertheless, for

individuals making the gesture, he graciously follows the time-honored custom. The pope prefers the smallest size, white silk chamois-lined *zucchetto*. He will, however, make the exchange only in private gatherings, not in larger settings.

---

* The Roman suppliers of vesture know of this preference and have *zucchetti* in stock ready for sale for persons who wish to purchase them. At the present rate, they sell for $65 US.

Mozzetta

The short cape that completely encircles the prelate is known as a *mozzetta*. In design, this cape is elbow length, with a cassock-style upright collar. The collar, however, is rounded rather than notched so that it fastens over the choir cassock in such a way as to overlap in the front in a V-shape or closed mode. The *mozzetta* is closed in front by a row of twelve silk-covered buttons.* The buttons, piping, and lining are always silk.

The *mozzetta* is one of the garments that is immediately associated with the hierarchy. From its earliest development in the thirteenth century until 1969, it was a hierarchical garment of jurisdiction. With the *motu proprio* of Paul VI,† the *mozzetta* was transformed from a pure symbol of ordinary jurisdiction to one of more universal episcopal dignity.‡

Only the Sovereign Pontiff may make use of velvet in his ecclesiastical vesture, including the *mozzetta*. Cardinals make use of watered silk when prescribed, silk, and merlino, which is a light wool blend similar to the material used in cassock making. The seasons are now the only factors that determine a change of material for the *mozzetta*. In the past, the liturgical calendar and times of mourning were factors as well, but now only changes in climate require vesture change. Patriarchs, by virtue of their automatic appointment as Assistants to the Papal Throne, as well as those archbishops singularly appointed to that title, make use of silk for their *mozzetta*. They may also make use of the material reserved for all other archbishops and bishops, light wool or merlino, in the appropriate color.

All lining, trim, facings, and buttons are traditionally worked in silk, unless otherwise prescribed if one is entitled a *mozzetta* by rescript as a canon or rector-primus. This holds true for the *monsignori* as well, were they still to hold a special, albeit rare, right to its use.

Prior to 1968, the *mozzetta* was forbidden to all titular bishops and archbishops. It had to be worn over the *mantelletta,* in a further restrictive manner, by all ordinaries when in the presence of a cardinal or the metropolitan of the province. It was also not permitted to be worn by ordinaries in the presence

---

* Representing the twelve Holy Apostles.
† Secretariat of State Directive No. 135705; and *On the Reform of Choral Dress,* Sacred Congregation for the Clergy (SRC), October 30, 1970.
‡ At the final session of the Second Vatican Council, Pope Paul VI felt that all bishops present were equal and that a differential in vesture precluded that equality. He later incorporated those feelings into the decree that abolished the *mantelletta* and permitted all clerics with episcopal dignity the unlimited use of the *mozzetta*.

of the cardinal legate of the pontiff, or, of course, the pope himself. Even cardinals had to first don a *mantelletta* before donning the *mozzetta* when in the presence of the pope.

Only the pope had the unlimited right to the *mozzetta*. Only the pope had the unlimited use of placing a stole over the *mozzetta* prior to 1969. Once the *mozzetta* was transformed from a garment signifying ordinary jurisdiction to one of episcopal dignity, all prelates with that dignity were also permitted use of the stole over the *mozzetta*. For instance, when attending ordinations in choir, they are now permitted to perform the imposition of hands on the *ordinandi* by simply donning the stole over the choir dress.

The *mozzetta*, it has been argued, draws from one of two early thirteenth-century sources: the *cappa magna* or the *almuce (capuce)*. The *mozzetta's* close identity to the *almuce* is through the hood. Some historians speculate that the hood of the *mozzetta* shortened as the *cappa magna* enlarged and became more dignified, but this appears not to be the case. The *cappa magna,* which still survives, encompasses a *mozzetta*, in a style almost exactly like that of the original *mozzetta*. In fact, if the top of the *cappa magna* were cut off, we would see the *mozzetta* of the pre-1968 modifications. At the time when the weather played so vital a role in the development of other clerical garb, so too it affected the great *cappa magna,* which, in the twelfth and thirteenth centuries, was quite voluminous in order to keep out the damp. As the warmth of summer approached, an abbreviated version developed, which, in present times, is called the *mozzetta*, from the Italian word *mozzare,* meaning "to cut" or "to shorten."

In 1969, a small hood, a remnant of the Middle Ages when it was necessary for warmth and protection, was abolished. It is the only change in the design of the *mozzetta* in six hundred years. Patriarchs, archbishops, and bishops make use of a purple *mozzetta*. The lining, trim, and buttons are amaranth-red silk. The cloth chosen for these *mozzette* must match the choir cassock. One may not mix a woolen *mozzetta* with a lighter merlino, just as cardinals may not mix silk with merlino.[*] Only patriarchs while in Rome and archbishops specifically honored with the title Assistant to the Papal Throne may make use of a silk *mozzetta* and choir cassock of purple hue. Both cassock and *mozzetta* in silk are marks of distinction of that rare title Assistant to the Papal Throne.

The *mozzetta* is now worn by all Bishops when vested in choir. The pectoral cross worn over the *mozzetta* is always suspended by the cord, red with gold for cardinals and green with gold for others with episcopal dignity.[†] The pectoral cross is never worn suspended from a chain over the *mozzetta*.

Often one hears the cape on the black house cassock referred to as a *mozzetta*. It should be understood that this cape is not the *mozzetta*, but rather forms, together with the cassocklike garb underneath, a separate item of vesture known as the simar. The two are not interchangeable terms.

By long-standing custom, when a bishop-designate has been nominated to the dignity of bishop, even prior to Episcopal Ordination or Consecration, he is permitted to assume the *mozzetta* over choir cassock and rochet. He may not, however, make use of any of the insignia such as the pectoral cross or ring.

The *mozzetta* of the pope is either red or white, the two proper colors of the papacy. In the past three pontificates, only the red *mozzetta* has been preferred by the incumbents. The *mozzetta* for the pontiff, in winter, is made of red velvet and

---

[*] Part of the problem of mixing materials of different weight is the color difference. Dyes adapt to materials differently, and a garment of lighter material may be lighter in hue than a garment of a heavier material.

[†] It is important to also review Chapter 33, Pectoral Cross.

trimmed in ermine.* It is now always lined in silk. In summer, the pope's *mozzetta* is of deep red satin; the button and piping are to match. The third *mozzetta* available to a pope is made entirely of white damask.† The white-damask *mozzetta* is worn only for a seven-day period, from Holy Saturday until Easter Sunday. Pope John XXIII was the most recent pontiff to opt for its use, yet Pope Pius XII made use of it annually. He also made use of a *mozzetta* made entirely of white ermine, with white silk buttons to fasten it. This was his own invention, preferred for its warmth, and he often wore it on the simar simply to ward off a chill. It was never a formal item of vesture and was peculiar to his pontificate, although subsequent popes would be free to adopt it.

The *mozzetta* of cardinals is scarlet, lined, trimmed, and piped in scarlet silk. In summer the cassock and *mozzetta* are silk (no longer watered silk); in winter, the *mozzetta* is made of merlino or another similar light woolen material. Until 1969, cardinals were permitted the use of scarlet watered silk (moiré) in the *mozzetta* and choir cassock as well as on the *fascia, zucchetto, biretta,* and *ferraiolo.* Moiré is still permitted for these other items of vesture, but not for the *mozzetta.* Cardinals no longer adapt the color of their choir dress to match the season or the occasion of mourning; this practice was abolished in 1969.

Clerics of nonepiscopal dignity who were formerly entitled to a purple or red *mozzetta* are no longer so entitled. The *mozzetta* is now entirely reserved for the episcopal dignity with the exception of certain canons or other clerics specifically granted this indult by right of a position they hold, such as benefices, rather than for a personal dignity. In all cases, the *mozzetta* must be made of black or gray wool, yet may, depending on the original papal rescript, have buttons, trim, lining, and piping in either red or purple. An example of such an indult would be that granted to a rector-primus of a(n) (arch)diocese (i.e., cathedral rector) but this is not a privilege that can be automatically assumed.‡

A *mozzetta* is also donned by the chaplains of the Equestrian Order of the Holy Sepulchre of Jerusalem and of the Order of Malta. These *mozzette* are always made in a material and color that matches the mantles of the lay knights. In the case of the Equestrian Order of the Holy Sepulchre, the *mozzetta* is made of creamy white wool, marked on the left shoulder with the blood-red Jerusalem cross, the emblem of the order. With the exception of color and texture, these *mozzette* are manufactured in the same fashion as the *mozzette* of the prelature. In some jurisdictions of the order, that is, in local regions, the stole has been incorrectly substituted for the *mozzetta.* It must be remembered that the *mozzetta* is a jurisdictional garment, whereas the stole is one of the sacred vestments. As such, for an ecclesiastical official of the order, the *mozzetta* would always be the proper vesture. The stole should be reserved for celebrants and concelebrants or by clerics vested in *mozzetta* if required to perform a sacred function at some point in a liturgy.

---

* Ermine is usually replaced by white rabbit fur. The present pontiff has chosen, up to the present, not to make use of this style of *mozzetta* although it was the more favored style of his five immediate predecessors except one, John Paul I.

† A white silk material with white silk embroidery; this type of mozzetta was worn each year during the Octave of Easter by Pope John XXIII.

‡ *Per Instructionem,* Secretariat of State Directive No. 135705; and *On the Reform of Choral Dress,* Sacred Congregation for the Clergy (SRC), October 30, 1970.

Ferraiolo

The Pauline modifications of 1969* made few changes to the ecclesiastical cape most commonly known as the *ferraiolo*. With the exception of change of color, as we will see, the privilege of the *ferraiolo* has gone unchanged.

The correct name for this garment is *ferraiolone*. At one time, there were two cloaks common to the clergy, the *ferraiolo* and the *ferraiolone*. The latter has long since fallen into disuse, whereas its name, being the easier of the two to remember, lives on. Sometimes, the English-speaking clergy refer to the *ferraiolo* as the *ferraiola*. This is inappropriate, as there has never been a garment by this name.

Because members of the Church have come, during the past hundred years, to refer to the ecclesiastical cape as the *ferraiolo*, I, too, will acquiesce for the sake of continuity; however, it should be noted that the only proper terminology for the ecclesiastical cape is the *ferraiolone*.

The *ferraiolo* is a cape that almost encircles the entire body. It may be worn both to appear to encircle the individual or thrown back behind the shoulders so as to drape down the back. This cape should always be made of a single piece of cloth, but often this is impossible. When the proper length

of cloth is not available, the *ferraiolo* should be constructed as to disguise the seams. Where the two pieces are joined, the cloth should never be seamed vertically in a manner that would make the garment appear to be in two separate united halves. When seamed, the *ferraiolo* must always appear to be one piece of cloth.

The ecclesiastical cape *(ferraiolo)* is properly worn from shoulder to heel. It should never be worn shorter. It has a large, flat collar, which is worn turned down, completely covering the shoulders. It is closed at the neck by two long ribbons, traditionally made of silk, which, when fastened, create a bow with two long tails down the front of the cassock. All members of the clergy, as well as theologians in seminary,† are permitted the *ferraiolo* although it is not used frequently by them. The only restrictions imposed by Rome are that of proper color and material.

Cardinals make use of a *ferraiolo* made entirely of scarlet watered silk (moiré). The ribbons are of

---

* Papal *Motu Proprio, Instruction on the Dress of Cardinals, Bishops and Lesser Prelates;* Paul VI, 1969.

† The *soprana* is proper to seminarians; however, with the Pauline modifications of 1969, it is apparent that the *ferraiolo* is now tolerated for theologians wishing to assume it, but it is doubtful that this privilege actually exists. Only wool should be used in its manufacture.

scarlet silk thread.* The material covering the broad collar is also of scarlet moiré. The *ferraiolo* of members of the Sacred College is always made fuller than those made for other members of the clergy. This is one of the vestural privileges bestowed upon the cardinalate, and anyone purchasing a *ferraiolo* for a cardinal should remind the manufacturer of this privilege. Cardinals always wear the *ferraiolo* draped forward over the shoulders and sleeves, fully covering the arms. When worn properly, the *ferraiolo* covers all but the center section of the simar.

Patriarchs, archbishops, and bishops make use of a purple silk *ferraiolo* in summer and light woolen one in winter, although, since 1969, the purchase of one silk *ferraiolo* seems to have become the norm. The use of watered silk for the *ferraiolo* is not permitted archbishops and bishops unless they have been granted the special dignity of Assistants to the Papal Throne, a dignity automatically bestowed upon noncardinalatial patriarchs. Patriarchs may make use of the watered-silk *ferraiolo*, in purple.

Of the *monsignori*, only the protonotaries, both apostolic de numero and supranumerary, are permitted the purple *ferraiolo*. This privilege is extended to both the summer (silk) and winter (broadcloth) capes, each with coordinating silk ribbons. The use of the purple *ferraiolo* for all others granted the title Monsignor is forbidden.† Therefore, all monsignors named after 1969 may make use only of the simple black woolen *ferraiolo* unless they are named to one of the two degrees of the class of protonotaries.

Prelates of Honor and Chaplains of His Holiness, priests, deacons, and theologians may make use of the black faille (a silklike cloth) *ferraiolo*, although a woolen *ferraiolo* would be more appropriate. It is traditional that the faille cape be made less full than that of the greater prelates, especially cardinals, and it should always be worn thrown back over the shoulder as to drape down the back. In so doing, the broad collar will hang loosely down off the shoulders, which is the appropriate manner for persons not entitled to the scarlet or purple *ferraiolo*.

HISTORY

The *ferraiolo* is a garment that was not designed for ecclesiastical use *per se*. It developed before the Renaissance as a knee-length cloak for use by all noble Romans. It entered the Church, officially, during the fifteenth century, when it was gradually lengthened and the various vesture colors were assigned to it.

Until 1969, the *ferraiolo* was mandatory for all papal audiences. Late in the last century, this regulation was implemented as the practice of attending the pontiff in choir gave way to the simar and the *ferraiolo* as a result of the rising popularity of the simar as more than simply the "house cassock," or vesture reserved for the residence. At present, the *ferraiolo* may be worn at papal audiences, as the 1969 modifications only made its use optional. Although it is the option of the wearer, few make use of this privilege. The *ferraiolo*, by *motu proprio* of Paul VI, should always be worn on nonliturgical solemn occasions. It should properly be worn at state and governmental functions to which the prelate or priests have been invited or to events known in the social world as "white tie" or "black tie" celebrations. "It is the proper dress at academic convocations, defending theses, making the Profession of Faith, the taking of an oath, the reception of

---

* The ribbons on all *ferraioli* must match the color of the cape. There can be no variance. Silk material is permitted the higher degrees of the prelature, whereas the woolen material or faille is to be used at all times by lesser prelates and the clergy.
† Inferior prelates who were granted their title prior to March 31, 1969, with its accompanying privileges, may retain them for their lifetime.

distinguished dignitaries, entertainments, lectures and banquets."[1]

Prior to 1969, the *ferraiolo* for religious prelates was identical in design but took on the color of their former habit, as did the choir dress. The former prelates *di mantelletta* and *di mantellone* were permitted the silk *ferraiolo*, purple during normal times and black during the vacancy of the See of Peter. In present times, priests and theologians may only make use of a black pure-silk *ferraiolo* by direct indult, or gift, from the Holy Father, which has not been granted in some time.

In the past, the *ferraiolo* used by cardinals differed by season, as did their choir attire. During the penitential season or during the vacancy of the papacy, cardinals donned a purple watered-silk *ferraiolo*. The ribbons, hem, and trim remained red silk. During the same period, patriarchs, archbishops, and bishops made use of a *ferraiolo* of black silk, whereas the ribbons, trim, and hem were of purple silk.

Even the pope makes use of a cape, but it should not be mistaken as a *ferraiolo*, as pontiffs have never made use of this form of vesture. The pope's cape is called, in Italian, *la cappa*, which simply means "cape." It is always made of scarlet wool or broadcloth. It is fastened not by ribbons but by a device known as a frog. The cloth has a capelet off the shoulders and is cut full in order to provide for ample room to move about. This cloak is not lined but is trimmed in gold and red silk cording very similar to that used for the pectoral-cross cords of cardinals.

N.B.: For prelates, the *ferraiolo* is always worn over the simar whereas for all others, it is worn over a cassock, with the *fascia*. The rochet or surplice is never worn with the *ferraiolo*.

Mantelletta

The short mantle, or *mantelletta*, is a garment of jurisdiction and, as such, has seen more changes and adaptations than most items of vesture in the Church. By design, the *mantelletta* should reach just below the knees of the wearer, though it was much longer in its primitive form. Prior to the Reformation, the garment was most commonly shin length. Today, one can see how the Renaissance *mantelletta* appeared close to its original design by studying the chimere, the garment of jurisdiction in the Church of England. Whereas the chimere had altered little from the original *mantelletta*, from which it developed, the Roman garment changed through the years to attain its present form. It took the name *mantelletta* once it had adapted to its present style.

In saying a garment is one of "jurisdiction," one is saying is that the garment is reserved for persons with specific jurisdiction, such as members of the Episcopacy. As the vestural privileges of the inferior prelates increased, the term *jurisdiction* was retained although for these inferior prelates who were permitted the use of the *mantelletta*, the jurisdictional privileges were purely honorific.

The Pauline modifications of 1969 greatly restricted the use of the *mantelletta*. What was formerly worn by all prelates—those with episcopal jurisdiction as well as those with honorary jurisdiction—was strictly reserved for the few Roman prelates who serve the Holy Father as Auditors of the Holy Roman Rota, the Promoter General of Justice, and the Defender of the Bond of the Apostolic Signatura, the Apostolic Protonotaries de Numero, the four clerics of the Camera, and certain canons who retained the privilege of the *mantelletta* by papal decree. All other prelates, regardless of rank and title, have no rights to the *mantelletta*. Even prelates who received the privilege of the *mantelletta* prior to 1969 are not permitted to retain it unless, of course, they are one of the group of prelates named above.

What exactly is the *mantelletta*, and what were its privileges prior to 1969? The *mantelletta* is a garment similar to the cassock in general shape but is only knee length; it has no buttons, being fastened by a hook-and-eye device at the neck. It has no sleeves but rather large slits for each arm to pass through. The *mantelletta* has a freestanding collar with a slight "V" cut rather than the square niche of the Roman collar. Either side of the front lining has a 6-inch-wide facing of silk of the same color and is designed in such a way as to assure that these two pieces invert to be seen at all times, most especially during movement, which added extra color during papal processions. All trim and lining are in silk. The facings are made of cloth or raw silk, and the slits for the sleeves are stitched with silk cording to prevent wear and tear. The *mantelletta* is made of silk for summer use and silk-trimmed light wool for winter use.

Although abolished for all but a handful of Roman prelates, the *mantelletta* was formerly associated with the entire prelature. Cardinals made use of several *mantellette*, having both the silk and woolen seasonal vesture as well as the penitential vesture of purple and rose color. The cardinal's *mantelletta* was of watered silk for all three colors. Patriarchs made use of purple watered silk, whereas archbishops and bishops made use of both the silk and the woolen vesture as well as the penitential black-silk *mantelletta* with purple facings.

Use of the *mantelletta* was prescribed by the *Ceremoniale*. It was required in the presence of the Holy Father at all times, as supreme jurisdiction was his alone. Cardinals always wore the *mantelletta* in Rome, under the *mozzetta*, but never made use of it outside Rome because members of the Sacred College had universal jurisdictional privileges, which made them subservient only to the pontiff.

Bishops were not required to use the *mantelletta* within their own jurisdiction, nor were metropolitans within their own see and province where they held jurisdiction. The *mantelletta* was worn, however, when a bishop was either not within his own diocese or when in the presence of a cardinal but still within his own jurisdiction. All titular bishops wore the *mantelletta* rather than the mozzetta at all times.

Former titular or honorary protonotaries apostolic had the privilege of the *mantelletta*, but that garb had to be made entirely of a black merlino (woolen) material. It was trimmed in black silk because purple was not permitted them. For this reason, honorary prelates of this degree were known as the "black protonotaries." Despite the "lack of color," this appellation was much sought after.

After the prelates of the episcopacy, the *mantelletta* was also the privilege of certain Roman honorary prelates. These prelates included the protonotaries apostolic, the votantes of the signatura, the auditors of the signatura and those holding the former title Domestic Prelate. They were known as the prelates *di mantelletta* because their household position entitled them to use this ecclesiastical garment.

Of course, in present times, only those prelates named in the previous paragraph retain the *mantelletta*, although the collective term prelates *di mantelletta* is no longer applied to them; that term was relegated to history by Pope Paul VI. It should be noted that the *mantelletta* was designed to cover the rochet, a garment used in place of a surplice at functions requiring "choir dress." The rochet, by papal decree, was never permitted to be uncovered. At times, the *mantelletta* was covered by the *mozzetta*, but vesting in such a way was restricted to prelates with episcopal dignity. The pectoral cross was worn over the *mantelletta* unless the *mozzetta* was also donned; in that case, however, it then was placed over the *mozzetta*.

At present, the *mantelletta* is no longer seen at the diocesan level. It is found only in Rome or during a papal visit when an official who is entitled to it would make use of it when accompanying the Holy Father. Strictly speaking, the *mantelletta* is now a Roman garment and should only be worn by persons entitled to it within the diocese of Rome. Canons were mandated to lay aside the purple *mantelletta* in 1969, and yet they are still seen making use of them all over Rome. For canons, the proper color for a *mantelletta* is now either gray or black, with purple trim or red trim. The purple *mantelletta*, as we have seen, has been maintained for only those prelates listed previously.

CHAPTER TWENTY-FOUR

Cappa Magna

The great cape known as the *cappa magna* has never been abolished, as has been thought by many persons, including present cardinals and bishops. It has been modified, to be sure, but remains an active item of vesture prescribed by Rome.

"The *cappa magna*, always without ermine, is no longer obligatory. It can be used only outside Rome, in circumstances of very special solemnity."* The *cappa magna* is the single item of vesture that the hierarchy and clergy believe to have been abolished in 1969. It was thought to be the "dinosaur of vesture," and yet Paul VI simply stated that its use should be reserved for the greatest and most solemn functions at the local churches (outside Rome), where a cardinal or bishop might preside. Ironically, the privilege of the *cappa magna* has been increased rather than abolished. In the past, it was purely a jurisdictional garment reserved for the use of an ordinary; today, it is the option of all bishops who might wish to make use of it on the most solemn occasions.

So few prelates make use of the *cappa magna* that little is known about it. The *cappa magna*'s history is as ancient as most items of vesture reaching back to the late ninth century, when it was used for warmth in monasteries in northern Italy and France. As bishops were called from the monastic tradition, this great winter cape was introduced into the liturgical vesture of the Church. Originally, it was a fur-lined garment, with the outer material and color matching the garb of the monastic habit of the house. It remained such until the twelfth century, when it assumed a duality of purpose, both functional and ceremonial. Although color and texture remained simple, the length and width was extended. The *cappa* was always fur lined out of necessity. As the hierarchy began to adapt necessity to liturgical function, the *cappa*'s fur also became classified. By the fourteenth century, ermine was reserved for cardinals and a chinchillalike fur for archbishops, with mink or other fur for bishops. By the mid-1800s, white fur (rabbit in most instances was officially designated as ermine) was permitted all ranks of the hierarchy. Until 1969, prelates raised from religious orders made use of *cappae* that reflected the color of their habits, as in the case of their choir vesture. Likewise, the fur of the *cappa* matched the color, as closely as possible, of their

---

* United States Catholic Conference translation; Papal *Motu Proprio, Dress and Insignia of Cardinals, Bishops and Lesser Prelates;* Paul VI, March 31, 1969, p. 5.

habit. Ermine was reserved for prelates raised from the diocesan priesthood.

"Cappa Magna literally means a large cope or cape. The word *cappa* is a term of low Latin said to be derived from *capine*, quia *capit* totum hominem—because it covers the whole person."[1] The *cappa* has always had a hood. Unlike the hood of the *mozzetta*, which shares a common origin with the *cappa*, the hood or the *cappa* is full size. Originally the entire *cappa* was lined in the same fur that formed the *mozzetta*-like segment of the *cappa*, but now it is lined with silk. The *cappa magna* was 15 feet long until 1952, when Pope Pius XII directed that it be shortened to 10 feet, the length that it remains today.

The design of the *cappa magna* has not altered drastically over time. It is meant to be a fully enveloping cape so that there is only one slit, down the center, which fastens at the neck by a hook-and-eye device. The *mozzetta*-like cape is placed over this, although some manufacturers in this century were able to make the garment into a one-piece cape. It was "entered" like a gothic chasuble, head first.

In winter, the *mozzetta*-like shoulder segment was made entirely of fur; in summer, it was made of the same material as the *cappa* itself. Cardinals make use of a scarlet watered-silk *cappa* at all times, as watered silk was not abolished for the *cappa magna* of cardinals; the fur, however, has been abolished.

Patriarchs, archbishops, and bishops, now both titular and residential, make use of a *cappa* of light wool. Patriarchs and archbishop Assistants to the Papal Throne do not assume a silk *cappa*, as would be their privilege with other vesture, as their privileges are restricted to Rome, and the *cappa* has been reserved for use outside the Eternal City.

Formerly, prelates who were raised to the Episcopacy from religious life adopted vesture appropriate to their new rank and dignity, retaining the colors of their order's habit, but this practice is no longer permitted. A *cappa magna* for a religious prelate,

therefore, would also be of the color and fabric appropriate to his new rank.

Prior to 1969, according to Roman etiquette, the *cappa magna* had many limitations placed upon its use. For instance, fur could be worn only in winter between the Feast of All Saints and Holy Saturday; silk or cloth replaced fur during the remainder of the year. When attending in choir, the ordinary was permitted to sit upon the *cathedra* only if vested in the *cappa magna*. If he entered his cathedral vested in choir dress with the *mozzetta*, he was to take the most prominent choir stall, leaving the *cathedra* vacant. Today, of course, these regulations have been abolished. The ordinary may take his *cathedra* at all times.

In photographs taken at papal functions prior to 1969, one will often see a fur or silk *cappa* without the train. Although it appeared that no train existed, it was present. It simply had to be bound by cords and rolled up behind the prelate. This practice followed etiquette that was formulated during the Renaissance, when the Papal Court was also a royal court. The bound *cappa magna* was worn by all prelates entitled to its use but inferior in rank to the presider (such as in the case of the pope as presider) or bishops in the presence of a cardinal. The bound *cappa*, a reflection of subservient jurisdiction, was abolished in 1969. In present times, only one bishop, the presider, has the right to the *cappa magna* on solemn occasions.

The Holy Father also makes use of the *cappa magna*, but the past two incumbents have made use of a great embroidered liturgical cope, instead of the traditional *cappa* reserved for them. The *cappa* of the pontiff is red velvet during winter and merlino during summer. Its length remains 15 feet, the length permitted prior to the directives of Pius XII. The pontiff has never made use of fur with the *mozzetta*. This *cappa magna* should not be confused with the simple red cape, or mantle, worn by the pope to this day for warmth in cooler weather.

CHAPTER TWENTY-FIVE

Rochet and Surplice

The rochet should never be confused with the surplice nor should they be viewed as interchangeable liturgical garments, despite their similar appearance and usage, because they have never been meant to be interchangeable.

ROCHET

The rochet is, first and foremost, a garment of jurisdiction. It is not, strictly speaking, a liturgical garment although it has always been worn during the liturgy if a prelate were not the presider or, as today, concelebrant. The rochet is always to be worn by a prelate when they are vested in choir. It is a prelate's foremost garment of choir dress. The *Roman Pontifical* has defined it as such for two centuries.

The rochet may be worn only by the pope, cardinals, patriarchs, archbishops, and bishops, and, by special rescript, the protonotaries apostolic de numero and certain canons. It may never be worn by the lower ranks of the *monsignori*, priests, seminarians, or by others vested as such for liturgical functions.

Although all clerics originally made use of the rochet, its earliest development is traced to the original alb. By the fourteenth century, during the pontificate of Benedict XII, it developed into a garment recognizable to us today. From that period onward, the rochet was forever restricted to the hierarchy. At present, by papal *motu proprio,* the rochet has been further restricted for use at liturgical functions where the prelate is attending the liturgy in choir dress.

The rochet takes its name from Old French and is also commonly known as the *rochetta,* from the Italian. Its origins, however, are from the Latin *rochettus* and from the High German *hrock,* both of which meant coat or tight cloak. Until the late eighteenth century, it was sometimes also referred to as the *fichu.* Although it is also pronounced as rock-et or ro-shet, as is the custom in the Anglican Church, the proper pronunciation remains ro-shay. The English pronunciation arose at the time of the Reformation, when some Roman influences were retained, but the Roman identity, such as the name, was Anglicized. As a result, the rochet began to be incorrectly pronounced as rock-et by members of the Church of England, a custom now reaching, inappropriately, into the Roman Church.

Although the rochet took on its proper form by the fourteenth century, it dates from the late eighth century. Until that time, the alb was the garment of many purposes and was worn for all functions. As it became clear that different functionaries required a distinct dress, so as to be vested in a manner that set them apart from the celebrant, the surplice and rochet began to develop. By the ninth century, the rochet was knee length, whereas the surplice remained longer in form. By the pontificate of Benedict XII, the rochet had become so identified with the expanded hierarchy that it became restricted to them. At that time, however, this garment was not restricted for liturgical functions alone because it still fundamentally remained a garment of jurisdiction utilized beyond the liturgy.

Prelates of all ranks, including, with time, the Papal Household functionaries holding the honorary titles of Monsignor, were permitted the rochet at all times when vested in choir cassock, in other words, when dressed in the color of rank.

From the fourteenth century, when it became officially reserved for prelates, until the *motu proprio* of Paul VI,* the rochet had to be covered at all times. Because the rochet symbolized the ordinary jurisdiction and authority of the wearer, it had to be covered slightly or completely as an act of reverence to the Sovereign Pontiff, who has universal jurisdiction and unlimited authority. Although a prelate was granted the privilege of this jurisdictional garment, the rochet, in turn, had to be covered to reflect the prelate's canonical deference to the pontiff. The rochet, therefore, was always covered by either the *mantelletta* and the *mozzetta* or by the *cappa magna*. When functioning as an official at the liturgy and, therefore, not vested in choir, a second garment, the simple surplice, had to be donned by that prelate, covering the rochet in part or totally.

Anyone doing research on Church ceremonies or history up until the time of the Second Vatican Council can see in photographs many prelates, usually a monsignor rather than a bishop, vested in purple, with a beautiful rochet partially covered by a cumbersome-looking surplice. This practice was the reminder to that prelate that his jurisdiction, rank, and honor were muted in the presence of the pope and that the pope alone had total authority and jurisdiction.

Today, a rochet is still always worn covered. It has been abolished as a privilege for all the *monsignori,* who would have needed to cover it by the surplice. Monsignors, priests, and seminarians always make use of a surplice, never the rochet. Cardinals, patriarchs, archbishops, and bishops must still all cover their rochet with a *mozzetta* or, on rare occasions, the *cappa magna*.

In the late nineteenth century, the practice of wearing choir dress, known in Italian as *abito paonazzo,* about town, to the opera, or to galas, as well as to attend the pope, was laid aside. The current practice of wearing academic dress (*abito piano*), consisting of simar and *ferraiolo*, was adopted for these and similar important functions by the late 1900s. In the past, one used to see a visiting cardinal in scarlet and a rochet, whereas today, one is more likely to see him properly vested in academic dress.

Design

The rochet's origins are with the ancient alb, and the rochet has remained true to those origins throughout its history. The sleeves of the rochet are always alblike and tight fitting; they are never bell-shaped or full.

After the changes in the vesture of the Church in 1968, many clerical clothing manufacturers, including those in Rome, took it upon themselves,

---

* Sacred Congregation of the Rites, *On the Reform of Choral Dress,* October 30, 1970. Secretariat of State Directive No. 135705. Papal *Motu Proprio, Dress and Insignia of Cardinals, Bishops, and Lesser Prelates;* Paul VI, 1969.

with no regard for historical accuracy or current Church directives and long-standing custom, to offer garments for sale that are not in keeping with the traditions and practices of the Church as outlined by the Holy Father's own personal decrees. With time, because no prohibitions had been placed on these clothiers to assure proper adherence to current practice, the garments that were sold, most especially the rochet, were no longer made according to the Church's rubrics. As a result, inappropriate garments took on an acceptance among the prelature and clergy when they should not legally have been.

Legally speaking, a cleric with episcopal dignity is never to don the surplice, no matter how fancy or dignified. He may only make use of the rochet. Having been clearly defined by Rome, this means that many prelates are in violation of the regulations of vesture without even knowing that they are so. What was frequently sold as a rochet is nothing more than a surplice. Any "rochet" made with bell-shaped or full sleeves is a surplice, no matter how fancy; it is not a rochet. Although many of these surplices are personally appealing, and, indeed, beautiful, some of very modern design, they are nothing more than surplices. The law of the Church* requires the jurisdictional garment of the rochet for all prelates with episcopal dignity, and prelates raised to this dignity need to be aware of this fact.

The rochet is now longer than a surplice, traditionally reaching below the knee, but not so long as the cotta. It is always to be made of linen, lace, or linen embroidery. It may be very simple in design or it may incorporate symbolism of rank, such as color.

The modern-style rochet incorporates the cross emblem and has some insertion of lace or embroidery, such as braiding. The traditional style, still the more popular everywhere but in the United States, makes use of lace or a linen/lace crochet. The yoke

is entirely of linen, whereas the base is worked in lace, usually with religious symbolism. The rubrics permitted no more than 12 inches of lace from yoke to base, but this allowance was relaxed in 1942. Today, some rochets are lace from breast to base. Prior to 1942, a good deal of linen would show below the *mozzetta*, especially if the *mantelletta* was not worn as well.

Both the modern style and the traditional style are permitted so long as they are both rochets. Both styles are permitted an 8-inch insert of either scarlet or amaranth-red silk for the cuffs, but this insert, too, is to be somewhat masked. The color is permitted due to the high rank of the prelate, and yet this prelate is reminded that this is still a jurisdictional garment, and all privileges of jurisdiction must be masked or muted in deference to the Holy Father. The traditional rochet makes use of a lace overlay. The modern style inserts the color cuff beneath the regular tight fit of the sleeves, resulting in some of it being visible from beneath. The practice of colored cuffs can be traced back to the fourteenth century.

The shoulders of the rochet were also permitted color. Prior to 1968, all rochets had a 4-inch by 2-inch notch for a color insert covered with lace—scarlet for cardinals and amaranth red for other prelates. Although this optional style is seldom seen in present times, it was not abolished in 1968 and may be incorporated into any rochet, traditional or modern, made today.

All rochets have a square-cut yoke or neck. They may also have a slit running in the center from neck to breast bone. The slit would then be tied closed with either white ribbon or, more commonly, by the ribbon appropriate in the color of rank. The pope makes use of a rochet made entirely of white,

---

* Secretariat of State Directive No. 135705 and Papal *Motu Proprio, Pontificalis Ritus;* Paul VI, June 21, 1968.

with all braid and lace inserts in white silk thread. In past pontificates, the traditional rochet was preferred, almost always worked in linen and silk.

Cardinals, archbishops, and bishops who were raised to the episcopal rank from religious life and who prefer the simplicity of the life within the order must don a rochet when vested in choir and when using the stole when not vested in the chasuble or cope.

Motu Proprio Pontificalis Ritus of 1968* introduced many changes in regulations governing the proper usage of the rochet. Today, to reinforce those directives, only individuals with episcopal rank are permitted use of the rochet; in fact, it is required of them, and the simple surplice, despite its dignity or appeal, must be laid aside.

During a period of extreme solemnity, as in the case of the death of the pontiff, all prelates retain their rochet, if entitled to it. In deference to the solemn tone of such an occasion, the tradition of the Church has been to substitute a rochet of great simplicity for the customary richly embroidered ones.†

Finally, the rochet should never be donned over the black cassock or the house cassock or simar. It is part of the choir dress of prelates and should be donned only over the choir cassock. The simple cassock or the colored trimmed simar is not a part of choir dress and should never be thought of as interchangeable items. Donning a rochet over anything other than a choir cassock is not only considered unacceptable, it is also forbidden by papal decree.

SURPLICE

The surplice is the most recognizable of liturgical garments. Similar to the rochet, it has its roots in the alb. Whereas the rochet retained its closeness in design to the alb, the surplice, with the exception of its long length, began to develop on its own rather quickly.

The surplice, or as it is known in Latin, *superpellicum*, meaning "a cloak worn over the skins or fur," came into general use in the Church by the eighth century. As a covering, it was meant to afford some degree of cleanliness and dignity when worn over the long precassock, fur-lined coat used at the time by everyone, including the laity.

"From the fourth to the eighth centuries, the alb was a very large vestment. Its generous size made the donning of the other vestments a difficult operation"[1] and was thus modified in time. Individuals who preferred the conical-shaped vestments used predominately in the fourth to the eighth centuries needed to develop a garment that retained its original fullness—thus the modern surplice. Ironically, this new garment was never worn under vestments but was used for the administration of the sacraments when vested in the cassock, which became popular simultaneously. By the eleventh century, the surplice was required for all liturgical functions if one was not vested in alb as celebrant. As such, it is one of the Church's oldest items of vesture, having been in continual use for more than one thousand years.

Soon the surplice took on various appearances, depending upon the locality and custom of the local Church. It remained almost floor length in the north and began to shorten in the south, due to the variances of climate. In the United Kingdom, today, the preference remains in both the Roman Church and the Anglican Church, for a longer calf-length surplice. This is a direct tie to the historically

---

* Ibid.

† During the entrance into the conclave of 1978, while the Church still mourned the death of Paul VI, a photograph of the procession of the Sacred College shows the Camerlengo and others in the simplicity of a simple rochet. It was not a surplice that had been substituted that day but a simple, dignified linen rochet that had been donned.

correct surplice of that region. In the south—in Spain, France, Italy, and thereby subsequently in the United States—the length of the surplice tends to be shorter, varying between hip length and knee length. The hip length style is most popular among seminarians who still make use of the surplice, as well as for choirs. This style came into vogue in the mid-1850s.

The surplice may have either a square-cut neck or a rounded neck. It may have bell-shaped sleeves or long full sleeves. The sleeves may even stretch to the hem of the garment, as in the case of the surplice in England. Traditionally, they are more simple in design. Made always of cotton, linen, or wool, they may be worked with lace or embroidery. Whichever the purpose, the surplice is required for all priests and seminarians who are vested in a cassock during liturgical functions, except in the case of a priest who is vested as concelebrant and dons the alb.

The most preferred or popular style surplice at present is known as the Vatican style because it is the style utilized by the Vatican's Masters of Ceremonies.* This so-called Vatican style is longer in length, reaching just below the knees. Most commonly made of light wool or wool blend, it is often ecru in color, not white.

The Vatican style, like all others, has full or bell-shaped sleeves. Some bands of embroidery, in a subdued fashion, as well as other emblems such as the cross or Celtic cross, are usually worked into each of the bottom regions and the sleeves. There are usually well-defined pleats as well. The elegance of this surplice is in its simplicity of design. It is never fancy. Known as the Vatican surplice, one can understand why it would not be too fancy. Always dignified, the functionaries surrounding the pope must never distract from him, the real focus of Vatican events.

Whichever style is preferred—be it the simpler style, lace embroidered, or the Vatican style—the surplice is the oldest and most recognizable item of vesture. At one time on the decline, as were so many other items of vesture, the surplice is once again in demand.

Finally, the surplice is always worn by a master of ceremonies over a cassock unless he is vested in alb.†

N.B.: Both the rochet and the surplice have indulgences attached to them. Prelates who don the rochet, and priests and seminarians (only) who don the surplice, so long as the appropriate prayers are sincerely recited, have an indulgence of one hundred days for each appropriate prayer said. (*The Sacred Penitentiary Apostolica;* Jan. 14, 1940—not abridged at later date.)

---

* The style is also known as either the Gammarelli or the Sorgenti (the two firms that specialize in them in Rome). Keep in mind, however, that there is no such thing as a Vatican-style rochet—only the surplice.
† The alb is more common in some regions, but should not be donned by an M.C. unless he serves also as concelebrant.

Mantellone, Crocia, and Soprana

MANTELLONE

Now abolished, the *mantellone* was one of the more colorful items of vesture in the Roman Church. It was seen in the diocese as well as within the Apostolic Palace.

The name *mantellone* is from Italian, meaning "a large, or great, mantle." It was designed to fully cover the purple choir cassock of the monsignors who were entitled to its use. Fastening with a hook-and-eye device at the neck, the *mantellone* had a stiff, upstanding collar. Although sleeveless, with 24-inch-long slits in which the arms could protrude, the *mantellone* did have visible remnants of the original sleeves in that it had full-length, 4-inch-wide strips that were attached to the shoulders and that fell to the floor. These former sleeves were referred to as "*mantellone* bands." Originally, they were 6 to 8 inches in width; however, with time, the width of the "bands" was limited to 4 inches.

The *mantellone* was always purple. It was trimmed and lined in reddish-purple silk known as amaranth red. The season determined its material—merlino in winter and silk in summer. The use of amaranth-red silk as facings, trim, and lining created an aura that enhanced the mystery of the garment. Monsignors entitled to its use became known as the prelates *di mantellone* and were always visible flashes of color at Vatican ceremonies. As they darted about on papal business, the "bands" and facings would flap in the wind, exposing the reddish-purple silk lining and trim.[*]

The *mantellone* was abolished by papal *motu proprio*[†] in 1969 and has been relegated to history and to the movies that depict historical Vatican life. This vestural garment was not part of the liturgical life of the Church; it was, strictly speaking, a livery garment. As such, it was the entitlement of papal honorees with the rank of chaplain[‡] and chamberlains to His Holiness who held the title Very Reverend Monsignor. These prelates were always seen in the attendance of the pontiff at Vatican and Lateran ceremonies and would be seen as chaplains to the diocesan bishop at important diocesan liturgical functions. It was the privilege of the prelates *di mantellone* to bear the train of the cape of the pontiff as well as the *cappa magna* of cardinals and diocesan bishops. They also were entitled to carry the

---

[*] Examples of this can be viewed in three Vatican-related films: *The Shoes of the Fisherman, The Cardinal,* and *The Scarlet and the Black.*
[†] Secretariat of State Directive No. 135705.
[‡] Not to be confused with the present title of Chaplain of His Holiness.

processional cross at all papal and important diocesan processions.

Individuals who were entitled to the *mantellone* were not also permitted the rochet, a jurisdictional garment permitted to members of the episcopacy and formerly to senior prelates with the title Domestic Prelate. These prelates *di mantellone* lost their title, rank, and privileges upon the burial of the pontiff who had nominated them. According to Roman legends, scores of hopes for higher rank in the Church, as well as the privileges of the inferior prelature, went into the crypt with the dead pope. Occasionally, the pope would confer the title Monsignor on one of the ranks of *di mantellone* for the bearer's lifetime, but this honor was rare and was usually conferred only on persons in the later stages of their lifetimes.

The privileges of the prelates *di mantellone* were restricted, by and large, to Rome, where they served in the Papal Household although, as we have seen, these prelates were also found at the diocesan level as well. Whereas all other members of the *monsignori* were entitled to full use of their privileges, the *di mantellone* were restricted. In use of the *ferraiolo*, they were not entitled to watered silk or purple. In heraldry, they made use of a black *galero* with purple *fiocchi* and cord; and in other articles of vesture, they were restricted to those used by simple priests.*

Finally, the *mantellone* was never worn at liturgical functions where the prelate was to take part in either the sacramental functions of his priesthood or in preaching. On these occasions, the prelate removed the *mantellone* and vested in surplice. He was never entitled to the rochet.

CROCIA

The *crocia*, or cloak, prior to 1969, was associated most with the prelates *di mantellone*. It was the vestural garment that these prelates donned when they were sent as special emissaries of the pope on important Household business, such as the mission announcing the bestowal of the Order of the Golden Rose upon a Catholic queen or Marian shrine, or when they were sent abroad to announce the conferral of the red hat on a foreign prelate. The *crocia* is also the proper formal garb for the members of the Sacred Roman Rota, and today it is most associated with these prelates. Within the Rota, it is called the *toga*, but this usage developed around 1920 as a slang term. In time, the proper appellation of *crocia* was forgotten by the Rota judges. Ironically, they are the only persons still entitled to its use.

Made of scarlet wool or merlino, trimmed and lined in scarlet silk, the *crocia* was worn under a second mantle of ermine.† The facings and cuffs are also of ermine for the higher classes and of red silk for the lower classes. Attached to the lower cape was a hood similar to that of the *cappa magna*, but it was never seen due to the secondary fur cape placed upon it. The *crocia* for the Rota members did not make use of the hood but was faced and cuffed in ermine‡ until the pontificate of Pope Pius IX. Red silk replaced ermine for the rotal judges on January 12, 1848, reserving ermine for individuals on a specific mission for the pope.

The original *crocia*, like the lining of the original cassock or pelisse, was completely made of ermine. This practice ended in the seventeenth century. The *crocia* of the prelates *di mantellone*, just as in the

---

* Except when in Rome, where they were permitted purple for their hosiery and violet cords for their *cappella*.
† The use of this second fur cape in the style of the *mozzetta* is not applied to the *crocia* as worn today by members of the Rota.
‡ Ermine is a soft white fur of great expense, often substituted with white rabbit. It always includes the black tails of the ermine to create the black-on-white appearance.

case of the *cappa magna* of other prelates, exchanged the ermine for scarlet silk during the summer season. The *crocia* of the Rota always remained the same, as the Rota does not sit in official session in summer. The front of the *crocia* of the Rota is closed by lace bands that form a circular collar around the neck and extend 8 inches, in two equal rectangular segments, down the front over the ermine. Its official name is *cravatta per uditore di Rota,* but it is known more familiarly as *la bavarola* (the baby's bib).

SOPRANA

Mention should be made at this point of the *soprana*, which closely resembles the *mantellone*. These two garments, although similar, were not interchangeable. The *soprana* was the overgarment for a Roman seminarian. It resembled the *mantellone* in design but did not include the "silk bands." The *soprana* was modeled after the *mantellone*, with its more ancient origins, and at a much later point in history; therefore, the bands of the *mantellone* were historical, whereas those of the *soprana* would have been presumptuous. The *soprana* also differed from the *mantellone* in material as well as color. Although many Roman seminaries made use of unique designs in their students' cassocks, the *soprana* remained simple, always full cut, unlike the *mantellone*, which had a narrow cut.

Whereas the *mantellone* was abolished directly by *motu proprio*, the *soprana* simply fell into disuse as the various changes in Church vesture were implemented. It has never been officially abolished, yet it is rarely, if ever, seen today. The *soprana* reached to the floor. It was traditionally made of black wool, sometimes with a black silk trim with facings of silk. Some Roman colleges made use of colored wool, matching the color of the trim to their institutions' cassocks in the place of silk. The *soprana* was fastened at the collar by a simple hook-and-eye device. It may still be seen in use at papal functions by some Roman seminarians.

Pontifical Hats

Hats for gentlemen in general fell out of vogue during the Kennedy presidency in the United States in the early 1960s. Studies have shown that after President Kennedy went hatless much of the time, so, too, did most of the men of the world (a trend that took root in the early 1960s but was almost universally accepted by the early 1970s). This fashion was reflected in the Church as well. Just as it became a trend to stop wearing the traditional hat for gentlemen in society and in the Church, wearing hats could as easily come back into fashion; no one can predict trends. As this is a historical treatise, I am including the pontifical hat in these pages, even if it is found to be of little modern relevance, in the event that future trends seek its return.

There is a difference between a pontifical hat and an ecclesiastical hat. The former is a hat worn by clerics during ordinary events in the function of their duties, whereas the ecclesiastical hats are those for liturgical or Church-related use. The ecclesiastical hats are the mitre, the *biretta,* and the *zucchetto,* each of which has a chapter devoted to it.

The pontifical hat is a "horse of a different color." Designed as a hat for everyday wear, like headgear the world over, it has fallen in disuse. Although never abolished and still seen from time to time, even in Rome one does not see the pontifical hat very often.

CAPPELLO ROMANO

The pontifical hat is also known as the *cappello romano,* or Roman hat, with a brim similar in shape to a large flying saucer and a derbylike crown. The rims of the brim are slightly turned up or rounded.

The *cappello romano* is made of either black beaver fur or black felt and is lined with white nylon or silk, as is the case with other male headgear. In years past, the heraldic color of each degree of the prelature was used for the lining: scarlet for cardinals; green for patriarchs, archbishops, and bishops; amaranth red, violet, or purple for the monsignorial ranks; and black or simple white for priests. This is still in practice if the purchaser wishes to pay for the extra cost involved in ordering a special lining. Today, however, the simple white silk or nylon lining is shared by all.

There is a marked difference, however, on the exterior, which marks the rank for the prelate.

Cardinals make use of the black beaver or felt *cappello.** Cords of red and gold threads line the brim, and entwined tassels or tufts of red silk and gold thread† fall to the left side. These cords and tufts are of the same material used to suspend the cardinal's pectoral cross.

Patriarchs, archbishops, and bishops make use of the same pontifical hat. The cords and tufts are of green silk and gold thread, the same as their pectoral-cross cords. The tufts are also worn on the left side. Until 1969, only archbishops and patriarchs made use of a green and gold cord and tufts, whereas bishops made use of green silk only. In an attempt to simplify practice, Pope Paul VI abolished the green cords and permitted the bishops the privilege of green and gold also.

The three grades of monsignor and the canons, unless by special rescript or indult that allows privileges contrary to the general practice, must make use of the same hat as that of simple priests—black felt or beaver fur, with no cords or tufts. Until 1969, canons were permitted a black and gold cord with similar tassels, and, of the twelve degrees of monsignor that existed at the time, the six highest grades wore a black *cappello* with cords and tufts of amaranth-red silk and gold, whereas the six lowest grades made use of purple silk and gold cord and tassels.

Until 1969, these pontifical hats could be worn only in the respective jurisdiction of the wearer or when privilege was granted to do so by special indult, as they were considered jurisdictional in nature. Outside one's jurisdiction, the simple, unadorned black *cappello* was required. In present times, one wishing to make use of a *cappello* may do so at any time during the ordinary functions of one's priesthood, according to the vestural changes ordered by Paul VI. The *cappello,* both prior to and after the Pauline 1969 *motu proprio,* can never take the place of a *biretta* or mitre, as it may never be considered liturgical headgear.

The Holy Father is now the only member of the hierarchy of the Church who is permitted a red plush or fur *cappello.* His cords are gold and have, in place of tufts, a series of golden weaves, or knots, around the base of the crown. The brim is turned slightly further upward than those of other *cappelli.* He makes use of the *cappello* when wearing either the white *greca* or pontifical red cape.

N.B.: One still sees, albeit predominately in Rome, the use of headgear when clergy are wearing the cassock through the streets. Often nonecclesiastical headgear is preferred, which, of course, is acceptable. The trilby, fedora, or beret, which is also known as the basque, is the most commonly seen. All three types are acceptable so long as they are black and the wearer knows that the pontifical hat, or *cappello romano,* is still permitted.

CAMAURO

The *camauro* is the fur-trimmed bonnet worn by the popes, and it is reserved for them alone. It can be seen in portraits of all the popes, from the eleventh century until our own times. The *camauro* is the original *biretta.* The *biretta,* however, developed along different lines over time, whereas the papal bonnet remained as it was originally designed. The original *camauro* was made of suede or soft leather, lined and trimmed in fur. Its purpose is to help keep out the bitter cold.

By the twelfth century, suede gave way to red velvet, and eventually the fur remained only as trim. The *zucchetto* is not worn under the *camauro* as it is under the *biretta,* a hat that the popes have never

---

* The scarlet beaver *cappello* with gold cording and braid was abolished by Paul VI in 1969.
† Recently, simple, cheap red cords have been offered in substitution for the prescribed red and gold for cardinals. This is not permitted by decree of Paul VI. Red and gold must be used.

made use of. Although nearly a century passed from the time a pontiff regularly wore the *camauro* (in 1860), Pope John XXIII resurrected it and made use of it on the most solemn occasions. Pius XII, who was not seen with the *camauro* in public, was vested with it, along with *mozzetta* and rochet, for the initial rites immediately after his death.

The *camauro* is made in two colors and materials: red velvet, lined in white silk and trimmed in white fur, for ordinary time and white damask, lined in white silk without fur, for the Octave of Easter. Pope John XXIII made use of each style, as many photographs illustrate. It has not been abolished and may be resurrected by the present, as well as any future, pope.

Ecclesiastical Cloaks

DOUILLETTE

The *douillette*, more commonly known as the *greca* or the *cappotto* in Italian, is a long, loose-fitting, double-breasted coat worn over the cassock or simar by seminarians, priests, and prelates, as well as by the Holy Father, in cooler climates and in Rome during winter months. In the English-speaking Church, it is simply known as the clerical or ecclesiastical overcoat.

The *douillette*, or *greca,* is designed to permit ample movement; therefore, it is not so tight-fitting as a circular-cut, double-breasted coat would be. It is made of light wool or silk. The lining depends upon the wearer and the climate; however, there may be no color seen from within or underneath. Fur or other ornaments are forbidden.

The *douillette* may be made in only two colors, black and white. White is reserved exclusively for the Holy Father; black is for everyone else entitled to wear it. When an indult has been provided for the substitution of white for traditional vesture colors for priests and prelates in warmer climates, this indult does not apply to the *douillette*, as an overcoat is unnecessary in warm climates.

The *douillette* has changed little since 1812, when it was officially adapted from civil wear (i.e., length-ened) for ecclesiastical wear. Strictly speaking, it is not a form of vesture in the same degree that the cassock or simar would be, but by tradition it is now governed by the same restrictions of good taste that apply to all church vesture.

The *douillette* came into the Roman Church through the lay world in France, but it was first widely adopted for ecclesiastical wear by the Oriental rite priests, who adopted the French double-breasted coat of the era for use when traveling. Thus the term *greca*, or *Greek*, which is always associated with the Oriental world, is used.

The greca is designed in a full cut and has either four or five sets of two buttons for closure (for a total of eight or ten buttons). The buttons must always be in the same color as the greca, as are the four sleeve buttons on the cuff.

The *douillette* should always be made amply to permit the comfortable use of the cassock and simar underneath. As is true with all overcoats for any gentleman, the *douillette* should always be worn closed, never left open.

CAPES

The cape has long been acceptable garb for outdoor use by clerics of all ranks. In more recent times, the types of capes permitted became defined. By 1832, the Vatican had set the norms for clerics wishing to make use of one type of cloak or another. In 1969, the *Motu Proprio* of Paul VI and the subsequent directive of enforcement by the Secretariat of State[*] limited the type of capes to be worn by the clergy in all ranks and classes.

Today, it is safe to say that a full-cut black woolen cape, without ornament or frill, is permissible. One who desires a cape or cloak should always avoid metallic closing devices, fringe, satin or silk facings, velvet used anywhere except the soft collar, and color, all of which have been abolished.

The large cloak with shoulder cape, full in cut and long in length, has been retained for winter use.

All ranks of the clergy, if preferring the long full cloak, must make use of this black cloak. Even cardinals, patriarchs, and other persons with episcopal dignity must now make use of the black cloak.

The cardinalatial scarlet cloak, known as the *taborro*, and its episcopal purple counterpart have been abolished.[†] Cardinals may not make use of a red woolen winter cloak nor may bishops make use of the purple cloak. The scarlet and purple silk linings of the coat or cloaks, as well as any color other than black, have also been abolished.

---

[*] Secretariat of State Directive No. 135705.
[†] Papal *Motu Proprio, Ut Sive Sollicite;* Paul VI, March 31, 1969.

Vesture Components

In studying items that were formerly important to prelatial dress, but whose use has either lapsed or been abandoned, it became apparent that they should be presented together in one final chapter on the section concerning vesture. The term *accessories* was chosen not to demean these items along the lines of everyday clothing, but to call forth an image that vividly depicts them as no longer essential to the vesture of prelates and priests of the Church.

ECCLESIASTICAL ACCESSORIES

The accessories now in abeyance, more so from lack of interest than from restriction by law, are the buskins, the ecclesiastical sandals, and the gauntlets. The buskins have not been abolished; in fact, no mention was made of them in the Pauline modifications other than to say that they were now optional. Once things are made optional, however, they generally tend to disappear from use.

The buskins, or *caligae*, are long silk stockings that fitted over the everyday stockings of a prelate when he was vested for a prelatial celebration. They can best be described as silk leggings that covered the leg from toe to knee. The buskins always matched the liturgical color: green for ordinary time and white for solemn feasts. They were introduced into the liturgy for purely functional reasons, like so many other items of vesture and sacred vestments, in order to protect the priests and, later, the bishops, from drafts. With time, the liturgical color was added to make ceremonial what was formerly functional. Soon silk was required for the manufacture of buskins. Before the eighth century, only the popes were permitted the buskins; thereafter, cardinals and, later, all bishops were also permitted their use.

During the Renaissance, it became the custom to bring ornamentation to the Church's vesture. The buskins were no exception. Although liturgical colors were assigned to them, the trim and ornamentation varied according to the rank of the prelate. For instance, cardinal-bishops were permitted gold with small gold tufts; cardinal-priests, gold with red silk; and cardinal-deacons, gold with simple red thread. The patriarchs made use of gold and green silk braiding, whereas the archbishops and bishops had simple gold seams. The protonotaries were not permitted gold at all; they made use of yellow seams.

The buskins completely covered the trousers. For persons with episcopal dignity, however, the buskins were put on at the altar while seated upon the fald-stool. Today, those few prelates making use of the buskins vest with them in the sacristy. The buskins were always worn with the ecclesiastical sandal, which was a soft silk slipper with varying degrees of embroidery. Often the coat of arms of the prelate was embroidered on the bridge of the shoe, which was made in colors to match both the buskin and the liturgical color of the day. These slippers developed for liturgical use by the fifth century. Prior to the thirteenth century, they were made of brown leather, nearly suede in quality, but by the Renaissance, silk universally replaced leather as the required material. The sandals, like the buskins, were formerly put on at the faldstool. In present time, however, they are donned in the sacristy by the few persons who still make use of them.

Only the pontiff can make use of velvet sandals, but this privilege has not been exercised since the last days of the pontificate of Pius XII. Today, the pontiff makes use of one design of shoe, the soft moroccan-leather slipper, for both everyday wear as well as for ecclesiastical wear.

The first accessory for ecclesiastical use to fall into disuse was the gauntlet, or liturgical glove. Like the buskins and sandals, the gauntlets have not been abolished but are rarely seen nonetheless. Another term for the gauntlet is the *pontifical glove*, as it is the glove worn by prelates when vested in pontificals. The gauntlet is a highly ornamented, richly embroidered glove worn by prelates of episcopal dignity when celebrating a pontifical Mass. The color always has to match the liturgical color of the day. The embroidery is traditionally in gold thread. Whereas the sandals and buskins are sometimes seen, the gauntlets are rarely, if ever, seen today. bishops complained long before the reforms that they were cumbersome and uncomfortable.

Gauntlets, like the buskins, developed out of necessity to help keep the hands of the bishop warm during long ceremonies in damp, cold medieval cathedrals. The episcopal ring always has to be seen, so if the gauntlets are worn, the ring must be worn over the glove.

The traditional design of the gauntlet extended beyond the wrist, where most gloves end. The gauntlet opened at the wrist to expand in a rectangular fashion up over the forearm. This extension was the most highly embroidered part of the gauntlet.

ORDINARY ACCESSORIES

Just as accessories developed for liturgical use out of necessity, so, too, did they develop for use in the ordinary life of the priest and prelate. The three most significant of these are the gloves, stockings, and shoes.

As the gauntlets developed for everyday use, so, too, did the gloves. As a rule, a cleric would make use of the gloves on the same occasions that a gentleman in civil life would do so. The difference between the two was the color and material used for the gloves of the prelates and, of course, the function, one ordinary and the other ceremonial.

At present, black and black alone may be worn by all clerics at all times when making use of gloves, with the exception of masters of ceremonies, who may make use of white cotton gloves when vested in cassock and surplice as diocesan master of ceremonies. There are no other exceptions beyond the Holy Father, who, of course, also makes use of white.

The use of only black or white was not always the case. Before 1969, there existed an entire hierarchy of colors and materials for the gloves worn by the prelature. Simplified, cardinals made use of red silk when vested "in choir" or in *cappa magna*, as well as when going about town. Bishops made use of purple silk for "choir" and *cappa magna*, but black silk for everyday wear. Protonotaries and canons made use of amaranth red and black, respectively, and purple and black for the lesser classes of the *monsignori*.

In present time, all priests and prelates make use of black gloves for everyday wear. If gloves are preferred by prelates for the liturgy, they must make use of the pontifical gauntlets, which may be worn only when vested in sacred vestments. If "in choir" or while wearing the *cappa magna*, they must now go without gloves. Colored gloves for all ranks of the clergy have been abolished.

Discussing the hosiery or stocking colors of the clergy seems trivial, but if this study is to be complete, these items must also be updated. The general rule is quite simple: All clerics must wear black hosiery at all times unless required to do otherwise as stated. This requirement precludes any and all personal preferences for specific colors, modern design, or the "discalced look" preferred by some persons. Black socks are to be worn at all times except when vested in choir dress or when celebrating Mass vested in choir cassock. At this time, cardinals must make use of the scarlet hosiery; patriarchs, archbishops, bishops, protonotaries apostolic (both grades), and prelates of honor make use of fuchsia or purple, as it is commonly called, hosiery. Chaplains of His Holiness and all others wear black at all times.*

---

* Secretariat of State Directive No. 135705.

Tenue de Ville

Although civil clothing or dress, that is, the clothing worn on the streets and in the classrooms, rectories, and chancelleries, does not come under the heading of vesture, a note should be made to clarify misconceptions regarding the official term for working clothing as *tenue de ville*.* Civil dress comprises primarily the clerical suit, the vest, or the clerical shirt. There has never been the same set of guidelines for these items as there has been with all other items of vesture. As a result, misconceptions and abuses have developed.

The only color proper to the clergy is black; in fact, black is more accurately defined as being colorless. Black has been used to define the symbolic or real poverty and humility of the Catholic clergy for the past nine centuries. Even the prelature, when not vested in ceremonial attire, don black at all times and on all public occasions.

Only in the tropics, by special papal indult, as we have seen with both the cassock and simar, is the use of white permitted in place of black. No other color has ever been permitted. Until the early 1970s, the tradition and symbolism of black vesture was carried over to civic attire as a matter of form and by accepted practice by the entire Roman

clergy. As civic attire was not the "official" garb of the clergy, no specific directives were indicated in the numerous changes made by Pope Paul VI. The Congregation of the Rites and the Councils (now abolished) and synods of local churches affirmed, over many centuries, the exclusive use of black as the vesture of the diocesan clergy and in the civic dress of the religious, as well.

In the 1970s and 1980s, clerical clothing manufacturers took it upon themselves to offer a "wider range" of colorful clothing options for the clergy. This was purely an appeal for new sales in an era when the clergy thought anything was possible, and many alternatives were introduced.

At the time of publication of this text, the Church officially recognizes only black and, for tropical weather, white as acceptable colors in vesture, including civic attire. Black or, in appropriate instances, white! The use of blue, celeste, gray (dark or light), brown, purple, beige, and all other colors for shirts, vests, or even suits is not the custom and practice of the Roman Church, and these

---

* *Tenue de ville* is the universally accepted term for business attire and civil or street clothing. Each refers to the business suit, shirt, and vest. *Ala Borghese* is a term used to describe casual clothes, an example of which would be trousers, shirt, and colored sweater.

colors have not been recognized by the Holy Father.*

The civic, or clerical, suit should be made of light wool, wool blend, or cloth appropriate to the climate and season. It should be completely black, never black on black, gray, charcoal, or any other color. The practice of the use of colors came into being at a time when the clergy were unsure of correct practice, and such practices were encouraged by ateliers for reasons of their own profit.

The *gilit* (Italian) or *gilet* (French) is a button-down vest with a Roman collar inserted in the stand-up collar. The buttons run from collar to notched bottom, and it is worn over the belt rather than tucked into the trousers. The buttons can be made of bone, plastic, or may be cloth-covered as in the case of the cassock front. Regardless of one's rank, the buttons are always black.

The *conottiera*, which is Italian for a sleeveless or false vest, similar to a dickey front, is also known more commonly by the English term *rabbi vest,* which should not be confused with the rabbi of the cassock. The *conottiera* is a smooth-fronted woolen or silk half-vest with Roman collar. It is a faux, or false, vest consisting of only the front half, fastening under the arms and strapped behind the back. The *gilet, conottiera,* or rabbi vest are very comfortable. It is used with the dress shirt, most commonly with french cuffs as they are worn during formal occasions, or at work, where the clerical suit would be more appropriate.

Tab shirts, always black, or black collarless shirts on which is affixed an "easy collar," that is, a collar combined with a false, black-notched guard to be attached by Velcro or other device, have become acceptable working attire for clerics and seminarians. These shirts wear out quickly, and care should be given to always keep them fresh and new in appearance. Colored tab or easy shirts, sometimes also referred to as "witness shirts," have never been an acceptable custom despite frequent use of various colors worldwide.

In the recent past, the practice of wearing colored shirts under the vest, most commonly but not exclusively blue, in devotion to Our Lady, has arisen. It is proper in these cases that whatever the preferred color of the shirt beneath the vest or gilet, the cuffs should be white, as only white shirts are to be worn under the cassock or clerical suit. Today, with the wide variety of clothing options, the purchase of a shirt of any desired color, as long as it has white cuffs, is quite possible. Whatever the desired color, no color should ever appear from beneath the suit, vest, cassock, or simar.

N.B.: It should go without saying that hose, shoes, leather belts, and/or all other accessories should be black and never flashy, regardless of one's rank in the Church.

---

* It should be noted that the episcopal conferences set the regulations for *tenue de ville* on clerical attire; however, Rome's directives should always carry proper weight in these deliberations. Therefore, unless otherwise directed, no matter how much one may admire a certain color, to make use of anything not prescribed or in keeping with the traditions of the Church is acting in self-interest alone and thus is not in accord with proper practice and would never be in keeping with the spirit of dignity of the clergy.

Sacred Vestments

In undertaking this study, I had no plans to include, other than simple definitions in the glossary, various items of sacred vestments. As sacred vestments form a study entirely different from the study of vesture and insignia, they should be dealt with in the fullest detail, with complete definition of present rubrics and historicity. It is, after all, a rich and unique discipline that deserves a fuller treatise. In completing this text, however, questions continually arose regarding the inclusion of a discussion on sacred vestments. Though not claiming expertise in this area, after investigations in Rome and with expert liturgists and Church historians, I offer the following brief, which sets forth the history, origin, and present regulations of many of the sacred vestments of the Latin Church. Other articles of vestments are defined briefly in the glossary section of this work.

HISTORIC ORIGINS

The historic, authentic origins of Christian sacred vestments are not with the Levitical priestly dress, as so many persons assume, but with the domestic dress of the mid-to-late Roman Empire. The modern gothic chasuble, for instance, may be traced to the poncholike cloak of the Roman citizen of the second century B.C. Rubanus Maurus of Mayence, in A.D. 850, wrote in his discourse *De Institutione Clericorum* that vestments of the Catholic Church were, in fact, applicable to the laws set forth for the high priesthood of Israel. This theory was soon debunked by Walafrides Stralo, a contemporary of the archbishop of Mayence, who, in A.D. 863, hypothesized on the Roman origins of all Church vestments existing at that time in his work *De Exordiis et Incrementes Rerum Ecclesiasticarum*. Historians have widely held to Stralo's opinions, grounded as they are in traceable detail and historical fact rather than fanciful hypothesis.

The first formal mention of specific vestments in the Church was made at the Council of Toledo in A.D. 633. Even then, this mention was veiled in the canons regarding the reinstatement of an unjustly condemned bishop, priest, or deacon to his former position. The ceremonial documents* decreed the formula, including which proper vestments and insignia to be solemnly re-presented to the reinstated cleric, for a public ceremony of reinstatement.

In A.D. 590, Pope St. Gregory the Great began a

---

* Canon 28, Council of Toledo, A.D. 633.

series of letters* that delineated the vestments that remained at that time in the gift of the Roman Pontiff. Specifically, these vestments were the dalmatic (*dalmatica*), the *pallium*, and the maniple. Today, the *pallium* remains the only historic vestment reserved as a gift from the Roman Pontiff. The maniple, which has since been abolished, long ago (in the twelfth century) entered into the domain of the vestments of the general clergy rather than reserved as a gift of the popes. The dalmatic became the symbol of the diaconate as early as the sixth century and was widely recognized as such by the eighth century.

Through the first six centuries of the Church, vestments developed from common cloaks of the era to something specifically sacred in character. By the sixth century, the Roman Pontiff began to delineate their importance and particularly their significance at the Sacred Liturgy. With time, customs, practices, and styles of the era began to play roles in their development.

Alb

The alb is the white gown donned by all clerics. It is the vestment reserved for all those at the altar. It is made of linen, light wool, or cotton blend. It is to entirely cover the body. The alb has always been made full, to comfortably cover the cassock, which is still officially required under the alb. This is not a custom adhered to by all, but it should be known that the fullness of the cut of all albs is such so as to be worn over a cassock.†

The alb gets its name from Medieval Latin *alba* (white), but originally it was known by many names. These include the *tunica talaris* (tight-fitting tunic), *talaris* and *toli* (ankle garb), and *camisia* (long white shirt). Until 1969, the alb was always made of either linen or the finest blend of wool. Modern, synthetic blends and fabrics arose only after the Pauline *Motu Proprio*,‡ which ironically made no

allowances for them. The use of synthetic fabrics was an "adaptation" or self-initiative of the vesture manufacturers and not a guideline of the Church.

The alb can be traced directly to the early Roman citizen who wore, as everyday garb, an alb covered by a cloak or tunic. Its origins, therefore, are ancient. It was first mentioned in writing "in a passage of Trebellius Pollio, who speaks of an *alba subserica* (half silken alb) mentioned in a letter sent from Valerian to Zosimus, Procurator of Syria (260–270 A.D.)."[1] Originally, the Roman tunic had no sleeves and was ornamented by colored stripes, added by the dye from herbs and vegetables; purple was used for the hierarchy of the Roman Empire. Sleeves were eventually added as fashion became more sophisticated. Pope St. Sylvester instituted the long-sleeved alb, which has remained in effect to the present day.

The alb must be white in color at all times. It may not be taupe, dark beige, or ecru, although wool, in its natural state, is light beige, which is considered white. The reason that this restriction remains in force is that Pope Innocent III, in A.D. 1207, laid aside whatever origins the alb may have had and decreed that the alb thenceforth would represent the purity of the clerical state. For one to don the alb would be a symbol of a cleric's baptismal state. The prayer applied to the alb and to which an indulgence has been granted, is as follows: *Purify me, O Lord and make me clean of heart, that washed in the blood of the Lamb, I may possess eternal joy.*

The alb is always made, as we have seen, of linen, wool, cotton blend or, by modern practice, synthetic

---

* Secret Vatican Archives collection.
† Whenever a cleric chooses not to wear the cassock beneath the alb, he should never wear an alb that has inserts of lace or embroidery. Long-standing custom and tradition of the Church, as binding as any law, discourage the showing of one's legs or trousers beneath an alb. The alb must cover the body entirely.
‡ *Roman Missal,* "General Instructions on Vestments," 1990. Secretariat of State Directive No. 135705.

fibers. The alb's design was not altered from the fourth century until the latter part of this century, when modern convenience and design allowed for the use of zippers, snaps, buttons, and tabs.

The alb, by its very nature and design, is meant to cover the entire body. It must cover completely the clerical collar or any other shirt. Newer designs are not only acceptable but welcomed in so far as new inventions and conveniences offer a better and longer-lasting garment; however, new designs cannot mean an adaption of long-standing, historical design simply to cater to one's own personal desires or preferences. As such, modern albs that are not white in color, with large bell or full-cut sleeves, or are cut in such a way as not to cover the clerical collar or shirt, are not in keeping with the practice, custom, and law of the Roman Church. By far the worst abuse of Church law and custom was seen recently in Rome, worn by a visiting American priest who donned his "alb" to concelebrate the Mass. Heads turned as this priest processed by the faithful in a white poncho—smaller and shorter than a chasuble, completely open all around, and reaching only to his knees. His flowered shirt was completely visible, as were his light blue slacks. Over this "alb," in an illegal fashion, was placed a stole of inappropriate seasonal color. Even persons present who would otherwise permit a personal "interpretation" of the rubrics were disgusted by this cleric's total abuse of Church law and practice.[*]

On a second occasion, this same priest likewise donned the illegal interpretation of the alb. On this occasion, however, it was within the Apostolic Palace at an intimate Mass celebrated by the Holy Father. As one of several concelebrants, he was not seen until the Communion Rite, at which time many highly placed eyebrows were raised. Never should behavior that outwardly illustrates disrespect for Church law be accepted simply out of one's determination to employ personal taste with regard to sacred vestments.[†]

The congregations of the Holy See, throughout time, have been vehemently firm in the requirements mandated for the alb, as it is primarily a sacred vestment that symbolizes the purity of the priesthood. Even at a time when flax and hemp, from which linen is made, could not be found locally, the congregations forbade substitution, not out of obstinacy, but out of fidelity to the decree of Innocent III, which remained in effect, practically unaltered, into the twentieth century.

The alb must always be long and of full cut. It must always have tight-fitting sleeves. It must always be white.[‡] It may have a square-cut neck, under which must then be worn the amice, or a tightly fitted neck as in the modern design. Both neck styles must mask the collar or clothing beneath. It should always be bound by a cincture or by the newer-designed insert tabs. Although cut full, it should never be worn in an unfolding, loose-fitting manner. A zipper or other modern closing device may not be visible on the modern alb; it must always be concealed.

CHASUBLE

The chasuble traces its origins to the Roman Empire, as well, but whereas the alb was adapted from the garb of the governing class, the chasuble is derived from the poncholike cloak of the worker who needed its protection from the elements. "The *casula* of the farmer, which ultimately became the *chasuble* of the early Church was a form of poncho

---

[*] *Concession of the Sacred Congregation of Divine Worship,* "Regarding the Chasuble Alb," May 1, 1971.

[†] Church law and custom, as laid down by papal decrees through the ages, have earned the respect due them, yet often such respect is not forthcoming, even from among the clergy.

[‡] Making an allowance for the whiteness of natural wool.

that allowed the farmer to work his fields even when it was raining because he could see down inside the front of his cloak to watch what he was doing. It had one seam in the front and a hood for working in bad weather."[2] In the earliest church, just as had been the case civilly as far back as 300 B.C., the original chasuble belonged solely to the peasant classes and workers. It was not until A.D. 350, some six hundred years after it was first recorded by Plautus, that all classes of Roman society began to adopt it. This acceptance was the direct result of the influence of the Church, which had adopted the *casula* for its own use shortly after Christ's Ascension.

The *casula* soon became differentiated once it was accepted by the society at large. Names such as *paenula* and *planeta* began to appear to refer to it. These garments were similar but not identical in nature. "The planeta was the handsomer and more costly habit worn in ordinary life at Rome alike by Senators and Popes."[3] The *casula* was simpler and more in keeping with its earlier origin, as a poncho or protective garb, and therefore remained identified with the simple clergy. The terms *planeta* and *paenula,* however, are not interchangeable. Similar in form but differentiated by ornamentation, the two developed independently of each other.

By the third century, the *casula* was worn by all Christians, men and women alike, but it was then limited for use by travelers of high rank. By a decree of Alexander Severus, the *casula* was forbidden women who were not a part of the official hierarchy of imperial Rome. At the same time, the *casula* and *paenula* were identified as sacred vestments and were additionally reserved for priests and bishops. Laity were no longer permitted the *casula* within a sacred space.

The earliest chasuble had a hood, a direct vestige of its origins as a protective garb, but the hood was abolished in A.D. 438 for sacred vestments. St. Mar-

tin of Tours wrote in the year of his death, A.D. 397, that "he was accustomed to celebrating mass in a tunic (alb) and amphibalus."[4] The *amphibalus* was the ancient name for the *paenula.*

At the Council of Toledo in A.D. 633, the chasuble was decreed a residential garb for all bishops and priests, deacons, and minor clerics. By the eighth century, the chasuble was restricted to bishops and priests, and the dalmatic was delegated as the official vestment for the diaconate.

The chasuble began as a simple cloak. By the sixth century, it was part of bishop's vesture, and soon became elaborate. The original form was conical, that is, free flowing and long. By the seventh century, colored bands and minor embroidery appeared. By the tenth century, embroidered cloth began to appear, and, by the fifteenth, elaborate designs and brocades began to influence the vestments of the Church in a large way. In the Vatican treasury, there is a beautiful display of Charlemagne's great dalmatic of richly embroidered cloth and brocade of silk and gold, which illustrates the early influence of expensive cloth for ceremonial use. Charlemagne's dalmatic is of eighth-century origins.

Originally, the *casula*, or chasuble, was very full in cut, often extending over the hands and to the ankle. This style required the help of assistants, who carefully guarded that the vestment would not catch fire during the lengthy rituals of the Church. As the bishops and priests moved about the sanctuary, they were attended by acolytes, who were sure to steer the vestment away from the many candles that illuminated the darkened medieval churches.

With the change of architectural style that permitted more natural light to enter the great cathedrals, along with a shift to ceremonies during the daylight hours, the need for acolyte assistants dropped off. The priest could function on his own, and yet this garb was still somewhat cumbersome.

The chasuble's style began to modify. From it developed the origins of the present Gothic-style chasuble—less full in cut and not as long at the arms and feet. The Gothic style has remained one of the two styles of chasuble acceptable in the Church for the past six hundred years.

During the Renaissance, the second most familiar style developed, the Roman style. This style has many other familiar names and gradations. It is known as the "fiddle-back" because it resembles the shape of a large bass fiddle. The Roman style is a high Renaissance development. The original Roman style is what we call today the Flemish style, that is, tapered or sculptured in front somewhat in a fiddle form, but cut broadly and entirely square on the reverse.

The Italians, and later the Spanish, adapted the true Roman style to mirror their own tastes and unique styles. The square-backed chasuble became the fiddle-back style, and the gold thread and silk were enhanced by brocade, embroidery, and rich embellishment, including images of Christ, Our Blessed Lady, and the Saints, as well as symbols of the Blessed Sacrament, the Holy Spirit, the angels, and other sacramental designs. During the period of time between the fifteenth and seventeenth centuries, masterpieces of artistry and great craft were produced. The workmanship exhibited a devotion to Christ and His Church likened to the works of Michelangelo, Fra Angelico, and Bernini. During the post-Renaissance period, the Gothic style fell into abeyance except within the monastery tradition, which continued its use and use of a style mimicking its ancient predecessor, the *casula* (derived from the word for "hut" or "tent").

As the craftsmanship of this earlier period waned, the Gothic chasuble once again rose in popularity. By the nineteenth century, it had become so popular that serious doubt arose as to whether it was acceptable at all, as it had not been seen publicly in the Latin Church for a few hundred years. The Congregation of Rites of the Roman Curia examined the issue and under binding decree declared that the Gothic chasuble was "improper and must be discontinued." The Gothic chasuble, however, had become so popular during the late eighteenth and early nineteenth centuries in England, Ireland, and the German states that bishops in these nations demanded a further review. Arguments continued until the Gothic chasuble was permitted. Thereafter, the Gothic chasuble would have to be made of rich cloth and embroidery so "as to not effect scandal."

The reverse occurred after the great Second Vatican Council. The Roman style, in its many forms, was laid aside in favor of the Gothic chasuble and various versions of it, but the Roman style has not been placed in abeyance. No edict or decree was issued to effect this change; however, a preference for the Gothic style became so widespread as to cause some persons to later say that it had been abolished. The maniple, however, has been abolished and may never be used by individuals who still make use of one of the Roman-style chasubles.*

Present rubrics state that all sacred vestments must be dignified, rich in quality, and deserving of the sacred function of which they form a part and in which they play a special role. They are to be of a design in keeping with the traditions of the Roman Catholic faith and practice. The wording permits for some modernizations, and, in fact, Paul VI welcomed them; however, these modernizations are never to be made at the initiation of or based upon the personal taste of one cleric or another. They are always to conform with the practice of the Holy Father and the decrees of the Roman Curia.

---

* The Pontifical Council *Ecclesia Dei* has granted the use of the maniple to the members of the Fraternity of St. Peter, who still retain pre-1969 vestments in the liturgy.

In present-day Rome, one sees full-cut Gothic-style vestments, reminiscent of the early *casula*. They reach to the ground, are ample in cut and long at the sleeve, and are most commonly made of silk, with gold threads throughout. They are very beautiful and are worn often by Pope John Paul II. Also, now, one sees a resurgence of the original Roman style, that is, the square-cut back and modified front, rich in embroidery and made of silk and gold. These Roman chasubles, too, are dignified and elegant but do not enjoy the widespread popularity of the rich Gothic chasubles.

The Second Vatican Council reinforced the dignity of the Sacred Liturgy and demanded of all the faithful a respect that should be freely given in worship and adoration of our Lord. The early post–Vatican II abuses of tradition and custom have, for the most part, ceased, and the practices originally anticipated, desired, and encouraged by the Council Fathers can now be seen reflected in dignified, elegant use of sacred vestments, especially in the chasuble.

An indulgence is attached to each sacred vestment if the bishop and priest don them solemnly and prayerfully, silently reciting the proper prayer assigned to it. For the chasuble, this prayer has been unaltered for five centuries: *My yoke is sweet and my burden light—grant that I may so carry it as to merit Thy grace.*

Long ago, the Church set aside specific colors to represent the various seasons, feasts, and celebrations of the liturgical year. In the Middle Ages, this was most often the only means for a largely illiterate people to know of an important change or event in the Church's life. This color system is not stagnant, yet changes are rare and develop more over the centuries than within one single pontificate. The accompanying reference chart lists the present rubrics governing seasons, many feasts, and ceremonies.

LITURGICAL COLORS OF THE LATIN RITE

The colors of sacred vestments in the Latin rite are listed below. Some variance might exist from country to country.

COLOR	SEASON		SYMBOLISM
GREEN	Ordinary time		Hope, Everlasting life, Fidelity
WHITE	Christmas, Easter, B.V.M. Feasts, Feasts of Virgins, The Chair of Peter	The Conversion of Paul, Birth of John the Baptist, All Souls,* Funerals*	Joy, Exuberance, Celebration, Resurrection, Victory, Purity, Innocence
GOLD AND SILVER†	For most solemn Feasts		Same as white
RED	Pentecost, Good Friday	Palm Sunday, Feast of Martyrs	Holy Spirit, Suffering of the Lord, of the Apostles, and for Martyrdom
VIOLET (PURPLE)	Advent, Lent	Funerals,* All Souls' Day*	Sorrow, Mourning, Repentance, Penance
BLACK	All Souls' Day	Funerals*	Mourning and Death
ROSE	Gaudete Sunday‡	Laetare Sunday‡	Subdued joy

* For funerals and All Souls' Day, the following colors are optional: white, violet, or black.
† Gold and silver may be substituted for white at any time; especially for the most solemn feasts.
‡ For Gaudete and Laetare Sundays, rose is to be substituted for violet whenever possible. At no other time is rose worn.

COPE

The cope is the second most recognizable of the sacred vestments. It is long and richly ornamented; thus it naturally calls attention to the celebrant who makes use of it. Originally, the cope was worn over the chasuble by clerics in procession until the procession reached the inside of the Church so that the clerics would be protected from rain and chilly weather. This custom explains its Latin name, *pluviale*, which means "rain catcher."

In the Middle Ages, the cope developed into a liturgical garment of its own accord, being used at ceremonies other than the Mass. As the materials and ornamentation of the chasuble developed, so, too, was the case with the cope. The large *capuce*, or hood, that covered the head until the eleventh century, fell into disuse later and soon became only ornamental. Today, the *capuce* takes several designs: round, octagonal, or even triangular, as it is only representative of the *capuce* that was once a functional hood.

Some modern designers have returned the actual *capuce*, or hood, to the cope, a practice that is not unwelcomed, historically speaking. It must be remembered, however, that a simple cope with *capuce*, void of all ornamentation, as is a trend with some designers, is not historical. At the time when the *pluviale* with *capuce* without ornamentation was in vogue, it was used solely to protect the cleric from inclement weather. It was discarded at the door of the church as improper for use inside. It was never, in this simplified early form, considered worthy of being used as a sacred vestment.

Persons who seek to recall the earliest origins of this vestment should be mindful that although it is always welcome to recall from within our own ancient traditions, to reach into those origins in many instances leads to a vestment neither worthy

of use in the sacred liturgy nor one that calls forth the vestment's true historical origins. Today's designers, being mindful of this, would be faithful to the historicity of the cope if they were to design a cope with *capuce* and made of rich cloth and ornamented in the fashion of the earliest period when the cope with *capuce* was accepted within the liturgies of the Church.

The cope should never be worn over the chasuble. It must always be worn either over the alb, a cassock and surplice, or over the rochet. It should always be worn over the stole as well. The cope should be fastened at the breast by a device simple in design.* The morse, an elaborate metallic ornament of large design used by persons of episcopal rank, has been laid aside by papal decree. A simple metallic or silk closure device was prescribed by Paul VI when he issued his directives on the pontificals in 1969.

The cope is worn at Vespers by the celebrant, at Benediction of the Blessed Sacrament, at Confirmation if outside the Mass, as archpriest at a First Mass, by the presiding prelate at the transfer of jurisdiction of a see (usually the retiring prelate, cardinal, or nuncio), and at the final commendation of a bishop or cardinal.†

DALMATIC AND TUNICLE

The dalmatic takes its name from Dalmatia, a historic region of Croatia, along the Adriatic Sea. In the early centuries of the Christian era, it was the garb of rank and prestige in civil society. Only privileged members of the community were entitled to the dalmatic, in much the same way as only persons

---

* Secretariat of State Directive No. 135705.
† The cope may still be used by priests, deacons, and even seminarians when necessary (for instance, when carrying the canopy above the Blessed Sacrament in procession).

of rank in ancient Rome were permitted to wear the purple cloak. The tunicle developed in the same design in ancient Rome, where it was worn within the villa, never to be seen outdoors. Ancient graffiti illustrate the tunicle as something akin to a lounging suit or caftan, showing it being worn during meals. Both garments had entered the Church by the fourth century. Their designs were almost identical. The only differences were in weight and, later on, in degree of ornamentation.

The dalmatic was granted to the Order of Deacons by Pope St. Sylvester in A.D. 332. Some scholars and historians argue that this granting was arbitrarily assigned to Sylvester and that Pope Symmachus of Sardo granted the privilege for the first time nearly two hundred years later in A.D. 507. It is impossible to ascertain who, indeed, was first to grant the dalmatic to the Order of Deacons, as documents directly citing this privilege have not been found. Certainly, what is important to note is the early origins of the dalmatic as well as its total acceptance by the early Church as a distinct vestment of importance for the Church.

The tunicle was accepted, officially, into the Church much later on. It was not adopted as an item of vesture in the Church until A.D. 829, when it was adapted from lapsed civil use in Rome and was later assigned to the rank of subdeacon (as the degrees of orders became more formalized). Bishops made use of the dalmatic and the tunicle as part of their required vesture beneath the chasuble from the thirteenth century until late in the twentieth. After 1969, the dalmatic became optional for bishops when celebrating the Mass or when donning the sacred vestments. The tunicle was abolished, but it must be understood that the dalmatic was not laid aside or abolished for bishops. It remains the right of all bishops to don the dalmatic under their chasuble to this day.

Design

Both the tunicle and dalmatic share a similar design. "The dalmatic is a vestment open on each side with wide sleeves and marked with two stripes."[5] It is rich in design and ornamentation and always matches the celebrant's chasuble in color, if not in identical cloth. The tunicle was always light in cloth and limited in ornamentation. It was reserved primarily for the Order of Subdeacon, which has now been abolished. It is not seen today as it no longer remains the privilege of the bishop.

STOLE

Like so many of the sacred vestments of the Church, the stole comes to us from a functional background. Its origins lie in the primitive scarf used both in life, to keep the neck and upper body warm, and in death, to cover the face before wrapping the body in the burial shroud.

St. Ambrose, in the year 386, wrote that St. Lazarus was wrapped in an *orarium*, or scarf, as he was laid in the crypt. *Orarium* is the original Latin word for the stole. By the fourth century, Roman society adopted the *orarium* as a sign of dignity similar to that of public honors. Persons entitled to use the *orarium* were awarded this honor for specific services to the state. Messengers of the emperor were entitled to the simple *orarium*. Individuals entitled to the use of a colored *orarium* over the *alba* were further identified for their heroic accomplishments.

By the sixth century, the *orarium* was used universally throughout the Latin rite. At Ravenna, the early Church mosaics depict the earliest use of the stole by the episcopacy.* By the Council of Mayence

---

* Mid-sixth century.

in A.D. 813, all clerics were required to wear the stole at all times.*

The early writers of the Church attach to it the symbolism of Christ washing the feet of the Twelve with the *orarium*, an act that signifies the stole's role of service and the jurisdiction of the priest over the faithful.

The word *stolé* is a Greek word derived from the early Greek word for towel, *stolas.* All clerics are entitled to the stole. Indeed, it is required of them when vested or performing the sacramental role of their office.

Deacons make use of stoles identical to both that of the office of priest and bishop. The only difference is the manner of wearing the stole. So as to illustrate that a deacon has not yet received the Order of Priesthood, he must wear his stole from the left shoulder, across the breast, to the right hip. Priests and bishops wear the stole around the back of the neck, with each side falling equally in front of them. It is proper that the stole be "reserved," that is, held in place, by either the cincture or the permanent folds of the modern design alb. It has never been, nor should it be, left free to move about the front of the alb.

The stole connotes the sacramental role of the cleric and therefore should be of a design that exhibits dignity, the same rule that applies to all sacred vestments.† Many modern designs are beautiful without having elaborate ornamentation or brocades; they are elegant in their simplicity. Some designs, however, just as some examples of ancient or medieval vestments likewise illustrate, are improper for use in presiding or participating in the sacramental life of the Church. Care should be given to bring elegance to the vestments, not gaudiness or profusely homespun preferences.

The stole known as the preaching stole, which is shorter, with a widening at the base of each side

and usually heavy with embroidery, has not been abolished. It is still available, although it is seldom seen today. A priest should never make use of a preaching stole when vested in alb and stole as concelebrant. This stole is reserved for preaching, therefore, over cassock and surplice.

The modern stole is long, usually reaching to the shinbone. It should never be more than 6½ inches (11.5 cm) in width. The cloth that is used is always of the best quality and often, both at the breast and at the base, tapestry or brocade in seasonal pattern or color is applied. The stole traditionally makes use of tassels or fringe of matching or coordinating colors.

Never may the stole be worn by the nonordained. It is reserved to the clergy as a mark of their special office, just as the *pallium* serves as a mark of the special office of the metropolitan.[6] A small band of lace or linen is often seen, but not universally accepted, over the stole, where it would fall on the back of the neck of the cleric. This addition developed late in the fifteenth century, only as a means to protect the stole from getting soiled. This band is, of course, optional.

Until 1969, the stole was never permitted to be worn over the *mozzetta* of persons entitled to it. Properly, the *mozzetta* had to be removed by a prelate attending "in choir," who now also wished to participate in the sacramental function of his office, such as co-consecration of a priest or bishop. As one will see in Chapter 21, Mozzetta, this jurisdictional garment could not be covered by the stole. Today, however, the rubrics permit the stole to be donned by those vested "in choir" if they are

---

* Nearly thirty years later, this was clarified by Rome, the stole being required only when the cleric was vested or performing the sacraments.

† Respect for the regulations, traditions, and customs of the Church is absolute and deserved.

to participate at some point of the liturgical or sacramental functions.

The stole that the popes make use of over the *mozzetta* when vested "in state" is always made of red silk with gold thread. It is elaborate in its design, often incorporating both emblems of a pope's patronal saints and his heraldic device, often hand-painted and worked in precious threads of gold. Until 1968, the stole worn by the popes in state was always in the design of the preaching stole; however, Paul VI began the custom of adopting the more modern design stole for himself when he vested in state, a practice that remains today.

Finally, as we have seen with other items of sacred vestments, a custom of prayer accompanies the donning of the stole. Assigned to this reverential act is the aforementioned indulgence. The traditional prayer is as follows: *Give me anew, O Lord, the stole of immortality, which I have lost by the prevarication of sin of our first parents, and although I am unworthy to approach the holy mysteries, may I yet merit eternal joy.*[7]

AMICE

The amice is a rectangular piece of linen with two linen or cotton strings at the upper corners by which the priest fastens it to the shoulders (over the cassock or clerical shirt) by crisscrossing the strings around and under his arms and waist. Sown into the amice is a cross, which the priest should always reverence prior to placing the vestment upon his shoulders. The amice entered the Church as a sacred vestment as early as A.D. 821 with St. Theodolph of Orleans. A modern adaptation of the traditional amice, without the length of strings, is now most popular. This amice either buttons or snaps as it closes at the upper chest and neck. The purpose of the amice is to completely cover the cassock or, in some modern circumstances, the clerical shirt, so that they are not visible while the priest is in sacred vestments. The word *amice* derives from the Latin verb *amicire*, which means "to cover."

The amice is to be placed upon the head with solemnity. After reverencing the cross, which is stitched into it, the priest should recite the proper prayer. The most ancient of these is, as follows: *Place upon my head, O Lord, the helmet of salvation for repelling the attacks of the evil one.* This prayer is a very vivid image of the priest's role as a soldier of Christ. Persons blessed with the opportunity of attending the present pope's private morning Mass within the Apostolic Palace, where they will see Pope John Paul II vest before them prior to celebrating the Mass, would see an amice of white linen and silk, somewhat larger than the traditional size, on which is emblazoned, in white silk damask, the coat of arms of the pope.

CHAPTER THIRTY-TWO

Rings

The episcopal ring is the symbol of a prelate's authority, and, for this reason, it must not be assumed by clerics not entitled to it. In the past two decades, it has become acceptable for priests and lesser prelates to wear jewelry. The most common type of jewelry seen is the signet ring, that is, the ring with the arms of the priest, and the class or school ring. The previous Codes of Canon Law forbade the wearing of rings or jewelry of any kind by clerics, other than those with episcopal rank.

The ring as an episcopal symbol of authority first appeared in the third century. By the fifth century, it was part of the episcopal insignia. Saint Isidore of Seville wrote in 637: "To the Bishop at his consecration is given a staff; a ring likewise is given him to signify pontifical honor or as a seal for secrets."[1] This is not surprising, as kings and princes were also given a ring of governance at their coronations, which were always ceremonies of religious consecration. Later, the ring took the additional symbolic meaning of a bishop's marriage to the Church and his spiritual parentage over the faithful of his diocese. The power of the ring is significant, as it binds priests and the faithful to the bishop and his teaching on all spiritual matters.

The ring is always worn on the fourth finger of the right hand, known as the ring finger. In the past, there were three distinct types of rings for each prelate. In present times, because of the cost, this is not often possible. The greatest of the proper rings is the pontifical ring, that is, the ring worn as a pontifical insignia for most solemn events. In the past, this ring was nearly always worn over the ceremonial glove. As such, it had an expandable base to fit both the finger and the gloved finger. The pontifical ring is also the most elaborate, often made of a precious stone with other precious or semi-precious stones framing it. As this is the most expensive of the episcopal rings, it has become customary for bishops and archbishops to bequeath their rings to prelates or priests for possible future use or to their dioceses for use by future ordinaries.

The gemmed ring is a more simplified version of the pontifical ring and contains an inexpensive single stone. Although it was historically distinct from the pontifical ring of the past, the modern desire for simplicity, as well as concern for cost, has seen this ring serve many prelates as both the pontifical or ceremonial ring and the standard gemmed ring.

The ordinary ring is for daily, nonceremonial use and most often contains the arms of the bishop. It is very similar to the signet ring for laymen. It may also be religious in design, worked in simple gold or silver. The ordinary ring should not be worn at liturgical functions.

RINGS OF THE POPE

The pope officially makes use of one ring only, the Fisherman's Ring. It is so called because it depicts the image of St. Peter casting his fishnet into the sea. The ring is always gold. The pope's pontifical name, that is, the name that he chose upon election, is engraved above or near the image of St. Peter. The actual Fisherman's Ring is not worn daily by the popes as it once was. The ring is kept in his apartment, and when necessary, it is used to seal papal decrees. A simplified version of the ring is worn on a daily basis. Pope John Paul II has chosen as his ordinary ring a simple band of hammered gold made into the form of the crucifix.

In the past, the "simple ring" was anything but simple. Pope Pius IX's ordinary ring was an inch in diameter and contained more than one hundred diamonds that formed his effigy in profile. Pope John XXIII preferred a simple cameo as his ordinary ring. This ring, too, was nearly an inch in length. The Fisherman's Ring was mentioned for the first time in 1265 when Pope Clement IV wrote to his nephew Piero Grossi concerning its use. In the past, when both the pope and all prelates wore pontifical gloves, the popes also made use of the pontifical ring that had the expandable base in order for the ring to fit onto the gloved finger. It was always made with a precious stone and, traditionally, was always elaborate. At the end of each pontificate, as the pontiff is consigned to history, the Cardinal-Camerlengo of the Church always destroys the Fisherman's Ring in the presence of members of the Sacred College. The Fisherman's Seal, a larger version of the same insignia that is used to seal large *bulla*, is also destroyed at the pope's death.

RINGS OF THE CARDINALS

After a new Cardinal has received the red hat* from the Holy Father, he receives the cardinal's ring. This ceremony has taken many forms. At present, the ring is presented to new cardinals at a Mass on the day following the consistory that created them cardinals.

Today, the cardinal's ring is gold, with a modernistic bas-relief design that depicts a scene from the public life of Christ. It is nearly 1 inch in circumference. As it is the ring given to the cardinals by the pope, it is also the ring most frequently worn by the cardinals during their remaining lifetimes, although a smaller ordinary ring would be appropriate for daily office work.

Ironically, this newer style of ring makes no use of a precious stone. The stone reserved for members of the Sacred College is the sapphire, and no other prelate may make use of it. The sapphire, with other precious stones surrounding it, was traditionally presented to cardinals when they were received into the Sacred College. The present pope (as well as future popes) has the right to return to the use of the sapphire, as its use was not abolished. Because cost is the significant factor for any change of style, it may be unlikely to see a return of the gift of the sapphire ring. Cardinals who prefer a gemmed ring and who may have inherited a predecessor's ring may nevertheless make use of it. However, although other stones have been given them, such

---

* In present times, the red *biretta*, not the red *galero*, is presented by the pope.

as the topaz, the only gem permitted the cardinal, by tradition, is the sapphire.

The ring that is granted to a new cardinal upon his elevation to the Sacred College remains the property of the Holy See until it has been redeemed by the newly named Cardinal who, during the week of ceremonies of the consistory, pays a tax to the Holy See, which enables him to bequeath his ring to his diocese, family, or, upon his death, to another priest.

RINGS OF THE PATRIARCHS, ARCHBISHOPS, AND BISHOPS

All bishops, archbishops, and patriarchs are entitled to the episcopal ring, but they may not assume it until it has been bestowed upon them at the ceremony of consecration. Bishops likewise make use of three rings: the pontifical, the gemmed, and the ordinary. As we have seen, the pontifical and the gemmed rings have often become one and the same due to cost factors and a desire for simplicity. Although this practice is a concession to modern necessity, it is nevertheless historically incorrect.

For persons properly making use of all three rings, only the sapphire is forbidden to patriarchs, archbishops, and bishops. The traditional stone for patriarchs, archbishops, and bishops is the amethyst, both for the pontifical ring, which would additionally be surrounded by semiprecious stones, and the ordinary gemmed ring, which would be of gold and which would have only the amethyst. The daily or ordinary episcopal ring should have a religious symbol or the arms of the prelate engraved upon it. Another common design for the rings of these prelates is the cameo, traditionally of the Madonna, which also makes for a beautiful and impressive episcopal insignia.

RINGS OF THE ABBOTS, CANONS, AND DOCTORS

Abbots are presented with the ring of abbatial office at the ceremony known as the Blessing of the Abbot. In the past, the ring used by abbots, especially mitred abbots, or those permitted the privilege of wearing the simplex mitre, was quite ornate. Today, however, the custom of a simple gold ring is preferred.

In addition, many privileges have been granted to canons throughout the years. Certain European Chapters of Canons have been given privileges, including use of the ring. It must always be simple in design and, in present times, it may never resemble the episcopal ring.

Likewise, persons who hold and enjoy a doctoral degree from a pontifical institution in a discipline related to the Church have the privilege of wearing the ecclesiastical doctoral ring on the finger known as the "prelatial finger," the finger specifically reserved for the episcopal rings of bishops.[*] The doctoral ring may have a gemstone setting, but the design of the ring itself may not be altered in any way by the wearer to suit personal tastes. The doctoral ring differs in its design by academic discipline and by each pontifical institution.

RINGS OF THE PRIESTS

Both regular and order priests receive the ring of profession when they take vows appropriate to their order. These rings are not rings of jurisdiction. As we have seen, with the exception of these rings, former Codes of Canon Law forbade jewelry to priests. Although modern influences now permit certain exceptions, it is best not to assume a ring

---

[*] The ring finger of the right hand.

that represents the fundamental authority of the bishops.

INDULGENCES AND REVERENCING THE RING

For centuries, the Church has granted an indulgence to Catholics who reverence the ring of the pope, cardinals, and other prelates. "The faithful who devoutly kiss the ring of the Sovereign Pontiff are granted an indulgence of 300 days; that of a Cardinal, an indulgence of 100 days; that of a Patriarch, Archbishop or Bishop, and a Prefect Apostolic, an indulgence of 50 days."[2]

In most modern Western nations, the act of reverencing or kissing the episcopal ring is discouraged by the prelates themselves. Many prelates feel personally uncomfortable as the apparent recipient of this deferential courtesy; others view it as arcane. Whatever their individual feelings, they do a great disservice to the faithful by discouraging this act of reverence. It must be remembered that the faithful are not personally reverencing an individual bishop but are symbolically showing their respect and fidelity to the apostles, whom each Bishop represents through episcopal succession. Sometimes, when a lay Catholic wishes to demonstrate this sign of respect, in accordance with long-standing local custom, it is often a source of sadness and confusion when a prelate pulls his hand away from that individual. A subsequent welcoming handshake or gesture is always appropriate, however it should not take the place of the reverencing of the ring when desired.

Under the most formal protocol regulations (and these should be adhered to on every possible occasion), the following procedures historically have been followed when reverencing the episcopal ring. For the Holy Father, all ladies traditionally curtsy or perform a slight "bob" while they kiss the pope's ring. When circumstances do not allow this reverence (especially during large crowded gatherings), a simple kiss of the ring is permitted. In more formal circumstances, such as during private or semiprivate audiences, gentlemen most formally genuflect, whereas ladies curtsy. Less formally, a simple bow to the ring is acceptable and, in fact, most common in large gatherings. Royalty has always been granted the privilege of bowing when reverencing the pope's ring; however, this has become somewhat of a moot point of protocol, as nearly everyone bows today, although it is improper to do so.

Reverencing of the Rings of the Prelature

As with the pope, the most formal protocol requires that everyone genuflect when they kiss a cardinal's ring. Although it is proper to do so, it is not always possible, and often due to nervousness or excitement, one might forget to do so. In any case, a bow would be acceptable, followed by a proper greeting. It is best to follow the cardinal's lead. He, of course, should always take care to put the individual at ease, while simultaneously reserving the dignity of his position.

All nuncios, pro-nuncios, and apostolic delegates, as well as personal papal legates, should be accorded this same respect within their own jurisdiction or during the duration of their special mission. Otherwise, they should be accorded the level of respect entitled to all other prelates of their own episcopal rank (archbishops, bishops, prefects apostolic, etc.) when they are outside their individual jurisdictions.

Metropolitan archbishops within their own province receive this same deference, as does a bishop within his own jurisdiction. Titular archbishops and bishops are accorded a bow, by both ladies and gentlemen, before reverencing the ring, although, as we have already seen, many local customs determine the procedures to be followed in a particular region or nation.

Although protocol procedures may seem somewhat obsolete or arcane, they are set to recognize the dignity of the position of the prelate as well as the role or function that he performs within the Church. Universal formulae prevent gaffes and confusion caused by local differences unknown to the faithful or to a visiting dignitary.

INDULGENCE CITATION

The faithful who devoutly kiss the ring of the Sovereign Pontiff are granted an indulgence of 300 days. Of a cardinal: an indulgence of 100 days; and of a patriarch, archbishop, bishop, or prefect apostolic: an indulgence of 50 days. (Sacred Congregation of the Holy Office, March 18, 1909/Sacred Penitentiary Apostolica Dec. 29, 1934 and Nov. 21, 1945: not abridged after Vatican Council II).

CHAPTER THIRTY-THREE

Pectoral Cross

The pectoral cross is a small cross, traditionally no more than 6 inches in length, made of precious metal and worn at the breast by the pope and all cardinals, bishops, and abbots. Its name derives from the Latin word *pectus* (breast), as this cross is suspended from the neck by either a metal chain or silk cord.

Unlike other items of vesture and insignia that reflect the jurisdiction of a prelate, the pectoral cross reflects the order of dignity of the office of bishop or abbot. It served originally as a reliquary of the True Cross, which, due to the singular import of this relic, encouraged the practice of wearing the relic close to the heart by the highest Church officials.

In time, the reliquaries became ornate as a means to bring further honor to this holy relic. Sadly, all pectoral crosses made today do not possess the relic of the True Cross. Nevertheless, Rome acknowledges the time-honored practice that each bishop should possess at least one pectoral cross that contains a relic of the True Cross. Anticipating that the supply of these relics would be exhausted, as early as 1889 the Holy See took steps to assure that each bishop receive at least one of these special reliquaries. "In reference to the relic of the True Cross con-tained in the pectoral cross, the Cardinal Vicar of Rome, by order of Leo XIII, in a letter to all Bishops bearing the date March 25, 1889, reminds them that since these relics may become exhausted, the pectoral cross of a deceased Bishop is to be transmitted to his successor as his lawful heir, the proper authorities of the vacant See are instructed to execute this injunction."[1]

"The pectoral cross is to be worn at all times by those with Episcopal dignity."[2] It is to be worn exposed at all times unless it is worn with the black clerical suit, also known as *tenue de ville* and unless the chasuble is worn, in which case it would then be properly worn beneath the vestment. With the black suit, the pectoral cross is to be suspended from the neck by a chain and should cross the breast and rest in the left suit-coat or vest pocket; it should never be worn hanging freely about the neck. A bishop may never go without the pectoral cross.

The pectoral cross must always be worn in full view by prelates with episcopal dignity when in simar or cassock. Until the late 1800s, bishops would conceal their individual pectoral crosses in the presence of the pope as deference to his rank and authority. Pope Pius IX, at the First Vatican Council, reminded the prelates present that the pectoral cross was not a jurisdictional insignia but rather an insignia of the Order of Bishop and, as such, was not to be concealed in his presence as if in deference to the one with supreme jurisdiction.* From the First Vatican Council onward, it was required that the pectoral cross be worn exposed by all bishops whenever they were when vested in cassock or simar, but that it should never be in view when they were wearing the chasuble.

With time, the norms governing the use of the insignia of the pectoral cross developed. For instance, a papal regulation was promulgated that required the pectoral cross to be of Latin form, in which the length is longer than the width of the two segments. After the Second Vatican Council and during the pontificate of Paul VI, who had a great love for modern art, some flexibility in the cross design was permitted. At one time, only the archbishop of Armagh (primate of all Ireland) and the patriarch of Lisbon, as well as the Oriental patriarchates, were permitted a pectoral cross other than the one of traditional Latin design. Armagh and Lisbon were permitted a double traverse bar in a design known as the archiepiscopal cross. In present times, the pectoral cross, remaining basically Latin in design, has many variations that include the modern as well as the more ancient, such as the Celtic cross. Extravagant design should be avoided at all times. Dignity comes from simplicity.

There are two divisions of the pectoral cross. One type is simple, known as the ordinary pectoral cross, and the other is ornate, known as the pontifical pectoral cross. It is customary for bishops to have one of each. If necessity does not permit a relic in both crosses in the prelate's possession, then the relic should be placed in the pontifical pectoral cross. This has been the custom for seven hundred years. What exactly are the differences between the two crosses?

PONTIFICAL CROSS

The pontifical cross is traditionally more ornate than the ordinary cross. It is always to be made of gold and must contain the reliquary.† Often there is room in the cross for relics of patronal saints as well. The pontifical cross traditionally is fitted with at least one gem, if not more. The stones permitted cardinals are the sapphire and the diamond, which are stones reserved exclusively for them, and the ruby. Patriarchs, archbishops, and bishops make use of the amethyst. The pontifical cross is usually made of filigree so as to appear ornate.

The pontifical cross is the only pectoral cross permitted for use with choir dress, in other words, over the *mozzetta*. The pontifical pectoral cross must always be suspended from the silk cord. It may never be suspended from the chain. Many prelates have been seen of late wearing the pontifical pectoral cross on a chain that is suspended from the neck and fastened on the button of the *mozzetta*, as if it were a simple cassock or simar. This practice is not in conformity with Rome. When vested in choir dress, the prelate must always suspend the pontifical pectoral cross from the silk cord.

For cardinals, the cord is made of red silk, intertwined with gold thread, terminating in a large red and gold tuft.‡ The cord consists of two strands that fasten to the cross itself. A sliding bezel of the same material is provided in order to make tight the segment of the cord that rests on the chest above the *mozzetta*. This bezel should be tightened to the collar and not worn lower on the chest. The tuft traditionally is worn no lower on the back than the bottom of the *mozzetta*; it should never hang below

---

* Pius IX's words were *"Fuori le croci!"* (Show the Cross!)

† This rule is a result of ancient custom; it is not mandated by Church law.

‡ Some members of the Sacred College have made do with a simple red cord. At all times, the red and gold silk cord with tufts is to be used.

the _mozzetta_. Patriarchs, archbishops, and bishops make use of a similar silk cord in the colors of green and gold, worn in the same fashion.

The cord and tuft for abbots is simple black, whereas that for abbots nullius is black with gold threads. Prior to 1969, certain minor prelates were entitled to pontificals, which included a pectoral cross without gems. The cords for these prelates varied by title and rank. The supranumerary proto-notaries wore a cord and tuft of amaranth-red silk, whereas the rank of _ad instar_ made use of one of purple silk. For protonotaries apostolic de numero, the cord and tuft were made of amaranth red and gold silk; for prelates nullius and abbots general, of green silk and gold thread, as for bishops. Canons made use of a black cord with gold thread, although the color of each canonry varied, depending upon the indult of concession upon their erection. Minor prelates conferred prior to 1969 have been permitted the right to retain this privilege although all the _monsignori_ created after the Pauline changes are not entitled to make use of this insignia.

ORDINARY CROSS

The ordinary pectoral cross is worn with cassock or simar and may or may not include a reliquary for the relic of the True Cross. It is traditionally simple in design. Permission was granted by Paul VI to permit modern artistic art form or to include ancient cross design, and the ordinary pectoral cross has tended to include both these styles.

The ordinary pectoral cross is worn with the black clerical suit and with the cassock and simar. It is always suspended from the chain. Although traditionally of gold, the ordinary pectoral cross may also be designed in silver. Some have been made of rich wood, but these beautiful crosses should be

reserved for areas of the world where the use of wood is considered more dignified than precious metal. In other words, the choice of materials should reflect the culture of the place if the choice is not the traditional gold.*

By decree of Pope Saint Pius X, abbots, even those without episcopal dignity, are to make use of the pectoral cross only within their jurisdictions. Pope Paul VI further restricted that practice to abbots nullius in his _Motu Proprio_ of March 31, 1969.

It is important to note that the pectoral cross should never be worn over the chasuble when an individual is vested for the liturgy. This practice has arisen but has been forbidden for centuries by the various congregations governing these matters. When a cleric is vested in alb, the pontifical pec-toral cross should be worn, but it is not mandatory to do so, although long-standing custom, as well as rubrics prior to 1969, requires the use of the pon-tifical pectoral cross. Therefore, the proper silk cord should be attached to the cross and placed over the alb—under the chasuble, yet visible when vested in cope.[3] Never should the chain be used while one is vested for the liturgy.

INDULGENCE CITATION

An indulgence of one hundred days is granted to bishops if they properly and devotedly recite the prayers prescribed in the _Roman Missal_ while vest-ing in pontificals. The same indulgence is granted to priests who devotedly recite the prayers pre-scribed to them for vesting in that which is proper to their office.

---

* The reason for this is simply that the greatest dignity should be exhibited with the bishop's pectoral cross, as it distinctly represents the office of a successor of the apostles.

CHAPTER THIRTY-FOUR

Crozier

The official name of the crozier is *baculus pastoralis,* or pastoral staff. Today, it may take many forms, but prior to the Second Vatican Council, the form of the crozier was strictly regulated. The crozier is traditionally made in three segments: the crook, the staff, and the pediment, or bottom shaft, which is always pointed, and which, when disassembled, permits an ease for storage and transportation.

The crozier is the senior ecclesiastical insignia that symbolizes the pastoral authority of bishops. The crozier's history can be traced to the Twelve Apostles, as legend has it that they carried large staffs, typical of the travelers of their time. "It had a prototype among the insignia of the priesthood of the Hittites and Babylonians."[1] The Roman astronomers made use of a crooked staff that bears an exact resemblance to the pastoral staff of the bishops of the early Church. "Other early (ninth century) writers argued in favor of the crozier being simply the decorated and specialized heir of the common walking sticks used in Churches as a support before the introduction of seats."[2]* It symbolizes Christ's love and protection for His people as a shepherd would watch over his sheep.

HISTORY

In the early Church, the crozier (now also seen spelled crosier) was made entirely of rugged wood, with a crook natural to the individual branch of the tree that was selected. By the third century, a smooth wooden staff was assumed by bishops, with the earliest origins of the rounded crook taking form. By the fourth century, the crozier became a part of the insignia of all bishops, including the Bishop of Rome. St. Isidore wrote that the crozier was presented to each newly consecrated bishop "that he may govern and correct those below him or to offer support to the weakest of the weak."[3] By the middle of the fifth century, the crozier was mentioned in an open letter to the bishops of Narbonne and Vienne by Pope Celestine I (della Campagnia) stressing the magisterial authority that the staff represented.

During the reign of Celestine, the crozier made entirely of wood was laid aside for persons with the episcopal dignity, not to be seen again in the Church for fourteen hundred years. The staff itself was made of the richest of local woods—ebony,

---

* A reference to the creation of new sees and the subsequent ceremonies that mark the assumption of jurisdiction by a bishop.

oak, or cypress, depending on the locality—whereas the crook, which by this time took on its distinct form, was made of soft pliable metal and gilt. By the seventh century, the knob, or orb, at the base of the crook became an acceptable addition. From the pontificate of Celestine I to that of Paul VI, the crozier was required to have the ornamental crook. By the Renaissance, the ornamentation became elaborate, always utilizing the most precious of metals and including gems as well. After the tenth century, the crozier made partially of wood, for the most part, disappeared.

Only abbots and abbesses, prelates nullius, and prelates apostolic were permitted the staff of wood. In fact, the metal or gilt crozier was forbidden them. During the twelfth century, the English baron bishops added the *penicillium*, or silk veil, which was attached to the orb, or knob, by a gilt hook. The use of the *penicillium* was widespread and was quickly adopted as official for all croziers. Its official purpose was to cover the metal of the staff to prevent it from tarnishing. (This reasoning or purpose was soon forgotten, as, by this time, the gauntlets or gloves were mandatory, making the *penicillium* ineffective.) The true purpose for its adoption was the added flair it provided the crozier, which by now also took its proper size of from 60 to 70 inches in height, the size that the crozier remains today. The *penicillium* was later regulated for the sole use of abbesses* who are entitled to pontificals, yet it can still be seen today as the main heraldic emblem granted by Rome for use by both abbesses and abbots, abbots nullius, and prelates nullius in their armorial bearings.

DESIGN

By the seventeenth century, the Holy See set forth regulations that stipulated, by rank and dignity, the materials and design permitted prelates regarding the privileges to the crozier. The pope had long ago laid aside the crozier. By the eleventh century, the theology of the universal jurisdiction of the Roman Pontiff was unquestioned; therefore, the pope did not make use of a staff that symbolized jurisdiction of the prelate bearing it, as his authority was over the Universal Church. "Innocent III explains further by saying that the Blessed St. Peter sent his staff to Eucharius, the first Bishop of Trèves, which staff is preserved with great reverence in its cathedral."[4] St. Thomas Aquinas confirmed this legend by citing the reception of this staff by the popes when they paid apostolic visits to Treves.[5] It was not until the pontificate of Paul VI that the pastoral staff returned for use by a pope.

Pope Paul wished to stress his rule as supreme pastor and, in adopting a pastoral staff to signify this desire, as well as to illustrate his role as bishop in unison with the entire episcopacy, commissioned the design of the present, well-known modern-style Pauline staff with crucifix. The pope's staff is made of silver and has, in place of the crook, a hammered-silver modern crucifix with corpus.†

Cardinals were restricted by custom, until 1969, to a crozier of gold or silver gilt (gold-plated silver). They are entitled to carry it worldwide as one of their unique privileges. Non-Oriental patriarchs were also entitled to bear a gilt or gold crozier. Members of the College of Cardinals also were permitted their crozier to be gem encrusted, traditionally at the orb of the crook.

---

* As late as the early 1900s, the *penicillium* was in vogue by a few abbots as well, but its adoption was not in conformity with Roman practices.
† Pope Paul wished to stress the pastoral dimension of the papacy, rather than its jurisdictional dimension, in assuming a pastoral staff. He did not assume a crozier *per se*. The pastoral staff of Paul VI was designed by the Italian sculptor Léllo Scorzelli. It was used by Pope Paul's two successors John Paul I and John Paul II until May 18, 1990, when the sculptor created a slightly different version of the staff and presented it to Pope John Paul II for his birthday.

Archbishops and bishops, as well as abbots nullius, were limited to a crozier of silver. Prelates of nonepiscopal dignity were entitled to a crozier only by specific indult; however, the crozier had to be very simple.

In present times, prelates of all ranks with episcopal dignity may make use of the crozier style of their choice, within accepted norms, of course. Minor prelates and abbesses* are no longer granted an indult to bear the crozier.

Thus we see a return, after fourteen hundred years, to the wooden crozier of various designs. The requirement for the crook has been somewhat relaxed to permit ethnic and regional artistic interpretation as well as modern artistic expression. Gold is no longer reserved for cardinals and patriarchs, nor is it limited to them. The incorporation of ivory and bronze has also come into vogue.

The modern crozier may vary from a representation of the traditional crooked staff to the wooden pastoral staff of the early Church Fathers. The crook itself was not abolished because of its early origins and should not be laid aside in the design of new crozier. On the modern crozier, it is proper to incorporate images and symbols, including the prelates' armorial bearings, which should be placed with dignity on the staff portion or at the base of the crook. It is also proper to incorporate representations of the Risen Lord, the Agnus Dei, Angels, the Shepherd and Lamb, etc., but these are best reserved for metal croziers. If armorial bearings are to be included on the crozier, they should be worked in enamel. Often the shield of arms is placed at each axis of the orb so as to be seen from each direction at the same time.

ENTITLEMENT

Only individuals with episcopal dignity are permitted the crozier and, in fact, it is presented to them at the ceremony of consecration to the episcopacy. It may never be assumed by others, except abbots.

The pope has universal jurisdiction and, therefore, need not carry a crozier. As we have seen, however, Pope Paul VI and his successors have chosen to bear the pastoral staff to stress their role as universal pastor. Technically, the pastoral staff is not a crozier.

Cardinals are permitted the crozier worldwide except within the patriarchal basilicas in Rome. The nuncio, pro-nuncio, or apostolic delegate of the Holy See may bear his crozier, by unlimited right, within the jurisdiction assigned him. Metropolitans are permitted unlimited use of the crozier within their own provinces, and residential archbishops and bishops are entitled to the same rights within their sees. Titular archbishops and bishops are also, of course, entitled to bear the crozier but only when they are the chief celebrant or presider at the liturgy. "The diocesan Bishop may allow a visiting Bishop to use the crozier in his diocese, but it is better not to do so, especially when the outsider officiates in the presence of the diocesan."[6] Of course, this position was not taken to include ceremonies, such as Ordinations or Confirmations, that required the visiting bishop's use of the crozier. Even the long-standing custom of requesting permission to bear the crozier within another's jurisdiction has lapsed. At present, only the chief celebrant with episcopal rank carries the crozier, although other persons present may certainly be entitled to do so by right of episcopal ordination. No one may make use of the crozier in the presence of the Holy Father.

The crozier is always carried by the prelate with the crook facing forward, a position that is referred to as "opened," in reference to that prelate's open

---

* Abbesses usurped this privilege during the High Middle Ages. It was not a privilege expressly granted them.

authority as bishop and not necessarily as open jurisdiction over that locality. Formerly, only the ordinary carried the crozier opened. All others entitled to carry the crozier carried it backward, a position that was also known as either "unopened" or "closed."

The crozier is properly grasped by the orb, or knob, at the base of the crook. All croziers make use of the same style knob, which is the point of juncture for the crook and staff segment. Some modern designs place ivory or marble bands high on the staff, and the tendency is to grasp the crozier at this point rather than at the orb. Even though there are no regulations governing this somewhat modern adaptation, etiquette defers to long-standing custom in all cases; therefore, one would recommend, primarily, grasping the crozier at the orb and then, secondarily, at these special bands of ivory or marble, but even then the hands should be placed at the uppermost segment of these bands.

The crook of the crozier must always be carried "open" by the prelate, but it should always be carried "closed" in procession by a vimp, or bearer, in deference to, and in recognition of, the bishop's jurisdiction. This practice also permits the diocesan master of ceremonies, when retrieving it, to hand it over to the bishop, smoothly assuring that he will always receive it "opened."

CHAPTER THIRTY-FIVE

Pallium

The *pallium*, as a nonecclesiastical garment, predates Christ by at least two hundred years, when it was worn as a simple garment of warmth in ancient Greece. The *pallium* was then much larger than we know it to be today; it covered the torso and flowed down to the ground. Histories of the earliest Christians described them as wearing a garb that was distinctly the *pallium*. Many references are made to St. Justin the Martyr, who was said to have worn a *pallium* at his death in A.D. 165.

This ancient *pallium* was woolen without ornament, and it stretched some 12 feet in length. It was worn about the shoulders down and around the right arm, reaching to the sandals, front and rear. As best as we can tell, it was approximately 9 inches in width.

Although it predates the Christian era, the *pallium* was soon adopted by the early Christians as a sign of their fidelity to Christ, as early Christian graffiti detail. Symbols then began to appear on *pallia*: first the fish and, in later centuries, the cross. By the third century, the *pallium* was worn by many Christians and much of the clergy. By the fourth century, it was adopted by the bishops of Rome.

Long before the popes adopted it for themselves, however, the *pallium* was worn as an ecclesiastical garment in the East. Its use by the laity had already begun to wane and once the popes officially adopted the *pallium* for themselves, the use of it by all Christians, especially the clergy, lapsed.

By the fifth century, the *pallium* was in the gift of the Roman pontiffs—reserved for the highest of Churchmen—and clearly a distinct vestment in its own right. By the ninth century, the *pallium* was reserved for metropolitans, archbishops, and bishops of singular distinction, and it was exclusively a gift of the popes.

Until the eleventh century, the *pallium* resembled the large ancient Greek design more so than its modern counterpart. After A.D. 1050, the *pallium*, especially in the north of Europe, began to narrow and soon became symbolic rather than functional, no longer used for warmth.

Some historians claim that the *pallium* was first made of linen—especially in the pre-Christian and early Christian eras—but there appears to be no solid evidence of this claim. In fact, one of the predominant factors in the development of the *pallium* was the need for a warm covering about the shoulders, which linen would not provide. By the pontificate of Pope Leo III (A.D. 798), *pallia* were required to be made of wool.

It is attributed, but no historical certainty can be given to the claim, that the ceremony of blessing two lambs on the Feast of St. Agnes (January 21), who would later give their wool for the creation of the *pallia,* began during the pontificate of John XIII (A.D. 965–972).

Agnes was an early fourth-century martyr (A.D. 304) who gave up her life for the Faith. Her name is the feminine diminutive of *agnus,* which is Latin for "lamb." Every year on the Feast of St. Agnes, two lambs are presented to the canons of the Basilica of St. John Lateran in Rome to be blessed. The lambs, in turn, are entrusted to the care of the Sisters of the Torre di Specchi, where they are kept until their wool is ready for shearing. In a colorful gathering, the lambs' wool is shorn, cleaned, and woven into the *pallia* to be presented to the new metropolitan archbishops of the world.

On the eve of the Feast of SS. Peter and Paul (June 29), the *pallia* are carried in great ceremony to the Crypt of St. Peter beneath the High Altar in the Vatican Basilica, where they are kept in a small silver gilt casket in a niche in the crypt's Altar of the Confession—visible from above on the main floor of the basilica as well as below from the *Christo Re* Altar at the base of the Confession. The next morning they are carried in procession at Mass for the investiture ceremony. Before they are placed in the altar niche, the pope solemnly blesses the *pallia* at the close of evening prayer (first Vespers).

Although every metropolitan is entitled to the *pallium* and is expected to make use of it within his jurisdiction, it is not automatically bestowed upon new archbishops. Within three months of their promotion to the position of metropolitan archbishops, the new metropolitans must request the

pallium from the Holy Father through his representative at the nunciature or legation of their own nation. This formal request is expected shortly after the arrival of the new metropolitan in his see.

The *pallium* is a symbol of jurisdiction and has been such since the fifth century, when it was reserved as a gift of the Roman Pontiff. Only metropolitans are entitled to the *pallium*; no other prelate, no matter how high in rank, is entitled to this jurisdictional vesture. Nevertheless, the popes have always reserved for themselves the right to present the *pallium* to nonmetropolitan archbishops and bishops as a sign of unique or singular honor to them. This is a rare honor, reserved to a few, and is seldom seen today; in fact, persons who still hold this unique honor are most likely to be the last as a decree of 1978 reserved the *pallium*, once and for all, to metropolitans and the Latin Patriarch of Jerusalem.

The *pallium* used to be bestowed by cardinals, primates, nuncios, or apostolic delegates in nations so far from Rome that it would be too costly, dangerous, or time consuming to travel to Rome. In present times, with the ease of jet-age travel, all new metropolitans are expected to be present in Rome for their investiture with the *pallium* on the next Feast of SS. Peter and Paul (June 29) that follows their promotion in rank and position.

The ceremony of investiture is simple. The celebration of the sacrifice of the Mass is always the liturgy in which this ceremony takes place. Following the Liturgy of the Word, yet before the Homily, which the Holy Father preaches, the metropolitans proceed to a place of prominence.* The secretary

---

* If the Mass is held outside in St. Peter's Square, the metropolitans stand along the bottom stair that leads to the pope's throne behind the altar. If the Mass is held in the basilica proper, they are to form a line or an arch before the Confession of St. Peter.

of the Congregation of Bishops, an archbishop himself, carries the *pallia* on a silver tray. Vested in choir, he climbs the steps to the throne and kneels before the pope, who then blesses it once again. One by one, the metropolitans are called forward by the Master of Ceremonies of the Holy Father. Each is escorted to the throne, where the pontiff is seated vested in mitre and chasuble and wearing the *pallium* (as he always must when in sacred vestments), which represents universal jurisdiction. Each metropolitan approaches the throne without the mitre but still wearing the *zucchetto*. He makes a sign of reverence to the pope, either a deep bow or genuflection, and then kneels before the pope, who says:

> *To the glory of almighty God and the praise of the Blessed Virgin Mary and of the apostles Peter and Paul, and of the Holy Roman Church, for the honor of the Church of [place], which has been placed in your care, and as a symbol of your authority as Metropolitan Archbishop: we confer on you the pallium taken from the tomb of Peter to wear within the limits of your ecclesiastical province.*
>
> *May this pallium be a symbol of unity and a sign of your communion with the Apostolic See, a bond of love, and an incentive to courage. On the day of the coming and manifestation of our great God and chief shepherd, Jesus Christ, may you and the flock entrusted to you be clothed with immortality and glory. In the name of the Father, and of the Son, and of the Holy Spirit.*

JURISDICTION

The *pallium* is worn by all metropolitans within their jurisdictions, therefore, within their ecclesiastical provinces.* They must wear it if vested in sacred vestments. They never make use of it when vested in choir or academic dress.

The Holy Father wears his *pallium* at all times, in all places, when vested in sacred vestments. His jurisdiction alone is universal. For this reason, only one prelate makes use of the *pallium* at a given liturgical celebration.

When the Holy Father is present, as his jurisdiction is universal, all prelates, regardless of rank or jurisdiction, forgo the *pallium*. In fact, when the Holy Father is present in a jurisdiction of a metropolitan, the metropolitan would not be entitled to use of the *pallium*. In all other circumstances, the prelate whose jurisdiction it is (i.e., primates in their land and metropolitans in their provinces) alone is entitled to the use of the *pallium*. Only one prelate may make use of the *pallium*, regardless of others who may have been invested with it and who are present. Cardinal-archbishops, patriarchs, and other metropolitans defer to the metropolitan of the place in this regard. Therefore, the honor is one of jurisdiction. Cardinals defer to the local metropolitans at functions that require the *pallium*. The metropolitan of the place defers his honor only when the Holy Father is present.[†]

In order to stress the jurisdictional nature of the *pallium*, rather than any personal honor that may be assumed by an individual prelate, as early as the eleventh century, it became the practice in the Church to require a transferred archbishop (one who already holds a *pallium* from his previous see) to request, within three months of his transfer, a *pallium* that is tied to the new jurisdiction. Thus it is

---

* Primates in certain nations make use of the *pallium* throughout that nation as they are, jurisdictionally, first among equals in that place. All patriarchs are additionally invested with the *pallium*, which bonds them closely to the See of Peter while recognizing their unique position and authority in the Church.

† Even apostolic nuncios who may have previously been vested with the *pallium* (but which is not generally the case) cannot deny the privilege of the *pallium* to the metropolitan of the place.

not uncommon for prelates to have two, perhaps three, *pallia* in their lifetime.

Practice

In the past, the *pallium* was donned only on certain solemn or festive days. As we have seen, it was only worn over the sacred vestments. These special days included Christmas, Epiphany, Palm Sunday, Holy Thursday, Holy Saturday, Pentecost, the Feast of St. John the Baptist, the Feast of the Twelve Apostles, the Feast of the Immaculate Conception, and the patronal feasts of the diocese, province, and cathedral seat, as well as numerous others.[1] But as we have seen, in present times the *pallium* may be worn when celebrating pontifically at a Mass within the metropolitan's jurisdiction.

Vesting with the Pallium

The *pallium* is the last of the sacred vesture to be donned by the metropolitan. The metropolitan should be assisted by the Deacon of the Eucharist. The deacon should properly fold the *pallium* so that, like the *infullae* of the mitre, it will fall gracefully after it is placed over the shoulders of the prelate.

The front and rear sections should be folded into three sections, with the base, or black portion, facing outward. The deacon should present the *pallium* as he would a stole so that the metropolitan will properly reverence the *pallium* with a kiss.* The prelate then bows his head, the deacon places the *pallium* over the head and, after adjusting it to have the still folded stems front and rear, unfolds the stems to drop gracefully into place.

The *pallium* is set with three gemmed pins of precious metal. The first of these pins is placed on the front cross embroidered in black wool. An eyelet of the same black wool is worked into the center of the cross to permit these pins to fasten easily. If there is a difference in style or degree of elabo-

rate design of the pins, the most prominent pin is placed in front. It is best, however, to have three identical pins. The second pin is placed at the neck on the circular section of the *pallium* over the left shoulder. The third pin is placed on the cross on the rear flap.

These three pins, some ancient historians claim, represent the three days in the tomb before Christ triumphed over death. Although there is no proof of this symbolic significance, it has provided a wonderful symbolic link to Christ's death and Resurrection. No other historic explanation for these practices exists although the pins have been in use for six hundred years.

Additional Privileges

The *pallium* is of such ancient and esteemed origins that those invested with it are permitted the privilege of being buried with it.

The present *Ceremonial of Bishops* states, "The body is to be dressed in the violet vesture and with the insignia prescribed for a stational Mass, including the pallium, if the Bishop has the right to wear it. If the Bishop had been transferred from another See or from other Sees and had received several pallia, these are to be placed in the coffin, unless he has instructed otherwise before his death."[2] Traditions outside the United States have included the placement of these additional *pallia* on pillows at the foot of the catafalque. This is a very European custom, but a very dignified and elegant procedure. These extra *pallia* could then be placed in the archives of the archdiocese involved or, under special directives of the late prelate, with the cathedral, his family, and so forth. It is most proper, however, for these *pallia* to be placed under the pillow of the deceased

---

* He may kiss it anywhere, but tradition calls for a reverence of the cross as the *pallium* is presented.

metropolitan and interred with him, as the jurisdiction of this prelate ceased at his death and the *pallium* bound to his person cannot be transferred to another because the *pallium* is of personal jurisdictional dignity.

Another privilege of the *pallium* is heraldic in nature. Individuals invested with the *pallium* may depict it, according to the customs and regulations of the heraldic science (see Chapter 10, Ecclesiastical Heraldry). If a prelate has been conferred multiple *pallia*, he may not depict more than one *pallium* in his arms.*

---

* A heraldic expert should always be consulted as there are strict procedures regulating ecclesiastical heraldry that must, by Church law, be adhered to. Representation of the *pallium* in arms is bound by these regulations.

Mitre

The mitre (or miter) is an early tenth-century addition to the vesture of the Roman Catholic Church. Its origins, however, are much more ancient. For a number of years, it was thought generally that the mitre was simply transferred from the ancient Jewish or Levitical High Priesthood because their headgear resembled, somewhat, the earliest depicted mitres of the Roman Church (ca. eleventh century). Scholars later learned, however, that the perceived bonds between these two forms of religious headgear did not exist.

It is now fairly certain that the mitre's origins can be traced to ancient Greece of the pre-Christian era. The mitre is most likely derived from the cap worn by athletes of ancient Greece, as Church historians now hypothesize. Its *infulae,* or the ribbons of the mitre, actually predated the cap itself. These ribbons were worn around the forehead, tied in the rear by knot, and left to dangle down the back, and, in the heat of summer, a soft cloth cap was placed under the bands to protect the competitors from the outdoor heat. The winners of the athletic competitions were presented a laurel wreath, which encircled the head. This wreath formed the earliest ornamentation of the mitre. This headgear quickly became identified as being that of a champion. As time went on, it was copied by others, including the priests of ancient Greece, for civil dress.

During the earliest centuries of the Christian era, no mention is made of anything that resembles the present mitre. With the exception of certain localities within Greece, which included the now-Christianized population, the mitre appeared lost to history.

By the tenth century, the Bishop of Rome Pope Leo VIII is mentioned as making use of a *mitros* for occasional nonliturgical events. Soon after, it became part of the regalia of the papacy, the predecessor of the *triregno* (soon to develop), and the senior emblem of papal authority.

By the middle of the eleventh century, the mitre became a gift for bishops of special distinction. The first bishop to be presented the mitre by the Supreme Pontiff was Eberhart of Trèves, an archbishop and primate, who received it, along with the title Primate, at the hands of Leo IX in A.D. 1049. Soon after, bishops all over Europe were depicted wearing the mitre. It is clear that many bishops did not receive their mitres at the hands of the pope, yet records in the Vatican Secret Archives illustrate, certainly, that some bishops did indeed receive mitres as a gift of subsequent popes.*

The earliest recorded presentation of the mitre to an abbot took place on August 10, 1061, when Pope Alexander II conferred it upon Elegius, Abbot of the Monastery of St. Augustine in Canterbury, who was present at the Papal Court for some months of that year.† This gift of the mitre to abbots was directly opposed by St. Bernard, who wrote diligently against the practice. His will and diligence tempered the acceptance and use of the mitre by abbots until his death on August 20, 1153. Thereafter, the mitre as prescribed by Rome became *de rigueur* for abbots, who quickly adopted its use for themselves.

After A.D. 1150, bishops were always depicted as wearing the mitre. It was accepted as both an ecclesiastical, as well as civil, headgear.

The clergy of Rome made use of the mitre as early as the ninth century. First mention of it appears in the citation of it being worn by Pope Leo VII. Within three generations, the mitre was reserved for use of only the pope and cardinals. They made use of it even prior to its "official" adoption by Leo VIII for the papacy. It bore the name *camelaucem* and somewhat resembled the later mitre. The *camelaucem* is a direct descendant of the ancient Greek *mitros,* and this clear link between the two is evident by the choice of the word *mitros* in identifying this headgear once it officially entered the Church's vesture as an emblem of rank.‡

The shape of the modern mitre developed in the twelfth century. Before that time, the peaks of the mitre were soft, more caplike. By the twelfth century, ecclesiastical art illustrates that the mitre had developed as we would recognize it today.

DESIGN

All mitres are formed in the same fashion despite variances in design. The mitre comprises two flat forms, two *infulae* (the flaps, or fanons), and the lining. The flat forms are sewn together at the lower base on their lateral edges. The two *infulae* are suspended from the rear form, where they are sewn to its base—equidistant from each other so as to look proportional. The seams of the lining should never appear. This basically forms the requirements for the creation of a mitre; however, we must now speak in terms of style, type, and ornamentation.

Style

Historically, there have been three distinct styles of mitre that were worn at specific liturgies and even, before 1969, at different points during a single liturgy. The *Ceremoniale Episcoporum* (the Ceremonial of Bishops) would clarify in the rubrics when each of these three mitres would be required. These three styles were the only ones permitted in the Roman Church: precious mitre (*mitra pretiosa*); the golden, or orphreyed, mitre (*mitra auriphrygiata*); and the simple mitre (*mitra simplex*). Although postconciliar practice has seen a proliferation of other styles, these three remain the styles of mitre in use in the Latin rite of the Roman Church. All the other "new styles" in one way or another have been adopted from one of these three, correctly or incorrectly.

---

* In discussions with Rev. Monsignor Charles Burns, Archivist, the Secret Vatican Archives, June 1990.

† Earlier authors who claim that the mitre was first given to an abbot in 1091 by Pope Urban II were not privy to the texts, which were discovered later, on Elegius of Canterbury. Reference: Secret Vatican Archives Collection.

‡ Ironically, the Eastern Church—which did not adopt the mitre but retained the soft cap, which later developed into a crown for ceremonial liturgical functions—saw the development of an ordinary head covering known as the *kamilauka,* a clear link to its earliest roots in Rome, not in the East, as often suspected.

PRECIOUS MITRE

The precious mitre is the most important mitre of the three. It is worn by the pontiff and all bishops on the most festive occasions in the life of the Church. It is called precious because it has always been richly embroidered, often embedded with gemstones. This mitre is still in use in the Church. Contrary to popular conception, this mitre was never abolished; in fact, it is still encouraged as the most festive of mitres. Of course, today, when rich embroidery would be too costly, some allowances are made.

The precious mitre is always covered in silk cloth, of white or silver, and is elaborately embroidered with silk and gold in filigree style or designs more elaborate in nature. Whenever possible, gemstones should be sewn into the filigree. In present times, this is both costly and undesirable for some, so the use of gems, by custom, has become optional. Where they are not used however, the filigree or embroidery should still be elaborate. The lining of the precious mitre is always red silk; no other color is permitted.

The *infulae* are made of the same silk cloth and embroidery identical to that on the mitre. When gems are encrusted upon the mitre, they should properly be included on the *infulae* as well. The lining of the *infulae* is also always of red silk. The tassels must be gold (not yellow), and not red, blue for Our Lady, or any other color. The precious mitre makes use of gold tassels only!

At the base of the *infulae*, within a space of 2 inches or less (5 cm), a place is to be reserved on each fanon, or *infula,* for the depiction of the prelate's coat of arms in either gold thread or in full color embroidery. Although this practice has always been a requirement of the precious mitre, it has not always been adhered to by prelates. This one mitre makes use of the heraldic device to link it, in a special way, to the ancient traditions when all episcopal insignia (chasubles, copes, crozier, etc.) were marked by the prelates' arms.*

In days past, when different mitres were prescribed throughout the Mass, the precious mitre was used at the beginning of the ceremony until the Introit, or Opening Prayer, during the incensation, the post-Communion lavabo, and during the procession and recessional. It was also worn on Gaudete and Laetare Sundays, also known as Pink or Rose Sundays.

GOLDEN, OR ORPHREYED, MITRE

More properly called the *mitra auriphrygiata,* the golden, or orphreyed, mitre is the mitre of gold cloth, with gold silk bands for edging and borders. Gold silk was used for the flat forms, and gold silk or real spun gold thread was used to form the tassels. The lining was always red silk. The *infulae* were formed by the use of the same gold silk material, with red silk for the lining. When gold silk cloth was not available or when it was not desirable, the use of white silk, sewn with gold threads in a simple pattern so as to allude to gold in appearance, was substituted. The lining was red silk.

Prior to the eighteenth century, the orphreyed mitre was always made of the finest white silk and included two bands, known as the *circulus* and the *titulus,* always richly embroidered in gold. The use of pure gold silk for the entire mitre did not come into vogue until the post-Napoleonic period, when the Roman-design mitre gained widespread popularity. The prelate's coat of arms is not to be included on the orphreyed mitre. This mitre was worn in Advent and Lent, except on the Rose Sundays, ember days, and penitential days, as well as at

---

* This practice has lapsed because of the cost involved and the unavailability of craftspersons to undertake it. Today, modern technology takes care of this problem through the inexpensive use of the computer, electronic scanner, and embroidery machines (For suppliers, see Appendix 18.).

the ordination of bishops and priests and the blessing of abbots.

SIMPLE MITRE

The simple mitre is also called the *mitra simplex* or *mitra simplex alba* and takes its name, like the previous two mitres, by way of its appearance. The simple mitre* is just that, pure white. It was exclusively made of silk damask or linen, but this practice has been changed in the post-conciliar Church. The simple mitre is always worn on Good Friday. It is worn at all funeral Masses and when a burial service is to take place outside the liturgy of the Mass, such as a prayer service or memorial. The simple mitre must always be worn in the presence of the Pope when concelebrating Mass. No other mitre is permitted.

The lining of the simple mitre may be either red or white silk. Only the simple mitre with white lining should be worn in the presence of the Holy Father, as custom and practice have dictated for four hundred years.

The *infulae* and lining of the simple mitre are traditionally red, with the exception of the damasked mitre and in the case of a white-lined simple mitre for use in the presence of the pontiff, in which case the *infulae* would be lined in white, whereas the tassels would remain red by custom.

One might think that the damasked mitre should be in a category of its own because of its richness and larger size; however, it remains primarily a *mitra simplex*. The *mitra damasco,* or damasked mitre, is made of white silk on white silk, so that, as in the case of all damask material, a design is formed without the use of color. For the past hundred years or more, there have been two patterns used for the creation of the damask material. The first forms a pattern of diamond shapes, building upward until the point of the mitre is reached, where a fleurs-de-lis is reproduced. The second, of carefree filigree style, is more in keeping with the common damask

design familiar in Rome and throughout Italy. Neither pattern has symbolic notions. Both styles simply follow the patterns commonly used since the 1850s. Remember, the damasked mitre must have no color at all.

The height of the damasked mitre must be mentioned. Although all other mitres are seen in varying heights, the damasked mitre is almost 16 inches (40 cm) in height. The lining and fringe are always white silk.

The damasked mitre is required by all cardinals when vested in mitre in the presence of the pope. No other mitre is permitted them when in the pope's presence. Cardinals are also buried with the damasked mitre. Although the damasked mitre is not reserved to members of the Sacred College, it is, as we have seen, required of them. This is not the case with patriarchs, archbishops, and bishops, who may also make use of it anytime that the rubrics call for the simple mitre.

Keep in mind that the arms of a bishop may only be represented on the precious mitre where custom requires its use. The *simplex* and the *simplex damasco* are not permitted heraldic devices.

For centuries, the popes also made use of a *mitra simplex*. It was made of silver cloth and had gold bands upon it. It was unique in style and was reserved for the pope; however, this practice ceased during the pontificate of Pius XI.

Type of Design

There are basically four types or forms of mitre design in common use today. These are the Roman, the Gothic, the Norman, and the Anglican.

---

* Most Church documents refer to only two types of mitre: simple and ornate. In such cases, the orphreyed and precious mitres are considered the same, properly defined as ornate. Only one precious or ornate mitre is worn at a time. Therefore, all other bishops present make use of the simple mitre when the ornate or precious mitre is worn by the presider.

ROMAN MITRE

The Roman mitre is also known as the Pontiff* design; however, it should most correctly be referred to as the former. It is the largest style as well as the heaviest. It is so called because it was "invented" or adopted by the hierarchy of the Roman Curia in the early seventeenth century.

The Roman mitre is octagonal in shape, if one can imagine such a thing for headgear. Its base is as a normal mitre would be, fitting tightly around the brow; it then rises high into octagonal shape. It is, therefore, tall and very wide at the top and narrow at the bottom. Because of its height, the Roman mitre is usually pinched closed at the top. This design flaw never seemed to detract from its popularity, which remained high until the late 1960s. It is still popular today with many of the hierarchy, but this style has been somewhat modified to be slightly shorter and more rounded. This more recent, classic, distinguished style is what best can be called the Pontiff-style mitre. It was made popular by Pope Pius XII and his immediate successors, John XXIII and Paul VI. Pope John Paul II has had several made during his pontificate and makes exclusive use of the Pontiff form. The Pontiff form is an adaptation of the Roman mitre and is more aesthetic in design, although the term "Pontiff mitre" is not known to many outside Rome.

GOTHIC MITRE

The Gothic mitre is the style most commonly seen today among the clergy worldwide. Although it is tall, it is not so tall as either the Roman mitre or the special damasked mitre. The Gothic mitre's peaks may be pointed sharply, as has become the custom by some designers, but it is more common for the Gothic mitre to harken back to its roots in the Late Middle Ages and be slightly rounded at the peak.

When worn, the gothic mitre appears to gracefully envelop the head in a circular fashion. It does not appear to dominate the head, as does the Roman style. The Gothic design is at its best when it is at least 8 inches in height. Its form can carry 10 inches, but then the peak should surely be rounded instead of pointed. The Gothic suits tall and shorter prelates alike and alludes to a greater sense of dignity.

Like the Pontiff mitre, which developed gracefully from the Roman form, yet more distinctly so as to place it in a category of its own, the Gothic Mitre developed from an earlier form, the original medieval mitre now called the Norman.

NORMAN MITRE

The Norman mitre developed at a time when the Normans had great political influence. Much of that period is reflected through their customs. Although the Norman mitre did not develop, *per se,* in Normandy, it developed during the era when the Normans had their greatest worldwide influence, thus its name. The Norman mitre was very low in design. It sat low on the brow so as to dominate the forehead. It rose only about 3 inches before it turned inward and upward to form a peak. The total height was never more than 6 inches. This design resulted most clearly from the design of the Greek *mitros* and the Roman *camelaucum,* which capped the head and was bound tightly at the forehead. By the twelfth century, as the ecclesiastical mitre took form, the Norman mitre remained closest to the crown of the head.

As the ceremonial role of the bishop continued to increase, and as the mitre took on a more prominent ecclesiastical role, it began to adapt. By the late fifteenth century, it grew into what we now know as the mitre.

---

* A term developed in the years following the close of the Second Vatican Council, when Pope Paul retained the large Roman-style mitre, whereas others laid it aside for a mitre of smaller, more ancient design.

ANGLICAN MITRE

The fourth form of mitre is the Anglican mitre, mentioned here because it is sold in the United States and Britain, in particular, to Roman clergy. It is a hybrid design that harkens back to the Norman roots of the ecclesiastical mitre yet does not fully abandon the Gothic design. It is shorter than the Gothic form, yet much larger than the Norman as a result of its unique very sharp peak and point. It gives the appearance of a low, thick hat with a quick, sharp thrust to the point. The name "Anglican" has been applied to it because of the hierarchy of the Anglican Church's affinity for it when it first came back into vogue in the early 1950s.

The present forms of mitre therefore developed from Norman to Gothic and from Gothic, modified through the ages, to the Anglican style. The Roman developed from the Norman, later adopting the Gothic form to a particularly unique Italian style, only still later to be modified into what is commonly referred to as the Pontiff, the most recent style or form of acceptable design.

Ornamentation

From the earliest existence of the *mitros,* the brow was always ornamental. The introduction of the *mitros* into Greek civil society came as a result of the admiration of the laurel-bedecked *mitros* of acclaimed athletes of the era. From the earliest of times, the *mitros* had an ornamented base.

By the tenth century, when the use of the *mitros* entered the Church of Rome, the base was richly embroidered in a way that resembled a diadem or crown and that reflected the important status of the bishop, in this case the Bishop of Rome, a role reflected in the civil world as well as in the Church. From this earliest of papal mitres developed the *triregno,* or papal tiara. As time went on, the crownlike effect of a gold and jewel-encrusted diadem surrounding the base of the mitre was modified to become a richly embroidered band surrounding the entire base, often imitating the original diadem. This band was called the *circulus,* as it completely encircled the brow of the Bishop of Rome.

Soon thereafter, by the twelfth century, when most bishops made use of the mitre, the *circulus* design was repeated from the base to the peak, front and rear, forming a band that was called the *titulus.* These two bands, the *circulus* and the *titulus,* formed the sole ornamentation of the mitre for four centuries. By the late Renaissance, the precious mitre came into usage, and the rubrics required far more ornamentation than the *circulus* and *titulus* could provide. These two bands, however, remained on the orphreyed mitre until it took on a solid golden form in the eighteenth century. Until that time, this mitre was white or silver, with golden *titulus* and *circulus* completing the "orphreyed" requirements. The simplex mitre never made use of the *titulus* or *circulus.*

Modern Practice

It must be first said that the three mitres described in detail above (precious, golden, and simplex) have never been abolished. With the close of the Second Vatican Council and the changes in vesture made by Paul VI (1968–69), the design of the mitre has also greatly changed.

Whereas some other items of vesture historically went unchanged until after the Second Vatican Council (when they were then, on a whim, changed or altered without historical precedent, most often by clothing manufacturers and not the Church herself), the mitre has always been adapting, changing, and modifying. Changes to it in the past two decades, therefore, do not cause upset or distaste because the mitre was not specifically required to remain in one form only. Although the design of the mitre has always been modified, the actual components of the mitre—that is, the two flat forms, two *infulae,* lining, and fringe—must never be altered. Clearly these components remain a tradition of the Church from the time of the introduction of the mitre until the present.

What then can be accepted as adaptable? First of all, the precious mitre should carefully follow the design as set forth. The choice of the size, degree of ornamentation, and style (Norman, Gothic, Pontiff, etc.) is one for the prelate to make.

The orphreyed mitre is now most commonly seen as white or silver-threaded cloth, with the golden *titulus* and *circulus* in place. Certainly this choice, or the choice of one made entirely of gold cloth, would be acceptable. The wide range of beautiful cloth makes it possible to have the richest of mitres for a very low cost. A white or gold damasklike cloth, with solid gold-silk lining, makes the richest appearing mitre one could find—certainly so in the rounded Gothic style.

The simplex mitre should always be white. Choices abound, however; for instance, the lining could be blue, white, gold, or red.* White symbols or white cloth could also be employed; however, with the simplex mitre, colored symbols or bands are forbidden.

The practice of matching the mitre with the vestments of the day has become a popular custom in the past twenty years. Historically, the mitre is developing; it is not static. Although the Curia long ago required only three types of mitre, we now see, by predominance of local custom, that matching mitres are part of the Church's heritage. These have almost become an expression of style in place of the precious mitre.

The real question should be, will this trend last? If so, the Curia will have to set more specific guidelines to govern this form of episcopal insignia.† The problem arises, as in the case of the liberalization of sacred vestments, that the designers often have little regard for decorum and dignity, as they are more concerned with sales revenues. As a result, throughout the Church, we have seen acceptance of items that are specifically not in keeping with Church customs and that do not always follow the rubrics of the Church. Local taste and whim have affected the design of sacred vestments, often with negative results. If "matching mitres" were expressly permitted without qualifications, those same abuses would result. At present, there exist three specific types of mitre, each warranting a variety of choices that should meet both the occasion and the desires of the prelate. Therefore, the incorporation of matching mitres into the official practice of the Church needs to be promulgated by Rome, not simply adapted to personal taste.‡ Such a change would most likely refer to these matching designs as "precious mitres," as they are most commonly worn when this mitre is prescribed. If this were to be the case, then manufacturers must be mindful of the need for precious cloth in both vestment and mitre.

There are, of course, some beautiful matching mitres. The key to their use by persons who are most concerned with historical accuracy is dignity, elegance, and decorum. It should be remembered that the mitre belongs to the episcopacy—the successors to Peter and the Twelve Apostles—and not to the individual who is privileged to wear it. Therefore, personal extreme taste, however well meaning, should never replace the established regulations of the Church in this matter.

---

* Only the white lining should be worn by bishops in the pope's presence.

† It must be remembered, after all, that the mitre is an episcopal symbol, and proper respect is always warranted.

‡ Some vestments have been incorporated to match the bishop's mitre without regard for good taste or the rubrics of the Church and clearly reflected personal taste rather than Church practice.

MISCELLANEOUS

Prior to the Pauline *Motu Proprio* of 1967–1969, the mitre had ceased to be the sole prerogative of the episcopacy in the gift of the Roman Pontiff. Over the centuries, individuals entitled to its use were extended to include certain privileged canons and the protonotaries de numero, supranumerary, and *ad instar participantium*. Of course, with the exception of the de numero protonotaries, they were limited to a simplex mitre. Only the de numero and supranumerary were permitted gold-fringed fanons, and the *ad instar participantium* were permitted red-fringed fanons. The de numero protonotaries were also entitled to the orphreyed mitre under the same rubrics.

Persons whose titles were conferred before 1969 were permitted the continued usage of the privileges, titles, and styles conferred by their *bulla* of appointment. It was made clear, however, that the mitre was henceforth restricted as a jurisdictional symbol reserved for the episcopacy; therefore, those lesser prelates entitled to it at appointment were encouraged to relinquish this particular privilege. Prior to 1969, the simple mitre permitted the de numero and supranumerary protonotaries was of linen and could be worn when officiating at funerals, whereas that for *ad instar participantium* was made of white silk damask.

Abbots are entitled to two mitres, the orphreyed and the simplex, unless by special rescript or papal indult; they were additionally entitled to the precious mitre. Nearly all Abbots have traditionally made use of the Norman style, as well as the *circulus* and *titulus* ornamentation, as a means of retaining their simple state and historical traditions, despite their individual jurisdictional authority as abbot. Abbots seldom made use of a heraldic device on their mitre's fanons, or *infulae,* as this would have been incorrect. They were not generally entitled to the precious mitre, which does permit the heraldic device; rather, they made use of the simplex mitre, which did not permit the incorporation of their heraldic emblem.

Finally, only the pope, cardinals, and bishops are entitled to be buried in the mitre: the pontiff in an orphreyed or simplex mitre,* cardinals in damask mitre, and bishops in a white linen or silk mitre. Abbots, protonotaries prior to 1969, and rescripted canons are not granted this privilege.

A special note should be made about the historic peculiarity of mitred abbesses. This practice in the hierarchy of women religious in no way links these holy women to the episcopacy, as this phenomenon came into vogue long after the mitre no longer was reserved for the episcopacy. The adoption of mitre, crozier, gloves, and rings by abbesses was more a sign of her rank within the monastery in the hierarchy of sisters than it was a link to the episcopacy. It reflected the use of hierarchical emblems common to the day but did not reflect the dignity or office that they signified.

N. B.: It must be remembered that although the mitre is a symbol of episcopal dignity and jurisdiction, it should never be placed on the casket of a dead prelate. If such a gesture is desired by the Church of that place, the *galero* should be the only symbol so placed.

---

* Not simplex in reality, but, in lieu of the orphreyed mitre, a white mitre traditionally embroidered with embellishment would be proper.

CHAPTER THIRTY-SEVEN

Metropolitan or Archiepiscopal Cross and the Processional Cross

METROPOLITAN CROSS

The metropolitan cross is always carried in procession before a metropolitan archbishop. It stands between 7 and 9 feet in height and has a second, smaller crossbar above, which supports the arms of the crucified Christ. The origin of this second arm lies in the representation of the small board, or plaque, on which was hung the inscription I.N.R.I., an abbreviation that stands for the Latin phrase *Iesus Nazarenus Rex Iudaeorum* (Jesus of Nazareth, King of the Jews). This second arm became larger and more decorative in the early centuries of the Church. For the Latin rite, this decorative embellishment of the Latin cross design resulted from the artistic efforts of early Christian heraldic artists. In the Renaissance, when much of the insignia took on a more decorative style, the second transverse arm was displayed more prominently. For the Oriental rites of the Church, as well as for the Orthodox Church, the representation of this second transverse arm had very early origins and was rooted in theology, not heraldry. Each type of metropolitan cross developed independently of the other.

The crucifix of the metropolitan cross is always ornate. It can be made of precious metals or fine wood and ivory, or a combination of each. Throughout the years, gems were added to the metropolitan cross, as they were also depicted on the heraldic representation of the cross granted to archbishops. Ironically, the representation of the gemstones in heraldry did not result from their inclusion on the actual metropolitan cross because the heraldic representation had earlier origins, but as heraldry played so important a role in official Church life, the use of gems on the actual metropolitan cross was adopted as well. In present times, the metropolitan cross very much resembles the cross of earlier generations. Some modifications have been seen, but the historical-style cross has been widely retained, even though modern art is accepted in all other areas of insignia.

The metropolitan cross is now also known as the archiepiscopal cross.* Prior to the Second Vatican Council, strict regulations governed the privileges of this cross, restricting it to metropolitan archbishops in all cases. Despite the former restriction of its use in church heraldry to represent only individuals with the rank of archbishop, the cross was later assumed for processions by the titulars as well.

---

* Also seen spelled today as archepiscopal.

Technically, the archiepiscopal cross and the metropolitan cross are interchangeable only in heraldry, reserving the actual use for processions to the metropolitan. Modern custom, however, extends the privilege to all persons with archiepiscopal rank.

Therefore, although originally of heraldic invention, the metropolitan cross has come into the Church as an insignia of rank. As such, it was first recorded in A.D. 1232 by Pope Gregory IX (Ugolino di Segni), who mandated that the metropolitan cross be extended as insignia to all metropolitan archbishops and to papal legates within the jurisdiction of their mission.[1] In regulations issued in canon 5 of the documents of the fourth Lateran Council, this privilege was extended permanently to the patriarchs of Constantinople, Alexandria, Antioch, and Jerusalem. The metropolitan cross is carried before the pope under his authority as Metropolitan of the Roman Province. The three-barred cross, known as the papal cross, was implemented in the fifteenth century by heraldic artists, but there is no legal precedence to authorize recognition of its creation, although actual examples of its use can be found in history. Even Pope John Paul II has made use of a three-barred cross; yet this acceptance does little to alter the history of the three-barred cross.

The metropolitan cross is now carried at the head of the procession of the metropolitan or other archbishops. The cross is carried with the *corpus** facing forward, as is the case with all procession crosses. Prior to the Second Vatican Council, the practice was to carry the cross with the *corpus* facing backward, that is, facing the metropolitan or archbishop who follows it.

PROCESSIONAL CROSS

Everyone, today, is familiar with the processional cross. It is seen extensively at processions at the local Church. Originally this cross was similar to the metropolitan cross but smaller and without the second transverse bar yet ornate and elaborate. It was reserved for bishops, abbots, and certain other prelates. At present, however, the processional cross is used in most liturgies.

The cross that is to be carried before the ordinary should not be the same processional cross used at all Church ceremonies. At a cathedral or other prominent churches, a second, more elaborate processional cross should always be reserved for the use of the bishop or visiting bishop. In smaller parish churches, of course, this is not always feasible.

The crucifer† should be vested in cassock and surplice even when this vesture is not the custom of the locality. Never should the cross be carried by either laymen, altar servers, seminarians, or clergy who are vested in civilian clothes. The alb is accepted vesture, however, for the crucifer in those churches where this garb is the sole vesture used there. Church law and long-standing custom require the crucifer to be vested in liturgical or choir vesture in deference to the high-ranking prelate who heads the procession. This requirement precludes the use of the alb except in the case of acolytes, who often make use of a modern alblike garb.

INDULGENCE CITATION

An indulgence of three years is granted to those who faithfully reverence the processional cross by a bow of the head and the following prayer, which is devotedly recited in silence: *By the sign of the Holy Cross, deliver us from our enemies, O Our God.* (Sacred Penitentiary Apostolica, Aug. 1, 1934).

---

* Metropolitan, archiepiscopal, and episcopal processional crosses must always include the *corpus.*
† Crossbearer.

CHAPTER THIRTY-EIGHT

Guidelines of Vesture and Insignia

When an invitation calls for "white tie," "*tenue de soirée,*" or "black tie," the corresponding dress for prelates and priests is referred to as "*abito piano.*" In the English-speaking world, the term is known as "academic dress." The term *abito piano* (academic dress) comprises specific items of vesture and insignia.

FOR CARDINALS

The simar with scarlet watered-silk (moiré) sash with fringe; the pectoral cross, with gems, suspended from the chain; the scarlet silk *ferraiolo;* the scarlet *zucchetto;* scarlet stockings; and the cardinalatial ring (Cardinals would not properly wear the *biretta* with academic dress but would make use of the black plush roman hat with red and gold cords and pompon on the brim. Because so few cardinals today make use of the black plush roman hat, the scarlet wool (winter) or silk (summer) *biretta* may be used).

FOR ARCHBISHOPS AND BISHOPS

The simar with purple sash with fringe; the pectoral cross, with gems, suspended from the chain; the purple *ferraiolo;* the purple *biretta* with purple tuft; purple stockings; and the episcopal ring.

FOR APOSTOLIC PROTONOTARIES DE NUMERO

The black cassock with amaranth-red piping; purple sash with fringe; purple *ferraiolo;* the black *biretta* with red tuft; purple stockings.

FOR APOSTOLIC PROTONOTARIES SUPRANUMERARY AND HONORARY PRELATES

The black cassock with amaranth-red piping; purple sash with fringe; black *ferraiolo;* black *biretta* with black tuft.

FOR CANONS (WITH PRIVILEGES)

Canons whose privileges have not been revoked and who enjoy the use of *abito piano* specific to their rank as canon, rather than *abito piano* of a lesser rank, may make use of the dress of protonotaries supranumerary.

FOR CHAPLAINS OF HIS HOLINESS

The black cassock with purple piping; purple sash with fringe; black *ferraiolo;* black *biretta* with black tuft.

FOR PRIESTS

The black cassock, black sash (optional); the black *ferraiola* (optional); the black *biretta* with black tuft.

N. B.: For priests and monsignors of all ranks, when "black tie" or "black tie optional" is the required dress, it would also be appropriate to wear the black clerical suit and black vest.

SAMPLE FORMAL OCCASIONS WHEN ACADEMIC DRESS (*ABITO PIANO*) WOULD BE APPROPRIATE

There exist numerous scenarios, both within the Vatican and throughout the world in individual dioceses, that would require the following of formal dress regulations. These occasions call for proper attention to the dignity of the event or the circumstances that surround them. Below are listed those most common to the reader. As a general protocol rule, the most formal "official" events of civil society would correspond to the use of *abito piano*.

Papal Audiences (private) *Ferraiolo optional*	Papal Concerts; General Audiences; Public Ceremonies *Ferraiolo optional*
State Dinners: the White House, royal palaces, government houses, the United Nations, etc.	During an official visit within one's jurisdiction; a program or visit to a diocesan high school or grade school, touring a Catholic hospital or other diocesan facilities on an official basis, etc.
Formal Dinners: annual Cardinal's Dinner, the Al Smith Dinner, dinners for special Catholic organizations, and embassy receptions	Meeting honored guests at an airport or during motorcades, etc.
Academic convocations and commencements, conferral of honorary degrees	Inaugural Celebrations: royal (for kings and princes), presidential, gubernatorial, mayoral, and any reception or dinner that would accompany these events
Acceptance of personal honors, awards, and testimonials	Press conferences, television addresses and interviews from either the residence, chancery, or other diocesan property
Parades: reviewing a parade or acting as grand marshal	Banquets, concerts, the opera or theater, wedding receptions, ground-breaking ceremonies (when nonliturgical), etc.

N. B.: When an occasion calls for "black tie optional" it is the option of the prelate to wear *abito piano* with or without the *ferraiolo,* or the black clerical suit with black vest, pectoral cross placed in the side pocket.

The Pauline *Motu Proprio* of the post–Vatican II era state that the *ferraiolo* should continue to be used on the most solemn of occasions, both Church (when academic dress is required) and state. This directive has not been adhered to as most clerics and members of the hierarchy believe the *ferraiolo* to be limited to Church-related academic ceremonies. It should always be worn at state occasions. In September of 1993, at the enthronement of the new king of Belgium, Albert II, members of the hierarchy present went without the *ferraiolo.* Likewise, at the installation of the fifth president of the French Fifth Republic, Jacques Chirac, on May 17, 1995, prelates present at the Elysée went without its proper use. The *ferraiolo,* according to papal directives, should be worn on all solemn occasions.

PART FIVE

THE PAPACY

A History of Papal Titles

The title Pope comes to us from the early Italian word *papa,* which means "father figure." It was first used to identify the Bishop of Rome, as well as other bishops, in A.D. 535 by Pope St. John I of Tuscany, although a minority of scholars claim this right for St. Leo I (A.D. 440–461). The title *Pontifex Maximus* (the Greatest Pontiff) was not adopted until 1464 by Pope Paul II—for himself and his successors.

The origins of the title *Pontifex Maximus* was first applied to each member of a "sacred" society in ancient Rome. This society was known as the College of Pontiffs because its earliest members were given the financial responsibility for the upkeep and care of a certain bridge that crossed the Tiber. The name derives from the Latin *pons,* which means "bridge." The College of the Pontiffs later became responsible for regulation of the worship of the gods, who were believed to control the calendar in the pre-Christian era. The original college included three members, each holding their office for life. Later the number was increased to sixteen. The head of this college was given the title *Pontifex Maximus.* He held this title for life and, once elected, was never again permitted to leave Rome. The Pope is still referred to as *Pontifex Maximus* in some official Church documents.

The title *Summus Pontifex* came into effect in A.D. 452, when Leo the Great adopted it not only for himself but for all important bishops and Catholic leaders. The title is a Christianized adaptation of the pagan title for Roman bureaucrats. Three centuries later, the title was dropped for all but the Bishop of Rome.

From the pontificate of John XIV (A.D. 983–984), all popes have laid aside their baptismal name for the one chosen in conclave. The popes sign all official documents with the papal name or names chosen at conclave, the designation or Roman numeral denoting the number of popes who previously had borne that same name, and the initials P.P., which represent the papal titles Pope and Pontiff. This practice has been in effect since the eighth century.

In A.D. 602, Pope Gregory I (Gregory the Great) adopted the title *Servum Servorum Dei* (Servant of the Servants of God) as well as the title *Consul Dei* (God's Council), but this latter title lapsed within fifty years of its adoption.

Leo the Great added the title Vicar of Peter, which was soon altered to the more theologically correct Vicar of Christ on Earth. Pope Siricius referred to himself and all bishops of Rome in documents as early as A.D. 387 by the words *in nobis Petrus* (Peter is in us), which was later clarified in the sixth century in more accurate theological terms as *Tu es Petrus!* (You are Peter!)

The title Sovereign of the Vatican City State, affirmed by the Lateran Treaty on February 11, 1929, is the most recent title of the Roman Pontiff.* Although the popes are now only sovereigns of the small Vatican City State, through nearly all of the history of the papacy, the successors to Peter have held secular legal authority as reigning sovereigns. The first pope to hold royal status, as well as Petrine authority, was Pope Milchiades. Emperor Constantine the Great ceded the Lateran Palace and all its sizable land holdings and revenues to this pope in A.D. 312. The emperor granted the original palace to the pope along with the title *Princips Lateranensis* (Prince of the Lateran Palace), which was the first noble title of noble or sovereign status for the bishops of Rome. Pope Innocent I began to affirm that royal status by adopting the linguistic practice reserved for sovereigns known as the "royal we" in A.D. 414. This linguistic practice of speaking formally in the plural to denote personal, as well as jurisdictional authority, continued until the close of the pontificate of Paul VI in 1978, thirteen hundred years later.

Finally, the term *Sedes Apostolici* (the Apostolic See) was applied to Rome, which enhanced its prestige and preeminence, by Pope Liberius in A.D. 360. The title has been applied to the See of Peter at Rome ever since.

---

* Additional titles are Father of Princes and Kings, and Rector of the World Upon Earth. The pope is known affectionately as *il Papa* and Holy Father, as *Santo Padre* in Italian, and more formally as Santissimo Padre (Most Holy Father). In Latin, the pope is known as *Beatissimus Pater.* However, the official titles remain: Bishop of Rome, Vicar of Jesus Christ, Successor to the Prince of the Apostles, Supreme Pontiff of the Universal Church, Patriarch of the West, Primate of Italy, Archbishop and Metropolitan of the Roman Province, Sovereign of the Vatican City State, and Servant of the Servants of God.

CHAPTER FORTY

A Chronology of the Popes and Ecumenical Councils

"You are Peter [rock] and upon this rock I will build my Church and all the powers of hell shall not prevail against it. And I will give you the keys to the Kingdom of Heaven."* With these words to His disciple Simon Bar-Jona, thereafter called Peter, Jesus Christ founded the institutions of the papacy (as it has come to be called) as well as the episcopacy (of which the See of Rome is foremost) to lead and to guide His Church on earth. Christ went on to clarify what He had desired for His Church when He invested Peter with the keys of the kingdom to illustrate that Peter and his successors would hold ultimate power over the Church and her faithful.

Since the birth of the Church, there have been 263 popes as Bishops of Rome. Saint Peter founded the Church at Rome and it was there that he was martyred for his faith as its first Bishop. Peter lies buried deep beneath the basilica that bears his name; very near the site of his martyrdom. The Egyptian obelisk now in the center of St. Peter's Square stood further within the Vatican confines during the first century of the Christian era. It was the obelisk that was the last image St. Peter saw as

he died for his faith, hanging upside down on a cross. He was crucified opposite that obelisk in the Vatican marshlands outside Rome; it has stood at the Vatican as a reminder of St. Peter's martyrdom for two thousand years. Each of his 262 successors recognize it as a fate they, too, could share in as witnesses to Christ in turbulent times.

To attest to the sanctity of the early Bishops of Rome, all but one of the first fifty-eight popes have been canonized; some of these raised to the Canon of the Mass as exemplars to all the faithful. In the centuries that followed, many more of the popes have been raised to the Odor of Sanctity,† including one from the twentieth century, St. Pius X (Giuseppe Sarto), who was canonized by Pius XII in 1954.

Our Lord vested Peter and his successors with authority over the Universal Church. Joining the popes in the exercise of this authority are the bishops of the world. Each is vested with the responsibility of governing the local churches in conjunction with the pope as Supreme Pastor. Together as a College, under the presidency of the reigning pope, they

---

* Matthew 16: 18–19.

† A term used to refer to those who have been canonized.

exercise a special teaching authority known as the *Magesterium*.

In addition to the daily exercise of papal and episcopal jurisdiction and authority throughout the centuries, there have also been twenty-one Ecumenical Councils, called to clarify a dogmatic teaching or to address doctrinal or pastoral practices. The origins of the Ecumenical Councils are rooted in the Council of Jerusalem (A.D. 51) under the presidency of St. Peter. At this council, the apostles decreed that converts to Christianity were not bound by the rigors of Judaic custom of the time.

There have been more than twenty-one councils in the life of the Church, but only twenty-one, from Nicaea I (A.D. 325) to Vatican II (1962–1965), can be called Ecumenical. "A council is never ecumenical unless it is confirmed or at least accepted as such by the Successor of Peter."[1] A council cannot be forced upon a pope nor can there be an appeal of a pope's decree to a council as a pope's edict supercedes all others. As only a pope brings legitimacy to a council under the terms of canon law, he likewise becomes its head and "presides over it either personally or through legates."[2] Of the twenty-one councils, each addressed major concerns of that historic era; many affecting the life of the faithful to the present day.

The accompanying table lists the Successors to the Prince of the Apostles. Also listed in separate entry form, for historic purposes, are the names of those known collectively to history as the "antipopes" (those whose election is in doubt or whose election was clearly illegal). Those legitimately elected popes who took up residence at the papal residence at Avignon, France, are also listed with appropriate notation.

A history of the twenty-one Ecumenical Councils of the Church, including the names of those who had convened them and which pope had ratified them, providing each with the canonical status of legitimacy, are also found below—along with a presentation of the issues addressed at each as well as those persons of prominence of the time who played a leading role at council sessions.

CHRONOLOGY OF THE POPES

SAINT PETER
Simon of Bethsaida (Galilee)
died ca. A.D. 64

St. Linus (*Tuscia*) ca. 67–76

St. Anacletus (*Rome*) ca. 76–ca. 91

St. Clement I (*Rome*) ca. 91–ca. 101

St. Evaristus (*Greece*) ca. 100–ca. 109

St. Alexander I (*Rome*) ca. 109–ca. 116

St. Sixtus I (*Rome*) ca. 116–ca. 125

St. Telesphorus (*Greece*) ca. 125–ca. 136

St. Hyginus (*Greece*) ca. 138–ca. 140

St. Pius I (*Aquileia*) ca. 140–ca. 155

St. Anicetus (*Syria*) ca. 155–ca. 166

St. Soter (*Campania*) ca. 166–ca. 174

St. Eleutherius, or Eleutherus (*Nicopolis*)
    ca. 174–ca. 189*

St. Victor I (*Africa*) 189–198

St. Zephyrinus (*Rome*) 198–217

St. Callistus I [often Calixtus] (*Rome*) 217–222

St. Urban I (*Rome*) 222–230

St. Pontian (*Rome*) 21 July 230–28 Sept. 235

St. Anterus (*Greece*) 21 Nov. 235–3 Jan. 236

St. Fabian (*Rome*) 10 Jan. 236–20 Jan. 250

St. Cornelius (*Rome*) Mar. 251–June 253

St. Lucius I (*Rome*) 25 June 253–5 Mar. 254

St. Stephen I (*Rome*) 12 May 254–2 Aug. 257

St. Sixtus II (*Greece*) Aug. 257–6 Aug. 258

St. Dionysius (birthplace unknown)
    22 July 259–26 Dec. 268

St. Felix I (*Rome*) 3 Jan. 269–30 Dec. 274

St. Eutychian (*Luni*) 4 Jan. 275–7 Dec. 283

St. Gaius, or Caius (*Dalmatia*) 17 Dec. 283–22 Apr. 296

St. Marcellinus (*Rome*) 30 June 296–304;
    d. 25 Oct. 304

St. Marcellus I (*Rome*) Nov./Dec. 306–16 Jan. 308

St. Eusebius (*Greece*) 18 Apr.–21 Oct. 310

St. Miltiades, or Melchiades (*Africa*)
    2 July 311–10 Jan. 314

St. Silvester I (*Rome*) 31 Jan. 314–31 Dec. 335

St. Mark (*Rome*) 18 Jan.–7 Oct. 336

St. Julius I (*Rome*) 6 Feb. 337–12 Apr. 352

Liberius (*Rome*) 17 May 352–24 Sept. 366

St. Damasus I (*Spain*) 1 Oct. 366–11 Dec. 384

St. Siricius (*Rome*) Dec. 384–26 Nov. 399

St. Anastasius I (*Rome*) 27 Nov. 399–19 Dec. 401

St. Innocent I (*Albano*) 21 Dec. 401–12 Mar. 417

St. Zosimus (*Greece*) 18 Mar. 417–26 Dec. 418

St. Boniface I (*Rome*) 28 Dec. 418–4 Sept. 422

St. Celestine I (*Campania*) 10 Sept. 422–27 July 432

St. Sixtus, or Xystus, III (*Rome*)
    31 July 432–19 Aug. 440

St. Leo I, "the Great" (*Tuscany*)
    Aug./Sept. 440–10 Nov. 461

St. Hilarus, or Hilary of Sardinia (*Sardinia*)
    19 Nov. 461–29 Feb. 468

St. Simplicius (*Tivoli*) 3 Mar. 468–10 Mar. 483

St. Felix III (II) (*Rome*) 13 Mar. 483–1 Mar. 492†

St. Gelasius I (*Africa*) 1 Mar. 492–21 Nov. 496

Anastasius II (*Rome*) 24 Nov. 496–19 Nov. 498

St. Symmachus (*Sardinia*) 22 Nov. 498–19 July 514

St. Hormisdas (*Frosinore*) 20 July 514–6 Aug. 523

St. John I (*Tuscany*) 13 Aug. 523–18 May 526

St. Felix IV (III) (*Samnium*) 12 July 526–22 Sept. 530

Boniface II (*Rome*) 22 Sept. 530–17 Oct. 532

John II (*Rome*) 2 Jan. 533–8 May 535

---

* The source for the dates of each pontificate is the *Annuario Pontificio* of the Holy See. The dates of the pontificates up to St. Eleutherius are estimated based on historic data and legend.

† The placement of the name of St. Felix of Rome, a martyr of the early Church, among the earliest lists of popes has caused confusion over all popes named Felix. Felix III is, in fact, Felix II; subsequent pontiffs by this name are likewise numbered incorrectly. Modern lists illustrate this error by placing the inaccurate designation with the name—as this is the officially accepted number of the pontificate—and adding the historically accurate numeral in parentheses.

St. Agapitus I (*Rome*) 13 May 535–22 April 536

St. Silverius (*Campania*) 8 June 536–11 Nov. 537;
   d. 2 Dec. 537

Vigilius (*Rome*) 29 Mar. 537–7 June 555

Pelagius I (*Rome*) 16 Apr. 556–3 Mar. 561

John III (*Rome*) 17 July 561–13 July 574

Benedict I (*Rome*) 2 June 575–30 July 579

Pelagius II (*Rome*) 26 Nov. 579–7 Feb. 590

St. Gregory I, "the Great" (*Rome*)
   3 Sept. 590–12 Mar. 604

Sabinian (*Tuscany*) 13 Sept. 604–22 Feb. 606

Boniface III (*Rome*) 19 Feb. –12 Nov. 607

St. Boniface IV (*Abruzzi*) 15 Sept. 608–8 May 615

St. Deusdedit [later Adeodatus I] (*Rome*)
   19 Oct. 615–8 Nov. 618

Boniface V (*Naples*) 23 Dec. 619–25 Oct. 625

Honorius I (*Campania*) 27 Oct. 625–12 Oct. 638

Severinus (*Rome*) 28 May–2 Aug. 640

John IV (*Dalmatia*) 24 Dec. 640–12 Oct. 642

Theodore I (*Greece*) 24 Nov. 642–14 May 649

St. Martin I (*Todi*) 5 July 649–17 June 653;
   d. 16 Sept. 655

St. Eugene I (*Rome*) 10 Aug. 654–2 June 657

St. Vitalian (*Segni*) 30 July 657–27 Jan. 672

Adeodatus II (*Rome*) 11 Apr. 672–17 June 676

Donus (*Rome*) 2 Nov. 676–11 April 678

St. Agatho (*Sicily*) 27 June 678–10 Jan. 681

St. Leo II (*Sicily*) 17 Aug. 682–3 July 683

St. Benedict II (*Rome*) 26 June 684–8 May 685

John V (*Syria*) 23 July 685–2 Aug. 686

Conon [birthplace unknown]
   21 Oct. 686–21 Sept. 687

St. Sergius (*Syria*) 15 Dec. 687–9 Sept. 701

John VI (*Greece*) 30 Oct. 701–11 Jan. 705

John VII (*Greece*) 1 Mar. 705–18 Oct. 707

Sisinnius (*Syria*) 15 Jan.–4 Feb. 708

Constantine (*Syria*) 25 Mar. 708–9 Apr. 715

St. Gregory II (*Rome*) 19 May 715–11 Feb. 731

St. Gregory III (*Syria*) 18 Mar. 731–28 Nov. 741

St. Zacharias (*Greece*) 3 Dec. 741–15 Mar. 752

Stephen II (III) (*Rome*)
   26 Mar. 752–26 Apr. 757*

St. Paul I (*Rome*) 29 May 757–28 June 767

Stephen III (IV) (*Sicily*) 7 Aug. 768–24 Jan. 772

Hadrian I (*Rome*) 1 Feb. 772–25 Dec. 795

St. Leo III (*Rome*) 26 Dec. 795–12 June 816

Stephen IV (V) (*Rome*) 22 June 816–24 Jan. 817

St. Paschal I (*Rome*) 24 Jan. 817–11 Feb. 824

Eugene II (*Rome*) 5 June 824–27 Aug. 827

Valentine (*Rome*) Aug.–Sept. 827

Gregory IV (*Rome*) late 827–25 Jan. 844

Sergius II (*Rome*) Jan. 844–27 Jan. 847

St. Leo IV (*Rome*) 10 April 847–17 July 855

Benedict III (*Rome*) 29 Sept. 855–17 Apr. 858

St. Nicholas I, "the Great" (*Rome*)
   24 Apr. 858–13 Nov. 867

Hadrian II (*Rome*) 14 Dec. 867–Nov. or Dec. 872

John VIII (*Rome*) 14 Dec. 872–16 Dec. 882

Marinus I (*Gallese*) 16 Dec. 882–15 May 884

St. Hadrian III (*Rome*) 17 May 884–mid-Sept. 885

Stephen V (VI) (*Rome*) Sept. 885–14 Sept. 891

Formosus (*Porto*) 6 Oct. 891–4 Apr. 896

Boniface VI (*Rome*) Apr. 896

Stephen VI (VII) (*Rome*) May 896–Aug. 897

Romanus (*Gallese*) Aug.–Nov. 897; d.?

Theodore II (*Rome*) Nov. 897

John IX (*Tivoli*) Jan. 898–Jan. 900

Benedict IV (*Rome*) May/June 900–Aug. 903

Leo V (*Ardea*) Aug.–Sept. 903; d. early 904

Sergius III (*Rome*) 29 Jan. 904–14 Apr. 911

Anastasius III (*Rome*) ca. June 911–ca. Aug. 913

Landus (*Sabina*) ca. Aug. 913–ca. Mar. 914

John X (*Imola*) Mar./Apr. 914–May 928 (deposed);
   d. 929

Leo VI (*Rome*) May–Dec. 928

Stephen VII (VIII) (*Rome*) Dec. 928–Feb. 931

John XI (*Rome*) Feb. or Mar. 931–Dec. 935
   or Jan. 936

---

* Stephen of Rome was elected to succeed St. Zacharias as Bishop of Rome in A.D. 752 but lived only four days before succumbing to a sudden illness. He was succeeded by another Stephen of Rome (the practice of changing one's name once elected had not yet begun), who was known as Stephen II. Historians, when later compiling the list of popes, began to recognize Stephen of Rome's proper place by adding the accurate numerical sequence in parentheses. This practice is continued with all popes named Stephen.

Leo VII (*Rome*) 3 Jan. 936–13 July 939
Stephen VIII (IX) (*Rome*) 14 July 939–late Oct. 942
Marinus II (*Rome*) 30 Oct. 942–early May 946
Agapitus II (*Rome*) 10 May 946–Dec. 955
John XII (*Tusculum*) 16 Dec. 955–14 May 964*
Leo VIII (*Rome*) 4 Dec. 963–1 Mar. 965
Benedict V (*Rome*) 22 May–23 June 964
   (deposed); d. 4 July 966
John XIII (*Rome*) 1 Oct. 965–6 Sept. 972
Benedict VI (*Rome*) 19 Jan. 973–July 974
Benedict VII (*Rome*) Oct. 974–10 July 983
John XIV (*Pavia*) Dec. 983–20 Aug. 984
John XV (*Rome*) mid-Aug. 985–Mar. 996
Gregory V (*Saxony*) 3 May 996–18 Feb. 999
Sylvester II Gerberto (*Auvergne*)
   2 Apr. 999–12 May 1003
John XVII, Siccone (*Rome*) 16 May–6 Nov. 1003
John XVIII, Phasianus (*Rome*) 25 Dec. 1003–June
   or July 1009
Sergius IV, Peter (*Rome*) 31 July 1009–12 May 1012†
Benedict VIII, Theophylactus (*Tusculum*)
   17 May 1012–9 Apr. 1024
John XIX (*Rome*) 19 Apr. 1024–20 Oct. 1032
Benedict IX, Theophylactus (*Tusculum*) 21 Oct.
   1032–16 July 1048‡
Silvester III, John (*Rome*) 20 Jan.–10 Mar. 1045;
   d. 1063§
Gregory VI, John Gratian (*Rome*) 1 May 1045–
   20 Dec. 1046; d. late 1047
Clement II, Suitger, Lord of Morsleben and Horn-
   burg (*Saxony*) 24 Dec. 1046–9 Oct. 1047

Damasus II, Poppo (*Bavaria*) 17 July–9 Aug. 1048
St. Leo IX, Bruno (*Alsace*)
   12 Feb. 1049–19 Apr. 1054
Victor II, Gebhard (*Swabia*)
   13 Apr. 1055–28 July 1057
Stephen IX (X), Frederick (*Lorraine*)
   2 Aug. 1057–29 Mar. 1058
Nicholas II, Gerard (*Burgundy*) 6 Dec. 1058–
   19 or 26 July 1061
Alexander II, Anselm da Baggio (*Milan*)
   30 Sept. 1061–21 April 1073
St. Gregory VII, Hildebrand (*Tuscany*)
   22 Apr. 1073–25 May 1085‖
Bl. Victor III, Desiderius (*Benevento*)
   24 May 1086–16 Sept. 1087
Bl. Urban II, Otto di Lagery (*France*)
   12 Mar. 1088–29 July 1099
Paschal II, Raniero (*Ravenna*)
   13 Aug. 1099–21 Jan. 1118
Gelasius II, Giovanni Caetani (*Gaeta*)
   24 Jan. 1118–29 Jan. 1119
Callistus II, Guido of Burgundy (*Burgundy*)
   2 Feb. 1119–14 Dec. 1124
Honorius II, Lamberto (*Fiagnano*)
   21 Dec. 1124–13 Feb. 1130
Innocent II, Gregorio Papareschi (*Rome*)
   15/16 Dec. 1130–24 Sept. 1143
Celestine II, Guido (*Citta di Castello*)
   14 Feb. 1143–8 Mar. 1144
Lucius II, Gerardo Caccianemici (*Bologna*)
   12 Mar. 1144–15 Feb. 1145

---

* The status of the pontificates of Leo VIII and Benedict V is in question. Historians agree that John XII had been deposed by the Council of Rome (A.D. 963). The question arises as to the legitimacy of this act of deposition. If it was an illegal act, then the two succeeding popes occupied the See of Peter as antipopes. If, however, this act was valid, then Leo would have been pope and Benedict, whose election was simultaneous to Leo's, would alone be antipope.

† Peter of Rome was elected to succeed John XVIII. As he was the first Peter to be elected since the Prince of the Apostles, he chose to adopt a name rather than his baptismal name so as not to assume himself to be as great as the first pope. This practice continues to the present day, with the exception of a few pontiffs who have retained their baptismal names.

‡ Benedict IX laid aside the papal throne in September 1044, only to resume it for two brief periods: 10 March–1 May 1045 and 8 Nov. 1047–16 July 1048. He died in A.D. 1055.

§ Silvester III is considered by some as an antipope because it was not made clear whether his predecessor Benedict IX was deposed legitimately or not. This holds true, as well, for both Gregory VI and Clement II.

‖ A period of twelve months without an election of a successor to Gregory VII existed. Urban II was elected one day short of a full year after Gregory's death.

Bl. Eugene III, Bernardo di Montemagno (*Pisa*)
15 Feb. 1145–8 July 1153

Anastasius IV, Corrado (*Rome*)
8 July 1153–3 Dec. 1154

Hadrian IV, Nicholas Breakspear (*England*)
4 Dec. 1154–1 Sept. 1159

Aleander III, Rolando Bandinelli (*Siena*)
7 Sept. 1159–30 Aug. 1181

Lcuius III, Ubaldo Allucingoli (*Lucca*)
1 Sept. 1181–25 Nov. 1185

Urban III, Uberto Crivelli (*Milan*)
25 Nov. 1185–19/20 Oct. 1187

Gregory VIII, Alberto de Morra (*Benevento*)
21 Oct.–17 Dec. 1187

Clement III, Paolo Scolari (*Rome*)
19 Dec. 1187–late Mar. 1191

Celestine III, Giacinto Bobone (*Rome*)
Mar./Apr. 1191–8 Jan. 1198

Innocent III, Lotario di Segni (*Anagni*)
8 Jan. 1198–16 July 1216

Honorius III, Cencio Savelli (*Rome*)
18 July 1216–18 Mar. 1227

Gregory IX, Ugolino di Segni (*Anagni*)
19 Mar. 1227–22 Aug. 1241

Celestine IV, Goffredo Castiglione (*Milan*)
25 Oct.–10 Nov. 1241

Innocent IV, Sinibaldo Fieschi (*Genoa*)
25 June 1243–7 Dec. 1254

Alexander IV, Rinaldo di Segni (*Anagni*)
12 Dec. 1254–25 May 1261

Urban IV, Jacques Pantaléon (*Troyes*)
29 Aug. 1261–2 Oct. 1264

Clement IV, Guy Foulques (*France*)
5 Feb. 1265–29 Nov. 1268

Bl. Gregory X, Teobaldo Visconti (*Piacenza*)
1 Sept. 1271–10 Jan. 1276

Bl. Innocent V, Peter of Tarentaise (*Savoy*)
21 Jan.–22 June 1276

Hadrian V, Ottobono Fieschi (*Genoa*)
22 July–18 Aug. 1276

John XXI, Petrus Iuliani (*Portugal*)
8 Sept. 1276–20 May 1277

Nicholas III, Giovanni Gaetano Orsini (*Rome*)
25 Nov. 1277–22 Aug. 1280

Martin IV, Simon de Brie (*France*)
22 Feb. 1281–28 Mar. 1285

Honorius IV, Giacomo Savelli (*Rome*)
2 Apr. 1285–3 Apr. 1287

Nicholas IV, Girolamo Masci (*Ascoli*)
22 Feb. 1288–4 Apr. 1292

St. Peter Celestine V, Pietro del Murrone (*Isernia*)
5 July–13 Dec. 1294; d. 19 May 1296

Boniface VIII, Benedetto Caetano (*Anagni*)
24 Dec. 1294–11 Oct. 1303

Bl. Benedict XI, Nicholas Boccasini (*Treviso*)
22 Oct. 1303–7 July 1304

Clement V, Bertrand de Got (*France*)
5 June 1305–20 Apr. 1314*

John XXII, Jacques d'Euse (*Cahors*)
7 Aug. 1316–4 Dec. 1334

Benedict XII, Jacques Fournier (*France*)
20 Dec. 1334–25 Apr. 1342

Clement VI, Pierre Roger (*France*)
7 May 1342–6 Dec. 1352

Innocent VI, Etienne Aubert (*France*)
18 Dec. 1352–12 Sept. 1362

Bl. Urban V, Guillaume de Grimoard (*France*)
28 Sept. 1362–19 Dec. 1370

Gregory XI, Pierre Roger de Beaufort (*France*)
30 Dec. 1370–27 Mar. 1378

Urban VI, Bartolomeo Prignano (*Naples*)
8 Apr. 1378–15 Oct. 1389†

---

* Popes from Clement V to Gregory XI removed themselves from Rome to the papal residence in southern France. This period of seventy-three years is known collectively as the Avignon Papacy.

† Immediately following the Avignon Papacy was a period known as the Western Schism, encompassing four pontificates—from Urban VI to Gregory XII—and three antipopes. It began as a jurisdictional argument between those who believed that the College of Bishops in general council superseded the universal authority of the pope and those who correctly adhered to papal supremacy. The Council at Florence and later at Pisa attempted to address the schism but it was not until the Council of Constance (A.D. 1414–1418) that the issue was resolved in favor of the papacy. At this same council, the antipope John XXIII was deposed and the legally elected, yet factional, Gregory XII abdicated so that a post-Schism conciliatory candidate could be elected.

Boniface IX, Pietro Tomacelli (*Naples*)
2 Nov. 1389–1 Oct. 1404

Innocent VII, Cosmo Migliorati (*Sulmona*)
17 Oct. 1404–6 Nov. 1406

Gregory XII, Angelo Correr (*Venice*) 30 Nov. 1406–
4 July 1415; d. 18 Oct. 1417

Martin V, Oddone Colonna (*Rome*)
11 Nov. 1417–20 Feb. 1431

Eugene IV, Gabriele Condulmer (*Venice*)
3 Mar. 1431–23 Feb. 1447

Nicholas V, Tommaso Parentucelli (*Sarzana*)
6 Mar. 1447–24 Mar. 1455

Callistus III, Alfonso Borgia (*Jativa, Valencia*)
8 Apr. 1455–6 Aug. 1458

Pius II, Enea Silvio Piccolomini (*Siena*)
19 Aug. 1458–15 Aug. 1464

Paul II, Pietro Barbo (*Venice*)
30 Aug. 1464–26 July 1471

Sixtus IV, Francesco della Rovere (*Savona*)
9 Aug. 1471–12 Aug. 1484

Innocent VIII, Giovanni Battista Cibo (*Genoa*)
29 Aug. 1484–25 July 1492

Alexander VI, Rodrigo de Borgia (*Jativa, Valencia*)
11 Aug. 1492–18 Aug. 1503

Pius III, Francesco Todeschini-Piccolomini (*Siena*)
22 Sept.–18 Oct. 1503

Julius II, Guiliano della Rovere (*Savona*)
1 Nov. 1503–21 Feb. 1513

Leo X, Giovanni de'Medici (*Florence*)
11 Mar. 1513–1 Dec. 1521

Hadrian VI, Adrian Florensz (*Utrecht*)
9 Jan. 1522–14 Sept. 1523

Clement VII, Giulio de 'Medici (*Florence*)
19 Nov. 1523–25 Sept. 1534

Paul III, Alessandro Farnese (*Rome*)
13 Oct. 1534–10 Nov. 1549

Julius III, Giovanni Ciocchi del Monte (*Rome*)
8 Feb. 1550–23 Mar. 1555

Marcellus II, Marcella Cervini (*Montepulciano*)
9 Apr.–1 May 1555

Paul IV, Gian Pietro Carafa (*Naples*)
23 May 1555–18 Aug. 1559

Pius IV, Giovan-Angelo de'Medici (*Milan*)
25 Dec. 1559–9 Dec. 1565

St. Pius V, Antonio Ghislieri (*Bosco*)
7 Jan. 1566–1 May 1572

Gregory XIII, Ugo Buonncompagni (*Bologna*)
14 May 1572–10 Apr. 1585

Sixtus V, Felice Peretti (*Grottammare*)
24 Apr. 1585–27 Aug. 1590

Urban VII, Giambattista Castagna (*Rome*)
15–27 Sept. 1590

Gregory XIV, Niccolo Sfondrati (*Cremona*)
5 Dec. 1590–16 Oct. 1591

Innocent IX, Giovan Antonio Facchinetti (*Bologna*)
29 Oct.–30 Dec. 1591

Clement VIII, Ippolito Aldobrandini (*Florence*)
30 Jan. 1592–5 Mar. 1605

Leo XI, Alessandro de'Medici (*Florence*)
1–27 Apr. 1605

Paul V, Camillo Borghese (*Rome*)
16 May 1605–28 Jan. 1621

Gregory XV, Alessandro Ludovisi (*Bologna*)
9 Feb. 1621–8 July 1623

Urban VIII, Maffeo Barberini (*Florence*)
6 Aug. 1623–29 July 1644

Innocent X, Giovanni Battista Pamphili (*Rome*)
15 Sept. 1644–1 Jan. 1655

Alexander VII, Fabio Chigi (*Siena*)
7 Apr. 1655–22 May 1667

Clement IX, Giulio Rospigliosi (*Pistoia*)
20 June 1667–9 Dec. 1669

Clement X, Emilio Altieri (*Rome*)
29 Apr. 1670–22 July 1676

Bl. Innocent XI, Benedetto Odescalchi (*Como*)
21 Sept. 1676–12 Aug. 1689

Alexander VIII, Pietro Ottoboni (*Venice*)
6 Oct. 1689–1 Feb. 1691

Innocent XII, Antonio Pignatelli (*Spinazzola*)
12 July 1691–27 Sept. 1700

Clement XI, Giovanni Francesco Albani (*Urbino*)
23 Nov. 1700–19 Mar. 1721

Innocent XIII, Michelangelo dei Conti (*Rome*)
8 May 1721–7 Mar. 1724

Benedict XIII, Pietro Orsini (*Gravina*)
29 May 1724–21 Feb. 1730

Clement XII, Lorenzo Corsini (*Florence*)
12 July 1730–6 Feb. 1740

Benedict XIV, Prospero Lambertini (*Bologna*)
17 Aug. 1740–3 May 1758
Clement XIII, Carlo Rezzonico (*Venice*)
6 July 1758–2 Feb. 1769
Clement XIV, Giovanni Ganganelli (*Rimini*)
19 May 1769–22 Sept. 1774
Pius VI, Gionangelo Braschi (*Cesena*)
15 Feb. 1775–29 Aug. 1799
Pius VII, Barnaba Chiaramonti (*Cesena*)
14 Mar. 1800–20 July 1823
Leo XII, Annibale della Genga (*Fabriano*)
28 Sept. 1823–10 Feb. 1829
Pius VIII, Francesco Castiglioni (*Cingoli*)
31 Mar. 1829–30 Nov. 1830
Gregory XVI, Bartolomeo Cappellari (*Belluno*)
2 Feb. 1831–1 June 1846
Pius IX, Giovanni Ferretti (*Senigallia*)
16 June 1846–7 Feb. 1878

Leo XIII, Gioacchino Pecci (*Anagni*)
20 Feb. 1878–20 July 1903
St. Pius X, Giuseppe Sarto (*Treviso*)
4 Aug. 1903–20 Aug. 1914
Benedict XV, Giacomo della Chiesa (*Genoa*)
3 Sept. 1914–22 Jan. 1922
Pius XI, Achille Ratti (*Milan*)
6 Feb. 1922–10 Feb. 1939
Pius XII, Eugenio Pacelli (*Rome*)
2 Mar. 1939–9 Oct. 1958
John XXIII, Angelo Roncalli (*Bergamo*)
28 Oct. 1958–3 June 1963
Paul VI, Giovanni Battista Montini (*Brescia*)
21 June 1963–6 Aug. 1978
John Paul I, Albino Luciani (*Belluno*)
26 Aug.–28 Sept. 1978*

JOHN PAUL II
"Gloriosamente Regnante,"
Karol Wojtyla
Born: 18 May 1920
Ordained to the Priesthood:
1 November 1946
Ordained a Bishop: 28 September 1958
Created a Cardinal-Priest in the Title of
San Ceasareo in Palatio: 26 June 1967
Elected Supreme Pontiff and Bishop of
Rome: 16 October 1978

---

* Although Saint Peter was known also as Simon Peter, Albino Luciani was the first pope to officially assume two names when he was elected pope in 1978. As John Paul I, he chose the name of the pope who had named him a bishop, John XXIII, and the pope who had named him a cardinal, Paul VI. The duality of his pontifical name surprised many and was so innovative that during his brief pontificate the press frequently included a hyphen (John–Paul I) to illustrate the uniqueness of his choice of names. With the exception of France, this style was not adopted by the press for his successor, the present pontiff, John Paul II.

THE ANTIPOPES

These men held uncanonical claims to the papal office. Their names are listed below with the dates of their illegitimate reigns.

St. Hippolytus, 217–235
Novatian, 251
Felix II, 355–22 Nov. 365
Ursinus, 366–367
Eulalius, 27 Dec. 418–419
Lawrence, 498; 501–505
Dioscorus, 22 Sept. 530–14 Oct. 530
Theodore, 687
Paschal, 687
Constantine, 28 June 767–769
Philip, 31 July 768; retired to his monastery
    on this day
John, 844
Anastasius, Aug. 855–Sept. 855
Christopher, July 903–Jan. 904
Boniface VII, June 974–July 974; Aug. 984–July 985
John XVI, Apr. 997–Feb. 998
Gergory, 1012
Benedict X, 5 Apr. 1058–24 Jan. 1059
Honorius II, 28 Oct. 1061–1072
Clement III, 25 June 1080–8 Sept. 1100

Theodoric, 1100
Albert, 1102
Sylvester IV, 18 Nov. 1105–1111
Gregory VIII, 8 Mar. 1118–1121
Celestine II, Dec. 1124
Anacletus II, 14 Feb. 1130–25 Jan. 1138
Victor IV, Mar. 1139–29 May 1138;
    submitted to Pope Innocent II
Victor IV, 7 Sept. 1159–20 Apr. 1164
Paschal III, 22 Apr. 1164–20 Sept. 1168
Callistus III, Sept. 1168–29 Aug. 1178;
    submitted to Pope Alexander III
Innocent III, 29 Sept. 1179–1180
Nicholas V, 12 May 1328–25 Aug. 1330
Clement VII, 20 Sept. (31 Oct.) 1378–25 Aug. 1330
Benedict XIII, 28 Sept. 1394–23 May 1423
Alexander V, 26 June 1409–3 May 1410
John XXIII, 17 May 1410–29 May 1415
    (deposition by Council of Constance ended the
    Western Schism; d. 22 Nov. 1419)
Felix V, 5 Nov. 1439–7 Apr. 1449

THE TWENTY-ONE ECUMENICAL COUNCILS OF THE ROMAN CATHOLIC CHURCH

Councils have not always been uniformly numbered. The numbering given below came into general use only after the Roman Edition of the Councils was issued under Pope Paul V (1605–21). The distinctive marks of an Ecumenical Council now required by canon law such as summons by the pope and definition of those entitled to vote, have only become established in the course of time and are subject to change in future pontificates.

PLACE NAME	YEAR(S)	CONVENED BY	PONTIFICATE	RATIFIED BY
1. Nicaea I	325	Emperor Constantine the Great	Silvester I, also present were Hosius of Cordoba and the Priests Vitus and Vincent	Silvester I
2. Constantinople I	381	Emperor Theodosius I	Damasus I	Debatable, either in 382 or after 490
3. Ephesus	431	Emperor Theodosius II	Celestine I	Celestine I
4. Chalcedon	451	Emperor Marcian	Leo I	Leo I
5. Constantinople II	553	Emperor Justinian	Vigilius	Debatable, either Vigilius or Gregory I The Great, 591
6. Constantinople III	680–81	Emperor Constantine III	Agatho, represented by the Priests Theodore and George and the Deacon John	Leo II, 682
7. Nicaea II	787	Empress Irene Charlemagne called the counter-Synod to Frankfurt in 794	Hadrian I, represented by the Bishop Peter and the Abbot Peter	Debatable, either by Hadrian I or after 866
8. Constantinople IV	869–70	Emperor Basil I	Hadrian II, represented by the Bishops Donatus, Stephen, and Marinus	Hadrian II

PARTICIPATION	SUBJECT/OUTCOME/TEACHING
About 250 bishops; only 5 from the West.	Nicene Creed (against Arius); consubstantiality of the Son with the Father. Twenty dogmas.
About 150 Eastern bishops.	Nicene-Constantinopolitan Creed: divinity of the Holy Spirit. Four dogmas.
About 250 Eastern bishops.	Solemn definition of the doctrine of the Incarnation of the divine Logos, and of the Virgin Mary as the "Mother of God" (against Nestorius who taught that the Virgin could be called only "Mother of Christ"). Condemnation of Monophysitism, Necessity of Grace (against Pelagius). Six dogmas.
About 630 Eastern bishops; from the West, only 5 papal legates.	The person of Christ contains two natures, without confusion, without change, without division, without separation (against the monophysite doctrine of Eutyches). Twenty-eight dogmas.
About 160 Eastern bishops, and about 10 from the West.	Against Origen and his teaching (e.g., creation from eternity and the ultimate restoration of *all* things): against the "Three Chapters" of the Nestorians.
174 Eastern bishops.	In Christ are two wills, one divine and one human (condemnation of Monothelitism). No dogma.
About 300 Eastern bishops.	Meaning and propriety of the veneration of images (against the Iconoclasts). Twenty dogmas.
102 Eastern bishops.	Rules of faith against current theological errors. Deposition of Photius, Patriarch of Constantinople. Twenty-seven dogmas.

Place Name	Year(s)	Convened By	Pontificate	Ratified By
9. Lateran I	1123	Calixtus II	Calixtus II	Calixtus II
10. Lateran II	1139	Innocent II	Innocent II	Innocent II
11. Lateran III	1179	Alexander III	Alexander III	Alexander III
12. Lateran IV	1215	Innocent III	Innocent III	Innocent III
13. Lyons I	1245	Innocent IV	Innocent IV	Innocent IV
14. Lyons II	1274	Gregory X	Gregory X	Gregory X
15. Vienne	1311–12	Clement V (Avignon)	Clement V	Clement V
16. Constance	1414–18	John XXIII at the instigation of Emperor Sigismund	John XXIII deposed during the Council: Gregory XII and Martin V	Martin V
17. Basle-Ferrara-Florence	1431–45	Eugene IV	Eugene IV	Eugene IV
18. Lateran V	1512–17	Julius II	Julius II, Leo X	Leo X
19. Trent	1545–63	Paul III	Paul III, Julius III, Pius IV	Pius IV
20. Vatican I	1869–70	Pius IX	Pius IX	Pius IX
21. Vatican II	1962–65	John XXIII	John XXIII, Paul VI	Paul VI

PARTICIPATION	SUBJECT/OUTCOME/TEACHING
Between 300 and 997 participants.	The controversy on Investiture: questions of moral teaching and Church discipline. Confirmation of the Concordat of Worms. Twenty-five dogmas.
Up to 1000 participants, including 800 abbots.	Against the schism of Anaclete II. Questions of moral teaching. Thirty dogmas.
300 bishops and 400 priests from the West.	Decree on papal elections (two-thirds majority). Against the Albigensians and Waldensians. Twenty-seven chapters.
412 bishops and 338 priests.	Questions of moral teaching and Church discipline. Against the Cathari, Albigensians, and Waldensians, and against Abbot Joachim of Calabria. Transubstantiation of the Eucharist. Annual confession and communion. Seventy chapters.
140 to 150 Western bishops.	Deposition of the Emperor Frederick II. Twenty-two chapters.
Some 500 bishops and 570 priests from East and West. The Emperor Michael Palaeologus also attended.	Reunion with the Greek Church. Regulations for the holding of Conclaves. Crusade. Thirty-one chapters.
Nearly 300 bishops from the West.	Dissolution of the Templars. Controversy over Franciscan poverty. Reform decrees.
32 cardinals, 183 bishops, 100 abbots, and 350 priests.	Settlement of the Western Schism. Decree *Sacrosancta* on the council's supremacy over the pope. Decree *Frequens* on the frequency of councils. More reform decrees. Election of Martin V. Against Wyclif and Hus: the latter burned.
About 150 Western, and several Eastern bishops. (At Ferrara 700 Greek bishops and theologians were present, and also the Emperor John VIII Palaeologus.)	Reunion with the Greek Church in 1439. Protocol of Union signed by 115 Western and 33 Eastern bishops, and by the Emperor John VIII Palaeologus. Union with the Armenians in 1439 and with the Jacobites in 1442.
15 cardinals, 79 bishops—almost all Italians.	Against the schismatic Council of Pisa. Ecclesiastical reforms.
70 bishops at the start, 252 at the final session.	Against Protestantism. Doctrine on Scripture and Tradition, Original Sin, Justification, the Sacraments and the Sacrifice of the Mass, the Veneration of Saints. Reform decrees.
774 bishops from all parts of the world.	The relationship between Faith and Reason. Papal Primacy and Infallibility.
More than 2300 bishops from all parts of the world.	Constitutions on the Liturgy and on the Church. Decrees on media of mass-communications, the Church in the modern world, and the non-Christian religions.

abbot A superior with jurisdiction over an abbey. Just as there are titular bishops, there are also titular abbots; their titular title is one of an abbey that no longer exists. The title Archabbot is given to those who have jurisdiction over archabbeys, a title of distinction for abbeys of particular import. Those having special ties with the Holy See are as follows: (1) *Abbots Nullius,* who, in addition to having jurisdiction over their abbey, have jurisdiction over an ecclesiastical territory with both clergy and faithful, called an abbey *nullius dioceoses* because its jurisdiction is independent of any diocese. The abbot nullius has quasi-episcopal powers of jurisdiction. Abbots nullius have a place in Papal Chapel and are named or confirmed by the pope. They are often nominated to a titular see as bishops. (2) *Abbots general or president* are those abbots with jurisdiction over their respective orders (and are therefore resident in their respective generalates) or over the "congregations" into which their order may be divided. (3) The *abbot primate* of the Benedictines is *primo inter pares* of all Benedictine abbots and resides in Rome. The Eastern rite counterparts of the abbot are a *hegumen* and an *archimandrite.* The term *abbot* is derived from the Greek word for father.

abito filetta Literally, a habit with frills and braids but, in reality, the manner to describe the most formal vesture for nonprelatial clerics and seminarians. It refers to ceremonies, most commonly in conjunction with the formal civil life of the Church rather than the ecclesiastical life.

abito paonazzo The Italian proper term applied to choral or **choir dress** (q.v.).

abito piano The vesture appropriate for formal, non-liturgical occasions consisting primarily of the simar, *ferraiolo, fascia, zucchetto,* and pectoral cross.

abito scuro The proper Italian-language term applied to a mode of dress for the laity that requires conservative, dark clothing. *Abito scuro* is required (yet not always adhered to) for all visiting the Holy Father in private for papal audiences, for Vatican concerts in the presence of the Holy Father, and for private visits with cardinals.

academic dress The English-language term applied to **abito piano** (q.v.).

accosted A heraldic term meaning side-by-side as it applies to the division of the shield and the placement of emblems.

achievement A heraldic term meaning a full coat of arms encompassing the crest, helmet, mantling, shield, motto, and, when rank permits, either the *galero* for ecclesiastics or the coronet, supporters, the pavilion, and the insignia of orders for the laity.

Acta Apostolicae Sedis The official document of the government of the Holy See, published annually. Pontifical laws are promulgated by publication in it and generally go into effect three months after publication. Before 1908 it was called *Acta Sanctae Sedis.* Papal honors for the clergy and the laity are first published here, and one cannot assume these titles and the honors associated with them until the publication of the nomination takes place.

addetti; addetti di segretaria; addetti tecnici   Staff of various grades and specialties within the departments of the Roman Curia.

ad limina apostolorum   The periodic visit, normally every five years, of the residential bishops to the pope to report on the conditions of their dioceses. The term translates "on the threshold," meaning the pilgrimage of the bishops to the tombs of Peter and Paul. The tradition of the *ad limina* visit dates to Pope St. Leo III (A.D. 810). The *ad limina* is divided into three parts: the visit to the pope, during which the visiting bishop reaffirms his fidelity to him; the visit to the apostles' tombs; and the report (known as *relatio*) that details all the statistics and activities of the diocese during the previous five years. Meetings with the appropriate curial offices is also a part of the *relatio*.

aiutante di studio   An official of the Roman Curia of a junior rank.

allocutio   The Italian term for an allocution or prolonged, formal address by the pope used for a select audience such as a head of state or government with their accompanying entourage, a group of pilgrims, or the **ad limina** (q.v.) visiting bishops of a particular region or province. Although the content of the allocution is released for general review and study, the intent is to speak to a specific audience in relation to topics of specific concern to them and to the Holy See.

altar   From the Latin *altus,* meaning high or exalted place of sacrifice. Reserved for worship, the altar is the table of the Eucharist on which are celebrated the Sacred Mysteries.

amice   The white linen cloth, with ties, used to cover the neck and collar of a cleric when wearing sacred vestments. *See also* Chapter 31, Sacred Vestments.

Annuario Pontificio   The yearbook of the Holy See's activities, consisting of all the official statistics of the Church. It is published by the Secretariat of State at the beginning of each year. It concerns itself primarily with the government of the Church and is printed in Italian. The *Annuario* becomes available for sale in February of each year.

antependium   The cloth of precious fabric or weaving that covers the entire front of the altar from the lowest part of the tabletop to the floor, Gospel side to Epistle side. These cloths were used during the Tridintine period and were continued as optional in the post–Vatican II period. Today, the *antependium* is most commonly changed to match the liturgical color. The most beautiful of these are those designed in the Renaissance or high Medieval motif. The usage of symbols, including those depicting Our Lord, the Blessed Sacrament, or Our Lady and the Saints are all acceptable, provided they are presented with dignity. There is no blessing of the *antependium*.

apostolic administrator   A prelate who is placed in charge of a canonical jurisdiction known as an apostolic administration. This title is also conferred upon a chargé of the Holy See in extraordinary cases, when also ruling a diocese or a part of it. Apostolic administrators, because they are extraordinary rulers of dioceses, either vacant or filled, either temporary or permanent, are named only if the normal rule of the dioceses or territory is in some way impeded. They may be named for disciplinary reasons, because of changes in national frontiers, or because of difficulties with civil governments.

apostolic brief   A less formal means of informing the faithful about matters concerning the Church, such as ecclesiastical grants and concessions, as well as administrative matters.

apostolic bull   A document that derives its name from the Latin *bulla,* meaning "leaden seal," which is used to imprint the reigning pope's insignia, or seal, on the document. The most solemn of the papal documents, the bull creates a prelate a cardinal (although the *biglietto* announces it). Bishops are officially appointed by the papal bull, as are other high-ranking officials. It is also the document that announces beatifications and canonizations.

Apostolic Chancery   The former office responsible for the issuance of papal bulls and briefs and for the guardianship of the Fisherman's Seal. In the reorganization of the Roman Curia by Pope Paul VI, the Apostolic Chancery was abolished, and its responsibilities were vested in the Secretariat of State.

Apostolic Constitution A formal papal document with the force of law used by the Holy Father to promulgate law. It is often abbreviated as "ap. cons."

apostolic delegate A prelate who most commonly holds a titular see as an archbishop and who represents the Holy See in a nation, but without diplomatic standing. He is tied to the Church of that nation and not its government.

apostolic delegation Permanent representation of the Holy See in a nation, but without diplomatic standing, either because the territory is not independent or because there are no diplomatic relations between that nation and the Holy See. The head of an apostolic delegation is a delegate, never a nuncio unless he holds this title by some other right or designation.

apostolic exhortation Known in Latin as *Adhortatio Apostolica,* a special address by the pope; used for the teaching of the faithful in such a way as to appear more potent in content, such as a homily. It is most commonly used as a means of reinforcing Church teaching on a well-defined dogma.

Apostolic Signatura The highest of the tribunals of the Roman Curia. It serves as the supreme court of the Vatican City State and the Church. It has competence over the lower courts and has jurisdiction in cases involving the personnel and decisions of the Sacred Rota. It was established by Pope Eugene IV in the fifteenth century.

apostolic succession The laying of hands, through episcopal ordination, from St. Peter to the present, forming a college of bishops that originated at the beginning of the Church and continues for all time.

archbishop (1) A bishop who, besides having jurisdiction over an archdiocese where he exercises immediate jurisdiction, exercises a certain authority and enjoys certain privileges of honor, having mediate jurisdiction over one or more dioceses, which, together with his own, compose an ecclesiastical province, and whose bishops are called suffragans,

whereas the archbishop in this case is called metropolitan. The metropolitan archbishop has a right to possess the pallium, which he must request of the pope within three months after his nomination. (Example: The ecclesiastical province of Philadelphia is composed of the archdiocese of Philadelphia, whose titular is the metropolitan archbishop, and whose suffragan dioceses are Allentown, Altoona-Johnstown, Erie, Greensburg, Harrisburg, Pittsburgh, and Scranton.) (2) The bishop of a nonmetropolitan archdiocese, called "immediately subject" to the Holy See. (3) The bishop of a residential diocese who has the personal title of archbishop (therefore addressed as "the archbishop-bishop of . . .") for one of the following reasons: (a) an honor bestowed by the pope; (b) if there is precedent that the titular of the particular diocese is a personal or titular archbishop (such as the suburbicarian sees surrounding Rome); (c) if the bishop is at the same time the head of a papal mission, such as a nuncio; (d) if he is at the same time coadjutor to an archbishop or, to all purposes, retains another residential archdiocese. (4) Titular archbishops who are consecrated with the title of an archdiocese that no longer exists, but the memory of which the Church keeps alive. (Such titles are generally given to nuncios, pronuncios, apostolic delegates, secretaries of Roman congregations, etc). All archbishops can be assistants at the papal throne; some archbishops have the title Primate.

archdiocese An ecclesiastical territory, ruled by an archbishop. It can be a metropolitan see (in which case it has one or more suffragan dioceses, forming with them an ecclesiastical province (e.g., Philadelphia, New York), or it can be immediately subject to the Holy See (neither having suffragan dioceses nor forming part of an ecclesiastical province).

archpriest A priest chosen to assist the local bishop or to substitute for him at specific functions. A cardinal-archpriest is that cardinal representing the Holy Father in specific responsibilities in Rome (i.e., Cardinal-Archpriest of the Roman Basilicas).

argent A heraldic term meaning silver; one of the two heraldic metals. It is always depicted as white.

armiger A heraldic term to connote one who is entitled to bear arms. Also known as armigerous.

attaché *Addetto,* a title of a junior official within the Secretariat of State and in the Roman congregations and councils.

attaché of nunciature *Addetto di Nunziatura,* the grade or level with which ecclesiastical diplomats begin their careers. *See also* Chapter 4, Papal Diplomacy.

Attivitá Della Santa Sede A publication of the Holy See that records the important events, dates, and appointments of the pope and Curia in the preceding year.

Aula della Udienze (Hall of Audiences) The modern audience hall to the left of St. Peter's Basilica and just behind the offices of the Congregation for the Doctrine of the Faith. Originally called the *Nervi,* it has since been renamed the Paul VI Audience Hall after the pope who ordered its construction.

azure A heraldic term for the color blue; one of the five principal heraldic colors.

baldachin (*baldachino*) (1) An ecclesiastical architectural term connoting the great canopy above the main altar of a cathedral or church. (2) The canopy of wood or marble that, in the past, surmounted the *cathedra* of a bishop. The continuation of this practice in new construction has been forbidden; however, the Church has been careful to reaffirm the historic significance of those already existing. (3) The cloth canopy in ecclesiastical or civil usage that connotes dignity, authority, and supremacy. Almost always fashioned of rich cloth, often embroidered, an example of a civil usage would be the canopy of a throne for an emperor, a king, or a prince. An ecclesiastical example would be the canopies over each of the cardinal-electors, in conclave, symbolizing equal authority during the *Sede Vacante.* Upon election, the canopies of all but the new pope were lowered as the first symbolic gesture of obedience to the new pope. Because of the increase in the size of the Sacred College, in relation to the small size of the Sistine Chapel, the canopies have not been used in the past two elections. They have not, however, been abolished. The term *baldachin* comes from the word

meaning "Baghdad," where, at the time, the most richly embroidered cloth originated.

base A heraldic term used to describe the bottom portion of a shield.

basilica (1) A term used to describe a kingly hall. When Emperor Constantine began building the first churches in Rome, the only architectural style with which he was familiar was that of the great ceremonial hall; thus, he copied this style for the first Catholic churches that were not previously built as private residences. A basilica always had a forecourt, with trees and a fountain, and a colonnade, or loggia, enclosing it. The great hall was attached to this loggia. A wonderful example of the basilica-style architecture is the Basilica of St. Paul Outside the Walls in Rome. (2) The churches of great importance in the life and history of the Church. There are two types: The major basilicas are those great churches in Rome. These include St. Peter's in the Vatican, St. Paul Outside the Walls, St. John Lateran, St. Mary Major, St. Lawrence Outside the Walls, and St. Sebastian, as well as the Basilica of the Holy Cross in Jerusalem. The minor basilicas are other important churches in Rome and throughout the world to which the successors of Peter have bestowed upon them the title of basilica. These churches have been recognized for specific historic and liturgical reasons and thus carry high honors and privileges. One of these includes the great papal symbol, the *ombrellino,* which originated as the canopy carried over the pontiff and which subsequently emerged, heraldically, as an honor reserved to the papacy. The most recently named basilica in the United States is the Basilica of the National Shrine of the Immaculate Conception in Washington, D.C.

basque A soft, black, beretlike hat worn by priests, seminarians, and religious brothers, most commonly in the southern European states. It takes its name from the region in France and Spain from where it came: Originally worn by Basque peasants, it is still worn by farmers of that region. The basque is never worn at liturgical functions. It is the counterpart of the *cappello romano,* albeit simpler; it does not take the place of the *biretta.*

bells Bells have been known throughout history as *Vox Deo* (the voice of God). The use of bells in the church can be traced to the eighth century. The largest used bell still in existence in Rome dates from 1093 in the campanile of San Benedetto in Piscinula in the Trastevere section of the city. During the era of the Papal States, an edict was issued that forbade the ringing of bells before seven in the morning; therefore, all of Europe, and later the world, adopted this practice, with the exception of the monasteries whose members may have been out in the field or dairies long before dawn and would need to be called back to chapel. Bells were used inside church during the Mass in place of (or simultaneous to) incense, primarily at the imposition and elevations, although they were rung in different rites at other times as well. The original purpose for the use of bells at Mass was to alert the sacristan to the part of the celebration of the Mass the priest was at; the sacristan, in turn, was waiting at the campanile so as to ring the tower bell to alert those who could not come to Mass, but who were praying at that same hour. The bell also served as a hurry call for field workers who could not attend Mass but who knew at the call of the bell that they could hurry to the door of the church to receive the Blessed Sacrament and quickly return to their chores. Many persons think that the use of bells during Mass have been abolished. This simply is not so. Their use has been optional for some time, but even papal ceremonies still make use of them. As one travels throughout the world, one would be surprised to see that bells at Mass are still widely employed. The outdoor bells of St. Peter's ring at different times for specific purposes. The largest of these is the famous Bell of the Arch of the Bells, which weighs ten tons and seldom rings. It is the sole bell that tolls the death of the pope, even to this day, and can be heard for miles around Rome.

benefice, ecclesiastical A consistorial benefice is one assigned in consistory, such as nomination to the episcopacy. More common in past eras than today, the benefice was a legal entity granted, in perpetuity, by authority of the Church (such as the pontiff, cardinals, or bishops); it consisted of the dignity of a sacred office with the right to enjoy the income connected with that office.

Benemerenti Medal A papal honor and decoration bestowed upon lay persons, Swiss Guardsmen, and low-level government officials during a state visit at the Vatican. *See also* Chapter 6, Papal Honors: Laity.

Bersaglieri The crack Italian regiment, known for their impressive headdress, with long horsetail ornamentation, who were traditionally sent to the Vatican by the Republican regime as an honor guard during the most solemn outdoor public occasions.

Biblioteca Privata (Private Library) Situated on the second floor of the Apostolic Palace, overlooking St. Peter's Square, this is the official office of the Holy Father, in which he receives his most important visitors.

Biglietto of the Secretariat of State The document by which certain papal appointments or nominations are brought to the attention of the consignee or honoree concerned. Notification by *biglietto*, which translates as "note," would include a prelate's nomination to the College of Cardinals.

biretta, cardinalatial A hat that is imposed on a new cardinal by the pope or, in former times, by a chief of state in certain Catholic countries.

bishop An ordinary who retains a diocese that is either residential (where he resides with jurisdiction over the faithful of the diocese) or titular. If a residential bishop asks the pope to be relieved of his duties and the permission is granted, he is officially transferred to a titular see. The only persons with episcopal consecration but without a see are the cardinals of the Order of Priests. Their titular dioceses become vacant with their creation as cardinals; also their residential dioceses are vacant, unless the pope gives permission to retain them, which is most often the case.

Black Nobility The political identification applied to those families of the sixty-one noble houses of Rome who remained loyal to the Roman pontiffs when Italy unified under the royal House of Savoy. The Blacks were those nobles who were appointed to the grandest posts of the old Papal Court prior to the modifications made by Pope Paul VI. In today's Vatican, these noble families continue to give service to the Church although several felt offended by the Church, in 1969, when many lost their privileged, time-honored Vatican ceremonial posts. The remainder, however, are often found represented in the government, administration, and economic affairs of the city-state. Some of these families are Lancellotti, Chigi, Torlonia, Sacchetti, Ruspoli, Colonna, Barberini, Orsini, Boncompagni, and Del Drago.

blazon A heraldic term for the official description of a coat of arms.

bordure A heraldic term describing a band or border that encircles the shield's edge, in some cases to appear as a frame for the shield.

bugia An episcopal candlestick with an elongated gilt handle. It was always made of gold or gilded silver for cardinals and patriarchs and silver for archbishops and bishops. It was abolished by Pope Paul VI in 1969 for use in the Latin rite. Its use developed simply out of necessity when cathedrals were too dark for the prelates to see and to read the order of the Mass. The *bugia* was always held to the right of the book and held a white beeswax candle. It was forbidden at Good Friday, for use by bishops when in the presence of cardinals or nuncios, and to priests altogether; nevertheless, in 1905, Pope Pius X granted the class of protonotaries the right to use a bronze *bugia* so long as they were the highest-ranking prelate present.

burse A receptacle for the corporal and paten when they are not in use prior to the Liturgy of the Eucharist. It is no longer mandatory. If used, however, the burse should be covered on the exterior with ornate cloth, which would match the color of the day. It would be lined in silk or like cloth. Approximately in the sixteenth century, the receptacle took on the form of a square, with one open side or pocket.

bussolanti The men in service to the pope, in former times, who served as his messengers and personal chamberlains. Their costume was one of red velvet and silk damask for ceremonial events, black for everyday use.

Camerlengo of the Holy Roman Church A member of the Sacred College, most often of the class of cardinal-bishops, who has been chosen by the Holy Father and given the main responsibility of governing the day-to-day affairs of the Church during the *Sede Vacante*. The Camerlengo officially proclaims the death of a pope and announces it to the Sacred College, the diplomatic corps, and to the world at large.

Camerlengo of the Sacred College An office responsible for the economic affairs of the Sacred College and all matters relating to that scope of responsibility. This post is held by a different cardinal, in turn, each year.

candles, ecclesiastical usage of The papal decree of December 1904, which has not been abrogated, requires that the Paschal candle and the two altar candles be made predominately of beeswax and that all other candles placed within the sanctuary should contain at least 60 percent of the same substance. The use of beeswax in the Church was twofold—functional and symbolic. Beeswax was, for centuries, the most reliable wax to use in making candles and thus served as a guarantee that light would illuminate the sanctuary. In a symbolic way, beeswax, made from the honeycomb of a type of bee that remains virginal until it stops secreting honey, is symbolic of both the purity of Our Lord and the Blessed Virgin.

The proper number of altar candles for cardinals celebrating pontifical Mass is nine and, for an archbishop or bishop, seven, the odd number candle being placed before the crucifix or processional-cross stand. For an ordinary mass, a cardinal has six, and archbishops and bishops have four (although six large candles have become the general norm for special celebrations in the Church). Priests celebrate all Masses with two altar candles. Six additional candles may be carried out into the sanctuary as the Consecration begins and remain there until the Sanctus. These candles are called "Sanctus torches" and are there, in place, to bring special reverence to the miracle that is about to take place. The Sanctus torches are carried in procession, two by two, and are led by one or two thurifers, who kneel between three bearers to the left and three to the right at the foot of the altar. The thurifers incense at the two elevations and at the Sanctus.

The use of candles, however, was never intended solely for illumination of the sanctuary; modern electricity would have made them redundant if this were so. From the earliest of times the use of candles was symbolic: (a) to show that Christ is the true light of the world, which enlightens every man coming into the world; (b) to illustrate the dignity, the great reverence, and splendor of the Sacred Mysteries; and (c) to awaken the faithful to the truth of Christ's message and the need for participation in Him. The rubrics mandated use of beeswax because of the purity of the wax, which symbolized the purity and humanity of Christ. Today, even though western countries have adopted modern technology of design, the specific requirement and traditions of the candle remain. Each church should bless the candles needed throughout the coming liturgical year on the feast of Candlemas (February 2).

A single candle is presented to a newly welcomed member of the Church at his or her baptism. Incorporated into the new rite is this prayer: *Receive the light of Christ. Parents and Godparents, this light is entrusted to you to be kept burning brightly. This child of yours has been enlightened by Christ. He (she) is to walk always as a child of the light. May he (she) keep the flame of faith alive in his (her) heart. When the Lord comes, may he (she) go out to meet Him with all the saints in the heavenly kingdom.*

canon law   The law in force in the Church. The Code of Canon Law was published by Benedict XV in 1917 and has been revised for both the Latin and the Oriental rites. The Latin Rite Code was revised and promulgated in 1983.

capo ufficio   The title of the head of the offices within the Curia but below that of prefect, president, secretary, and regent. The equivalent in commerce would be "supervisor."

cardinal   A title of great honor to those prelates who form the Senate of the Church and to whom is entrusted the election of the Roman Pontiff. *See also* Chapter 1, Sacred College.

cartouche   A heraldic term describing the oval-shaped shield that is employed for the depiction of arms for ladies and for ecclesiastics. In Italian heraldic practice, the cartouche was customary for papal, cardinalatial, and episcopal arms.

cathedra   A Greek word for "seat," which serves as the official seat or throne of a residential bishop. The Holy Father speaks *ex cathedra* to the world as teacher and Bishop. The local bishop has the right to the *cathedra* in his diocese, and visiting prelates must be granted permission for its use, even when the ordinary is not present. The Roman Chair of St. Peter is the See where the successor of the Prince of the Apostles resides with supreme jurisdiction over the whole world. The terms *ex cathedra, cathedraticum,* and *cathedral* are derivatives.

cathedral   A church which serves as the seat of the local bishop (ordinary) and wherein his teaching authority technically rests (*magisterium*). In former times, a cathedral was not also a parish church. If it were, it would technically be a procathedral (a parish church, used as a cathedral by the local bishop), but this has not been the case for some time. The pastor of a cathedral is known as *rector-primus,* for he is the pastor of the first, or primary, Church of the diocese.

celebret   The document of a diocesan bishop or superior of a religious order affirming that a priest under his jurisdiction is in good standing.

ceremoniere   Italian term for the Papal Master of Ceremonies.

chancel   The area of a church around the altar, so called because it once was entirely separated from the congregation by a *cancellae* or railing.

chapel   The term for a small place of worship and prayer often attached to a cathedral, basilica, or great church, or within a building not reserved exclusively for worship (i.e., the residence of a bishop; a Catholic hospital, school, or other facility; the Apostolic Palace; etc.). The word *chapel* comes to us from the early Church where it was first applied to the hall attached to the Church of St. Martin of Tours in France. St. Martin died in A.D. 397 after a heroic life. The cape he wore as a soldier, and which he gave to a beggar, an act that triggered his conversion and vocation, is enshrined as a holy relic in this hall. The word for *cape* in Italian is *cappa*. The term applied to this hall which was the repository for St. Martin's *cappa* was *cappella*, which translates in both French and English as *chapel*. Chapel has been used to describe small sacred places of worship from this time to the present day.

Chapel of Matilda   The chapel in the rooms of Pope Gregory XIII in the Vatican, which is the site of the annual Lenten retreat for cardinals and Curia officials. At one time it was also the site for the annual New Year's Day Mass for the diplomatic corps accredited to the Holy See.

chief   A heraldic term used to describe the top segment of a shield encompassing the top one third of the shield. The chief is reserved for prominent emblems such as membership in an order of knighthood.

chirograph   A formal message in the pope's own handwriting.

choir dress (*abito paonazzo*)   For the prelature, choir dress is the most formal vesture of the Church for both liturgical and nonliturgical events. In most cases, however, choir dress should be reserved for use exclusively at the liturgy. Although choir dress may be appropriate at nonliturgical events, it would be more appropriate for *abito piano* to be donned after a liturgical event and before any "social" event were to begin. There are occasions, however, when use of choir dress at nonliturgical functions is permissible. Choir dress always consists of the scarlet or purple choir cassock and *fascia*, the rochet, the *mozzetta*, the *zucchetto*, the *biretta*, and the pectoral cross.

cincture   In speaking of liturgical vestments, the cincture is a linen or silk rope, with knots, tassels, or tufts at each end, which is used to gird or bind the alb. It must be clear that we are not speaking of the *fascia*, or sash, reserved for the cassock/soutane, or simar when we refer to the cincture. From generation to generation, the colors permitted the cincture have changed. Today, the rubrics define white as acceptable. In the past, the cincture most commonly took on the liturgical color of the day. Several prayers can be said

silently as the cincture is placed around the waist. The most ancient formula is *Gird (or Bind) me O Lord, with the cincture of purity and extinguish in my loins the heat of concupiscence that the virtue of continence and charity may abide in me,* a certain reference to the priest's marriage to Christ.

cochlear   A small golden spoon formerly used by the celebrants to measure the exact amount of water to be commingled with the wine at the offertory. In the seventeenth century, it became quite ornate. It has since been abolished.

Code of Canon Law   The codified law of the Church that governs practice and behavior in matters of faith, morals, teaching, and government. The Pontifical Council for the Interpretation of the Legislative Texts is responsible for the authentic interpretation of canon law. The Code for the Latin rite was updated in 1983.

College of Cardinals   The ensemble of all the cardinals, constituting the pope's senate. There are three orders of cardinals, of whom the members of the first (cardinal-bishops) and the last (cardinal-deacons) reside in Rome. The cardinals who do not reside in Rome are of the Order of Priests. They assist the pope in the supreme government of the Church and are given a church, in Rome, as their titular church.

competence of the sacred congregations   The Code of Canon Law specifies the ordinary competence of the offices of the Curia. Their extraordinary competence is that which is given them by the pope *ex audientia Sanctissimi. See also* Chapter 2, Roman Curia.

conclave   The meeting of all the cardinals to elect a pope. The word derives from the Latin *con* (with) and *clavis* (key), which refers to the locked nature of the gathering of cardinals. The term *conclave* is also applied to the election of the Prince Grand Master of Malta. *See also* Chapter 1, Sacred College, and Chapter 8, Sovereign Military Order of Malta.

concordat   The most formal of papal documents between the Church and a state. The concordat takes the form of a treaty and grants to the Church special and unique privileges in regard to the Church and the faithful in that country.

congregations   A term applied to the religious orders, sometimes subdivided into congregations, such as the Swiss Congregation and the American Cassinesse Congresses of the order of St. Benedict. A number of abbeys form a congregation.

congregations, Roman   The nine ecclesiastical departments (once commonly called *dicasteries* or ministries) that assist the pope in the universal government of the Church. Together with the councils, tribunals, commissions, and offices, they form the Roman Curia. *See also* Chapter 2, Roman Curia.

congress of congregations   A convocation of the Curia, which can be either ordinary or plenary.

consistory   A meeting of the cardinals and other prelates under the presidency of the pope. If only the pope and the cardinals take part, it is called a secret consistory. Bishops also attend a semipublic consistory, and a public consistory admits the presence of other ecclesiastics and laymen. New cardinals are created and their nomination is published in consistory, though both not necessarily in the same consistory. There are two types of consistory: the extraordinary and the ordinary. The ordinary consistory occurs regularly when the pope turns to those cardinals at Rome for consultation on important matters of the Church. The extraordinary consistory occurs when the reigning Pope convokes a meeting of all cardinals worldwide who are summoned for consultation on specific or serious issues facing the Church and for nominations of new members to the College. Pope John Paul II has convoked extraordinary consistories five times between 1978 and June 1994. *See also* Chapter 1, Sacred College.

consistorial allocution   A discourse of the pope, in consistory, in which he brings the important current events to the attention of the cardinals.

consultori della congregazioni   Those senior prelates and other ecclesiastical and lay specialists who serve as consulters to the various congregations, councils, and offices of the Roman Curia.

counterpotent   A heraldic fur as depicted opposite **potent** (q.v.).

countervair   One of the heraldic furs depicted in the reverse of **vair** (q.v.).

cravatta nera   The Italian term (literally "black tie") applied to formal events where tuxedo (for men) and formal dress (for women) would accompany **abito piano** (q.v.) or *tenue de ville* for clerics. *Cravatta bianca* ("white tie") is the term applied to events where the most formal of attire, often including decorations and orders, is worn by all.

cruciform   A term applied to church architecture when the edifice is designed in the shape of a cross. This style became popular in the post-Romanesque period and was characterized by the transept (or crossbar), which originally served as additional exits but which later developed into devotional areas.

cuculla   The long habit of several religious orders but best known as the impressive habit for Knights of the Sovereign Order of Malta. For the order's knights, the *cuculla* is black, with a white cowl and cuffs. It is emblazoned with the white maltese cross and is worn at religious ceremonies.

declaration   An official document that offers an explanation or definition of a code or law of the Church.

decoration bar   A term derived from both the military and diplomatic world to describe the proper ordering of the miniature decorations or awards granted an individual for wear by the laity on formal attire and by the clergy on the cassock or simar. In actuality, the miniatures can be placed on a golden bar, sewn together on a central pin, or suspended from a hanging gold chain. Local custom and personal taste are the only deciding factors; however, one must always place decorations that have been awarded in proper order; not to do so causes offense or embarrassment at formal ceremonies. *See also* Chapter 6, Papal Honors: Laity, and Chapter 7, Papal Honors: Clergy.

decretal letters (*litteras decretales*)   Letters reserved for the official promulgation of beatifications and canonizations.

dexter   A heraldic term used to describe the right side of a shield of arms, although appearing as the left side as one observes the arms.

diplomatic dress   A term, applied to the most formal governmental or state receptions, that calls for guests to don the diplomatic braided uniform, national costume, or white tie with decorations. For clerics of all ranks, *abito piano* with *ferraiolo* would always be required.

east   The mandatory direction churches faced until recently. East was symbolic of the Resurrection, just as the sun rises in the east each day. The old English word for *resurrection*, or *rising*, was *east*.

ecclesiastical signatures   Signatures of members of the hierarchy of the Church, which have been regulated by historic precedence and custom. For centuries, the popes have signed their papal names in Latin rather than Italian. Pope John Paul II, as pope, would sign his name *Ioannes Paulus II,* but as Bishop of Rome, he would sign his name *Giovanni Paolo II.* Further, all pontiffs include the two post-nominal initials that designate that they, and they alone, are successors to Peter: *P.P.,* for *Pope* and *Pontiff,* follow the papal name on all documents, including the first notarized parchment documenting their election to the papacy. The present pope's signature appears, therefore, as *Ioannes Paulus P.P. II.* (John Paul, Pope and Pontiff, II).

Members of the Sacred College must sign their names inclusive of their titles. As such, each cardinal's signature comprises his baptismal name, the *cardinalatial* title, and his surname. Cardinal John Doe would therefore always sign his name as *John Cardinal Doe.* He may, by custom, abbreviate the title as *John Card. Doe,* although he may never abbreviate it simply as *John C. Doe.*

Patriarchs, archbishops, and bishops sign their names in full, as would any priest or layman; however, they always begin their signatures by making the sign of the cross before their baptismal names, as part of their own signatures. This is something cardinals do not do. Cardinals were not always bishops prior to the 1960s, and the use of the cross as part of a signature was always reserved for those with episcopal dignity. After the 1960s, this custom was not extended to cardinals. With modern computer graphics, the cross (✠) is now also added in typeface as it appears below the actual signature. In writing to these prelates, however, one does not include the cross. This symbol is applied to these prelates by themselves only and not by others to them. Abbots also enjoy this privilege; however, inferior prelates, priests, seminarians, and laymen do not.

The use of *junior* or its customary abbreviations *Jnr.* or *Jr.,* as well as the post-nominal use of Roman numerals (except for the Roman Pontiff) that designate a linear relationship (father to son or one bishop to another), are inappropriate for those with Holy Orders and should be avoided at all times. Whenever a cleric is firmly committed to an outward sign of his relationship to his father it is always proper for the father to assume the designation (such as *senior, Snr.,* or *Sr.*), whereas the ecclesiastical son goes without any designation from the time of ordination onward.

encolpium   A cross or reliquary worn upon the breast as a pectoral cross or icon for Eastern rite bishops.

encyclical   An encyclical is a letter addressed to all Christendom, for the defense and increase of spiritual life. Generally, encyclicals do not contain infallible definitions (*ex cathedra*), but their directives are often obligatory and contain doctrinal teachings. They always derive their name from the first Latin words of the text.

eparch   A residential ordinary of the Oriental rite.

ermine   A heraldic term describing one of the six base furs employed historically in arms. It appears as white fur with black tails.

erminois   A heraldic term used to describe the fur that appears as gold with black spots.

escutcheon   A heraldic term describing a small shield placed in the center of the main arms. It is used by ladies of rank who bear their own arms or by two families of rank that have merged their arms, names, lands, and titles.

exarch   An ordinary of the Oriental rite corresponding to the vicar apostolic of the Latin rite. He is a titular bishop.

ex cathedra   An expression used when the pope speaks infallibly as head of Christendom on matters of faith and morals.

exempt religious orders   Those religious orders that are not subject to the jurisdiction of the local bishop, but are immediately dependent on the pope.

Fabric of St. Peter's, Commission of the   A commission that provides maintenance of the Vatican Basilica.

falda   A vestment of white silk, reaching to the floor, which the pope traditionally wore in solemn ceremonies. It was worn whenever he donned pontifical vestments. There were also two kinds: one, which the pope wore when vested in *mozzetta* and stole for a secret consistory and when vested to receive visiting heads of state; the other, and longer one, which he wore with pontificals. Although it is seldom seen today, the *falda* has not been abolished. It dates from the early fifteenth century, its name deriving from the Italian meaning "train."

faldstool   A highly decorative, but backless chair, used by bishops during certain ceremonies and for the bishop celebrating the Mass if he is not the ordinary for whom is reserved the *cathedra.* The faldstool is no longer officially mentioned in the *Ceremonial of Bishops;* however, it is still widely in use. The cushion for cardinals was always made of silk or silk damask and merlino (wool) for bishops and was always in the appropriate liturgical color.

fanon (*fanone*)   A vestment proper to the pope that he uses when he celebrates a pontifical Mass. It consists of a double *mozzetta* of silk and gold. The first goes under the stole, whereas the second goes over the chasuble. This vestment has not been abolished, but it has not been seen for some time. It dates from the first century of the Church and was the ancient predecessor of the amice. It took the form we see today as early as in the twelfth century. In the fifteenth century, it was reserved as a "pontifical" for the pope.

fichu   The original name for the garment known today as the rochet. *See also* Chapter 25, Rochet and Surplice.

field   A heraldic term used to describe the surface of the shield on which is placed emblems (ordinaries).

Fisherman's Ring   The papal ring, which has a setting especially cut to serve as a seal, yet is not actually worn by the pope. Its design bears the figure of the apostle Peter standing in a bark in the act of casting a fishnet. The Prefect of the Papal Household is its custodian.

fistula   A golden, silver, ivory, or glass tube formerly used by all clerics to communicate the Precious Blood during Mass. This device ceased to be the privilege of all clerics and communicants by 1385. Nevertheless, it remained one of the means by which the popes received the Precious Blood, especially when not celebrating Mass. It was abolished in the pontificate of John XXIII. Its origins reach to the practices of the early Eastern Church, which allowed the use of reeds as straws so as not to spill the Precious Blood. Considered to be sacred after use, these reeds were then burned after each use.

flabellum   A pontifical fan, familiar to all Catholics "of a certain age." These fans, or *flabella,* which originated in Byzantium, were used at all papal ceremonies in the procession of the pope. They were originally developed to keep insects from the Eucharist and the ministers; during the Renaissance, they developed into beautiful embellishments at the Papal Court. Made of leather, they were covered in crimson velvet and gold and were topped by white ostrich plumes. The *flabella* were embroidered with the arms of the reigning pontiff. Abolished by Paul VI, along with many other appointments from the Papal Court, the *flabellum* can be seen in the Papal Court exhibit at the Lateran Palace, which opens only on the first Sunday of each month.

forum, external   The expression used to indicate the jurisdiction of the Church over the external acts of the faithful.

Forum, internal   The expression used to indicate the Church's jurisdiction over the consciences of the faithful. Such jurisdiction can be exercised sacramentally, as in the case of a penitent absolved in confession, or extrasacramentally, as in the case of the rehabilitation of a person who has been under censure.

Fra   A title derived from *frater,* meaning "religious brother." The title Fra is applied most commonly today to the professed Knights of the Order of

Malta. For example, the Prince Grand Master incorporates this religious title into his official title: His Most Eminent Highness, Fra Andrew W. Bertie, The Prince Grand Master of the Sovereign Military Order of St. John of Jerusalem, of Rhodes, and of Malta.

galero The great red cardinalitial hat with tassels, which was not worn but was only placed on the head of new cardinals during the ceremonies of the public consistory, then stored away. Today it is still utilized in the arms of cardinals, patriarchs, archbishops, bishops, lesser prelates, and priests who make use of a *galero* of the colors appropriate to their individual ranks. *See also* Chapter 12, Ecclesiastical Precedence.

gamberi colli Sarcastic Roman slang meaning "the shrimps," referring to the Teutonic Seminary's German students, who wore red cassocks.

generalates, or general curias The headquarters, in Rome, of all the religious orders, congregations, and institutes, at which the superiors general (or their equivalent) and their staffs reside.

gorget A Swiss term used to define the white plait or pleated ruff collar, a remnant from the Renaissance, which was worn by many officials within the Vatican prior to 1969. Today, it is worn only by the Swiss Guard, on the more solemn occasions, on their ceremonial uniform.

Gregorian indulgence The ancient practice, confirmed by the Church on March 15, 1884, regarding the sanctity of the altar of the Church of St. Gregory on the Coclian Hill in Rome. It was said that a soul in Purgatory would immediately become liberated for Heaven if a Mass was said for that specific deceased upon this church's altar.

gremial An oblong or rectangular cloth used by the bishop while ordaining, confirming, or when washing the feet of the Twelve on the Holy Saturday Vigil Mass. It was formerly used by the bishops during the lavabo at Mass and during times when perhaps the chasuble would get soiled. It is used today for the same purpose, but it first came into use in the fourteenth century. It is made of linen, sometimes also silk, with trim of lace. Today, long linen strings extend from it

so that it can be tied around the girth of the bishop if need be. It is never blessed.

gules A heraldic term used for the color red.

humeral veil A veil, about 5 feet in length and 2½ feet in width, of color and fabric to match the sacred vestments, most especially the cope. It is used by the celebrant to cover his hands when handling the monstrance, or *ostensorium*, during the elevation and benediction or during solemn Eucharistic processions.

immediately subject to the Holy See A canonical term used to refer to an archdiocese that is not a metropolitan see or also a diocese that is not a suffragan see.

impalement A heraldic term used to describe the union of two separate coats of arms onto one shield so as to become one device. An ordinary of a diocese may impale his personal arms with those of his diocese, but this custom is not mandatory. Likewise, a husband and wife may impale their arms if both parties are armigerous.

in nigris *See* **nigris, in.**

incense, use of Usage of incense in sacred ceremonies preceded the birth of Christ. The Church has always made use of incense in the liturgy because of its symbolism in according great honor and respect. The Magi presented incense to the Christ child as one of their gifts. The Church makes use of this aromatic mineral because its sweet-smelling vapors signify the practice of prayer: *Let my prayer, O Lord, be directed like incense unto Thy holy sight.* It has long symbolized the fire and flame of holy charity, which should consume each Christian, and its sweet smell represents the cleanliness of Christ diffused deep within our hearts. Incense is burned in a device known as a thurible, which is traditionally made of ornate metal. The thurible can be either carried in procession, in which case the attendant carrying the incense would be known as a thurifer, or it may be suspended in the sanctuary, where it would be left to burn throughout the liturgy.

Institute for Religious Works (*Istituto per le Opere di Religione*) Office of credit and banking in the Vatican, most widely known as the Vatican Bank. Originally established to assist religious orders, based in Rome, with the work of their orders abroad.

institutes, secular Institutes whose members are the faithful who are not properly tied to the canonical state of religious, but also aim toward evangelical perfection through the voluntary practice of the three evangelical counsels (poverty, chastity, and obedience). Their apostolates are modern and varied. Members wear no particular habit, nor are they bound to a life of community. They make private vows, more properly called semipublic, which bind in conscience. They remain seculars (clerical or lay, according to the state that they adopt) both in fact and in law.

kamilauka The Eastern-rite headdress that is stiff and cylindrical in form. For the celibate clergy, it may be covered by the black veil-like hood known as a *klobuk*.

kissing of the palms The act of kissing the palms of the hands of a newly ordained priest. Those persons who devotedly attend the first Mass of a newly ordained priest may gain an indulgence of seven years, or a plenary indulgence if they are related to the third degree to the newly ordained, if they receive the sacrament of penance and received the Eucharist and have prayed for the intentions of the pope. Those persons who reverently and devotedly kiss the palms of the hands of the newly ordained, where the sacred oils have just been placed in anointing, receive an indulgence of one hundred days under the same conditions. This grant may be bestowed both after ordination and the first Mass.

Latin briefs to princes Formal letters from the Secretariat of State, on behalf of the pontiff, to heads of state and government. Known as "briefs to princes" because monarchy was formerly the predominate form of government. *See also* Chapter 2, Roman Curia.

law, canon *See* **law, canon.**

legate A title defining a personal representative of the pope. A cardinal-legate is the highest degree of papal representative and is one who is traditionally designated to represent the Holy Father at a short-term international event.

letters: apostolic, ordinary, pontifical, decretal Bulls that concern the canonization of saints and other important statements.

Librarian and Archivist of the Holy Roman Church A post held by a cardinal who serves as head of the historic Vatican libraries and Secret Vatican Archives.

livery colors In heraldry, the two main colors of one's heraldic device that were used in the dress of one's staff in Europe. The color purple was used as a livery or household color for clerics in the household of a cardinal even when his household did not hold monsignorial rank.

maniple A cloth of linen used in ancient Rome to wipe away perspiration and moisture from the hands and brow and from the mouth after eating. From it developed our present-day napkin at table and the purificator at Mass. Servants made use of it after meals to clean vessels. It was carried on the wrist in some localities, or on the hand, and eventually made its way to the Mass. It is now abolished as a sacred vestment. Over time, it developed from linen to raw silk, matching the color and fabric of the chasuble. It long ago lost its significance and, by the fourteenth century, became purely symbolic. It was as ornamented as the chasuble and was made with two linen or silk strings to tie together to ensure a tight fit. The maniple was one of the items laid aside by the decree of Pope Paul VI.

maniturgium A fine linen cloth, often embroidered with fine lace or some insignia, used by a newly ordained priest after the anointing with holy oils. It was removed from the Rite of Ordination but is often still used by the newly ordained when they return to the sacristy to clean their hands. This *maniturgium* is then put aside by the priest to be used to place in the hands of his deceased mother before burial. Often two were used, one for each parent.

major archbishop A title used to denote a special status over a people beyond the normal jurisdictional limits of an archdiocese. A major archbishop (such as Lvov in the Ukraine) is given precedence after patriarchs but before the college of archbishops. Otherwise, all things remain consistent with the residential archbishops; however, major archbishops have the additional precedence, respect, and esteem of patriarchs because of the character of their position as the head of a rite or of a national Church.

major basilicas (patriarchal) of Rome The Arch-basilica of St. John Lateran, the Archbasilica of St. Peter in the Vatican, the Liberian Basilica of St. Mary Major, the Basilica of St. Paul Outside the Walls, and the Basilica of St. Lawrence. A cardinal-archpriest is assigned to each of the first three.

major prelates Also known as greater prelates, a term used to refer to patriarchs, archbishops, bishops, abbots nullius, and prelates nullius. All other prelates are known as minor or inferior prelates.

marriage "ratum et non consummatum" A marriage "ratified but not consummated."

marshal of the Holy Roman Church and guard of the conclave The highest office a layman can have in ecclesiastical matters. He is in charge of defending the independence and the exterior secrecy of a conclave.

master of ceremonies The title of the priest who governs the Office for Liturgical Celebrations of the Supreme Pontiff.

maunch A heraldic device that is depicted as a sleeve with enlarged cuff, such as that in the arms of Pio Cardinal Laghi.

metropolitan *See* **archbishop.**

military ordinariate A jurisdiction similar to that of a residential archdiocese that provides for the care of souls in the armed forces of each nation. The chaplains of the armed forces staff it, and it has a military ordinary at its head as a residential (arch)bishop.

military staff The pontifical Swiss Guard.

minutante A post in the Roman congregations, a high-ranking administrative secretary.

monsignor From the French *monseigneur,* meaning "My Lord," this title of honor is accorded to all archbishops and bishops (although in the United States it is not used by these prelates); by the Protonotaries Apostolic de Numero and Supranumerary, by Prelates of Honor, and by Chaplains of His Holiness. In the civil world, the title Monseigneur is always accorded to royal princes and the highest ranks of the nobility, and, for them, precedes the Christian name, rather than the surname.

morion Part of the colorful Swiss Guard costume, the morion is the heavy, ornate metal helmet in either gray, but called white, which is used for the highest ceremonial events, or black, for less important occasions. The morion is not worn at all times but, when worn, usually makes use of plumage as well.

motu proprio A term meaning "by personal initiative," applied to those pronouncements, usually of significant import, which are written and decreed by a pontiff's own personal design. These pronouncements were first employed by Pope Innocent VIII in 1489.

narthex The area of the original basilica-style buildings that served as the porch area off the atrium. In time, this developed into the indoor vestibule of today's churches.

nave The principle section of a church, best identified as the area between the vestibule and the altar railing or steps. It derives its name from the *naos* of the Greeks, which translates as the central area of the Greek temples. It is also said that the ancient bark, or ship, *Navis,* which resembled a large nave of a church, was the reason for the adoption of this term in church architecture; however, it is more likely that the Greek origins are more accurate.

nigris, in A Roman term applied to prelates who are vested in the simple black cassock rather than in the red-trimmed black simar of their rank when at home, at work, or in unofficial life.

novena A period of nine days of prayer and/or special devotion. The nine days symbolize the nine days of prayer (*novenus*) between the Ascension of Our Lord and Pentecost.

novendialia The period of nine days between the burial of a pontiff and the entering into conclave. On each day the cardinals gather to offer a solemn Mass in memory of the dead pontiff, and prayers for the resurrection of his soul are sung.

oecumene The origin of the term *ecumenical* from the Greek, meaning "the Latin world." Originally, as well as currently, used to refer to the Ecumenical Patriarch of Constantinople.

offices Part of the Roman Curia, together with the congregations, councils, commissions, and tribunals.

officiale   A post in the Roman congregations. There are major and minor categories and various grades of each.

or   A heraldic term used to describe gold; one of the two heraldic metals. It is depicted as yellow.

orders, equestrian   Papal honors bestowed upon the laity.

ordinary   The generic name of the ecclesiastical superior who exercises ordinary jurisdiction: the bishop in the diocese, the vicar apostolic in the Vicariate Apostolic, the prelate nullius in a Prelature Nullius, etc.

ordinary ecclesiastical affairs   Those matters that affect the normal affairs of the Church are under the care and governance of the Second Section of the Secretariat of State.

ostensorium   Commonly known as the monstrance, a large vessel of precious metal used for the adoration of the most Blessed Sacrament and for processions. It has a base of rounded metal or ornamentation with three legs. The stem is an elongated version of the chalice. Emanating from the central glass medallion, in which is placed the *lunnula* (*luna* or *lunette*) that contains the Blessed Sacrament, are rays of gold, silver, ivory, or enamels, which form a circular array around the central *lunnula*. Some designs incorporate Gothic architectural features rather than the baroque sunburst, whereas others incorporate modernistic artistic expression. The rubrics call for an ostensorium of precious metal and dignified appearance, permitting at the same time the possibility of proper adoration of the Blessed Sacrament. Although a double-sided glass *lunnula* is generally used, officially the rubrics still require a *lunette* made of one side of glass (to permit view) and the rear of gold or silver with gilt on the inside, which would touch against the Blessed Sacrament.

palafrenieri   A term for the former papal grooms. It also provided the name of the Vatican's parish church—Sant'Anna dei Palafrenieri.

pall   A term used for two items of vestment in the Church. The first is that which covers the chalice at all times until the liturgy has progressed to the point of consecration. Whenever the chalice is not directly being used, even for an instant, the pall must be placed, covering the mouth of the cup. It should always be made of linen. If it cannot be entirely of linen, then the portion that touches the chalice should be of linen. Embroidery is permitted only on the upper, or exposed, section of the pall. The second use for the term *pall* is applied to the covering, used at burial, that is placed over the casket of the deceased. In the United States, the preferred color is white, with emblems matching the vestments of the priests. In other countries, black or violet is still in use. In some European nations, the emblem of the deceased's family, such as their heraldic device, is emblazoned upon white cloth.

papable (*papabile*)   A term applied to those cardinals considered favored for possible election to the papacy.

papal decrees   Documents issued by the Roman Curia and approved by the pope.

papal documents, letters   A term that encompasses the following types of written papal communications: apostolic constitution, encyclical, bull, brief, apostolic and ordinary letters, motu proprio.

papal encyclicals   The richest and most colorful documents of the Church, issued primarily as the teaching authority (*magisterium*) of the Church in a manner to clarify the Church's position on issues of the modern world. Each encyclical takes its name from the first two (or more) Latin words of the text.

Papal Household   Those prelates, priests, and laymen with specific duties in the Vatican, or those who have received an outstanding honor from the pope. *See also* Chapter 3, A Look into the Papal Household and Papal Family.

Papal Master of Ceremonies   The chief Master of Ceremonies responsible for the good performance of liturgical ceremonies.

papal theologian   A post formerly known as "Master of the Sacred Palace." This post in the Church is traditionally held by a Dominican priest who serves the pope, the Secretariat of State, and the Curia on matters of theological import.

pappeggianti   A term, long since forgotten, which referred to those cardinals, in more political times, who pushed the applications of one of their number, for political considerations, to election to the papacy.

pasokh The term used for the pastoral staff (crozier) of a bishop of the Oriental rites. It usually is either in the form of a tau cross or in the form of the caduceus (two dueling serpents), which, unlike the commonly felt evil symbolism of snakes and serpents, has come to symbolize, in the Eastern rites, the biblical connotation of "having the wisdom of serpents." The *pateressa*, from the Greek, is the name of the staff of bishops of the Greek Orthodox Church.

patriarch The title of an ecclesiastical dignitary, superior to that of primate or archbishop. Apart from the pope, who has the title Patriarch of the West, the only patriarchs are Venice, Lisbon, the East Indies (Goa), the West Indies, resident in Spain but vacant since 1963, the patriarchs of the Oriental rite in union with the Holy See, both titular and residential. The patriarchs form a college of their own and are automatically named "Assistants to the Throne." The institution of the patriarchate is of ancient origin and existed in the earliest times of the Church. The patriarchs, not members of the Sacred College, take precedence before all other prelates including the archbishops, and, in keeping with their singular traditions, are accorded great respect. Each patriarch presides over his rite's faithful as father and bishop and is accorded, in canon law, the highest esteem.

Pauline Chapel (*Cappella Paolina*) One of the most beautiful of the Vatican chapels, the Pauline Chapel is situated adjacent to the Sala Regia and is the site of the Mass of the Holy Spirit, the Mass of the Cardinal-Electors, prior to entry into conclave. It served popes as their private chapel in former centuries.

Pauline privilege A law concerning the marriage between two non-Christians who later divorce, while one of the two converts to Catholicism and who seeks to remarry another from within the faith (canons 1143–1150).

Penitentiary, Apostolic The first-ranking of the ecclesiastical tribunals of the Roman Curia.

personal prelature A canonically structured ecclesiastical authority established for the purpose of the pastoral care of a missionary area or a special group within the Church. To date, the Holy Father has erected only one personal prelature, that of *Opus Dei*. The personal prelature has the right to establish its own seminaries and to educate the faithful under its authority in accord with the law (canons 294–297).

Peter's Pence The practice, begun by King Canute of England in the eleventh century, of taxing each Catholic annually as a donation to the pope for his charities. Today, Peter's Pence is an optional donation by the faithful; due to the ongoing annual deficit of the Holy See, it is used to offset operating expenses.

petition A term that indicates an official request for some favor or nomination to be granted by the Holy See.

piatto cardinalice The term traditionally applied to the salaries of cardinals in the service of the Curia. This should not be confused with the now defunct *Rotulus cardinalitius,* which was an annual stipend from a special fund, common for all the cardinals, which was generated from Mass stipends.

Pinacoteca Vaticana The pink brick palazzo, commissioned by Pope Puis XI, serving as the art gallery for works of art from the later centuries.

Pink (Rose) Sundays The third Sunday of Advent, known as *Gaudete,* and the fourth Sunday of Lent, known as *Laetare,* so called because on those days the cardinals, who wore scarlet the year-round, donned rose (pink)-colored, red-trimmed vesture, signifying the joy felt within the two solemn seasons of the year. *Gaudete* means expressed or exuberant joy. *Laetare* means internal joy, a joy of anticipation felt within the solemn season of Lent. Vestments, traditionally violet during these seasons, were also exchanged for rose (pink), thus carrying with them the name of Pink or, more accurately, Rose Sundays.

plenary A monthly meeting of the congregations.

plenary indulgence The eradication of all temporal debt and punishment due to God's justice because of our sins after their forgiveness. The term is derived from the Latin *indulgentia,* which means pardon.

plena signatura A plenary meeting of the cardinals and prelates who are members of the Apostolic Signatura.

Pontiff, Supreme The successor of St. Peter who received from Christ the supreme power (primacy of honor and of jurisdiction) over the Universal Church, to be passed onto his successors.

pontificals A term applied to certain insignia (ring, crozier, pectoral cross, etc.) used today exclusively by those with episcopal dignity but previously used by the honorary prelature in certain classes as well. The term derives from the use of these articles at pontifical High Mass at which they would have officiated.

pontifical academies A world-renowned company of scholars under the direction of the Holy See. Appointment as a Pontifical academician carries with it a lifetime appointment and the title "Excellency." The greatest scientists of each age are commonly appointed to the academy, regardless of their faith.

pontifical almoner An archbishop resident in Vatican City who is responsible for the care of those seeking succor from the Holy See. He is also responsible for the issuance of the colorful parchments certifying that the Holy Father has bestowed his blessing upon the faithful who had requested it. The almoner is also known as the archbishop-elemosiniere or, in the Italian, as *Elemosiniere di Sua Santitá*.

porporati The title applied, in past eras, to newly created cardinals during the ceremonies of the "opening" and "closing of the mouth." This title was used in reference to them only during these ceremonies.

potent A heraldic term applied to a fur serving as a division of a shield.

precedence, establishment of The precedence of dignitaries is established by the Prefecture of the Papal Household. Within the College of Cardinals, it depends on the respective orders. For cardinal-bishops, precedence is set from the date of their promotion to a suburbicarian see. For other cardinals, precedence is derived from the date of their elevation; for cardinals created in the same consistory, precedence is derived from the original placement of their names on the official list of nomination.

predilla The term applied to the platform of stone or marble, three or four steps in height, upon which rests the altar of worship.

prefect apostolic The priest (generally of an order) placed as ordinary over a prefecture apostolic. He is not invested with episcopal dignity.

prefecture apostolic An ecclesiastical circumscription that constitutes the first step in the organization of the ecclesiastical hierarchy in a determined territory.

prelate Besides bishops and other high dignitaries, the term *prelate* includes all those priests, secular or religious, who have jurisdiction in the external forum or who have received the honorary title Honorary Prelate from the Holy See. From the Latin *praeferre* (to come before), the term implies jurisdiction. The ranks of the prelature were modified in 1969 (*Regimini Ecclesiastae*) by Pope Paul VI. Today, generally speaking, prelates of episcopal rank are cardinals, patriarchs, archbishops, bishops, and consecrated abbots. Those prelates with jurisdiction but without the episcopal dignity are the prelates nullius and prelates apostolic. Prelates without either episcopal dignity and jurisdiction are known as inferior prelates. These prelates compose the ranks of the monsignorial titles, including protonotary apostolic (three classes), prelates of honor, and chaplains of His Holiness.

prelate nullius The ordinary of a prelature nullius who exercises quasi-episcopal jurisdiction and is empowered to confer confirmation. Prelates nullius are named by the pope and are sometimes titular bishops.

prelature nullius In comparison with an abbey nullius, the territory with the clergy and faithful, separated from every diocese and in which the prelate nullius exercises quasi-episcopal jurisdiction.

prerogative of place A nicety of protocol, which, sadly, is not always honored today. In nations where there is no longer, or never has been, a primate, the first see created would hold the honors and privileges of *primus inter pares* (first among equals). As such, the holder of that see would be accorded the senior privileges of protocol unless a higher-ranking cleric, such as a cardinal, were present at the same function. In such cases, the prerogative of place of a primate or senior archbishop would be muted. Among his own peers, however, the holder of that see would receive the honors of protocol as the first among equals.

primate Today, the title conferred by the Holy See to one of the metropolitan archbishops of a region or nation, often the most historic and most ancient. The title Primate is one of honor and precedence, not one of jurisdiction. The primate is *primus inter pares* among the metropolitan archbishops of the region, for he normally does not have jurisdiction over them. Because of their preeminence, the national primates are generally also members of the College of Cardinals.

primacy of Peter and of his successors An absolute primacy of honor and of jurisdiction reserved to the office of the pope.

privilège du blanc (*the white privilege*) Vatican protocol requires a strict observance of dress for persons visiting the Holy Father in private audience or attending the funeral or installation of a pope. For women over the age of eighteen, this requirement is a conservative black dress with a black mantilla. The white privilege is a special diplomatic privilege reserved for Catholic queens and the Grand Duchess of Luxembourg. All other women, regardless of their rank, must wear black. Today, only the queen of Spain, the two queens of Belgium—Queen Fabiola, widow of the late King Baudouin, and Queen Paola, wife of King Albert II—along with Queen Maria José of Italy and the Grand Duchess of Luxembourg, hold this privilege.

privileges of doctors Those priests and prelates who have received a doctoral-level degree from a pontifical institution have the following privileges not permitted other clerics: They may wear the ring, even when not of episcopal dignity, on the prelatial finger; it may be a gemmed ring, depending on the ring bestowed on the candidate for the doctorate by the institution. The doctoral *biretta*, always a four-horned cap, may be worn with a colored tuft appropriate to the academic discipline. The doctoral *biretta* may never

be substituted, however, for the simple ecclesiastical *biretta*, even by the hierarchy. The doctoral *biretta* is positively restricted for use at academic settings, never during liturgical or social functions where the ecclesiastical *biretta* would be expected.

protonotaries apostolic Prelates, divided into two categories: (1) *protonotaries apostolic de numero*, a college of seven prelates with various specific functions in Rome; (2) *protonotaries apostolic supranumerary*, the honorary protonotaries, a papal honor, and the highest of the monsignorial titles awarded by the Holy Father, outside Rome. Prior to the *motu proprio Pontificalis Domus*, these prelates were also the canons of the Roman pontifical basilicas. There were, additionally, *protonotaries ad instar participatinum*, but with the reforms of Pope Paul VI, only the first two divisions remain. Vicars general in dioceses have the title Protonotary Apostolic Supranumerary *ipso iure*.

province A regional grouping of a religious order or of a religious congregation.

province, ecclesiastical The union of two or more dioceses, of which one is the metropolitan archdiocese and the others are suffragan dioceses.

purificator A cloth used to clear the chalice of dust before adding the water and wine, to wipe the fingers or lips of the celebrant, or to clean the lip of the chalice when more than one person is to drink from it in order to avoid the spread of germs. It is to be made entirely of linen, white in color, and should be 10 inches in length. The purificator may have some embroidery upon it; however, this is restricted to white in color. The use of a purificator is also prescribed by the rubrics for the lavabo. No other cloth should be used, as seems to be the rising custom in some places. Only the linen purificator, not one made of terry cloth or other materials, is proper. The medieval name *mundatory* was used for the purificator until the late 1800s.

purpure One of the heraldic colors; used to describe purple.

qualificator A scholar in the service of the Congregation for the Doctrine of the Faith for the examination of sacred doctrine. Traditionally, qualificators make use of one of the other titles of the officials of the Roman Curia.

raccolta A text prepared under the scrutiny of the Penitentiary of the Holy See, which defines the prayers, practices, and devotions that have attached to them, by official bull of the Holy See, the indulgences of the Church for the faithful. Also known by the Latin title *Enchiridion Indulgentiarum.*

Radio Vatican The radio station of the Vatican that broadcasts daily in many languages. It is directed by the Jesuit Fathers and has its headquarters in Vatican City. Its primary mission is to bring the Word of God and the work of the Holy Father to the world.

regent A senior post in the Apostolic Penitentiary and Apostolic Chancery equivalent to the post of secretary in the congregations.

religious A term used to refer to the religious orders, congregations, or institutes, clerical or lay. This term is also used to designate the members of these same canonical bodies. Under the law, religious are divided into different categories that correspond to their juridical distinction or to the historic development of the religious life: (1) *Orders (regulars),* whose members make solemn vows and are called regulars or nuns (female). They are further distinguished as canons regular (Premonstaratesians and Croziers), monks (Benedictines, Cistercians), mendicants (Dominicans, Franciscans, Augustinians, and Carmelites), and clerics regular (Theatines, Barnabites, and Jesuits). Congregations have members who make simple vows and are called *simple religious.* (2) *Religious of pontifical right,* who enjoy papal recognition and approval (with at least the canonical rating of "decree of praise," and *religious of diocesan right,* which are instituted by the local ordinary with permission of the Holy See. (3) *Clerical religious,* nearly all of whom are priests, and *lay religious,* when the members are not priests or when only some of the members are priests, the remaining being of the lay state.

rescript A term for a paper of some official affair in a congregation or an office of the Curia. It may be the answer to a question or a dispensation, or in reply to a request for favors, having effect for the individual or group to whom it is addressed.

reverencing the Blessed Sacrament The practice, as old as the Church, of showing proper and truly devout reverence for the Blessed Sacrament. Attached to the act of reverence, known as the genuflection, are the following indulgences. An indulgence of three hundred days is granted if the faithful recite a prayer of adoration to the Blessed Sacrament such as *Jesus, my God, I adore Thee here present in the Sacrament of Thy love.* When the Blessed Sacrament is exposed and the faithful reverence on both knees, an indulgence of five hundred days is granted if a prayer of adoration accompanies this act despite the common incorrect belief that this practice was abolished. If an additional sign of reverence to the Blessed Sacrament, such as the blessing of oneself, is made while passing a church, an indulgence of three hundred days is granted. Many of these practices are viewed by some to be out of date, yet they still remain an active part of the Church's tradition.

riasa The floor-length, full-cut cloak worn by Eastern rite clergy over the cassock. For prelates, it can be lined, trimmed, and faced in the appropriate colors of each rank of the prelature for everyday use. For an Eastern rite cardinal, a shade of scarlet that corresponds to the scarlet of the choir vesture of the Sacred College is used.

rites of the Church In the Catholic Church, there are the Latin and Oriental liturgical rites. The Latin rite is by great predominance that of the Roman rite, but there are also the Ambrosian rite of the archdiocese of Milan and the particular ancient rites of several religious orders (although in abeyance since Vatican Council II). The Oriental (or Eastern) rites are Antiochian, Alexandrian, Byzantine, Chaldean, and Armenian.

rogito The term applied to a document (only one per pontificate) that officially consigns a dead pope to history and that accompanies him to the grave. The *rogito* cites historic information (such as his baptismal and family name, the name of his pontificate, the dates of importance in his life), and it often makes reference, in elaborate Latin text, to specific papal decrees promulgated during his pontificate. It may or may not also accompany him to his grave.

Roman Curia The ensemble of all the congregations, councils, tribunals, commissions, secretariats, and offices of the Holy See that compose the central government of the Church.

Roman pilgrimage A religious pilgrimage to Rome made by the faithful, who intentionally and piously pray at the holiest sites in the city, while also remembering, in prayer, the intentions of the Holy Father, and who gain a plenary indulgence on the day of their departure if they receive the Sacrament of Penance while in Rome and if they receive the Eucharist.

Room of Tears The Gospel side of the Sistine Chapel, known also as the Chapel of Tears, which serves as both its sacristy and as the vesting room for the new pontiff. It is in the Room of Tears that the newly elected Pope is led to shed his scarlet vesture and to don the vesture and insignia of the successor of Peter.

Rota, Sacred Roman One of the three ecclesiastical tribunals of the Roman Curia. It is the ordinary court of appeals of the Holy See and is the court of cassation in matters concerning the validity of marriage.

rotal studies A three-year course of studies at the Sacred Rota for the formation of rotal lawyers, who are priests assigned as future judges, promoters of justice, and defenders of the bond. *See also* **studium.**

rubrics The rules governing the exterior action of liturgy, both public and private, such as the correct timing, place, manner, and formula in observing the rites and ceremonies of the Church. The word *rubric* derives from the Latin word for red (*rubrica*) because all directives regarding the liturgy and ceremonies are presented in red above the text. The ancient origins of the term *rubric* can be traced to the laws of the Roman empire. Each imperial decree placed the title of a new law in red as the heading of the announcement of the law. From this derives present usage of the legal term *rubric.*

sable A heraldic color used to describe black.

sanctuary (1) The area of a church around the altar, where the Sacred Mysteries occur; also known as the chancel or the apse. (2) In civil law, the concept that citizens could seek refuge, or sanctuary, in a church from the civil authorities. In old English Common Law, the terms for such sanctuary were set by custom, and penalties were set forth for those abusing this privilege.

sang A heraldic term used to describe blood red.

sanpietrini The workmen employed by the Commission of the Fabric of St. Peter's who are responsible for the care and upkeep of the Vatican basilica and for preparing the basilica for sacred functions. They also are responsible for preparing the Apostolic Palace for the conclave, as well as having the honor of lowering the deceased pontiff into his crypt. Also sometimes seen as *sampietrini.*

scoufia The Eastern rite headdress for everyday wear (corresponding to the *biretta*) and of varying colors. It is a soft cap by design.

scrutatores The title of a cardinal elector who, during conclave, serves as an official counter of each ballot and who announces the results of each round of balloting to his brethren cardinals.

secretary of congregation The first-ranking prelate of a Roman congregation after the cardinal-prefect. He normally has archiepiscopal dignity.

secretary of embassies The title of one of the lesser prelates, not to be confused with the *segretario per le ambasciate,* who was one of the former lay private chamberlains participating.

Sede Vacante The period between the death of a pope and the election of his successor. It begins officially with the burial of the pope, at which time those papal honors that were conferred *ad vitam* (meaning for the life of the reigning pope) cease to exist. The *Sede Vacante* extends to the moment when the new pontiff officially accepts election.

sedia gestatoria The portable throne used for centuries to carry the pope aloft during processions during the most solemn occasions. Although the last two popes have not made use of the *sedia,* it has not been abolished and may very well reappear as the Holy Father ages. The *sedia* is carried by twelve members of the Holy Father's personal household, properly known as both *sediarii* and *palafrenieri.* The *sedia* originated in Byzantium.

See, Apostolic The see of the pope, Bishop of Rome, Vicar of Christ.

Signatura Apostolica *See* **Apostolic Signatura**.

signature A monthly meeting of the cardinal major penitentiary with his consultors.

Sistine Chapel In recent history, the site of the election of a new pope; where the Papal Chapel was often held; where deceased pontiffs are traditionally placed on view for the Curia and Papal Household to pay their respects before being carried in state, into St. Peter's Basilica. The famous Sistine Chapel choir sings at the services held there.

smoking An English word derived from *smoking jacket,* incorporated into the French language and used to designate a type of formal dress for laymen. It is seen most commonly in Europe in the social world, yet it also appears frequently in the diplomatic world to specify required dress as black tie, or evening jacket. The French refer to black tie as "*smoking,*" and much of official life in Europe has adopted this usage. The word *smoking* would appear on the lower-left side of an invitation to denote proper dress.

society without vows A canonical designation for the associations of clergy and/or of the laity who have dedicated themselves to their own perfection. They do not take solemn vows, nor do they make vows such as do the Maryknolls, Paulists, and Vincentians. They should not be considered as a society or congregation of religious; however, they do assume a similar vocation of life.

S.P. Ap. The appropriate abbreviation for the Sacred Penitentiary Apostolic, the body of the Church under whose domain falls the regulation and bestowal of indulgences as prescribed by the Holy See. The abbreviation always appears prior to the date of issuance of the appropriate decree.

staff of governance The symbolic term used to describe the crozier at the moment it is passed by the proper ecclesiastic authority to a new bishop or archbishop when assuming his new jurisdiction.

stemma; stemme The Italian terms applied, in the singular and plural, to a coat of arms.

states of perfection This term includes both religious (orders, congregations, clerical, and lay) and societies without vows, as well as secular institutes.

studium A two- or three-year course of studies at one of the congregations (Congregation for Institutes of Consecrated Life and for Societies of Apostolic Life) or at the Sacred Rota in order to progress to one of the competent offices of these Curia departments.

subdatary First prelate of the former apostolic datary, ranking after the cardinal datary.

subdean of the college of cardinals The cardinal-bishop second in line of seniority in the Order of Cardinal Bishops. With the death of the dean, he automatically succeeds and adds the diocese of Ostia to the one he holds presently.

subsecretary of congregation The first-ranking prelate after the secretary of a congregation.

substitute secretary of state A high post in the Secretariat of State.

suburbicarian diocese The name given to the seven dioceses in the immediate surroundings of Rome and whose titulars are the six cardinals of the Order of Bishop. They are Albano, Frascati, Palestrina, Porto e Santa Rufina, Sabina e Poggio Mirteto, and Velletri-Segni. There is also Ostia, which is held by the cardinal-dean, together with the diocese that he already had before assuming the deanship.

suffragan sees Those dioceses of an ecclesiastical province so called in relation to their metropolitan see. They are suffragans because their ordinaries have suffrage in provincial councils.

superior general The head of a religious order, congregation, or institute. Most commonly superiors general reside in Rome during their terms of office and enjoy certain protocol privileges normally reserved for prelates.

supplica *See* **petition**.

Supreme Pontiff *See* **Pontiff, Supreme**.

Sylvester, Order of St. One of the lay awards or orders granted to the faithful for service to the Church. *See also* Chapter 6, Papal Honors: Laity.

terna A list that is formulated by the pope's legate in each nation (nuncio, pro-nuncio, delegate, etc.) for the purpose of naming a priest a Bishop. The name is derived from the Latin, meaning "three names." Each of the candidates is carefully investigated. If it is for a bishop's appointment in the Latin rite, the *terna* is forwarded to the Congregation for the Bishops (or for the mission territories to the Congregation for the Evangelization of the Peoples). In the Oriental rites, the *terna* is forwarded to the Congregation for the Oriental Churches. *See also* Chapter 2, Roman Curia.

thabor An ornamental stand made entirely of either precious metal or carved wood, on which rests the Blessed Sacrament when exposed for veneration without the solemn monstrance.

tincture A heraldic term for color.

titles of kinship Those fraternal appellations used by the pope when openly addressing members of the hierarchy of the Church. These include "Most Venerable" or "Esteemed Brother" (cardinals); "Venerable Brother" (bishops); and "Beloved Son" (all other clerics).

titular churches Those churches in Rome that are the titular churches of cardinal-priests. The titular churches of the cardinal-deacons are also sometimes so called. A titular church can also refer to a titular diocese or archdiocese.

transept The cross-aisle of the cruciform style church, usually before the chancel or sanctuary begins. It may contain seating or serve as a passageway. Also known as the crossing.

treasurer of the Apostolic Chamber A former title of the Apostolic Chamber. The treasurer was the third-ranking of the now defunct prelates *di fiocchetto*.

tribunals *See* Chapter 2, Roman Curia.

tronetto The thronelike single seat in the rear of the papal limousine. Today, the papal limousine has an electric *tronetto* that can be raised to afford spectators a better view of the pope.

uniat or **uniate** Those Christian communities of the Eastern rites, as distinguished from Latin rite, yet Catholic, which are in union with the Holy See.

unio primaria Title given to an institution of a religious to which are affiliated other similar associations scattered throughout the world.

Urbi et Orbi The blessing (meaning "to the city and to the world") that the pope imparts, on special occasions, to Rome and to the entire world, with a plenary indulgence attached, even if received over the radio or television.

vair One of the heraldic furs. It is depicted as rows of small shields, each row inverted against the previous.

Vatican The territory that holds the legal status of the Vatican City State. It also comprises the official residence of the pope. The name is derived from the ancient Latin word *Vaticinia*, meaning the oracles that were pronounced by the priests of the temple of Apollo. *Montes Vaticani* (the Vatican Hill), adjacent to the Janiculum, and *Ager Vaticanus* (the lowlands or meadows) form the area stretching from St. Peter's north of the Tiber.

Vatican City The sovereign state that came into existence in 1929 with the Lateran Treaty and that guarantees to the pope free exercise of his high ministry. It is governed in the name of the pope by a commission of cardinals and high-ranking laymen. Pope Pius XII named a cardinalatial commission for the state's government, as has Pope John Paul II. At various times in its history, a lay governor, usually from the Roman Black Nobility, has been appointed in lieu of a cardinalatial commission. The spiritual jurisdiction of the state, and the Vatican basilica with its Chapter of Canons, today is exercised by the cardinal-archpriest of the Vatican basilica who, for this reason, also has the title Vicar General of His Holiness for Vatican City, a title formerly in the domain of the Augustinians.

Vatican Polyglot Press A printing house in the Vatican that was established by papal decree in 1926. It has typefaces of almost every language on earth and is responsible for the printing of official documents.

Vatican State citizenship Citizenship in the Vatican City State is now restricted to members of the Sacred College resident in Rome, nuncios, and other senior diplomats serving the Holy See, and, in unique circumstances, cardinals and other senior ecclesiastics outside Italy. At one time, Vatican citizenship was extended to all members of the Sacred College. Citizenship entitles an individual the privilege of carrying the coveted Vatican diplomatic passport.

vert One of the heraldic colors; used to describe green.

veste filetta Same as **abito filetta** (q.v.).

vicariate apostolic The second stage toward the establishment of a regular ecclesiastical hierarchy in a region or mission, which comes after prefecture apostolic and before diocese. The vicar apostolic is always a titular bishop.

vicariate of Rome Because the pope has the care of the Church of the whole world, he cannot personally govern the diocese of Rome, his own diocese. He therefore names a cardinal as his vicar for Rome (a nomination that does not cease with the pope's death), who exercises ordinary jurisdiction, with the same powers of a residential bishop, in his place.

vicariate of Vatican City Vatican City, while forming part of the diocese of Rome (whose bishop is the pope, but whose government is entrusted to the cardinal-vicar), is exempt from the jurisdiction of the cardinal-vicar of Rome. A special vicar general is appointed specifically for Vatican City; he has jurisdiction also over the pontifical Lateran Palace and the pontifical villa of Castel Gandolfo. Today, along with the Vatican basilica, with its canonical house, Vatican City depends on the cardinal-archpriest of the Basilica of St. Peter as vicar general.

Vice Camerlengo of the Holy Roman Church Formerly, the first-ranking post of the now-defunct prelates *di fiocchetto*; now always a post held by an archbishop.

vice-gerent of Rome One of several assistants to the vicar for Rome. He is usually an archbishop and is equivalent to other diocesan auxiliary bishops. There are traditionally more than one who assist the cardinal vicar for Rome.

vimp The veil or shoulder cape of silk material, often matching the liturgical vestments of the day, but most frequently in white or gold, and worn by two attendants, traditionally dressed in cassock and surplice, who follow a prelate in order to receive from the master of ceremonies the mitre and the crozier. It should not be confused with the humeral veil, which is reserved for use by the clergy. The vimp has threads of silk or cotton that tie at the neck. Often, inside pockets are provided for the hands to move easily in order to grasp the episcopal insignia. It is not permitted to have uncovered human hands touch the episcopal insignia during ceremonies, and the vimp is donned to avoid this. The term *vimps* refers to those designated to wear a vimp for a liturgical ceremony.

APPENDIXES

All appendixes have been reproduced faithfully from the original documents. The appendixes have not been edited for style or grammar; no corrections, additions, or changes have been made to the text. Inconsistencies in style and usage among individual documents reflect the preferences of the original sources. Several of the appendix documents appear in excerpted form, reproducing only that text which is relevant to this study.

The Vacancy of the Apostolic See

CHAPTER I: THE POWER OF THE SACRED COLLEGE OF CARDINALS DURING THE VACANCY OF THE APOSTOLIC SEE

1. During the vacancy of the Apostolic See, the government of the Church is entrusted to the Sacred College of Cardinals for the sole despatch of ordinary business and of matters which cannot be postponed, and for the preparation of everything necessary for the election of the new Pope, within the terms and limits indicated in this our Constitution.

2. The Sacred College therefore during this period has no power or jurisdiction in matters which pertained to the Supreme Pontiff during his lifetime, but such matters are to be reserved totally and exclusively to the future Pontiff. We therefore declare null and void any act of power or jurisdiction pertaining to the Roman Pontiff during his lifetime which the College of Cardinals might see fit to exercise, beyond what is expressly permitted in this our Constitution.

3. We further lay down that the Sacred College of Cardinals may make no dispositions concerning the rights of the Apostolic See and of the Roman Church, nor permit any elements of these rights to lapse, either directly or indirectly, even though it be to solve disputes or to deal with acts perpetrated against these same

rights after the death of the Pontiff. All are to take care to defend these rights.

4. In the same way, while the Apostolic See is vacant, laws issued by the Roman Pontiff can in no way be corrected or modified, nor can anything be added, nor a dispensation given from a part of them, especially with regard to the ordering of the election of the Supreme Pontiff. Should anything be done or even merely attempted against this disposition, by our Supreme Authority we declare it null and void.

5. Should there arise doubts concerning the meaning of the prescriptions contained in this our Constitution, or concerning the manner of putting them into issuing a judgment concerning the same belongs to the College of Cardinals, to which we grant the faculty of interpreting doubtful or controverted points, and we establish that should it be necessary to discuss these or other similar questions, excepting the act itself of electing the Pontiff, it suffices that the majority of the Cardinals present should agree on the same opinion.

6. In the same way, should there be a question which, in the view of the majority of the assembled Cardinals, cannot be postponed

until another time, the Sacred College may similarly act according to the majority opinion.

CHAPTER II: THE CONGREGATIONS OF THE CARDINALS

7. While the See is vacant and until the entry into the Conclave, there are two kinds of Congregations of the Cardinals, and of them alone, namely: a General Congregation, that is one of the whole Sacred College, and a Particular Congregation. The General Congregations must be attended by all the Cardinals who are not legitimately prevented from doing so, as soon as they are informed of the vacancy of the Apostolic See. However, Cardinals who have completed their eightieth year are granted the faculty of taking part or not. The Particular Congregation is made up of the Cardinal Camerlengo of the Holy Roman Church and of three Cardinals, one from each order, chosen by lot from among all those who have the right to elect the Pope in accordance with paragraph 33 of the present Constitution. The office of these three Cardinals, who are called "Assistants", ceases completely on the third day after the entry into the Conclave, and their place is taken, similarly by ballot, by three others every three days. During the Conclave, more important matters are if necessary dealt with by the assembly of the Cardinal electors, while ordinary affairs continue to be dealt with by the Particular Congregation of the Cardinals. In the General and Particular Congregation, during the vacancy of the Apostolic See, the Cardinals are to wear the usual black cassock with piping and the red sash.

8. In the Particular Congregations only questions of lesser importance which arise from day to day or from moment to moment are to be dealt with. But should there arise more serious questions requiring a more detailed examination, these must be submitted to the General Congregation. Moreover, what has been decided, resolved or refused in one Particular Congregation cannot be revoked, altered or granted in another; the right to do this belongs solely to the General Congregation, and with a majority vote.

9. The General Congregations of the Cardinals will be held in the Apostolic Vatican Palace or, if circumstances demand it, in another place judged more suitable by the Cardinals. At these Congregations the Dean of the Sacred College presides or, in his absence, the Subdean. Should one or both of these be unable to enter the Conclave because they have completed eighty years of age, the assembly of the Cardinal electors which may take place there, on the basis of paragraph 7, will be presided over by the senior Cardinal, according to the usual order of the precedence.

10. Votes in the Congregations of the Cardinals, when matters of great importance are concerned, are to be expressed not by word of mouth but in a way which preserves secrecy.

11. The General Congregations preceding the entry into the Conclave, and therefore called "preparatory", are to be held daily, beginning on the day which shall be fixed by the Camerlengo of the Holy Roman Church and the three senior Cardinals in each order, including those days on which the obsequies of the deceased Pontiff are celebrated. This shall be done in order to enable the Cardinal Camerlengo to hear the opinion of the Sacred College and to communicate to it what is considered necessary or

suitable, and in order that the individual Cardinals may be able to express their opinions on problems that present themselves, to ask for explanations in cases of doubt and to make suggestions.

12. During the first General Congregations the first part of the present Constitution, "The Vacancy of the Apostolic See", will be read out, and at the end of the reading all the Cardinals present will take an oath concerning the observance of the prescriptions contained therein and the observance of secrecy. This oath, which shall also be taken by Cardinals who arrive later and subsequently take part in these Congregations, shall be read out by the Cardinal Dean, in the presence of the other Cardinals, according to the following formula:

> *We, Cardinals of the Holy Roman Church, Bishops, Priests and Deacons, promise, bind ourselves and swear, as a body and individually, to observe exactly and faithfully all the norms contained in the Apostolic Constitution* Romano Pontifici Eligendo *of the Supreme Pontiff Paul VI, and scrupulously to observe secrecy concerning everything that shall be dealt with or decided in the Congregation of the Cardinals, both before and during the Conclave, and concerning anything that in any way may pertain to the election of the Roman Pontiff.*
>
> Next, each Cardinal will say: *And I, N. Cardinal N., promise, bind myself and swear.* And, placing his hand on the Gospels, he will add: *So Help me God and these Holy Gospels which I touch with my hand.*

13. In one of the Congregations immediately following, the Cardinals, according to a pre-arranged agenda, shall take decisions on the more urgent matters regarding the beginning of the Conclave; that is to say they shall:

a. fix the day, hour and manner in which the body of the deceased Pontiff shall be taken into the Vatican Basilica, there to be exposed for the homage of the faithful;

b. make all necessary arrangement for the obsequies of the deceased Pontiff, which shall be performed for nine consecutive days, and decide when they are to begin;

c. nominate two separate Commissions each consisting of three Cardinals; the first shall designate those who are to enter the Conclave for the various services and who shall be responsible for the same; it shall carefully consider whether any conclavist should be admitted according to norm 45 of the present Constitution; it shall also make diligent enquiries concerning the suitability of all the conclavists. The second Commission shall take charge of the preparation and enclosing of the Conclave and of the preparation of the cells;

d. examine and prove the expenses of the Conclave;

e. read the documents left by the deceased Pontiff for the Sacred College of Cardinals, should any such exist;

f. arrange for the breaking of the Fisherman's Ring and of the lead Seal under which Apostolic Letters are despatched;

g. distribute by lot to the electors the cells of the Conclave, unless the ill-health of one or other of the electors should make other arrangements advisable;

h. fix the day and hour of entry into the Conclave.

CHAPTER III: CONCERNING CERTAIN OFFICES DURING THE VACANCY OF THE APOSTOLIC SEE

14. In accordance with the intention of the Apostolic Constitution *Regimini Ecclesiae universae,* all the Cardinals in charge of the departments of the Roman Curia, and even the Cardinal Secretary of State, relinquish the exercise of their office at the death of the Pontiff, with exception of the Camerlengo of the Holy Roman Church, the Major Penitentiary and the Vicar General for the Diocese of Rome, who continue to exercise their ordinary functions, submitting to the Sacred College of Cardinals matters that have to be referred to the Supreme Pontiff (7).

15. Should the offices of Camerlengo of the Holy Roman Church or of Major Penitentiary be vacant at the death of the Pontiff, or before the election of his successor, the Sacred College shall provide as soon as possible for the election of the Cardinal or Cardinals as the case may be, and they shall hold office until the election of the Pontiff. In each of the cases mentioned, election takes place through a secret vote of all Cardinals present, by the use of cards which shall be distributed and collected by the Masters of Ceremonies, who will then open them in the presence of the Camerlengo and of the three Cardinal Assistants, if it is a matter of electing the Major Penitentiary; or in the presence of the said three Cardinals and of the Secretary of the Sacred College, if it is a matter of electing the Camerlengo. Whoever receives the greatest number of votes will be elected and will have *ipso facto* all the relevant faculties. In the case of an equal number of votes, the Cardinal belonging to the higher order or, if both are in the same order, the one first made a member of the Sacred College, will be appointed. Until the Camerlengo is elected, his functions are carried out by the Dean of the Sacred College, who can without any delay take the decisions that circumstances demand.

16. If during the vacancy of the Apostolic See the Vicar General for the Diocese of Rome should die, the Vicegerent in the office at the time shall have every faculty, authority and power which belonged to that Vicar for the exercise of his office and which the Pontiff himself normally grants temporarily to the Vicegerent when the office of Vicar is vacant and until he names the new Vicar. Should there not be a Vicegerent or should he be unable to exercise his office, the Auxiliary Bishop who is senior by appointment will carry out the functions.

17. It is the task of the Camerlengo of the Holy Roman Church during the vacancy of the Apostolic See to take charge of and administer the goods and temporal rights of the Holy See, within the help of the three Cardinal Assistants, and after learning the views of the Sacred College, once only for less important matters, but on each occasion when more serious matters arise. Hence, as soon as he is informed of the death of the Supreme Pontiff by the Prefect of the Papal Household, the Camerlengo of the Holy Roman Church will officially ascertain the Pontiff's death, in the presence of the Papal Master of Ceremonies, of the Cleric Prelates of the *Reverenda Camera Apostolica* and of the Secretary Chancellor of the same, who shall draw up the official death certificate. It is also the task of the Camerlengo: to place the seals on the private apartment of the Pontiff; to inform the Cardinal Vicar of the death, upon which the latter will inform the People of Rome by a special notification; to take possession of the Apostolic Vatican Palace and, either

in person or through a delegate, of the Palaces of the Lateran and of Castelgandolfo, and to act as custodian and administrator of the same; to decide, after consulting the heads of the three orders of Cardinals, all matters concerning the burial of the Pontiff, unless the latter during his lifetime had manifested his wishes in this regard; and, in the name of and with the consent of the Sacred College, to deal with all matters that circumstances suggest for safeguarding the rights of the Apostolic See and for its proper administration.

18. The Cardinal Major Penitentiary and his Officials, during the period in which the Apostolic See is vacant, can perform what was laid down by our Predecessor Pius XI in the Apostolic Constitution *Quae Divinitus* of 25 March 1935 (8).

19. The Dean of the Sacred College for his part, as soon as he is informed of the death of the Pontiff by the Prefect of the Papal Household, shall inform all the Cardinals, convoking them for the Congregations of the Sacred College, and convoking all those having the right thereto for entry into the Conclave at the appropriate time. He will also communicate the news of the death of the Pontiff to the Diplomatic Corps accredited to the Holy See and to the Heads of the respective Nations.

20. As is laid down in the Apostolic Constitution *Regimini Ecclesiae Universae,* during the period that the Apostolic See is vacant the Substitute of the Secretariat of State or Papal Secretariat continues to carry out the duties of his office, for which he is responsible to the Sacred College of Cardinals (9).

21. In the same way, during the period of vacancy the office and relevant powers of Papal Representatives do not lapse.

22. The Almoner of His Holiness will also continue to carry out works of charity according to the same criteria followed during the lifetime of the Pontiff; and he will be dependent upon the Sacred College of Cardinals until the election of the new Pope. It will be the task of the Cardinal Camerlengo of the Holy Roman Church to issue the relative mandate for this.

23. During the vacancy of the Apostolic See, all the civil power of the Supreme Pontiff concerning the government of Vatican City State belongs to the Sacred College of Cardinals, which however will be unable to issue decrees except in cases of urgent necessity and solely for the time in which the Holy See is vacant. Such decrees will be valid for the future only if the new Pontiff confirms them.

CHAPTER IV: FACULTIES OF THE SACRED CONGREGATIONS AND TRIBUNALS OF THE ROMAN CURIA DURING THE VACANCY OF THE APOSTOLIC SEE

24. During the period of vacancy, the Sacred Roman Congregations have no faculty in those things that *Sede plena,* they can only deal with and carry out *facto verbo cum Sanctissimo* or *ex Audientia Sanctissimi* or *vigore specialium et extraordinariarum facultatum* which the Roman Pontiff is accustomed to grant to their Prefects or Secretaries.

25. On the other hand the ordinary faculties proper to each Sacred Congregation do not cease at the death of the Pontiff. We lay down, however, that the Sacred Congregations are only to make use of these faculties in order to grant requests of minor importance, while more serious or controverted matters, if they can be postponed, must be exclusively reserved to the future Pontiff. If such matters admit of

no delay, they can be entrusted by the Sacred College of Cardinals to the Cardinal who was Prefect until the death of the Pontiff (10) and to the other Cardinals to the same Congregation, to whose examination the Pontiff would probably have entrusted them. They will be able to decide *per modum provisionis,* in such circumstances, until the election of the Pontiff, what they judge most fitting and appropriate for the preservation and defence of ecclesiastical rights and traditions.

26. The Supreme Tribunal of the Apostolic Signatura and the Tribunal of the Sacred Roman Rota, during the vacancy of the Holy See, continue to deal with cases according to their proper laws, with due regard however for the prescriptions of the Code of Canon Law contained in Canons 244, § 1, and 1603, § 2.

CHAPTER V: THE OBSEQUIES OF THE ROMAN PONTIFF

27. After the death of the Roman Pontiff, the Cardinals will celebrate his obsequies for nine consecutive days, according to the *Ordo exsequiarum Summi Pontificis vita functi;* this document, together with the *Ordo sacrorum rituum Conclavis,* forms an integral part of the present Constitution.

28. If the burial takes place in the Vatican Basilica, the relevant official document is drawn up by the Notary of the Chapter of the Basilica. Later, a delegate of the Cardinal Camerlengo and a delegate of the Prefect of the Papal Household shall separately draw up documents certifying that the burial has taken place. The first mentioned delegate shall do so in the presence of the *Reverenda Camera Apostolica* and the second in the presence of the Prefect of the Papal Household.

29. If the Roman Pontiff should die outside Rome, it is the competence of the Sacred College of Cardinals to make all necessary arrangements for the fitting and reverent transfer of the body to the Vatican Basilica of Saint Peter's.

30. No one is permitted to take photographs of the Supreme Pontiff in his apartment, whether on his sickbed or after death, or to record his words on tape to reproduce them afterwards. If anyone, after the death of the Pope should wish to take photographs of him for the sake of documentation, he shall seek permission from the Cardinal Camerlengo of the Holy Roman Church, who will not however permit the taking of photographs of the Supreme Pontiff except attired in the pontifical vestments.

31. Before or during the Conclave, no part of the private apartment of the Supreme Pontiff is to be lived in.

32. If the deceased Supreme Pontiff has made a will concerning his property, letters and private documents and has named a personal executor thereof, it is the concern of the executor to decide and carry out, according to the mandate received from the testator, matters concerning the private property and writings of the deceased Pontiff. The executor will give an account of the task he has carried out only to the new Supreme Pontiff.

The Election of a Pope

New rules for the election of a Pope were released by Pope Paul VI Nov. 13 (though, as is typical with such documents, they were formally dated Oct. 1, 1975). The Pope reaffirmed "the principal whereby the election of the Roman pontiff is by ancient tradition the competence of the Church of Rome, that is, of the Sacred College of Cardinals which represents her." But at the same time, he said he found it necessary "to proceed to the revision of certain norms concerning the election . . . so that they may fit the present-day situation and correspond to the good of the church." The new document containing rules for the election is an apostolic constitution entitled, "Romano Pontfici Eligendo." On the following pages the chapter appears that details the rules for the election discussing the membership of the conclave, the secrecy to be maintained by the conclave, the manner of voting, other matters such as politicking, and the proclamation and coronation of the new pontiff. (The portion of the constitution which does not appear here included an introduction and a discussion of Vatican policy during the vacancy of the Apostolic See. Official Vatican translation.)*

33. The right to elect the Roman pontiff belongs solely to the cardinals of the Holy Roman Church, excluding in accordance with the law previously published[1] those who the moment of entry into the conclave have already completed their 80th year. The maximum number of cardinal electors must not exceed one hundred and twenty. Any intervention by any other ecclesiastical dignitary or lay power of whatsoever degree and order is absolutely excluded.

34. If the Roman pontiff should die during the celebration of a general council or of a synod of bishops taking place in Rome or in any other place in the world, the election of the new pontiff is to be made solely and exclusively by the cardinal electors specified above, and not by the council or the synod of bishops. For this reason we declare as null and void any acts that would in any way temerariously presume to modify the electoral system or body. Moreover, the same council or synod of bishops, at whatever stage it may be, must be considered as suspended, *ipso iure*, as soon as certain notification is received of the death of the pontiff. It must therefore without delay close any meeting, congregation or session and desist from compiling or preparing any decrees or canons, under pain of nullity of the same. Neither

---

* Grateful acknowledgement to *Origins* for providing the publication of the original Vatican English translation.
1. Cf. Paul VI, M.P. *In Gravescent Aetatem*, II. 2., *AAS* 62, (1970), p. 811.

the council nor the synod can continue for any reason, even though it be very serious and worthy of special mention, until the new pontiff has been canonically elected and has given permission for it to be resumed or continued.

35. No cardinal elector can be excluded from the active and passive election of the supreme pontiff because of, or under the pretext of, whatsoever excommunication, suspension, interdict or any other ecclesiastical impediment; these censures, for the effects of such an election only, are to be considered as suspended.

36. A cardinal of the Holy Roman Church who has been created and published in a consistory has immediately by this very fact the right to elect the pontiff, even if he has not yet received the biretta or been given the ring proper to cardinals or taken the usual oath of fidelity. On the other hand, cardinals who have been canonically deposed or who have renounced the cardinalate with the permission of the pontiff do not have this right. Moreover, during the vacancy of the see the Sacred College of Cardinals cannot readmit or rehabilitate them.

37. We lay down moreover that after the death of the pontiff the cardinal electors who are present must wait fifteen full days for those who are absent; the faculty is also granted to the Sacred College of Cardinals to defer entry into the conclave for a few more days. But once a maximum period of twenty days has elapsed all the cardinal electors present are obliged to enter the conclave and proceed to the election.

38. However, should some cardinal electors arrive before the new pastor of the church has been elected, they shall be allowed to take part in the election at the stage it has reached.

39. All the cardinal electors who have been convoked by the cardinal dean, or by another cardinal in his name, for the election of the new pontiff, are required, and indeed in virtue of holy obedience, to give their assent to the announcement of convocation and to proceed to the place designated for the election, unless they are detained by infirmity or by some grave impediment, which must however be recognized as such by the Sacred College of Cardinals.

40. If it should happen that a cardinal having the right to vote does not wish to enter the conclave or, once having entered, leaves it without a clear reason of illness, attested to under oath by doctors and confirmed by the major part of the electors, the others shall proceed freely to the election, without waiting for him or readmitting him to the same election. But if a cardinal elector is constrained to leave the conclave because of illness, the election can proceed without his voting; if however he wishes to reenter the conclave after his health is restored, or even before, he must be readmitted. Moreover, if a cardinal elector leaves the conclave for some other grave reason, recognized as such by the majority of the electors, he can return to the conclave while it is in progress.

THE CONCLAVE AND THOSE WHO TAKE PART THEREIN

41. The election of the Supreme Pontiff must take place in the conclave—which is normally arranged in the Vatican Palace or, for special reasons, in another place—after the conclave has been enclosed. The nullity of the election established in this regard by Gregory XV or by any other pontifical decree is however removed.

42. By "conclave" are understood those clearly defined places, having as it were the character of a sacred retreat, where, after the invocation of the Holy Spirit, the cardinal electors choose

the supreme pontiff, and where they and the other officials and assistants, together with any conclavists there may be, remain night and day until the election has taken place, without having any dealings with extraneous persons or things, according to the modes and norms that follow.

43. Besides the cardinal electors, there shall enter the conclave the secretary of the Sacred College, who acts as secretary of the conclave; the vicar general of the Roman pontiff for Vatican City, with one or more assistants, as the Sacred College shall decide, for the care of the sacristy; and the papal master of ceremonies and assistants, for the fulfillment of their proper task. In addition, the cardinal dean, or the cardinal taking his place, is permitted to bring with him an ecclesiastic to act as his assistant.

44. There shall also be present a number of priests from the religious clergy, in order to make confessions possible in the principal languages; two doctors, one a surgeon and the other a general physician, with either one or two medical assistants; the architect of the conclave and two technicians (cf. nos. 55 and 61). All of these persons will be chosen by the majority of the cardinals on the proposal of the camerlengo and of the three cardinal assistants. There will also be added an appropriate number of other persons to take care of the needs of the conclave; these will be named by the appropriate commission of cardinals as mentioned in no. 1 3c.

45. The cardinal electors will not be entitled to bring with them any conclavist or personal assistant, whether clerical or lay. This can be conceded only in particular cases and as an exception, for the reason of serious illness. In such a case a request must be made to the cardinal camerlengo, explaining the reason. He will refer the matter to the relevant commission of cardinals, which will give its decision and, if the request is allowed, will make the most careful inquiries about the persons proposed for this task.

46. All the officials and other assistants of the conclave, whether ecclesiastics or lay, as well as any conclavists, must, under the responsibility of the camerlengo of the Holy Roman Church, take an oath in Latin or in another language, after each of them has understood the scope of the oath and the meaning of the formula. Hence a day or two before the entrance into the conclave they will swear before the secretary of the conclave and the papal master of ceremonies, who shall have been delegated for this task by the camerlengo—and who in their turn shall have first taken an oath before the camerlengo—*using the following formula translated as necessary into various languages:

> *I, N.N., promise and swear that I will observe inviolable secrecy about each and every matter concerning the election of the new pontiff which has been treated or defined in the congregations of the cardinals, and also concerning what takes place in the conclave or place of election, directly or indirectly concerning the balloting and concerning every other matter that may in any way come to my knowledge. I will not violate this secret in any way, either directly or indirectly, either by signs, words or writing, or in any other manner. Moreover I promise and swear not to use in the conclave any type of*

---

* Formula of the oath to be taken by the secretary of the conclave and by the papal master of ceremonies: *I.N.N., touching the holy gospels, promise and swear that I will be faithful to each and every disposition of the Sacred College of Cardinals and that I will carry out my office diligently and faithfully. Moreover I promise and swear that I will observe inviolable secrecy on each and every . . .* (there follows the text of the formula of the oath of the officials of the conclave, given above).

transmitting or receiving instrument, nor to use devices designed in any way for taking pictures; and this under pain of excommunication latae sententiae *reserved* specialissimo modo *to the Apostolic See, should the above norm be violated. I will maintain this secret conscientiously and scrupulously even after the election of the pontiff has taken place, unless a special faculty or an explicit authorization be granted to me by the same pontiff.*

In like manner I promise and swear that I will never give my help or support to any interference, opposition or any other form of intervention whereby the civil powers of any order and degree, or any group or individual persons, would wish to interfere in the election of the Roman pontiff.

So help me God and these holy gospels which I touch with my hand.

47. Any officials or any other lay assistants who may leave the conclave, only because of manifest and obvious illness, attested to under oath by the doctors, and with the consent given *eorum onerata conscientia* by the cardinal camerlengo and by the three cardinal assistants, may not return for any reason at all; but should it be necessary, at the same time as the sick persons leave other individuals may enter in their place, provided that they are legitimately approved and accepted and have taken the oath.

48. Should a cardinal elector who has brought a conclavist with him die in the conclave, his conclavist must immediately leave and may not be taken into the service of another cardinal elector during the same conclave.

ENTRY INTO THE CONCLAVE

49. When the obsequies of the deceased pontiff have been performed according to the prescriptions and the conclave has in the mean-time been prepared, the cardinal electors shall assemble on the day appointed in Saint Peter's Basilica, or, according to circumstances, in another place, where the ceremonies laid down by the *Ordo Sacrorum Rituum Conclavis* will take place. Immediately after the celebration of the Mass in the morning or, if it seems more opportune, in the afternoon of the same day, the entry into the conclave will take place. When the entry has been made into the chapel the appropriate prayer is said, and when the order *extra omnes* from the chapel has been given the second part of the present constitution is read, namely "The Election of the Roman Pontiff." Then all the cardinal electors take an oath according to the following formula, which is read aloud by the dean or by the cardinal who is first in order and seniority:

All we cardinal electors present in this conclave, as a body and as individuals, bind ourselves and swear to observe faithfully and scrupulously all the prescriptions contained in the Apostolic Constitution of the Supreme Pontiff Paul VI Romano Pontifici Eligendo, issued on October 1, 1975. We likewise promise, bind ourselves and swear that whichever of us by divine disposition is elected Roman Pontiff will not cease to affirm, defend and if necessary vindicate integrally and strenuously the spiritual and temporal rights and the liberty of the Holy See. Above all, we promise and swear to observe with the greatest fidelity and with all persons, including any conclavists, the secret concerning everything that in any way relates to the election of the Roman Pontiff and concerning what takes place in the conclave or place of the election, directly or indirectly concerning the scrutinies; not to break this secret in any way, either during the conclave or after the election of the new pontiff, unless we are given a special faculty or explicit authorization from the same future pontiff. Likewise, not to accept in any way from any civil authority, under any pretext, the task of imposing the veto or *exclusiva*, even under the form of a simple wish, and not to be known a veto which may in any way make known to us; never to lend aid or favor to any interference, opposition or any other form of intervention, whereby the secular authorities of whatever order and degree or whatsoever group or individual persons would wish to interfere in the election of the Roman pontiff.

Each of the cardinal electors will then say: *And, I N. Cardinal N., promise, bind myself and swear*, and, placing his hand on the gospel, will add: *So help me God and these holy gospels which I touch with my hand.*

After this the cardinal dean or the cardinal who is first in order and seniority gives a brief address to those present, exhorting them to carry out the election in the manner prescribed and with the right intention, having before their eyes solely the good of the universal church.

50. When all this has been completed, the prefect of the papal household, the special delegate of the Pontifical Commission for Vatican City and the commandant of the Swiss Guard, who by virtue of this constitution are entrusted with the guarding of the conclave, will take the oath according to the prescribed formula* before the cardinal dean or the senior cardinal and in the presence of all the cardinal electors. The same will be done by the cleric prelates of the *reverenda camera apostolica*, the protonotaries apostolic *de numero participantium* and the auditors of the Sacred Roman Rota, who are entrusted with guarding and inspecting whatever is brought into or taken out of the conclave. All of these persons will be assisted by the papal masters of ceremonies.

51. All the cardinal electors will then proceed to the cells assigned to them, with the exception of the camerlengo and the three cardinal assistants, who remain in the chapel in order to proceed with the enclosing of the conclave. In the meantime, all the officials of the conclave and the other assistants shall as soon as possible take the oath prescribed above if they have not already done so, in the presence of the secretary of the conclave and the papal master of ceremonies, who are delegated for this task by the camerlengo of the Holy Roman Church.

52. Finally, when a suitable signal has been given by order of the cardinal dean or of the senior cardinal, the camerlengo and the three cardinal assistants, together with the papal master of ceremonies, with the other ceremonial assistants, the architect of the conclave and the two technicians, shall carefully search the various areas of the conclave, in order that no extraneous person shall remain inside. For this reason they shall inspect all the assistants of the conclave, including any cardinal electors' conclavists, to ensure that no one extraneous to the conclave has been included among them. For the purpose of this check they shall be assembled in the chapel, where a roll-call shall be taken.

53. While the enclosure of the conclave is being ensured from within, it must, after a careful inspection, also be ensured from without, by the prefect of the papal household, the special delegate of the Pontifical Commission for Vatican City and the commandant of the Swiss Guard, in the presence of the dean of the cleric

---

* Formula of the oath: *I, N. N., promise and swear to carry out my office diligently and scrupulously, according to the norms laid down by the supreme pontiffs and the dispositions given by the Sacred College of Cardinals. So help me God and these holy gospels which I touch with my hand.*

prelates of the *reverenda camera apostolica,* together with the secretary chancellor, deputed by the camerlengo, the masters of ceremonies and the architects. The keys shall then be given to the special delegate of the Pontifical Commission for Vatican City.

54. Two separate documents are to be drawn up regarding the internal and external closure, the first by the papal master of ceremonies, which must be signed by the secretary of the conclave and by the papal master of ceremonies acting as notary in the presence of two assistant masters of ceremonies acting as witnesses; the other must be drawn up by one of the cleric prelates of the *reverenda camera apostolica,* deputed by the cardinal camerlengo of the Holy Roman Church, at the office of the special delegate of the Pontifical Commission for Vatican City, with the signatures of the prefect of the papal household, the special delegate and the commandant of the Swiss Guard.

Observance of the Secret Regarding Everything that Takes Place in the Conclave

55. The cardinal camerlengo and the three cardinal assistants *pro tempore* are bound to maintain careful vigilance, making frequent visits either personally or through others to the various areas of the conclave, to ensure that the enclosure thereof is not violated in any way. During these visits there shall always be present two technicians who by the use, if necessary, of appropriate modern equipment will test for the presence of the instruments mentioned in no. 61. Should anything of the sort be discovered, those responsible are to be expelled from the conclave and subjected to grave penalties in the judgment of the future pontiff.

56. After the enclosure of the conclave, no one may be admitted to speak to the cardinal electors and the other persons in the conclave except in the presence of the prelates entrusted with the guarding of the same, and such persons must speak distinctly and in a language which can be understood. Should anyone enter the conclave secretly, he is *ipso facto* to be deprived of every honor, rank, office and ecclesiastical benefice, or, depending upon the condition of the person concerned, subjected to appropriate penalties.

57. We likewise lay down that no letters or written matter of any sort, including printed matter, may be sent to those in the conclave, not excluding the cardinal electors, and, especially, from the conclave to those outside, unless each and every such written document has first been examined by the secretary of the conclave, with the prelates delegated for the guarding of the conclave. However, an exception to this rule is made for the exchange of letters, which shall be free and unhindered, between the apostolic penitentiary and the cardinal major penitentiary present inside the conclave; therefore such letters, bearing the official seal, will not be subjected to scrutiny and examination.

    Furthermore, we explicitly prohibit the sending of newspapers or periodicals into or out of the conclave.

58. The assistants of the conclave also are obliged carefully to avoid whatever may in any way directly or indirectly violate secrecy, whether by words, by writings, by signs or in any other manner, under pain of excommunication *latae sententiae* reserved to the Apostolic See.

59. In particular, we forbid the cardinal electors to reveal to their assistants or to any other person information directly or indirectly regarding the

voting and what has been dealt with or decided concerning the election of the pontiff in the congregations of the cardinals, either before or during the conclave.

60. We further order the cardinal electors, *graviter onerata ipsorum conscientia,* to preserve secrecy concerning these matters even after the election of the new pontiff has taken place, and we remind them that it is not licit to break the secret in any way unless a special and explicit faculty has been granted by the pontiff himself. We desire that this command be extended to all the other persons participating in the conclave who, in good or bad faith, may have come to the knowledge of what took place in the conclave.

61. Finally, in order that the cardinal electors may protect themselves from the indiscretion of others and from possible trickery that might be exercised upon their independence of judgment and freedom of decision, we absolutely forbid the introduction into the conclave, under whatsoever pretext, or the use, should they have been introduced, of technical instruments of whatsoever kind for the recording, reproduction or transmission of voices and images.

THE CARRYING OUT OF THE ELECTION

62. On the morning following the enclosing of the conclave, after the signal, the cardinal electors who are not prevented by illness, meet in the designated chapel, where they concelebrate or assist at Mass. At the end of the Mass and after the Holy Spirit has been invoked the election is immediately begun; it must be carried out in only one of the three ways or forms described below, otherwise it is to be considered null and void, though what is laid down in Number 76 remains in force.

63. The first manner, which can be entitled *by acclamation* or *by inspiration,* occurs when the cardinal electors, as it were through the inspiration of the Holy Spirit, freely and spontaneously, unanimously and aloud, proclaim one individual as supreme pontiff. This form of election, however, can take place only in conclave and after its enclosure, and must be made by the use of the word *eligo,* pronounced in an intelligible manner or expressed in writing if a person is unable to utter it. It is further necessary that this form of election should be accepted unanimously by each and every cardinal elector present in the conclave, including the sick who remain in their cells, without the dissent of any individual and without there having previously been any special agreement concerning the name of the person to be elected. Thus, for example, should one of the cardinal electors spontaneously and without any previous special agreement say: "Most Eminent Fathers, in view of the singular virtue and probity of the Most Reverend N.N., I would judge him worthy to be elected Roman pontiff and I now choose him as Pope," and all the others without exception should follow his example, repeating in an intelligible way the word *eligo,* or, should anyone be unable to do so, expressing it in writing, the person thus unanimously indicated without previous special agreement would be the Pope canonically elected according to this manner of election.

64. The second way, called *by delegation,* takes place when, in certain particular circumstances, the cardinal electors entrust to a group of their members the power of electing, on behalf of them all, the pastor of the Catholic Church. In this case also, each and every cardinal elector without exception present in the already enclosed conclave, having decided, without

any dissenting vote, to proceed by delegation, entrusts the election to some of the fathers, who shall be of an uneven number, from a minimum of nine to a maximum of fifteen, signing for example the following formula: "In the name of the Lord. Amen. In the year . . . , on the . . . day of the month of . . . , we, the cardinal electors present in this conclave (there follow the names of each elector) individually and jointly have decided and do decide to carry out the election by delegation, and in agreement, unanimously and without any dissent we elect as our delegates the most eminent fathers . . . , to whom we grant the full faculty and power to provide the Holy Roman Church with its pastor, in this manner, namely . . ." And here it is necessary that the cardinal electors making the delegation should clearly indicate the manner and the form whereby the delegates are to proceed to the election and what is required in order that this election should be valid, such as, for example, whether they should first propose to the entire body of electors the person whom they intend to elect, or whether they should carry out the election directly; whether all the delegates should agree upon the same person or whether they should nominate only a member of the electoral body or also someone outside it, etc.

It will further be necessary to state the period of time for which the cardinal electors intend to grant the representatives the power of electing; and then the following or similar words will be added: "And we promise to regard as supreme pontiff the person whom the delegates shall have decided to elect according to the aforementioned form."

When they have received this mandate with the above clauses, the delegates proceed to a separate and enclosed place, having first clearly stated, in order to be more free in speaking, that they do not intend to give their consent by any pronouncement or words unless they also expressly put it down in writing. After the delegates have proceeded to the election according to the manner prescribed for them and the election has been promulgated in the conclave, the one who has been thus elected is canonically and truly Pope.

65. The third and ordinary manner of electing the Roman Pontiff is *by scrutiny.* In this regard we fully confirm the law sanctioned in ancient times and faithfully observed ever since, which establishes that for the valid election of the supreme pontiff two-thirds of the votes are necessary. In the same way, we will to maintain in force the norm laid down by our predecessor Pius XII which prescribes that in addition to two-thirds of the votes there must always be one additional vote.[2]

66. Election by scrutiny takes place in three phases, of which the first, which may be called the *pre-scrutiny,* comprises: 1.) the preparation and distribution of the cards by the masters of ceremonies, who give at least two or three to each cardinal elector; 2.) the drawing by lot, from among all the cardinal electors, of three scrutineers, of three persons charged with collecting the votes of the sick, called for the sake of brevity *infirmarii,* and of three revisers; this drawing of lots is carried out publicly by the junior cardinal deacon, who draws out nine names, one after another, of those who shall carry out these tasks; 3.) the completion of the cards, which must be carried out secretly by each cardinal elector, who will write down, as far as possible in writing that cannot be identi-

---

2. Cf. Apostolic Constitution *Vacantis Apostolicae Sedis,* 68: *AAS* 38 (1946), p. 87.

fied as his, the name of the person he chooses, taking care not to write other names as well, since this would make the vote null; 4.) the folding of the cards, which is done down the center of each card in such a way that the card is reduced to the width of about one inch.

67. For this phase of election by scrutiny the following dispositions must be borne in mind: *a.)* the card must be rectangular in shape, and must bear in the center of the upper half, in print if possible, the words *eligo in summum pontificem;* on the lower half there must be a space left for writing the name of the person chosen; thus the card is made in such a way that it can be folded in two; *b.)* if in the drawing of lots for the scrutineers, *infirmarii* and revisers there should come out the names of cardinal electors who because of infirmity or other reasons are unable to carry out these tasks, in their place the names of others who are not impeded are to be drawn. The first three drawn will act as scrutineers, the second three as *infirmarii* and the last three as revisers; *c.)* during the voting, the cardinal electors must remain alone in the chapel, and therefore, immediately after the distribution of the cards and before the electors begin to write, the secretary of the conclave, the papal master of ceremonies and the assistant masters of ceremonies must leave the chapel. After their exit the junior cardinal deacon shall close the door, opening and shutting it again each time this is necessary, as for example when the *infirmarii* go to collect the votes of the sick and when they return to the chapel.

68. The second phase, the scrutiny properly so called, comprises: 1.) The placing of the cards in the appropriate receptacle; 2.) the mixing and counting of the cards; 3.) the scrutiny of the votes. Each cardinal elector, in order of precedence, having written on and folded his card, holds it up so that it can be seen and carries it to the altar, at which the scrutineers stand and upon which there is placed a receptacle, covered by a plate, for receiving the cards. Having reached the altar, the cardinal elector kneels, prays for a short time and then rises and pronounces aloud the following form of oath: "I call to witness Christ the Lord who will be my judge, that my vote is given to the one who before God I consider should be elected." He then places the card on the plate, with which he drops it into the receptacle. Having done this, he bows to the altar and returns to his place.

If because of infirmity any of the cardinal electors present in the chapel should be unable to go to the altar, the last of the scrutineers goes to him and he, having pronounced the above oath, hands the folded card to the scrutineer, who carries it in full view to the altar and omitting the prayer and oath places it on the plate, with which he drops it into the receptacle.

69. If there are sick cardinal electors remaining in their cells, the three *infirmarii* go to them with a box which has a slit in the top through which a folded card can be inserted. Before giving the box to the *infirmarii,* the scrutineers open it publicly, so that the other electors can see that it is empty; they are then to lock it and place the key on the altar. The *infirmarii,* taking the locked box and an appropriate number of cards on a small tray, then go to the sick electors, each of whom takes a card, writes his vote in secret, folds the card and, after taking the above oath, puts it through the slit into the box. If any sick elector is unable to write, one of the three *infirmarii* or another cardinal elector chosen by the sick man, having taken an oath before the *infirmarii* concerning the observance

of secrecy, carries out the above procedure. The *infirmarii* then take the box back into the chapel and the scrutineers, having opened it, are to count the cards contained therein and, after ascertaining that their number corresponds to the sick electors, are to place them one by one on the plate and with this drop them all together into the receptacle. In order not to prolong the voting process unduly, the *infirmarii* may complete their own cards and place them in the receptacle immediately after the senior cardinal, and then go to collect the votes of the sick in the manner indicated above while the other electors cast their votes.

70. After all the cardinal electors have placed their cards in the receptacle, the first scrutineer shakes the receptacle several times in order to mix them, and immediately afterwards the last scrutineer proceeds to count them, picking them out of the receptacle in full view and depositing them in another empty receptacle previously prepared for this purpose.

    If the number of cards does not correspond to the number of electors the cards must all be burned and a second vote taken at once; if however the number of cards does correspond to the number of electors, there follows the scrutiny of the cards, which takes place in the following manner.

71. The scrutineers sit at a table placed in front of the altar. The first of them takes a card, unfolds it, notes the name of the person chosen and passes the card to the second scrutineer, who in his turn notes the name of the person chosen and passes the card to the third, who reads it aloud and in an intelligible manner, so that all the electors present can make a note of the vote on a sheet of paper prepared for the purpose. He himself writes down the name read from the card.

If during the scrutiny of the votes the scrutineers should discover two cards folded in such a way as to appear to have been filled in by one elector, if these cards bear the same name they are counted as one vote; if however they bear different names, neither of the votes will be valid; however, in neither of the two cases is the voting annulled.

When all the votes have been scrutinized, the scrutineers add up the sum of votes obtained by the different names, and write them down on a separate sheet of paper. As he reads out the individual cards, the last scrutineer pierces each one with a threaded needle through the word *eligo* and places it on the thread, so that the cards can be more carefully preserved. After the names have been read out, the ends of the thread are tied in a knot, and the cards thus joined together are placed in an empty receptacle or on one side of the table.

72. There then follows the third and last phase, also known as the *post-scrutiny,* which comprises: 1.) The counting of the votes; 2.) the checking of the same; 3.) the burning of the cards.

    The scrutineers add up all the votes that each individual has received, and if no one has reached the majority of two-thirds plus one the Pope has not been elected in this voting; if however the result is that someone has obtained two-thirds of the votes plus one, the canonically valid election of the Roman pontiff has taken place.

    In either case, that is, whether the election has resulted or not, the revisers must proceed to the checking both of the cards and of the notes of the votes made by the scrutineers, in order to make sure that these latter have performed their task exactly and faithfully.

    Immediately after the checking and before the cardinal electors leave the chapel, all the cards are to be burnt by the scrutineers, with the assistance of the secretary of the conclave and the masters of ceremonies, who have meanwhile been summoned by the junior cardinal deacon. If however a second vote is to take place immediately, the cards from the first voting will be burned only at the end, together with the cards from the second voting.

73. In order that secrecy may be more securely observed, we order each and every cardinal elector to surrender to the cardinal camerlengo or to one of the three cardinal assistants whatsoever kind of notes he may have in his possession concerning the result of each scrutiny. These notes are to be burnt together with the cards.

    We further lay down that at the end of the conclave the cardinal camerlengo of the Holy Roman Church shall draw up a document, to be approved also by the three cardinal assistants, stating the result of the voting of each session. This statement, which is to be kept in the archives, shall be placed in a sealed envelope, which may be opened by no one unless the supreme pontiff gives explicit permission.

74. Confirming the dispositions of our predecessors, Saint Pius X[3] and Pius XII,[4] we decree that both in the morning and in the afternoon, after a voting session which does not result in an election, the cardinal electors shall proceed immediately to a second one, at which they shall again cast their votes. No account shall be taken of the votes cast in the previous sessions. In the second session all the formalities of the previous one are to be observed, with the difference that the electors are not bound to take a fresh oath or to elect new scrutineers, *infirmarii* and revisers; what was done in this regard in the first session will be valid for the second one also, without the need for repetition.

75. Everything that has been laid down above concerning the manner of carrying out the voting must be diligently observed by the cardinal electors in all the sessions, which are to take place each day, in the morning and in the afternoon, after the carrying out of the sacred rites and the recitation of the prayers laid down in the *Ordo Sacrorum Rituum Conclavis* mentioned above.

76. Should the cardinal electors have difficulty in agreeing upon the person to be elected, in this case, when the sessions have been carried out for three days in the form described above (Numbers 65 ff.) and no result has been achieved, the sessions are suspended for a maximum of one day in order to allow a pause for prayer, free discussions among the voters and a brief spiritual exhortation given by the senior cardinal in the order of deacons. The voting sessions are then resumed according to the same form and after seven sessions, if the election has not taken place, there is another pause for prayer, discussion and an exhortation given by the senior cardinal of the order of priests.

    Another series of seven sessions is then proceeded with, and, if a result has still not been reached, is followed by a fresh pause for prayer, discussion and an exhortation given by the senior cardinal in the order of bishops. At this point the cardinal camerlengo of the Holy Roman Church will consult the electors concerning the manner of proceeding. The criterion of requiring, for an effective vote, two-thirds of the votes plus one must not be abandoned, unless all the cardinal electors unanimously, that is with no exception, express themselves in favor of a different criterion,

---

3. Cf. Apostolic Constitution *Vacante Sede Apostolica*, 76: *Pii X. Pontificis Maximi Acta*, III, pp. 280–281.

4. Cf. Apostolic Constitution *Vacantis Apostolicae Sedis*, 88: *AAS* 38 (1946), p. 93.

which may consist of the *delegation* (cf. Number 64) or of the absolute majority of votes plus one, or of balloting between the two who in the session immediately preceding have gained the greatest number of votes.

77. Should the election be conducted in a manner different from the three procedures described above (cf. Numbers 63 ff.) or without the conditions laid down for each of the same, it is for this very reason null and void (cf. Number 62), without the need for any declaration, and gives no right to him who has been thus elected.

78. We lay down that the dispositions concerning everything that precedes the election of the Roman pontiff and concerning the conduct of the election itself are also to be observed in full if the Apostolic See should become vacant as a result of the resignation of the Supreme Pontiff.

Matters to be Observed and Matters to be Avoided in the Election of the Roman Pontiff

79. As did our predecessors, so do we also censure and condemn the detestable crime of simony in the election of the Roman pontiff, and we inflict excommunication *latae sententiae* upon all those guilty of it. However, at the same time we confirm the disposition of our predecessor Saint Pius X which removed the nullity of simoniacal election laid down by Julius II or by any other pontifical decree, in order that the validity of the election of the Roman pontiff may not be challenged for this reason.[5]

80. Also in confirmation of the prescriptions of our predecessors, we forbid anyone, even though he be a cardinal, during the lifetime of the pontiff and without having consulted him, to deliberate on the election of his successor, promise votes or make decisions in this regard in private meetings.

81. In the same way, we wish to confirm the provisions sanctioned by our predecessors for the purpose of excluding any external intervention in the election of the supreme pontiff. In virtue of holy obedience and under pain of excommunication *latae sententiae,* therefore, we again forbid each and every cardinal elector, present and future, and likewise the secretary of the conclave, and all other persons taking part in the conclave, to accept under whatsoever pretext, from whatsoever civil authority, the task of proposing the *veto* or *exclusiva,* even in the form of a simple wish, or to reveal such either to the entire electoral body assembled together or to individual electors, in writing or by word of mouth, directly and personally or indirectly through others, both before and during the conclave. We intend this prohibition to include every possible interference, opposition and desire whereby the secular authorities of whatever order and degree or whatever group or individual persons would wish to interfere in the election of the pontiff.

82. The cardinal electors shall further abstain from any form of pact, agreement, promise or other commitment of whatever kind which could oblige them to give or not to give their vote to a certain person or persons. If this should in fact be done, even under oath, we decree that it shall be null and void and that no one shall be bound to observe it; and we hereby inflict excommunication *latae sententiae* upon the transgressors of this prohibition. We do not however have the intention of forbidding the

5. Cf. Apostolic Constitution *Vacante Sede Apostolica,* 79: *Pii X. Pontificis Maximi Acta,* III, p. 282.

exchange of views concerning the election during the period in which the see is vacant.

83. We likewise forbid the cardinals to enter into any compromise before the election or to undertake commitments of common accord to which they agree to be bound should one of them be elevated to the pontificate. These promises too, should any in fact be made, even under oath, we declare null and void.

84. With the same insistence as was shown by our predecessors we earnestly exhort the electors that in electing the pontiff they should not let themselves be guided by friendship or aversion, or be influenced by favor or respect towards anyone, or be forced by the intervention of persons in authority or by pressure groups, by the suggestion of the mass media, or by force, fear or the seeking for popularity. But, having before their eyes solely the glory of God and the good of the church and after imploring God's help, they shall give their vote to the person whom they judge to be more suited than the others to govern the universal church fruitfully and usefully.

85. During the celebration of the conclave the church is united in a very special manner with the pastors and especially with the cardinal electors of the supreme pontiff, and implores from God a new head as a gift of his goodness and providence. In fact, according to the example of the first Christian community spoken of in the Acts of the Apostles,[6] the universal church, spiritually united with Mary the Mother of Jesus, must "persevere in one mind in prayer"; thus the election of the new pontiff will not be something unconnected with the people of God and reserved only to the college of electors but will be in a certain sense an act of the whole church.

We therefore lay down that in all cities and other places, at least the more important ones, after the death of the Pope has been announced and solemn obsequies have been celebrated for him, there shall be offered humble and assiduous prayers to the Lord, that he may enlighten the electors and make them so like-minded in their task that a speedy, unanimous and fruitful election may take place, as is required by the salvation of souls and the good of the whole Catholic world.

86. We also ask him who is elected not to refuse the office to which he has been elected for fear of its weight, but to submit himself humbly to the design of the divine will. For God who imposes the burden sustains him with His hand, lest he be unequal to bearing it; in conferring the heavy task upon him, God also helps him to accomplish it and, in giving him the dignity, He grants him the strength lest in his weakness he should fall beneath the weight of his office.

THE ACCEPTANCE, PROCLAMATION AND CORONATION OF THE NEW PONTIFF

87. When the election has been canonically carried out, the junior cardinal deacon summons into the hall of the conclave the secretary of the conclave, the papal master of ceremonies and the assistant masters of ceremonies; the cardinal dean, or the cardinal who is first in order and seniority, in the name of the whole college of electors then asks the consent of the one who has been elected with the following words: "Do you accept your canonical election as Supreme Pontiff?" And, immediately after the declaration of consent, he asks him: "By what name do you wish to be called?" Then

---

6. Cf. Acts 1:14.

the papal master of ceremonies acting as notary and with two assistant masters of ceremonies acting as witnesses draws up a document concerning the acceptance of the new pontiff and the name taken by him.

88. After the acceptance, the person elected, if he has already received episcopal ordination, is immediately bishop of the Church of Rome, true pope and head of the College of Bishops; and *ipso facto* he acquires and can exercise full and absolute jurisdiction over the whole church.

Should the person elected not already be a bishop, he shall immediately be ordained bishop.

89. When the formalities provided for in the *Ordo Sacrorum Rituum Conclavis* have been carried out, the cardinal electors, according to the manner laid down, approach to make their act of homage and obedience to the newly elected supreme pontiff. When this has been done, an act of thanksgiving to God is made, after which the senior cardinal deacon proclaims to the waiting people the new pontiff, who immediately imparts the apostolic blessing *Urbi et Orbi*.

If the person elected is not already a bishop, homage is given to him and the proclamation made to the people only after he has been ordained bishop.

90. If the person elected should be residing outside the conclave, the norms contained in the above-mentioned *Ordo Sacrorum Rituum Conclavis* are to be observed.

Should the newly elected supreme pontiff not already be a bishop, as mentioned in Numbers 88 and 89, his episcopal ordination shall be performed according to the usage of the church by the dean of the sacred college of cardinals or, in his absence, by the subdean or, should he too be prevented from doing so, by the senior cardinal bishop.

91. We lay down that the conclave, as far as the canonical effects dealt with in Number 56 are concerned, should come to an end immediately after the new supreme pontiff has been elected and has given assent to his election; and, if he is not a bishop, after his episcopal ordination (cf. Numbers 88 and 89). We therefore decree that from that moment the newly-elected supreme pontiff may be approached by the substitute of the Secretariat of State or Papal Secretariat, the secretary of the Council for the Public Affairs of the Church, the prefect of the papal household and whoever else needs to consult the elected pontiff on matters of immediate necessity.

92. Finally, the pontiff will be crowned by the senior cardinal deacon, and, within an appropriate time, will take possession of the Patriarchal Archbasilica of the Lateran, according to the ritual prescribed.

All these things we lay down and prescribe after careful and mature reflection; and, declaring abrogated, as provided for above, the apostolic constitutions and orders issued in this regard by the Roman pontiffs, we wish this constitution of ours to have full effect now and in the future, in such a way that everything that has been described and laid down therein should be religiously observed by all concerned and therefore should come into force, notwithstanding whatsoever disposition to the contrary, even though worthy of very special mention. If anyone therefore, knowingly or unknowingly, should act in a manner different from what we have prescribed, we order that such action is to be considered null and void.

Given in Rome, at Saint Peter's, on the first day of the month of October in the year 1975, the thirteenth of our pontificate.

Pastor Bonus

I. GENERAL NORMS

The Notion of Roman Curia

Art. 1—The Roman Curia is the complex of dicasteries and institutes which help the Roman Pontiff in the exercise of his supreme pastoral function for the good and service of the whole Church and of the particular Churches. This strengthens the unity of the faith and the communion of the people of God and promotes the mission proper to the Church in the world.

The Structure of the Dicasteries

Art. 2—§ 1. By the word "dicasteries" are understood the Secretariat of State, Congregations, Tribunals, Councils and Offices, namely the Apostolic Camera, the Administration of the Patrimony of the Apostolic See, and the Prefecture for the Economic Affairs of the Holy See.

§ 2. The dicasteries are juridically equal among themselves.

§ 3. Attached to the institutes of the Roman Curia are the Prefecture of the Papal Household and the Office for the Liturgical Celebrations of the Supreme Pontiff.

Art. 3—§ 1. Unless they have a different structure in virtue of their specific nature or some special law, the dicasteries are composed of the cardinal prefect or the presiding archbishop, a body of cardinals and of some bishops, assisted by a secretary, consultors, senior administrators, and a suitable number of officials.

§ 2. According to the specific nature of certain dicasteries, clerics and other faithful can be added to the body of cardinals and bishops.

§ 3. Strictly speaking the members of a congregation are the cardinals and the bishops.

Art. 4—The prefect or president acts as moderator of the dicastery, directs it and acts in its name.

The secretary, with the help of the undersecretary, assists the prefect or president in managing the business of the dicastery as well as its human resources.

Art. 5—§ 1. The prefect or president, the members of the body mentioned in art. 3, § 1, the secretary, and other senior administrators and consultors are appointed by the Supreme Pontiff for a five-year term.

§ 2. Once they have completed seventy-five years of age, cardinal prefects are asked to submit their resignation to the Roman Pontiff, who will provide, all things considered. Other moderators and secretaries cease from office, having completed seventy-five years of age; members, when they have completed eighty years of age; those who are attached to any dicastery by reason of their function cease to be members when their function ceases.

Art. 6—On the death of the Supreme Pontiff, all moderators and members of the dicasteries cease from their function. The chamberlain of the Roman Church and the major penitentiary are excepted, who expedite ordinary business and refer to the College of Cardinals those things which would have been referred to the Supreme Pontiff.

The secretaries see to the ordinary operations of the dicasteries, taking care of ordinary business only; they need to be confirmed in office by the Supreme Pontiff within three months of his election.

Art. 7—The members of the body mentioned in art. 3, § 1, are taken from among the cardinals living in Rome or outside the city, to whom are added some bishops, especially diocesan ones, insofar as they have special expertise in the matters being dealt with; also, depending on the nature of the dicastery, some clerics and other Christian faithful, with this proviso that matters requiring the exercise of power of governance be reserved to those in holy orders.

Art. 8—Consultors also are appointed from among clerics or other Christian faithful outstanding for knowledge and prudence, taking into consideration, as much as possible, the international character of the Church.

Art. 9—Officials are taken from among the Christian faithful, clergy or laity, voted for their virtue, prudence, and experience, and for the necessary knowledge attested by suitable academic degrees, and selected as far as possible from the various regions of the world, so that the Curia may express the universal character of the Church. The suitability of the applicants should be evaluated by test or other appropriate means, according to the circumstances.

Particular Churches, moderators of Institutes of Consecrated Life and of Societies of Apostolic Life will not fail to render assistance to the Apostolic See by allowing their Christian faithful or their members to be available for service at the Roman Curia.

Art. 10—Each dicastery is to have its own archive where incoming documents and copies of documents sent out are kept safe in an organized system of "protocol" in accordance with modern methods.

Procedure

Art. 11—§ 1. Matters of major importance are reserved to the general meeting, according to the nature of each dicastery.

§ 2. All members must be called in due time to the plenary sessions, held as far as possible once a year, to deal with questions involving general principles, and for other questions which the prefect or president may have deemed to require treatment. For ordinary sessions it is sufficient to convoke members who are in Rome.

§ 3. The secretary participates in all sessions of the meeting with the right to vote.

Art. 12—Consultors and those who are equivalent to them are to make a diligent study of the matter in hand and to present their considered opinion, usually in writing.

So far as opportunity allows and depending on the nature of each dicastery, consultors can be called together to examine questions in a collegial fashion and, as the case may be, present a common position.

For individual cases, others can be called in for consultation who, although not numbered among the consultors, are qualified by their special expertise in the matter to be treated.

Art. 13—Depending on their own proper field of competence, the dicasteries deal with those matters which, because of their special importance, either by their nature or by law, are reserved to the Apostolic See and those which exceed the competence of individual bishops and their conferences, as well as those matters committed to them by the Supreme Pontiff. The dicasteries study the major problems of the present age, so that the Church's pastoral action may be more effectively promoted and suitably coordinated, with due regard to relations with the particular Churches. The dicasteries promote initiatives for the good of the universal Church. Finally, they review matters that the Christian faithful, exercising their own right, bring to the attention of the Apostolic See.

Art. 14—The competence of dicasteries is defined on the basis of subject matter, unless otherwise expressly provided for.

Art. 15—Questions are to be dealt with according to law, be it universal law or the special of the Roman Curia, and according to the norms of each dicastery, yet with pastoral means and judgements, attentive both to justice and the good of the Church and especially to the salvation of souls.

Art. 16—Apart from the official Latin language, it is acceptable to approach the Roman Curia in any of the languages widely known today.

For the convenience of the dicasteries, a centre is being established for translating documents into other languages.[36]

Art. 17—General documents prepared by one dicastery will be communicated to other interested dicasteries, so that the text may be improved with any corrections that may be suggested, and, through common consultation, it may even be proceeded in a coordinated manner to their implementation.

Art. 18—Decisions of major importance are to be submitted for the approbation of the Supreme Pontiff, except decisions for which special faculties have been granted to the moderators of the dicasteries as well as the sentences of the Tribunal of the Roman Rota and the Supreme Tribunal of the Apostolic Signatura within the limits of their proper competence.

The dicasteries cannot issue laws or general decrees having the force of law or derogate from the prescriptions of current universal law, unless in individual cases and with the specific approval of the Supreme Pontiff.

It is of the utmost importance that nothing grave and extraordinary be transacted unless the Supreme Pontiff be previously informed by the moderators of the dicasteries.

Art. 19—§ 1. Hierarchical recourses are received by whichever dicastery has competence in that subject matter, without prejudice to art. 21, § 1.

§ 2. But questions which are to be dealt with judicially are sent to the competent tribunals, without prejudice to arts. 52–53.

Art. 20—Conflicts of competence arising between dicasteries are to be submitted to the Supreme Tribunal of the Apostolic Signatura, unless it pleases the Supreme Pontiff to deal with them otherwise.

Art. 21—§ 1. Matters touching the competence of more than one dicastery are to be examined together by the dicasteries concerned.

To enable them to exchange advice, a meeting will be called by the moderator of the dicastery which has begun to deal with the matter, either on his own initiative or at the request of another dicastery concerned. However, if the subject matter demands it, it may be referred to a plenary session of the dicasteries concerned.

The meeting will be chaired by the moderator of the dicastery who called the meeting or by its secretary, if only the secretaries are meeting.

§ 2. Where needed, permanent interdicasterial commissions will be set up to deal with matters requiring mutual and frequent consultation.

---

[36][As yet—December 1992—, the Translation Centre has not been established. (Editors' note.)]

The Meetings of Cardinals

Art. 22—By mandate of the Supreme Pontiff, the cardinals in charge of dicasteries meet together several times a year to examine more important questions, coordinate their activities, so that they may be able to exchange information and take counsel.

Art. 23—More serious business of a general character can be usefully dealt with, if the Supreme Pontiff so decides, by the cardinals assembled in plenary consistory according to proper law.

The Council of Cardinals for the Study of Organizational and Economic Questions of the Apostolic See

Art. 24—The Council of Cardinals to Study the Organizational and Economic Questions of the Apostolic See consists of fifteen cardinals who head particular Churches from various parts of the world and are appointed by the Supreme Pontiff for a five-year term of office.

Art. 25—§ 1. The Council is convened by the cardinal secretary of state, usually twice a year, to consider those economic and organizational questions which relate to the administration of the Apostolic See, with the assistance, as needed, of experts in these affairs.

§ 2. The Council also considers the activities of the special institute which is erected and located within the State of Vatican City in order to safeguard and administer economic goods placed in its care with the purpose of supporting works of religion and charity. This institute is governed by a special law.

Relations with Particular Churches

Art. 26—§ 1. Close relations are to be fostered with the particular Churches and with the conferences of bishops, seeking out their advice when preparing documents of major importance that have a general character.

§ 2. As far as possible, documents of a general character or having a special bearing on their particular Churches about be communicated to the bishops before they are made public.

§ 3. Questions brought before the dicasteries are to be diligently examined and, without delay, an answer or at least a written acknowledgement of receipt, insofar as this is necessary, should be sent.

Art. 27—Dicasteries should not omit to consult with papal legates about business affecting the particular Churches where the legates are serving, nor should they omit to communicate to the legates the results of deliberations.

"Ad limina" Visits

Art. 28—In keeping with venerable tradition and the prescriptions of law, bishops presiding over particular Churches approach the tombs of the Apostles at predetermined times and on that occasion present to the Roman Pontiff a report on the state of their diocese.

Art. 29—These kinds of visits have a special importance in the life of the Church, making as they do the apogee of the relationship between the pastors of each particular Church with the Roman Pontiff. For he meets his brother bishops, and deals with them about matters concerning the good of the Churches and the bishops' role as shepherds, and he confirms and supports them in faith and charity. This strengthens the bonds of hierarchical communion and openly manifests the catholicity of the Church and the unity of the episcopal college.

Art. 30—The *ad limina* visits also concern the dicasteries of the Roman Curia. For through these visits a helpful dialogue between the bishops and the Apostolic See is increased and deepened, information is shared, advice and timely suggestions are brought forward for the greater good and progress of the Churches and for the observance of the common discipline of the Church.

Art. 31—These visits are to be scrupulously and appropriately prepared so that they proceed well and enjoy a successful outcome in their three principal stages—namely, the pilgrimage to the tombs of the Princes of the Apostles and their veneration, the meeting with the Supreme Pontiff, and the meetings at the dicasteries of the Roman Curia.

Art. 32—For this purpose, the report on the state of the diocese should be sent to the Holy See six months before the time set for the visit. It is to be examined with all diligence by the competent dicasteries, and their remarks are to be shared with a special committee convened for this purpose so that a brief synthesis of these may be drawn up and be readily at hand in the meetings.

The Pastoral Character of the Activity of the Roman Curia

Art. 33—The activity of all who work at the Roman Curia and the other institutes of the Holy See is a true ecclesial service, marked with a pastoral character, a service that all must discharge with a deep sense of duty and desire to serve, as it is a sharing in the world-wide mission of the bishop of Rome.

Art. 34—Each individual dicastery pursues its own end, yet they cooperate among one another. Therefore, all who are working in the Roman Curia are to do so in such a way that their work may come together and be forged into one. Accordingly, all must always be prepared to offer their services wherever needed.

Art. 35—Although any work performed within the institutes of the Holy See is a sharing in the apostolic action, priests are to apply themselves as best they can to the care of souls, without prejudice however to their own office.

The Central Labour Office

Art. 36—According to its own terms of reference, the Central Labour Office deals with working

conditions within the Roman Curia and related questions.

Regulations

Art. 37—To this Apostolic Constitution is added an *Ordo servandus* or common norms setting forth the ways and means of transacting business in the Curia itself, without prejudice to norms of this Constitution.[37]

Art. 38—Each dicastry is to have its own *Ordo servandus* or special norms setting forth the ways and means of transacting business within it.

The *Ordo servandus* of each dicastery shall be made public in the usual manner of the Apostolic See.

II. THE SECRETARIAT OF STATE

Art. 39—The Secretariat of State provides close assistance to the Supreme Pontiff in the exercise of his supreme function.

Art. 40—The Secretariat is presided over by the Cardinal Secretary of State. It contains two sections, the first being the *Section for General Affairs,* under the direct control of the substitute, with the help of the assessor; the second being the *Section for Relations with States,* under the direction of its own secretary, with the help of the undersecretary. Attached to this latter section is a council of cardinals and some bishops.

The First Section

Art. 41—§ 1. It is the task of the First Section in a special way to expedite the business concerning

---

[37][The *Ordo servandus* was published on 04-02-1992 under the title of *Regolamento generale della Curia romana,* in AAS 84 (1992) 202–267; it is in force as of 08-06-1992. The *Regolamento* has also been reprinted as a separate publication (Città del Vaticano, Libreria editrice Vaticana, 1992, 76 p.). (Editors' note.)]

the daily service of the Supreme Pontiff; to deal with those matters which arise outside the ordinary competence of the dicasteries of the Roman Curia and of the other institutes of the Apostolic See; to foster relations with those dicasteries and coordinate their work, without prejudice to their autonomy; to supervise the office and work of the legates of the Holy See, especially as concerns the particular Churches. This section deals with everything concerning the ambassadors of States to the Holy See.

§ 2. In consultation with other competent dicasteries, this section takes care of matters concerning the presence and activity of the Holy See in international organizations, without prejudice to art. 46. It does the same concerning Catholic international organizations.

Art. 42—It is also the task of the First Section:

1° to draw up and dispatch apostolic constitutions, decretal letters, apostolic letters, epistles, and other documents entrusted to it by the Supreme Pontiff;

2° to prepare the appropriate documents concerning appointments to be made or approved by the Supreme Pontiff in the Roman Curia and in the other institutes depending on the Holy See;

3° to guard the leaden seal and the Fisherman's ring.

Art. 43—It is likewise within the competence of this Section:

1° to prepare for publication the acts and public documents of the Holy See in the periodical entitled *Acta Apostolicæ Sedis;*

2° through its special office commonly known as the *Press Office,* to publish official announcements of acts of the Supreme Pontiff or of the activities of the Holy See;

3° in consultation with the Second Section, to oversee the newspaper called *L'Osservatore Romano,* the Vatican Radio Station, and the Vatican Television Centre.

Art. 44—Through the *Central Statistical Office,* it collects, organizes, and publishes all data, set down according to statistical standards, concerning the life of the whole Church throughout the world.

The Second Section

Art. 45—The Section for Relations with States has the special task of dealing with heads of government.

Art. 46—The Section for Relations with States has within its competence:

1° to foster relations, especially of the diplomatic kind, with States and other subjects of public international law, and to deal with matters of common interest, promoting the good of the Church and of civil society by means of concordats and other agreements of this kind, if the case arises, while respecting the considered opinions of the bishops' conferences that may be affected:

2° in consultation with the competent dicasteries of the Roman Curia, to represent the Holy See at international organizations and meetings concerning questions of a public nature;

3° within the scope of its competence, to deal with what pertains to the papal legates.

Art. 47 § 1. In special circumstances and by mandate of the Supreme Pontiff, and in consultation with the competent dicasteries of the Roman Curia, this Section takes action for the provision of particular Churches, and for the constitution of and changes to these Churches and their groupings.

§ 2. In other cases, especially where a concordat is in force, and without prejudice to art. 78, this Section has competence to transact business with civil governments.

III. The Congregations

The Congregation for the Doctrine of the Faith

Art. 48—The proper function of the Congregation for the Doctrine of the Faith is to promote and safeguard the doctrine on faith and morals in the whole Catholic world; so it has competence in things that touch this matter in any way.

Art. 49—Fulfilling its function of promoting doctrine, the Congregation fosters studies so that the understanding of the faith may grow and a response in the light of the faith may be given to new questions arising from the progress of the sciences or human culture.

Art. 50—It helps the bishops, individually or in groups, in carrying out their function as authentic teachers and doctors of the faith, a function that carries with it the duty of promoting and guarding the integrity of that faith.

Art. 51—To safeguard the truth of faith and the integrity of morals, the Congregation takes care lest faith or morals suffer harm through errors that have been spread in any way whatever.

Wherefore:

1° it has the duty of requiring that books and other writings touching faith or morals, being published by the Christian faithful, be subjected to prior examination by the competent authority;

2° it searches out writings and opinions that seem to be contrary or dangerous to true faith, and, if it is established that they are opposed to the teaching of the Church, reproves them in due time, having given authors full opportunity to explain their minds, and having forewarned the Ordinary concerned; it brings suitable remedies to bear, if this be opportune.

3° finally, it takes good care lest errors or dangerous doctrines, which may have been spread among the Christian people, do not go without apt rebuttal.

Art. 52—The Congregation examines offences against the faith and more serious ones both in behaviour or in the celebration of the sacraments which have been reported to it and, if need be, proceeds to the declaration or imposition of canonical sanctions in accordance with the norms of common or proper law.

Art. 53—It is to examine whatever concerns the privilege of the faith, whether in law or in fact.

Art. 54—Documents being published by other dicasteries of the Roman Curia, insofar as they touch on the doctrine of faith or morals, are to be subjected to its prior judgement.

Art. 55—Established within the Congregation for the Doctrine of the Faith are the Pontifical Biblical Commission and the International Theological Commission, which act according to their own approved norms and are presided over by the cardinal prefect of this Congregation.

The Congregation for the Oriental Churches

Art. 56—The Congregation for the Oriental Churches considers those matters, whether concerning persons or things, affecting the Oriental Catholic Churches.

Art. 57—§ 1. The patriarchs and major archbishops of the Oriental Churches, and the president of the Council for Promoting Christian Unity, are *ipso iure* members of this Congregation.

§ 2. The consultors and officials are to be selected in such a way as to reflect as far as possible the diversity of rites.

Art. 58—§ 1. The competence of this Congregation extends to all matters which are proper to the Oriental Churches and which are to be referred to the Apostolic See, whether concerning the structure and organization of the Churches, the exercise of the functions of teaching, sanctifying and governing, or the status, rights, and obligations of persons. It also handles everything that has to be done concerning quinquennial reports and the *ad limina* visits in accordance with arts. 31–32.

§ 2. This however does not infringe on the proper and exclusive competence of the Congregations for the Doctrine of the Faith and for the

Causes of Saints, of the Apostolic Penitentiary, the Supreme Tribunal of the Apostolic Signatura, or of the Tribunal of the Roman Rota, as well as of the Congregation for Divine Worship and the Discipline of the Sacraments for what pertains to dispensation from a marriage *ratum et non consummatum*.

In matters which also affect the faithful of the Latin Church, the Congregation will proceed, if the matter is sufficiently important, in consultation with the dicastery that has competence in the same matter for the faithful of the Latin Church.

Art. 59—The Congregation pays careful attention to communities of Oriental Christian faithful living within the territories of the Latin Church, and attends to their spiritual needs by providing visitators and even a hierarchy of their own, so far as possible and where numbers and circumstances demand it, in consultation with the Congregation competent for the establishment of particular Churches in that region.

Art. 60—In regions where Oriental rites have been preponderant from ancient times, apostolic and missionary activity depends solely on this Congregation, even if it is carried out by missionaries of the Latin Church.

Art. 61—The Congregation proceeds in collaboration with the Council for Promoting Christian Unity in matters which may concern relations with non-Catholic Oriental Churches and with the Council for Inter-religious Dialogue in matters within the scope of this Council.

The Congregation for Divine Worship and the Discipline of the Sacraments

Art. 62—The Congregation for Divine Worship and the Discipline of the Sacraments does whatever pertains to the Apostolic See concerning the regulation and promotion of the sacred liturgy, primarily of the sacraments, without prejudice to the competence of the Congregation for the Doctrine of the Faith.

Art. 63—It fosters and safeguards the regulation of the administration of the sacraments, especially regarding their valid and licit celebration. It grants favours and dispensations not contained in the faculties of diocesan bishops in this subject matter.

Art. 64—§ 1. By effective and suitable means, the Congregation promotes liturgical pastoral activity, especially regarding the celebration of the Eucharist; it gives support to the diocesan bishops so that the Christian faithful may share more and more actively in the sacred liturgy.

§ 2. It sees to the drawing up and revision of liturgical texts. It reviews particular calendars and proper texts for the Mass and the Divine Office for particular Churches and institutes which enjoy that right.

§ 3. It grants the *recognitio* to translations of liturgical books and adaptations of them that have been lawfully prepared by conferences of bishops.

Art. 65—The Congregation fosters commissions or institutes for promoting liturgical apostolate or sacred music, song or art, and it maintains relations with them. In accordance with the law, it erects associations which have an international character or approves or grants the *recognitio* to their statutes. It contributes to the progress of liturgical life by encouraging meetings from various regions.

Art. 66—The Congregation provides attentive supervision to see that liturgical norms be accurately observed, abuses avoided, and that they be eradicated where they are found to exist.

Art. 67—This Congregation examines the fact of non-consummation in a marriage and the existence of just cause for granting a dispensation. It receives all the acts together with the *votum* of the bishop and the remarks of the defender of the bond, weighs them according to its own special procedure, and, if the case warrants it, submits a petition to the Supreme Pontiff requesting the dispensation.

Art. 68—It is also competent to examine, in accordance with the law, cases concerning the nullity of sacred ordination.

Art. 69—This Congregation has competence concerning the cult of sacred relics, the confirmation of heavenly patrons and the granting of the title of minor basilica.

Art. 70—The Congregation gives assistance to bishops so that, in addition to liturgical worship, the prayers and pious exercises of the Christian people, in full harmony with the norms of the Church, may be fostered and held in high esteem.

The Congregation for the Causes of Saints

Art. 71—The Congregation for the Causes of Saints deals with everything which, according to the established way, leads to the canonization of servants of God.

Art. 72—§ 1. With special norms and timely advice, it assists diocesan bishops, who have competence to instruct the cause.

§ 2. It considers causes that have already been instructed, inquiring whether everything has been carried out in accordance with the law. It thoroughly examines the causes that have thus been reviewed, in order to judge whether everything required is present for a favorable recommendation to be submitted to the Supreme Pontiff, according to the previously established classification of causes.

Art. 73—The Congregation also is competent to examine what is necessary for the granting of the title of doctor to saints, after having received the recommendation of the Congregation for the Doctrine of the Faith concerning outstanding teaching.

Art. 74—Moreover, it has competence to decide everything concerning authenticating holy relics and preserving them.

The Congregation for Bishops

Art. 75—The Congregation for Bishops examines what pertains to the establishment and provision of particular Churches and to the exercise of the episcopal function in the Latin Church, without prejudice to the competence of the Congregation for the Evangelization of Peoples.

Art. 76—This Congregation deals with everything concerning the constitution, division, union, suppression, and other changes of particular Churches and of their groupings. It also erects military ordinariates for the pastoral care of soldiers.

Art. 77—It deals with everything concerning the appointment of bishops, even titular ones, and generally with the provision of particular Churches.

Art. 78—Whenever it is a matter of dealing with civil governments, either in establishing or modifying particular Churches and their groupings or in the provision of these Churches, this Congregation must only proceed in consultation with the Section for Relations with States of the Secretariat of State.

Art. 79—Furthermore, the Congregation applies itself to matters relating to the correct exercise of the pastoral function of the bishops, by offering them every kind of assistance. For it is part of its duty to initiate general apostolic visitations where needed, in agreement with the dicasteries concerned and, in the same manner, to evaluate their results and to propose to the Supreme Pontiff the appropriate actions to be taken.

Art. 80—This Congregation has competence over everything involving the Holy See in the matter of personal prelatures.

Art. 81—For the particular Churches assigned to its care, the Congregation takes care of everything with respect to the *ad limina* visits; so it studies the quinquennial reports, submitted in accordance with art. 32. It is available to the bishops who come to Rome, especially to see that suitable arrangements are made for the meeting with the Supreme Pontiff and for other meetings and pilgrimages. When the visit is completed, it communicates to the bishops in writing the conclusions concerning their dioceses.

Art. 82—The Congregation deals with matters pertaining to the celebration of particular councils as well as the erection of conferences of bishops and the *recognition* of their statutes. It receives the acts of these bodies and, in consultation with the dicasteries concerned, it examines the decrees which require the recognition of the Apostolic See.

The Pontifical Commission for Latin America

Art. 83—§ 1. The functions of the Commission is to be available to the particular Churches in Latin America, by counsel and by action, taking a keen interest in the questions that affect the life and progress of those Churches; and especially to help the Churches themselves in the solution of those questions, or to be helpful to those dicasteries of the Curia that are involved by reason of their competence.

§ 2. It is also to foster relations between the national and international ecclesiastical institutes that work for the regions of Latin America and the dicasteries of the Roman Curia.

Art. 84—§ 1. The president of the Commission is the prefect of the Congregation for Bishops, assisted by a bishop as vice-president.

They have as counselors some bishops either from the Roman Curia or selected from the Churches of Latin America.

§ 2. The members of the Commission are selected either from the dicasteries of the Roman Curia or from the *Consejo episcopal latinoamericano,* whether these last be from among the bishops of Latin America or from the institutes mentioned in the preceding article.

§ 3. The Commission has its own staff.

The Congregation for the Evangelization of Peoples

Art. 85—The functions of the Congregation for the Evangelization of Peoples is to direct and coordinate throughout the world the actual work of spreading the Gospel as well as missionary cooperation, without prejudice to the competence of the Congregation for the Oriental Churches.

Art. 86—The Congregation promotes research in theology of the mission as well as in spirituality and pastoral work; it likewise proposes principles, norms, and procedures, fitting the needs of time and place, by which evangelization is carried out.

Art. 87—The Congregation strives to bring the people of God to work effectively at the missionary task, by their prayers and the witness of their lives, by their active work and contributions, well aware of their duty and filled with missionary spirit.

Art. 88—§ 1. It takes steps to awaken missionary vocations, whether clerical, religious, or lay, and advises on a suitable distribution of missionaries.

§ 2. In the territories subject to it, it cares for the education of the secular clergy and of catechists, without prejudice to the competence of the Congregation for Seminaries and Institutes of Studies concerning the general programme of studies and the universities and other institutes of higher education.

Art. 89—Within its competence are mission territories, the evangelization of which is committed to suitable institutes and societies and to particular Churches. For these territories it deals with everything pertaining to the establishment and change of ecclesiastical territories and to the provision of these Churches, and it carries out the other functions that the Congregation of Bishops fulfills within the scope of its competence.

Art. 90—§ 1. With regard to members of institutes of consecrated life, whether these are erected in the mission territories or are just working there, the Congregation enjoys competence in matters touching those members as missionaries, individually and collectively, without prejudice to art. 21, § 1.

§ 2. Those societies of apostolic life that were founded for the missions are subject to this Congregation.

Art. 91—To foster missionary cooperation, even through the effective collection and equal distribution of subsidies, the Congregation chiefly uses the Pontifical Missionary Works, namely, the Society for the Propagation of the Faith, the Society of St. Peter the Apostle, and the Holy Childhood Association, as well as the Pontifical Missionary Union of the Clergy.

Art. 92—Through a special office, the congregation administers its own funds and other resources destined for the missions, with full accountability to the Prefecture for the Economic Affairs of the Holy See.

The Congregation for the Clergy

Art. 93—Without prejudice to the right of bishops and their conferences, the Congregation examines matters regarding priests and deacons of the secular clergy, with regard to their persons and pastoral ministry, and with regard to resources available to them for the exercise of this ministry; and in all these matters the Congregation offers timely assistance to the bishops.

Art. 94—It has the function of promoting the religious education of the Christian faithful of all ages and conditions; it issues timely norms so that catechetical lessons be conducted according to a proper programme; it maintains a watchful attention to the suitable delivery of catechetical instruction; and, with the assent with the Congregation for the Doctrine of the Faith, it grants the prescribed approbation of the Holy See for catechisms and other writings pertaining to catechetical instruction. It is available to catechetical offices and

international initiatives on religious education, coordinates their activities and, where necessary, lends assistance.

Art. 95—§ 1. The Congregation is competent concerning the life, conduct, rights, and obligations of clergy.

§ 2. It advises on a more suitable distribution of priests.

§ 3. It fosters the ongoing education of clergy, especially concerning their sanctification and the effective exercise of their pastoral ministry, most of all in the fitting preaching of the Word of God.

Art. 96—This Congregation deals with everything that has to do with the clerical state as such for all clergy, including religious, in consultation with the dicasteries involved when the matter so requires.

Art. 97—The Congregation deals with those matters that are within the competence of the Holy See:

1° whether concerning presbyterial councils, colleges of consultors, chapters of canons, pastoral councils, parishes, churches, shrines, or concerning clerical associations, or ecclesiastical archives and records;

2° concerning Mass obligations as well as pious wills in general and pious foundations.

Art. 98—The Congregation carries out everything that pertains to the Holy See regarding the regulation of ecclesiastical goods, and especially for the correct administration of those properties; it grants the necessary approvals and *recognitiones* and it further sees to it that serious thought is given to the support and social security of the clergy.

The Pontifical Commission for Preserving the Patrimony of Art and History

Art. 99—At the Congregation for the Clergy there is a Commission that has the duty of acting as curator for the artistic and historical patrimony of the whole Church, namely, the Pontifical Commission for Preserving the Patrimony of Art and History.

Art. 100—To this patrimony belong, in the first place, all works of every kind of art of the past, works that must be kept and preserved with the greatest care. Those works whose proper use has ceased are to be kept in a suitable manner in museums of the Church or elsewhere.

Art. 101—§ 1. Outstanding among valuable historical objects are all documents and instruments referring and testifying to pastoral life and care, as well as to the rights and obligations of dioceses, parishes, churches, and other juridical persons in the Church.

§ 2. This historical patrimony is to be kept in archives or also in libraries and everywhere entrusted to competent curators lest testimonies of this kind be lost.

Art. 102—The Commission lends its assistance to particular Churches and conferences of bishops and together with them, where the case arises, sees to the setting up of museums, archives, and libraries, and ensures that the entire patrimony of art and history in the whole territory is properly collected and safeguarded and made available to all who have an interest in it.

Art. 103—In consultation with the Congregation for Seminaries and Educational Institutions and the Congregation for Divine Worship and the Discipline of the Sacraments, the Commission has the task of striving to make the people of God more and more aware of the need and importance of conserving the artistical and historical patrimony of the Church.

Art. 104—The president of the Commission is the cardinal prefect of the Congregation for the Clergy, assisted by the secretary of the Commission. Moreover, the Commission has its own staff.

The Congregation for Institutes of Consecrated Life and for Societies of Apostolic Life

Art. 105—The principal function of the Congregation for Institutes of Consecrated Life and for Societies of Apostolic Life is to promote and supervise in the whole Latin Church the practice of the evangelical counsels as they are lived in approved forms of consecrated life and at the same time the work of societies of apostolic life.

Art. 106—§ 1. The Congregation erects and approves religious and secular institutes and societies of apostolic life, or passes judgement on the suitability of their erection by the diocesan bishop. It also suppresses such institutes and societies if necessary.

§ 2. The Congregation is also competent to establish, or, if need be, to rescind, the unions or federations of institutes and societies.

Art. 107—The Congregation for its part takes care that institutes of consecrated life and societies of apostolic life grow and flourish according to the spirit of their founders and healthy traditions, faithfully follow their proper purpose and truly benefit the salvific mission of the Church.

Art. 108—§ 1. It deals with everything which, in accordance with the law, belongs to the Holy See concerning the life and work of the institutes and societies, especially the approval of their constitutions, their manner of government and apostolate, the recruitment and training as well as the rights and obligations of members, dispensation from vows and the dismissal of members, and the administration of goods.

§ 2. However, the organization of philosophical and theological studies and other academic subjects comes within the competence of the Congregation for Seminaries and Institutes of Studies.

Art. 109—It is the function of this Congregation to establish conferences of major superiors of men and women religious, to grant approval to their statutes and to give great attention in order that their activities are directed to achieving their true purpose.

Art. 110—The Congregation has competence also regarding eremetical life, the order of virgins and their associations as well as other form of consecrated life.

Art. 111—Its competence also embraces the third orders and associations of the faithful which are erected with the intention that, after a period of preparation, they may eventually become institutes of consecrated life or societies of apostolic life.

The Congregation for Seminaries and Educational Institutions[38]

Art. 112—The Congregation for Seminaries and Educational Institutions gives practical expression to the concern of the Apostolic See for the training of those who are called to holy orders, and for the promotion and organization of Catholic education.

Art. 113—§ 1. It is available to the bishops so that in their Churches vocations to the sacred ministry may be cultivated to the highest degree, and seminaries may be established and conducted in accordance with the law, where students may be suitable trained, receiving a solid formation that is human and spiritual, doctrinal and pastoral.

§ 2. It carefully gives great attention that the way of life and programme of the seminaries is in full harmony with the idea of priestly education, and that the superiors and teachers, by the example of their life and sound doctrine, contribute their utmost to the formation of the personality of the sacred ministers.

§ 3. It is also to erect interdiocesan seminaries and to approve their statutes.

Art. 114—The Congregation makes every effort to see that the fundamental principles of Catholic education as set out by the magisterium of the Church be ever more deeply researched, championed, and known by the people of God.

It also takes care that in this matter the Christian faithful may be able to fulfill their duties by striving to bring civil society to recognize and protect their rights.

Art. 115—The Congregation sets the norms by which Catholic schools are governed. It is available to diocesan bishops so that, wherever possible, Catholic schools be established and fostered with the utmost care, and that in every school appropriate undertakings bring catechetical instruction and pastoral care to the Christian pupils.

Art. 116—§ 1. The Congregation labours to ensure that there be in the Church a sufficient number of ecclesiastical and Catholic universities as well as other educational institutions in which the sacred disciplines may be pursued in depth, studies in the humanities and the sciences may be promoted, with due regard for Christian truth, so that the Christian faithful may be suitably trained to fulfill their own functions.

§ 2. It erects or approves ecclesiastical universities and institutions, ratifies their statutes, exercises higher supervision on them and exercises great attention so that the integrity of the Catholic faith is preserved in teaching doctrine.

§ 3. With regard to Catholic universities, it deals with those matters that are within the competence of the Holy See.

§ 4. It fosters cooperation and mutual help between universities and their associations and serves as a resource for them.

---

[38][The Congregation never formally used this name. On 26 February 1989, a few days before the coming into force of PB (1 March 1989), its soon-to-be new name was changed to "Congregation for Catholic Education (for Seminaries and Educational Institutions)" (letter of the Secretariat of State, prot. no. 236.026). See commentary on c. 360 for details. (Editors' note.)]

IV. THE TRIBUNALS

The Apostolic Penitentiary

Art. 117—The competence of the Apostolic Penitentiary regards the internal forum and indulgences.

Art. 118—For the internal forum, whether sacramental or non-sacramental, it grants absolutions, dispensations, commutations, validations, condonations, and other favours.

Art. 119—The Apostolic Penitentiary sees to it that in the patriarchal basilicas of Rome there be penitentiaries in sufficient numbers supplied with the appropriate faculties.

Art. 120—This dicastery is charged with the granting and use of indulgences, without prejudice to the right of the Congregation for the Doctrine of the Faith to review those things concerning dogmatic teaching on them.

The Supreme Tribunal of the Apostolic Signatura

Art. 121—The Apostolic Signatura functions as the supreme tribunal and also ensures that justice in the Church is correctly administered.

Art. 122—This Tribunal adjudicates:

1° complaints of nullity and petitions for total reinstatement against sentences of the Roman Rota;

2° in cases concerning the status of persons, recourses when the Roman Rota has denied a new examination of the case;

3° exceptions of suspicion and other proceedings against judges of the Roman Rota arising from the exercise of their functions;

4° conflicts of competence between tribunals which are not subject to the same appellate tribunal.

Art. 123—§ 1. The Signatura adjudicates recourses lodged within the peremptory limit of thirty useful days against singular administrative acts whether issued by the dicasteries of the Roman Curia or approved by them, whenever it is contended that the impugned act violated some law either in the decision-making process or in the procedure used.

§ 2. In these cases, in addition to the judgement regarding illegality of the act, it can also adjudicate, at the request of the plaintiff, the reparation of damages incurred through the unlawful act.

§ 3. The Signatura also adjudicates other administrative controversies referred to it by the Roman Pontiff or by dicasteries of the Roman Curia, as well as conflicts of competence between these dicasteries.

Art. 124—The Signatura also has the responsibility:

1° to exercise vigilance over the correct administration of justice, and, if need be, to censure advocates and procurators;

2° to deal with petitions presented to the Apostolic See for obtaining the commission of a case to the Roman Rota or some other favour relative to the administration of justice;

3° to prorogate the competence of lower tribunals;

4° to grant its approval to tribunals for appeals reserved to the Holy See, and to promote and approve the erection of interdiocesan tribunals.

Art. 125—The Apostolic Signatura is governed by its own law.

The Tribunal of the Roman Rota

Art. 126—The Roman Rota is a court of higher instance at the Apostolic See, usually at the appellate stage, with the purpose of safeguarding rights within the Church; it fosters unity of jurisprudence, and, by virtue of its own decisions, provides assistance to lower tribunals.

Art. 127—The judges of this Tribunal constitute a college. Persons of proven doctrine and experience, they have been selected by the Supreme

Pontiff from various parts of the world. The Tribunal is presided over by a dean, likewise appointed by the Supreme Pontiff from among the judges and for specific term of office.

Art. 128—This Tribunal adjudicates:

1° in second instances, cases that have been decided by ordinary tribunals of the first instance and are being referred to the Holy See by legitimate appeal;

2° in third or further instance, cases already decided by the same Apostolic Tribunal and by any other tribunals whatever, unless they have become a resiudicata.

Art. 129—§ 1. The Tribunal, however, judges the following in first instance:

1° bishops in contentious matters, unless it deals with the rights or temporal goods of a juridical person represented by the bishop;

2° abbots primate or abbots superior of a monastic congregation and supreme moderators of religious institutes of pontifical right;

3° dioceses or other ecclesiastical persons, whether physical or juridical, which have no superior below the Roman Pontiff;

4° cases which the Supreme Pontiff commits to this Tribunal.

§ 2. It deals with the same cases even in second and further instances, unless other provisions are made.

Art. 130—The Tribunal of the Roman Rota is governed by its own law.

V. THE PONTIFICAL COUNCILS

The Pontifical Council for the Laity

Art. 131—The Pontifical Council for the Laity is competent in those matters pertaining to the Apostolic See in promoting and coordinating the apostolate of the laity and, generally, in those matters respecting the Christian life of laypeople as such.

Art. 132—The president is assisted by an advisory board of cardinals and bishops. Figuring especially among the members of the Council are certain Christian faithful engaged in various fields of activity.

Art. 133—§ 1. The Council is to urge and support laypeople to participate in the life and mission of the Church in their own way, as individuals or in associations, especially so that they may carry out their special responsibility of filling the realm of temporal things with the spirit of the Gospel.

§ 2. It fosters joint action among laypeople in catechetical instruction, in liturgical and sacramental life as well as in works of mercy, charity, and social development.

§ 3. The Council attends to and organizes international conferences and other projects concerning the apostolate of the laity.

Art. 134—Within the parameters of its own competence, the Council performs all activities respecting lay associations of the Christian faithful; it erects associations of an international character and provides approval or *recognitio* for their statutes, saving the competence of the Secretariat of State. As for secular third orders, the Council deals only with those matters concerning their apostolic activities.

The Pontifical Council for Promoting Christian Unity

Art. 135—It is the function of the Pontifical Council for Promoting Christian Unity to engage in ecumenical work through timely initiatives and activities, labouring to restore unity among Christians.

Art. 136—§ 1. It sees that the decrees of the Second Vatican Council pertaining to ecumenism are put into practice.

It deals with the correct interpretation of the principles of ecumenism and enjoins that they be carried out.

§ 2. It fosters, brings together, and coordinates national and international Catholic organizations promoting Christian unity, and supervises their undertakings.

§ 3. After prior consultation with the Supreme Pontiff, the Council maintains relations with Christians of Churches and ecclesial communities that do not yet have full communion with the Catholic Church, and especially organizes dialogue and meetings to promote unity with them, with the help of theological experts of sound doctrine. As often as may seem opportune, the Council deputes Catholic observers to Christian meetings, and to Catholic meetings it invites observers from other Churches and ecclesial communities.

Art. 137—§ 1. Since the council deals with matters which by their very nature touch on questions of faith, it must proceed in close connection with the Congregation for the Doctrine of the Faith, especially if declarations and public documents have to be issued.

§ 2. In dealing with important matters concerning the separated Eastern Churches, the Council must first hear the Congregation for the Eastern Churches.

Art. 138—Within the Council there is a Commission to study and deal with matters concerning the Jews from a religious perspective; the president of the Council presides over the Commission.[39]

The Pontifical Council for the Family

Art. 139—The Pontifical Council for the Family promotes the pastoral care of families, protects their rights and dignity in the Church and in civil society, so that they may ever be more able to fulfill their duties.

Art. 140—The president is assisted by an advisory board of bishops. Figuring above all among the members of the Council are laypeople, both men and women, especially married ones, from all over the world.

Art. 141—§ 1. The Council works for a deeper understanding of the Church's teaching on the family and for its spread through suitable catechesis. It encourages studies in the spirituality of marriage and the family.

§ 2. It works together with the bishops and their conferences to ensure the accurate recognition of the human and social conditions of the family institution everywhere and to ensure a strong general awareness of initiatives that help pastoral work for families.

§ 3. The Council strives to ensure that the rights of the family be acknowledged and defended even in the social and political realm. It also supports and coordinates initiatives to protect human life from the first moment of conception and to encourage responsible procreation.

§ 4. Without prejudice to art. 133, it follows the activities of institutes and associations which seek to work for the good of the family.

The Pontifical Council for Justice and Peace

Art. 142—The ideal of the Pontifical Council for Justice and Peace is that justice and peace in this world may be strengthened in accordance with the Gospel and the social teaching of the Church.

Art. 143—§ 1. The Council makes a thorough study of the social teaching of the Church and takes pains to see that this teaching is widely spread and put into practice among people and communities, especially regarding the relations between workers and management, relations that must come to be more and more imbued with the spirit of the Gospel.

§ 2. It collects information and research on justice and peace, about human development and violations of human rights; it ponders all this, and,

---

[39][The name of the Commission is the Commission for Religious Relations with the Jews. (Editors' note.)]

when the occasion offers, shares its conclusions with the groupings of bishops. It cultivates relationships with Catholic international organizations and other institutions, even ones outside the Catholic Church, which sincerely strive to achieve peace and justice in the world.

§ 3. It works to form among peoples a mentality which fosters peace, especially on the occasion of the World Peace Day.

Art. 144—The Council has a special relationship with the Secretariat of State, especially whenever matters of peace and justice have to be dealt with in public by documents or announcements.

The Pontifical Council "Cor unum"

Art. 145—The Pontifical Council "Cor unum" shows the solicitude of the Catholic Church for the needy, in order that human fraternity may be fostered and that the charity of Christ be made manifest.

Art. 146—It is the function of the Council:

1° to stimulate the Christian faithful as participants in the mission of the Church, to give witness to evangelical charity and to support them in this concern;

2° to foster and coordinate the initiatives of Catholic institutions that labour to help peoples in need, especially those who go to the rescue in the more urgent crises and disasters, and to facilitate their relations with public international organizations operating in the same field of assistance and good works;

3° to give serious attention and promote plans and undertakings for joint action and neighbourly help serving human progress.

Art. 147—The president of this Council is the same as the president of the Pontifical Council for Justice and Peace, who sees to it that the activities of both institutes are closely coordinated.

Art. 148—To ensure that the proposals of the Council are more effectively put into effect, among members of the Council are men and also women representing Catholic beneficent institutions.

The Pontifical Council for the Pastoral Care of Migrants and Itinerant People

Art. 149—The Pontifical Council for the Pastoral Care of Migrants and Itinerant People brings the pastoral concern of the Church to bear on the special needs of those who have been forced to leave their native land or who do not have one. It sees to it that these matters are considered with the serious attention they deserve.

Art. 150—§ 1. The Council works to see that in the particular Churches refugees and exiles, migrants, nomads, and circus workers receive effective and special spiritual care, even, if necessary, by means of suitable pastoral structures.

§ 2. It likewise fosters pastoral solicitude in these same Churches for sailors, at sea and in port, especially through the Apostleship of the Sea, over which it exercises ultimate direction.

§ 3. The Council has the same concern for those who work in airports or airplanes.

§ 4. It tries to ensure that the Christian people come to an awareness of the needs of these people and effectively demonstrate their own brotherly attitude towards them, especially on the occasion of the World Migration Day.

Art. 151—The Council works to ensure that journeys which Christians undertake for reasons of piety, study, or recreation contribute to their moral and religious formation, and it is available to the particular Churches in order that all who are away from home receive suitable spiritual care.

The Pontifical Council for Pastoral Assistance to Health Care Workers

Art. 152—The Pontifical Council for Pastoral Assistance to Health Care Workers shows the solicitude of the Church for the sick by helping those who serve the sick and suffering, so that their apostolate of mercy may ever more respond to people's needs.

Art. 153—§ 1. The Council is to spread the Church's teaching on the spiritual and moral aspects of illness as well as the meaning of human suffering.

§ 2. It lends its assistance to the particular Churches to ensure that health care workers receive the help of spiritual care in carrying out their work according to Christian teachings, and especially that in turn the pastoral workers in this field may never lack the help they need to carry out their work.

§ 3. The Council fosters studies and actions which international Catholic organizations or other institutions undertake in this field.

§ 4. With keen interest it follows new health care developments in law and science so that these may be duly taken into account in the pastoral work of the Church.

The Pontifical Council for the Interpretation of Legislative Texts

Art. 154—The function of the Pontifical Council for the Interpretation of Legislative Texts consists mainly in interpreting the laws of the Church.

Art. 155—The Council is competent to publish authentic interpretations of universal laws of the Church which are confirmed by pontifical authority, having heard in questions of major importance the views of the dicasteries concerned by the subject matter.

Art. 156—This Council is at the service of the other Roman dicasteries to assist them in order to ensure that general executory decrees and instructions which they are going to publish are in confor-

mity with the prescriptions of the law currently in force and that they are drawn up in a correct juridical form.

Art. 157—Moreover, the general decrees of the conferences of bishops are to be submitted to this Council by the dicastery which is competent to grant them the *recognitio,* in order that they be examined from a juridical perspective.

Art. 158—At the request of those interested, this Council determines whether particular laws and general decrees issued by legislators below the level of the supreme authority are in agreement or not with the universal laws of the Church.

The Pontifical Council for Inter-religious Dialogue

Art. 159—The Pontifical Council for Inter-religious Dialogue fosters and supervises relations with members and groups of religions that do not carry the Christian name as well as with those who are in any way endowed with religious feeling.

Art. 160—The Council fosters relations, including suitable dialogue, with adherents of other religions. It promotes timely studies and conferences to develop mutual information and esteem, so that human dignity and the spiritual and moral riches of people may be advanced. The Council sees to the formation of those who engage in this kind of dialogue.

Art. 161—When the subject matter so requires, the Council must proceed in the exercise of its own function in consultation with the Congregation for the Doctrine of the Faith, and, if need be, with the Congregations for the Oriental Churches and for the Evangelization of Peoples.

Art. 162—This Council has a Commission, under the direction of the president of the Council, for fostering relations with Muslims from a religious perspective.

The Pontifical Council for Dialogue with Non-Believers

Art. 163—The Pontifical Council for Dialogue with Non-Believers shows the pastoral solicitude of the Church for those who do not believe in God or who profess no religion.

Art. 164—It promotes the study of atheism and of the lack of faith and religion, looking into their causes and their consequences with regard to the Christian faith, so that suitable assistance may be given to pastoral action through the work especially of Catholic institutions of higher learning.

Art. 165—The Council sets up dialogue with atheists and unbelievers whenever they agree to sincere cooperation, and it is represented by true specialists at conferences on this matter.

The Pontifical Council for Culture

Art. 166—The Pontifical Council for Culture fosters relations between the Holy See and the realm of human culture, especially by promoting discussion with various contemporary institutions of learning and teaching, so that secular culture may be more and more open to the Gospel, and specialists in the sciences, literature, and the arts may feel themselves called by the Church to truth, goodness, and beauty.

Art. 167—The Council has its own special structure. The president is assisted by an advisory board and another board, composed of specialists of various disciplines from several parts of the world.

Art. 168—The Council on its own undertakes suitable projects with respect to culture. It follows through on those which are undertaken by various institutes of the Church, and, so far as necessary, lends them assistance. In consultation with the Secretariat of State, it shows interest in measures adopted by countries and international agencies in support of human culture and, as appropriate, it is present in the principal organizations in the field of culture and fosters conferences.

The Pontifical Council for Social Communications

Art. 169—§ 1. The Pontifical Council for Social Communications is involved in questions respecting the instruments of social communication, so that, even by means of these instruments, human progress and the news of salvation may be advanced for the benefit of secular culture and mores.

§ 2. In carrying out its functions, the Council must proceed in close connection with the Secretariat of State.

Art. 170—§ 1. The chief function of this Council is to arouse the Church and the Christian faithful, in a timely and suitable way, to action in the many forms of social communication, and to sustain them in it. It takes pains to see that newspapers and periodicals, as well as films and radio or television broadcasts, are more and more imbued with a human and Christian spirit.

§ 2. With special solicitude the Council looks to Catholic newspapers and periodicals, as well as radio and television stations, that they may truly live up to their nature and function, by transmitting especially the teaching of the Church as it is laid out by the Church's magisterium, and by spreading religious news accurately and faithfully.

§ 3. It fosters mutual relations with Catholic associations active in social communications.

§ 4. It takes steps to make the Christian people aware, especially on the occasion offered by the World Communications Day, of the duty of each and every person to make sure that the media be of service to the Church's pastoral mission.

VI. The Administrative Services

The Apostolic Camera

Art. 171—§ 1. The Apostolic Camera, presided over by the cardinal chamberlain of the Holy Roman Church, assisted by the vice-chamberlain and the other prelates of the Camera, chiefly exercises the functions assigned to it by the special law on the vacancy of the Apostolic See.[40]

§ 2. When the Apostolic See falls vacant, it is the right and the duty of the cardinal chamberlain of the Holy Roman Church, personally or through his delegate, to request, from all administrations dependent on the Holy See, reports on their patrimonial and economic status as well as information on any extraordinary business that may at that time be under way, and, from the Prefecture for the Economic Affairs of the Holy See he shall request a financial statement on income and expenditures of the previous year and the budgetary estimates for the following year. He is in duty bound to submit these reports and estimates to the College of Cardinals.

The Administration of the Patrimony of the Apostolic See

Art. 172—It is the function of the Administration of the Patrimony of the Apostolic See to administer the properties owned by the Holy See in order to underwrite the expenses needed for the Roman Curia to function.

Art. 173—This Council is presided over by a cardinal assisted by a board of cardinals; and it is composed of two sections, the Ordinary Section and the Extraordinary, under the control of the prelate secretary.

Art. 174—The Ordinary Section administers the properties entrusted to its care, calling in the advice of experts if needed; it examines matters concerning the juridical and economic status of the employees of the Holy See; it supervises institutions under its fiscal responsibility; it sees to the provision of all that is required to carry out the ordinary business and specific aims of the dicasteries; it maintains records of income and expenditures and prepares the accounts of the money received and paid out for the past year, and it draws up the estimates for the year to come.

Art. 175—The Extraordinary Section administers its own moveable goods and acts as a guardian for moveable goods entrusted to it by other institutes of the Holy See.

The Prefecture for the Economic Affairs of the Holy See

Art. 176—The Prefecture for the Economic Affairs of the Holy See has the function of supervising and governing the temporal goods of the administrations that are dependent on the Holy See, or of which the Holy See has charge, whatever the autonomy these administrations may happen to enjoy.

Art. 177—The Prefecture is presided over by a cardinal assisted by a board of cardinals, one of whom is the president, with the collaboration of the prelate secretary and the general accountant.

Art. 178—§ 1. It studies the reports on the patrimonial and economic status of the Holy See, as well as the statements of income and expenditures for the previous year and the budget estimates for the following year of the administrations mentioned in art. 176, if need be, inspecting books and documents.

§ 2. The Prefecture compiles the Holy See's consolidated financial statement of the previous year's expenditures as well as the consolidated estimates of the next year's expenditures, and submits these at specific times to higher authority for approval.

---

[40][Cf. Ap. Const. *Romano pontifici eligendo,* in this appendix, pp. 1086–1141. (Editors' note.)]

Art. 179—§ 1. The Prefecture supervises financial undertakings of the administrations and expresses its opinion in concerning projects of major importance.

§ 2. It inquires into damages inflicted in whatever manner on the patrimony of the Holy See, and, if need be, lodges penal or civil actions to the competent tribunals.

VII. THE OTHER INSTITUTES OF THE ROMAN CURIA

The Prefecture of the Papal Household

Art. 180—The Prefecture of the Papal Household looks after the internal organization of the papal household, and supervises everything concerning the conduct and service of all clerics and laypersons who make up the papal chapel and family.

Art. 181—§ 1. It is at the service of the Supreme Pontiff, both in the Apostolic Palace and when he travels in Rome or in Italy.

§ 2. Apart from the strictly liturgical part, which is handled by the Office for the Liturgical Celebrations of the Supreme Pontiff, the Prefecture sees to the organization and progress of papal ceremonies and determines the order of precedence.

§ 3. It arranges public and private audiences with the Pontiff, in consultation with the Secretariat of State whenever circumstances so demand and under whose direction it arranges the procedures to be followed when the Roman Pontiff meets in a solemn audience with heads of State, ambassadors, members of governments, public authorities, and other distinguished persons and dignitaries.

The Office for the Liturgical Celebrations of the Supreme Pontiff

Art. 182—§ 1. The Office for the Liturgical Celebration of the Supreme Pontiff is to prepare all that is necessary for the liturgical and other sacred celebrations performed by the Supreme Pontiff or in his name and supervise them according to the current prescriptions of liturgical law.

§ 2. The master of papal liturgical celebrations is appointed by the Supreme Pontiff to a five-year term of office; papal masters of ceremonies who assist him in sacred celebrations are likewise appointed by the secretary of state to a term of the same length.

VIII. THE ADVOCATES

Art. 183—Apart from the advocates of the Roman Rota and the advocates for the causes of saints, there is a roster of advocates who, at the request of interested parties, are qualified to represent them in their cases at the Supreme Tribunal of the Apostolic Signatura and to offer assistance in hierarchical recourses lodged before dicasteries of the Roman Curia.

Art. 184—Candidates can be inscribed in the roster by the cardinal secretary of state, after he has consulted a commission stably constituted for this purpose. Candidates must be qualified by a suitable preparation attested by appropriate academic degrees, and at the same time be recommended by their example of a Christian life, honourable character, and expertise. If these qualities happen to be lacking at a later date, the advocate shall be struck off the roster.

Art. 185—§ 1. The body called "Advocates of the Holy See" is composed mainly of advocates listed in the roster of advocates, and its members are able to undertake the representation of cases in civil or ecclesiastical tribunals in the name of the Holy See or the dicasteries of the Roman Curia.

§ 2. They are appointed by the cardinal secretary of state to a five-year term of office on the recommendation of the commission mentioned in art.

184; for serious reasons, they may be removed from office. Once they have completed seventy-five years of age, they cease their office.

IX. THE INSTITUTIONS CONNECTED TO THE HOLY SEE

Art. 186—There are certain institutes, some of ancient origin and some not long established, which do not belong to the Roman Curia in a strict sense but nevertheless provide useful or necessary services to the Supreme Pontiff himself, to the Curia and the whole Church, and are in some way connected to the Apostolic See.

Art. 187—Outstanding among institutes of this kind is the Vatican Secret Archives, where documents of the Church's governance are preserved first of all so that they may be available to the Holy See itself and to the Curia as they carry out their own work, but then also, by papal permission, so that they may be available to everyone engaged in historical research and prove to be sources of information on all areas of secular history of all the regions that have been closely connected with the life of the Church in centuries gone by.

Art. 188—In the Vatican Apostolic Library, established by the Supreme Pontiffs, the Church has a remarkable instrument for fostering, guarding, and spreading culture. In its various sections, it offers to scholars researching truth a treasure of every kind of art and knowledge.

Art. 189—To seek the truth and to spread it in the various areas of divine and human sciences there have arisen in the bosom of the Roman Church various academies, as they are called, outstanding among which is the Pontifical Academy of Sciences.

Art. 190—In their constitution and administra-tion, all these institutions of the Roman Church are governed by their own laws.

Art. 191—Of more recent origin, though partly based on certain examples of the past, are the Vatican Polyglot Press; the Vatican Publishing House and its bookstore; the daily, weekly and monthly newspapers, among which *L'Osservatore Romano* stands out; Vatican Radio; the Vatican Television Centre. These institutes, according to their own regulations, come within the competence of the Secretariat of State or of other agencies of the Roman Curia.

Art. 192—The Fabric of Saint Peter's labours, according to its own regulations, to care for matters concerning the Basilica of the Prince of the Apostles, with respect to the preservation and decoration of the building and behaviour among the employees and pilgrims who come into the church for sight-seeing. Where necessary, the superiors of the Fabric act in harmony with the chapter of that basilica.

Art. 193—The Office of Papal Charities carries on the work of aid of the Supreme Pontiff toward the poor and depends directly upon him.

We decree the present Apostolic Constitution to be firm, valid, and effective now and henceforth, that it shall receive its full and integral effects from the first day of the month of March of 1989, and that it must in each and everything and in any manner whatsoever be fully observed by all those to whom it applies or in any way shall apply, anything to the contrary notwithstanding, even if it is worthy of most special mention.

Given in Rome, at Saint Peter's, in the presence of the cardinals in consistory assembled, on the vigil of the solemnity of the Holy Apostles Peter and Paul, 28 June in the Marian Year 1988, the tenth of Our pontificate.

JOHN PAUL II

Apostolic Letter of Pope Paul VI Renovating the Organization of the Papal Household

The "Pontifical Household" came into being in the course of centuries through a slow and complex process of adaptation to the requirements of the person of the Pope and his mission. It has always constituted an organism of unique decorum and usefulness for the Chair of Peter, the spiritual center of the Catholic Church and the See of the Vicar of Jesus Christ on earth.

Accordingly, the Pope, as visible head of the Catholic Church and as the sovereign of a temporal state recognized by the civil authorities of various nations, chose for himself at all times a number of loyal and capable persons, ecclesiastics as well as lay, who could worthily meet the demands of the liturgy, culminating in the most solemn sacred ceremonies of certain occasions in the life of the Church, as well as the many needs of the temporal state.

Owing, however, to the evident developments and changes of modern times, many of the functions once entrusted to the members of the Pontifical Household have now lost their meaning, and though they continue to exist as purely honorary offices, they are no longer in keeping with the concrete realities of the times. On the other hand, the religious mission of the Roman pontificate has day by day taken on new forms and dimensions. As a result, a realistic view of things demands, though painfully at times, as we said at our first meeting with the members of the nobility and of the Roman patricians, that the Apostolic See make a careful selection from its heritage of institutions and customs and retain that which is essential and vital. It should be added that in the entire Church, particularly after the Second Vatican Council, as well as in world public opinion, a more attentive and, we would say, a more jealous sensitivity has gained ground to the pre-eminence of clearly spiritual values, to the demands of truth, order and realism and to a respect for that which if efficacious, functional and reasonable, as opposed to that which is merely nominal, decorative and external.

It seems to us that at this time the make-up of the Pontifical Household should also conform to these deeply felt needs and should faithfully reflect the reality of things, emphasizing on the one hand, the essentially spiritual mission of the Roman Pontiff and, on the other, his unique role even in the areas of civil and international life.

We therefore desire that the members of the Pontifical Household, including both the chapel—which is at the service of the Pope in his capacity as the spiritual head of the Catholic religion—as well as the family—which is at the service of the Pope as a sovereign, that is to say, as the head of a society possessing a juridical personality publicly recognized by states and international organizations and with the right of active and passive representation—that all the members exercise effective functions and activities in the spiritual and temporal fields, thus providing an updated version—in keeping with the conditions and demands of the day—of the time-honored reality that led in the past to the constitution of the various offices of the court.

Thus our ancient and well-deserving court, which will henceforth be called by its original and noble name of "Pontifical Household," will continue to shine forth in its true prestige, made up of ecclesiastics and laymen who, in addition to their peculiar competence and authority, have distinguished themselves with noteworthy service in the areas of the apostolate, culture, science and the professions for the good of souls and the glory of the name of the Lord.

Accordingly, after having heard the opinion of our collaborators, we establish and decree the following regarding the "Pontifical Household:"

THE PONTIFICAL HOUSEHOLD

One

1. The "Pontifical Household" is made up of members of the clergy and the laity who form, on the one hand, the chapel and, on the other, the Pontifical family, ecclesiastical and lay.

2. The chapel is composed of members of the various categories of the Church and the People of God—bishops, priests and laymen—as well as of representatives of those called by the Holy

Father to assist him in the exercise of his lofty functions and his immediate associates.

3. The pontifical family is composed of members of the Catholic laity holding posts of special responsibility and qualified representation in the service of the Supreme Pontiff in the exercise of his mission as head of the Apostolic See and sovereign of the Vatican City State. It also includes the ecclesiastics who assist him more directly in this office as well as his closest associates.

Two

The "Pontifical Household" is entrusted to the direction of the Prefect of the Apostolic Palace. It is his task to convene the members of the household for the respective religious and civil ceremonies referred to in No. 4, to establish their functions, to watch over the order and the carrying out of these ceremonies, according to the special norms referred to in No. 5, and to provide for their requirements, in agreement with the Secretariat of State.

Three

1. All the members of the "Pontifical Household," ecclesiastics and laymen, are appointed by the Pope.

2. The terms of office of the members of the chapel and of the pontifical family are regulated for ecclesiastics by the norms set down by the Apostolic Constitution *Regimini Ecclesiae universae* (No. 2, paragraph 5, AAS 59, 1967, p. 891) and by other special regulations already in force or to be issued in the future. For laymen, the term of office is five years.

   The duration in office may be extended by the Holy Father.

3. The term of office expires when the Apostolic See becomes vacant, though the obligation

remains to be available, according to the functions of each member, for the normal carrying on of ordinary business and of the various ceremonies celebrated during this period, according to the pertinent instructions of the Sacred College.

4. No office in the "Pontifical Household" is hereditary.

Four

1. Ceremonies in which the members of the "Pontifical Household" take part are of a religious and of a civil nature.

2. Religious ceremonies are either solemn (e.g., coronation of the Pontiff, public consistories, papal chapels, canonizations) or ordinary.

3. Civil ceremonies consist either of audiences of an official nature (granted to sovereigns, heads of state, premiers and foreign ministers; the presentation of credentials by ambassadors and ministers accredited to the Holy See) or of a non-official nature.

Five

The Prefect of the Apostolic Palace will issue, with the approval of His Holiness, appropriate rules for religious and civil pontifical ceremonies as well as for the dress to be worn by ecclesiastical and lay members of the chapel and the family of the "Pontifical Household."

Six

1. The pontifical chapel, in addition to the members of the ecclesiastical pontifical family referred to in no. 7, #1, is constituted as follows:

   - Members of the various orders of the Sacred College of Cardinals.
   - Patriarchs, archbishops, bishops and eparchs, assistants to the throne, be they of the Latin or of the Oriental rites.
   - The vice chamberlain of the Holy Roman Church.
   - The superior prelate of each of the Sacred Congregations, the secretary of the Supreme Tribunal of the Signature, the dean of the Sacred Roman Rota.
   - The regent of the Sacred Apostolic Penitentiary.
   - The regent of the Apostolic Chancellery.
   - The superior prelate of the three secretariats.
   - The president of the Pontifical Commission for Social Communications.
   - The abbot of Montecassino and the abbots general of the Canons Regular and of the monastic Orders.
   - The superior general or, in his absence, the procurator general of each of the mendicant Orders.
   - The auditors of the Sacred Roman Rota.
   - The votanti of the Apostolic Signature.
   - The members of the chapters of the three patriarchal basilicas.
   - The consistorial advocates.
   - The Pastors of Rome.
   - The clerics of the Pontifical Chapel (cf. no. 6, #5).
   - The immediate associates of the Pope.

2. The above mentioned persons take part in religious celebrations presided over by the Pope or taking place in his presence (cf. No. 4, #2) and they occupy the places assigned to them according to an established order of precedence.

3. In the papal procession, which will likewise be regulated by the special norms referred to, the above listed categories will be represented on each occasion by only two members, except in the case of the Pastors of Rome who can have a larger representation.

4. The following offices and titles of the pontifical chapel are abolished: Palatine Cardinals; Prelates of the Fiocchetto; Princes Assistants to the Throne; Majordomo of His Holiness; Minister of the Interior; Knight Commander of the Holy Spirit; Roman Magistrate; Master of the Sacred Hospice; Honorary Chamberlains in abito paonazzo; Privy Chaplains and Honorary Privy Chaplains; Privy Clerks; Confessor of the Pontifical Family; Candle-bearing Acolytes; Ordinary Pontifical Chaplains; Master Porters of the Virga Rubea; Custodian of the Sacred Tiara; Macebearers; Apostolic Messengers.

5. The clerics of the pontifical chapel, directed by the papal master of ceremonies, assist the Holy Father at the altar. Members of the suppressed categories of Privy and Honorary Privy Chaplains, Privy Clerks, Candle-bearing Acolytes, Ordinary Pontifical Chaplains and Master Porters of the Virga Rubea also form part of this group.

THE PONTIFICAL FAMILY

Seven

The pontifical family consists of ecclesiastic and lay members.

1. The ecclesiastical pontifical family is made up as follows:

   • The substitute secretary of state and the Secretary of the Cypher.

   • The secretary for the Council for the Public Affairs of the Church.

   • The almoner of His Holiness.

   • The vicar general of His Holiness for Vatican City (cf. no. 7, #5).

   • The president of the Pontifical Ecclesiastical Academy.

   • The theologian of the Pontifical Household (cf. No. 7, #4).

   • The secretary of Briefs to Princes.

   • The secretary of Latin Letters.

   • The apostolic protonotaries.

   • Prelates of the antechamber (cf. No. 7, #11).

   • Masters of pontifical ceremonies.

   • Honorary prelates of His Holiness (cf. No. 7, #6).

   • Chaplains of His Holiness (cf. No. 7, #6).

   • The apostolic preacher.

2. The lay pontifical family is made up as follows:

   • The assistants to the throne.

   • The delegate of Vatican City State.

   • The general counselor of Vatican City State.

   • The commander of the Guard of Honor of the Pope (cf. No. 9).

   • The commander of the Swiss Guards.

   • The commander of the Palatine Guard of Honor.

   • The commander of the Pontifical Gendarmes.

   • The consultors of Vatican City State.

   • The president of the Pontifical Academy of Sciences.

   • The gentlemen-in-waiting of His Holiness (cf. No. 7, #7).

   • The Procurators of the Sacred Apostolic Palace.

- The attaches of the antechamber (cf. No. 7, #7).
- The immediate associates of the Pope.

3. The following offices and titles of the Pontifical Family are abolished: Palatine Cardinals; Palatine Prelates (Majordomo of His Holiness, Master of the Chamber, Auditor of His Holiness); Master of the Sacred Hospice; Head Messenger of the Sacred Apostolic Palace; Head Riding Master of His Holiness; General Superintendent of the Post Office; Bearers of the Golden Rose; Secretary for Embassies, Esente of the Noble Guards; Honorary Chamberlains in abito paonazzo; Honorary Chamberlains extra Urbem; Privy Clerks; Ordinary Pontifical Chaplains; Confessor of the Pontifical Family, Privy Steward.

4. The Master of the Sacred Apostolic Palace retains his office and will be called the Theologian of the Pontifical Household.

5. The title of privy chamberlain is abolished. For those who until now held this title, the following is set down: the privy almoner and the sacristan of His Holiness remain in office but are known respectively as the almoner of His Holiness and the vicar general of His Holiness for Vatican City. The Secretary of Briefs to Princes and the Secretary of Latin Letters, to whom apply the norms of the Apostolic Constitution *Regimini Ecclesiae universae,* No. 134 (AAS, *op. cit.,* p. 927) remain in office and retain their specific title. The following titles and offices are abolished: Cupbearer; Secretary for Embassies and of the Wardrobe; the services of the antechamber formerly rendered by these persons will now be performed by the two antechamber prelates referred to in No. 7, #11. The title and office of Sub-Datary are abolished.

6. Domestic prelates and supernumerary privy chamberlains continue to form part of the pontifical family as well as of the chapel, but they are now called respectively Honorary Prelates of His Holiness and Chaplains of His Holiness according to the provisions in No. 8.

7. Likewise, the Privy and Honorary Chamberlains of Cape and Sword remain in office but are known as Gentlemen-in-waiting of His Holiness. The Bearers of the Chair (bussolanti) also remain in office but have the title of Attaches of the Antechamber.

8. The members of the lay pontifical family do not take part in pontifical procession or in the ceremonies of the chapel, although they assist at the sacred pontifical rites from a specially reserved place.

9. The Assistants to the Throne are at the service of the Prefect of the Apostolic Palace. It is their task to be host on the occasion of the more solemn civil ceremonies referred to in No. 4, #3, and to offer their assistance in the performance of the duties of the lay pontifical family.

10. The Prefect of the Apostolic Palace may entrust special assignments to the Consultors of Vatican City State on the occasion of the more solemn civil ceremonies.

11. The two antechamber prelates render daily service in the pontifical antechamber. Appointed by the Supreme Pontiff, their office expires when the Apostolic See becomes vacant.

Eight

Honorary ecclesiastical titles from now on include only the three categories of Apostolic Protonotaries (numerary and supernumerary), Honorary Prelates of His Holiness and Chaplains of His Holiness. All the other categories are abolished.

Nine

The corps of the Pontifical Noble Guard takes on the name of Guard of Honor of the Pope. From now on, its service will be honorary in the pontifical ceremonies of a civil and official nature referred to in No. 4, #3, according to special instructions issued by the Prefect of the Apostolic Palace. The number of the guards, their enrollment and manner of service are laid down in suitable updated internal rules.

Ten

All services of honor and of order in the Pontifical Household is maintained by the following pontifical corps:

• The Swiss Guards.

• The Palatine Guard of Honor.

• The Pontifical Gendarmerie.

Eleven

According to requirements, a corps of attaches will insure a service of order during the various religious and civil ceremonies of the Pontifical Household. These are appointed for a five-year term by the Prefect of the Apostolic Palace, who will also determine their particular functions.

We order that what has been by us decreed in this Motu Proprio remain and be observed, notwithstanding any contrary dispositions.

Given in Rome, at St. Peter's, on March 28 in the year 1968, the fourth of our pontificate.

L'Election du Grand Maitre

Counseil Complet d'Etat du 8 Mai 1962 L'Election

Le 8 mai 1962 le Conseil Complet d'Etat s'est réuni dans la Villa Magistrale de l'Aventin pour procéder à l élection du LXXVIIe Prince et Grand Maître.*

Selon l'Art. 22 de la Charte Constitutionnelle en vigueur avaient droit de vote:

a) le Lieutenant de Grand Maître:

- S. Exe. le Vén. Bailli Fra' *Ernesto Paternò Castello;*

b) les autres Membres Profes du Souverain Conseil:

- Comm. Fra' *Enrico Mantalto di Fragnito*, Représentant du Grand Prieuré de Rome;

- S. Exe. le Vén. Bailli Fra' *Renato Galleani d'Agliano*, Représentant du Grand Prieuré de Lombardie et Venise;

- Comm. Fra' *Fulco Galletti di S. Cataldo*, Représentant du Grand Prieuré de Naples et Sicile;

- S. Exe. le Vén. Bailli Fra' *Alfonso M. de Vesque-Püttlingen*, Représentant du Grand Prieuré de Bohème;

- Comm. Fra' *Ottone de Grisogono*, Représentant du Grand Prieuré d'Autriche;

c) le Prélat de l'Ordre:

- S. Exe. Mgr. *Carlo Alberto Ferrero di Cavallerleone*, Archevêque tit. de Trébizonde, Bailli Grand-Croix d'Honneur et de Dévotion;

d) les Grands Prieurs:

- S. Exe. le Vén. Bailli Fra' *Raimondo del Balzo di Presenzano*, Grand Prieur de Rome;

- S. Exe. le Vén. Bailli Fra' *Nicola Galleani d'Agliano*, Grand Prieur de Lombardie et Venise;

- S. Exe. le Vén. Bailli Fra' *Marzio Pignatelli Aragona Cortes*, Grand Prieur de Naples et Sicile;

- S. Exe. le Chevalier de Justice *Giovanni Trapp*, Prince Grand Prieur d'Autriche.

e) Les Baillis Profes:

- S. Exe. le Vén. Bailli Fra' *Antonio Hercolani Fava Simonetti:*

- S. Exe. le Vén. Bailli Fra' *Ferdinando di Thun e Hohenstein;*

---

* *Bulletin Officiel du Grand Magistère de l'Ordre S.M.H. de Malte*, Rome, May 1962.

f) deux Chevaliers profès, expressément délégués au Conseil para chacun des Grands Prieurés:

- Chevalier de Justice *Angelo M. Mazzaccara di Celenza e Carlantino dei Mazzaccara,* élu par le Chapitre du Grand Prieuré de Rome le 12-3-1962;

- Comm. Fra' *Giuseppe Dalla Torre del Tempio di Sanguinetto,* élu par le Chapitre du Grand Prieuré de Rome le 12-3-1962;

- Comm. Fra' *Angelo de Mojana di Cologna,* élu par le Chapitre du Grand Prieuré de Lombardie et Venise le 24-3-1962;

- Chevalier Fra' *Vincenzo Morelli di Popolo di Ticineto,* élu par le Chapitre du Grand Prieuré de Lombardie et Venise le 24-3-1962;

- Comm. Fra' *Nicola Mastelloni di Salza di Capograssi,* élu par le Chapitre du Grand Prieuré de Naples et Sicile le 10-3-1962;

- Comm. Fra' *Giuseppe Salazar,* élu par le Chapitre du Grand Prieuré de Naples et Sicile le 10-3-1962;

- Chevalier de Justice *Goffredo Ervino Gudenus,* élu par le Chapitre du Grand Prieuré d'Autriche le 6-3-1962;

- Chevalier de Justice *Roderich von Schnehen,* élu par le Chapitre du Grand Prieuré d'Autriche le 6-3-1962;

- S.A.S. le Bailli Grand-Croix d'Obédience Prince *Charles de Schwarzenberg,* President du Conseil de Régence du Grand Prieuré de Bohème.

g) les Régents des Sous-Prieurés:

- Chevalier de Justice *Hubertus von Ballestrem,* Régent du Sous-Prieuré de Ste Hedvige.

h) les Représentants des Associations Nationales:

- S. Exe. le Chevalier de Justice *Oberto Pallavicini,* Président de l'Association Hongroise;

- S. Exe. le Bailli Grand-Croix d'Obédience Comte *Lazy Henckel von Donnersmarck,* President de l'Association Silésienne;

- S. Exe. le Bailli Grand-Croix d'Obédience *Quintin Jermy Gwyn,* President de l'Association Canadienne;

- S. Exe. le Chevalier probaniste d'Obédience Dom *Carlos Tasso de Saxe-Coburgo e Braganca,* Président de l'Association de San Paul et du Brésil méridional;

- S. Exe. le Bailli Grand-Croix d'Honneur et de Dévotion Baron *Rudolk von Twickel,* Président de l'Association Rhénano-Westphalienne;

- S. Exe. le Bailli Grand-Croix d'Honneur et de Dévotion Lord *Robert Crichton Stuart,* Président de l'Association Britannique;

- S. Exe. le Bailli Grand-Croix d'Honneur et de Dévotion Prince *Guy de Polignac,* Président de l'Association Francaise;

- S. Exe. le Bailli Grand-Croix d'Honneur et de Dévotion Comte *de Vila Flor e de Alpedrinha,* Président de l'Association Portugaise.

S. Exe. le Grand Chancelier Don *Enzo di Napoli Rampolla,* Prince *de Resuttano,* Bailli Grand-Croix d'Obédience, et le Chevalier de Grâce Magistrale *Filippo Spada,* Secrétaire de la Chancellerie, Ministre Plénipotentiaire, étaient présents en qualité respectivement de Secrétaire et « amanuensé » du Conseil.

Empêchés par de graves raisons de santé les Baillis Profès Fra' Antonio Hercolani Fava Simonetti et

Fra' Ferdinando di Thun Hohenstein n'ont pu prendre part au Conseil.

Après avoir assisté à la Messe du Saint-Esprit, célébrée dans la Chapelle de la Villa Magistrale par le Prélat de l'Ordre, les Electeurs se sont rendus dans la Grande Salle du Conseil. Toutes portes closes, par le Gardien du Conseil Nob. Carlo Lovera di Castiglione des Marquis de Maria, Bailli Grand-Croix d'Obédience, S. Exe. le Vén. Lieutenant de Grand Maître a invité chacun des Electeurs à prêter serment et a fait observer que tous les assistants étaient tenus au secret. Les opérations de vote ont alors commencé. Le résultat des scrutins ayant désigné le Comm. Fra' Angelo de Mojana di Cologna, le nom de l'élu a été aussitôt communiqué à la Légation de l'Ordre Souverain près le Saint-Siège pour être soumis à l'approbation du Souverain Pontife.

En exprimant leurs félicitations au nouveau Prince et Grand Maître, les Electeurs ont anticipéles voeux que formule ici la Réau nom de tous les membres de l'Ordre.

Son Altesse Eminentissime Fra' Angelo de Mojana, fils de Don Francesco et de Donna Giuseppino, née Nasalli Rocca di Corneliano, soeur du regretté Cardinal Archevêque de Bologne, naquit à Milan le 13 août 1905.

Il fit des études classiques au Lycée « Zaccaria » des Pères Barnabites et obtint, en 1928, sa licence en droit à l'Université de Milan.

Avocat au barreau, il se spécialisa en droit civil et commercial, se consacrant surtout aux problèmes du travail en tant que consulteur de l'Organisation des Industriels de Milan.

En décembre 1940 il fut recu dans l'Ordre de Malte en qualité de Chevalier d'Honneur et de Dévotion et prit la direction des institutions hospitalières de l'Ordre en Lombardie: en premier lieu de l'hôpital-sanatorium mil-itaire « Sant'Anna », à Côme, et de la maison de convalescence « Villa Giovio », à Camerlata di Como. Il collabora à l'érection du nouveau sanatorium « Villa Soldo », à Orsenigo, et en assuma la direction jusqu'en mai 1950.

Ayant fait à la même époque Profession des voeux simples, il fut nommé représentant du Grand Prieuré de Lombardie et Venise au Souverain Conseil, charge qu'il occupa jusqu'en avril 1955.

Durant son mandat au Souverain Conseil et pendant les années qui suivirent, il fut membre de nombreuses Commissions, dont celle pour l'étude et la révision du Code de Rohan pour le rendre plus conforme aux exigences de l'époque actuelle, Commission qu'il présida en 1954 et pour laquelle il rédigea un prohet intégral. Pendant la Lieutenance de S. Exe. le Vén. Bailli Fra' Ernesto Paternò Castello il prit part à la Commission pour l'étude de L'amendement de la Charte Constitutionnelle et pour la rédaction du Code et de la Régle.

Conseil Complet d'Etat du 12 Mai 1962

Le Serment Du Grand Maitre

Le samedi 12 mai, les Membres du Conseil Complet d'Etat ont assisté à la Messe, célébrée par S. Exe. le Prélat de l'Ordre dans la Chapelle de la Villa Magistrale, et se sont réunis ensuite dans la Salle du Conseil en présence de Son Eminence le « Cardinalis Patronus » Paolo Giobbe.

Aprés la récitation des prières rituelles S. Exe. le Grand Chancelier Don Enzo di Napoli Rampolla. Prince de Resuttano, donna lecture de la lettre du Cardinalis Patronus communiquant le « Nibil obstat » de Sa Sainteté à l'élection du Comm. Fra' Angelo de Mojana di Cologna à la charge de Prince et Grand Maître.

Aprés la prestation de serment du Nouveau Chef de l'Ordre, S. Exe. le Vén. Bailli Fra' Ernesto

Paternò Castello prononça un discours dans lequel il félicitait l'élu de son accession à la Grande Maîtrise, charge qu'il mérite par ses qualités d'intelligence et de coeur autant que par son attachement à l'Ordre et sa spiritualité profondément chrétienne. L'orateur poursuivit en retraçant brièvement l'histoire de l'Ordre pendant les sept années de sa lieutenance et remercia nommément tous ceux qui ont collaboré avec lui.

Son Altesse Eminentissime le Prince et Grand Maître a répondu en ces termes:

Eminence Révérendissime, Excellences, mes chers Confrères,

La confiance exprimée par le vote qui m'a désigné, 77ème Grand Maître de notre Ordre a créé dans mon âme une grande inquiétude: la conaissance intime de la faiblesse de mes mérites et de l'insuffisance de mes talents, me fait craindre de n'être pas à la hauteur des graves devoirs que vous m'avez assignés.

Le trouble qui m'a envahi au moment de mon élévation à une si haute charge, et l'émotion qui m'a dominé à cet instant ont pu trouver un allègement dans la confiance absolue et sereine en la Providence Divine qui, après avoir voulu, par l'expression de votre volonté bien pesée, daigner jeter un regard sur ma personne, ne manquera certainement pas de m'assister dans les jours à venir, puisque l'infinie Bonté de Dieu ne trompe jamais ceux qui s'adressent à Elle avec confiance, offrant généreusement leurs efforts, leurs peines et leurs aspirations dans l'accomplissement quotidien des tâches qui leur ont été données.

Cette confiance, qui atténue mon trouble profond, se fortifie dans la certitude que mes travaux prochains seront soutenus par la collaboration étroite, sincère, fervente et généreuse du groupe des Confrères que vous représentez si dignement dans ce Conseil Complet d'Etat, et particulièrement par les personnes autorisées que vous-mêmes désignerez comme mes collaborateurs les plus proches et qui assumeront avec moi les plus hautes responsabilités

dans le gouvernement de l'Ordre, accomplissant leur action pour la réalisation des buts de charité et d'amour qui forment le caractère, immuable depuis près de mille ans des Chevaliers de l'Ordre de Saint Jean.

L'aide du Pontife Romain, qui est notre consolation à tous, en même temps que les soins paternels de S.S. Pie XII de Vénérée Mémoire et la sollicitude manifestée par S.S. Jean XXIII henreusement régnant, a confirmé, par l'auguste approbation de la nouvelle Charte Constitutionnelle, l'actualité de notre Ordre.

Certain d'interpréter les sentiments du nouveau Gouvernement de l'Ordre, tel qu'il sera formé prochainement par le Chapitre Général, sentiments partagés à l'unanimité par tous les membres de l'Ordre répandus dans le monde, mais unis par la même foi dans nos idéaux les plus élevés, j'épreuve le grand désir d'exprimer au Souverain Pontife notre reconnaissance filiale et de confirmer solennellement notre dévotion inaltérable au Siège de Pierre et à l'Eminentissime « Cardinalis Patronus », qui en est le Représentant autorisé dans l'Ordre.

Au moment où je me prépare à prendre les rênes de notre Ordre permettez-moi, mes chers Confrères, d'élever une pieuse pensée à la Mémoire de mon Prédécesseur, S.A. E.me le Prince et Grand Maître Ludovico Chigi Albani della Rovere, à qui je suis lié par le souvenir depuis le début de mon activité plus étroite au service de l'Ordre.

Une pensée émue également à l'adresse de S.E. le Vén. Bailli Fra' Antonio Hercolani, qui ne peut malheureusement prendre part à notre réunion aujourd'hui; lui qui a rendu pendant cinq lustres de si grands et précieux services à l'Ordre, et dont la trempe si forte et généreuse a été ébranlée au cours de sa Lieutenance difficile et laborieuse, je lui souhaite fraternellement toute consolation possible dans l'épreuve douloureuse qu'il traverse en ce moment.

Au nom de toute la grande famille des Chevaliers de Malte et à titre personnel, je désire adresser de façon toute spéciale en cette circonstance solennelle, l'expression de mes sentiments les plus reconnaisants à S.E. le Vén.

Bailli Fra' Ernesto Paternò Castello, qui a dirigé l'Ordre en qualité de Lieutenant de Grand Maître au cours de ce dernier septennat, pendant lequel il a atteint des résultats fondamentaux qui ont permis à l'Ordre de s'asseoir sur des bases plus solides, plus sûres, plus adaptées aux conditions changées de l'époque, tout en respectant son caractère propre et traditionnel.

Les grands efforts que S.E. le Lieutenant de Grand Maître Fra' Ernesto Paternò Castello, a déployés en des circonstances non certes faciles, se concrétisent surtout dans la structure modifiée de l'Ordre moyennant la nouvelle Charte Constitutionnelle et l'étude approfondie du nouveau Code.

Même les observateurs les plus superficiels se seront rendu compte de l'importance décisive de l'oeuvre accomplie par la Lieutenance Paternò, action qui a posé les bases essentielles pour le nouvel épanouissement de l'Ordre, à l'intérieur comme à l'extérieur, et qui a fait naître de nouvelles Oeuvres de bienfaisance.

Mais je croirais manquer à un devoir essentiel si je n'exprimais devant cette illustre assemblée à mon Vénérable Confrère, les sentiments de ma reconnaissance personnelle pour les preuves multiples de sollicitude affectueuse, réconfortante et fraternelle, ou plus exactement, paternelle qu'il a bien voulu me donner en chaque occasion, et pour la confiance qu'il m'a accordée en me permettant de vivre intensément la vie de l'Ordre et de collaborer à l'oeuvre la plus haute et significative à laquelle sa Lieutenance était appelée spécifiquement.

Que ces sentiments de gratitude de tous les Chevaliers, et tout particulièrement les miens, Excellence, nous donnent l'assurance du souvenir impérissable et reconnaissant, qui nous animera sans trêve, et nous encouragera à poursuivre le chemin que Votre Excellence a suivi avec tant d'abnégation et avec un si louable esprit de sacrifice.

Chers Confrères,

En exprimant mon acceptation de la charge que votre vote m'a conférée, j'ai invoqué l'aide de la Divine Providence par l'intercession de notre Céleste Protectrice et de notre Patron Saint Jean Baptiste: mais j'ai aussi demandé votre union de coeur et votre collaboration.

Je réitère maintenant cette invocation: soyez tous à mes côtés à tout moment par votre activité et votre conseil, dans la concorde sincère, ouverte et loyale.

Ce n'est qu'en agissant de concert, avec des sentiments de charité, de justice et de compréhension, que nous pourrons être sûrs que La puissante intercession de nos Saints Patrons nous obtiendra du Trés Haut l'abondance de dons spirituels qui alimentera nos énergies afin de nous permettre d'accomplir nos devoirs, de surmonter les obstacles qui se trouveront sur notre chemin et d'atteindre le couronnement de nos efforts.

O Bienheureuse Vierge du Philerme, et vous Saint Jean Baptiste, jettez sur nos efforts un regard bienveillant, fortifiez-nous dans le travail, fondez-nous en une seule flamme d'amour aspirant au bien de notre Ordre et à la sérénité de son avenir!

Au terme de cette allocution S. Exe. le Lieutenant de Grand Maître sortant imposa le Collier au nouveau Chef de l'Ordre, geste qui exprime symboliquement et substantiellement le passage des pouvoirs.

Son Eminence le « Cardinalis Patronus » prenant alors la parole fit observer d'abord que la charité est le but principal de l'Ordre, tant pour son propre bien que pour celui de l'Eglise. Il exprima ensuite sa satisfaction de voir rétablie cette concorde si nécessaire aux activités fructueuses. Après avoir adressé ses félicitations et ses voeux les plus chaleureux au nouveau Grand Maître il lui a cité les paroles de Notre Seigneur à Simon « Dux in altum » (Luc V. 4) qui devraient être le programme de son gouvernement.

Les travaux étant terminés le Grand Chancelier, en sa fonction de Secrétaire, donna lecture de la formule de clôture du Conseil Complet d'Etat.

Aussitôt après la cérémonie le nouveau Chef de l'Ordre fit parvenir au Souverain Pontife l'expression de ses sentiments de dévotion filiale indéfectible. En réponse Sa Sainteté Jean XXIII a daigné accorder la Bénédiction Apostolique au Prince et Grand Maître, ainsi qu'à l'Ordre tout entier.

CHAPITRE GENERAL: 13 MAI 1962

ELECTION DU SOUVERAIN CONSEIL ET DE LA CHAMBRE DES COMPTES

Le dimanche 13 mai, Une Messe d'actin de grâces, suivie du « Te Deum » a été célébrée dans la Chapelle de la Ville Magistrale par S. Exe. Mgr. Carlo Alberto Ferrero di Cavallerleone, Prélat de l'Ordre. Son Altesse Eminentissime le Prince et Grand Maître y assistait, du trône qui lui est réservé, tandis que les autres Chevaliers Profés occupaient les stalles placées dans le choeur. Invités de'honneur à cette célébration étaient les membres du Corps Diplomatique accrédités près l'Ordre Souverain, qui se trouvait ainsi représenté par: S. Exe. l'Ambassadeur Francisco Gomez de Llano, Envoyé Extraordinaire et Ministre Plénipotentiaire d'Espagne; S. Exe. l'Ambassadeur Luis F. Lanata Coudy, Envoyé Extraordinaire et Ministre Plénipotentiaire du Pérou; S. Exe. l'Ambassadeur Bartolomeo Migone, Envoyé Extraordinaire et Ministre Plenipotentiaire d'Italie; S. Exe. l'Ambassadeur Santiago de Estrada, Envoyé Extraordinaire et Ministre Plénipotentiaire d'Argentine; S. Exe. l'Ambassadeur Pedro de Yurrita Maury, Envoyé Extraordinaire et Ministre Plénipotentiaire de Guatemala; S. Exe. l'Ambassadeur Fernando Aldunate Errazuriz, Envoyé Extraordinaire et Ministre Plénipotentiaire de Chili; S. Exe. l'Ambassadeur Dario Echandia, Envoyé Extraordinaire et Ministre Plénipotentiaire de Colombie; S. Exe. l'Ambassaderu Henrique de Souza Gomes, Envoyé Extraordinaire et Ministre Plénipotentiaire du Brésil; S. Exe. l'Ambassadeur Johannes Coreth, Envoyé Extraordinaire et Ministre Plénipotentiaire d'Aut-

riche; S. Exe. l'Ambassadeur A. Bermudez Milla, Envoyé Extraordinaire et Ministre Plénipotentiaire de Honduras; Monsieur Pastor C. Filartiga, Chargé d'Affaires de Paraguay; Monsieur Alexandre Ammoun, Attaché de la Légation du Liban.

Les autres personnalités présentes étaient: les Chevaliers Electeurs, les hauts dignitaires du Grand Magistére et les missions diplomatiques de l'Ordre Souverain près le Gouvernement Italien, sous la conduite de leurs Chefs respectifs S. Exe. le Comte Stanislao Pecci et S. Exe. le Baron Gabriel Apor de Altorja.

La Messe terminée, Son Eminence Révérendissime Paolo Giobbe, Cardinalis Patronus, a fait son entrée dans l'église où, arrivé au bas de l'autel et revêtu de la chape, il entonna le « Te Deum », repris par toute l'assistance. A l'issue de la cérémonie religieuse les membres du Corps Diplomatique ont été présentés à Son Altesse Eminentissime le Prince et Grand Maître.

Aprés un court intervalle, durant lequel une légère collation fut servie dans le jardin d'hiver, les Chevaliers Capitularies se sont réunis dans la Salle du Conseil pour prendre part au Chapitre Général, selon l'Art. 21 de la Charte Constitutionnelle en vigueur.

Sauf les Baillis Profés Fra' Antonio Hercolani Fava Simonetti et Fra' Ferdinando di Thun e Hohenstin, absent pour raison de santé, et le Chevalier d'Honneur et de Dévotion Comte Bonabes Eugène de Rougé, obligé de partir, le Chapitre Général était composé de:

a) Son Altesse Eminentissime Fra' *Angelo de Mojana di Colgna,* Prince et Grand Maître;

b) les autres membres du Souverain Conseil:

- Comm. Fra' *Enrico Montalto di Fragnito,* Représentant du Grand Prieuré de Rome;

- S. Exe. le Vén. Bailli Fra' *Renato Galleani*

d'Agliano, Représentant du Grand Prieuré de Lombardie et Venise;

- Comm. Fra' *Fulco Galleti di S. Cataldo,* Représentant du Grand Prieuré de Naples et Sicile;

- S. Exe. le Vén. Bailli Fra' *Alfonso M. de Vesque-Püttlingen,* Représentant du Grand Prieuré de Bohème;

- Comm. Fra' *Ottone de Grisogono,* Représentant du Grand Prieuré d'Autriche;

- Bailli Grand-Croix d'Honneur et de Dévotion Baron *Clens von Oer* Représentant des Associations Nationales;

- Grand-Croix de Grâce et de Dévotion Vicomte *Furness,* Représentant des Associations Nationales;

- S. Exe. le Bailli Grand-Croix d'Obédience Don *Enzo di Napoli Rampolla,* Prince *de Resuttano,* Grand Chancelier;

- Bailli Grand-Croix d'Obédience Nob. *Carlo Lovera di Castiglione,* des Marquis *de Maria,* Receveur du Commun Trésor;

c) le Prélat de l'Ordre:

- S. Exe. Mgr. *Carlo Alberto Ferrero di Cavallerleone,* Archevêque tit. de Trébizonde, Bailli Grand-Croix d'Honneur et de Dévotion;

d) les Grands Prieurs:

- S. Exe. le Vén. Bailli Fra' *Raimondo del Balzo di Presenzano,* Grand Prieur de Rome;

- S. Exe. le Vén. Bailli Fra' *Nicola Galleani d'Agliano,* Grand Prieur de Lombardie et Venise et Grand Commandeur;

- S. Exe. le Vén. Bailli Fra' *Marzio Pignatelli Aragona Cortes,* Grand Prieur de Naples et Sicile;

- S. Exe. le Chevalier de Justice *Giovanni Trapp,* Prince Grand Prieur d'Autriche;

e) les Baillis Profes:

- S. Exe. le Vén. Bailli Fra' *Ernesto Paternò Castello,* (les deux autres Baillis profes appartenant à cette catégorie étaient absents pour la raison mentionnée plus haut);

f) deux Chevaliers profes délégués au Chapitre par chacun des Grands Prieurés:

- Chevalier de Justice *Angelo M. Mazzaccara di Celenza e Carlantino dei Mazzaccara,* élu par le Chapitre du Grand Prieuré de Rome le 12-3-1962;

- Comm. Fra' *Giuseppe Dalla Torre del Tempio di Sanguinetto,* élu par le Chapitre du Grand Prieuré de Rome le 12-3-1962;

- Chevalier Fra' *Vincenzo Morelli di Popolo di Ticineto,* élu par le Chapitre du Grand Prieuré de Lombardie et Venise le 24-3-162;

- Comm. Fra' *Nicola Mastelloni di Salza di Capograssi,* élu par le Chapitre du Grand Prieuré de Naples et Sicile le 10-3-1962;

- Comm. Fra' *Giuseppe Salazar,* élu par le Chapitre du Grand Prieuré de Naples et Sicile le 10-3-1962;

- Chevalier de Justice *Goffredo Ervino Gudenus,* élu par le Chapitre du Grand Prieuré d'Autriche le 6-3-1962;

- Chevalier de Justice *Roderich von Schnehen,* élu par le Chapitre du Grand Prieuré d'Autriche le 6-3-1962;

- S.A.S. le Bailli Grand-Croix d'Obédience Prince *Charles de Schwarzenberg,* President du Conseil de Régence du Grand Prieuré de Bohème;

g) les Régents des Sous-Prieurés:

- Chevalier de Justice *Hubertus von Ballestrem*, Régent du Sous-Prieuré de Sainte Hedvige;

h) les Représentants des Associations Nationales:

- S. Exe. le Chevalier de Justice *Oberto Pallavicini*, Président de l'Association Hongroise;
- S. Exe. le Bailli Grand-Croix d'Obédience Comte *Lazy Henckel von Donnersmarck*, Président de l'Association Silésienne;
- S. Exe. le Bailli Grand-Croix d'Obédience *Quintin Jermy Gwyn*, Président de l'Association Canadienne;
- S. Exe. le Chevalier probaniste d'Obédience Dom *Carlos Tasso de Saxe-Coburgo e Braganca*, Président de l'Association de S. Paolo et Brésil Méridional;
- S. Exe. le Bailli Grand-Croix d'Honneur et de Dévotion Baron *Rudolf von Twickel*, Président de l'Association Rhénano-Westphalienne;
- S. Exe. le Bailli Grand-Croix d'Honneur et de Dévotion Lord *Robert Crichton Stuart*, Président de l'Association Britannique;
- S. Exe. le Bailli Grand-Croix d'Honneur et de Dévotion Prince *Guy de Polignac*, Président de l'Association Francaise;
- S. Exe. le Bailli Grand-Croix d'Honneur et de Dévotion Comte de *de Vila Flor e de Alpedrinha*, Président de l'Association Portugaise.

Après la récitation de la prière habituelle, la séance a débuté par la vérification de la légitimité du mandat de chacun des présents et par la désignation d'un Secrétaire, en la personne du Grand Chancelier; de deux scrutateurs: le Chevalier de Justice Goffredo Ervino Gudenus et le Chevalier probaniste d'Obédience Dom Carlos Tasso de Saxe-Coburgo e Braganca; d'un « amanuensé », le Secrétaire de la Chancellerie Chevalier de Grâce Magistrale Filippo Spada, Ministre Plénipotentiaire, qui tous quatre prêterent le serment du secret à garder aussi après la conclusion du Chapitre. Ces opérations terminées Son Altesse Eminentissime le Prince et Grand Maître prononça l'allocution suivante:

« *Excellence Révérendissime, Excellences, mes chers Confrères.*

C'est pour la première fois depuis 186 ans que se réunit le Chapitre Général de l'Ordre de Malte, puisque le dernier fut tenu en 1776, sous la présidence du Grand Maître de Rohan.

Cet événement est d'une importance historique et montre la pleine efficience que l'Ordre a retrouvée après les vicissitudes causées par la perte de l'Ile de Malte, les pérégrinations du XIXe siècle d'un groupe toujours plus restreint de Chevaliers sous la conduite de plusieurs Lieutenants successifs, jusqu'à la reconstitution de la Grande Maîtrise, charge conférée au Lieutenant Ceschi a Santa Croce.

Les événements récents de la vie de l'Ordre vou sont connus et je pense qu'il n'est pas besoin de les rappeler ici.

Je me contenterai donc de relever qu'après la mort de mon prédécesseur le 76me Prince et Grand Maître Fra' Ludovico Chigi Albani della Rovere et l'ouverture de la lieutenance intérimaire du Vén. Bailli Fra' Antonio Hercolani Fava Simonetti, advint en avril 1955 l'élection d'un Lieutenant de Grand Maître en la personne du Vén. Bailli Fra' Ernesto Paternò Castello di Carcaci. Cette Lieutenance a eu comme mandat spécial la rédaction d'une nouvelle Charte Constitutionnelle, du Code et de la Règle, mandat qui a été exécuté d'abord par la préparation de la Charte Constitutionnelle promulguée le 8 décembre 1956 et mise en vigueur ad experimentum, puis par l'étude des amendements de la même Charles et du Code. Sur la base des travaux accomplis par la Lieutenance la présente Charte Constitutionnelle fut promulguée, ayant été approuvée par Bref Apostolique du 24 juin 1961, tandis que le projet du Code fut préparé; projet cont a été approuvé ad experimentum l'extrait qui a permis de procéder à la convocation da Conseil Complet d'Etat pour l'élection du 77me Prince et Grand Maître, ainsi que la réunion du présent Chapitre Général pour l'élection des titulaires des hautes charges et des conseillers qui composent le Souverain Conseil, selon les dispositions des articles 18 et 20 de la Charte Constitutionnelle actuellement en vigueur.

A l'ouverture du Chapitre Général il m'incombe également de vous exposer l'état actuel de l'Ordre: celui-ci se compose de 5 Grands Prieurés, à savoir ceux de Rome, de Lombardie et Venise, de Naples et Sicile, de Bohème et d'Autriche: du Sous-Prieuré de Ste Hedvige et de 26 Associations Nationales, dont 13 européennes, 12 américaines et une asiatique (Philippines).

Au 31 décembre 1961, date du dernier recensement officiel, l'Ordre comptait au total 7,567 membres dont:

3.538 appartenants aux trois Grands Prieurés italiens,

350 au Grand Prieuré d'Autriche,

17 au Grand Prieuré de Bohème,

2,850 aux 26 Associations Nationales et

802 inscrits au Gremio Religionis.

Les Oeuvres de l'Ordre sont nombreuses et leur liste a été publiée en 1961 dans le Cahier N. 1, que vous connaissez tous, ce qui me dispense de les énumérer ici en détail.

Comme vous savez le Chapitre Général est l'assemblée suprême de notre Order, 11 est composé des représentants de ses différentes classes et de ses organismes et se réunit périodiquement afin de procéder aux élections capitulaires, de traiter des problèmes les plus importants de l'Ordre, aussi de nature constitutionnelle, et de formuler les programmes de son activité.

Mais le Chapitre Général actuel, en harmonie avec ce qui a été établi par le décret du Conseil n. 9041. Répertoire Général du 28 février 1962, doit se limiter à l'élection des hautes charges, des 4 Conseillers effectifs et des 2 Suppléants, qui constituent le Souverain Conseil, ainsi que des membres de la Chambre des Comptes, en spécifiant nommément le Président, et tout ceci selon les dispositions des articles 20, 21 et 25 de la Charte Constitutionnelle en vigueur.

Mes chers Confrères en vous invitant à bien vouloir passer au vote en toute liberté de conscience, à seule fin de former un organisme efficient qui réellement m'assiste dans le gouvernement de l'Ordre, je vous exhorte, dans l'exercice de cette action spéciale et de grande responsabilité comme Chevaliers de St. Jean, à toujours tendre exclusivement au bien de notre Ordre et à sa prospérité.

Je prie maintenant l'Exe.me Prélat de l'Ordre de bien vouloir donner lecture du rapport sur l'état spirituel de l'Ordre.»

Secretariat of State Directive N.364118

DAL VATICANO, 7TH JANUARY, 1956*

The Secretariat of State of His Holiness presents its compliments to the Right Honourable The Lord Lyon King of Arms, and, in acknowledging the communication addressed to the Secretary of the Commissions Araldica per la Corte Pontificia under date of 25th November, 1955, has the honour to transmit the enclosed Memorandum which contains an outline of ecclesiastical usages regarding coats-of-arms.

The Secretariat of State of His Holiness avails itself of this occasion to assure The Right Honourable The Lord Lyon King of Arms of its most distinguished consideration.

MEMORANDUM

1. The use of a coat-of-arms for Bishops and inferior Prelates of the Catholic Church possessed of territorial jurisdiction derives from the *seal* with which they authenticated official acts issued by them. Such usage consequently has an origin diverse from that of other coats-of-arms.

2. Such a coat-of-arms was formerly composed of the Shield alone, without ornaments. These latter were added gradually during the feudal period and customs. The Arms could be the original Arms of the Bishop's or Prelate's family; they could also, however, be different, or even be partially varied—but in this last case such variation or difference need not influence the proper Arms of the family, since the Bishop's or Prelate's Arms had a *personal character* inherent to the bearer's function. At present, the Holy See in practice considers such Arms to be personal.

3. The ornaments (Crozier, Mitre, etc.) added to such Arms have not generally been the subject of particular legislation by the Holy See. They are the result of local traditions of various countries during various historical periods, and of particular social needs; but they were always tolerated as optional according to the uses of each nation. However, the displaying of Mitre and Crozier at the upper corners of the Shield is not forbidden, as it is a precise indication of Episcopal character, although they are not in common use in the Roman Church and Court. For this reason, local tradition may be followed regard-

---

* Since the issuance of this decree, papal *motu proprio* have required further changes. These changes are faithfully documented in Chapter 10.

ing the use of the precious Mitre (*mitra pretiosa*) for Bishops and of the simple Mitre (*mitra simplex*) for Abbots, in Scotland.

4. The Holy See actually and formally admits, as ornaments for ecclesiastical coats-of-arms, only: the Hat surrounding the Shield, and the Cross standing behind the Shield, as determined hereafter:

(A) BISHOPS—Shield with Roman Hat (formerly green, now also black), with green cords and twelve green tassels—one, two, three—descending at either side of the Shield: Between the Hat and the top of the Shield, a simple Episcopal Cross, the foot projecting below the bottom of the Shield.

(B) ARCHBISHOPS—Shield with Hat as above, with twenty green tassels—one, two, three, four—descending at either side of the Shield: Between the Hat and the top of the Shield, the Cross which is the Archiepiscopal Cross with double crossbar.

(C) CARDINALS—The Shield is surmounted by a red Hat with red cords and thirty red tassels interwoven with gold thread, disposed equally at either side of the Shield, one, two, three, four, five. Provided the Cardinal possesses Episcopal character, the Arms also bear the Cross as for other Archbishops and Bishops.

(D) PRELATES—Participating, Supernumerary and *ad instar* Protonotaries Apostolic have over their Shield a *crimson* Hat with cords and tassels of the same colour, disposed: one, two, three (twelve tassels altogether). The use of Crozier or Mitre is *espressly forbidden* in the Arms.

   Titular and Honorary Protonotaries have a Hat with tassels similarly disposed, but all *black*.

Domestic Prelates have a Hat with tassels as above, but of *purple* colour.

5. ABBOTS—In the British Commonwealth, there are four Abbacies *nullius dioceseos,* but in Scotland there is none. Such Abbots, being also titular Bishops, and having moreover as Abbots territorial jurisdiction, use the same heraldic insignia as Bishops (see above, 4(A)).

   Abbots, however, who have no territorial jurisdiction outside their Abbey, such as the Abbots of Scotland, bear over the Shield a black Hat with black tassels disposed one, two (six in all): except the case of particular privilege granted by the Holy See to particular Abbeys or Abbots.

   No pontifical disposition exists with regard to Priors of Abbeys. Local usage and the internal Constitutions of each Order may furnish indications in this matter for each case.

6. The Holy See also concedes the use of Arms to National Ecclesiastical Colleges, Pontifical Universities, and other such bodies, but in these cases the text of the pontifical concession must be followed both for the disposition of the heraldic figures and for the ornaments.

7. Finally, each Diocese may have its own coat-of-arms, distinct from that of the Bishop, and generally used during the vacancy of the See. Such Arms nearly always have a historical or traditional origin, and there is therefore no intervention on the part of the Holy See.

TO THE CORPORATION OF THE KINGS, HERALDS AND PURSUIVANTS OF ARMS OF THE COLLEGE OF ARMS

Whereas it has been represented unto me that the prelates and other clergy of the Roman Catholic Church have customarily used certain insignia in connection with their personal Armorial Bearings, but that such insignia is not at present recorded in the College of Arms.

And that whereas it now seems expedient that when granting personal Armorial Ensigns to prelates and other clergy of the Roman Catholic Church the appropriate insignia may be shown with their Arms.

I, Bernard Marmaduke, Duke of Norfolk, Knight of the Most Noble Order of the Garter, Knight Grand Cross of the Royal Victorian Order, Earl Marshal and Hereditary Marshal of England and One of Her Majesty's Most Honourable Privy Council, do hereby authorize and require you to record these Presents and the annexed schedule detailing the insignia abovementioned accordingly and for so doing this shall be your Warrant.

Given under hand and Seal this 17th day of July 1967.
Norfolk, E.M.

Schedule of insignia which may be used in connection with the personal arms of prelates and clergy of the Roman Catholic Church, except where a Pontifical Concession details particular insignia. In such cases the text of the decree should be followed. The figures in the text refer to the illustrations in the margin.

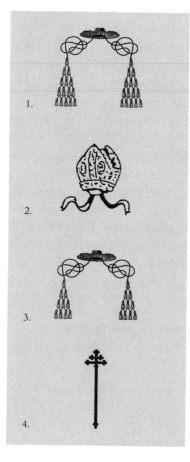

1.

2.

3.

4.

CARDINALS

Above the arms is placed a red hat having fifteen tassels interwoven with gold thread on either side (1).

ARCHBISHOPS

Above the arms is placed a mitre (mitra pretiosa) (2) and/or a green hat having ten tassels pendent on either side (3). Behind the arms is placed a double-traversed cross (4) in pale.

DIOCESAN AND TITULAR BISHOPS & ABBOTS NULLIUS DIOCESEOS

Above the arms is placed a mitre (mitra pretiosa) (2) and/or a green hat having six tassels pendent on either side (5). Behind the arms is placed either a single traversed cross (6) or a crozier (7) either in pale or in bend.

ABBOTS

Above the arms is placed a mitre (mitra simplex) (8) or a black hat having three tassels pendent on either side (9). Behind the arms is placed a golden crozier (5) either in pale or in bend.

PROTONOTARIES APOSTOLIC AND VICARS PREFECTS & ADMINISTRATORS APOSTOLIC

Above the arms is placed a crimson hat having six tassels pendent on either side (10).

RELIGIOUS SUPERIORS GENERAL OR PROVINCIAL AND HONORARY OR TITULAR PROTONOTARIES APOSTOLIC

Above the arms is placed a black hat having six tassels pendent on either side (11).

DOMESTIC PRELATES TO THE POPE

Above the arms is placed a violet hat having six tassels pendent on either side (12).

PRIVY CHAMBERLAINS AND PRIVY CHAPLAINS TO THE POPE

Above the arms is placed a black hat having six violet tassels pendent on either side (13).

CANONS

Above the arms is placed a black hat having three tassels pendent on either side (9).

PRIESTS

Above the arms is placed a black hat having one tassel pendent on either side (14).

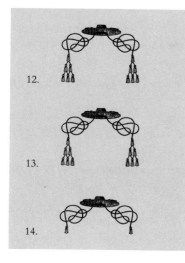

12.

13.

14.

N.B.: If any of the above prelates or clergy are cardinals of the Roman Catholic Church, then they substitute the cardinal's hat (1) for that which they would otherwise use.

Note: The illustrations have been enhanced faithfully from the original to clarify the presentation of the insignia displayed.

A Decree

Forbidding the Use of Civilities of Nobility in the Inscriptions and Coats of Arms of Bishops

Keeping fully in mind those precepts governing the use of titles and insignia of the families of the nobility in episcopal inscriptions and coats of arms, which for a long time have been in force—namely, since the Apostolic Constitution "Militantis Ecclesiae" of the 19th December, 1644, and the Consistorial Decree of the 15th January, 1915—Our Most Holy Lord Pius, by the providence of God Pope PIUS XII, considers on careful reflection that secular titles and marks of nobility of this kind have become divorced from their ancient legal foundations, and are not in keeping with the present-day conditions of the world; and has decided that the time has come for the old patterns to be changed, and for new ones to be laid down.

Hence, by this present Consistorial Decree, Our Most Holy Lord has deemed fit to decree, that all Ordinaries should in future refrain entirely from employing titles of nobility, (and from using) coronets, or other marks of a secular character, on their seals, insignia or coats of arms, as also in inscriptions on letters and edicts, even if such things belong by right to the Episcopal or Archiepiscopal See.

Anything to the contrary, even if worthy of the most particular mention, in no way withstanding.

Given at Rome, from the Palace of the Sacred Consistorial Congregation, the 12th day of May, 1951.

FR. A. I. CARD. PIAZZA, etc.,
Secretary

Istruzioni

Per i Camerieri Secreti Soprannumerari
e i Camerieri d'Onore in Abito Paonazzo

1. Il Cameriere Segreto soprannumerario (*cubicularius intimus adlectus supra numerum*) ed il Cameriere d'Onore in abito paonazzo (*cubicularius honorarius*) fanno parte della Famiglia Nobile di Sua Santità godono del titolo di *Monsignore*.

2. Tre sono gli abiti propi ed uguali per ambedue le suddette classi dei Camerieri ecclesiastici.

3. Il primo consta: *a)* della veste talare paonazza senza coda, coi paramani alti quindici centimetri, asole, bottoni e orlatura di seta paonazza; *b)* della fascia di seta paonazza larga dodici centimetri e pendente alle due estremità circa cinquanta centimetri sul lato sinistro, con appesi due fiocchi del medesimo colore; *c)* del mantellone sovrapposto alla veste talare, con le mostre interne, larghe venti centimetri, e l'orlatura di seta paonazza; *d)* del collare di seta paonazza; *e)* delle calze nere e scarpe con fibbie d'argento; *f)* del coppello con cordone e fiocchi neri. Gli Ablergati inviati a portare la berretta cardinalizia hanno il privilegio del cordone, fiocchi e calze paonazze durante la loro missione.

   La stoffa della veste e del mantellone è di panno o lana: nell'estate può essere anche di seta.

4. Il secondo, detto *Croccia,* è un'ampia soprav-veste di lana rossa con larghe maniche fino all'avambraccio con rivolti di seta rossa, alla quale si sovrappone una cappa con cappuccio pure di lana rossa, foderata internamente di seta rossa ed esternamente di aimellino nell'inverno e di seta rossa nell'estate. Quest'abito s'indossa sopra l'abito descritto nell'articolo precedente senza però il mantellone.

5. Il terzo abito è quello che comunemente dicesi *Piano* e consta: *a)* della veste talare nera senza coda, con asole, bottoni e orlatura di seta paonazza; *b)* della fascia di seta paonazza larga dodici centimetri, guarnita nelle estremità, pendenti al lato sinistro per circa cinquanta centimetri, di frangia di seta dello stesso colore; *c)* del ferraiolone nero di lana, o seta; *d)* del collare di seta paonazza; *e)* della calze nere e scarpe con fibbie d'argento; *f)* del cappello con cordone e fiocchi neri. Riguardo agli Ablegati vedi art. 3°.

6. Il primo abito s'indossa nel servizio dell'Anticamera Pontificia ed anche nelle sacre funzioni, avuto però riguardo alle prescrizioni liturgiche. Il secondo nelle Cappelle e Cortei Papali, nei Concistori pubblici, quando si fa l'ora di turno nell'esposizione del Ssño Sacramento nel Palazzo Apostolico e dall'Ablegato apostolico nella

cerimonia dell'imposizione della berretta cardinalizia. In tutte le altre occasioni nelle quali o si debba, come alla presenza di Sua Santità, o convenga portare i distintivi del proprio grado, si mette l'abito *Piano*.

7. I Camerieri Segreti soprannumerari e d'Onore rimangono soggetti alia giurisdizione del proprio Ordinario. Facendo essi parte di qualche Capitolo non hanno, per il loro titolo, diritto a precedenza o privilegio; possono però indossare in Coro ed in ogni altro atto o funzione capitolare la veste talare paonazza con relativa fascia, sovrapponendo i distintivi proprî del Capitolo, purchè le costituzioni o l'abito corale del Capitolo stesso non lo impediscano.

8. Nelle Cappelle Papali e nei Concistori pubblici fanno essi parte del Corteo, purchè indossino la *Croccia,* e procedono dopo gli Avvocati Concistoriali. Nelle Cappelle Papali, che hanno luogo nella Sistina in Vaticano, seggono in piccoli banchi di fronte al trono di Sua Santità, nella Basilica Vaticana sugli scalini laterali dell'Altare Papale.

9. Spetta ai Camerieri Segreti soprannumerari ed in loro vece anche ai Camerieri d'Onore in abito paonazzo, portare i due flabelli, quando Sua Santità incede in Sedia Gestatoria; agli uni ed agli altri appartiene altresì portare le dodici torce quando il Sommo Pontefice dà la Benedizione con il Ssmo Sacramento, e sorreggere le aste del baldacchino nelle processioni nelle quali Sua Santità segue a piedi il Ssmo Sacramento.

10. I Camerieri Segreti soprannumerari e i Camerieri d'Onore invitati a prestar servizio nell'Anticamera Pontificia debbono stare i primi nell'Anticamera segreta, i secondi in quella d'onore, ossia nella sala del Trono; coadiuvare, insieme ai Camerieri di Spada e Cappa, nel ricevere ed intrattenere, ciascuno nella propria Anticamera, le persone ammesse all'udienza; portare ambasciate, plichi, ecc., il Cameriere d'Onore fino alla soglia dell'Anticamera segreta, il Cameriere Segreto dentro la medesima e vice-versa, stare a disposizione del Maestro di Camera: e, in assenza di lui, del Cameriere Segreto ecclesiastico partecipante di servizio. Alla presenza del Santo Padre, come aitresì in servizio, non è permesso di portare lo zucchetto.

11. I Camerieri Segreti hanno la precedenza sopra quelli d'Onore e questi, come i primi, prendono la precedenza tra di loro secondo l'anzianità di nomina.

12. Nell'accompagnare il Santo Padre, quando il servizio di Anticamera è doppio, i due Camerieri d'Onore in abito paonazzo seguono immediatamente i due Camerieri d'Onore di Spada e Cappa, come i Camerieri Segreti vanno immediatamente dopo i Camerieri Segreti di Spada e Cappa. In caso diverso il Cameriere Segreto e quello d'Onore in abito paonazzo vanno di conserva prendendo il primo la destra e seguono immediatamente il Cameriere Segreto e d'Onore di Spada e Cappa.

13. I Camerieri Segreti e d'Onore, che avranno prestato servisio di Anticamera durante l'anno, riceveranno dal Maestro di Camera due medaglie d'argento nella ricorrenza della festa dei Ss. Apostoli Pietro e Paolo.

14. I Camerieri Segreti e d'Onore dovranno ogni anno, nel mese di settembre, informare la Segreteria di Stato della loro residenza, anche perchè i loro nomi siano iscritti nell'*Annuario Pontificio*.

15. Nel caso in cui per volontà Sovrana un Cameriere Segreto o d'Onore fosse cancellato dall'albo del rispettivo ceto, egli cessa *ipso facto* di goderne il titolo, i privilegi, ecc., ed è obbligato, appena avuta cognizione della misura presa

a suo carico, di rimandare immediatamente alla Segreteria di Stato il biglietto di nomina.

16. I Camerieri Segreti e d'Onore cessano di far parte della Corte Pontificia e perdono in conseguenza titolo, privilegi e distintivi, alla morte del Sommo Pontefice, dopo la tumulazione delle auguste spoglie. Desiderando di essere ascritti alla Corte del Successore dovranno farne domanda.

IL SOSTITUTO DELLA SEGRETERIA DI STATO
DI SUA SANTITÀ

ISTRUZIONI DELLA SEGRETERIA DI STATO SUGLI ABITI E GLI STEMMI DEI CARDINAL, VESCOVI E DEI PRELATI★

Par. 19—Per i Protonotari Apostotici soprannumerari e per i *Prelate d'Onore* di Sua Santità si aboliscono la mantelletta paonazza, la fascia con i fiocchi, le calze di colore, le fibbie sulle scarpe e il fiocco rosso sulla berretta.

Si conservano, invece, la talare paonazza, la talare filettata senza pellegrina e la fascia con frangia. Occorrendo, sulla talare paonazza si indosserà la cotta, non griccia, anziché il rocchetto.

Il ferraiolo paonazzo, sebbene non obbligatorio, si conserva per i Protonotari Apostolici soprannumerari, ma non per i Prelati d'Onore.

Par. 20—Per i Cappellani di Sua Santità si conserva la veste talare filettata, con relativa fascia paonazza, da usarsi anche nelle cerimonie sacre.

La veste paonazza, il mantellone dello stesso colore, la fascia con i fiocchi e le fibbie sulle scarpe sono aboliti.

★(cfr. *Acta Apostolicae Sedis.* 61 [1969], p. 338)

552. *Sacred Congregation of the Clergy Circular Letter*

Per Instructionem, *on the reform of choral vesture*

30 OCTOBER 1970: AAS 63 (1971) 314–315; NOT 8 (1972) 36–37

The Instruction *Ut sive sollicite,* which the Cardinal Secretary of State issued on 31 March 1969 by order of Pope Paul VI, directed this Congregation for the Clergy to make rules, consistent with that Instruction, for the choral vesture and titles of canons, holders of benefices, and pastors.[1]

This Congregation has consulted the Latin-rite conferences of bishops concerned, compared their decisions, and submitted them to review by the papal Secretariat of State. The Congregation in virtue of the present Circular Letter now entrusts to the same conference of bishops the task of simplifying choral vesture. They are to be guided by the following universal rules:

1. This Letter abolishes all, even centuries-old and immemorial privileges, in keeping with the directives of the Motu Proprio *Pontificalia insignia,* 21 June 1968,[2] and the Instruction *Ut sive sollicite,* 31 March 1969.[3]

2. Only those canons who are bishops may wear the purple mozzetta. Other canons are to wear a black or grey mozzetta with purple trim. Cler-

ics holding benefices are to wear a black or grey mozzetta and pastors are to use only the stole.

3. Canons, clerics holding benefices, and pastors are also forbidden to use any of the following insignia, which are still in use in some places: the *mantelletta,* the sash with tassles, red stockings, shoes with buckles, purple cloak, rochet, miter, staff, ring, pectoral cross.

4. Everything in the Apostolic See's documents already mentioned concerning cardinals and bishops applies also, in due proportion, to other categories of ecclesiastics.

Each conference of bishops is given the power to put into effect gradually, while respecting the requirements of law, the aforementioned directives contained in the documents of the Apostolic See and in the present Letter.

---

[1]No. 35 [DOL 551 no. 4532].
[2]See AAS 60 (1968) 374–377 [DOL 549].
[3]See AAS 61 (1969) 334–340 [DOL 551].

Vestments

GENERAL INSTRUCTION OF THE ROMAN MISSAL, IV: § 297–310

297. In the Church, the Body of Christ, not all members have the same function. This diversity of ministries is shown outwardly in worship by the diversity of vestments. These should therefore symbolize the function proper to each ministry. But at the same time the vestments should also contribute to the beauty of the rite.

298. The vestment common to ministers of every rank is the alb, tied at the waist with a cincture, unless it is made to fit without a cincture. An amice should be put on first if the alb does not completely cover the street clothing at the neck. A surplice may not be substituted for the alb when the chasuble or dalmatic is to be worn or when a stole is used instead of the chasuble or dalmatic.

299. Unless otherwise indicated, the chasuble, worn over the alb and stole, is the vestment proper to the priest celebrant at Mass and other rites immediately connected with Mass.

300. The dalmatic, worn over the alb and stole, is the vestment proper to the deacon.

301. Ministers below the order of deacon may wear the alb or other vestment that is lawfully approved in each region.

302. The priest wears the stole around his neck and hanging down in front. The deacon wears it over his left shoulder and drawn across the chest to the right side, where it is fastened.

303. The cope is worn by the priest in processions and other services, in keeping with the rubrics proper to each rite.

304. Regarding the design of vestments, the conference of bishops may determine and propose to the Apostolic See adaptations that correspond to the needs and usages of their regions.

305. In addition to the traditional materials, natural fabrics proper to the region may be used for making vestments; artificial fabrics that are in keeping with the dignity of the liturgy and the person wearing them may also be used. The conference of bishops will be the judge in this matter.

306. The beauty of a vestment should derive from its material and design rather than from lavish ornamentation. Representations on vestments should consist only of symbols, images, or pictures portraying the sacred. Anything out of keeping with the sacred is to be avoided.

307. Variety in the color of the vestments is meant to give effective, outward expression to the

specific character of the mysteries of the faith being celebrated and, in the course of the year, to a sense of progress in the Christian life.

308. Traditional usage should be retained for the vestment colors.

a. White is used in the offices and Masses of the Easter and Christmas seasons; on feasts and memorials of the Lord, other than of his passion; on feasts and memorials of Mary, the angels, saints who were not martyrs; All Saints (November 1), John the Baptist (June 24), John the Evangelist (December 27), the Chair of St. Peter (February 22), and the Conversion of St. Paul (January 25).

b. Red is used on Passion Sunday (Palm Sunday) and Good Friday, Pentecost, celebrations of the Lord's passion, birthday feasts of the apostles and evangelists, and celebrations of martyrs.

c. Green is used in the offices and Masses of Ordinary Time.

d. Violet is used in Lent and Advent. It may also be worn in offices and Masses for the dead.

e. Black may be used in Masses for the dead.

f. Rose may be used on *Gaudete* Sunday (Third Sunday of Advent) and *Laetare* Sunday (Fourth Sunday of Lent).

The conference of bishops may choose and propose to the Apostolic See adaptations suited to the needs and culture of peoples.

309. On solemn occasions more precious vestments may be used, even if not of the color of the day.

310. Ritual Masses are celebrated in their proper color, in white, or in a festive color; Masses for various needs and occasions are celebrated in the color proper to the day or the season or in violet if they bear a penitential character; votive Masses are celebrated in the color suited to the Mass itself or in the color proper to the day or season.

552. Sacred Congregation for the Rites Instruction

Pontificalis ritus, *on the simplification of pontifical rites and insignia*

21 JUNE 1968: AAS 60 (1968) 406–412; NOT 4 (1968) 246–252

Esteem for the pontifical rites and care over them are matters of centuries-old standing. These rites provide a symbol of the honor by which the bishop's dignity is to be acknowledged in the Church and they place clearly before the faithful the mystery of the Church itself.

The *Caeremoniale Episcoporum,* a collection of the norms required for pontifical celebrations made by papal authority, is evidence of the Church's continuing attentiveness regarding rites to be celebrated by a bishop.

The *Caeremoniale* preserves venerable traditions belonging to the ancient celebrations in which priests, deacons, and ministers perform their ministry when a bishop presides and the congregation of the faithful is present. In many places, however, it contains matters that are obsolete and not in keeping with our own times.

Reform of the liturgy was meant to bring the rites once again to a noble simplicity and to authenticity as signs. Once begun many bishops insistently requested that pontifical celebrations and insignia also be simplified.

Not everything in the *Caeremoniale Episcoporum* can be revised before completion of the definitive reform of the Order of Mass, the divine office, and the liturgical year. But careful reflection on the matter led to the conclusion that it is now timely to establish certain measures that, while preserving the dignity of pontifical rites, will also mark them with simplicity. Therefore the following matters are ordered to be changed or introduced at once.

I. PRIESTS AND MINISTERS IN A CELEBRATION WITH THE BISHOP

A. Priests and Ministers in a Concelebrated Mass

1. The preeminent manifestation of the Church is most clearly expressed in the eucharist at which the bishop presides, surrounded by his college of priests and ministers, with the people taking an active part. To show this more clearly it is especially fitting, now that concelebration has been restored, for priests to be present with the bishop at a solemn celebration and concelebrate with him, in

accord with an ancient tradition in the Church.

So that priests who hold some higher rank may have more opportunity to concelebrate with the bishop:

a. One of the concelebrants may perform the function of assistant priest.

b. When no deacons are present, two of the concelebrants may replace assistant deacons.[1]

B. Assistant Priest and Deacons

2. It belongs to the assistant priest to stand by the bishop's side as he reads. When the bishop is not at the altar, however, a server holds the book in front of him.

3. As a rule, priests of higher rank assist the bishop at the chair. It is permissible, however, for a deacon to do so and to perform the ministries of the assistant deacons; if necessary, the deacon and subdeacon of the Mass may fulfill these functions.

C. Deacons and Subdeacons

4. At a celebration with a bishop presiding, the reality of orders and ministries should stand out clearly. Therefore, deacons and subdeacons, if any are present, should not be excluded from serving as the deacon at the altar and the subdeacon for Mass.

5. Several deacons, clad in their proper vestments, may exercise their ministry, each taking a part in this ministry.

6. When a bishop celebrates a Mass without singing, it is fitting that he be assisted by at least one deacon, vested in amice, alb, cinc-ture, and stole; the deacon reads the gospel and assists at the altar.[2]

7. If all the deacons and subdeacons called for by the rubrics are not available on Holy Thursday at the chrism Mass, fewer suffice. If none at all are available, some of the concelebrating priests are to carry the oils.

D. Canons Present in Choir

8. At a pontifical Mass of a bishop the canons are always to wear a canon's choral vesture.

E. Lesser Ministers

9. Ministers who assist the bishop at the throne are not to wear a cope.

II. Chair or Throne of the Bishop

10. The honored and traditional name for the chair of the bishop is the *cathedra*.

11. From now on there is to be no baldachin over the bishop's chair; but the valuable works of art from the past are to be preserved with utmost care. Further, existing baldachins are not to be removed without consultation with the commissions on liturgy and art.

12. Depending on the design of each church the chair should have enough steps leading up to it for the bishop to be clearly visible to the faithful and truly to appear as the one presiding over the whole community of the faithful.

---

[1]See *Rite of Concelebration* nos. 18 and 19.
[2]See *Ritus servandus in celebratione Missae* (1965) no. 44.

13. In all cases there is to be only a single episcopal chair and the bishop who sits on it is the one who is celebrating or presiding pontifically at the celebration. A chair is also to be provided in a convenient place for any other bishop or prelate who may be present, but it is not to be set up as a *cathedra*.

III. SIMPLIFICATION OF SOME OF THE PONTIFICAL VESTURE AND INSIGNIA

14. A bishop who wears an alb as required by the rubrics need not wear the rochet under the alb.

15. Use of the following is left to the bishop's choice:
    a. buskins and sandals;
    b. gloves, which may be white on all occasions if he prefers;
    c. the morse (*formale*) worn over the cope.

16. The following are to be dropped:
    a. the episcopal tunicle previously worn under the dalmatic;
    b. the silk lap-cloth (*gremial*); another gremial is retained, if it serves a purpose, e.g., for the performance of anointings;
    c. the candle (*bugia*) presented to the bishop for readings, unless it is needed;
    d. the cushion for kneeling during the rites.

17. In keeping with ancient tradition, the bishop is to retain the dalmatic when he celebrates solemnly. In addition he is to wear it in a recited Mass at the consecration of a bishop, the conferral of orders, the blessing of an abbot or an abbess, the blessing and consecration of virgins, the consecration of a church and an altar. But for a reasonable cause he may omit wearing the dalmatic under the chasuble.

18. In each liturgical service a bishop is to use only one miter, plain or ornate depending on the character of the celebration.

19. Any bishop who, with the consent of the local bishop, celebrates solemnly may use the episcopal staff.

20. Only a single cross is to be carried in a procession, to increase the dignity of the cross and its veneration. If an archbishop is present, the cross will be the archiepiscopal cross, to be carried at the head of the procession, with the image of Christ crucified facing forward. The recommended practice is to stand the processional cross near the altar so that it serves as the altar cross. If this is not done, the processional cross is put away.

IV. THINGS TO BE CHANGED OR ELIMINATED IN EPISCOPAL RITES

A. Putting on and Taking off Vestments

21. In any liturgical ceremony a bishop vests and unvests in a side chapel or, if there is none, in the sacristy, at the chair, or, if more convenient, in front of the altar. Vestments and insignia, however, are not to be laid on the altar.

22. When a bishop presides in a side chapel at an hour of the office suited to the time of day, he wears the chasuble right from the start of the office.

B. The Book of the Gospels

23. The Book of the Gospels, preferably distinct from the book of other readings, is carried by the subdeacon at the beginning of Mass. After the bishop celebrant has kissed the altar and the Book of the Gospels, this is left on the altar at the middle. After saying the prayer, *Almighty God, cleanse thy heart,* the deacon takes the Book of the Gospels before asking the bishop's blessing for the singing of the gospel.

C. Liturgy of the Word in a Mass At Which a Bishop Presides Without Celebrating

24. When, in keeping with no. 13, a bishop presides at a Mass without celebrating, he may do all those things in the liturgy of the word that usually belong to the celebrant.

D. Things to be Eliminated

25. The bishop is no longer greeted by a genuflection but by a bow. In carrying out their service the ministers stand rather than kneel before him, unless kneeling is more practical.

26. The washing of the bishop's hands within a liturgical rite is carried out by acolytes or clerics, not by members of the bishop's household.

27. All prescriptions in the *Caeremoniale Episcoporum* on forming a circle of assistants in front of the bishop or on certain parts recited in alternation are abolished.

28. Also to be abolished is the previous tasting of the bread, wine, and water prescribed in the *Caeremoniale.*

29. If a bishop presides at a canonical hour before Mass, he omits those preparatory prayers for Mass that the *Caeremoniale* prescribes during the chanting of the psalms [lib. II, cap. viii, no. 9].

30. In a Mass at which a bishop presides without celebrating, the celebrant, not the bishop, blesses the water to be poured into the chalice at the offertory.

31. The bishop may omit use of the miter and staff as he goes from one place to another when there is only a short space between them.

32. A bishop does not use the miter, unless he already has it on, for the washing of the hands and the receiving of incensation.

E. Blessings by a Bishop

33. The blessing after the homily mentioned in the *Caeremoniale* is abolished.

34. When, in keeping with the provisions of law, a bishop bestows it, the papal blessing with its formularies replaces the usual blessing at the end of Mass.

35. The cross is not to be brought to an archbishop when he gives the blessing.

36. A bishop is to take the staff before he begins the blessing formulary, so that this is not interrupted. Thus in this instance the raising and extension of the hands prescribed in the *Ritus servandus* no. 87 are omitted.

    An archbishop is to put the miter on before the blessing.

37. After the blessing, the bishop, with miter and staff, reverences the altar, as he is leaving. If he has the right to wear the pallium, he does not take it off at the altar but in the sacristy.

V. PRELATES OF LESS THAN EPISCOPAL RANK; OTHER CLERICS; OTHER LITURGICAL RITES

38. All the points in this Instruction on simplifying pontifical vesture, insignia, and rites and on matters to be eliminated or modified apply in due measure to prelates or clerics of less than episcopal rank who by law or by privilege are entitled to certain pontifical insignia.

39. The suppressions and changes that have been decreed here apply also to all liturgical services celebrated by other clerics.

Pope Paul VI on 10 June 1968 approved this Instruction drawn up by the congregation of Rites and the Consilium, confirmed it by his authority, and ordered its publication, setting 8 September 1963, the feast of the Birth of the Blessed Virgin Mary, as its effective date.

554. Paul VI, Motu Proprio

Inter eximia episcopalis, *on the pallium*

11 May 1978: AAS 70 (1978) 441–442; Not 14 (1978) 319–320

The pallium, received from the revered tomb of St. Peter,[1] is deservedly included among the special insignia of the bishop's office. It is one of those marks of honor that the Apostolic See has from earliest times accorded to Churches and their heads, first throughout Europe, then throughout the world. The pallium, "a symbol of archiepiscopal power,"[2] "belongs *de iure* only to an archbishop,"[3] since, through its bestowal the fullness of the pontifical office is conferred along with the title of archbishop."[4] As historical records show,[5] however, the popes have continued the early practice of honoring episcopal sees with the dignity of the archiepiscopal pallium as a grant in perpetuity in order to enhance the standing of such Churches because of the renown of the place, the antiquity of the Churches, and their unfailing reverence toward the See of Peter. Furthermore, the popes have also followed the practice of conferring the pallium as a personal privilege to reward the exceptional merits of illustrious bishops.[6]

Vatican Council II, however, has decreed that new and effective norms are to specify the rights and privileges of metropolitans.[7] We have accordingly decided to revise the privileges and practices related to the granting of the pallium in order that it might serve as a distinctive symbol of the power of the metropolitan.[8]

We have received and taken into consideration the opinions of the Roman curial congregations involved and of the commissions for the revision of the code of canon law and of the Eastern code of canon law. Of set purpose and by our own supreme apostolic authority, we now decree that for the entire Latin Church the pallium hereafter belongs exclusively to metropolitans and the Latin-rite patriarch of Jerusalem.[9] We abolish all privileges and customs now applying either to particular Churches or to certain bishops as a personal prerogative.

As to the Eastern Churches, we repeal canon 322 of the Motu Proprio *Cleri sanctitati*.[10]

---

[1] See PR, pars prima, *ed. typica* (Rome, 1962) 62.
[2] CIC can. 275.
[3] Benedict XIV, *De Synodo dioecesana* lib. 2, 6, no. 1.
[4] Benedict XIV, Ap. Const. *Ad honorandum,* 27 March 1754, §17.
[5] See Benedict XIV, *De Synodo dioecesana* loc. cit.
[6] See Benedict XIV, Ap. Const. *Inter conspicuos,* 29 Aug. 1744, no 18.
[7] See CD no. 40: AAS 58 (1966) 694; ConstDecrDecl 318.
[8] See CIC can. 275.
[9] See Pius IX Apostolic Letter *Nulla celebrior,* 23 July 1947: *Acta Pii IX,* pars. 2, vol. 1, 62.
[10] See AAS 67 (1957) 529.

We permit archbishops and bishops who already have received the pallium, however, to use it as long as they continue as pastors of the Churches now entrusted to them.

In the case of the episcopal ordination of a pope-elect who is not yet a bishop, wearing of the pallium is granted by law to the cardinal dean of the college of cardinals[11] or else to that cardinal to whom the rite of ordination is assigned according to the Apostolic Constitution *Romano Pontifici eligendo.*[12]

The effective date for these norms is the date of their publication in the *Acta Apostolicae Sedis.*

We command that whatever has been decreed by this Motu Proprio is ratified and established, all things to the contrary notwithstanding, even those deserving explicit mention.

---

[11]See CIC can. 239, §2.
[12]See AAS 67 (1975) 644–645.

553. Sacred Congregation for Divine Worship Concession

La Sacrée Congrégation, *allowing use of the chasuble-alb*

1 MAY 1971: NOT 9 (1973) 96–98, FRENCH*

A petition conforming to the General Instruction of the Roman Missal no. 304 has been addressed to the Congregation for Divine Worship to authorize wearing of the chasuble-alb with the stole over it in liturgical celebrations. This is a loose-fitting priestly vestment that entirely envelops the celebrant's body and thus replaces the alb.

1. This proposal seems to be consistent with the general principles on liturgical vestments, as determined by the General Instruction of the Roman Missal no. 297. In particular:

   a. The prominence given to the stole by reason of its being worn over the chasuble-alb puts due emphasis on the hierarchic ministry of the priest, namely, his role as presiding over the assembly *in persona Christi* (See Introduction no. 4; Text no. 60).

   b. Since it is so ample that it covers the celebrant's entire body, the chasuble-alb maintains the sacredness of things used in the liturgy and adds an element of beauty, if it is of graceful design and good material.

2. Taking into account the diversity of pastoral situations, the Congregation for Divine Worship therefore authorizes use of this vestment under the following conditions.

   a. For the usual celebration of Mass, particularly in places of worship, the traditional liturgical vestments are to continue in use: the amice (when needed to cover the neck completely), the alb, the stole, and the chasuble, as required by the General Instruction nos. 81(a), 298, and 299. It is preferable to ensure the observance of this prescription, but at the same time not to refuse to meet legitimate needs of the present day.

   b. For concelebration, the General Instruction (no. 161) has confirmed the faculty granted to concelebrants, except for the principal concelebrant, to wear just the alb with the stole over it. This makes for a certain

---

*SCDW, Prot. N. 1937/71, to France, the same concession was extended to other conferences of bishops.

simplicity but at the same time respects the dignity and sacredness of the liturgical service. It is proper in concelebrations that the principal concelebrant wear the vestments listed here in no. 2(a).

c. The chasuble-alb may be worn in concelebrations for Masses with special groups, for celebrations outside a place of worship, and for other similar occasions where this usage seems to be suggested by reason of the place or people involved.

d. As to color, the only requirement for use of the chasuble-alb is that the stole be of the color assigned to the Mass.

3. We should add that the approval of a new type of vestment must not put an end to the creativity of artisans and vestment makers regarding the design or the material and color of vestments. But all their efforts must respect the twofold requirement formulated by the General Instruction no. 297 and repeated here in no. 1(a) and (b): to give proper emphasis to the celebrant's ministry and to ensure the sacredness and beauty of the vestments.

551. Secretariat of State Instruction

Ut sive sollicite, *on the vesture, titles, and insignia of cardinals, bishops, and lesser prelates*

31 MARCH 1969: AAS 61 (1969) 334–340

In conscientious fulfillment of his obligation to watch over the universal Church and in his efforts to carry out the directives and teachings of Vatican Council II, Pope Paul VI has devoted his attention even to the outward symbols of ecclesiastical life. His intention has been to adapt such externals to the altered conditions of the present time and to relate them more closely to the spiritual values they are meant to signify and to enhance.

The issue at hand is disquieting to our contemporaries. It involves harmonizing, without giving in to conflicting, extreme demands, propriety and dignity with simplicity, practicality, and the spirit of humility and poverty. These qualities must above all characterize those who, by their admittance to ecclesiastical office, have received a clear duty of service to the people of God.

Prompted by such considerations, the Pope in the last two years has seen to the issuance of norms on the dress and other prerogatives of cardinals (see SC Ceremonies, Decree, 6 June 1967, Prot. N. 3711), the Motu Proprio *Pontificalis Domus*, 28 March 1968, on the composition of the papal household, the Motu Proprio *Pontificalia insignia*, 21 July [June] 1968, on pontificals,[a] and the related Decree of the Congregation of Rites, Prot. N. R.32/968, on the same date.[b]

Pope Paul, however, wished to change even more extensively the regulations on the vesture, titles, and coats-of-arms of cardinals, bishops, and prelates of lesser rank. He therefore ordered a special commission of cardinals and the papal Secretary of State to study the issue thoroughly, taking into account both established custom, contemporary usage, and the spiritual values connected with various symbols of ecclesiastical life, even though they are external nonessentials.

The consultation of this commission is the basis of the present Instruction. In an audience granted to me, the Cardinal Secretary of State, 28 March 1969, Pope Paul VI approved this

---

[a]See DOL 549; AAS mistakenly has 21 July 1968 as the date.
[b]See DOL 550 [the document is an instruction, not a decree].

Instruction and set 13 April 1969, Low Sunday, as its effective date.

All things to the contrary notwithstanding, even those deserving explicit mention.

PART ONE: DRESS

A. Cardinals

1. The following continue in use: the cassock of red wool or similar material, with sash, piping, buttons, and stitching of red silk; the mozzetta of the same material and color as the cassock but without the small hood.

    The *mantelletta* is abolished.

2. The black cassock with piping and red-silk stitching, buttonholes, and buttons, but without the oversleeves, also continues in use.

    The elbow-length cape, trimmed in the same manner as this cassock, may be worn over it.

3. The sash of red watered-silk, with silk fringes at the two ends, is to be worn with both the red cassock and the red-trimmed black cassock.

    The sash with tassels is abolished.

4. When the red cassock is worn, red stockings are also worn, but are optional with the red-trimmed black cassock.

5. The dress for ordinary or everyday use may be the plain black cassock. The stockings worn with it are to be black. The red *collare* [rabat or rabbi] and the skullcap of red watered-silk may be worn even with the plain black cassock.

6. The red watered-silk biretta is to be used only with choral dress, not for everyday wear.

7. Use of the red watered-silk cloak [*ferraiuolo*] is no longer obligatory for papal audiences and ceremonies held with the pope present. Its use is also optional in other cases, but should always be restricted to particular solemn occasions.

8. The great cloak of red wool [*tabarro*] is abolished. In its place a decent black cloak, even with cape, may be used.

9. The red cardinalatial hat [*galero*] and the red plush hat are abolished. But the black plush hat remains in use, to which, when warranted, red and gold cord and tassels may be added.

10. Use of red shoes and buckles, even silver buckles on black shoes, is abolished.

11. The rochet of linen or similar material is retained. The surplice or cotta is never to be worn over the rochet.

12. The *cappa magna*, without ermine, is no longer obligatory; it can be used only outside Rome, on very solemn occasions.

13. The cord and chain for the pectoral cross are retained. But the cord is to be worn only with the red cassock or sacred vestments.

B. Bishops

14. By analogy with what has been laid down for cardinals, bishops keep the purple cassock, the mozzetta without the small hood, and the black cassock with red piping and buttons.

    The mozzetta may be worn anywhere, even by titular bishops.

    The purple *mantelletta* or cloak is abolished.

The red-trimmed black cassock with its other red ornaments is no longer obligatory as ordinary dress. The small cape may be worn over it.

15. With regard to the sash, stockings, ordinary dress, *collare* [rabat], skullcap, biretta, *ferraiuolo,* cloak [*tabarro*], buckles, rochet, *cappa magna,* cord and chain for the pectoral cross, the rules laid down in nos. 3–8 and 10–13 are to be followed.

16. The black plush hat with green cord and tassels, which is to be the same for all bishops, both residential and titular, is retained.

17. Like all other bishops, those appointed from religious orders and congregations will use the purple cassock and the black cassock, with or without red trimmings.

C. Lesser Prelates

18. The higher-ranking prelates of the offices of the Roman Curia who do not have episcopal rank, the auditors of the Rota, the promoter general of justice, and the defender of the bond of the Apostolic Signatura, apostolic protonotaries *de numero,* papal chamberlains, and domestic prelates retain the purple cassock, the purple *mantelletta,* the rochet, the red-trimmed black cassock without cape, the purple sash with fringes of silk at the two ends, the purple *ferraiuolo* (nonobligatory), and the red tuft on the biretta.

    The silk sash with tassels, purple stockings, and shoe-buckles are abolished.

19. For supernumerary apostolic protonotaries and for honorary prelates of His Holiness, the purple *mantelletta,* the silk sash with tassels, purple stockings, shoe-buckles, and the red tuft on the biretta are all abolished.

The purple cassock, the red-trimmed black cassock without cape, and the silk sash with fringes are retained. If necessary, the unpleated surplice [cotta] may be worn over the purple cassock, in place of the rochet.

The purple *ferraiuolo,* although not obligatory, is retained for supernumerary apostolic protonotaries, but not for honorary prelates of His Holiness.

20. Chaplains of His Holiness keep the purple-trimmed black cassock with purple sash and other ornaments. It is to be worn also in sacred ceremonies.

    The purple cassock, the purple *mantellone,* the sash with tassels, and shoe-buckles are abolished.

21. The titles called "titles of kinship," which the pope uses in reference to cardinals, bishops, and other ecclesiastics, will be limited to the following: for a cardinal, "Our Esteemed Brother"; for a bishop, "Esteemed Brother"; for others, "Beloved Son."

22. For cardinals the title "Eminence" and for bishops, "Excellency," may still be used and the adjectival phrase "Most Reverend" added.

23. The simple titles "Lord Cardinal" and the Italian *Monsignore* may be used to address a cardinal and a bishop either orally or in writing.

24. "Most Reverend" may be added to the title *Monsignore* in addressing bishops.

25. For the prelates listed in no. 18, "Most Reverend" may also be added to the title *Monsignore.*

    For the dean of the Roman Rota and the secretary of the Apostolic Signatura, the title "Excellency" may be used but without "Most

Reverend." The same applies to the vice-chamberlain of the Holy Roman Church.

26. For supernumerary apostolic protonotaries, honorary prelates, and chaplains of His Holiness the title *Monsignore,* preceded where applicable by "Reverend," may be used.

27. In formal letters, the expressions "kissing the sacred purple," "kissing the sacred ring" may be omitted.

28. Cardinals and bishops are granted the right to have a coat-of-arms. The use of coats-of-arms must conform to the rules of heraldry and must be simple and clear.

    The episcopal staff and the miter in coats-of-arms is suppressed.

29. Cardinals are allowed to have their coats-of-arms affixed to the outside of their titular or diaconal church.

    The portrait of the titular cardinal is to be removed from such churches. Inside, near the main door, a plaque is permitted with the name of the titular cardinal inscribed in a manner suited to the style of the building.

ADDITIONAL PROVISIONS

30. With regard to the dress and titles of cardinals and patriarchs of the Eastern rites, the traditional usages of their individual rite are to be followed.

31. Patriarchs of the Latin rite who are not cardinals are to dress like other bishops.

32. Papal legates, whether bishops or not, are to conform to the rules already given for bishops.

    But within their own jurisdiction they may use the sash, skullcap, biretta, and *ferraiuolo* of watered silk.

    They will be accorded the title "Esteemed Brother" referred to in no. 21, only if they are bishops.

33. Prelates *nullius,* abbots *nullius,* apostolic administrators, vicars, and prefects apostolic who are not bishops may dress like bishops.

34. In the matter of forms of address conferences of bishops may lay down suitable rules conforming to local usages, but they are to take into account the norms and rules contained in the present Instruction.

35. Concerning the dress and titles of canons, holders of benefices, and pastors, the Congregation for the Clergy will issue pertinent rules for the future that are in keeping with the reason for this Instruction, namely, to reduce everything in this matter to a simpler form.

Secretariat of State Directive N. 135705

Instruction, sur les habits, les titres et les blasons des Cardinaux, des Evêques et des Prélats inférieurs

Dans l'exercice attentif de sa vigilance sur toute l'Eglise, et suivant les indications et l'esprit du Deuxième Concile due Vatican, Sa Sainteté le Pape Paul VI n'a pas manqué de prendre en examen certaines formes extérieures de la vie ecclésiastique, afin du'elles répondent davantage aux circonstances changeantes des temps et traduisent mieux désormais les valeurs spirituelles supérieures qu'elles doivent exprimer et promouvoir.

Il s'agit, comme on le sait, d'une matière à laquelle la mentalité moderne est particulièrement sensible, et où il faut, en se gardant des extrêmes, savoir concilier la convenance et le décorum avec la simplicité, et le caractère pratique avec l'esprit d'humilité et de pauvreté, qui doit toujours briller chez ceux-là surtout qui, revêtus de charges ecclésiastiques, ont une responsabilité spéciale au service du peuple de Dieu.

C'est sur la base de ces critères qu'au cours des deux dernières années le Saint-Père a fait publier successivement des règles sur les habits et autres prérogatives cardinalices (Protocole n. 3711 de la Sacrée Congregation Cérémoniale, du 6 juin 1967),

un Motu proprio sur la réorganisation de la Maison pontificale ("Prontificalis Domus", du 28 mars 1968), et un autre Motu proprio, complété par une Instruction de la S. Congrégation des Rites, sur l'usage des insignes pontificaux ("Pontificalis Insignia", du 21 juin 1968; Instruction N. R. 32/968, de la même date).

Voulant maintenant renouveler ultérieurement et plus largement la discipline des habits, des titres et des blasons des Cardinaux, des Evêques et des Prélats inférieurs, Sa Sainteté a chargé une Commission cardinalice et la Secrétairerie d'Etat d'étudier la chose avec diligence, en tenant compte à la fois et dans une juste mesure de la tradition, des exigences d'aujourd'hui et des valeurs plus profondes que comportent certaines formes de vie, même extérieures et contingentes.

Le fruit de ce travail est la présente Instruction, que le Saint-Père a daigné approuver dans l'audience accordée Cardinal Secrétaire d'Etat le 28 mars 1969, disposant qu'elle entre en vigueur le Dimanche *in Albis,* 13 avril 1969.

Première Partie: Les Habits

A. *Pour les Cardinaux*

1. La soutane de laine rouge (ou étoffe similaire) est conservée, avec revers, bordures, coutures et boutons de soie rouge; est conservée également la mozette de mêmes tissu et couleur que la soutane, mais sans le petit capuchon.

   Le mantelletta est abolie.

2. La soutane filetée est conservée, avec bordures, coutures, boutonnières et boutons de soie rouge, mais sans les surmanches.

   On pourra porter sur cette soutane le camail, fileté comme la soutane.

3. Tant avec la soutane rouge qu'avec la soutane filetée on portera la ceinture de soie moirée rouge, avec frange de soie aux deux extrémités.

   La ceinture à glands est abolie.

4. Le port de la soutane rouge comporte celui des bas de même couleur. L'usage de ceux-ci est facultatif avec la soutane filetée.

5. L'habit ordinaire pourra être la soutane noire; non filetée, avec bas noirs.

   Le "collare" rouge et la calotte de soie rouge moirée peuvent se porter également avec la soutane non filetée.

6. On ne fera usage de la barrette de soie rouge moirée qu'avec l'habit de choeur et on ne s'en servira pas comme d'un couvre-chef ordinaire.

7. L'usage du ferraiuolo de soie rouge moirée n'est plus obligatoire pour les audiences pontificales ni pour les cérémonies qui se déroulent en présence du Saint-Père. Il est facultatif également dans les autres cas et devra de toutes façon être limité à des circonstances particulièrement solennelles.

8. Le grand manteau rouge (*tabarro*) est aboli. On pourra le remplacer par un manteau noir, orné au besoin d'un camail.

9. Le chapeau rouge (*galero*) et le chapeau de feutre rouge sont abolis.

   Le chapeau de feutre noir est conservé. S'il y a lieu, il pourra etre orné, mais seulement du cordon et des glands rouge et or.

10. L'usage des chaussures rouges est supprimé, ainsi que l'usage des boucles, y compris celles d'argent sur les chaussures noires.

11. Le rochet de lin (ou tissu analogue) est conservé. On n'endossera jamais le surplis par-dessus le rochet.

12. La *cappa magna* ne comportera plus l'hermine et cessera d'être obligatoire. On ne pourra en faire usage désormais qu'en dehors de Rome, dans des circonstances très particulièrement solennelles.

13. L'usage du cordon et de la chaîne pour la croix pectorale est conservé. On ne se servira du cordon qu'avec la soutane rouge ou avec les ornements sacrés.

B. *Pour les Evêques*

14. D'une manière analogue à ce qui est prévu pour les Cardinaux, les Evêques conservent la soutane violette et la mozette, sans capuchon, et la soutane filetée.

    La mozette pourra être portée partout, même par les Evêques titulaires.

    La mantelletta est abolie.

    La soutane filetée n'est plus obligatoire comme habit ordinaire. Elle pourra être portée avec un camail.

15. Pour ce qui concerne la ceinture, les bas, l'habit ordinaire, le *collare,* la calotte, la barrette, le ferraiuolo, le manteau, les boucles, le rochet, la cappa magna, le cordon et la chaîne pour la croix pectorale, on suivra les critères indiqués aux Nos. 3–8 et 10–13.

16. On conserve l'usage du chapeau de feutre noir, avec cordon et glands verts, égal pour tous les Evêques, résidentiels et titulaires.

17. Les Evêques provenant d'Orders et de Congrégations religieuses feront usage de la soutane violette, de la soutane filetée et de la soutane noire non filetée, semblables en tout à celles des autres Evêques.

C. *Pour les Prélats inférieurs*

18. Pour les Prélats Supérieurs des Dicastères de la Curie Romaine non revêtus de la dignité épiscopale; pour les Auditeurs de Rote; pour le Promoteur de Justice et le Défenseur du lien de la Signature Apostolique; pour les Protonotaires Apostoliques *de numero* et les quatre clercs de la Chambre Apostolique, on conservera la soutane violette, la *mantelletta* violette, le rochet, la soutane filetée sans le camail, la ceinture violette avec frange de soie aux deux extrémités, le ferraiuolo violet (non obligatoire) et le pompon rouge sur la barrette.

    Sont abolis la ceinture à glands, les bas de couleur et les boucles sur les chaussures.

19. Pour les Protonotaires Apostoliques surnuméraires et pour les Prélats d'Honneur de Sa Sainteté, sont abolis: la mantelletta violette, la ceinture à glands, les bas de couleur, les boucles sur les chaussures et le pompon rouge sur la barrette.

    Sont conservés: la soutane violette, la soutane filetée sans le camail et la ceinture à frange. Au besoin on endossera sur la soutane violette le surplis non plissé, au lieu du rochet.

    Le ferraiuolo violet, sans être obligatoire, est conservé pour les Protonotaires Apostoliques surnuméraires, mais non pour les Prélats d'Honneur.

20. Pour les Chapelains de Sa Sainteté, on conserve la soutane filetée avec ceinture violette, dont ils feront usage également dans les cérémonies sacrées.

    La soutane violette, le manteau de même couleur, la ceinture à glands et les boucles des chaussures sont abolis.

II.ème Partie: Titres et blasons

21. Les "titres de parenté" utilisés par le Souverain Pontife à l'égard des Cardinaux, des Evêques et des autres ecclésiastiques, seront, respectivement, les seuls suivants:

    > "venerabilis frater noster"
    > "venerabilis frater"
    > "dilectus filius".

22. On pourra toutefois employer, pour les Cardinaux et les Evêques, respectivement, le titre d'Eminence et d'Excellence, même suivi du qualificatif "Révérendissime".

23. En s'adressant directement à un Cardinal ou à un Evêque, on pourra utiliser, respectivement, les simples appellatifs "Monsieur le Cardinal" et "Monseigneur".

24. Le titre de "Monseigneur" attribué aux Evêques dans la conversation directe pourra être accompagné du qualificatif "Très Révérend".

25. Pour les Prélats mentionnés au n. 18 le titre

de "Monseigneur" pourra être accompagné de "Très Révérend".

Pour le Doyen de la Rote et le Secrétaire de la Signature Apostolique, on pourra aussi employer le titre "Excellence", sans "Révérendissime". Ceci vaut également pour le Vice-Camerlingue de la Sainte Eglise Romaine.

26. Pour les Protonotaires Apostoliques surnuméraires et les Chapelains de Sa Sainteté, on pourra employer le titre de "Monseigneur", précédé éventuellement de "Révérend".

27. Dans les phrases protocolaires, on peut supprimer les expressions "baiser la pourpre sacrée", "baiser le saint anneau."

28. L'usage du blason est autorisé pour les Cardinaux et les Evêques.

L'écu du blason devra tenir compte des lois de l'héraldique; il sera simple et lisible.

On supprimera du blason la reproduction de la crosse et de la mitre.

29. Dans les églises de leur titre on Diaconie, les Cardinaux peuvent mettre, à l'extérieur, leur blason. De ces églises on enlévera le tableau due Cardinal titulaire. A l'intérieur de ces églises, à proximité de la porte principale, peut être indiqué le nom du Cardinal titulaire, sur une plaque en harmonie avec le style de l'édifice sacre.

DISPOSITIONS ADDITIONNELLES

30. Pour ce qui concerne les habits et les titres des Cardinaux et des Patriarches des Rites orientaux, on suivra les usages traditionnels propres à ces Rites.

31. Les Patriarches de Rite latin, qui ne seraient pas Cardinaux, s'habilleront comme les autres Evêques.

32. Les Représentants Pontificaux, revêtus ou non de la dignité épiscopale, se conformeront à ce qui a été décidé ci-dessus pour les Evêques.

Toutefois, dans leur territoire, ils pourront utiliser la ceinture, la calotte, la barrette et le ferraiuolo de soie moirée.

Aux mêmes Prélats on ne donnera le titre "Vénérable Frère", dont il a été question au n. 21, que s'ils sont revêtus de la dignité épiscopale.

33. Les Prélats et les Abbés "Nullius", les Administrateurs Apostoliques, les Vicaires et les Préfets Apostoliques non revêtus de la dignité épiscopale pourront s'habiller comme les Evêques.

34. En matiére de titres, les Conférences Episcopales pourront donner des normes opportunes, qui tiendront compte des usages locaux et des dispositions et critères contenus dans la présente Instruction.

35. Pour les habits et les titres des chanoines, des bénéficiers et des curés, des normes appropriées seront promulguées par la S. Congrégation pour le Clergé, selon les critères de simplification contenus dans le présent document.

Du Vatican, le 31 Mars 1969

From *Reform of the Use of Pontifical Insignia*

APOSTOLIC LETTER ISSUED MOTU PROPRIO, POPE PAUL VI
PONTIFICALIA INSIGNIA: JUNE 21, 1968; EFFECTIVE SEPTEMBER 8, 1968*

Thus it happens that in our time there are many clerics who, even if they do not have the episcopal rank, still enjoy the privilege of the pontifical insignia, in varying form and extent, in accord with the norms established in the Code of Canon Law, in the apostolic letter *Inter multiplices* issued motu proprio by our predecessor St. Pius X, on February 21, 1905, or in the apostolic constitution *Ad incrementum,* issued by our predecessor, Pope Pius XI, on August 15, 1934.

Recently, however, the Second Vatican Ecumenical Council explained, with new clarity the dignity and functions of bishops in the Church and distinguished more plainly between bishops and priests of the second order. The Council, moreover, in speaking to liturgical celebrations, decreed that "the rites should be distinguished by a noble simplicity . . . should be within the people's powers of comprehension, and normally should not require much explanation."[2] The elements which are introduced into sacred celebrations are signs used to signify invisible divine realities;[3] they must

therefore be easily and, so far as possible, directly understood by the faithful, so that the latter may be led to higher things.

For this reason, among the norms governing the restoration of the sacred liturgy, there is also an appropriate decision "that the use of pontificals be reserved to those ecclesiastical persons who have episcopal rank of some particular jurisdiction."[4] The spirit and the conditions of our time make much of the authenticity of signs, and it is necessary that liturgical rites should be marked by a noble simplicity. Therefore, authenticity must certainly be restored in the use of the pontifical insignia, which manifest the dignity and the office of being a shepherd to the people of God.

To implement the will of the holy Council, by

---

* Excerpted from the original in context to what applies directly to this study.
[2]*Ibid.,* art. 34: AAS 56 (1964) 109.
[3]Cf. *ibid.,* art. 33: AAS 56 (1964) 108.
[4]*Ibid.,* art. 103: AAS 56 (1964) 133.

our apostolic authority, at our own initiative, and with certain knowledge we decree the following:

1. In accord with the decision of art. 130 of the Constitution on the Sacred Liturgy, we direct that in the future the pontifical insignia be used only by the following prelates, in addition to bishops, who, although they lack the episcopal rank, enjoy true jurisdiction:

    (a) legates of the Roman Pontiff;

    (b) abbots and prelates who have jurisdiction in a territory distinct from any diocese (cf. canon 319, #1; canon 325, C.I.C.);

    (c) apostolic administrators who have a permanent appointment (canon 315, #1);

    (d) regular abbots *de regimine,* after they have received the abbatial blessing (canon 625).

2. The following, even though they do not possess episcopal rank, may also use the pontifical insignia, with the exception of the cathedra and staff:

    (a) apostolic administrators who have a temporary appointment (canon 351, #2, n. 2; cf. also canon 308);

    (b) vicars apostolic and prefects apostolic (canon 308).

3. The prelates named in n. 1 and 2 enjoy the abovementioned rites only in their own territory and while they hold office. Abbots primate and abbots general of monastic congregations, however, may use the pontifical insignia, while they hold office, in all the monasteries of their order or congregation. Other regular abbots *de regimine,* have the same right in any monastery of their order, but with the consent of the abbot or the conventual prior of that monastery.

4. Regular abbots *de regimine,* who have received the abbatial blessing and who are entered upon the government of their monastery, and titular abbots may use the pontifical insignia in any monastery of their order or congregation, but with the consent of the abbot or conventual prior of that monastery.

5. Other prelates who do not have episcopal rank, but who were named before the issuance of this apostolic letter, continue to enjoy the privileges of certain pontifical insignia which were granted to them under any title, whether personally or as members of a corporate body, and which they now enjoy. They may, however, give up these privileges spontaneously in accord with the law.

6. In view of the recent decrees of the Sacred Ecumenical Council and the principles we have explained concerning the genuineness of signs in sacred celebrations, prelates named in the future, with the exceptions mentioned in n. 1 and 2 above, will not have the faculty of using the pontifical insignia.

7. What is said here concerning prelates holds also for other clerics who use the pontifical insignia under any title.

8. The norms contained in this apostolic letter will take effect beginning September 8 of this year.

We command that everything decreed in this apostolic letter, issued at our own initiative, shall be firm and ratified, anything to the contrary, even worthy of the most special mention, notwithstanding.

Given at Rome, at St. Peter's, June 21, 1968, the sixth year of our pontificate.

PAUL VI

SACRED CONGREGATION OF RITES

INSTRUCTION, ON THE SIMPLIFICATION OF PONTIFICAL RITES AND INSIGNIA

Pontifical rites have been held in great esteem and have been preserved with great care over the centuries. Not only do they indicate the honor which is shown in the Church to the sacred order of bishops, but they also proclaim to the faithful the mystery of the Church itself.

Even in recent periods the Ceremonial of Bishops shows how much the Church has been concerned with the practice of rites celebrated by a bishop. This book gathered together, by authority of the Supreme Pontiffs, the norms necessary for directing pontifical services.

This book preserves the venerable traditions of ancient liturgical services in which, with the bishop presiding and in the presence of the assembled people, priests, deacons, and servers exercise their ministry. Yet it also contains elements that are obsolete and out of harmony with our age.

On this account, now that the liturgical restoration has begun to return sacred rites to a noble simplicity and to an authenticity of sign, many bishops have urgently asked that pontifical services and pontifical insignia should be simplified.

After thorough consideration, it appears that the Ceremonial of Bishops cannot be totally revised before the definitive restoration of the ordinary of the Mass, the divine office, and the liturgical year has been completed. But it seems appropriate now to make certain decisions so that pontifical rites may be simpler while maintaining their dignity. Therefore the following changes or restorations are prescribed:

I. Priests and Ministers at Pontifical Service

(A) PRIESTS AND MINISTERS AT A CONCELEBRATED MASS

1. To achieve more effectively that preeminent manifestation of the Church which is expressed so clearly in the Eucharist when the bishop presides, surrounded by his college of priests and by his ministers and with the active participation of the people, it is most suitable that—with the restoration of concelebration—priests should join as concelebrants with the bishop who solemnly celebrates, in accord with the venerable tradition of the Church.

   To give a greater opportunity for priests of higher rank to concelebrate Mass with the bishop:

   (a) One of the concelebrating priests should serve as assistant priest;

   (b) In the absence of deacons, two of the concelebrants may take the place of the assistant deacons.

(B) ASSISTANT PRIEST AND ASSISTANT DEACONS

2. It is the office of the assistant priest to stand next to the bishop when the latter reads. A server, however, should hold the book before the bishop when he reads, except when he is at the altar.

3. Priests of higher dignity should ordinarily assist the bishop at the cathedra. Nevertheless, deacons or, if necessary, even the deacon and subdeacon of the Mass may assist the bishop at the cathedra and perform the ministry of assistant deacons.

(C) DEACONS AND SUBDEACONS

4. To express clearly the genuineness of orders and ministries in the celebration of the

Eucharist over which the bishop presides, it is preferable not to exclude true deacons and subdeacons, if present, from the office of deacon and subdeacon of the Mass.

5. Several deacons, if they are present and wearing their vestments, may distribute the various ministries among themselves.

6. When a bishop celebrates a low Mass, it is proper that at least one deacon assist him. Vested in amice, alb, cincture, and stole, the deacon reads the Gospel and serves at the altar.

7. If the required deacons and subdeacons are not available at the Mass of the Chrism on Holy Thursday, a smaller number may assist. If not even these can be had, some of the concelebrating priests should carry the oils.

(D) CANONS WHO ASSIST IN CHOIR

8. At the pontifical Mass of a bishop, the canons should always vest in their choral dress.

(E) LESSER MINISTERS

9. Ministers who serve the bishop at the cathedra should not wear copes.

II. The Seat or Cathedra of the Bishop

10. The seat of the bishop is called by the venerable and traditional name, cathedra.

11. In the future a canopy should not be placed above the cathedra. Nevertheless, precious works of art handed down from past centuries should be carefully preserved. Existing canopies, moreover, should not be removed until the liturgical commission and the commission on sacred art have been consulted.

12. The number of steps of the cathedra should be so designed that, depending on the structure of the particular church, the bishop may be easily seen by the faithful and may truly appear to preside over the entire community of the faithful.

13. There should always be only one episcopal cathedra and the bishop who celebrates or who presides over the celebration should occupy it. If other bishops or priests are present, seats should be prepared for them in a suitable place, but these should not be erected in the form of a cathedra.

III. Simplification of Certain Vestments and Pontifical Insignia

14. The bishop who, according to the rubrics, vests in the alb, is not bound to wear the rochet under the alb.

15. At his own choice, the bishop may use:

    (a) buskins and sandals;

    (b) gloves; if he prefers, gloves of white color may always be used;

    (c) the morse worn on the cope.

16. The following are abolished:

    (a) the tunic of the bishop, which has hitherto been worn under the dalmatic;

    (b) the silk gremial; the other gremial is retained when it is truly useful, for example, at anointings;

    (c) the candle which is brought to the bishop when he reads from a book, unless this should be necessary;

    (d) the cushion placed before the bishop when he genuflects.

17. According to an ancient tradition, the bishop should wear the dalmatic when he celebrates solemnly and also at low Masses

for the consecration of a bishop, the conferral of orders, the blessing of an abbot, the blessing of an abbess, the blessing and consecration of virgins, the consecration of a church and of an altar. Nevertheless, for reasonable cause he may omit the wearing of the dalmatic under the chasuble.

18. In the course of a single liturgical service, the bishop should use only one mitre; according to the character of the service, this will be either a simple or an ornate mitre.

19. Any bishop who celebrates pontifically may use the staff with the consent of the bishop of the place.

20. Only a single cross should be carried in a procession, in order to give greater dignity and reference to the cross. If the archbishop is present, this will be the archepiscopal cross, carried at the head of the procession with the image of the Crucified facing forward. It is desirable to place the cross, which has been carried in the procession, near the altar, so that it may serve as the cross of the altar. Otherwise it should be put away during the service.

IV. Certain Changes and Suppressions in the Pontifical Rites

(A) VESTING

21. The bishop puts on the sacred vestments for any liturgical service, or removes them in the secretarium or, if there is none, in the sacristy, or even at the cathedra or, according to circumstances, before the altar. The vestments and insignia, however, should not be placed on the altar.

22. If before Mass the bishop presides in the secretarium at an hour of the office, appropriate to the time of the day, he wears the chasuble from the beginning of the hour.

(B) BOOK OF GOSPELS

23. It is desirable that the book of Gospels be separate from the book of Epistles; it is carried by the subdeacon at the beginning of Mass. After the celebrating bishop has kissed the altar and the book of Gospels, the latter is left upon the altar in the center. After the deacon has said Munda cor meum, he takes the book from the altar before he seeks the bishop's blessing for the singing of the Gospel.

(C) LITURGY OF THE WORD AT THE MASS AT WHICH THE BISHOP PRESIDES WITHOUT CELEBRATING

24. When the bishop, according to n. 13, presides at Mass without celebrating, he may perform all the functions in the liturgy of the word which are ordinarily done by the celebrant.

(D) SUPPRESSIONS

25. The bishop is saluted by all with a bow, not with a genuflection. Similarly, the ministers stand before him in the performance of their office, unless convenience dictates otherwise.

26. In liturgical services, acolytes or clerics, rather than the bishop's servants, should minister when he washes his hands.

27. All the prescriptions of the Ceremonial of Bishops concerning the circles to be made by the canons before the bishop and concerning the alternate recitation of certain texts are abolished.

28. Likewise the tasting of bread, wine, and water, prescribed in the Ceremonial of Bishops is abolished.

29. If the bishop presides at a canonical hour before Mass, he omits the prayers of preparation which the Ceremonial of Bishops prescribes for recitation during the psalms.

30. When the bishop presides at a Mass without celebrating, the celebrant rather than the bishop blesses the water to be poured into the chalice at the offertory.

31. The bishop need not use the mitre and staff when he goes from place to place, if the distance is short.

32. The bishop does not wear the mitre, unless he already has it on, when he washes his hands or when he receives an incensation.

(E) EPISCOPAL BLESSING

33. The blessing after the homily, described in the Ceremonial of Bishops, is abolished.

34. When the bishop imparts the papal blessing, in accord with the law, this blessing with its formulas takes the place of the usual blessing at the end of the Mass.

35. The cross is not held before the archbishop when he gives the blessing.

36. The bishop should take the staff before he begins the formula of blessing, so that the latter will not be interrupted. In this case he does not raise and extend his hands, as prescribed in the Ritus servandus, n. 87.

    The archbishop, moreover, should also receive the mitre before the blessing.

37. After the blessing, the bishop salutes the altar while wearing the mitre and holding the staff. If he has the right to use the pallium, he takes this off in the secretarium rather than at the altar.

V. Prelates Who Do Not Have Episcopal Rank, Other Clerics, and Other Liturgical Services

38. Everything in this instruction concerning the simplification of certain pontifical vestments, insignia, and rites, as well as various suppressions and changes, holds also, with the proper adaptations, for prelates or clerics who lack the episcopal rank but who by law or privilege have the use of certain pontifical insignia.

39. The suppressions and changes also affect all liturgical services celebrated by other clerics.

This instruction was prepared by the Sacred Congregation of Rites and the Consilium for the Implementation of the Constitution on the Sacred Liturgy.

On June 10, 1968, the Supreme Pontiff, Pope Paul VI, kindly approved it, confirmed it by his authority, and ordered that it be published, determined at the same time that it should take effect beginning September 8, 1968, the feast of the birth of the Blessed Virgin Mary.

BENNO CARDINAL GUT,
Prefect of S.R.C.,

✠ FERDINAND ANTONELLI,
Archbishop of Idicren,
Secretary of S.R.C.

Rome, June 21, 1968

Bollettino No. 183, Giovedì 8 giugno 1967

(678/67) NUOVE DISPOSIZIONI PER I CARDINALI

In vista del Concistoro per la creazione di nuovi Cardinali, indetto del Santo Padre Paola VI, per il 26 giugno p.v., la Congregazione Cerimoniale ha riesaminoto la questione delle prerogative e, soprattutto degli abiti dei Cardinali, nell'intento di semplificarli in armonia col desiderio espresso durante il Concilio Vaticano II°.

In particolare, con l'approvazione del Santo Padre, sono stabilite le seguenti modifiche che entreranno in vigore con il prossimo Concistoro.

1) NON VI SARA'PIU'DIFFERENZA TRA GLI ABITI DEI CARDINALI ASSUNTI DAL CLERO SECOLARE E QUELLI PROVENIENTI DA ORDINI RELIGIOSI, ANCHE MENDICANTI.

2) IL GALERO E'SEMPRE IL SIMBOLO DELLA DIGNITA' CARDINALIZIA; MA NON S'IMPONE NELLA CERIMONIA D'INVESTITURA.

3) RIMANE UNA SOLA CAPPA MAGNA ED UN UNICO FERRAIOLO: DI SETA ONDATA ROSSA. LA CAPPA MAGNA NON SI DISPIEGA NELLE CERIMONIE ALLA PRESENZA DI SUA SANTITA'.

4) SONO ABOLITE LE ORLATURE D'ORO DEL MANTELLO O TABARRO, E COSI'PURE I FIOCCHI DI CARNUTIGLIA D'ORO DELLA FASCIA IN USO CON LA SOTTANA ROSSA. QUESTI ULTIMI TUTTAVIA SARANNO SOSTITUITI DA FIOCCHI DI SETA.

5) E'SOPPRESSO L'UFFICIO DI GENTILUOMO.

6) E'SOPPRESSO L'UFFICIO DI CAUDATARIO. I SUOI SERVIZI SARANNO PRESTATI DAL MEDESIMO ECCLESIASTICO CHE FA DA SEGRETARIO O "MINISTER ASSISTENS" DEL CARDINALE E CHE VESTIRA'SEMPRE IN SOTTANA E FASCIA NERA, CON COTTA O FERRAIOLO DI SETA NERA, A SECONDA CHE SI TRATTI DI CERIMONIE RELIGIOSE O CIVILI. E'ABOLITA LA CROCCIA.

7) E'ABOLITO L'USO DEL FERRAIOLINO PER IL CAMERIERE.

La Congregazione Cerimoniale, infine, ha preparato un elenco completo degli oggetti che, in base alle nuove disposizione, formeranno il vestiario d'un Cardinale.

Sacra Congregazione Cerimoniale

Nota degli abiti
occorrenti agli Em.mi e Rev.mi
Signori Cardinali

- Sottana di lana (o stoffa simile) rossa, con mostra, orlature, cucitura e bottoni di seta rossa.

- Mantelletta e mozzetta del medesimo tessuto.

- Fascia di seta ondata rossa (*moirée*), con due frocchi (uno per ciascuna estremità), da usarsi sulla sottana rossa.

- Rocchetto di lino.

- Cappa magna di seta ondata rossa, con petto ed interno del cappuccio di seta rossa semplice (con pelli d'ermellino nell'inverno).

- Cordone di seta rossa intrecciato d'oro per la Croce pettorale.[1]

- Zucchetto e Berretta di seta ondata rossa.

- Sottana con orlature, cuciture, asole e bottoni di seta rossa (per ogni tempo).

- Fascia di nastro di seta ondata rossa, con frangia di seta alle due estremità (da usarsi con la sottana pïana).

- Ferraiolone di seta ondata rossa, con mostre e bavero di seta rossa (da usarsi sulla sottana pïana).

- Mantello (tabarro) con mantellina, di panno rosso e bavero di velluto rosso, con mostre di seta rossa.

- Cappello di felpa rossa con fascia e nappe di seta rossa fregiate di oro, cordoncini e orlature di oro.[2]

- Cappello di felpa nera con fascia e nappe come sopra.

- Collare e calze rosse.

- Scarpe rosse con fibbie dorate.[3]

- Scarpe nere con fibbie dorate.

- Fazzoletto grande di seta rossa (per avvolgere indumenti).

---

[1] La Croce pettorale si porta dai Cardinali sopra la Mozzetta. Usando la Cappa magna si porta sotto la medesima. La catena d'oro per la Croce pettorale si usa soltanto sull'abito piano.

[2] Il cappello di felpa rossa si usa con l'abito cardinalizio rosso. Quello di felpa nera si usa con l'abito pïano, in occasione di Udienze, Congregazioni, Visite di formalità, ecc.

[3] Le scarpe rosse si usano soltanto nei Pontificali, nelle Assistenze in Paramenti sacri ed ogni volta che l'Eminentissimo si reca al proprio Titolo o Diaconia.

Il Venerdì Santo si usano le scarpe nere, e non si porta l'anello.

Sacra Congregazione Cerimoniale

Corteo processionale del Papa col Clero in Sacri Paramenti*

- Sergente della Guardia Svizzera Pontificia.
- Bussolanti.
- Procuratori di Collegio.
- Confessore della Famiglia Pontificia—Predicatore Apostolico.
- Procuratori Generali degli Ordini Mendicanti, che ne hanno il privilegio.
- Chierici della Cappella Pontificia in croccia.
- Cappellani Communi Pontifici, che portano, se conforme al rito della cerimonia, Mitre preziose e Triregni: in questo caso il Gioielliere custode dei Triregni incede a sinistra.
- Chierici Segreti.
- Cappellani d'Onore.
- Cappellani Segreti.
- Avvocati del Sacro Concistoro.
- Camerieri d'Onore *in abito paonazzo*.
- Camerieri Segreti Ecclesiastici Soprannumerari.
- Cappellani Cantori pontifici, se conforme al rito della cerimonia.
- Prelati Votani e Referendari della Segnatura Apostolica.
- Prelati Chierici della Rev. Camera Apostolica.

- P. Maestro del S. Palazzo con a sinistra il P. Commissario del S. Offizio.
- Prelati Uditori della Sacra Romana Rota.
- Due Cappellani Segreti che portano, se conforme al rito della cerimonia, Metra e Triregno.
- Maestro del Sacro Ospizio Apostolico.
- Decano della Segnatura Apostolica, turiferario.
- Prelati Votanti de Segnatura, accoliti, e fra loro il Prelato Uditore de Rota, Crocifero.
- Due Maestri Ostiari di « Virga rubea » quasi ai lati del Crocifero.
- Prelato Uditore di Rota, Suddiacono ministrante, in mezzo al Diacono e Suddiacono greci, nella Messa Papale.

---

*Questo è il Corteo Sacro ordinariamente in uso per le Messe Papali, per le Canonizzazioni, per l'apertura e chiusura della Porta Santa. Le processioni della Coronazione, della Candelora, della Domenica della Palme, del Giovedì Santo, del *Corpus Domini,* dei primi Vesperi Papali hanno alcune varianti, piuttosto rituali.

N.B.: The papal procession today has been simplified extensively to include only the Papal Master of Ceremonies and his assistant, the Prefect of the Papal Household, those cardinals, bishops and archbishops present, and the pontifical Swiss Guard. For the most solemn papal ceremonies, the reorganized Papal Household, as it is presently constituted, would follow a similar professional organization (utilizing the new titles and positions) as the one described herein.

- Prenitenzieri Apostolici preceduti da due chierici con le bacchette.
- Abati generali che ne hanno il privilegio.
- Abati *nullius.*
- Commendatore de S. Spirito in Sassia, a destra dell'Abate digniore.
- Vescovi, Arcivescovi.
- Vescovi, Arcivescovi Assistenti al Soglio Pontificio.
- Patriarchi.
- Ai lati del Sacro Collegio: due Cursori Apostolici con le mazze.
- Cardinali Diaconi, Preti e Vescovi, ciascuno col Caudatario.

- Altri due Cursori Apostolici, con le mazze.
- Principe Assistente al Soglio e a destra il Vice-Camerlengo de Santa Romana Chiesa.
- I Due Cardinali Diaconi assistenti, e fra loro il Cardinale Diacono ministrante nella Messa Papale.
- Il Prefetto ed il secondo Maestro della Cerimonie Apostoliche.
- Comandante della Guardia Palatina d'Onore, *a sinistra,*—Comandante della Guardia Svizzera Pontificia, *a destra.*
- Esente della Guardia Nobile di servizio, *a sinistra,*—Segretario per le Ambasciate, *a destra.*
- Latore della Rosa d'oro, *a sinistra,*—Soprainten-dente Generale alle Poste Pontificie, *a destra.*

SEDIA GESTATORIA

PORTATA DE DODICI SEDIARI IN ZIMARRA

A) Foriere Maggiore dei SS. PP. AA.
B) Cavallerizzo Maggiore di Sua Santità.
C) Esente Aiutante Maggiore della Guardia Nobile.
D) Cadetto Aiutante della Guardia Nobile.
E) Otto Prelati Referendari della Segnatura Apostolica per le aste del Baldacchino, se la funzione lo richiede.
F) Mazzieri Pontifici.
G) Capitano Comandante della Guardia Nobile di Sua Sontità.
H) Un Tenente della Guardia Nobile.
K) Due Camerieri Segreti Soprannumerari con i Flabelli.
L) Otto Esenti della Guardia Nobile.
M) Sei Guardie Svizzere con gli spadoni.
N) Sottoforiere dei SS. PP. AA.
O) Dodiei Sediari.

- Prelato Decano della S. R. Rota per la Mitra, in mezzo ai due Camerieri Partecipanti di servizio per il manto.

- Domestico—Aiutante di Camera—Archiatro Pontificio—Decano di Sala.

- Gruppo di Cantori della Cappella Sistina, se la funzione lo richiede.

- Uditore della Reverenda Camera Apostolica—Tesoriere della Reverenda Camera Apostolica—Maggiordomo di Sua Santità.

- Assessori e Segretari delle SS. Congregazioni.

- Segretario del Tribunale della Segnatura Apostolica.

- Sostituto della Segreteria di Stato.

- Protonotari Apostolici di numero partecipanti, col Maestro di Camera di Sua Santità a sinistra del seniore dei medesimi.

- Protonotari Apostolici Soprannumerari e « ad instar ».

- Reggente della Cancelleria Apostolica.

- Superiori Generali degli Ordini Mendicanti, che ne hanno il privilegio.

- Corpo della Guardia Nobile di Sua Santità al ritorno dalla cerimonia.

- Sediari in sovrappiù di quelli che portano la Sedia Gestatoria col Sotto-Decano di Sala.

- Picchetto della Guardia Palatina d'Onore.

- *Coppie di Guardie Svizzere fiancheggiano il Corteo.*

Eccettuati i militari ed i casi qui preveduti, nel Corteo processionale, tutti coloro che precedono la Sedia Gestatoria debbono incedere per due, coloro che la seguono per quattro.

Il Corteo processionale è regolato dai Maestri delle Cerimonie Apostoliche, per la parte di servizio assegnata a ciascuno di loro da Monsignor Prefetto.

Oltre le persone nominatamente sopra indicate ai loro posti, nessun altro dovrà unirsi al Corteo processionale per qualsiasi titolo o motivo.

Il presente « Corteo processionale del Papa col Clero in sacri paramenti », sottoposto all'approvazione del Sommo Pontefice Paolo VI daMons. Segretario della S. C. Cerimoniale nell'udienza del 3 marzo 1964, è stato approvato da Sua Santità ed entra in vigore in data odierna.

Si ordina la piena esecuzione delle disposizioni in esso contenute.

Dalla Sede della S. Congregazione Cerimoniale, 5 maggio 1964.

Eugenio Card. Tisserant
Decano del Sacro Collegio Prefetto

✠ Gennaro Verolino
Arcivescovo Tit. di Corinto
Segretario

Resources

A Suggested Guide to Authentic Suppliers of Vesture and Insignia

Italy

FLORENCE

Instituto Cristo Re
Villa Martelli
via di Gricigliano, 52
I-50069 Sieci, Italy
TEL: 39-55-83-09-622

ROME

Apostolato Liturgico
(Pie Discepole del Divin Maestro)
via Liberiana, 16 *(across from St. Mary Major)*
00185 Rome
TEL & FAX: 39-6-481-4794
(fax after hours)

Barbiconi
via S. Caterina da Siena, 58-60
00186 Rome
TEL: 39-6-679-49-85
FAX: 39-6-684-07-99

DeRitis
via dei Cestari, 48
00186 Rome
TEL: 39-6-68-65-843

Euroclero
Piazza del Sant'Uffizio, 4
via del Sant'Uffizio, 31
00193 Rome
TEL: 39-6-68-67-988
FAX: 39-6-68-69-148

Fratelli Mango
via Del Mascherina, 15
00193 Rome
TEL: 39-6-68-30-85-75

Gammarelli
(Ditta Annibale Gammarelli)
via S. Chiara, 34
00186 S. Chiara, 34
TEL: 39-6-654-1314

Anna Maria Gaudonzi
(Oggetti Sacri)
Piazza della Minerva, 69A
00186 Rome
TEL: 39-6-679-04-31

Mondo Cattolico
(Mosaics)
Piazzo Pio XII, 12
00193 Rome
TEL: 39-6-68-69-297

Spain

Manufacturas Bermejo Roma
Barcelona, 2 Spain
TEL: 34-3-317-5080 or 34-3-318-1791

Talleres De Arte Granda
(Suppliers of Precious Gold and Silver Sacred Vessels)
Serrano 56
28001 Madrid, Spain
TEL: 275-90-15 or 435-07-08
   or
San Severo 6
28042 Madrid, Spain

United Kingdom

Wippell & Company*
(Linen Clerical Collars)
P.O. Box 1
88 Buller Road
Exeter, EX4 1DQ
United Kingdom
TEL: 03292-54234
   or
11 Tufton Street
London *(near Westminster Abbey)*

* Although these collars are referred to as military collars, used primarily for British military uniforms, they are perfect for use under the cassock or inside a gilet vest. Similar linen collars are now available at Gammarelli in Rome. Both suppliers provide easy care linen rather than the former material, which required more attention.

United States

The Holy Rood Guild
(Sacred Vestments)
St. Joseph's Abbey
Spencer, Massachusetts 01562
TEL: 508-885-8750 or 9882
FAX: 508-885-3999

The House of Hanson
(Sacred Vestments and Vesture)
4223 W. Irving Park Road
Chicago, Illinois 60641
TEL: 800-522-1457 or 312-372-8750

Sister Mary Isabel, R.S.M.
(custom mitres for bishops; not sold commercially)
Convent of Mercy
273 Willoughby Avenue
Brooklyn, New York 11205
TEL: 718-622-5840

Mr. Larry Montefusco
(embroidered coat of arms for the infulae of precious mitres, sacred vestments, cathedra cushions, etc.)*
Impressions Recognition Awards
8342 State Road, Unit 1
Philadelphia, Pennsylvania 19136
TEL: 215-333-3510
FAX: 215-333-3512

* For the mitre infulae, a good color sample of the heraldic art and the outside material of each infulae is required before it is sewn.

Renzetti & Magnarelli
Clerical Apparel
2216 South Broad Street
Philadelphia, Pennsylvania 19145
TEL: 215-339-0558
FAX: 215-463-0161

A SUGGESTED GUIDE TO AUTHENTIC DESIGNERS AND ARTISTS IN THE SCIENCE OF ECCLESIASTICAL HERALDRY

For the Infulae on Mitres and Sacred Vestments

Apostolato Liturgico
(Pie Discepole del Divin Maestro)
via Liberiana, 16 *(across from St. Mary Major)*
00185 Rome
TEL & FAX: 39-6-481-4794 *(fax after hours)*

Heraldic Engravers

RINGS, CATHEDRA ARMS, ENAMELS, STATIONERY GOODS

Benneton Graveur, Paris
75 Boulevard Malesherbes
75008 Paris, France
TEL: 33-43-87-57-39
FAX: 33-43-87-13-68

Cartier
Stationery and Engraving Department
2 East 52nd Street
New York, New York 10022
TEL: 212-753-0111

Heraldists

Resources named are known by the author and publisher to maintain the high standards set by the Secretariat of State in the presentation of new arms for ecclesiastics and papal honorees. Although there are others who may be so qualified, they are not personally known by the author and therefore do not receive the same endorsement. It is always best to discuss the design of one's arms with several heraldic artists. When commissioning such individuals, please be certain to follow the rubrics put forth in Chapter 10, Ecclesiastical Heraldry.

S.E.R. Mons. Bruno B. Heim, D.D.*
Titular Archbishop of Xanto
Zehnderweg, 31
CH-4600 Olten
Switzerland

* Semi-retired.

Alex Garey
Lelli–Garey, Ltd.
Piazza Farnese, 104
Rome, Italy
TEL: 39-6-688-01-890
FAX: 39-6-688-00-186

James–Charles Noonan, Jr.*
Post Box 634
Gwynedd Valley, Pennsylvania 19437

* Specialist in ecclesiastical arms.

Carl Alexander von Volborth
Academe Internationale d'Heraldique
4 bis Bvd. De Glatigny
F-78000 Versailles, France

Heraldic Suppliers

This listing represents those nations that legally confer letters patent for armorial bearings for individuals, institutions, and corporations, civil and ecclesiastic. Applications should be made direct to the appropriate national office. Switzerland also grants arms under specific conditions, as do many monarchial forms of government. This list represents those nations that have formal offices prepared to receive applications.

The Chief Herald of Canada
Heraldry Directorate
Government House (Rideau Hall)
1 Sussex Drive
Ottawa, Ontario K1A-OA1
CANADA

The Chief Herald of Ireland
2 Kildare Street
Dublin, Ireland

The College of Arms
Queen Victoria Street
London, EC4V-4BT
England, The United Kingdom

The Lord Lyon, King of Arms
and the Court of the Lord Lyon
H.M. New Register House
Edinburgh, EH1-3YT
Scotland, The United Kingdom

Cronista Rey Des Armas
Decano Del Cuerpo
Calle de Atocha, 91
Madrid, 12 SPAIN

PLATE CAPTIONS

PLATE 1. Pio Cardinal Laghi, Prefect of the Congregation for Catholic Education and Seminaries, presents a formal address of goodwill at the Mass opening the academic year, 1994. His Eminence greets the Holy Father at the close of his remarks. The Holy Father wears the pontiff-design mitre, gold chasuble, and all-white alb. His Eminence wears the scarlet *zucchetto* and the gold gothic chasuble. *Courtesy Arturo Mari.*

PLATE 2. As Cardinal Sodano receives the red *biretta* from Pope John Paul II, visible in the background is a tray of *zucchetti* and *birette*—each bearing the name of the recipient, each having been sent by the new cardinal to the Papal Master of Ceremonies. Cardinal Sodano prefers the lace rochet. Master of Ceremonies Mons. Piero Marini wears the Gammarelli surplice. *Courtesy Arturo Mari.*

PLATE 3. During the ceremonies of consistory in which cardinal-designates become full members of the Sacred College, new cardinals make the Profession of Faith, publicly renewing their faith commitment and the bond of loyalty they share to the pope. Over six thousand visitors and guests gathered in the Paul VI audience hall to witness their rise to the College of Cardinals in November, 1994. *Courtesy Arturo Mari.*

PLATE 4. This magnificent photograph shows the Sacred College in full panoply. In the front row, second from right, is former Secretary of State Agostino Cardinal Casaroli. To his left is the late Sebastiano Cardinal Baggio, and to his right Pierre Cardinal Sfeir of the Maronites in vesture proper to his rite. Cardinal Willebrands is in the second row; the Archbishop of Paris, Cardinal Lustiger, sits in the fifth. This photo, like no other, illustrates proper cardinalatial choral (choir) dress, including that for the Oriental rites. *Courtesy The National Geographic Society, photograph by James L. Stanfield.*

PLATE 5. Cardinal Keeler of Baltimore receives the cardinalatial ring at the hands of Pope John Paul II in the Vatican Basilica of St. Peter, November, 1994. *Courtesy Arturo Mari.*

PLATE 6. In the conclave of 1963, the cardinals gathered to elect Giovanni Montini who took the name, Paul VI. At the close of conclave, Paul VI celebrated Mass with the College members. This scene has great historic value. It illustrates the *cappa magna*. Although shorter in length today, the garb is still part of the vesture of bishops although very few know this fact. In the foreground, two inferior prelates are vested in the *mantellone*, a vestural item now abolished. The cardinal to the left, preparing to ascend for the *embracio,* is the famous Giuseppe Siri of Genoa. Monsignor Dante, a prelate *di mantelletta* and protonotary de numero, assists a cardinal who kneels in homage before Paul VI. The row of seated cardinals is significant in that the election of 1963 was the last in which the collapsible canopies were used. These were later abolished by Pauline *motu proprio. Courtesy Carlo Bavagnoli.*

PLATE 7. Pope John Paul II places the cardinalatial ring on the finger of a newly named cardinal in November, 1994. The pope's throne is placed across the entrance to the tomb of St. Peter known as the *Confessio. Courtesy Arturo Mari.*

PLATE 8. Cardinals gather in St. Peter's Basilica to concelebrate Mass with Pope John Paul II. Each is vested in the tallest of mitres—the *damasco* or damasked mitre, which is required of them in the pope's presence. In the background is the Swiss Guard Halberdier who wears the black, semi-formal morion (headdress) with red plumage. *Courtesy Arturo Mari.*

PLATE 9. The beautiful red and yellow flowers contrast the purple vestment of the chasuble of the cardinals concelebrating Mass with Pope John Paul II. *Courtesy Arturo Mari.*

PLATE 10. Before the *Pietà*, Michelangelo's magnificent sculpture of the lifeless Christ in His Mother's lap, the Holy Father, Pope John Paul II, gathers around him the newly named members of the Sacred College, November, 1994. *Courtesy Arturo Mari.*

PLATE 11. Seated before Pericle Fazzini's sculpture of the *Risen Christ* in the Paul VI audience hall, John Paul II presents the first of his discourses to the new cardinals. *Courtesy Arturo Mari.*

PLATE 12. A close study of this photograph illustrates topics discussed in *The Church Visible.* During the Mass of the Rings of the consistory of June 29, 1991, one can see those prelates known as metropolitan archbishops, those members of the hierarchy responsible for larger areas and peoples. They gather here to receive the *pallium.* In the next row, standing behind them, are those cardinals present in Rome. Then appear senior members of the Curia,

archbishops and bishops, and their assistants. To the right stand two bishops dressed in the *riasa* and *kamilauka* of the Oriental rite. *Courtesy Arturo Mari.*

PLATE 13. Roger Cardinal Mahony arrives at his titular church, Ss. Quattro Coronati, to take canonical or legal possession. As he enters, he is vested in choir dress. He later will vest in sacred vestments to celebrate his first Mass as titular protector of this church and her faithful. His Eminence venerates the crucifix presented to him by a local bishop. Behind the cardinal is Archbishop Justin Rigali, now archbishop of St. Louis, Missouri, who is a native of Los Angeles, California. *Courtesy Arturo Mari.*

PLATE 14. Roger Cardinal Mahony, archbishop of Los Angeles, signs the notary document transferring titular title of the church, Ss. Quattro Coronati, to him after taking formal possession of this church during consistory week, June, 1991. *Courtesy Arturo Mari.*

PLATE 15. Dignitaries of the Church and state officials gather for a moment of relaxation in the Vatican gardens to honor Angelo Cardinal Sodano on the occasion of his elevation to the Sacred College, June, 1991. *Courtesy Arturo Mari.*

PLATE 16. Three old friends gather in the Belvedere gardens near the Vatican museums to celebrate the elevation of Cardinal Sodano to the Sacred College, June, 1991. At right, Cardinal Sodano talks with Cardinal Casaroli, center, who preceded Cardinal Sodano in the office of Secretary of State. The much beloved Dean of the College of Cardinals, Bernardin Cardinal Gantin, appears at left. *Courtesy Arturo Mari.*

PLATE 17. Cardinals present in Rome are presented to the Orthodox Ecumenical Patriarch Bartholomew I during his three-day visit to Pope John Paul II, June, 1995. Cardinal Sodano makes each presentation. Partially hidden is the Dean of the College, Cardinal Gantin. Following him are the remaining cardinal-bishops including Cardinals Casa-roli and Ratzinger. Also visible are Cardinals Baum and Keeler of the United States. *Courtesy Arturo Mari.*

PLATE 18. Colonel Alois Estermann leads his regiment in salute to the Holy Father as he enters the great balcony above the portals of St. Peter's Basilica. Estermann, a Swiss national, is well known at the Vatican for his fidelity, as well as his profes-sionalism. The commander is vested in the ceremo-nial dress uniform of his rank, including maroon tunic and knee breeches. It is this color that the ear-liest Swiss Guards employed for their uniform. The commander also wears the star of the Order of St. Gregory (partially hidden) and the neck ribbon of a Commander of the Pian Order. In the background, before the Bernini colonnade, are Italian police also serving as Guard of Honor to Pope John Paul II on Christmas morning. *Courtesy Arturo Mari.*

PLATE 19. On parade each Christmas and Easter morning, the Swiss Guard regiment at the Vatican dons its ceremonial dress uniform. Carrying the halberd, or spear-like staff, which gives the guards-men their official title *Halberdiers,* this uniform also includes the white gorget and the white (known as gray) morion with red ostrich plumage. Those who have been in service for some time may receive the papal decorations of the *Cross Pro Ecclesia et Pontifice* and the *Benemerenti Medal,* award of which must be earned. *Courtesy Arturo Mari.*

PLATE 20. Snapped to attention at the arrival of a visiting head of state in the San Damasco Court-yard of the Apostolic Palace, the regiment of Swiss Guards in full ceremonial dress salutes the official visitors. Each guardsman carries a concealed firearm for use if the need arises. *Courtesy Arturo Mari.*

PLATE 21. On Christmas and Easter mornings, as well as during the many events surrounding the death, burial, and election of popes, the Italian Presidential Guard is dispatched to Vatican City as a sign of respect and deference by the Italian govern-ment. Their magnificent uniforms, complete with red and blue plumed tricorn hats for the regiment, and red and blue swan feathers on a bicorn cap for the officers, are most impressive. When they appear in St. Peter's Square with blue capes thrown over the shoulder to reveal a red lining, the crowds burst into applause at the sight of a military display from a bygone era. *Courtesy Arturo Mari.*

PLATE 22. October, 1978: The pope and cardi-nals gather in the Sistine Chapel to concelebrate the first mass of the pontificate of John Paul II. The newly elected pope mandated that the conclave continue for an additional day following election so that he and the cardinals could make a spiritual retreat together. *Courtesy UPI/Bettmann Archives.*

PLATE 23. In 1978, Pope John Paul I felt some-what overburdened by the thought of the cere-monies attached to a papal coronation and therefore sought a more simplified installation ceremony. Fol-lowing the investiture with the *pallium* of universal jurisdiction, the pontiff received each of the cardi-nals for the exchange of the Kiss of Peace. Seen here, John Paul I had a warm word of thanks and a prayer for each cardinal who approached the seated pope. One month later, John Paul II repeated the simpler ceremony while he reminded the Church that the more historic coronation had not been abolished and could properly return in the future. *Courtesy Fotografia Felici.*

PLATE 24. The Mass of the Rings in St. Peter's Square, June 29, 1991. From the main balcony is hung the tapestry bearing the present pope's coat of arms. The white central section bearing the arms is replaced after each papal election to depict the new pope's arms. Below is the throne of the pope, who is flanked on either side by the newly named cardi-nals awaiting the presentation of their cardinalatial rings. In the forefront is the altar. To each side, the new archbishops await the gift of the *pallium*. To the left appear the Curia cardinals, archbishops and bishops, priests, and seminarians. To the right appear the diplomatic corps accredited to the Holy See. *Courtesy Arturo Mari.*

PLATE 25. Jacques Cardinal Martin, Prefect-Emeritus of the Papal Household, and one of the closest associates of Pope John Paul II, lies in repose inside his Vatican apartment. Within one hour of death, the Holy Father came to pray at his friend's bier. Here, he blesses the deceased. Out of respect, the Holy Father removes his own *zucchetto* (skull-cap). The cardinal is properly vested in the damask mitre, the scarlet choir cassock, stockings, and *zuchetto*. He is vested also in the purple chasuble reserved in burial for cardinals. The popes are buried in red and gold sacred vestments. *Courtesy Arturo Mari.*

PLATE 26. New Year's Address: Each January, the Holy Father receives all those diplomats accredited to the Holy See, who present to him their collective greetings and good wishes. Likewise, the Holy Father uses this gathering as an opportunity to inform the world's politicians of his feelings and his plans for the coming year. Here, the Dean of the Diplomatic Corps at the Holy See presents the address to Pope John Paul II. *Courtesy Arturo Mari.*

PLATE 27. Her Majesty Elizabeth II and HRH the Duke of Edinburgh pay a state visit to Pope John Paul II. This was the queen's third visit to the Apostolic Palace. Her Majesty and the duke wear state ceremonial dress. Although a queen, Elizabeth is not entitled to wear white as she is not a Roman Catholic. The *privilège du blanc* is reserved to Catholic queens and the Grand Duchess of Luxembourg. Greeting the queen in the San Damasco Square are the lay officials of the Papal Household, including Gentlemen of His Holiness. *Courtesy Arturo Mari.*

PLATE 28. President and Mrs. Ronald Reagan during their state visit to the Vatican. Mrs. Reagan,

although not a Catholic, exhibited much respect for Vatican traditions by donning a full-length black dress and black lace mantilla. *Courtesy Arturo Mari.*

PLATE 29. During one of their last joint foreign tours, the Prince and Princess of Wales pay a visit to the Holy Father, who welcomed them both warmly in the private library of the pope's formal apartments. *Courtesy Arturo Mari.*

PLATE 30. Papal Household officials escort the Grand Duke and Duchess of Luxembourg and their entourage through St. Peter's Square to the diplomatic seating area for the installation Mass of John Paul I, September, 1978. *Courtesy Fotografia Felici.*

PLATE 31. The present Prefect of the Papal Household, Bishop Dino Monduzzi, with the official household staff of the pope. Shown here at the courtyard entrance at Castel Gandolfo, the pope's summer residence, the bishop is flanked by the Gentlemen of His Holiness in their chain of office and various orders and decorations. *Courtesy Arturo Mari.*

PLATE 32. Pope John Paul II signs all bulls that bear his name, such as nominations to the Sacred College, canonizations, promotions to the episcopacy, creation of new dioceses, and so on. These documents are richly illustrated and have great historic value. *Courtesy Arturo Mari.*

PLATE 33. The Secretary of State signs, on behalf of the pontiff, all concordats or treaties with Catholic nations and heads of state. Here, Cardinal Casaroli signs a concordat with the minister of the prince of Monaco. This concordat was sealed between the Holy See and the Principality of Monaco, a Catholic sovereign state. *Courtesy Arturo Mari.*

PLATE 34. This photograph illustrates the proper method of wearing a nonpapal decoration of the highest class, the Grand Cross for ecclesiastics. Often churchmen are called to accept and wear civil decorations and orders. Properly, the sash should be worn beneath the cape of the simar, not over it. The pectoral cross should be placed above the ribbon, as well. The star, or plaque, of the order (not shown) can be worn pinned to the cape of the simar. *Courtesy Arturo Mari.*

PLATE 35. This photograph illustrates the presentation of a lesser civil decoration upon a cleric. The rank of commander is worn around the neck while the star, or plaque, of the order is worn at the chest. *Courtesy Arturo Mari.*

PLATE 36. The entrance into the conclave of 1958, which resulted in the election of Angelo Roncalli, John XXIII, included a cardinal-elector; his personal secretary, wearing the traditional *ferraiolo;* and an officer of the now-abolished papal Noble Guard with his unique uniform and helmet. *Courtesy Fotografia Felici.*

PLATE 37. The Prince Assistant to the Papal Throne and Master of the Conclave (titles now abolished) locks the outer doors of the conclave area at the same moment that the predecessor of the title of Prefect of the Papal Household locks the inner doors. A wax seal and ribbon was placed across each lock to assure security during the days of conclave. The prince's costume, a vestige of the Papal Court, is on display at the Lateran Palace Papal Court Museum. *Courtesy Fotografia Felici.*

PLATE 38. As seen in other photographs of the conclave of 1958, the entrance into conclave included a Noble Guard officer and the priest-secretary of the cardinal. This image best illustrates the now-abolished ceremonial *fascia,* which included a gold tuft, for cardinals and the simple rochet of mourning (not to be confused with the simple surplice) appropriate for the period of *Sede Vacante. Courtesy Fotografia Felici.*

PLATE 39. Preparing for voting, the Master of Ceremonies and other court officials speak to the cardinals as they begin the scrutiny preparation for the conclave of 1958. *Courtesy Fotografia Felici.*

PLATE 40. The arms of Pope John Paul II as designed by Archbishop Bruno B. Heim. All papal arms include the tiara and the crossed keys, which mark the pope's legal and spiritual authority over the Church of Christ. The shield of John Paul II is unique in that it breaks with heraldic tradition by utilizing the initial, "M," rather than one of the Marian symbols to represent Our Blessed Mother. Pope John Paul II insisted on keeping this design which he used as cardinal-archbishop of Cracow. The off-center golden cross is symbolic of Christ's Own Cross and the "M" is so placed not only to bring honor to the Mother of God, but also to show how she faithfully stood at the foot of the cross on Calvary. *Courtesy Carl Alexander von Volborth/New Orchard Editions/Villiers House and Archbishop Bruno B. Heim.*

PLATE 41. The arms of Albino Luciani, who served the Church as Pope John Paul I for twenty-eight days in 1978. In chief (the top third of the shield and the place of honor) is the Lion of St. Mark, which was included in this pontiff's arms as he came to the papacy as Patriarch of Venice, the See of St. Mark. The shield proper depicts the symbolic terrain of the pope's mountain home in Northern Italy. *Courtesy Secretariat of State, Vatican City.*

PLATE 42. Paul VI preferred an Italianate-style shield in red. The charges (a term used to describe images upon the shield) that he chose for his arms were likewise symbolic. The six cones represent mountains, a play on his family name of Montini and his origins from the north of Italy. The fleurs-de-lis are symbolic of Our Lady, and, by the specific choice of three, also symbolic of the Blessed Trinity. Paul VI insisted upon the artistic depiction of the actual tiara presented to him by the people of Milan, from where he came to the papacy, which was indeed most unique in design. After the ceremonies marking his coronation, Paul VI sent the tiara to the United States. It is now on permanent display at the Basilica of the National Shrine of the Immaculate Conception in Washington, D.C. *Courtesy Secretariat of State, Vatican City.*

PLATE 43. The arms chosen by John XXIII for himself were designed by his secretary, then Monsignor Bruno B. Heim, who worked alongside the pontiff when he served as nuncio to Paris. John XXIII had definite ideas about his coat of arms and took great care in its design. In chief is the Lion of St. Mark, as he too came to the papacy as Partiarch of Venice. The shield proper is a mixture of symbolism of family, origin, and faith. The tiara shown here is likewise a realistic interpretation of the actual tiara preferred by John XXIII. *Courtesy Secretariat of State, Vatican City.*

PLATE 44. Because of the length of the pontificate of Pius XII, there are many renditions of this pope's arms available for study. This particular example is noteworthy for its beauty and style. The arms of Pius XII were the last to follow the artistic treatment popular from the High Rennaissance until the Second Vatican Council. The charges (figures/symbols) are depicted realistically, rather then symbolically. With its ornate border and embellishments, the shield also reflects an earlier age. As in the cases of Paul VI and John XXIII, the tiara depicted here is an actual representation of the one preferred by Pius XII. There are several styles available, most of them now housed in the Papal Treasury. *Courtesy Secretariat of State, Vatican City.*

PLATE 45. The tiara and crossed keys are the emblem of authority of the Roman Curia, as well as the adopted symbol of affinity with Rome. Heraldically, the tiara represents the authority of the popes: militant, penitent, and triumphant. It also has been said to represent their universal episcopate, jurisdictional supremacy, and temporal power. The two keys represent Peter, who was given them by Christ, and the power they hold over Heaven and earth. This device has seen many artistic representations through the centuries. *Courtesy Maria-Helena Bedoya/Maria Mocnik.*

PLATE 46. The pontifical (red and gold) *ombrellino* is the emblem of the basilicas. When it appears above and behind the cross keys of the Holy See, together these form the legal seal of the interregnum, a period between popes known as the *Sede Vacante*. This emblem appears during *Sede Vacante* on the postage stamps, coins, and letterhead of the Holy See. *Courtesy Carl Alexander von Volborth/New Orchard Editions/Villiers House.*

PLATE 47. The arms of His Eminence Pio Cardinal Laghi are a fine example of modern heraldic, ecclesiastical art. In particular, note the treatment and design of the cardinalatial *galero*. The hat is Italian in design and appears fuller than those used in North American coats of arms. It offers a balance to the overall achievement. The placement of the *fiocchi*, so as to begin at the top of the shield and to fall just to the curve of the shield's base, adds to this balance. The motto is depicted in the modern style without an actual ribbon. Behind the cardinal's shield is the jewelled archiepiscopal cross with two crossbars. The charge in chief (that is, the emblem in the place of honor) is the symbol of the cardinal's home. The shield proper includes a scarlet maunch, representing a cardinal's arm, holding a full fishing net over an open sea to represent the scriptural phrase that bishops are to be "fishers of men." The lake is also representational of the cardinal's surname. *Courtesy Pio Cardinal Laghi.*

PLATE 48. The arms of His Eminence John Cardinal Krol, while still archbishop of Philadelphia. The arms of the cardinal depicted here include those of the archdiocese of Philadelphia in a method known as marshalling, or the joining of both personal and diocesan arms. Although seen more commonly today than not, this practice is not mandatory and, in fact, is rare outside the United States. The flat *galero* is the style preferred by American heraldic artists. *Courtesy Alex Garey.*

PLATE 49. The arms of a patriarch comprise his personal shield (or heraldic device), the archiepiscopal cross behind the shield, the *galero* of green with two green *fiocchi* at the brim, and fifteen green *fiocchi* on either side of the shield in rows of one, two, three, four, and five. Since ca. 1850 gold thread has appeared in patriarchal arms intertwined in the green cording and the *fiocchi*. There are no legal grounds for this embellishment, however. *Courtesy Carl Alexander von Volborth / New Orchard Editions / Villiers House.*

PLATE 50. The arms of archbishops, both residential and titular, consist of the shield or personal armoral device of the prelate placed upon the archiepiscopal cross. Ensigned above the cross and shield is a *galero* of green with two green *fiocchi* at the brim and ten green *fiocchi* suspended from green cords on either side of the shield. The cords emanate from the brim in as elaborate a fashion as is desired by both the bearer and the artist. Unlike patriarchs, no gold thread can be utilized in the cording and *fiocchi* of archbishops. *Courtesy Carl Alexander von Volborth / New Orchard Editions / Villiers House.*

PLATE 51. It has become more prevalent in the second part of this century to depict an archbishop's or bishop's arms without the use of the *galero*. It is forbidden to depict a cardinal's and a patriarch's arms without the *galero*, as the *galero* and appropriate *fiocchi* alone identify the bearer's rank. Archbishops and bishops, residential and titular, however, can lay aside the *galero* if they so choose because the archiepiscopal and the episcopal crosses behind the shield properly identify the bearer's rank. One of the finest examples of this style of heraldic design is the arms of Archbishop Bruno B. Heim, renowned heraldist, Church diplomat, and author whose family arms appear placed upon the archiepiscopal cross of his rank in the Church. *Courtesy Archbishop Bruno B. Heim.*

PLATE 52. The arms of a bishop, both residential and titular, are depicted with a shield or personal armoral device of the bearer over a jewelled episcopal cross of one crossbar. Ensigned above the cross and shield is the episcopal *galero* of green with two green *fiocchi* at the brim. Emanating from inside the brim is cording of green in as elaborate a fashion as desired, terminating on either side of the shield in six green *fiocchi*. *Courtesy Carl Alexander von Volborth / New Orchard Editions / Villiers House.*

PLATE 53. The arms of an abbot, and those of provosts, replace the archiepiscopal or episcopal cross with the veiled (*studarium*) crozier. At one time, like cardinals, archbishops and bishops, the abbots and provosts were entitled to the mitre along with the crozier and *galero*. Use of the mitre for all persons has been abolished (although it is still permitted for the arms of dioceses). While the mitre and crozier have been abolished for all other ranks, the crozier is permitted to abbots and provosts. However, it must appear as veiled. In place of the mitre is the black *galero*, identical to that of bishops in all respects but color. Black is required for abbots and provosts. *Courtesy Carl Alexander von Volborth / New Orchard Editions / Villiers House.*

PLATE 54. The arms of the abbot nullius and prelate nullius of the hierarchy are depicted as a mix between bishops and abbots. The color of the *galero* and the number and placement of the *fiocchi* are the same as for bishops. In place of the episcopal cross, however, is the veiled crozier reserved for abbots, provosts, abbots nullius, and prelates nullius. *Courtesy Carl Alexander von Volborth / New Orchard Editions / Villiers House.*

PLATE 55. The posts in the former Papal Court that carried with them the honorific *Prelates di Fiocchetto,* because of their high rank within the Vatican hierarchy, have been abolished. These four high offices of the Curia, including Vice Chamberlain or Vice Camerlengo, did not carry with them the rank of episcopal dignity, yet, because these posts were sufficiently important, additional awards of vesture and heraldry were granted. For the *prelates di fiocchetto,* so called because one of their perks was the grant of red *fiocchi* on the livery of their horses to distinguish them from other honorary prelates, a special *galero* of violet was provided. On the brim were two scarlet *fiocchi.* Emanating from inside the crown of the hat in a fanciful style were scarlet cords that terminated in ten scarlet *fiocchi* on either side of the shield. Because of their beauty, heraldic authors continue to identify this special heraldic design. It must be clear that this privilege and the posts to which it was attached were abolished in 1969 by Paul VI. *Courtesy Carl Alexander von Volborth / New Orchard Editions / Villiers House.*

PLATE 56. Protonotary apostolic (de numero and supranumerary): Now the highest class of the honorary prelature, the protonotaries apostolic retain some heraldic privileges, the foremost among these being the grant of the violet *galero* with scarlet cording and *fiocchi.* Only six *fiocchi* are suspended on either side of the bearer's shield. *Courtesy Carl Alexander von Volborth / New Orchard Editions / Villiers House.*

PLATE 57. Prelates of Honor of His Holiness are ensigned by a violet *galero* with violet cords and *fiocchi.* Six *fiocchi* are suspended on either side of the bearer's shield. All clerics have the right to depict membership in either the Sovereign Order of Malta or the Equestrian Order of the Holy Sepulchre of Jerusalem, if appropriate. The proper method for the inclusion of these orders is discussed in Chapter 10. *Courtesy Carl Alexander von Volborth / New Orchard Editions / Villiers House.*

PLATE 58. One of the loveliest heraldic attributes granted to the clergy is the ensign of the black *galero* with violet cords and *fiocchi* of the class, Chaplains of

His Holiness. The contrast between the black velvet hat and the clerical violet is very impressive. Sadly, because so few priests realize that it is their privilege to adopt and bear arms, those who receive the lowest title of honorary prelature seldom realize that this privilege has been granted to them by many successive popes. To this class, six violet *fiocchi* are suspended on either side of the shield in rows of one, two, and three. *Courtesy Carl Alexander von Volborth / New Orchard Editions / Villiers House.*

PLATE 59. Canons maintain many privileges due them by their special position and by virtue of the bull of appointment, which often included a grant of still further privileges. Therefore, the arms of canons seen in archives of the Church and of local dioceses, or on grave markers in ancient churches, tend to vary without rhyme or reason. As a general rule, the popes granted a black *galero* with three black *fiocchi* suspended on either side of the shield. Because of the common practice of promoting canons of prestigious basilicas to a higher title simultaneously, one will also see a "canon's arms" depicted with the *galero* and *fiocchi* of apostolic protonotaries or of another high office. The artistic representation of the *fiocchi* seen here is acceptable, of course, yet the more formal design is more prevalent. *Courtesy Carl Alexander von Volborth / New Orchard Editions / Villiers House.*

PLATE 60. The arms of deans, vicars forane, and vicars episcopal, jurisdictional posts of the Church, are ensigned by a black *galero,* black cords, and two black *fiocchi* suspended on either side. Artists have depicted these either one on top of the other or side by side. It is the choice of the heraldic artist and the bearer to design placement of the two *fiocchi.* *Courtesy Carl Alexander von Volborth / New Orchard Editions / Villiers House.*

PLATE 61. The arms of a priest are ensigned by a black *galero* with two black *fiocchi* on the brim and one *fiocchi* suspended on either side of the shield.

Heraldic artists have had great fun attempting to glamorize priests' arms. Some depict the cords longer with many twists and turns, while others depict them more simply. Either is correct so long as the design follows custom and form and so long as the bearer is pleased by the final result.

N.B.: No heraldic treatment has been devised for permanent deacons, although such directive will need eventually to be laid down. Perhaps a black *galero* devoid of *fiocchi,* both on the brim and below, would suffice as the heraldic representation of this office in Holy Orders. *Courtesy James-Charles Noonan, Jr. / S. Buchanon.*

PLATE 62. The arms of the present Prince Grand Master of the Sovereign Order of St. John of Jerusalem, Rhodes, and Malta, Fra Andrew W. Bertie. The personal arms of His Highness appear quartered with those of the order: the order's arms appear in the first and fourth quarters and the prince's in the second and the third. The shield rests on the insignia of the order, the white Maltese cross. Encircling the shield, intertwining with the arms of the cross, is the Grand Master's chain of office from which hangs the cross of the order in miniature. The entire achievement is placed below a mantle of black ermine-lined velvet and the Grand Magistral crown. *Courtesy Grand Magistral Palace, the Order of Malta.*

PLATE 63. The arms of the Sovereign Order, its official seal, is quite similar to that of the Prince Grand Master. It differs in that the shield of the order, a field of red with a white cross, stands alone. The shield is mounted on the Maltese cross, surrounded by a white rosary. In place of the traditional crucifix, it terminates in a white Maltese cross. Behind the achievement are four military banners (*drapeau*) of the order. *Courtesy Grand Magistral Palace, the Order of Malta.*

PLATE 64. The arms of the Grand Master of the Equestrian Order of the Holy Sepulchre of Jerusalem, His Eminence Giuseppe Cardinal Caprio.

Depicted here in monochrome, this is the proper representation of a cardinal's arms when not reproducing a cardinal's heraldic device in full color. The cardinal quarters his arms with those of the order. The use of this design of Roman *galero* illustrates another beautiful style, which also connotes elegance and balance. This design of *galero* is, however, more akin to the present day *cappello romano* than the original pilgrim's hat. Nevertheless, it is quite beautiful. The cardinal's personal motto appears on a scroll at the base of the device while his title and the name of the order itself appear in Latin below, complementing the overall balance to the heraldic achievement. *Courtesy of Giuseppe Cardinal Caprio.*

PLATE 65. The arms of the Equestrian Order of the Holy Sepulchre of Jerusalem are elegant in their simplicity. The shield is white (silver) with only one charge (or symbol)—the blood-red Jerusalem cross, the emblem of the order. Above the shield is ensigned a golden helmet with a breastplate of gold, likewise marked with a red cross. The helmet is wreathed in laurel of natural colors. Behind the shield are two white banners, each bearing a red cross, unfurled upon crossed staffs. The achievement is supported by two angels robed in red and blue dalmatics, one carrying a pastoral staff, the other a banner. The order's motto: *Deus Lo Vult,* God Wills It, appears below on an Italianate scroll. *Courtesy Grand Magistral Palace, the Equestrian Order of the Holy Sepulchre of Jerusalem.*

PLATE 66. A simple knight of the Order of the Holy Sepulchre can depict one's membership heraldically by the placement of the ribbon and insignia of the order (and that of Malta) below the shield. One may also chose to depict membership by placing the cross of either order (or both, if a member of both) alongside the shield or in close proximity to it. The senior classes of each order have unique privileges in regard to the heraldry, discussed in Chapter 10. *Courtesy James-Charles Noonan, Jr./S. Buchanon.*

PLATE 67A. Although reminiscent of the diplomatic dress of a past era, the uniform of the Knights of the Collar of the Order of Christ, the highest order that a pope can bestow, is rarely seen in modern times. This is because the honor is reserved for Catholic kings who, while visiting the Vatican, normally prefer to wear the official dress or uniform of their native countries. This rare award carries with it, however, the privilege of this Napoleonic-era uniform. There are no living recipients of this honor, the last being Baudouin I, King of the Belgians. *Courtesy Archives of the Secretariat of State, Vatican City.*

PLATE 67B. The grand collar of the Supreme Order of Christ is composed of two gold filigree chains joined together by alternating filigree knots and white enamel medallions upon which are emblazoned the papal tiara and crossed keys. The badge of the order, a distinct white enameled red-and gold-trimmed cross, is suspended below a full military trophy and golden cannons. *Courtesy Archives of the Secretariat of State, Vatican City.*

PLATE 68A. Like the Knights of the Collar of the Supreme Order of Christ, Knights of the Order of the Golden Spur are most commonly heads of state and therefore make little use of the uniform which has gone unchanged in two hundred years. The tunic is deep red with two rows of gold buttons on which is emblazoned the insignia of the order. The trousers are black with gold military stripes. Napoleonic epaulets, sword, and chapeau complete the uniform. *Courtesy Archives of the Secretariat of State, Vatican City.*

PLATE 68B. At one time the insignia of the order consisted of an eight-point gold enameled cross suspended from a ribbon of red and silver moiré silk. After the Lateran Treaty (1929), the golden collar was substituted for the ribbon. The central medallion of the badge is white enamel with the crowned monogram of the Mother of God. Below the bottom arm of the cross is suspended the golden spur. *Courtesy Archives of the Secretariat of State, Vatican City.*

PLATE 69A. The impressive uniform of the Knight Grand Cross of the Order of Pius IX is still widely worn at the Vatican and in the dioceses of the world. Its design is that of the nineteenth-century diplomatic dress. Blue in color, the uniform is made entirely of wool with the exception of the collar and cuffs which are worked in gold leaf on embroidered red velvet. The trousers have a gold-threaded military stripe on the outside leg. The degree of embroidery depends on the rank of the honoree. Grand Cross, seen here, includes a gold leaf motif on the breast, the waist, and tailcoat. A sword and chapeau complete the uniform. *Courtesy Archives of the Secretariat of State, Vatican City.*

PLATE 69B. The insignia of the order is not done justice in photographs and illustrations. It should be seen personally so as to appreciate fully the craftmanship and vivid color of this award. The insignia consists of an eight-rayed blue enamel star. Between each ray are gold flames. On the central medallion of white enamel is the monogram of the order's founder, Pius IX. A gold circle closes the medallion, upon which appears the motto of the order. The ribbon is midnight blue with two red stripes toward each end. Here, one sees the ribbon of the rank, Grand Cross. *Courtesy Archives of the Secretariat of State, Vatican City.*

PLATE 70A. The uniform of the Knights of St. Gregory the Great is a fixture both in Rome and in the local Church. It is based on the diplomatic costume of the late nineteenth and early twentieth centuries. The tailcoat and trousers are made of deep green wool with silver embroidery, the degree of which depends on the rank of the honoree. The motif is oak leaf. A plumed silk hat, gloves, and sword complete the uniform. *Courtesy Archives of the Secretariat of State, Vatican City.*

PLATE 70B. The ribbon of the order is distinctive: red moiré silk with edges of yellow silk. The badge of the order is an eight-point red enamel cross with gold balls at the tip of each point. The central medallion consists of blue enamel, upon which appears the image of St. Gregory the Great in gold. Surrounding the image is a circle of gold, upon which is worked the order's motto: *Pro Deo et Principe*, For God and Prince. *Courtesy Archives of the Secretariat of State, Vatican City.*

PLATE 71A. The style of uniform for the Order of Pope St. Sylvester is identical to those of the orders of Pius IX and St. Gregory the Great in all but color and decorative motif. The cloth used for this uniform in known as "Sylvester" black, a deep black. The motif is oak leaf but worked in gold; the degree of elaborateness depends on the rank of the honoree. A sword, silk chapeau, and gloves complete the uniform. *Courtesy Archives of the Secretariat of State, Vatican City.*

PLATE 71B. The ribbon of the Order of Pope St. Sylvester is recognizable by its number of stripes and color scheme. Black in composition, a red central stripe and two red borders create an image of red, black, red, black, red. The insignia comprises a white enamel eight-point cross. Between each arm appears a golden flame. On a field of midnight blue enamel appears the effigy of the order's patron, St. Sylvester, worked in gold. Encircling this effigy is the name of the order worked in gold. *Courtesy Archives of the Secretariat of State, Vatican City.*

PLATE 72. On parade in St. Peter's Square, an officer of the Pontifical Swiss Guard is seen wearing both the *Cross Pro Ecclesia et Pontifice* and the *Benemerenti Medal*. Both are suspended from the colors of the Vatican City State, gold and silver (yellow and white). Paul VI preferred the modernistic representation of the Greek cross, so the design was changed

from a more traditional military cross. The larger of the two insignia seen here is the *Cross Pro Ecclesia,* the smaller being the *Benemerenti Medal.* The basic design for both awards has remained the same since Paul VI's pontificate. However, in each pontificate, the seal and name of the reigning pope replaces that of his predecessor. One can, therefore, receive these awards from successive popes. *Courtesy Arturo Mari.*

PLATE 73. Awaiting the arrival of the pope at the Wednesday general audience at the Paul VI Audience Hall, the lay dignitaries of the Papal Household, known as Gentlemen of His Holiness, are seen dressed in *tenue pontificale,* including the distinctive chain of office and other Church and civil awards. The conferral of the title, Gentleman of His Holiness, carries with it the privilege of attending to the pope for one week (or more) each year. *Courtesy Arturo Mari.*

PLATE 74. On the afternoon following his installation as pope, Pope John Paul I received Their Serene Highnesses Rainier III, Prince of Monaco, and his late wife, Princess Grace. The royal couple were always welcome visitors at the Vatican. Here, the late pope presents gifts to the prince and princess. On the table are the gifts of the princely family to the newly elected pope. Princess Grace is dressed in a full-length black dress and mantilla. Although a Catholic princess, she was not entitled to the *privilège du blanc.* She wears the Order of St. Charles (partially visible), Monaco's highest award and one of the most beautiful in the world. The sovereign prince wears *tenue pontificale.* In addition to the miniatures of all the awards he has been given during his reign (Prince Rainier is one of the most highly decorated persons alive), he wears two chains: the collar of the Golden Spur of the Holy See and the collar of the Grand Master of the Order of St. Charles of Monaco. *Courtesy Fotografia Felici.*

PLATE 75. Their Serene Highnesses Rainier III, Sovereign Prince of Monaco, and Albert, Crown

Prince, after the *Te Deum* marking Monaco's national day. Prince Rainier wears the star of the Order of the Golden Spur. He is one of the few living recipients of the second-highest papal order and is never seen in official dress without it. His other insignia include the collar of the Grand Master of the Order of St. Charles (the principality's highest honor), the star of Grand Officer of the French Legion of Honor, and numerous military campaign medals. Prince Albert wears the sash and star of the Grand Cross of the Order of St. Charles and the star of the Legion of Honor. He is also a member of the orders of Malta and the Holy Sepulchre. *Courtesy Palais-Princier de Monaco.*

PLATE 76. Also on the afternoon following his installation as pope, John Paul I met with the heads of state and royal guests who had gathered in Rome to witness the ceremonies marking his election to the papacy. Here, the late King Baudouin I of Belguim (a much loved and respected figure by the Vatican) is seen wearing the grand collar and star of the Order of Christ. Because he held many ranks in the military of his own nation, Baudouin did not make use of the ceremonial uniform of the Order of Christ. *Courtesy Fotografia Felici.*

PLATE 77. The king and queen of Spain meet with Pope John Paul II shortly after his installation, October, 1978. Queen Sofia wears the *privelège du blanc* and the *Cross Pro Ecclesia et Pontifice* and the Spanish Order of Carlos III. Juan Carlos I, although entitled to the Order of Christ, has not as yet received it. He wears the grand collar and star of the Order of Pius IX. *Courtesy Fotografia Felici.*

PLATE 78. The President of Italy, Oscar Luigi Scalfaro (center), introduces a noble and Knight Grand Cross of the Order of Pius IX, seen here in the insignia and uniform of that order, to His Holiness, Pope John Paul II, during a general audience at the Vatican. President Scalfaro is seen wearing the grand collar of the Order of Pius IX and the grand cross of the Order of Merit of Italy. One can see in this photograph the degree of embroidery on the uniform of the rank, Grand Cross. *Courtesy Arturo Mari.*

PLATE 79. In 1991, Pope John Paul II decreed that women are entitled to membership in all classes of three pontifical orders. Here, the secretary for the Rapport with the States of the Vatican Secretariat of State, His Excellency, the Most Reverend Archbishop Jean-Louis Tauran, presents the insignia of dame commander to Her Royal Highness, Princess Françoise de Lobkowicz at the Apostolic Nunciature in Paris, March 21, 1995.

N.B.: It might be suggested that as women are now honored by all classes of the papal orders of Pius IX, St. Gregory the Great, and Pope Saint Sylvester, a proper uniform consistent with the history of the vesture of these orders should be decreed. It is suggested that the cue be taken from the habit changes of the Academie Française. The *habit vert,* as it is called, retained the tunic for female honorees but substituted a full-length skirt for the trousers. The Holy See might follow this prescription for female recipients of the pontifical orders. A second option is the mandate of *tenue pontificale:* black mantilla, full-length black dress, and black gloves, along with the insignia of the order awarded. *Courtesy His Serene Highness Prince Edouard de Lobkowicz.*

PLATE 80. His Most Eminent Highness, the Prince Grand Master of the Sovereign Order of St. John of Jerusalem, Rhodes, and Malta (the Knights of Malta), greets each of the guests at the ceremonies marking their national feast day. As Prince Grand Master, Fra Andrew Bertie is the senior knight of the order and makes use of a special tunic and collar. The ladies seen here wear *tenue pontificale,* that is, black full-length dress and mantilla, while the knights wear orders and decorations of various nations. *Courtesy Grand Magistral Palace, the Order of Malta.*

PLATE 81. The Villa Malta on the Aventine Hill is the smallest nation on earth, forming part of the properties of the Sovereign Order of Malta. Here the villa is seen from the gardens, the site of the annual St. John the Baptist feast day luncheon for diplomats and Churchmen. *Courtesy Grand Magistral Palace, the Order of Malta.*

PLATE 82. His Eminence Pio Cardinal Laghi, *patronus* of the order, with the senior Marquis Pallavicini at the the luncheon following the national day celebrations at the Villa Malta on the Aventine Hill. The Marquis Pallavicini wears the ceremonial uniform of a professed bailiff. Cardinal Laghi appears in scarlet cassock and additionally wears the collar of bailiff of the order. *Courtesy Grand Magistral Palace, the Order of Malta.*

PLATE 83. Bishop Donato de Bonis is seen here with the Grand Master and an African diplomat accredited to both the Sovereign Order and to the Holy See at the luncheon following the national day celebrations at Villa Malta on the Aventine Hill. *Courtesy of the Grand Magistral Palace, the Order of Malta.*

PLATE 84. Bishop Donato de Bonis, prelate of the Order of Malta, is seen here with a Knight Grand Cross of Justice at the ceremonies marking the order's national day, the feast of St. John the Baptist. Bishop de Bonis is vested in choir dress with the violet choir cassock, *fascia, mozzetta, zucchetto,* and the rochet. He also wears the collar of a Knight of Justice over his pectoral cross. The lay knight wears the ceremonial dress uniform of his rank in the order. *Courtesy Grand Magistral Palace, the Order of Malta.*

PLATE 85. His Eminence Giuseppe Cardinal Caprio, Grand Master of the Equestrian Order of the Holy Sepulchre of Jerusalem, seen here in his library at the order's headquarters in the sixteenth-century Palazzo dei Pentitenzieri on the via della Conciliazione, the grand boulevard leading into St. Peter's Square. His Eminence is vested in academic dress (*abito piano*) and also wears the collar of the office of Grand Master and the star of Grand Cross. For those prelates entitled to the star, or plaque, of

any order, this photo of Cardinal Caprio depicts the proper placement of the decoration. *Courtesy Grand Magistral Palace, the Equestrian Order of the Holy Sepulchre of Jerusalem.*

PLATE 86. Then regent of the Papal Household, Monsignor (now Bishop) Dino Monduzzi escorts the 77th Grand Master to pay his respects to the newly elected Pope John Paul I, September, 1978. Also escorting Prince Angelo Di Mojana is one of the papal Gentlemen of His Holiness seen wearing the much coveted chain of office of this Papal Household position. *Courtesy Fotografia Felici.*

PLATE 87. The uniform of the Knights of the Equestrian Order of the Holy Sepulchre consists of a black velvet breastplate embroidered with a gold oak leaf border, collar, and cuffs. The remainder of the dress uniform is made of creamy white wool and sports gold epaulets and striped trousers. Over the uniform, the knights wear a calf-length white mantle with the red Jerusalem cross emblazoned on the right shoulder. Knights also make use of a black beaver chapeau with red cochade and white plumes. A sword and spurs complete the official dress uniform. *Courtesy Rocco L. and Barbara Martino.*

PLATE 88A. A Knight Grand Cross of the Equestrian Order during the early nineteenth century. Seen here by Italian portraitist C. Sogni, the nobleman Alfredo Uboldo wears the formal dress uniform of the order, which has gone unchanged for two centuries. *Courtesy Rocco L. and Barbara Martino.*

PLATE 88B. The insignia of the Equestrian Order of the Holy Sepulchre of Jerusalem. The neck ribbon and insignia of the rank of commander, which includes the black silk moiré ribbon and the blood-red enamel Jerusalem cross (the emblem of the order), is suspended from a military trophy in gold, consisting of the cuirass emblazoned with the Jerusalem cross and six individual flags (known as colors), cannons, and a mace. A plumed helmet surmounts the trophy. There are two stars, or plaques, of the order: the rank of Grand Officer (center) and Grand Cross. *Courtesy Rocco L. and Barbara Martino.*

PLATE 89. This whimsical nineteenth-century painting, *Perplexed,* by Georges Croegaert Paris (1848–1920), actually presents an accurate study of the vesture of the Church common before the Second Vatican Council. From left to right: A Dominican, raised to the rank of bishop, retained the color of his order's habit but adopted the cassock and *mozzetta* (the simar had not been widely accepted as daily attire until the late 1900s). The *fascia* and trim are amaranth red. The Dominican prelate also received the French royal decoration of that era: The Holy Spirit. The cardinal next to him wears the choir cassock with train (as do all others). This train was abolished in 1969. A canon with the vestural privilege of ermine is seated behind the table. Beside him is seated an archbishop-nuncio who wears the golden tuft on the *fascia.* Only nuncios, cardinals, and patriarchs were permitted the golden tuft.

An archbishop appointed Assistant to the Papal Throne completes this arcane scene. Only the Assistants to the Papal Throne were entitled to purple watered silk vesture. In fact, that purple was much deeper in hue than all other archbishop's and bishop's vesture. The red Moroccan leather, silver buckled shoes have been abolished (1969). *Courtesy Kurt F. Schon, Ltd., New Orleans.*

PLATE 90. Pope John Paul II stands in the doorway of his study at Castel Gandolfo, the pope's summer residence in the Alban Hills southeast of Rome, awaiting the arrival of the Japanese imperial couple. This photo superbly illustrates papal vesture for everyday use: the white silk simar, the white watered silk *fascia* with gold fringe and papal arms in full-color representation (The pope is the only prelate of the Church permitted the inclusion of heraldry upon the *fascia.*), the gold pectoral cross suspended from the gold chain, and the white watered silk *zucchetto. Courtesy Arturo Mari.*

PLATE 91. A rare moment! In naming Anthony Bevilacqua to the office of cardinal, Pope John Paul II took the rare step in naming two living cardinals of the same see. Here, in the inner courtyard of the North American College in Rome, Anthony Cardinal Bevilacqua is congratulated by his immediate predecessor—the famous John Cardinal Krol. Both are properly vested in the simar, scarlet watered silk *fascia* and *zucchetto,* with the pectoral cross properly suspended from the chain. Cardinal Krol has always preferred a silken material in the manufacture of his simar. He is one of the few who still make use of the silk over the more common light wool. *Courtesy Arturo Mari.*

PLATE 92. On the morning of his elevation to the Sacred College, Angelo Cardinal Sodano meets with callers and well-wishers. Here, he embraces Giuseppe Cardinal Caprio, Grand Master of the Equestrian Order of the Holy Sepulchre of Jerusalem. Cardinal Sodano is vested in scarlet. It could not be said that he is vested "in choir" as this form of dress also requires the rochet and the *mozzetta.* Cardinal Caprio is vested in *abito piano,* or academic dress. *Courtesy Arturo Mari.*

PLATE 93. Angelo Cardinal Sodano, Secretary of State of His Holiness, on the day of his elevation to the Sacred College. Here, dressed in the scarlet choir cassock with watered silk cuffs and *fascia,* and a precious pectoral cross of sapphires and gold with the proper gold and scarlet silk cord, he greets a cardinal of the Oriental rite who is vested in the cardinalatial simar and the *scoufia* of the Oriental Church made of scarlet watered silk. *Courtesy Arturo Mari.*

PLATE 94. Bishops of the Catholic Church. This photograph, taken in 1992 in the Paul VI Audience Hall, depicts the archbishops and bishops present vested properly in choir dress. A close study illustrates the various forms of rochet. In particular, those seated in the first five rows make use of the green and gold cord for the pectoral cross proper for choir dress, while those behind them, vested in academic dress (or *abito piano*) properly make use of the chain. Although only one prelate can be seen carrying the *biretta,* choir dress still requires its use. *Courtesy Arturo Mari.*

PLATE 95. During an outdoor Mass in St. Peter's Square, Alfons Cardinal Stickler, former head of the Vatican Library, shown here as a bishop, vested in choir dress with *biretta,* takes a moment to untangle his rosary. The size of the *biretta's* tuft depends upon the manufacturer. In Rome they tend to be quite large, while in the United States they tend to be somewhat smaller. *Courtesy The National Geographic Society, photograph by James L. Stanfield.*

PLATE 96. During the ceremonies marking their rise to the Sacred College, November, 1994, five new cardinals stand for the Profession of Faith. Each is vested in choir dress proper to his rank. The *zucchetto* is not worn until the pope places both it and the "red hat," the cardinalatial *biretta,* on the head of each. A cardinal-designate from the Oriental rite of the Church stands at far left. Oriental rite choir dress consists of the scarlet choir cassock under a scarlet *riasa* over which falls the pectoral cross. Although the hood was abolished for the *mozzetta,* it was not for the *riasa.* This hood would be lowered before receiving the *zucchetto* and *biretta* at the hands of the pope. In the case of Oriental cardinal-designates, it is the scarlet *scoufia* that is conferred by the pope. Also seen here are the two currently acceptable styles of rochet: lace and linen. *Courtesy Arturo Mari.*

PLATE 97. Pope John Paul II, dressed in state *mozzetta* of red silk and the embroidered stole, greets diplomats at an ambassador's presentation of credentials at the Vatican. *Courtesy Arturo Mari.*

PLATE 98. Pope John Paul II arrives at the sacristy of St. Peter's Basilica on the morning of his installation as pope. He is accompanied by his secretary of the time. On this solemn occasion, the pope's simar is made wholly of white watered silk. It is the only time the Holy Father has made use of white watered silk for the entire fabrication of the simar during his pontificate. Tradition dictates that white watered silk be used for the cuffs of the simar, as well as for the *fascia* and *zucchetto.* Pope John Paul II also makes use of a simple rochet, the red state *mozzetta,* and the Paul VI state stole in the form of a preaching stole. His secretary, also a protonotary apostolic de numero, makes use of the violet choir cassock and *mantelletta* over a simple surplice. *Courtesy Fotografia Felici.*

PLATE 99. Three of the canons of St. Peter's, each of whom are also apostolic protonotaries de numero, greet the Holy Father at the entrance of St. Peter's Basilica. The pope carries the *aspergillium,* or holy water sprinkler. Each of the canons touches it and then blesses himself by making the Sign of the Cross. This photo also illustates the *mantelletta,* the garb now reserved for this class of honorary prelates and certain canons. Under it, they wear the rochet rather than a surplice and the violet choir cassock. *Courtesy Arturo Mari.*

PLATE 100. John Paul II greets each member of the Sacred Rota, or Church court, at their annual meeting with him inside the Apostolic Palace. Over the ermine collar of the amaranth red and violet *crocia* is the lace band known in Italian as the *cravatta per uditori di Rota. Courtesy Arturo Mari.*

PLATE 101. The annual visit of the judges of the Rota of the Catholic Church. Once each year, the senior prelates of the Church's court pay their official visit to the pope. Here in the pope's library inside the Apostolic Palace, John Paul II is flanked by the *uditori* (auditors) in their magnificent vesture, known as the *crocia,* of violet silk and amaranth red satin. The famous collar of lace adds to the color of the costume. The *crocia* is worn over the cassock as a civil judge would wear his court robes over a business suit. The *uditori* are still permitted the red tuft on the black, red-piped *biretta. Courtesy Arturo Mari.*

PLATE **102.** On the feast of the Epiphany, January 6, Pope John Paul II consecrates priests to the episcopacy. It is one of the most beautiful of Vatican ceremonies. Here the pope vests a newly consecrated bishop with the mitre. Pope John Paul II is seen here wearing a gold pontiff-design mitre; the *pallium,* the symbol of his universal jurisdiction; the papal ring; and the chasuble. Partially seen in the foreground are two croziers, each intended for a new bishop. Monsignor Piero Marini, Papal Master of Ceremonies, is seen in the center of the photograph. He wears a Vatican-style surplice. *Courtesy Arturo Mari.*

PLATE **103.** At the conclusion of the Mass of the Rings, November, 1994, the newly elevated cardinals process down the center aisle of St. Peter's Basilica. Each of the new cardinals wears the damask mitre appropriate to cardinals while in the presence of the pontiff and the purple chasuble proper for Advent. *Courtesy Arturo Mari.*

PLATE **104.** Archbishop Justin Rigali, then Secretary for the Office of Bishops (now Archbishop of St. Louis, Missouri) kneels before the Holy Father at the Mass of the Pallium. Pope John Paul II blesses the silver tray containing those *pallia* to be vested on the metropolitans of the Church named to those special posts during the previous year. The Holy Father wears one of his favorite pontiff-design mitres, tall in height with an extremely wide aperture. *Courtesy Arturo Mari.*

PLATE **105.** Of the various styles of mitre, the golden or orphreyed mitre is the least seen today. It has never been abolished. However, the updated rubrics make no specific mention of it. This mitre usually took the fuller Roman style. Here, the Most Reverend John J. Graham, retired auxiliary bishop of Philadelphia, wears the orphreyed mitre to ordain the deaconal class of Philadelphia, 1993. The bishop also wears a richly tapestried chasuble in the gothic style and carries the traditional crozier. *Courtesy James-Charles Noonan, Jr.*

PLATE **106.** During the Episcopal Ordination Mass of the Epiphany, cardinals in choir dress don the stole of priest and bishop to lay hands on the heads of those nominated to the office of bishop. The newly created bishops kneel as the cardinals, in turn, pray over each new bishop. *Courtesy Arturo Mari.*

PLATE **107.** Laying prostrate before the *Confessio,* or Confession of St. Peter, the opening to the tomb of the Prince of the Apostles, are the newly named bishops on the feast of the Epiphany. *Courtesy Arturo Mari.*

PLATE **108.** John Paul II, on a throne above the *Confessio,* or Confession of Peter, during a Mass at Christmas, 1994. The Holy Father is surrounded by beautiful live decorations. The *sanpietrini* under the direction of Cardinal Noè, President of the Fabric of St. Peter's Basilica, clean and decorate the basilica and are responsible for its continued upkeep. *Courtesy Arturo Mari.*

PLATE **109.** Pope John Paul II vests an African archbishop with the *pallium,* the symbol of this prelate's jurisdiction in the ecclesiastical territory under his care at home, known as a metropolitan province. Only the pope may wear the *pallium* throughout the world, as he alone has universal jurisdiction. This occasion is the only time this prelate will be seen wearing his *pallium* in the pope's presence, as no one is entitled to do so at any time other than at its receipt from the hands of the pope. *Courtesy Arturo Mari.*

PLATE **110.** Pope John Paul II is seen carrying the pastoral staff as he walks in procession behind the Blessed Sacrament at the annual Corpus Christi procession in June, 1995. The Holy Father is wearing a cape clasped by a morse of gold, over a white linen alb. Monsignor Piero Marini, Papal Master of Ceremonies, stands behind the pontiff. A deacon carries the monstrance, or *ostensorium*. As custom requires, his hands and arms are covered by an ornate cloth known commonly as a vimp, yet this term is more English vernacular than of historic origin. *Courtesy Arturo Mari.*

PLATE **111.** Pope John Paul II kneels in adoration and prayer before the Blessed Sacrament during the Corpus Christi procession, June, 1995. Because of the pain resulting from a broken hip, the Holy Father did not walk the length of the entire procession as has always been his custom. Rather, a special vehicle was outfitted for him so to be seen by the crowds of the faithful who participate in this procession each year. *Courtesy Arturo Mari.*

PLATE **112.** During the great Second Vatican Council, cardinals of all three classes are vested in the sacred vestments appropriate to their class: cope for cardinal-bishops, chasuble for cardinal-priests, and dalmatic for cardinal-deacons. This practice is no longer strictly followed at all liturgies, but the vestural distinctions still remain. Each cardinal wears the damask mitre, still required for members of the Sacred College in the presence of the pope. *Courtesy Viking Penguin, a division of Penguin Books USA Inc. From* The Council *by Lothar Wolleh and Emil Schmitz. Copyright © 1966 by the Viking Press, renewed.*

PLATE **113.** Pope Paul VI during the closing ceremonies of the Second Vatican Council. Here, the pope wears the great cope embroidered in gold, which always bears the arms of the reigning pope. It is clasped by the morse, now abolished for non papal vestments. Paul VI also is seen wearing the full *falda* or special papal alb, which the present pope, John Paul II, does not prefer. On either side of the pope are the cardinal-deacons vested in scarlet and the dalmatic of their class in the Sacred College.

The Papal Master of Ceremonies, Monsignor (later Cardinal) Dante, stands in the foreground. As an apostolic protonotary de numero, he was then entitled to the pectoral cross and ring (neither are now permitted this class of prelate). Also noteworthy: Before the Pauline changes of 1969, those entitled to the lace rochet were also to cover it in the presence of the pope by a lace surplice. Monsignor Dante is seen here following this now-abolished edict. *Courtesy Viking Penguin, a division of Penguin Books USA Inc. From* The Council *by Lothar Wolleh and Emil Schmitz. Copyright © 1966 by the Viking Press, renewed.*

PLATE **114.** At the Paul VI Audience Hall, Pope John Paul II envelopes a small child in his red cape. All other prelates must make use of black capes, if the cape is their preference. Only the pope makes use of the red cape. It is piped in the same red and gold cording used for the pectoral cross cords of cardinals. A filigree "frog" or closure device is made of the same material. *Courtesy Arturo Mari.*

PLATE **115.** The *privilège du blanc* reserved for Catholic Queens and the Grand Duchess of Luxembourg is that diplomatic privilege which negates special Vatican protocol calling for women to be dressed entirely in black when they are presented to the pope. Only Catholic Queens and the Grand Duchess of Luxembourg are granted the privilege of wearing white. Here, Juan Carlos and Sophia, the king and queen of Spain, visit John Paul I shortly after his installation ceremonies as pope, September, 1978. *Courtesy Arturo Mari.*

PLATE **116.** A rare opportunity to discuss informally over lunch those issues that still affect the relationship between the Roman Catholic and Orthodox Churches. This special luncheon (*pranzo*) took place at the Vatican during the rare three-day meeting between Pope John Paul II and Bartholomew I, Ecumenical Greek Orthodox Patriarch. The Greek prelates wear the *riasa* and the *kamilauka;* the Latin prelates wear daily attire known as *abito piano. Courtesy Arturo Mari.*

PLATE 117. His Eminence Adam Cardinal Maida, archbishop of Detroit, as he arrives at the annual Cardinal's Dinner of the Catholic University of America accompanied by board of regent's members, Leonard F. Charla and Elizabeth Du Mouchelle. In January, 1995, Cardinal Bevilacqua was the gala's host in the City of Brotherly Love. Cardinal Maida is seen here in *abito piano,* the most formal nonliturgical dress for the clergy. Consisting of the scarlet watered silk *ferraiolo, fascia,* and *zuchetto* for cardinals, he also wears the black, scarlet-trimmed simar, the pectoral cross, and the cardinalatial ring. The scarlet *biretta* would also be proper for such a formal event. *Courtesy Colleen Boyle Sharp.*

PLATE 118. Pope John XXIII vested in state dress comprising the red velvet and ermine *mozzetta,* the state stole embroidered with the pope's personal coat of arms and icons of the saints, the cameo ordinary ring preferred by John for daily use in place of the Fisherman's Ring, the white lace *falda,* and the white silk *zucchetto. Courtesy Fotografia Felici.*

PLATE 119. Pope John XXIII is the most recent pontiff to make use of the ancient *camauro* of red velvet and ermine, and the white damask and ermine *mozzetta,* April 18, 1963. *Courtesy Fotografia Felici.*

PLATE 120. Pope John XXIII is the last pontiff but one to make use of the *triregno.* The Vatican Treasury has several historic examples of the triple tiara. Here, the pope gives his apostolic blessing: *Urbi et Orbi.* Partially visible is his preferred madonna cameo ring. The rich gold on the silver cape is closed by a jeweled morse. *Courtesy Fotografia Felici.*

PLATE 121. Pope Pius XII, seen here in 1952, made use of a white ermine *mozzetta* fastened by white silk cassock buttons. This *mozzetta* was not a formal item of vesture for the papacy. In fact, it had

not been used by any of his predecessors. Pius XII keenly felt the chill and damp of the Roman winters and preferred this self-designed *mozzetta* over all others. Because it was not a formal item of vesture, it was not addressed in the changes of Paul VI from 1967 to 1969. Therefore, it is free to return in the future should a pontiff wish it, but this is unlikely. Pius XII is also seen wearing the short *falda* over his silk simar. *Courtesy Fotografia Felici.*

PLATE 122. John Paul I, the smiling pope of September, 1978, is seen here shortly after his installation ceremony. John Paul I wears the mitre preferred by his predecessor Paul VI late in his pontificate; the *pallium,* symbolizing his universal jurisdiction; the chasuble; and the staff of Paul VI designed by Lello Scorzelli. He is the most recent pope to use the *sedia gestatoria,* as Pope John Paul II does not prefer it. In the future, as this or any other, pope's stamina slows, the *sedia* will make its return to the Vatican. It is presently on exhibit at the Lateran Palace Papal Court Museum. *Courtesy Arturo Mari.*

PLATE 123. The *Urbi et Orbi* (To the City and World) blessing is given from the central balcony of the facade of St. Peter's Basilica high above the chief portal of the church, each Christmas and Easter Day. Pope John Paul II has made the event his own by including messages to all the peoples of the world in their own tongues—often exceeding fifty-four languages and dialects. Partially seen, hanging over the balcony, is the coat of arms of the present pontiff. The pope is wearing one of the pontiff-design mitres familiar to him, while two cardinal-deacons wear the damask mitre of their office as cardinals. Each of the cardinals is vested in dalmatic, the sacred vestment of their class in the Sacred College. The Papal Masters of Ceremonies and the ever-present television camera accompany the pope. *Courtesy Arturo Mari.*

ENDNOTES AND BIBLIOGRAPHY

ENDNOTES

PART ONE: AT THE VATICAN

Chapter One SACRED COLLEGE

1. Peter C. van Lierde. *What Is a Cardinal?* New York: Hawthorne Books Inc., 1964, p. 14.
2. Ibid., p. 16.
3. *The Code of Canon Law, A Text and Commentary.* Ed. James A. Coriden et al. Mahwah, NJ: Paulist Press, 1985, p. 287.
4. Peter C. van Lierde. *What Is a Cardinal?* New York: Hawthorne Books, Inc., 1964, p. 59.
5. Ibid., p. 74.
6. *The Code of Canon Law, A Text and Commentary,* Ed. James A. Coriden et al. Mahwah, NJ: Paulist Press, 1985, p. 289.
7. Ibid., p. 287.
8. Ibid.
9. Ibid., p. 291.
10. Ibid., p. 683.
11. Canon, 350 § 1.
12. AAS, 53 (1961), p. 198.
13. *The Code of Canon Law, A Text and Commentary.* Ed. James A. Coriden et al. Mahwah, NJ: Paulist Press, 1985, p. 288.
14. Ibid.
15. Peter C. van Lierde. *What Is a Cardinal?* New York: Hawthorne Books, Inc., 1964, p. 33.
16. John Travis. *Quiet Revolution, Pope Uses Cardinals as a Think Tank.* Catholic News Service Report, Thursday, June 23, 1994.
17. Ibid.
18. Official Ceremonial, Archdiocese of New York, February 4, 1946.
19. Ibid.
20. Ibid.
21. *Nights of Sorrow, Days of Joy.* Ed. Richard Daw. Washington, DC: 1978, pp. 42–43.
22. Ibid., p. 44.
23. George Seldes. *The Vatican Yesterday, Today, Tomorrow.* New York: Harper Brothers, 1934, p. 81.
24. Ibid., p. 85.
25. *The Code of Canon Law, A Text and Commentary.* Ed. James A. Coriden et al. New York: Paulist Press, 1985, p. 270.
26. Paul VI. Papal *Motu Proprio On the Vacancy of the Apostolic See,* 1975, I, art. 4.
27. Ibid., II, art. 12.
28. Paul VI. Papal *Motu Proprio On Electing the Roman Pontiff,* October 1, 1975.
29. Ibid., art. 56.
30. Ibid., art. 62.
31. Ibid.
32. Ibid., art. 64.
33. Ibid., art. 66.
34. Ibid.
35. Ibid., art. 88.
36. This translation is an unofficial text, worked from the original *In Exsequiis Cardinalium Defunctorum,* translated where appropriate from the original Latin and Italian in order to provide English-speaking (arch)dioceses the procedures for proper burial for a member of the Sacred College under the protocol of Rome. It is not meant in any way as an official text, translation, or authorized version of the original, which was provided, and permission graciously given, by the Rt. Rev. Monsignor Piero Marini, Master of Ceremonies of His Holiness Pope John Paul II (1992). As of the publication of this text, to the author and publisher's knowledge, no official English translation exists for this rite. Translations have been provided by a panel of Rome-based, English-speaking priests, knowledgeable in Latin, Italian, and the present mode of prayer for the English language.
37. The use of the terms *Option I* and *Option II* for the appropriate orations, prayers, and parts of the Mass results from a differential in the two base languages of the original Vatican text. Option I is a translation from the Latin, whereas Option II is the translation provided from the Italian.

This terminology is also provided throughout when referring to the options available in use of psalms or antiphons. Most commonly, Option I in these cases refers to the English text, whereas Option II refers to the Latin Chant mode used at the Vatican for the Burial Rite of Cardinals.

Chapter Two   ROMAN CURIA

1. John Paul II, the Apostolic Palace, Vatican City.
2. Nicholas Hilling. *Procedure at the Roman Curia.* New York: Joseph F. Wagner, Co., 1907, p. 110.
3. *Romanum decet Pontificem,* June, 1692.
4. *Romanus Pontifix,* April, 1678.
5. *Regiminir Ecclesiae Universae,* March 1968.
6. *Integral Servandae,* December 7, 1965.
7. Apostolic Constitution: *Romano Pontifici.*
8. *Dei Providentis,* May 1, 1917.
9. Peter C. van Lierde. *The Holy See at Work.* New York: Hawthorne Books, Inc., 1962, p. 67.
10. *Pastor Bonus,* June 28, 1988.
11. *1995 Catholic Almanac,* Ed. Felician A. Foy. Huntington, IN: Our Sunday Visitor Publishing Division, Our Sunday Visitor, Inc., 1994, p. 145.
12. Kenneth L. Woodward, *Making Saints.* New York: Simon and Schuster, 1990, p. 98.
13. Ibid.
14. *1995 Catholic Almanac.* Ed. Felician A. Foy. Huntington, IN: Our Sunday Visitor Publishing Division, Our Sunday Visitor, Inc., 1994, p. 146.
15. Ibid., p. 146.
16. Ibid., p. 146.
17. *Acta Apostolicae Sedis,* vol. 46 (1954), p. 315.
18. Peter C. van Lierde. *The Holy See at Work,* New York: Hawthorne Books, Inc., 1962, p. 129.
19. Ibid., p. 133.
20. Ibid.
21. Ibid.
22. Ibid.
23. Ibid.
24. *1995 Catholic Almanac.* Ed. Felician A. Foy. Huntington, IN: Our Sunday Visitor Publishing Division, Our Sunday Visitor, Inc., 1994, p. 147.
25. Ibid., p. 148.

Chapter Three   THE PAPAL HOUSEHOLD AND THE PAPAL FAMILY

1. A. G. Dickens. *The Courts of Europe.* New York: Greenwich House, 1977, p. 213.
2. George Bull. *Inside the Vatican.* New York: St. Martin's Press, 1982, pp. 77–78.
3. *1995 Catholic Almanac.* Ed. Felician A. Foy. Huntington, IN: Our Sunday Visitor Publishing Division, Our Sunday Visitor, Inc., 1994, p. 149.
4. Jacques Martin. *Heraldry in the Vatican.* Gerrards Cross, UK: Van Duran Publishers, 1987, p. 31.

Chapter Four   PAPAL DIPLOMACY

1. George Bull. *Inside the Vatican.* New York: St. Martin's Press, 1982, pp. 127–128.
2. *Annuario Pontificio.* Libreria Editrice Vaticana, 1992, p. 1758.
3. Ibid.
4. Ibid.
5. Ibid., p. 1759.
6. George Bull. *Inside the Vatican.* New York: St. Martin's Press, 1982, pp. 131–132.

Chapter Five   SWISS GUARD

1. Corrado Pallenberg. *Inside the Vatican.* New York: Hawthorne Books, Inc., 1960, p. 227.
2. Antonio Serrano. *The Swiss Guard of the Popes.* Dachau: Bayerland, 1992, p. 45.
3. Ibid., p. 70.
4. John S. Brennan. *Protecting the Pope, The History of the Swiss Guards.* Liguorian, May 1992, p. 51.
5. The Press Information Office, Vatican City.
6. Corrado Pallenberg. *Inside the Vatican.* New York: Hawthorne Books, Inc., 1960, p. 228.
7. John S. Brennan. *Protecting the Pope, The History of the Swiss Guards.* Liguorian, May 1992, p. 50.
8. Antonio Serrano. *The Swiss Guard of the Popes.* Dachau: Bayerland, 1992, p. 139.
9. Ibid.
10. Corrado Pallenberg. *Inside the Vatican.* New York: Hawthorne Books, Inc., 1960. p. 225.

PART TWO: PAPAL HONORS

Chapter Six   PAPAL HONORS: LAITY

1. George Seldes. *The Vatican Yesterday, Today, Tomorrow.* New York: Harper Brothers, 1934, p. 227.
2. H. E. Cardinale. *Orders of Knighthood, Awards of the Holy See.* Gerrards Cross, UK: Van Duran Publishers, 1983, p. 63.
3. Ibid., p. 66.
4. Ibid., p. 30.
5. Robert Werlich. *Orders and Decorations of All Nations.* Washington, DC: Quaker Press, 1974, p. 441.
6. *Annuario Pontifico,* 1992.
7. *Acta Apostolicae Sedis,* 1940.
8. H. E. Cardinale. *Orders of Knighthood, Awards of the Holy See.* Gerrards Cross, UK: Van Duran Publishers, 1983, p. 56.
9. *1995 Catholic Almanac.* Ed. Felician A. Foy. Huntington, IN: Our Sunday Visitor Publishing Division, Our Sunday Visitor, Inc., 1994, p. 596.
10. "Noblesse Pontificale," *Dynastie,* no. 18., Octobre 1986, Paris, p. 7.

Chapter Seven   PAPAL HONORS: CLERGY

1. *Reform of the Use of Pontifical Insignia,* June 21, 1968.

2. Henry J. McCloud. *Clerical Dress and Insignia of the Roman Catholic Church.* Milwaukee: The Bruce Publishing Co., 1948, p. 33.
3. Ibid.
4. Francis J. Weber. "Monsignorial Appointments in the U.S.A.," *American Ecclesiastical Review,* p. 114.
5. Ibid.

Chapter Nine EQUESTRIAN ORDER OF THE HOLY SEPULCHRE OF JERUSALEM

1. From the Investiture program of the Eastern Lieutenancy of the United States, September 28, 1991.
2. Ibid., p. 4.
3. H. E. Cardinale. *Orders of Knighthood, Awards of the Holy See.* Gerrards Cross, UK: Van Duran Publishers, 1983, p. 104.
4. Ibid., p. 105.
5. Ibid.

Chapter Ten ECCLESIASTICAL HERALDRY

1. Carl Alexander von Volborth. *Heraldry, Customs, Rules and Styles.* London: New Orchard Press, 1991, p. vii.
2. Bruno B. Heim. *Heraldry in the Catholic Church.* Gerrards Cross, UK: Van Duran Publishers, 1981, p. 19.
3. Carl Alexander von Volborth, *Heraldry, Customs, Rules and Styles.* New Orchard Press, 1991, p. vii.
4. Bruno B. Heim. *Heraldry in the Catholic Church.* Gerrards Cross, UK: Van Duran Publishers, 1981, p. 20.
5. Ibid., p. 43.
6. Ibid., p. 45.
7. Ibid., p. 50.
8. Ibid., p. 54.
9. Bruno B. Heim, to author, in a telephone conversation, May 24, 1992.
10. Ramon John Hartshyn. *The Canadian Heraldic Authority,* August 1990, p. 3.

PART THREE

Chapter Thirteen ECCLESIASTICAL PROTOCOL AND ETIQUETTE

1. Mary Jane McCaffree and Pauline Innis. *Protocol, A Complete Handbook of Diplomatic, Official and Social Usage.* Englewood Cliffs, NJ: Prentice Hall, 1977. pp. xi.
2. Ibid., p. ix.

PART FOUR: VESTURE AND INSIGNIA

Chapter Fifteen CASSOCK

1. John Walsh. *The Mass and Vestments of the Catholic Church.* New York: Benzinger Brothers, 1916, p. 454.
2. John A. Nainfa. *Costume of Prelates of the Catholic Church.* Baltimore: John Murphy and Company, 1926, p. 44.
3. Henry J. McCloud. *Clerical Dress and Insignia of the Roman Catholic Church.* Milwaukee: The Bruce Publishing Co., 1945, p. 54.
4. Ibid., p. 49.

Chapter Twenty ZUCCHETTO

1. John Walsh. *The Mass and Vestments of the Catholic Church.* New York: Benzinger Brothers, 1916, p. 454.

Chapter Twenty-two FERRAIOLO

1. J. A. Nainfa. *Costumes of Prelates of the Catholic Church.* Baltimore: John Murphy and Co., 1926, p. 90.

Chapter Twenty-four CAPPA MAGNA

1. J. A. Nainfa. *Costume of Prelates of the Catholic Church.* Baltimore: John Murphy and Co., 1926, p. 90.

Chapter Twenty-five ROCHET AND SURPLICE

1. John Walsh. *The Mass and Vestments of the Catholic Church.* New York: Benzinger Brothers, 1916, p. 454.

Chapter Thirty-one SACRED VESTMENTS

1. John Walsh. *The Mass and Vestments of the Catholic Church.* New York: Benzinger Brothers, 1916, p. 388.
2. Edward N. West. *Outward Signs.* New York: Walker & Co., 1989, p. 145.
3. John Walsh. *The Mass and Vestments of the Catholic Church.* New York: Benzinger Brothers, 1916, p. 417.
4. Ibid.
5. Ibid., p. 460.
6. Ibid., p. 406.
7. Ibid., p. 410.

Chapter Thirty-two RINGS

1. Henry J. McCloud. *Clerical Dress and Insignia of the Roman Catholic Church.* Milwaukee: The Bruce Publishing Co., 1948, p. 131.
2. Ibid., p. 133.

Chapter Thirty-three PECTORAL CROSS

1. John Walsh. *The Mass and Vestments of the Catholic Church.* New York: Benzinger Brothers, 1916, p. 441.
2. Sacred Congregation of the Rites (SRC), No. 4035 ad 1.
3. *Missale Romanum Ritus.* Serv. Tit. I, No. 4; and *Ceremoniale Ep.,* I, XXIX, 3.

Chapter Thirty-four CROZIER

1. John Walsh. *The Mass and Vestments of the Catholic Church.* New York: Benzinger Brothers, 1916, p. 442.
2. Ibid.
3. Ibid.
4. Ibid., p. 443.
5. St. Thomas Aquinas. *Sumna Theologi-*

cae, Senten, IV, question 3; article 3.

6. J. A. Nainfa. *Costume of Prelates of the Catholic Church.* Baltimore: John Murphy and Co., 1926, p. 156.

Chapter Thirty-five PALLIUM

1. Henry S. McCloud. *Clerical Dress and Insignia of the Roman Catholic Church.* Milwaukee: The Bruce Publishing Co., 1948, p. 130.

Chapter Thirty-seven
METROPOLITAN OR ARCHIEPISCOPAL CROSS AND THE PROCESSIONAL CROSS

1. Augustine. *Liturgical Law,* p. 61.

2. *Ceremonial of Bishops,* (ICEL). Collegeville, Minn.: The Liturgical Press, 1989, p. 315.

PART FIVE: THE PAPACY

Chapter Forty CHRONOLOGY OF THE POPES AND ECUMENICAL COUNCILS

1. *1995 Catholic Almanac.* Ed. Felician A. Foy. Huntington, IN: Our Sunday Visitor Publishing Division, Our Sunday Visitor, Inc., 1994, p. 146.

2. Ibid.

BIBLIOGRAPHY

GENERAL BIBLIOGRAPHY

Alberigo, Giuseppe. *Cardinalatato e Collegialita.* Florence: Vallecchi, 1969.

Archdiocese of New York Informational Release on the College of Cardinals, February 4, 1946.

The Bishop and the Liturgy. U.S. Catholic Conference. Washington, 1986.

Brennan, John S. "Protecting the Pope, The History of the Swiss Guard." *Liguorian,* May 1992, pp. 46–51.

Buehrle, Marie C. *Rafael Cardinal Merry del Val.* Milwaukee: Bruce Publishing Co., 1957.

Bull, George. *Inside the Vatican.* New York: St. Martin's Press, 1982.

Carnahan, Ann. *The Vatican.* New York: Farrar Strauss & Co., 1949.

Cattaneo, E. *Il culto cristiano in occidentale.* Rome: Editrice Leonina, 1994.

Ceremonial of Bishops. Collegeville, Minn.: The Liturgical Press, 1989.

Chappin, Marcel. *La Chiesa Antica e Medievale.* Rome: Editrice Gregoriana, 1992.

Cheetham, Nicolas. *The History of the Popes.* New York: Dorset Press, 1992.

Ciofalo, Andrew C. *The Pilgrimage for Peace.* South Hackensack, N.J.: Custombook Inc., 1965.

Coriden, James A., et al. *The Code of Canon Law, A Text and Commentary.* New York: Paulist Press, 1985.

Coughlan, Joseph. *Inside the Vatican.* New York: Gallery Books, 1990.

Dues, Greg. *Catholic Customs and Traditions: A Popular Guide.* Mystic, Conn.: Twenty-third Publications, 1990.

Hebblethwaite, Peter. *Pope John XXIII, Shepherd of the Modern World.* Garden City, N.Y.: Image Books, 1984.

Hebblethwaite, Peter, et al. *The Vatican.* New York: Vendome Press, 1980.

Hilling, Nicholas. *Procedure at the Roman Curia.* New York: Joseph F. Wagner Co., 1907.

Hofmann, Paul. *O, Vatican: A Slightly Wicked View of the Holy See.* New York: Congden and Weed, Inc., 1984.

Huizing, Peter. Edited by Knot Walf. *The Roman Curia and the Communion of Churches.* New York: Seabury Press, 1979.

Hynes, Harry G. *Privileges of Cardinals.* Washington, DC: The Catholic University Press, 1945.

Jung-Inglessis, E. M. *St. Peter's.* Florence: Scala Books, 1980.

Kittler, Glenn D. *The Papal Princes.* New York: Funk and Wagnalls, 1960.

Korn, Frank J. *Country of the Spirit . . . Vatican City.* Boston: St. Paul Editions, 1982.

Liturgy Documents: A Parish Resource, 3d ed. Chicago: Liturgy Training Publications, 1991.

Martin, S. J., Michael. *The Roman Curia.* New York: Benzinger Brothers, 1913.

Mathieu-Rosay, Jean. *La Véritable Histoire des Papes.* Paris: Jacques Grancher Editions, 1992.

McDowell, Bart. *Inside the Vatican.* Washington, DC: The National Geographic Society, 1991.

Murphy, Francis X. *This Church, These Times: Roman Catholic Church Since Vatican II.* Chicago: Follett Publishing, 1980.

Nights of Sorrow, Days of Joy. Edited by Richard W. Daw. Washington, DC: National Catholic News Service, 1978.

Nuovo Dicionario di Liturgico. Rome: Editrice Paolina, 1986.

Pallenberg, Corrado. *Inside the Vatican.* New York: Hawthorne Books, Inc., 1960.

"Le Pape a Lourdes." *Point De Vue Images Du Monde,* No. 1829. 19 Aout 1983, pp. 1–12.

Paro, Gino. *The Right of Papal Legation.* Washington, DC: The Catholic University Press, 1947.

Parsons, Reuben. *Studies in Church History,* 6 vols. New York: Pustet & Co., 1896.

Pecker, Eric. *John XXIII.* New York: McGraw-Hill Book Company, 1959.

Popek, Alfonse S. *The Rights and Obligations of Metropolitans.* Washington, DC: Catholic University Press, 1947.

The Pope's Visit: Time-Life Special Report. New York: Time Inc., 1965.

Reese, Thomas J. *Archbishop.* Cambridge, Mass.: Harper and Row, 1989.

Robinson, John M. *Cardinal Consalvi.* London: The Bodley Head, 1987.

Seldes, George. *The Vatican: Yesterday, Today and Tomorrow.* New York: Harper and Brothers, 1994.

Serrano, Antonio. *Die Schweizergarda der Päpste.* Dachau: Bayerland, 1992.

Thornton, Francis B. *Our American Princes.* New York: G. P. Putnam's Sons, 1963.

Tierney, Brian. "The Pope and Bishops: An Historical Survey." *America,* March 5, 1988, pp. 230–237.

van Hoek, Kees. *Pope Pius XII, Priest and Statesman.* New York: Philosophical Library, 1945.

van Lierde, Peter C. J. *The Holy See at Work: How the Catholic Church Is Governed.* New York: Hawthorne Books, Inc., 1962.

van Lierde, Peter C. J., and A. Giraud. *What Is a Cardinal?* New York: Hawthorne Books, 1964.

Vaughn, John S. *The Purpose of the Papacy.* London: Sands and Co., 1910.

Walsh, Michael. *The Secret World of Opus Dei.* London: Grafton Books, 1989.

Weber, Francis J. "Monsignorial Appointments in the U.S.A." *The American Ecclesiastical Review,* (date unknown), pp. 113–120.

West, Edward N. *Outward Signs: The Language of Christian Symbolism.* New York: Walker & Co., 1989.

Woodward, Kenneth L. *Making Saints.* New York: Simon & Schuster, 1990.

HERALDRY

Bräundle-Falkensee, Helmut. *Christian Symbols, in European Heraldry and Order-concerns.* Vienna: (privately printed), 1991.

Brooke-Little, J. P. *Boutell's Heraldry.* London: Frederick Warne and Company, 1973.

Canadian Heraldic Authority. Rideau Hall, Ottawa, 1990.

Elvins, Mark T. *Cardinals and Heraldry.* London: Buckland Publications, 1988.

Foster, Joseph. *The Dictionary of Heraldry, Feudal Coats of Arms and Pedigrees.* New York: Arch Cape Press, 1989.

Fox-Davies, Arthur Charles. *Art of Heraldry.* London: Bloomsbury Books, 1906/1986.

Friar, Stephen. *Dictionary of Heraldry.* New York: Harmony Books, 1987.

Heim, Bruno B. *Heraldry in the Catholic Church.* Gerrards Cross, UK: Van Duran Publishers, 1981.

———. *Or & Argent.* Gerrards Cross: Colin Smythe, 1994.

Louda, J., and M. Maclagan. *Heraldry of the Royal Families of Europe.* New York: Clarkson N. Potter, Inc., 1981.

Martin, Jacques. *Heraldry in the Vatican.* Gerrards Cross, UK: Van Duran Publishers, 1987.

Neubecker, Ottfried. *Heraldry: Sources, Symbols, and Meaning.* New York: McGraw-Hill Book Co., 1976.

Puttock, A. G. *A Dictionary of Heraldry and Related Subjects.* New York: Arco Publishing, Inc., 1985.

von Volborth, Carl Alexander. *Heraldry: Customs, Rules and Styles.* London: New Orchard Editions–Villiers House, 1991.

Woodcock, Thomas, and J. M. Robinson. *Oxford Guide to Heraldry.* Oxford: Oxford University Press, 1988.

PONTIFICAL HONORS

Bander van Duren, Peter. *The Cross on the Sword.* Gerrards Cross, UK: Van Duran Publishers, 1987.

Bradford, Ernie. *Knights of the Order.* New York: Dorset Press, 1972.

Bulletin Officiel. Rome: Grand Magistral Palace, 1965.

Bulletin Officiel du Grande Magistère de L'Ordre S.M.H. de Malte. Rome: Grand Magistral Palace, May, 1962.

Cardinale, H. E. *Orders of Knighthood, Awards and the Holy See.* Gerrards Cross, UK: Van Doran Publishers, 1983.

Catholic Almanac. Edited by Felician A. Foy. Huntington, IN: Our Sunday Visitor, Inc., 1992.

The Catholic Encyclopedia. Edited by Robert C. Broderick. Nashville: Thomas Nelson Publishers, 1986.

Catholic Encyclopedia. Edited by Peter M. J. Stravinskas. Huntington, IN: Our Sunday Visitor, Inc., 1991.

Ceremonial: The Equestrian Order of the Holy Sepulchre of Jerusalem. Vatican City: Sacred Congregation of the Rites, July 25, 1962.

Chaffanjon, A., and B. G. Flavigny. *Ordres et Contre-ordres de Chevalerie.* Paris: n.p., 1982.

Constantinian Chronicler (#1). Buckinghamshire: Colin Smythe, May, 1990.

Dorling, H. Taprell. *Ribbons and Medals.* London: Fortress Publications, Inc., 1983.

Felice y Quadremy, S. *Ordenes de Cavalleria Pontificias.* Mallorca, 1950.

Friar, Stephen. *Dictionary of Heraldry.* New York: Harmony Books, 1987.

Guiraud-Darmais, Jacques. *Ordres et Décorations Monégasques.* Monaco: Palais de Monaco, 1985.

King, E. J. *The Knights Hospitaller in the Holy Land.* London: Metheun, 1939.

A Modern Crusade. Rome: Grand Magistral Palace.

Mericka, Vaclav. *Book of Orders and Decorations.* London: Hamlyn Publishing Group, 1975.

L'Osservatore Romano, English weekly edition No. 29. 18 July 1988, p. 11.

Prochozka, Freiherr von. *Oesterreiches Ordenshandbuch.* Munich: Klenau, 1974.

Prokopowski, Rudolf. *Ordre Souverain et Militaire Jeroselymitais de Malte.* Vatican City: Cité du Vatican Editions "Ecclesia," 1950.

"A Rome: L'Intronisation du 78e Grand Maître de L'Ordre Souverain de Malte." *Point De Vue Images Du Monde,* No. 2074. 29 Avril 1988. pp. 1–8.

Revista Internazionale. Rome: Grand Magistral Palace, 1989.

Revista Internazionale, Numero Speciale

1988. Rome: Grand Magistral Palace, 1988.

"La Royaume du Vaticane." *Dynasty, Le Magazine des Grande Familles,* 3 Octobre 1986, pp. 4–7.

Seward, Desmond. *Italy's Knights of St. George.* Gerrards Cross, UK: Van Duran Publishers, 1986.

van der Veldt, James. *Ecclesiastical Orders of Knighthood.* Washington: The Catholic University of America Press, 1956.

Werlich, Robert. *Orders and Decorations of All Nations,* 2d ed. Washington: Quaker Press, 1974.

PROTOCOL

Baldridge, Letitia. *Of Diamonds and Diplomats.* Boston: Houghton Mifflin Company, 1968.

McCaffree, Mary Jane, and Pauline Innis. *Protocol: The Complete Handbook of Diplomatic, Official and Social Usage.* Englewood Cliffs, N.J.: Prentice-Hall, Inc., 1977.

Measures, Howard. *A Manual for Usage in Writing and in Speech.* Toronto: MacMillan Company of Canada.

Oliveri, Mario. *The Representatives: The Real Nature and Function of Papal Legates.* Gerrards Cross, UK: Van Doran Publishers, 1981.

Serres, Jean. *Le Protocole et les Usages.* Paris: Presses Universitaires de France.

Woods, John R., and Jean Serres. *Diplomatic Ceremonial and Protocol: Procedures and Practices.* New York: Columbia University Press.

VATICAN DOCUMENTS

Annuaire Pontifical Catholique. Archdiocese of Paris, 1906.

Annuario Pontificio. Vatican City: Liberia Editrice Vaticano, 1992/1994.

Bollettino, nuove disposizioni per i Cardinali. Vatican City, 1967.

The Ceremonial to be observed by a new most Eminent Prince upon his promotion to the Cardinalate. Rome: The Vatican Press, 1898.

Corteo Processionale Del Papa Col Clero in Sacri Paramenti. Sacra Congregazione Cerimoniale. Vatican City: Tipografia Poliglotta Vaticano, 1964.

Instruction sur les habits, les titres et les blasons des Cardinaux, des Evêques et des Prélates inférieurs. Secretariat of State No. 135705. Vatican City: 13 Avril 1969.

Istruzioni per i Camerieri Segreti Soprannumerari e i Camerieri D'Onore in Abito Paonazzo. Vatican City: Secretariat of State, 1969.

Memorandum (No. 364118): Secretariat of State, The Vatican to Lord Lyon King of Arms (UK). 7 January 1956.

Nota degli abito occorrenti agli Em.mi e Rev. mi Signori Cardinali. Vatican City: Sacra Congregazione Cerimoniale.

On the Papal Household (Pontificalis Domus). Vatican City: *Motu Proprio* Pope Paul VI, March 28, 1968.

Reform of the Use of Pontifical Insignia (Pontificalia Insignia). Vatican City: *Motu Proprio* Pope Paul VI, June 27, 1968.

Regimini Ecclesiae Universae (Apostolic Constitution concerning the Roman Curia). Vatican City: *Motu Proprio* Pope Paul VI, August 15, 1967.

Romano Pontifici Eligendo (On Electing the Roman Pontiff). Vatican City: *Motu Proprio* Pope Paul VI, October 1, 1975.

Sacrosanctum Concilium (Constitution on the Sacred Liturgy). Vatican City: December 4, 1963.

Sapientia Christiana (Apostolic Constitution on Ecclesiastical Universities and Faculties).

Vatican City: *Motu Proprio* Pope John Paul II, 1979.

Simplification of Pontifical Rites and Insignia (Pontificales Ritus). Vatican City: Congregation of Rites, June 21, 1968.

Tres Abhinc Annos. Vatican City: *Motu Proprio* Pope Paul VI, May 4, 1967.

VESTURE

Constitutiones Apostolicae Recentiores De Protonotariis Apostolicis Praelatis Urbanis Et Alliis Qui Nonnullis Privilegiis Praelatorum Propriis Fruuntur. Vatican City: Typis Polyglottis Vaticanis, 1956.

Dolby, Anastasia. *Church Vestments.* London: Chapman and Hall, 1868.

Instruction on the Dress of Cardinals, Bishops, and Other Prelates. Washington, DC: U.S. Catholic Conference, March 31, 1969.

Norris, Herbert. *Church Vestments.* London: J. M. Dent and Sons, 1949.

McCloud, Henry J. *Clerical Dress and Insignia of the Roman Catholic Church.* Milwaukee: The Bruce Publishing Company, 1948.

Montault, Barbier de. *Le Costume et les usages ecclésiastiques selon la tradition Romaine.* Paris: (privately published), 1889.

Nainfa, John A. *Costume of Prelates of the Catholic Church, According to the Roman Etiquette.* Baltimore: John Murphy and Company, 1926.

Oliva, Laurent. *Vêtements Ecclésiastiques.* Paris, 1910.

Pugin. *Glossary of Ecclesiastical Ornaments.* London, 1868.

Roulin, Dom E. A. *Vestments and Vesture.* London: Sands and Company, 1931.

Walsh, John. *The Mass and Vestments of the Catholic Church.* New York: Benzinger Brothers, 1916.

INDEXES

NAME INDEX

Note: Page numbers followed by an *f* indicate figures; those with an *n* indicate footnotes; those with *pl.* indicate color plates (with page number of legend in parentheses).

SUBJECT INDEX

Note: Page numbers followed by an *f* indicate figures; those with an *n* indicate footnotes; those with *pl.* indicate color plates (with page number of legend in parentheses).

James-Charles Noonan, Jr. was born in the city of Philadelphia in 1958. He received his education in the archdiocesan school system in Philadelphia through the secondary level when he entered LaSalle University, a Christian Brothers institution, in Philadelphia. He went on to earn a degree in International Relations and Political Science, a pre-foreign service degree program, in 1980. As a specialist in diplomatic, social, business, and church protocol, he went on to consult for many international organizations, including numerous official bodies of the Roman Catholic Church. He has been awarded numerous honors in his lifetime, including six orders of knighthood, as a result of his unique expertise in protocol.

In 1987, inspired by his lifelong friend, the late Jacques Cardinal Martin, who served the papacy for forty years and who ended his service in the Curia as Prefect of the Papal Household—governing the official life of the Holy Father—Mr. Noonan began research in the Secret Vatican Archives on a study of the post-Vatican II era Church vis-à-vis her protocol and ceremonial life, a scope of study never before undertaken. Encouraged by senior members of the Church's hierarchy, including numerous members of the Sacred College of Cardinals, Mr. Noonan's intended study rapidly expanded to include a wealth of years of valuable research materials and papal documents. Some of these were never before opened for a wider, serious academic study.

Mr. Noonan was received eleven times inside the Apostolic Palace including one visit at which the Holy Father presented a *zucchetto* to him with the words, "accept this as a sign of fidelity for your endeavor." The author's love, devotion, and fidelity to Pope John Paul II and to the institution of the papacy is well known inside the Vatican and far beyond its territorial frontiers.

In 1992, he entered priestly formation, initially being posted to Saint Charles Borromeo Seminary, Philadelphia, and then to the Pontifical Gregorian University in Rome. With a personal need to return home to the United States, his formation program was interrupted during which time this completed work was offered for publication. It has been a long, inspirational journey for him, one blessed by the hand of God. Mr. Noonan never fails to offer public thanks for all that has been given him.

In large measure due to the scholarship of *The Church Visible* and his years of research and academic enterprise within the Vatican Secret Archives—the "memory of the Church," The Catholic University of America in Washington has awarded Mr. Noonan a scholarship in the doctoral program in the School of Religious Studies as a lay scholar of Church History, one of the finest programs in this discipline in the academic world. At the completion of this doctoral studies, with the help of God, he will return to complete his priestly formation. Towards this holy end, he seeks a remembrance in the prayers of all the readers of *The Church Visible*.